Alcohol

Its production, properties, chemistry, and industrial applications; with chapters on methyl alcohol, fusel oil, and spirituous beverages

Charles Simmonds

Alpha Editions

This edition published in 2020

ISBN : 9789354037573

Design and Setting By
Alpha Editions
www.alphaedis.com
email - alphaedis@gmail.com

As per information held with us this book is in Public Domain.
This book is a reproduction of an important historical work. Alpha Editions uses the best technology to reproduce historical work in the same manner it was first published to preserve its original nature. Any marks or number seen are left intentionally to preserve its true form.

TC
S

ALCOHOL

Its Production, Properties, Chemistry, and Industrial Applications

WITH CHAPTERS ON METHYL ALCOHOL, FUSEL OIL, AND SPIRITUOUS BEVERAGES

BY

CHARLES SIMMONDS, B.Sc.

Analyst in the Government Laboratory, London

15948
22/2/21

MACMILLAN AND CO., LIMITED
ST. MARTIN'S STREET, LONDON
1919

PREFACE

IN this volume has been collected information which, it is hoped, will be found useful to those persons—a numerous class—who have occasion to employ alcohol scientifically or industrially in their various callings.

Widely scattered through scientific and technical literature are many facts and figures concerning alcohol, which in one way or another are of interest and importance not only to the professional chemist, the physicist, or the scientific investigator, but also to the manufacturer, the engineer, the technical student, the industrial research worker, and the user of a motor-car. To many among these it will, doubtless, be a convenience to have the various facts, or the most important of them, brought together and made readily accessible in a single volume such as the one now presented.

Half humorously, sulphuric acid was formerly said to be an index of national prosperity. Possibly, at the present day, industrial alcohol is an even better index. But be that as it may, the importance of alcohol to manufactures is undoubted; and in view of this, the question of industrial alcohol and its applications, both here and abroad, has been dealt with at some length. A chapter on methyl alcohol has been included, since this product is closely associated with ordinary alcohol in technical practice.

A question which may tend to become prominent in the near future is the use of alcohol as a fuel in internal-combustion engines. Another is the production of synthetic alcohol, either from calcium carbide or from the ethylene present in coke-oven gas. Some consideration has been given to these matters in Chapters II and IX.

The author's cordial thanks are due to the Government Chemist, Sir J. J. Dobbie, F.R.S., for permission to use various data obtained in the Government Laboratory, and to the Controller of H.M Stationery Office as regards the alcohol tables in Chapter VI and much of the material utilised in compiling Chapter XII. Fo blocks of illustrations he wishes also to thank Messrs. Egrot an Grangé, Paris; Messrs. Blair, Campbell, and McLean, Glasgow Messrs. The Haslam Foundry Co., Derby; and the Editor of th *Journal of the Institute of Brewing* (Figs. 2–9).

June, 1919.

CONTENTS

CHAPTER I

CHAPTER II

CHAPTER II—*cont.*

CHAPTER III

CHAPTER IV

CHAPTER V

CHAPTER VI

CHAPTER VII

CHAPTER VIII

CHAPTER VIII—*cont.*

CHAPTER IX

CHAPTER X

CHAPTER XI

CHAPTER XI—*cont.*

CHAPTER XII

Temperatures are expressed in Centigrade degrees, except where otherwise indicated.

LIST OF TABLES

LIST OF ILLUSTRATIONS

TABLE OF ABBREVIATIONS EMPLOYED IN THE REFERENCES

ABBREVIATED TITLE.	JOURNAL.
Allgem. Brau.-Hopf. Zeit.	Allgemeine Brau- und Hopfen-Zeitung.
Amer. Chem. J.	American Chemical Journal.
Amer. J. Physiol.	American Journal of Physiology.
Annalen	Justus Liebig's Annalen der Chemie.
Annali. Chim. Appl.	Annali di Chimica Applicata.
Ann. Chim. Anal.	Annales de Chimie Analytique.
Ann. Chem. Pharm.	Annalen der Chemie und Pharmazie.
Ann. Chim. Phys.	Annales de Chimie et de Physique.
Ann. Falsif.	Annales des Falsifications.
Ann. Inst. Pasteur	Annales de l'Institut Pasteur.
Arbeit. Kais. Gesund.	Arbeiten der Kaiserliche Gesundheitsamt.
Arch. d. Sci. Phys. et Nat. Geneva	Archives des Sciences Physiques et Naturelles. Geneva.
Arch. Farmacol. Sperim.	Archivio di farmacologia sperimentale e scienze affini.
Arch. of Neurol.	Archives of Neurology.
Arch. Pharm.	Archiv der Pharmazie.
Arkiv Kem. Min. Geol.	Arkiv für Kemi, Mineralogisch Geologi.
Apoth. Zeit.	Apotheker-Zeitung.
Ber.	Berichte der Deutschen chemischen Gesellschaft.
Biochem. J.	Biochemical Journal.
Biochem. Zeitsch.	Biochemische Zeitschrift.
B.P.	British Patent.
Brewers' J.	Brewers' Journal.
Bull. Agric. Intell.	Bulle in of the Bureau of Agricultural Intelligence and of Plant Diseases.
Bull. Assoc. Chim. Sucr.	Bulletin de l'Association des Chimistes de Sucre et de Distillerie.
Bull. Soc. chim.	Bulletin de la Société chimique de France.
Bull. Soc. Chim. Belg.	Bulletin de la Société chimique de Belgique.
Bull. U.S. Bur. of Standards	Bulletin of the Bureau of Standards (U.S.A.).
Chem. and Metall. Eng.	Chemical and Metallurgical Engineering.
Chem. News	Chemical News.
Chem. Tr. J.	Chemical Trade Journal.
Chem. Weekblad.	Chemisch Weekblad.
Chem.-Zeit.	Chemiker-Zeitung.
Chem. Zentr.	Chemisches Zentralblatt.
Compt. rend.	Comptes rendus hebdomadaires des Séances de l'Académie des Sciences.
Compt. rend. Soc. Biol.	Comptes rendus hebdomadaires de Séances de la Société de Biologie.
Compt. rend. trav. Lab. Carlsberg	Comptes rendus des Travaux de Laboratorie de Carlsberg.
Deutsch. Archiv f. Klin. Med.	Deutsches Archiv für Klinische Medizin.
Die Chem. Industrie.	Die Chemische Industrie.
D.R.-P.	Deutsches Reichs-Patent.

Abbreviated Title.	Journal.
Eighth Int. Cong. Appl. Chem.	Eighth International Congress of Applied Chemistry, Proceedings.
Gilb. Ann.	Gilbert's Annalen.
Helv. Chim. Acta.	Helvetica Chimica Acta.
J. Amer. Chem. Soc.	Journal of the American Chemical Society.
J. Chem. Soc.	Journal of the Chemical Society.
J. Gas Lighting	Journal of Gas Lighting.
J. Inst. Brewing	Journal of the Institute of Brewing.
Journ. de Phys.	Journal de Physique.
J. Phys. Chem.	Journal of Physical Chemistry.
J. Physiol. path.	Journal de Physiologie et de Pathologie générale.
J. Russ. Phys. Chem. Soc.	Journal of the Physical and Chemical Society of Russia.
J. Soc. Chem. Ind.	Journal of the Society of Chemical Industry.
Mitt. K. Materialprüf.	Mittheilungen aus dem Königlichen Materialprüfungsamt zu Gross-Lichterfelde West.
Neu. Jahrb. Pharm.	Neues Jahrbuch der Pharmazie.
Pflüger's Archiv.	Archiv für das gesammte Physiologie des Menschen und der Thiere.
Pharm. J.	Pharmaceutical Journal.
Pharm. Zeit.	Pharmazeutische Zeitung.
Pharm. Zentr.-h.	Pharmazeutische Zentralhalle.
Phil. J. Sci.	Philippine Journal of Science.
Phil. Mag.	Philosophical Magazine (The London, Edinburgh and Dublin).
Phil. Trans.	Philosophical Transactions of the Royal Society of London.
Pogg. Ann.	Poggendorff's annalen der Physik und Chemie.
Proc. Roy. Soc.	Proceedings of the Royal Society.
Proc. Sco. Exp. Biol. Med.	Proceedings of the Society for Experimental Biology and Medicine.
Scient. Proc. Roy. Dublin Soc.	Scientific Proceedings of the Royal Dublin Society.
Skand. Arch. Physiol.	Skandinavisches Archiv für Physiologie.
Trans. Chem. Soc.	Transactions of the Chemical Society.
Trans. Roy. Soc. Edin.	Transactions of the Royal Society of Edinburgh.
U.S. Dep. Agr. Bull.	United States Department of Agriculture Bulletins.
U.S.P.	United States Patent.
Wochensch. Brau.	Wochenschrift für Brauerei.
Zeitsch. anal. Chem.	Zeitschrift für analytische Chemie.
Zeitsch. angew. Chem.	Zeitschrift für angewandte Chemie
Zeitsch. Elektrochem.	Zeitschrift für Elektrochemie.
Zeitsch. ges. Brauw.	Zeitschrift für das gesammte Brauwesen.
Zeitsch. Nahr. Genussm.	Zeitschrift für Untersuchung der Nahrungs- und Genussmittel.
Zeitsch. physikal. Chem.	Zeitschrift für physikalische Chemie, Stöchiometrie und Verwandtschaftslehre.
Zeitsch. Spiritusind.	Zeitschrift für Spiritusindustrie.
Zentr. Biochem. Biophys.	Zentralblatt für Biochemie und Biophysiologie.
Z. ges. Schiess.- u. Sprengstoffw.	Zeitschrift für des gesammte Schiess und Sprengstoffwessen.

ALCOHOL

CHAPTER I

INTRODUCTORY

"Alcohol."—The word "alcohol" is derived from the Arabic *al-koh'l*, denoting native antimony sulphide, which substance, in the form of an impalpable powder, has long been used by Eastern women for darkening the eyebrows and eyelashes. This custom is mentioned in Ezekiel (xxiii, 40), and also in the Second Book of Kings (ix, 30).

In course of time the word came to be used for fine powders generically. Thus in alchemical writings we find such expressions as the "alcohol of Mars" (powdered iron), "alcohol of sulphur" (powdered brimstone), and so on. Paracelsus speaks of antimony which has been changed into the alcohol—that is, reduced to fine powder; and in mentioning tartar, the sediment deposited from wine, he remarks: "*Alcool, id est tartarus resolutus in minutas partes.*" Even in comparatively modern pharmacy, "*alcohol ferri,*" or "*ferrum alcoholisatum,*" still denoted a powder of iron.

Primarily, therefore, "alcohol" indicated a dye or stain in the form of fine powder, and afterwards any fine powder. Exactly how the word came to be applied to the spirit obtained from wine is not very definitely known, though it is easy to understand how the change probably came about. Certain of the finest powders were obtained by the method of sublimation, and the resemblance of this process to the distilling of wine, whereby the finer part of the wine was obtained free from grosser particles, may well have suggested calling the spirit the "alcohol" of wine. In fact, a quotation from Querectanus given by Schorlemmer[1]—"*spiritus vini alcoholisatus circulationibus*"—indicates that the strengthening of spirits of wine by rectification was also called alcoholisation. As late as 1773, in Baumé's "Chymie Experimentale," alcohol is defined as meaning primarily "powders of the finest tenuity," and secondarily as "spirits of wine rectified to the utmost degree."[2]

Another suggestion is that the phrase "*vinum alcalisatum,*" applied to spirit of wine distilled over potassium carbonate, through

[1] "Rise and Development of Organic Chemistry," p. 94.
[2] Wootton's "Chronicles of Pharmacy," 1, 327.

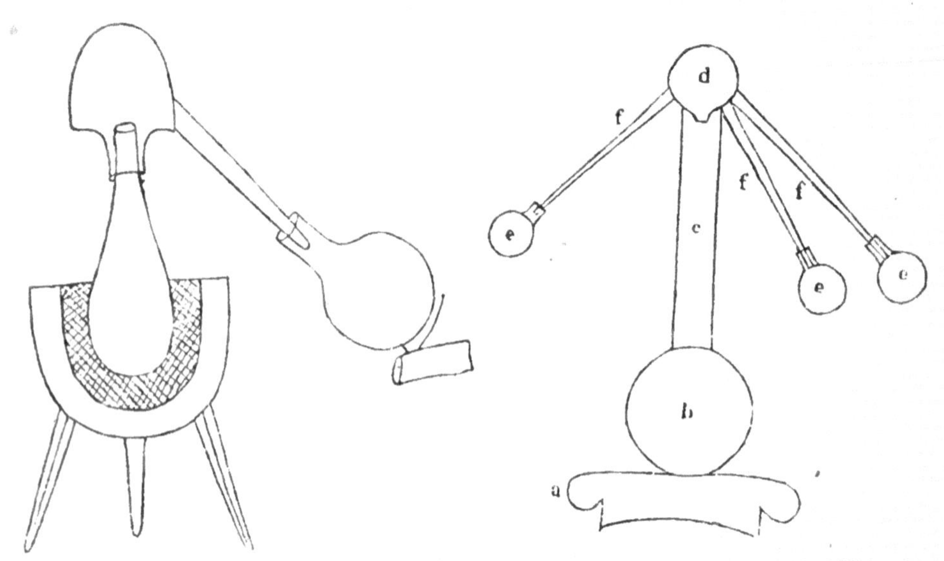

FIG. 1.—FORMS OF DISTILLATION APPARATUS EMPLOYED BY THE ALEXANDRIANS.

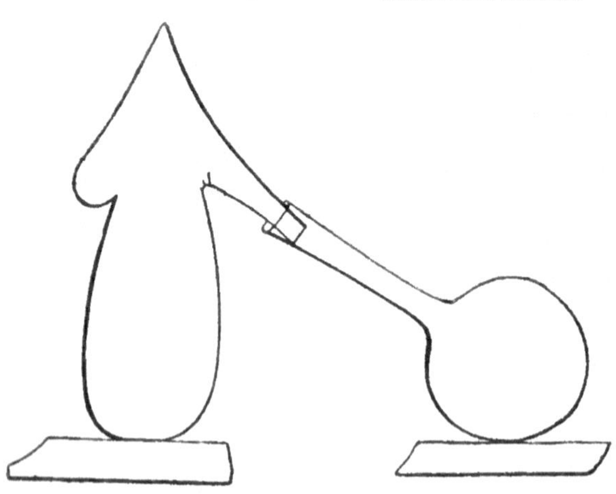

FIG. 2.—ALEMBIC AND RECEIVER FIGURED BY ZOSIMUS OF ALEXANDRIA.

FIG. 3.—ANCIENT STILL USED by KALMUCK TARTARS.
The still is constructed of clay. A tube of cane or wood connects the head with the receiver. Used for distilling koumiss.

some confusion came to be written "*vinum alcoholisatum*," which afterwards became *alcohol vini*.[1] The expression "*vini alcool, vel vinum alcalisatum*," occurs in Andreas Libavius's "Alchymia," published in 1597. Later, Boyle,[2] describing the distillation of spirit from potassium carbonate ("white calx of tartar") and quicklime, says that "the phlegmatic part of the spirit of wine is soaked up by the alcalizate salt, and the inflammable part is freed from it . . . there-

[1] Roscoe and Schorlemmer's "Chemistry," **3**, i, 284.

[2] *Opera*, **1**, 333.

fore, this alcohol of wine we peculiarly call the alcalizate spirit of wine."

Early history.—Passing from the word to the thing signified, it is safe to say that spirituous drinks have been known from time immemorial. Fermented liquors, including wine, beer, and mead, were familiar to the ancients. Distillation appears to have been known to the Chinese from a period in the remote past, and they may perhaps have distilled wine, thus obtaining alcohol from it; but the usually accepted belief is that the Arabian chemists were the discoverers of alcohol from wine. E. O. von Lippmann[1] has recently contended that the discovery of alcohol probably took place in Italy, the article being first mentioned in an Italian work

FIG. 4.—PRIMITIVE STILL USED IN TAHITI.

The body of the still is a large stone hollowed to form a pot; the head is formed of a hollowed-out log. In this is inserted a long bamboo cane, which passes through a trough or gutter filled with cold water to serve as a condenser.

FIG. 5.—ANCIENT STILL USED IN CEYLON.

The still is of earthenware; *a*, *b*, form the alembic and head luted together; *d*, *e*, are the receiver and refrigerator, in one piece, connected with the head by a bamboo, *c*.

FIG. 6.—ANCIENT FORM OF STILL USED IN PERU.

The still is an earthen pot, having a hole in the side near the top, through which passes a wooden gutter as shown, connecting with the receiver. A pan filled with cold water is placed on the top, and luted to the pot with clay; this pan acts as a condenser. The spirit vapour condenses on the bottom of the pan, falls into the gutter, and passes out to the receiver.

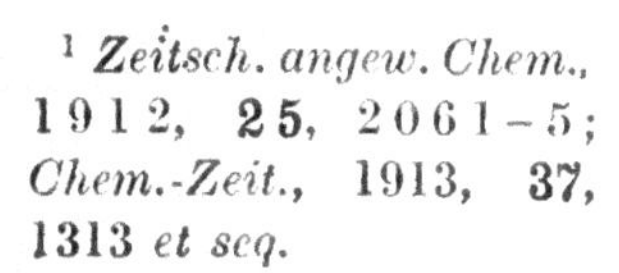

[1] *Zeitsch. angew. Chem.*, 1912, **25**, 2061-5; *Chem.-Zeit.*, 1913, **37**, 1313 *et seq.*

of the ninth or tenth century. A mention of it is also said to be found in a manuscript of the twelfth century from the *Mappa clavicula*. Apart from this, however, there does not appear to be any trustworthy evidence of the production of alcohol from wine earlier than the thirteenth century. As the first definite indication, Berthelot quotes from Marcus Grecas' "Book of Fires" a method of distilling *aqua ardens* from "a black wine, thick and old." This book, he states, could not be of earlier date than 1300.

FIG. 7.—STILL USED IN THIBET AND BHOTAN.

A, an earthenware vessel in which the "chong" for distillation is placed; *B*, another vessel open at the bottom; *C*, the receiver; *D*, an iron basin filled with cold water to serve as condenser; *e*, *e*, *e*, staves of wood on which *C* rests. The spirit vapour rises through *B*, is condensed on the convex bottom of the basin *D*, and falls into *C*. *f* is the fireplace, and *g*, *g*, openings for the reception of similar apparatus.

There is little doubt, however, that distilled alcoholic beverages had been obtained from materials other than wine at a period far anterior to this. A number of examples have been collected by T. Fairley,[1] who quotes Hoeffer's "Histoire de Chimie," Morewood's "Inebriating Liquors," and various other works as his authorities. Thus arrack, distilled from toddy, has been known in India since at least 800 B.C., and in Ceylon from "time immemorial." Toddy itself is a fermented liquor obtained from rice and various palms. In China, rice, millet, and other grains yield

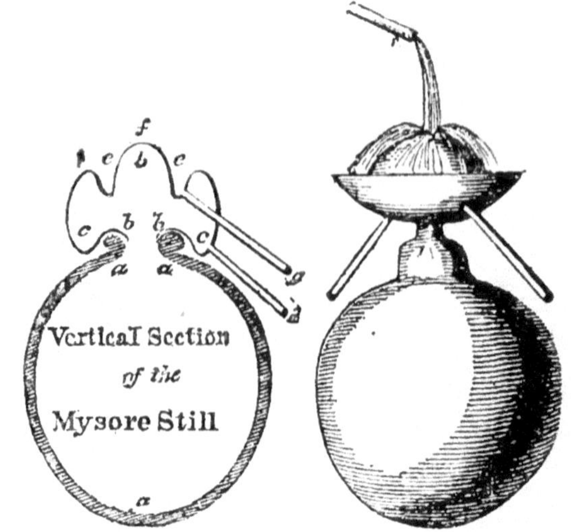

FIG. 8.—ANCIENT STILL USED IN SOUTHERN INDIA.

The still is of either earthenware or metal. It is charged with fermented liquid from rice, molasses, or palm sap; then placed in a hole in the ground, and heated by a fire underneath. The vapour is condensed by a stream of cold water which runs off through the tube *g*, whilst the condensed liquid passes out through the lower tube.

[1] *Analyst*, 1905, **30**, 294; *J. Inst. Brewing*, 1907, **13**, 559.

the fermented liquor *tar-asun* or *tchoo*, from which a distilled liquor, *sautchoo*, was obtained long before the Christian era. Similarly, *sochu* was distilled in very ancient times from the well-known Japanese drink *saké*, obtained by fermenting rice. The *koumiss* of the Tartars in Central Asia, and the *kephir* used by the Caucasians, are the fermented milk of mares and other animals, and have from "very ancient" times yielded distilled liquors known respectively as *arika* and *skhou*. In this country, Taliesin, a Cymric bard of the

FIG. 9.—DISTILLING APPARATUS.

From a German edition of Geber's works dated 1710. The same apparatus is figured Braunschwick's "Das Buch zu Distillieren," dated 1512.

sixth century, sings the praises of distilled mead in the "Mead Song":—

> "Mead distilled I praise,
> Its eulogy is everywhere . . ."

With respect to this, however, it is only fair to say that "Taliesin" is regarded by some scholars as a purely mythical personage, and they consider many of the poems in the "Book of Taliesin" to be of much later date than the sixth century.

Distillation is seldom referred to by Greek or Roman writers. Aristotle, however, states[1] that "sea-water can be rendered potable by distillation; wine and other liquids can be submitted to the same process. After they have been converted into humid vapours they return to liquids." But if these views of Aristotle were applied in practice it was apparently done secretly. Nicander,

[1] "*Meteorology*," lib. II, chap. ii.

about 140 B.C., mentions water distilled from roses in an "ambix"—this name being the Greek word which, with the Arab prefix "al," gives us our word "alembic." Condensing apparatus is said to have been invented and used at Alexandria as early as the first century of the Christian era. The first exact description of apparatus for distillation in this part of the world, however, is given by Zosimus of Alexandria, in the fourth century. A figure of the alembic and receiver described by Zosimus, and said to have been copied from the ancient temple of Memphis, is given in Fairley's articles,[1] and is reproduced here, with several others.

Von Lippmann[2] contends that although distillation apparatus was known to the Greek alchemists in Alexandria as early as the first century A.D., there was very little progress shown in condensing the vapour until the sixth or seventh century, so that the production of liquids with low boiling points was impracticable. It is true that at that period an "aqua vitæ" was known, but according to von Lippmann this was not spirit of wine; it was an ancient Egyptian "elixir of life." Even as late as the year 1120, Al Khazini expressly declared that olive oil was the specifically lightest liquid known. This would not, however, exclude alcohol of 50 to 60 per cent. strength.

Aromatic herbs were much used in Arab pharmacy, and a process for distilling water from such herbs is described in writings attributed to Geber, probably about the end of the ninth century; whilst later a physician of Cordova, Albucasis, gave an exact description of a distillation apparatus as applied in the preparation of medicines, which may perhaps have included spirits of wine. In any case, towards the end of the thirteenth century *aqua vini* had acquired the reputation of a valuable medicine. In Italy, it was sold as a general heal-all about the year 1250, and in more northern countries about 1400. Indeed for some centuries this medicinal use was the chief application of the spirit obtained from wine. The knowledge of it was spread into France and abroad by Arnaud de Villeneuve (Arnold of Villa Nova), Raymond Lully, and others. The processes were often kept secret, under severe penalties, in the hands of the priests, or of religious orders.

Wootton[3] puts the matter thus:—

"Albucasis, a Spanish Arab of the eleventh century, is supposed from some obscure expressions in his writings to have known how to make a spirit from wine; but Arnold of Villa Nova, who wrote in the latter part of the thirteenth century, is the first explicitly

[1] *loc. cit.* [2] *Chem.-Zeit.*, 1912, **36**, 655.
[3] *Chron. of Pharmacy*, **1**, 329.

to refer to it. He does not intimate that he had discovered it himself, but he appears to treat it as something comparatively new. *Aqua vini* is what he calls it, but some name it, he says, *aqua vitæ* . . . and golden water. It is well called water of life, he says, because it strengthens the body and prolongs life. He distilled herbs with it such as rosemary and sage, and highly commended the medicinal virtue of these tinctures."

Whatever may be the facts as to the earliest mention of distilled alcohol, one thing is clear. The recognition of alcohol as a constituent of all fermented beverages such as wine, beer, and mead depended on the possibility of separating it, and followed upon the improvements in distillation effected by the Alexandrians. As already indicated, the use of dehydrating agents in obtaining stronger spirit from weaker has long been practised; the method was known to Raymond Lully and to Basil Valentine, who both describe the employment of calcined tartar (potassium carbonate) for the purpose. It is interesting to note, in view of the importance of alcohol in medicine, that Lully terms it *consolatio ultima corporis humani*. Other names which the substance has received at one time or another are *aqua ardens*, *aqua vitæ*, *aqua vitis*, *spiritus vivus*, and *mercurius vegetabilis*. Lully, indeed, waxes quaintly enthusiastic about his teacher Arnold's *aqua vitæ*: it is "of marveylous use and commoditie a little before the joyning of battle to styre and encourage the soldiers' minds." "The taste of it exceedeth all other tastes, and the smell all other smells," he says. Against this, by way of contrast, we may put Shakespeare's lines: "O thou invisible spirit of wine, if thou hast no name to be known by, let us call thee devil." (*Othello*, Act II, Scene 3.)

As regards the early use of alcohol in this country, "usquebagh," a spirit of native origin, is stated by Scarisbrick,[1] though the authority is not given, to have been probably manufactured in Ireland about 1100 A.D. Brandy, according to the same writer, may have been received from France as early as the twelfth or thirteenth century; but the earliest trustworthy mention of spirit imports is of arrack ("huraca") brought to South Britain by Genoese merchants in the fifteenth century. The item "to a woman for bringing *aqua vitæ*, 3*s*. 4*d*.," occurs in an account of the privy purse expenses of Henry VII. Distilling had become known in the English monasteries, and alcohol figured in the pharmacopœias of the period as a stimulant and curative agent in disease. By 1530 alcohol formed a recognised article of English diet. "Spyrites of the buttrye" was a common phrase for spirits of

[1] "Spirit Assaying," p. 47.

wine, which was also referred to as "brennynge watir" and "watir of lijf."

Alcohol may have been introduced into Scotland from Ireland in the twelfth century, but there appears to be no proof of its manufacture there till towards the end of the fifteenth century. The earliest reference so far traced occurs in the Scottish Exchequer Rolls for the year 1494–5, where a certain friar, Brother John Cor, is directed to be supplied with eight bolls of malt *ad faciendum aquavite* for the use of the Scottish king.[1] In 1498, the king, James IV., making a tour of his dominions, fell ill at Dundee, and a barber-surgeon called in to treat him prescribed alcohol. Hence in the accounts of the Lord High Treasurer of Scotland the entry occurs :—"*Item to the barbour that brocht aquavite to the king in Dunde be the kingis command— I X shillings.*"

In the time of the Tudor kings, Scotch whisky obtained a considerable reputation in England. Thenceforward the knowledge and practice of distillation became gradually more widespread, and eventually the manufacture of spirits attracted the attention of the tax-gatherer. It was in due time brought under official scrutiny, and made a source of revenue by means of licences and excise duties.

Of the subsequent landmarks in the history of alcohol production, we may note here the introduction of distillation with direct steam by Sir A. Perrier at Cork in 1822. Much more important, however, was the introduction of the "patent" or Coffey still, by means of which it became possible to produce alcohol of high strength and purity at a single distillation, carried on as a continuous process. This still was invented by Aeneas Coffey in 1831, and patented in 1832.

Composition of alcohol.—As to the question, What *is* alcohol ? there was more or less speculation during the seventeenth and eighteenth centuries, but it was not till towards the close of the latter period that much was definitely proved. Stahl (1660–1734) regarded alcohol as a very light, attenuated oil, united by an acid to a larger quantity of water than was present in ordinary oils. Kunckel, however (1630–1702), gives excellent reasons why it cannot be an oil. It mixes with water, does not dissolve sulphur, and does not form a soap with alkali.

Another view (Junker) was that alcohol consisted of phlogiston united simply with water, since it was found that only water was produced when alcohol was burnt. Boerhaave also (1757) found that the product of combustion was pure water. Nevertheless, the

[1] Scarisbrick, *loc. cit.*, p. 48.

"oil" idea still had its partisans. Lémery[1] considered alcohol as the oily part of wine, but rarefied by the acid salts of the wine. Macquer[2] gives both views, but adopts that of pure phlogiston without oil. He correctly regards the oily residue, left when alcohol (of wine) evaporates, as an impurity of the alcohol.

In Fourcroy's *Traité de Chimie* (*An* 11 *de la République*) another question is raised. Does alcohol pre-exist in wine, or is it formed during the boiling when wine is distilled? The author indicates that the former view was that held by the older chemists; the more modern *savants* considered that wine contained two "principles," respectively characterised by (i) much hydrogen, and (ii) very little carbon; and that during distillation of the wine these combined to form alcohol. In 1806, however, Fourcroy[3] no longer supports either this opinion or the oil theory. He regards alcohol as a product of the fermentation of sugar, which has been reduced to a "simpler term."

Lavoisier's analysis.—It was Lavoisier's analysis of alcohol in 1781, supplemented by de Saussure's analyses (1807–1813), which settled the question of the composition of alcohol. Lavoisier, whose other researches had disposed of the phlogiston theory, found that 1 lb. of spirit of wine yielded on combustion:—

	Onces.	Gros.	Grs.
Carbon	4	4	37½
Inflammable gas (hydrogen)	1	2	5½
Water, ready formed	10	1	29

The analysis was made by burning alcohol in a bell-jar filled with oxygen and placed over mercury, and estimating the carbon dioxide formed and the quantity of oxygen consumed. Lavoisier regarded the results as indicating that alcohol was a compound of carbon and hydrogen united with ready-formed water. The figures indicate, of course, an aqueous alcohol. According to P. Guichard,[4] if we leave aside the water and calculate the carbon and hydrogen percentages, the result is 51·85 per cent. of carbon and 13·36 per cent. of hydrogen, as compared with the theoretical quantities 52·17 and 13·04 per cent. respectively.

Discussing the results in 1793, Lavoisier concluded that the carbon and hydrogen contained in alcohol are not present in the form of oil; they are combined with such a proportion of oxygen as makes them soluble in water.

A more definite proof that oxygen is a constituent of alcohol

[1] *Chimie*, 1754. [2] *Dict. de Chimie*, 1779. [3] "Philosophie Chimique."
[4] "Traité de Distillerie," Vol. III. The quantities expressed in modern figures are given as: Carbon, 149·5785 grams, Hydrogen, 38·5325 grams.

came later from de Saussure, who took up the study in 1807–1813. He made analyses by various methods, including Lavoisier's combustion process, decomposition in a eudiometer, and finally by a process of passing the alcohol through a tube heated to redness. Lowitz had meanwhile (1796) shown how a strong alcohol could be obtained by treatment of rectified spirit of wine with freshly-heated potassium carbonate, so that de Saussure could work with a much less aqueous product than was at Lavoisier's disposal. From the results obtained with his red-hot tube experiments, he deduced the composition of alcohol to be :—

Carbon	57·57 per cent.
Oxygen	28·47 ,,
Hydrogen	13·96 ,,

The analysis is notably less exact than Lavoisier's as regards carbon and hydrogen, but more complete in respect of oxygen. Subsequent analyses by Gay-Lussac, Dumas, and Boullay established the composition more precisely.

Fig. 10.—Dr. Thomas Willis, 1621–1675.

Synthesis of alcohol.—The first chemical synthesis of alcohol has generally been attributed to Berthelot, who, in 1854, obtained it from olefiant gas by absorbing this gas in sulphuric acid, diluting the product, and distilling it. Meldola has shown, however, that our own countryman, Henry Hennell, had succeeded in effecting this synthesis some twenty-six years previously. In a paper communicated to the Royal Society in 1827, Hennell indicates that he had identified sulphovinic acid (ethyl sulphuric acid) in a quantity of sulphuric acid given him by Faraday, which had absorbed eighty times its volume of olefiant gas ; and in a subsequent paper (1828) he describes how he had distilled sulphovinic acid with water and a little sulphuric acid, and proved that it was decomposed into sulphuric acid and alcohol. Since alcohol is a product of living organisms, Meldola claims for Hennell "a place not inferior to that of Wöhler" (who synthesised urea in the same year, 1828), "as being among the first to produce an organic compound independently of the living organism."[1] Alcohol was not, however, at that time regarded as a vital product in the same sense as urea was, and hence Hennell's achievement did not attract the same attention as did the synthesis of urea.

It is, however, on the biological or biochemical questions arising out of the study of alcoholic fermentation that the most interesting and important results have accrued. With a brief historical outline and a general indication of these results and their significance we may fitly close this introductory sketch of our subject.

FIG. 11.—G. E. STAHL, 1659–1734.

Fermentation.—Although the production of spirits from grain was known in Europe as early, perhaps, as the eleventh or twelfth century, and fermented liquors have been used since the dawn of history, only very vague and general ideas were prevalent as to the nature of the fermentation process. To the alchemists, almost any action between two substances, especially when gas was evolved, formed a "fermentation."

In the seventeenth century, Willis's view of fermentation was current (1659). A ferment is a body in a state of decomposition, with energetic motion of its particles; this motion it can impart to another body which is capable of fermentation. This view was upheld by Stahl (1697), according to whose opinion fermentation was a matter of the decomposition of a fermentable body into its

[1] "The Chemical Synthesis of Vital Products," p. 1. See also a detailed discussion in *J. Soc. Chem. Ind.*, 1910, **29**, 737.

components, which then re-combined in a different manner to form new substances. For example, sugar might thus be disintegrated into its constituent particles, and these then re-united to form alcohol. A body in such a state of internal motion as that supposed by Willis could communicate this motion to another which was itself at rest, provided that the latter body was one fitted for the change. Thus was explained the propagation of fermentation from one liquid to another.

Towards the end of the seventeenth century, Leeuwenhoek, with a home-made microscope of 150 diameters magnifying power, found that yeast was composed of small round or oval particles. He described these in letters to the Royal Society (1680), and may thus be said to have laid the foundation of researches on fermentation by means of the microscope. The further use of this instrument in such researches might have cut short many controversies during the next century and a half, but it appears to have been neglected. Desmazières in 1826 found that a film taken from beer was composed of elongated cells which he designated *Mycoderma cerevisiæ*. It is not clear, however, that he looked upon these as fermentative agents.

Fig. 12.—Justus von Liebig, 1803–1873.

Van Helmont's discoveries (1648) that in fermentation a gas, as well as alcohol, was produced, and that a ferment was necessary to start the process, were important steps in the elucidation of fermentation phenomena. So also was the identification by MacBride (1764) of the gas in question as Black's "fixed air" (carbon dioxide). Cavendish (1766) found that the proportion of this "fixed air" yielded by sugar on fermentation was 57 per cent.; and Lavoisier showed by numerous experiments that sugar was decomposed almost quantitatively into alcohol and carbon dioxide.[1]

The nineteenth century brought forth the famous scientific controversy between Pasteur and Liebig as to the cause of fermentation; and it brought also the definite settlement of the question. Hitherto the phenomenon had been regarded as essentially a chemical one; yeast was a chemical reagent, not a living organism. Even in 1810, Gay-Lussac, discussing the researches of Lavoisier,

[1] "Traité élémentaire de Chimie," 1793.

Fabroni, and Thenard, treats the matter essentially from the chemical point of view. It had been tacitly assumed that fermentation can begin and continue without the aid of oxygen. Gay-Lussac, however, considered that oxygen was certainly necessary, since grape juice preserved by heat in closed bottles began to ferment at once when exposed to the air, but showed no fermentation in absence of air. That the air contained living organisms capable of setting up the fermentation was not, apparently, suspected.

The microscope, however, presently threw further light on the problem. In 1836, Cagniard-Latour[1] recognised that yeast was a living organism, reproduced by budding, and probably a plant; alcoholic fermentation was looked upon as due to its vegetative activity. Kützing, of Nordhausen, arrived at the same result: yeast is not a chemical compound, but a vegetable organism. Also Schwann,[2] about the same time (1837), came to a similar conclusion from experiments on heated air and boiled liquids, confirmed by subsequent microscopical examination. Turpin (1838) confirmed the accuracy of Cagniard-Latour's observations and deductions.

FIG. 13.—LOUIS PASTEUR, 1822-1895.

The views of the three microscopists, however, were very strongly contested by the most distinguished chemists of the period—Berzelius and von Liebig. Berzelius regarded fermentation as a catalytic process. On Liebig's view, ferments are unstable nitrogen-containing substances, formed by the action of air upon plant juices containing sugar. These easily-decomposable ferments are in a condition of constant degradation or decay; by their decomposition a corresponding chemical motion is imparted to the atoms of the

[1] *Ann. Chim. Phys.*, 1838, **68**, 206.

[2] *Pogg. Ann.*, 1837, **41**, 184.

sugar; and thus the sugar is itself decomposed, with production of alcohol. This, it will be seen, embodies Stahl's theory.

A sort of reconciling link between the two opposed views—the vitalistic and the chemical—was put forward by Mitscherlich (1841). He regarded fermentation as produced by a vegetable organism (yeast), but through a sort of contact-action, not through the vital activities of the yeast.

By about the middle of the century more and more evidence had accumulated in favour of the vegetative nature of yeast, and even Berzelius had now become satisfied of this. Liebig's authority, however, was very great in the scientific world, and opinion was still divided between the vitalistic and the purely chemical theory of fermentation.

Eventually, through Pasteur's researches, the former view prevailed. Liebig's theory—that yeast arises by the action of atmospheric oxygen on some special nitrogenous constituent of the fermenting liquid—Pasteur disproved by growing a crop of yeast in a synthetic culture medium containing an ammonium salt as the sole nitrogenous constituent. Also he showed that whenever fermentation occurred there was a simultaneous growth of yeast in the liquid. Moreover, alcohol and carbon dioxide were not, as Liebig had assumed, the only products of fermentation; succinic acid and glycerol were also produced. Pasteur showed, further, that each kind of fermentation (alcoholic, lactic, butyric, etc.) required its special kind of micro-organism. Alcoholic fermentation, he concludes, is an act correlated with the life and organisation of the yeast-cells, not with their death and decay. Nor is it a mere contact-phenomenon, for then the transformation of the sugar would take place without anything being either given up to the yeast or taken away from it; whereas experiment showed definitely that something was given up to the yeast by the sugar. "No fermentation without life," was Pasteur's verdict. But he also said: "If I am asked in what consists the chemical act whereby the sugar is decomposed and what is its real cause, I reply that I am completely ignorant of it."

Later on, the aphorism, "no fermentation without life," proved to be, in strictness, untenable. The idea that alcoholic fermentation was due to an enzyme elaborated by the yeast-cell, and not immediately to the life-processes of the cell itself, had been put forward by Traube as early as 1857. Liebig himself had referred to the possibility, and Pasteur saw no objection to it.[1] No satisfactory evidence of this, the true explanation, was, however, forth-

[1] See "Studies on Fermentation," p. 327 (English edition, 1879).

coming until towards the close of the century, when Buchner, as mentioned later on, succeeded in supplying the proof. But the aphorism is only too wide by a single stage. "Without life no enzymes, and without enzymes no fermentation" would be true, so far as our present knowledge goes.

Pasteur's work, however, was fundamental, and of much wider import than the settlement of this particular controversy. It has had an outstanding influence upon the development of the brewing and distilling industries. Not only so; it was destined to have a far-reaching effect upon the welfare of the whole human race, and to this aspect of the matter a few words may now be specially devoted.

In 1854, Pasteur was appointed Dean of the newly-established *Faculté des Sciences* at Lille, in which town distilling had then become an important industry. About two years later he was consulted by a distiller, M. Bigo, in reference to certain difficulties and disappointments that had been met with in the manufacture of alcohol from beetroot. This fortunate circumstance it was which directed the genius and acumen of Pasteur to those studies of fermentation which have helped to make his name immortal. It is a matter of common knowledge that to Pasteur is due the explanation of alcoholic fermentation as a process correlative with the life and organisation of the yeast-cell. But it is perhaps less generally recognised that by these "Etudes sur la Bière" and "Etudes sur le Vin," and their subsequent ramifications and extensions, the boundaries of natural science have been advanced beyond all that could have been foreseen, and that incalculable benefits have thereby been conferred upon humanity. Pasteur's researches upon alcoholic fermentation, at first concerned with the "maladies" of beer, wine, and vinegar, led directly to the more definitely pathological investigations of silkworm disease and anthrax. The proof that these are bacterial ailments was followed by the production of "vaccines," and by those further studies of infectious diseases and the nature of immunisation which have had so enormous an influence upon the development of medicine, surgery, and sanitation. Pasteur's later work was the direct outcome of his researches on alcoholic fermentation; it was in large measure rendered possible by the experience and *technique* acquired in those researches; and it laid the foundation of the subsequent wonderful developments which have taken place in the spheres of preventive medicine and hygiene. "Modern surgery, like preventive medicine, is a child of the fermentation industries."[1]

[1] Dr. H. T. Brown, *J. Inst. Brewing*, 1916, **22**, 301.

Nor was this result a mere lucky consequence, accidental and unexpected. Pasteur, at all events, foresaw the possible future application of his new ideas to the etiology of infectious and contagious diseases. "Man has it in his power to cause parasitic diseases to vanish from the face of the earth," he wrote in his studies of the silkworm disease. He foresaw this possibility, and he laboured towards its attainment; and on the foundations which he laid, developed and extended by other workers, the whole superstructure of modern bacteriology has been erected.

If the abuse of alcohol as a beverage has been fraught with much misery to the world, on the other side of the account may well be put the indisputable and inestimable benefits which have accrued to the human race through the reduction or elimination of disease by discoveries which had their origin in the study of alcoholic fermentation.

Of the developments which have occurred since Pasteur's researches, Buchner's account of "Alcoholic Fermentation without Yeast-cells," published in 1897, is one of the outstanding phases.[1] It is so, because of the evidence it affords that fermentation is not, or is not necessarily, a direct outcome of the vital action of yeast-cells, but rather a chemical action due to an intermediate, non-living product (enzyme) first elaborated by the living cell, but separable from it. Buchner proved that juice pressed out from yeast, and containing none of the cells, can induce alcoholic fermentation in solutions of sugar, and that during the process there is no growth of yeast-cells in these solutions. Further important studies of the enzymes, leading to suggestive theories as to their mode of action, their molecular correspondence with the substances they act upon (Fischer's "lock and key" analogy), and their bearing upon the mechanism of immunisation from disease (Ehrlich) are of wide general interest; but they belong to the domain of physiology rather than to that of alcohol production. One further name, however, may be mentioned here, namely, that of E. C. Hansen, who from the year 1879 onwards investigated the life-history of individual alcohol-producing yeasts, and developed the method of procuring a pure yeast by cultivation from a single mother-cell.

Recalling the numerous developments in science and industry which directly or indirectly have followed from the study of alcoholic fermentation; remembering their present importance, and realising their implications of future progress; we may justifiably acquiesce in, and indeed applaud, the remark of the enthusiast: *Omnis scientia ex cerevisiâ.*

[1] *Ber.*, 1897 to 1900; vols. **30** to **33**.

CHAPTER II

OUTLINE OF THE PRODUCTION OF ALCOHOL

THE ordinary alcohol of commerce (ethyl alcohol) is chiefly obtained by the fermentation of some form of sugar through the action of yeast. The sugar may be already existent in the raw materials employed; it is so, for instance, in grape juice, beet juice, and molasses. Other raw materials, however, may not contain sugar as such, or may contain it in trivial quantities only. Thus in cereals and potatoes, which are some of the chief sources of alcohol, the utilisable substance is starch; and in sawdust or wood-pulp, other sources, it is wood-cellulose. But whether starch or cellulose, the material must be converted into sugar before it can be fermented by yeast to produce alcohol.

Starch, in fact, is the source of by far the larger part of the sugar from which alcohol is eventually obtained, and it will be useful to give forthwith, in a few words, a preliminary idea of the chief process by which this raw material is converted into the finished product. The various phases of the operation will afterwards be dealt with in greater detail.

The starchy material is first ground, and heated with water to gelatinise the starch. This forms the "**mash**," which is then saccharified by means of malt, the conversion of starch into sugar being effected through the action of an enzyme, *diastase* (*amylase*), which is present in the malt. The resulting liquid is now known as the "**wort**"; it is essentially a solution of sugar (maltose) with dextrin and other ingredients obtained from the starchy material.

Next, the wort is fermented by adding yeast ("pitching"). As a result of the fermentation, the sugar is converted into alcohol through the action of certain other enzymes (*maltase*; *zymase*) which are present in the yeast. The fermented alcoholic liquid is termed the "**wash.**" Finally, the wash is distilled to separate the alcohol, and the latter, if necessary, is subsequently "rectified" by further distillation to such a degree of strength and purity as may be desired.

If molasses or other sugar-containing material is being u
instead of starch, the preliminary saccharification stages are,
course, unnecessary. A solution of the material is prepared
contain a suitable proportion of sugar, and fermented directly.

We now proceed to describe more fully the materials and
cesses employed, and the principles underlying the various o
tions.

I.—MATERIALS EMPLOYED

The possible sources from which alcohol can be obtained are very numerous, since any substance containing either sugar or starch may be used for the purpose. Moreover, not only sugar and starch, but wood and other cellulose-containing materials are also in use as sources of alcohol, and synthetic alcohol from hydrocarbons is emerging out of the purely experimental stage and becoming, or promising soon to become, a regular commercial product.

Sugar and starch, however, are foodstuffs, and they, or the substances containing them, may for this reason sometimes and in some places be too expensive for use in making alcohol. Thus comparatively little wheat is employed for the purpose anywhere. Potatoes are very largely used on the Continent for making alcohol, but in this country scarcely at all. They command here a higher price for ordinary consumption than the distiller will pay. He finds maize and molasses more economical, in spite of the fact that they are not indigenous products, whilst potatoes are so. Moreover, many of the substances which contain starches and sugars do not contain a sufficient proportion to make it profitable, in normal circumstances, to use them in spirit manufacture.

Hence, in spite of the great number of articles from which it is possible to obtain alcohol, the materials actually employed to any large extent are comparatively few. They may be grouped into the following classes :—

(*a*) Starch-containing materials.
(*b*) Sugar-containing materials.
(*c*) Cellulosic substances.
(*d*) Synthetic materials.

A tabular botanical summary of the first two classes will be found at the end of this section (p. 22).

(*a*) **Materials containing starch.**—Of these, cereals and potatoes are the principal substances used in making alcohol.

The chief cereals employed for the purpose are barley, maize, oats, rice, rye, and wheat. Naturally they vary in their content starch, and in large distilleries the calculations as to yield are ed upon analysis of the actual consignments of grain in use. average values may be taken as approximately the following :—

	Starch, per cent.
Barley	60
Maize	63
Oats	53
Rice	67
Rye	63
Wheat	65
Green malt	40
Dry malt...	68

Barley is used in large quantities for malting and in the making of potable spirits. For industrial alcohol, it is too expensive to be used by itself on a large scale.

Wheat, for the same reason, is employed to a relatively small extent, and chiefly for special spirits. On the Continent, for instance, malted wheat is used for making "Geneva" spirit, and also in brewing certain kinds of beer.

Maize is used very largely, both in Europe and in America. It is so easily grown in the latter country, and stands storage and carriage so well, that it has become pre-eminently a raw material for distillers' use.

Oats are rather extensively employed in this country, and **rye** on the Continent ; whilst **rice** is often cheap enough to be used on a large scale, here and abroad. Other kinds of grain used to an important extent are **millet,** and **sorghum grain** or **dari.**

Potatoes contain on an average about 20 per cent. of starch, the amount ranging usually from 15 to 24 per cent. They are very largely used on the Continent for the making of alcohol. In Germany, where about eight million acres of land are devoted to potato cultivation, more than four-fifths of the total alcohol produced (84 million gallons in 1913) is derived from potatoes, of which some 3 million tons *per annum* are used for this purpose. In Russia the principal sources of alcohol are potatoes and rye.

Not much alcohol is produced from potatoes in France, where the chief raw materials are sugar-beet, molasses, maize, and wine. In this country, barley, oats, maize, rice, and molasses are the main substances used. Maize is the principal starchy source of alcohol in the United States.

In the tropics, starch plants such as **cassava** (manioc) and **arrowroot** are comparable with potatoes as regards starch yield, and are expected to become more and more important as sources of alcohol. Manioc, in fact, is already employed to some extent in Europe for the purpose. The cassava tubers are about 8 to 10 lb. in weight.

They contain approximately 25 per cent. of starch, and from 4 to 6 per cent. of fermentable sugars.

An acre of ground yielding a crop of five tons of potatoes will furnish about one ton of starch, equivalent to 160 gallons of absolute alcohol theoretically, or approximately 130 gallons in practice. From barley and oats, the yield of starch per acre of land is much less, lying between one-third and one-half of the foregoing quantity. Maize, taking the average yield at 27½ bushels (56 lb.) per acre, and the starch *plus* sugar at 65 per cent., will give 1000 lb. of fermentable matter for each acre. An average acre of cassava, however, is stated to yield 10 tons of tubers, giving about 5000 lb. of extractable starch,[1] or more than double the amount obtained from an average acre of potatoes.

(*b*) **Materials containing sugar.**—A considerable quantity of alcohol is obtained by fermenting the juice of sugar-beets. In France, the amount thus produced is about one-third to one-half of the total output of alcohol. The better varieties of beets contain from 12 to 16 per cent. of fermentable sugar; but the beets used for fermentation purposes may be, and often are, less rich in sugar than those employed for beet-sugar manufacture. Consequently, the yield of alcohol varies considerably, ranging from 11 to 24 gallons per ton of roots. The yield of roots per acre is usually from 12 to 20 tons.

Molasses, both cane and beet, are another considerable source of alcohol. In cane-sugar molasses, the total amount of sugars, calculated as dextrose, ranges from about 52 to 67 per cent., and beet-sugar molasses contain from 48 to 53 per cent. of sucrose. The theoretical yield of alcohol from dextrose is 51·1 per cent., and from sucrose 53·8 per cent.; and the practical yield is about 83 per cent. of the theoretical in each case. One gallon of absolute alcohol is obtainable from 2·2 gallons of cane molasses of average sugar-content 57·7 per cent. and specific gravity 1·47, or from 2·5 gallons of beet molasses containing 50 per cent. of sugar. It has been calculated that the total quantity of alcohol obtainable from the world's production of cane- and beet-molasses would be about 200 million gallons.[2] The actual quantity obtained is uncertain, but is, of course, very much less than this.

Cane-sugar juice and palm sap.—In the tropics and sub-tropics cane-sugar juice, as well as the cane molasses, serves as a source of alcohol both for industrial purposes and for making spirituous beverages such as rum and tafia. The juice of sorghum stalks is

[1] *Press Bulletin, No.* 63, Bureau of Science, Manila, 1917.
[2] Heriot, *J. Soc. Chem. Ind.*, 1915, **34**, 339.

likewise employed to some extent for similar purposes. Both the sugar-cane and the sorghum stalks yield 65 to 70 per cent. of juice, which contains 12 to 16 per cent. of sugars.

The sap of certain varieties of palm, especially the nipa palm and the coco palm, is also an important actual and potential source of alcohol. In the Philippine Islands there are more than 100,000 acres of nipa palm swamp, and in British North Borneo as much or more, relatively small parts of which are yet worked. The sap has an average sugar-content of 15 per cent., and it is calculated that the yield of sap in a season is about 30,000 litres per hectare of land. The total production of alcohol in the Philippines is about $2\frac{1}{2}$ million gallons a year, of which nine-tenths is obtained from nipa sap; and it is estimated that 50 million gallons of alcohol could be produced each season.

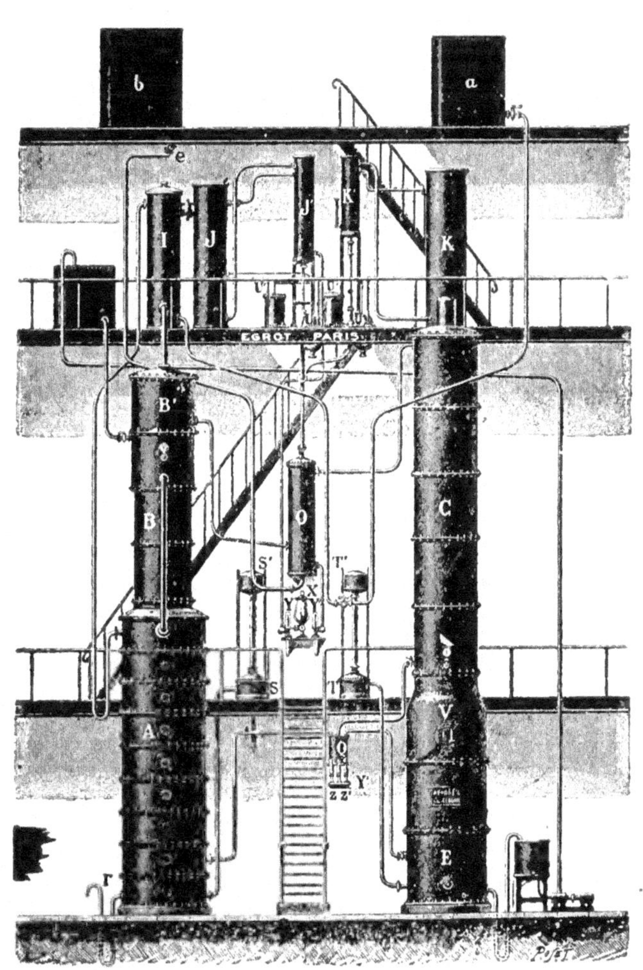

FIG. 14.—STILL FOR COMBINED DISTILLATION AND RECTIFICATION OF WINE.

A, distilling column. *B*, column for preliminary purification. *B'*, column for concentration of foreshots. *C*, rectifying column. *I*, pre-heater. *J*, *K*, condensers. *J'*, *K'*, refrigerators. *a*, *b*, backs for wine and water, respectively (Egrot and Grangé, Paris).

Wine; fruits.—In wine-producing countries a large quantity of alcohol is obtained by the distillation of wine, both for the making of brandy and the production of industrial alcohol. Surplus stocks of wine are thus used up, the inferior kinds serving for the manufacture of the highly-rectified alcohol used in the arts, and the better qualities for the distillation of brandy. Similarly, other sugar-containing fruits besides the grape, either surplus produce or over-ripe or damaged stocks, are in some countries regularly fermented and distilled as a source of alcohol.

Of other, less important, sugar- or starch-containing materials it will suffice to mention **artichokes,** which contain 16 to 18 per cent. of fermentable matter in the form of lævulose and inulin; **sweet potatoes,** used in the Azores and West Indies for alcohol-making, and containing about 27 per cent. of starch and sugar; and **asphodel** (Italian "*porrazzo*"), a starch-containing tuber common in the Mediterranean area, where it has been used as a source of industrial alcohol. It is claimed that an acre of asphodel plants yields eight tons of the tubers, from which at least 107 gallons of alcohol could be produced, but some difficulties appear to have been met with in the rectification. The **Sotol** plant, which grows abundantly in N. Mexico and W. Texas, and is employed in the making of alcohol, is said to yield from 18 to 25 gallons (presumably U.S. gallons) of 90 per cent. spirit per ton. **Sisal** waste, left after removal of the hemp fibres, has been used for the production of alcohol in Yucatan; the leaves contain about 12 per cent. of sugars.

A review of the plants from which alcohol is obtained has been compiled by J. H. Holland;[1] the table given below has been summarised from this compilation. Many of the materials mentioned are of only minor importance, but the table may be found useful for reference. Oats, wheat, buckwheat, and millet are not included in the original.

Plants used as Sources of Alcohol.

Plant.	Botanical Name.	Where found or used.
1.—Fruits:—		
Grape-vine	*Vitis vinifera*, Linn.	Widely distributed.
Apple	*Pyrus malus*, Linn.	Widely distributed.
Pear	*Pyrus communis*, Linn.	Widely distributed.
Peach	*Prunus persica*, Benth. & Hook.	Widely distributed.
Cherry	*Prunus cerasus*, Linn.	Germany; Caucasus.
Plum	*Prunus domestica*, Linn.	Germany; Caucasus.
Prune	*Prunus domestica*, var. *Juliana*.	Germany; Caucasus.
Strawberry Tree	*Arbutus unedo*, Linn.	Corsica; Italy; Greece.
Banana	*Musa sapientum*, Linn.	West Indies; E. & C. Africa, etc.
Date Palm	*Phœnix dactylifera*, Linn.	Syria, Egypt, Nubia, etc.
Carob	*Ceratonia siliqua*, Linn.	Cyprus.
Cashew	*Anacardium occidentale*, Linn.	Mozambique.
Prickly Pear	*Opuntia*, spp.	S. America.
C. African or Desert Date.	*Balanites ægyptiaca*, Delile.	Nigeria.
Pine-apple	*Ananas sativas*, Schult. f.	Malay States.
Mulberry	*Morus nigra*, Linn.	Caucasus.
Mulberry	*Morus alba*, Linn.	Kashmir.
Jambolana	*Eugenia jambolana*, Lam.	India, Ceylon, etc.

[1] *Kew Bulletin*, 1912, 113–130.

Plants used as Sources of Alcohol—*continued.*

II.—Roots, Tuberous-roots, and Root-stocks :—

Plant.	Botanical name.	Where found or used.
Potato	*Solanum tuberosum*, Linn.	Widely distributed.
Beet-root	*Beta vulgaris*, Linn.	Widely distributed.
Sweet Potato	*Ipomœa batatas*, Linn.	S. America, W. Indies, etc.
Cassava, bitter	*Manihot utilissima*, Pohl.	Tropics.
Cassava, sweet	*Manihot palmata*, var. *Aipi*, Muell.-Arg.	Tropics.
Arrowroot	*Maranta arundinacea*, Linn.	W. Indies, C. America, etc.
Artichoke	*Helianthus tuberosus*, Linn.	Europe; N. America.
Mescal Maguey	*Agave*, spp.	Mexico.
Yam	*Dioscorea sativa* and *D. alata*, Linn.	Tropical Africa, W. Indies, etc.
Tchirish.	*Asphodelus ramosus*, Linn., and *A. albus*, Willd.	S. Europe; Algeria.

III.—Grain :—

Plant.	Botanical name.	Where found or used.
Barley	*Hordeum vulgare*, Linn.	Europe, America, etc.
Rye	*Secale cereale*, Linn.	N. Europe, etc.
Maize	*Zea Mays*, Linn. var.	U.S.A., etc.
Sorghum, Dari, or Guinea Corn.	*Sorghum vulgare*, Pers.; *Andropogon sorghum*, var. *vulgaris*, Hack.	Manchuria, Europe, etc.
Rice	*Oryza sativa*, Linn.	Asia; Europe; America.
Ragi	*Eleusine coracana*, Gærtn.	India.
Millet	*Panicum miliaceum*.	Asia; Africa; Europe.
Oats	*Avena sativa*, var.	N. Europe.
Wheat	*Triticum vulgare*, var.	Widely distributed.
Buckwheat	*Fagopyrum esculentum*.	Europe; America.

IV. Stems :—

Plant.	Botanical name.	Where found or used.
Sugar Cane.	*Saccharum officinarum*, Linn.	Tropics.
Sugar Corn	*Zea Mays*, Linn.	U.S.A.
Sugar Sorghum.	*Sorghum saccharatum*, Mœnch.	India; China; Japan; N. America.
Grass Trees, or Black Boys.	*Xanthorrhœa Preisii*.	Australia.
Sotol	*Dasylirion texanum*, Schult.	Mexico.
Date Palm.	*Phœnix dactylifera*, Linn.	India.
Wild Date	*Phœnix sylvestris*, Roxb.	India.

V. Leaves :—

Plant.	Botanical name.	Where found or used.
Utschkui.	*Heracleum sphondylium*, Linn.	Europe and N. Asia.
Sisal Hemp or Henequen.	*Agave rigida*, Mill., var. *sisalana*, Pers.	Yucatan.

VI. Inflorescences :—

Plant.	Botanical name.	Where found or used.
Palmyra or Black Run Palm.	*Borassus flabellifer*, Linn.	Tropical Africa; India; Burma; Ceylon.
Cocoa-nut Palm	*Cocos nucifera*, Linn.	India; Philippines.
Buri Palm	*Corypha elata*, Roxb.	India; Philippines.
Gomuti or Sugar Palm.	*Arenga saccharifera*, Labill.	Philippines; Java; Siam.
Nipa Palm	*Nipa fruticans*, Wurmb.	Philippines, India, etc.
Sago Palm	*Caryota urens*, Linn.	Trop. Asia; Malaya.
Mahwa	*Bassia latifolia*, Roxb.	India; Burma.
Pulque Maguey	*Agave atrovirens*, Karw.	Mexico.

To the foregoing may be added acorns and horse chestnuts,

recently examined by Baker and Hulton.[1] In both cases the yield of alcohol was about 27 per cent. of the dried peeled kernels, corresponding with about 12 per cent. of the fresh material (deprived of the outer green shell). The starch of the peeled acorns was 43·4–44·3 per cent., and of the chestnuts, 15·2–39·0 per cent. The total sugars were: Acorns, 6·8–8·3; chestnuts, 10·6–20·2 per cent.

(*c*) **Alcohol from wood.**—Cellulose, which constitutes about 50 per cent. of wood, can be partially resolved into dextrose and other sugars by treatment with acids under pressure. After neutralisation of the acid, the sugars, or the greater part of them, can be fermented with yeast, and the resulting alcohol separated by distillation. On the ground of economy, sawdust or other wood waste is the material employed.

The process was developed on a laboratory scale by Classen at the University of Aix-la-Chapelle, and was subsequently tried as a manufacturing experiment at Chicago. It was there found that about 300 lb. of fermentable sugars could be obtained from one ton of pine sawdust. Following these demonstrations, a company (The Classen Lignin Co.) was formed to work the process commercially, and four plants were erected in America for the purpose.

So far as the production of alcohol is concerned, success has been met with, undoubtedly. Thus a plant established at Georgetown, S. Carolina, was reported in 1911 to have run for more than a year, producing upwards of 2,000 gallons of alcohol per day.[2] Nevertheless, it appears that by 1914 only one of the four plants remained in operation, and the process was still regarded as in an experimental stage.[3] The industry has also been tried experimentally in this country, but apparently was not able to compete successfully with the established methods.

Though simple in principle, the process presents various technical difficulties in operation. Since 1914, however, improvements have evidently been made in working it in the United States. According to one authority, a method is now in operation at Fullerton, Louisiana, whereby a yield of 8·6 gallons of 95 per cent. alcohol is obtained per cord of sawdust or common wood waste. Taking pine wood at 920 lb. per cord of 128 cubic feet, this yield works out to 21 gallons per ton. It is stated that the quality of the alcohol is very good, much of it being used in perfumery.

[1] *Analyst*, 1917, **42**, 351.

[2] *J. Ind. Eng. Chem.*, 1911, **3**, 439.

[3] See "By-products of the Lumber Industry," by H. K. Benson, p. 57 (Washington: Govt. Printer, 1916).

The output of this plant is said to be 2,000 gallons per day. The Georgetown distillery, mentioned above, was later (1918) turning out 2,500 gallons. On account of the demand for alcohol in making munitions of war, the process was no doubt remunerative at that time, but it remains to be seen whether in normal circumstances alcohol so produced will be able to hold its own against that from molasses and other sources.

According to Mr. C. F. Cross, the difficulties have been so far overcome as to allow of alcohol being produced on the large scale at a very low cost. Under the most favourable conditions, however, the yield of alcohol actually obtained represents only about 8 per cent. of the cellulose content of the wood.[1] Larger yields, however, are possible ; and wood waste must be considered a very important raw material for the potential production of alcohol in well-timbered countries. The manufacture is described in greater detail further on (p. 90).

Considerable quantities of alcohol are now being made from the waste liquor produced in the manufacture of wood pulp by the "sulphite" process. This waste liquor contains from 1½ to 2 per cent. of fermentable sugars, arising from the action of sulphites on the wood ; and alcohol is produced from these sugars by neutralising the liquor, fermenting, and distilling it. In Norway, two plants are now (1918) in operation for this purpose, whilst in Sweden four are working, and three more are being erected. About one million gallons of alcohol *per annum* are being turned out by the four Swedish instalments. In Germany thirteen factories have been built for the same purpose, and probably are now in actual working. There are also two plants in the United States, and one in Switzerland.[2] To develop the manufacture of this "sulphite spirit" in Sweden, it has been proposed officially that the production and sale of denatured alcohol for the propulsion of motors and for other technical purposes shall be reserved as far as practicable to the sulphite spirit factories. Further, these establishments are to have the exclusive right of denaturing their alcohol with benzol.

Alcohol from wood usually contains an appreciable quantity of methyl alcohol, and in this country such a product could only be used for making methylated spirit or other variety of denatured alcohol, not for making beverages.

Peat has been advocated as a possible source of cheap alcohol

[1] *J. Soc. Chem. Ind.*, 1917, **36**, 532.
[2] B. Johnsen, *ibid.*, 1918, **37**, 131.

in the United Kingdom.[1] So far, however, this material has not been used commercially for the purpose.

(*d*) **Synthetic alcohol from calcium carbide or acetylene.**—It has now become commercially practicable to prepare alcohol synthetically, as well as by the fermentation methods. The raw material employed is the hydrocarbon gas acetylene, C_2H_2—or rather calcium carbide, which readily yields acetylene on treatment with water.

Acetylene can be converted into ethylene, C_2H_4, or into aldehyde C_2H_4O, either of which substances can furnish alcohol.

Calcium carbide, CaC_2, is obtained by heating a mixture of coke and lime in the electric furnace.

Another carbide is said to have been produced which yields ethylene directly, instead of acetylene, when treated with water. The particulars have not been disclosed.

II.—THE BIOCHEMICAL AGENTS: ENZYMES; MALT; YEAST.

Enzymes.

As already indicated (p. 17), enzymes play a very important part, both in the production of sugar from starch and in the conversion of sugar into alcohol. They are nitrogenous compounds, either albuminoids or very closely related to albuminoids in composition, which occur in all living organisms, whether animal or vegetable. Their function in the organism appears generally to be to attack insoluble materials intended for the sustenance of the animal or plant, converting them into more soluble and more diffusible substances, and thus making them more available for nutrition. *Ptyalin*, for example, the enzyme contained in saliva, and also *amylopsin*, present in the juice of the pancreas, both have the power of converting insoluble starch into soluble sugar. They thus resemble diastase in their action. The *pepsin* of the gastric juice, and the *trypsin* of the pancreas, each converts insoluble proteids into simpler proteoses and peptones, rendering them more fit for absorption; whilst *lipase*, which occurs in the pancreas and also in various seeds, splits up fats into glycerol and fatty acids. The *zymase* of yeast converts sugar into alcohol and carbon dioxide; the *maltase* of malt transforms the 12-carbon sugar maltose into the 6-carbon sugar dextrose.

Thus the enzymes can be classified into groups according to the kind of action which they exert. Chief among these groups for

[1] Motor Union Fuels Committee, *Report*, p. 50.

our present purpose are (i) the diastatic enzymes, which hydrolyse starch; (ii) the inverting enzymes, which transform cane-sugar into invert-sugar, or maltose into dextrose; (iii) the alcohol-producing enzymes, *e.g.*, zymase and its co-enzyme; and (iv) the proteolytic enzymes, which convert proteins into simpler bodies such as peptones and amino-acids.

Enzymes are soluble in water, and are coagulated by heat. From their aqueous solutions excess of alcohol separates them as amorphous, white precipitates, as also does ammonium sulphate. The precipitated enzymes are dissolved by glycerol, and these solutions can be preserved for a considerable time: the solutions in water soon decompose. When completely dry, the enzymes may be exposed to temperatures as high as 100 to 125° without destruction of all their characteristic properties; but in aqueous solution a temperature of 80 to 90° usually destroys their activities. They act at ordinary or slightly elevated temperatures; below 0° their activity is suspended, and it is lessened at about 60°, though they are not all equally sensitive to the effects of heat. There is a limited range of optimum temperature for every enzyme; thus diastase acts best at about 50–55°, and invertase at about 55°.

One notable fact about enzymes is that a very small quantity will suffice to transform a relatively enormous amount of the substance acted upon. Thus one part of invertase (sucrase), according to O'Sullivan and Tompson, can invert 200,000 parts of cane-sugar. In this respect, the enzymes resemble catalysts, and they are also similar in the fact that they are very sensitive to the presence of certain chemical substances, such as hydrocyanic acid, formaldehyde, and mercury salts, which render them inactive, much as catalysts are "poisoned" by minute quantities of certain bodies.

Another remarkable fact is that a given enzyme can only act upon a certain class of substances: it has its own specific action. Diastase hydrolyses starch, but not proteids; pepsin attacks proteids, but not starch. Neither of these will split up fats; whilst lipase, which does this, cannot break up either carbohydrates or proteids. Further, there are several examples of sugars, which exist in two optically isomeric forms, and of which one isomer is susceptible to the attack of an enzyme, while the other remains unaffected. Thus *d*-glucose is fermented by certain yeasts, but *l*-glucose is not. These facts suggest that there is a close resemblance in structure between an enzyme and the substance which it attacks. They have led to the hypothesis that the molecular configuration of the enzyme and that of the sugar it ferments are complementary, so that "the one may be said to fit the other as a key fits a lock" (E. Fischer), or "as male and female screw" (Pasteur). Nothing, however, is actually known of the molecular structure of the enzymes.

According to Adrian Brown,[1] the enzyme invertase in its action on cane-sugar combines with the sugar to form a molecular compound, which does not decompose instantaneously, but exists for a perceptible interval of time before final disruption. O'Sullivan and Tompson had previously shown that the activity of invertase in the presence of cane-sugar survives a temperature which completely destroys it if cane-sugar is not present, and they regarded this as indicating the existence of a combination of the enzyme and sugar molecules.[2] Wurtz[3] had also shown that the enzyme papain appears to form an insoluble compound with fibrin previous to the hydrolysis of the latter.

It may be noted that in modern enzyme terminology the ending "ase" is used to denote an enzyme, the first part of the name indicating the substance *attacked* by the enzyme. Thus the enzyme malt*ase* attacks the sugar malt*ose*; lact*ase* attacks lact*ose*; and so on. Hence the modern term for diastase is *amylase* (*amylum*, starch), and for invertase, *sucrase*, since this enzyme attacks sucrose. But the older terms are frequently used, especially the long-established ones, like diastase.

Diastase (amylase).—The principal diastatic enzyme is the amylase or diastase of malt—that is, of germinated barley. It was the first enzyme to be isolated. Persoz and Payen[4] effected the separation so far back as the year 1832, though the diastase obtained was only a very impure product.

Barley which has not germinated contains a different form of amylase ("barley diastase"), termed by Brown and Morris "translocation diastase," since its function appears to be the conversion of starch deposited in one part of the plant into sugar for transference to another part, where it is again deposited as starch. The ordinary malt amylase was termed "diastase of secretion," as it is chiefly formed during the germinating process by secretion from the scutellum of the embryo. (See under "Malt," p. 38).

Malt amylase quickly dissolves starch, converting it first into dextrins and then into maltose. It acts best at a temperature of about 50—55° (122—131° F.). At about 80° (176° F.) it becomes inactive, and begins to coagulate.

Enzymes of the amylase or diastase class, however, are by no

[1] *Trans. Chem. Soc.*, 1902, **81**, 388. [2] *Ibid.*, 1890, **57**, 865.
[3] *Compt. rend.*, 1880, **91**, 787. [4] *Ann. Chim. Phys.*, 1833, [ii], **53**, 73.

means confined to barley. They are found widely distributed through the vegetable kingdom, in foliage leaves and ungerminated seeds, particularly in the aleurone layers of the seed-coats. In some small Continental distilleries, for instance, alcohol is made from raw rye, without malt of any kind, whether barley-malt or other. The diastase present in the raw grain suffices to saccharify the starch during the mashing operation. Similarly, it has been found that the bran of wheat has a high diastatic power, sufficient to allow of bran being employed technically as a saccharifying agent of starchy materials in fermentation operations.[1]

Persoz and Payen obtained their diastase by heating a cold-water extract of malt to 70°, filtering from coagulated proteins, and precipitating the diastase by adding a large quantity of absolute alcohol to the filtrate. The diastase was then further purified by re-solution in water and re-precipitation with alcohol: after drying at 40—50°, it was obtained as a white, tasteless powder.

A much better preparation is obtained by Lintner's method. This consists in concentrating a strong water-extract of malt by freezing, and pressing out the extract from the ice through a filter-cloth; the injurious effects of heat upon the enzyme are thus avoided. The diastase is precipitated from the concentrated extract by addition of ammonium sulphate.

J. B. Osborne[2] has carried out an investigation in which the diastase was prepared by an elaborate method involving repeated dialysis, "salting out" with ammonium sulphate, and several precipitations by alcohol. The purest sample thus obtained had the following elementary composition:—

Ash	0·66	per cent.
Organic portion:		
Carbon	52·5	,,
Hydrogen	6·7	,,
Nitrogen	16·1	,,
Oxygen	22·8	,,
Sulphur	1·9	,,
	100·0	,,

This composition agrees closely with that of a protein body. Naturally, the exact composition depends upon the degree of purity reached in the diastase prepared; thus one of Lintner's preparations showed much less nitrogen and much more oxygen than the foregoing, namely, nitrogen 10·4 per cent., and oxygen 34·5 per cent. Osborne's purest diastase had a diastatic power of 600,

[1] U.S. P. 1178039; see *J. Inst. Brewing*, 1918, **24**, 26.
[2] *J. Amer. Chem. Soc.*, 1895, **17**, 587–603.

expressed in terms of Lintner's scale, or six times that of the most active preparation obtained by Lintner himself.

Purified malt amylase (diastase) with a much higher diastatic power than Osborne's has, however, been obtained by Sherman and Schlesinger,[1] working as follows.

Ground malt was extracted with two and a half times its weight of cold water, dilute alcohol, or a very dilute solution of sodium monophosphate, for one and a half to two hours at a temperature of about 10°. The extract was then decanted or filtered, and dialysed in collodion bags against ten times its volume of cold water (temperature 7–15°) for 25 to 42 hours, with two or three changes of the dialysate ; next it was filtered, and an equal volume of alcohol or acetone added. The precipitate produced was discarded, and further alcohol or acetone added in quantity sufficient to bring the final concentration up to 65 or 70 per cent. The precipitate thus obtained was separated and dried in a partial vacuum over sulphuric acid at about 10°. So far as practicable, this temperature was maintained throughout the operations, and in any case the temperature was not allowed to rise above 20°.

Of a number of specimens thus prepared, 13 had diastatic powers equivalent to 1200–1800 on Lintner's scale, and seven gave values corresponding with 1800–2300. Even these values, though the highest yet recorded for malt amylase, were lower than those obtained by the authors with pancreatic amylase. The product (from malt) was a yellowish-white substance giving the typical protein reactions, and under the ultramicroscope it had the appearance of a colloid. It coagulated when heated in aqueous solution ; the coagulum gave a violet-blue, and the solution a rose-red, biuret reaction. The most active specimen contained about 14 per cent. of nitrogen.

Diastase when quite dry can withstand a temperature of 150°, becoming inactive at about 158°.

Solutions of amylase for keeping are best prepared, according to Chrzaszcz and Joscht[2] by extracting malt, not with the usual solvents (water, alcohol, acetone, chloroform), but with aqueous glycerin, aqueous pyridine (3–6 per cent.) or quinoline water The glycerin is preferably used at a concentration of about 50 per cent., but any strength between 20 and 90 per cent. can be employed.

Extracts prepared with these media, and containing 5 to 8 per cent. of diastase, have been tested as regards their starch-liquefying power, saccharifying power, and dextrin-forming power. The results show that there is no definite relation between the liquefying

[1] *J. Amer. Chem. Soc.*, 1913, **35**, 1617–1623. [2] *Biochem. Zeitsch.*, 1917, **80**, 211.

power of amylase and its saccharifying power; this suggests that these two functions may be due to different enzymes. The dextrin-forming power varies mainly in accordance with change of liquefying power, but the results are not conclusive as to the relationship between the two functions.

Cytase (cellulase) is another enzyme found in germinating barley. It attacks the cellulose walls of the cells which enclose the starch, softening or dissolving them, and thus allowing the diastase to obtain access to the starch and exert its solvent action upon the latter.

Sucrase (invertase) is an enzyme present in yeast, and also in malt. It hydrolyses cane-sugar, converting it into "invert-sugar," a mixture of dextrose and lævulose. The optimum temperature for this action is 55–60°, and the enzyme is rendered inactive at 75°. It can be obtained from yeast by drying the latter at 105° and extracting it with cold water, the solution being then precipitated by adding an excess of alcohol. The dried enzyme may be heated for some time at 140–150° without destroying its properties.

Maltase is another enzyme which occurs in malt, and also in many yeasts. Croft Hill obtained it from ordinary brewery yeast by extracting the dried material with a dilute solution of sodium hydroxide and toluene.[1] It attacks maltose, transforming it into the simpler sugar dextrose, the optimum temperature for this effect being 40°. At about 50–55°, it is rendered inactive. Maltase is not very soluble in water. It exerts its maximum activity in faintly acid solutions, but is very sensitive towards alkalinity or excess of acid.

Zymase is the enzyme, secreted in the yeast-cells, which directly produces alcohol from dextrose and from lævulose. It will be seen that from the point of view of alcohol production the action of all the foregoing enzymes—cytase, diastase, maltase, and sucrase—is, as it were, a preparatory action, bringing the material into a form in which it can be attacked by the zymase. Cytase facilitates the action of diastase upon starch up to a certain point; diastase transforms starch into maltose, and maltase converts this into dextrose; sucrase changes cane-sugar into dextrose and lævulose; and it is the two final products, dextrose and lævulose, which are attacked by zymase and converted into alcohol. Zymase does not itself transform either starch or cane-sugar directly.

The enzyme is contained in the liquid contents of the yeast-cells, but it cannot pass through the cell wall, and hence can only be

[1] *Trans. Chem. Soc.*, 1898, **73**, 634.

obtained by rupturing the cells. A method of doing this was published by E. Buchner in 1897,[1] and it marks a great step forward in our knowledge of the fermentation processes. In separating the cell-sap or "yeast juice," fresh brewing-yeast, freed from adherent water by pressure, was ground up with quartz sand and kieselguhr in order to rupture the cells. The resulting plastic mass was then mixed with water and squeezed through cloth in a hydraulic press, at a pressure of 400 to 500 atmospheres. The juice thus expressed was a slightly opalescent, yellow liquid, which when mixed with solutions of dextrose, grape-sugar, cane-sugar, or maltose rapidly fermented them, although no organism visible under a high magnifying power was present, nor could such be detected even when the solutions had been fermenting for some days. Furthermore, the fermenting power was still retained after the juice had been filtered through a Berkefeld filter, which would retain any organisms of the size of yeast-cells; and also after being dialysed through parchment-paper. Thus the fermentation was not due directly to the action of yeast-cells. Moreover, the yeast juice could induce the fermentation even when powerful protoplasmic poisons such as chloroform and sodium arsenite were present, so that it was not a case of the fermentative activity being due to particles of living protoplasm. In fact, the fermentative power was shown to be due, not directly to any vital process, but to a chemical or enzyme action of some constituent of the yeast juice, and this enzyme Buchner termed "zymase."

Harden and Young subsequently found that by submitting yeast juice to filtration through a Chamberland filter coated with a film of gelatin a residue was left upon the filter. But—a very remarkable fact—neither this residue by itself, nor the filtrate by itself, was capable of setting up alcoholic fermentation. When, however, the two portions were reunited, the mixture produced almost as active a fermentation as the original juice.[2] The active constituent of the filtrate is designated the "co-enzyme"; the enzyme is contained in the colloidal residue left on the filter. There is evidence in favour of the view that the co-enzyme is probably acetaldehyde, though at present this cannot be stated with certainty.[3]

Zymase, or at least a solid preparation containing active zymase, may be obtained as an amorphous powder by precipitating yeast juice with alcohol, or with a mixture of alcohol and ether, or with acetone. One volume of juice, for example, is poured into ten

[1] *Ber.*, 1897, **30**, 117; also vols. **31**, **32**, and **33**.
[2] A. Harden, "Alcoholic Fermentation," Chap. IV.
[3] Harden, *Biochem. J.*, 1917, **11**, 64.

volumes of acetone, the mixture rapidly centrifuged, and the liquid decanted; the precipitate is washed with acetone and with ether, and then dried over sulphuric acid. The resulting amorphous, white powder does not dissolve completely in water, but is nearly all soluble in a mixture of water and glycerol containing from 2·5 to 20 per cent. of the latter: the solution thus obtained is practically as active as the original juice in effecting alcoholic fermentation.

Zymase appears capable of withstanding a temperature of 100° for six hours at least, since dried yeast which has been thus treated, and so deprived of the power of growth and reproduction, is still able to ferment sugar and to furnish an active juice.

Endotryptase is a proteolytic enzyme which occurs in yeast. Like zymase, it is formed within the cells, and cannot be extracted until the cell is ruptured; it is therefore found in yeast juice. It converts yeast albumin into simpler products—tyrosin, leucin, etc.—and is of interest because it is believed to have a digestive action upon the zymase of the fresh juice. This would explain the otherwise puzzling fact that the juice quickly loses its fermentative power—in the course of a day or more, according to the temperature at which it is kept.

Hexosephosphatase is the term applied by Harden to a hydrolytic enzyme which is considered to be present in yeast. Its *rôle* in fermentation is to decompose hexosephosphate into the hexose sugar and free phosphate.[1]

Lactase, an enzyme which hydrolyses milk-sugar, occurs in kephir ferment and in a few culture yeasts, but not in ordinary yeast, which therefore is unable to ferment milk-sugar. It converts lactose into *d*-glucose and *d*-galactose.

Reductase.—Yeast possesses marked reducing power towards certain substances—*e.g.*, methylene-blue and sodium selenite—and it is considered that this property is due to an enzyme which has been termed "reductase." It seems probable from recent work that this substance plays an important part in the phenomenon of alcoholic fermentation.[2]

Carboxylase.—This is the name applied to an enzyme, present in yeast, which has the property of fermenting pyruvic acid.[3] The latter substance is an intermediate compound formed during the alcoholic fermentation of sugar.

The **proteolytic enzymes** of malt are of considerable

[1] "Alcoholic Fermentation," 1911, p. 49.
[2] Harden and Norris, *Biochem. J.*, 1914, **8**, 100.
[3] C. Neuberg, *Biochem. Zeitsch.*, 1915, **71**, 1.

importance, inasmuch as they break down the complex proteins of the grain into simpler products, namely, albumoses, peptones, and amides, thus rendering them soluble and diffusible, and making them available as nutrients of the yeast during the subsequent fermentation process. There appear to be two of these enzymes in malt, one a **peptase,** which converts the albumins into albumoses; the other a **tryptase,** which effects a more complete transformation into amides and amino-bodies such as asparagine. The former acts rapidly, and has its optimum temperature at 51°; the tryptase action is slower, and the most favourable temperature is a little lower—namely, between 45° and 50°. Both act best in a slightly acid medium; alkalis retard their action.

Three proteolytic enzymes have also been found in yeast.[1] They are analogous to, but differ in some particulars from, proteolytic enzymes of the animal organism. They comprise (i), a yeast *pepsin,* which can degrade proteins to peptones, but not further; (ii), a yeast *tryptase,* which does not act on the proteins of yeast itself, but can degrade certain proteins, such as acid albumins, gelatin, and caseinogen, into peptides and amino-acids; and (iii), a yeast **ereptase,** which readily degrades peptones and polypeptides into amino-acids.

The only other sucroclastic enzyme that need be mentioned here is **melibiase,** which is contained in "bottom" yeasts, but not in yeasts used for "top" fermentation. It inverts the sugar melibiose, itself a product of the partial hydrolysis of raffinose, found in sugar-beets and also in barley. Hence the bottom yeasts can ferment raffinose completely, whereas the top fermentation yeasts cannot do so.

"Phosphatese."—Before leaving the subject of enzyme action we may note that in some cases this action has been shown to be reversible, effecting a synthesis or condensation instead of a hydrolytic decomposition. Thus by acting upon dextrose with maltase, Croft Hill[2] obtained evidence of the production of maltose (or isomaltose; Emmerling[3]). Lipase, which decomposes fats (esters of glycerol), can synthesise the ester ethyl butyrate from ethyl alcohol and butyric acid; and other instances of reverse action are known.

Of these may be mentioned that of the enzyme "phosphatese," which can be separated from the zymase complex. It synthesises the hexosephosphate of yeast.[4]

[1] K. G. Dernby, *Biochem. Zeitsch.*, 1917, **81**, 109.
[2] *Trans. Chem. Soc.*, 1898, **73**, 634. [3] *Ber.*, 1901, **34**, 600.
[4] Euler, Ohlsen, & Johanssohn, *Biochem. Zeitsch.*, 1917, **84**, 402.

Malt.

Malt is grain, usually barley, in which germination has been artificially induced, allowed to proceed as far as may be desired, and then stopped by a moderate drying of the grain at the ordinary temperature (" green malt "), followed in general by a slow application of heat (kilned malt). Maize, oats, rye, and wheat are also malted, but are generally used in conjunction with more or less barley malt.

The effect of malting is to develop the enzymes of the barley grain ; to modify the texture of the grain by converting the hard, tough corn into a friable, mealy one ; and in the case of kilned malt, to produce a pleasant aromatic or biscuity flavour together with a certain amount of amber or brown colour. To the brewer of beer the flavour and colour of the malt are of importance, but they are of no particular consequence to the distiller of alcohol.

When barley planted in the earth germinates naturally, the process is started by absorption of moisture from the soil. In a similar manner, the maltster sets up artificial germination of the grain by moistening it and exposing it to suitable conditions of temperature and aeration. We are here concerned chiefly with the biological changes which take place in the grain during this germination—that is, during the growth of the embryo or rudimentary plantlet contained in the barley corn. Before discussing these changes, however, it is desirable to give a short account of the manufacturing operations through which the barley passes in the course of being converted into malt.

Malting.—The screened barley is first steeped in water for a period which varies from two to four days, according to the nature of the barley and the temperature of the water. During this steeping it absorbs about one-half of its weight of water, and the grains become softened. Generally the water is drained off and replaced two or three times during the steeping, and for distillery malts it is a common practice to add calcium bisulphite or other antiseptic to prevent the development of harmful micro-organisms. For brewery malts there is less necessity to use antiseptics, because, apart from any effect which the subsequent kilning may have upon moulds and bacteria, these organisms are destroyed later on, when the wort is boiled and hopped ; whereas neither boiling nor hopping is required by distillers' worts.

The steeped barley is next "couched," that is, spread out in a frame, or in a levelled heap a foot or more in depth upon the malt-house floor. Here it begins to germinate. It absorbs oxygen and gives off carbon dioxide; the temperature commences to rise; and the surface of the corns shows an exudation of moisture ("sweating"). The grain is turned over now and then to aerate it and to equalise the temperature; and presently, as the growth of the embryo proceeds, a small, white rootlet appears at the end of the corn ("chitting"). When the temperature reaches 15° to 17° the couch or heap is broken down and spread into a thinner layer, varying in depth according to the season of the year ("flooring"). Whilst the grain continues to germinate it is well turned over two or three times a day; and when the growth has proceeded far enough the heap is spread more thinly, to allow of the grain gradually drying or "withering." Should the drying be too rapid, sprinkling with water is resorted to as a corrective. The necessity for this is shown by the rootlets becoming flaccid before sufficient growth has been obtained; and the amount of growth is judged by the distance to which the "acrospire" or "plumule"—the leaflet part of the young plant—has pushed its way under the husk from the base towards the apex of the corn. The temperature is not allowed to rise above 15·5°.

When the process of withering is complete, the product, now known as "green" malt, is removed to the drying-kiln, unless it is to be used in the green state. Here it is gradually dried more completely, first at a low temperature (27 to 38°), and exposed to a current of air. The temperature is then slowly raised until the required degree is reached at which the malt is to be finished: this may vary from about 60° to 88° or even 110°, according to the kind of kiln used and the variety of malt required. This operation of kiln-drying usually occupies three or four days.

The length of time during which germination is allowed to proceed depends upon the purpose for which the malt is required. Malts intended for brewing are left on the "floor" for about seven to ten days ("short" malt). Malts for distillery and vinegar-making purposes are allowed to germinate much longer—about twenty days—in order to produce more diastase ("long" malt).

In **"pneumatic"** malting, the essential feature is a systematic aeration of the malt during the germinating stage by means of a current of air which, passing through a spray of water, warm or cold as desired, can be regulated as regards its moisture and temperature. The steeped grain is contained in revolving cylinders through which the air-current is led: this does away with the necessity for hand-labour in "turning" the grain, and saves much floor-space. The plentiful supply of fresh air, itself more or less purified by the washing it has received, keeps the malt free from moulds.

A. R. Ling[1] has shown that when green malt is kept for some hours at a stage where it still contains from 10 to 15 per cent. of moisture, combination occurs between the amino-compounds and the carbohydrates containing free carbonyl groups; and when the products are heated in the final stages of kilning they are decomposed, giving rise to colouring and flavouring matters.

Changes which occur during germination.—We owe to Brown and Morris the first satisfactory exposition of the principal chemical and morphological changes which go on in the barley grain during the early stages of germination. These investigators studied chiefly the carbohydrate constituents of the grain, and the manner in which these were transformed, rendered assimilable by the growing plantlet, and transferred from one part of the corn to another in subserving the plantlet's needs.[2] Later, Brown and Escombe further elaborated these studies;[3] and still later, with other coadjutors (McMullen and Millar) extended them to the investigation of the transformation and migration of the protein constituents of the grain.[4] These researches are well worth reading in the original accounts by those interested; all that can be done here is to give a short summary of the chief results, in so far as they are germane to present purposes.

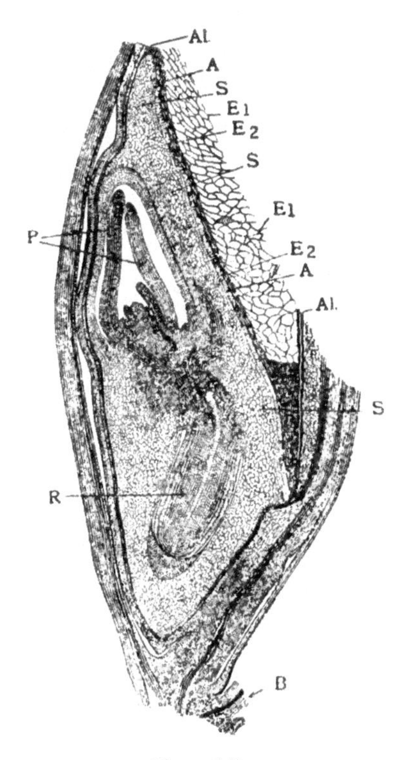

FIG. 15.

Median section through proximal end of a grain of barley, showing embryo and a little of the endosperm. (Reproduced by permission from *Trans. Chem. Soc.*, 1890, **57**.)

P, plumule (acrospire) of embryo.
R, radicle " "
S, scutellum.
A, secretory epithelium.
Al, aleurone cells of endosperm.
E_1, starch " " "
E_2, depleted " " "
B, basal bristle of grain.

The main bulk of the barley

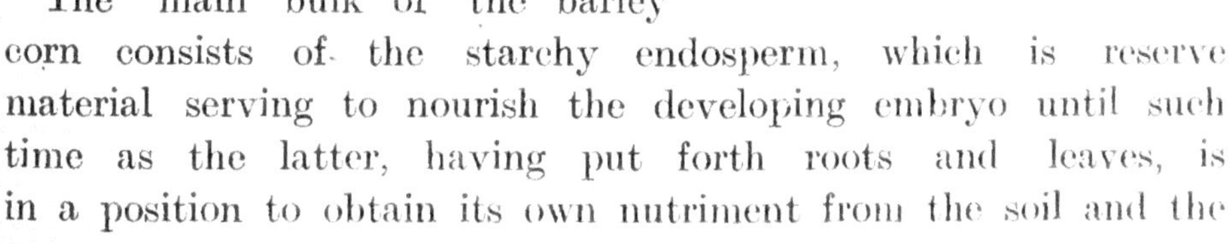
corn consists of the starchy endosperm, which is reserve material serving to nourish the developing embryo until such time as the latter, having put forth roots and leaves, is in a position to obtain its own nutriment from the soil and the

[1] *J. Soc. Chem. Ind.*, 1908, **27**, 1033.

[2] "Researches on the Germination of some of the Gramineæ," *Trans. Chem. Soc.*, 1890, **57**, 458 *et seq.*

[3] *Proc. Roy. Soc.*, 1898.

[4] *Trans. Guinness Research Laboratory*, 1906; pt. ii, 284.

air. The embryo itself is situated at one end of the corn. It is not structurally connected with the endosperm, but only in close apposition to it, kept in place by the integument which surrounds both. But the endosperm is a hard, compact mass; the starch granules are packed tightly in the endosperm cells; and these cells themselves are invested with a cellulose membrane, forming the cell-walls. The question is, exactly how, and in what form, does the hard starchy mass reach the developing germ? What are the changes which are invoked in it, to allow of its being transported from one part of the corn to another, and to arrive in such a condition that it can be absorbed and assimilated by the young plantlet? These are the questions to which the investigators above-mentioned, with others, have in large measure supplied the answer.

The part of the embryo which is in contact with the starchy endosperm is a sort of partition-wall; a cellular structure known as the *scutellum*, which bears on its surface a remarkable *epithelium* containing a layer of elongated (columnar) cells, termed the *secretory layer*. Also, surrounding the endosperm and in contact with the starch cells, there is a layer of tissue consisting of square cells, and known as the *aleurone layer*. When moisture is absorbed by the grain and germination commences, one of the early changes is the secretion, in part by the scutellar epithelium and in part by the aleurone layer, of an enzyme, *cytase*, which is capable of attacking the cellulose walls of the starch cells and either destroying them completely, or at least partly dissolving them and rendering them softer and more permeable to liquids. This enzyme gradually invades the whole of the endosperm, disintegrating the cell-walls, and thus producing what, in malting, is technically termed the "modification" of the endosperm, by which the corn is rendered mealy and friable.

The scutellar epithelium, moreover, secretes a yet more important enzyme, namely, *amylase* (diastase). Brown and Morris were able to demonstrate this experimentally by removing the embryo entirely from the barley corn, and cultivating it on gelatin impregnated with starch, and on other nutrient media. One or two typical experiments out of a large number made may be quoted here.

First, it was shown that diastase is secreted by the *growing* embryo. Fifty embryos were removed from barley corns and germinated on moistened glass wool. After growing for a time, the embryos were macerated in a suitable volume of water, and a definite quantity of the liquid was allowed to act upon a solution of soluble starch. If diastase were present it would convert some of the starch to maltose, and a measure of the amount could be obtained by weighing the copper oxide precipitated when the liquid was heated with an alkaline copper sulphate solution. The total diastatic power of these fifty embryos was thus found to be represented by 148 milligrams of cupric oxide, and of another fifty germinated on gelatin, 163 milligrams ; whereas the diastatic power of a similar number of *ungerminated* embryos was found to be *nil* or very small, only 5 milligrams of cupric oxide being obtained, and this quantity was possibly within the limits of error under the conditions of the experiment. Diastase had therefore been produced in relatively large quantity in the embryos during their germination.

Also it was shown that the power of secreting the diastase was localised in the scutellar epithelium. For on removing the latter, and cultivating the embryo on starch-gelatin, it was found to have lost its power of dissolving the starch granules. This was not due to the embryo having also lost its power of growth, because the embryo, deprived of its epithelium as before, still grew readily when *sugar*, instead of starch, was included in the culture-medium. The ground-tissue of the scutellum could absorb the soluble and readily-assimilable sugar ; but in the absence of the epithelium no diastase was produced, and consequently the insoluble starch could not be attacked and dissolved.

Diastase, therefore, is elaborated by the scutellar epithelium during the growth of the embryo. It attacks the starch of the endosperm, and renders it soluble, so that the products can now diffuse through the water present and reach the embryo, there to serve as aliment for the young plant. The attacking of the starch has been facilitated, and indeed made possible, by the previous softening action of the cytase on the starch cell-walls, as the latter in their normal state are not permeable to the diastase.[1]

By experiments on somewhat similar lines to those described, it has further been shown that during germination there is also a transference of a part of the *nitrogenous* constituents of the barley grain from the endosperm to the embryo. Thus in barley which had been on the malting-floor for nine days, about one-third of the tc al endosperm nitrogen was found to have migrated to the embr[illegible] . There is, in fact, a development of *proteolytic enzymes* (pept[illegible] and tryptase) during germination, and these convert a prop[illegible]on of the insoluble proteins of the grain into simpler subs[illegible]s, such as proteoses, peptones, and amino-acids. These

[1] S[illegible]so Mann and Harlan on the "Morphology of the Barley Grain," *U.S.* [illegible] *Agr. Bull.*, No. 183 (1915). A reprint of this is given in *J. Inst. Brew*[illegible] 16, **22**, 73.

proteolytic enzymes, there is good reason to believe, are, like the diastase and cytase, secreted by the scutellar epithelium.

The simpler products into which the protein is converted are soluble in water, and hence in malt there is a larger proportion of soluble nitrogenous bodies than in the original barley; in fact nearly double as much. Thus Bungener and Fries found the "soluble" nitrogen in a specimen of barley to be 0·355 per cent., and in the malt made from it, 0·642 per cent. The total amounts of nitrogen in the barley and malt were 1·69 and 1·58 per cent. respectively. The importance of the production of soluble nitrogenous compounds during malting lies in the fact that they pass into the wort when the malt is mashed, and serve as nitrogenous nutriment for the yeast during the subsequent fermentation.

Summing up, then, we find that during the germination of barley, enzymes of three classes are secreted by the embryo: (1) a cellulose-dissolving enzyme *cytase*, which attacks the walls of the starch cells and makes them permeable to diastase; (2) a diastatic enzyme, *malt-amylase* or *diastase*, which can convert starch into sugars and other soluble matters; and (3) proteolytic enzymes, *peptase* and *tryptase*, which convert a portion of the insoluble proteins of the grain into simpler, soluble nitrogenous substances. By these means the whole solid contents of the endosperm can be broken down and utilised by the young plant.

"The art of the maltster," Dr. H. T. Brown remarks, "consists in directing, co-ordinating, and limiting these natural physiological processes of interaction between the embryo and endosperm, and making them as far as possible subservient to a particular end"—namely, the production of a friable malt, which will yield the maximal amount of extract of the right composition for the special purpose in view.

This purpose is not the same for the distiller as for the brewer. It has already been seen that the former uses "long" malt, which has been germinated for a more extended period than the brewer's "short" malt, and has therefore produced more diastase. The aim of the distiller is to produce alcohol; that of the brewe is to make a beverage which contains as essential ingredients nc only alcohol but other substances derived from starch, namely d trins and malto-dextrins. These impart "body" and palate-ful ss to the beer, and provide material for the secondary ferm tion which it undergoes in the cask. In fact the flavour and c cter of beer depend quite as much on the presence of unf nted dextrins and other extractive matters as they do on the f nted alcohol which the beverage contains. Hence the brewer not want completely to convert all the starch of his grain into sugar: his wort must not be wholly fermentable. The brewer's malt is therefore not germinated to produce the maximum of diastase, and moreover it is heated on the kiln to a temperature which destroys much of the diastase that has been formed. On the other hand, the distiller wishes to convert the whole of his starchy material into alcohol; any not so converted is mere loss. He looks upon his malt as, essentially, a source of diastase, used for the purpose of transforming the starch of raw cereals or of potatoes as completely as possible into fermentable sugars.

Hence distillery malts are usually germinated long enough to produce the maximum amount of diastase, and are preferably used as "green" malts, or, if kilned at all, only at the lowest practicable temperature. The higher the temperature used in drying the malt, the greater is the loss of diastatic power. This is especially so if the heat is applied too quickly, while the malt still contains much moisture; because diastase when moist is very sensitive to the action of heat. Green malt, however, can only be employed to a limited extent for making malt whisky, since the special flavour of this is due mainly to the use of kilned malt. In distilleries which make compressed yeast, too, a proportion of kilned malt is employed.

Ordinarily, the diastatic power of green malt is from 110° to 125° (Lintner's scale). In brewery malts it is reduced by the kilning process to less than one-fourth of this amount, ranging generally from 20° to 40°. Distillery malts, and also malts used by vinegar-makers, have usually a diastatic power of 80° upwards.

Diastatic power of malt ("Lintner value").—This is determined in a conventional manner by allowing an extract of the malt, prepared under standard conditions, to act upon a 2 per cent. solution of soluble starch for an hour at 21·1° (70° F.). The quantity of starch converted is then estimated from the volume of the converted liquid required to reduce a given volume (5 c.c.) of Fehling's solution. So long as the maltose produced does not exceed 45 per cent. of the starch used, this maltose may be taken as a measure of the diastatic activity of the extract (Kjeldahl). The *modus operandi* recommended by the Malt Analysis Committee of the Institute of Brewing is as follows.[1]

Twenty-five grams of ground malt are extracted with 500 c.c. of pure distilled water for three hours at 21·1°, and filtered. The first 100 c.c. of the filtrate are rejected. Of the perfectly bright

[1] *J. Inst. Brewing*, 1906, **12**, 6.

residual filtrate, 3 c.c. are allowed to act on 100 c.c. of a 2 per cent. solution of soluble starch at 21·1° for an hour in a 200 c.c. flask.

Decinormal alkali (10 c.c.) is then added in order to stop further diastatic action, the liquid cooled at 15·5°, made up to 200 c.c. with distilled water at the same temperature, well shaken, and titrated against 5 c.c. portions of Fehling's solution, ferrous thiocyanate solution being used as indicator.

The method of titration (Ling) is carried out in the following manner :—

Five c.c. of Fehling's solution (34·64 grams of crystallised copper sulphate, 70 grams of sodium hydroxide, and 175 grams of sodium potassium tartrate, per litre) are accurately measured into a 150 c.c. boiling flask, and raised to boiling over a small naked Bunsen flame. The converted starch solution is added from a burette, at first in small quantities of about 5 c.c., the mixture being kept rotated and boiled after each addition until reduction of the copper salt is complete, which is ascertained by rapidly withdrawing a drop of the liquid with a glass rod and bringing it at once in contact with a drop of the indicator on a porcelain or opal glass slab. Then if x denotes the number of c.c. of the converted solution required to reduce the 5 c.c. of Fehling's liquid, and y the number of c.c. of malt extract contained in 100 c.c. of the same converted solution (200 c.c.),

$$\text{Diastatic power} = \frac{1000}{xy}.$$

A gravimetric method of determining diastatic activity has been proposed by Sherman, Kendall, and Clark,[1] which they state is capable of greater accuracy than Lintner's method.

Soluble starch can be prepared by various methods. Lintner obtained it by allowing potato starch to remain in contact with 7·5 per cent. hydrochloric acid for seven or eight days. Brown and Morris, using 12 per cent. acid, obtained a similar product in twenty-four hours. Starch thus treated, and washed free from acid, dissolves in hot water without forming a viscid paste. To prepare it by Lintner's method for the foregoing determination, purified potato starch is mixed with about twice its weight of hydrochloric acid, sp. gr. 1·037, at the ordinary temperature (15–18°), and allowed to act for seven days, stirring up every day. The acid is then poured off, the starch washed very thoroughly by decantation with water until free from acid, filtered on a Buchner filter, and drained as dry as practicable at the filter pump ; then

[1] *J. Amer. Chem. Soc.*, 1910, **32**, 1082

spread on a new porous plate, and dried as quickly as possible at a temperature of about 43°. The starch is then triturated in a porcelain mortar and rubbed through a fine hair sieve. It is dissolved in boiling water in the proportion of 2 grams per 100 c.c., and cooled to 21·1° for use in the experiment as above described. The solution should not be gelatinous, should be neutral to litmus, and should show only a negligible reduction of Fehling's solution.

If the malt is found to have a diastatic power exceeding 50, less than 3 c.c. of the malt extract must be taken, and the experiment repeated.

Alternatively, the "Lintner value" of malt is often determined by a comparative series of test-tube experiments carried out as follows. Eight or ten clean test-tubes, of about 2 cm. internal diameter, are arranged in a stand suitable for placing in a water-bath. In each of the tubes 10 c.c. of the 2 per cent. solution of soluble starch are placed, and the temperature brought to 21·1° by immersing the stand in a bath kept at this temperature. Quantities of 0·1, 0·2, 0·3 . . . c.c. of the malt extract, prepared as already described, are run into the tubes, so that each tube receives 0·1 c.c. more than the preceding one. The time is noted, the contents of each tube well mixed, and all are kept in the bath at 21·1° for exactly an hour. At the end of this period 5 c.c. of Fehling's solution are mixed with the contents of each tube. The whole are then heated in a boiling water-bath for ten minutes, and allowed to settle. In the series of tubes there will usually be found some in which the sugar produced has been insufficient to reduce the whole of the Fehling's reagent, so that the supernatant liquid is blue; and also others in which the reduction is complete, and the liquid is colourless or yellow. In particular, two neighbouring tubes will be found, one showing under-reduction and the other exact reduction or over-reduction, from which the quantity, x, of malt extract just necessary for the reduction can be judged. Then, taking the diastatic power of 0·1 c.c. of malt extract (1 to 20) as 100, the diastatic power of the sample is given by $\frac{0{\cdot}1 \times 100}{x}$.

From this value 1·5 is deducted on account of reducing sugars in the extract.

An "iodine method" of determining diastatic power is described by Sherman, Kendall, and Clark.[1]

A standard starch paste is prepared by suspending a quantity of air-dry potato starch, equivalent to 10 grams of anhydrous starch, in 100 c.c. of cold water; this suspension is added to a

[1] *J. Amer. Chem. Soc.*, 1910, **32**, 1073.

quantity of water, sufficient to make up the total volume to 1 litre, which has meanwhile been heated nearly to boiling under a reflux condenser; then the whole is boiled for two hours under the condenser, and allowed to cool.

Portions of 250 grams of this standard paste (= 2·5 grams of anhydrous starch) are placed in flasks of 350–400 c.c. capacity immersed in a water-bath kept at 40°, and the desired amount of the enzyme preparation introduced together with 20 c.c. of water. The contents of the flask are well mixed, and digestion is continued at 40° until 0·25 c.c. of the mixture yields no coloration with 5 c.c. of a standard dilute iodine solution. Tests are made with varying amounts of the enzyme solution until that amount is found which completes the conversion in 30 minutes (± 1 minute).

The diastatic power is expressed as the weight of starch (2·5 grams) divided by the weight of enzyme preparation required to digest it under the prescribed conditions.

The iodine solution is prepared by dissolving 2 grams of iodine and 4 grams of potassium iodide in 250 c.c. of water, and diluting 2 c.c. of this solution to 1 litre.

The values obtained are, very roughly, about three times the values given by Lintner's method.

Extract value.—The procedure recommended by the Malt Analysis Committee mentioned above is as follows:[1]

Fifty grams of the ground malt are mashed in a beaker of about 500 c.c. capacity with 360 c.c. of distilled water previously heated to 67·8–68·3° (154–155° F.). The beaker is covered with a clock-glass, and placed in a water-bath, so that its contents are kept at a temperature of 65·5° (150° F.) for fifty-five minutes. The mash is stirred at intervals of about ten minutes during this time. The temperature is then raised to 68·3° during five minutes, and the whole mash washed into a flask graduated at 515 c.c. (The extra 15 c.c. is to compensate for the volume of the "grains.") After being cooled to 15·5°, the contents are made up to the mark with distilled water at the same temperature, well shaken, and filtered through a large ribbed paper. The specific gravity of the filtrate is then determined at once, at 15·5° compared with water at that temperature.

If preferred, the mashing can be carried out directly in the 515 c.c. flask. In this case, the mash should be shaken at intervals of about ten minutes.

The excess of the specific gravity over that of water (taken as

[1] *J. Inst. Brewing*, 1906, **12**, 5.

1000), multiplied by 3·36, gives the extract value in brewers' lb. per standard quarter of malt.

Determination of starch, etc., in distillery materials.—Three grams of the ground grain are heated in a pressure bottle with 30 c.c. of water and 25 c.c. of a 1 per cent. lactic acid solution for two hours at 135°. The liquid is now cooled to 70–80°, and shaken up with 50 c.c. of hot water; then cooled to the ordinary temperature and made up to 250 c.c. The flask is shaken well several times during the course of half an hour, and then the liquid is filtered. To 200 c.c. of the filtrate 15 c.c. of hydrochloric acid (sp. gr. 1·125) are added, and the mixture heated for two hours in a boiling water-bath under a reflux condenser. After cooling the solution, it is nearly neutralised, and made up to 500 c.c. The dextrose in 25 c.c. of this is estimated gravimetrically with Fehling's copper solution, and the result multiplied by 0·9 gives the corresponding quantity of starch and other fermentable material (Reinke).

YEAST

The yeast-plant is a unicellular vegetable organism without chlorophyll, belonging to the genus *Saccharomyces* (Reess). Since they contain no chlorophyll, the yeasts, like other fungi, cannot obtain their carbon by decomposing carbon dioxide. On the contrary, they elaborate this gas and evolve it, absorbing oxygen at the same time.

Ordinary brewer's yeast seen under the microscope is found to consist of spherical or ovoid cells, either free or united in simple or branching rows. These rows are produced by the budding-off of daughter-cells from a single parent cell; and as this is the chief method of reproduction, the yeasts are classed among the "budding fungi"; but they are capable also of reproduction by the formation of spores. The genus *Saccharomyces*, in fact, is restricted to organisms which can form spores.

For technical purposes, the yeasts may be divided into two groups, the "cultivated" yeasts and the "wild" yeasts. The first includes those which have been used from time out of mind in the operations of brewing. They belong to one species only, namely, *Saccharomyces cerevisiæ*. There are, however, many races and varieties of this species, differing quite notably in certain of their properties, such as the degree to which they can carry on fermentation, the rapidity with which they can bring that process about, and the flavour of the product obtained thereby. Of these "cultivated" yeasts there are two main types, one known as "top fermentation" yeast, the other as "bottom fermentation" yeast. These are so called because the former rises and collects on the surface of the fermenting liquid, whereas the latter falls to the bottom. "Top" yeast is the variety used in this country; whilst "bottom" yeast is employed on the Continent and elsewhere in the making of "lager" beer.

"Wild" yeasts are a numerous group. They occur wild in nature, and often on the surface of fruits—as, for instance, the wine yeasts which are present on the skins of grapes, and which set up fermentation of the "must" or grape-juice in the making of wine.[1] As these wild yeasts occur in the air, they may find their way into the brewery, where they may cause much inconvenience, since some of them are obnoxious. In the distillery, they are less a source of trouble than are bacteria and moulds, since the relatively high temperature at which fermentation is carried out is not favourable to the development of the wild yeasts.

Classification.—At one time the shape of the yeast-cells as seen under the microscope was taken as the basis of classification. Thus *S. cerevisiæ* included those yeasts of which the cells were approximately spherical, whilst those with elliptical cells were named *S. ellipsoideus*, and those the cells of which had the shape of a sausage were assigned to the species *S. Pastorianus*. It is true that the shapes mentioned are more or less characteristic of the respective species, but further study of the yeasts has shown that under certain conditions of cultivation the shapes of the cells may change, and one kind of yeast may temporarily assume the form of another. Hence the classification by shape alone was found to be misleading. More trustworthy methods were worked out by Hansen—to whom is also due the process by which pure yeast of any variety can be obtained by cultivation from a single cell of that variety (see p. 48).

Having by this process obtained pure yeasts of different kinds, Hansen found that each species could only develop spores between certain definite temperatures, and those temperatures were different for the various kinds of yeast. He recognised three distinct species of spore-forming *Saccharomycetes*, namely *S. cerevisiæ*, *S. Pastorianus*, and *S. ellipsoideus*, the first being the cultivated yeasts, the other two wild yeasts. These could be further subdivided into varieties, which were distinguished as *S. cerevisiæ* I., *S. cerevisiæ* II., and so on. At the following temperatures, no spores are formed by the

[1] It should be mentioned, however, that certain of the wine yeasts are now regularly cultivated.

six varieties named, but they are produced at temperatures intermediate between the extremes given :—

	No spores at	
S. cerevisiæ I	9°	or 37·5°
S. Pastorianus I	0·5	„ 31·5
„ II	0·5	„ 29
„ III	4	„ 29
S. ellipsoideus I	4	„ 32·5
„ II	4	„ 35

The yeast *S. cerevisiæ* I, it may be mentioned, was isolated from a "top" yeast used in an Edinburgh brewery.

Hansen also found that when these six varieties of yeasts were cultivated at temperatures at which they could all form spores, the time required for the commencement of spore-formation was different for the various organisms. This is illustrated for two temperatures in the table subjoined :—

	Time elapsing before spores are formed.	
	At 11–12°	At 25°
S. cerevisiæ I	10 days.	23 hours.
S. Pastorianus I	89 hours.	Less than 26 „
„ II	77 „	25 „
„ III	less than 7 days.	28 „
S. ellipsoideus I	„ 4½ „	21 „
„ II	„ 5½ „	27 „

Spore-formation occurs best when young and vigorous yeast is spread in thin layers on a moist surface—*e.g.*, on slices of carrot or potato, or better, on a plaster of Paris block standing in distilled water—and kept at a suitable temperature. To obtain the young cells the yeast is cultivated for some time in beer wort, and then a few drops of this are mixed with some fresh wort and incubated at 25–26° for twenty-four hours.

If then it is required to ascertain whether a specimen of ordinary brewery "top" yeast, *S. cerevisiæ* I, is contaminated with any of the above five wild yeasts, the specimen may be tested by first obtaining a culture of young cells as just described, and then finding the time required for spore formation when a little of the culture is incubated at 11–12° on a plaster of Paris block.

The block used for this purpose has the shape of a truncated cone, and is placed in a glass vessel provided with a cover. To be trustworthy, the experiment must be made with sterilised apparatus. The covered glass vessel containing the dry block is therefore wrapped in paper and heated in an air-oven for 1½ hours to a temperature of about 110°. After cooling, the paper is removed, and the cover raised a little to allow of a small quantity of the yeast culture being placed here and there on the top of the block.

about 25°, or alternatively at the ordinary temperature. In the course of two or three days, or more, according to the temperature, active fermentation will have set in, and after a week or so enough yeast will have been formed to allow of a larger quantity of wort being "pitched." This in its turn produces a still larger amount of yeast. Hence, given that precautions are taken to prevent contamination during the operations, any desired quantity of pure yeast can be obtained from the original single cell.

Special propagating apparatus, designed for the preparation of a regular supply of pure yeast on the foregoing principles, is installed in many breweries and distilleries.

Single-cell yeasts are employed with good results in distilleries and in numerous Continental and American breweries, but their application to English "top-fermentation" brewing has been less satisfactory, on account of the difficulty of obtaining a good secondary fermentation in casks when such yeast is used.

Yeasts are sometimes referred to as being of the "Saaz" type or the "Frohberg" type. The former term indicates yeasts which have a relatively small "attenuating" power—that is, which produce a low percentage of alcohol, about 8 per cent. by volume, or 14 per cent. of proof spirit; whereas Frohberg-type yeasts have a greater attenuating power, producing about 11 per cent. of alcohol, or 19 of proof spirit. More of the malto-dextrins are fermented by the "Frohberg" than by the "Saaz" types of yeast.

Two well-known yeasts largely used abroad for distillery fermentations are known as "Race II" and "Race XII." They were developed in Germany, and have given very good results in distillery practice by reason of their ability to ferment rapidly worts of high strength. Race II is a top yeast of the Frohberg type, distinguished chiefly by its large cells; it is well adapted for the fermentation of strong mashes, and has a good power of resistance to the inhibiting effect of the high proportion of alcohol produced. The use of a quick-fermenting yeast is advantageous, because on account of its rapid growth it suppresses bacteria and wild yeasts. Also a dilute wort is relatively more costly for distillation than one yielding more alcohol in the same volume; hence the advantage of a yeast which will rapidly ferment the more concentrated worts.

Mention may also be made here of the "Annam yeast," *S. anamensis*, which has been employed in distilleries using the amylo-process (p. 79) for fermenting mashes saccharified by moulds. This yeast is especially useful because it ferments sugars at the same temperature as the mucors (moulds) require which are employed to saccharify the mash, namely at 35–38°. It can therefore be used together with the moulds, so that saccharification and fermentation can go on simultaneously. The organism was isolated from a mixture of wild yeasts found on the sugar-cane in Cochin China. Its cells are normally oval, though some small, spherical ones may be present. The optimum temperature for spore-formation is 33°, at which temperature spores form in nine hours; the lower limit of temperature is 12°, with fifty hours as the time of spore-formation, and the upper limit 35°, when twelve hours are required for the production of spores. *S. anamensis* ferments and assimilates dextrose, lævulose, galactose, sucrose, maltose, and raffinose. Lactose is assimilated, but only slightly fermented.[1]

To produce alcohol in quantity, yeast must not only live, but grow. "Alcoholic fermentation never occurs without simultaneous organisation, development, and multiplication of cells, or the continued life of cells already formed" (Pasteur). Suitable nutriment must therefore be supplied, so that the cells may increase and multiply. What is suitable nutriment for yeast? A knowledge of the substances which go to form the tissues and contents of yeast-cells will partly answer the question, and this brings us to a consideration of the chemical constituents of yeast.

Composition of yeast.—A notable feature of yeast is the large proportion of nitrogenous substances which it contains. The quantity varies a good deal, apparently according to the conditions of nutrition under which the yeast has been grown; but in general more than one-half of the dry substance consists of proteins and other nitrogenous bodies. The proximate constituents other than nitrogen compounds include glycogen, gum, mucilage, fat, resinous matters, and cellulose, together with a good proportion of mineral ingredients. As showing the average composition of *dry* yeast the following analysis may be given:—

	Per cent.
Proteins, peptones, amides, etc.	51·8
Gum and other carbohydrates	29·5
Fat	1·0
Mineral matters	11·0
Cellulose and other constituents, by difference	6·7
	100·0

In pressed yeast—that is, yeast practically free from extraneous moisture—there is from 70 to 80 per cent. of water present, mainly in the cells. The following analysis of brewery yeast gives particulars of the soluble nitrogenous bodies present.[2]

[1] H. Will, *Zeitsch. ges. Brauw.*, 1913, **36**, 576.
[2] F. P. Siebel, *J. Inst. Brewing*, (Abst.), 1916, **22**, 398.

Brewery yeast.	Per cent.
Water	76·41
Soluble nitrogenous bodies	1·12
Insoluble „ „	11·35
Mineral matters	1·65
Resinous matters	0·08
Fat, cellulose, etc. (difference)	9·39
	100·00

Soluble nitrogenous bodies.	Per cent.
Albumins	0·16
Albumoses	0·05
Peptones	0·11
Amides	0·80
	1·12

A number of ultimate analyses of the organic portion of dry yeast have been published: the average of several of these is subjoined :—

	Per cent.
Carbon	48·3
Hydrogen	6·6
Nitrogen	10·6
Oxygen (including a little sulphur and phosphorus)	34·5
	100·0

The inorganic constituents of yeast consist almost wholly of phosphates. Of these, potassium phosphate forms by far the largest part, the remainder being made up of magnesium and calcium phosphates, which, with a little sulphate and silicate and a small quantity of iron compounds, practically complete the tale of mineral ingredients. According to Lintner, the average composition of the ash left on incinerating yeast is as follows :—

	Per cent.
Potassium oxide (K_2O) (including a little sodium oxide)	33·5
Magnesia (MgO)	6·1
Lime (CaO)	5·5
Iron oxide (Fe_2O_3)	0·5
Phosphoric acid (P_2O_5)	50·6
Sulphuric acid (SO_3)	0·6
Silica (SiO_2)	1·3
Ingredients not determined	1·9
	100·0

It may be gathered from these analyses that yeast requires for its growth a supply of both organic and inorganic nutriment, especially nitrogen- and potassium-compounds, and phosphorus. Moreover, as already seen, it contains no chlorophyll, and therefore must obtain its carbon in some soluble and assimilable form, since it cannot get it from carbon dioxide like green plants do. As regards the nitrogen, this can be supplied by ammonium sulphate, fluoride, or other ammonium salt ; but it is found that yeast grows more actively if its nitrogenous nutriment is furnished in an organic form—*e.g.*, as amino-compounds, amides, and peptones. Now these are precisely the substances which, as we have seen in connection with the germination of malt, are produced by the action of proteolytic enzymes upon the insoluble proteins of malt and other grain. In fact, malt wort, containing as it does these assimilable nitrogen compounds, soluble carbon nutriment in the form of sugar, and phosphates, with potassium, magnesium, and calcium salts, is a very excellent medium for the nourishment of yeast. Much the same can be said of grape juice also. Occasionally, however, and especially when a large proportion of brewing-sugar or of unmalted grain is used in making the wort, there is a deficiency of suitable nutriment; and this deficiency is corrected by adding special preparations of "yeast foods."

Yeast can be "acclimatised" to the presence of antiseptics such as sulphurous acid and hydrofluoric acid, and can be cultivated to withstand the effects of these up to a certain degree. Advantage is taken of this property in helping to keep distillery "wash" free from bacteria and wild yeasts, which are much more susceptible to the action of antiseptics. Distillery yeasts can be accustomed to grow actively in the presence of hydrofluoric acid or ammonium fluoride to the extent of 0·2 per cent. of the fermenting liquid—a proportion which is quite effective in destroying bacteria. Also a slightly acid "wash" encourages the development of distillery yeasts, but is unfavourable to bacteria and brewery yeasts; hence it is common in distillery practice, even where hydrofluoric acid is not used, to acidify the wash with lactic acid or sulphuric acid. Further, distillery yeasts develop best at a temperature (24–27°) much higher than that most favourable to brewery yeasts (about 15·6°).

By successive culture in worts of gradually increasing strength yeast can, up to a certain point, be accustomed to tolerate more and more alcohol, and its ability to ferment more concentrated worts is thus developed. This property is applied in the method of fermentation known as the "Molhant" process, used abroad in the distillation of molasses.

The zymase activity of yeast, whereby the hexose sugars (dextrose, lævulose) are converted into alcohol, can be completely suppressed by means of toluene, without preventing the action of the maltase. It is thus possible to investigate the maltase activity of yeast without the complications arising from simultaneous fermentation produced by the zymase. Schönfeld and Krumhaar found in the course of such studies that by adding toluene in the proportion of 8 per cent. of the volume of the liquid, the complete suppression of fermentation could be ensured.[1]

Antiseptics in general will prevent fermentation when present in relatively large amount; but many, on the other hand, have a

[1] *Wochensch. Brau.*, 1917, **34**, 157; *J. Inst. Brewing*, 1918, **24**, 36.

stimulating effect if present in only minute proportion. Thus mercuric chloride at a concentration of more than 1 in 20,000 inhibits fermentative action, but at 1 in 300,000 or less it has a favourable influence. Salicylic acid in the proportion of more than 0·1 per cent. has a deterrent effect, whereas less than one-sixth of this amount acts as a stimulant. Phenol is inhibitive at a concentration of more than 0·5 per cent., and stimulative at less than 0·1 per cent. Minute amounts of other toxic substances, such as strychnine, nicotine, and carbon disulphide, have also been found to favour fermentation.

Enzymes of yeast.—It is to these important substances that yeast owes its inverting and fermentative properties. They include sucrase (invertase), zymase, maltase (glucase), lactase, hexosephosphatase, reductase, carboxylase, melibiase, and endotryptase, as well as proteolytic enzymes, which have already been mentioned in the general description of the enzymes. But yeasts of different species do not all contain the same enzymes, and hence different yeasts behave differently towards the various sugars. A particular yeast may ferment one sugar but not another. So far as is known at present, only three of the aldo-hexose sugars, namely, dextrose, *d*-mannose, and *d*-galactose, are directly fermentable by yeast, and only one keto-hexose, viz., lævulos . According to E. F. Armstrong, all yeasts which ferment dextrose also attack mannose and lævulose. Most yeasts can invert, and then ferment, cane-sugar, because the enzyme sucrase (invertase) is of common occurrence in the yeasts. On the other hand, the enzyme lactase is absent from the majority of yeasts, and hence these are incapable of fermenting milk-sugar. *S. fragilis* and kephir ferment are exceptions to this : they contain lactase, and can bring about the fermentation of lactose.

The following synopsis shows at a glance how the more common sugars are affected by a number of yeast-species. Fermentation is indicated by the sign +, absence of it by the sign O :—

Yeast.	Dextrose.	Lævulose.	Mannose.	Galactose.	Maltose.	Cane-sugar.	Milk-sugar.
S. cerevisiæ	+	+	+	+	+	+	O
S. cerevisiæ Carlsberg	+	+	+	+	+	+	O
S. Pastorianus	+	+	+	+	+	+	O
S. ellipsoideus	+	+	+	+	+	+	O
S. Marxianus	+	+	+	+	O	+	O
S. exiguus	+	+	O	+	O	+	O
S. Ludwigii	+	+	+	O	O	+	O
S. anomalus	+	+	+	O	O	+	O
S. fragilis	+	+	+	+	O	+	+
S. anamensis	+	+	?	+	+	+	slt.
Kephir ferment	+	+	+	O	O	+	+

A number of observations on the sensitiveness of the chief enzymes of ordinary yeast towards various reagents are recorded by T. Bokorny.[1] Thus as regards the **invertase,** yeast placed in absolute alcohol for several days showed no loss of inverting power when removed. On the other hand, the invertase is destroyed in twenty-four hours by a 1 per cent. solution of caustic soda, though not by a 5 per cent. solution of formaldehyde. Towards acids also it is fairly stable. Fifty per cent. alcohol destroys the **zymase** activity within twenty-four hours, but 20 per cent. does not. Sulphuric or hydrochloric acid of 1 per cent. strength also destroys the activity within twenty-four hours, as do lactic, acetic, and butyric acids at 5 per cent. strength, though not at 2 per cent. Ammonia solution at a concentration of 0·05 per cent. destroys the zymase activity within forty-eight hours, and formaldehyde at 1 per cent. does so within twenty-four hours. Solutions of neutral salts at concentrations below 10 per cent. are harmless, and in some cases beneficial. As regards **maltase** activity, 1 per cent. caustic soda solution destroys this in a few hours, but 0·02 and 0·1 per cent. solutions have no appreciable effect in twenty-four hours. Within the same period, 10 per cent. alcohol, 1 per cent. acetic, lactic, or hydrochloric acid, or 0·1 per cent. formaldehyde, all act deleteriously.

"Permanent" yeast.—Zymin or permanent yeast ("acetone yeast") is a dry preparation obtained by well mixing finely-divided pressed brewers' yeast (500 grams) with acetone (3 litres) for ten minutes to destroy the vitality of the yeast-cells, and then filtering the mass and draining it with the filter-pump. The yeast is then again mixed with acetone (1 litre) for two minutes, filtered, drained, roughly powdered, and well kneaded with ether (250 c.c.) for three minutes, after which it is once more filtered and drained, and then spread on filter paper or porous plates and allowed to dry in the air for an hour. Finally, it is dried for twenty-four hours at 45°.

The product is a nearly white powder in which the yeast-cells are dead, and which therefore cannot grow and reproduce itself. Its cell-walls, however, are intact, and its sugar-fermenting enzyme, zymase, is still active ; so that even after keeping for years it will, when ground up and placed in a suitable sugar solution, induce a vigorous alcoholic fermentation.

T. Bokorny has recently described a method of preparing permanent yeast which appears to have some advantages. According to this writer, yeast-cells may be killed, without destroying the activity of the zymase, by treatment with dilute solutions (0·1 to 0·5 per

[1] *Zeitsch. angew. Chem.*, 1916, **29**, Ref. 319.

cent.) of sulphuric acid, or of various other agents, including formaldehyde, sodium or ammonium fluoride, ferrous sulphate, ammonium oxalate, potassium chlorate, ether, and chloroform.

Continued action of the toxic solution, however, ultimately affects the zymase also. By washing out the solutions with water, and drying the yeast, permanent yeast preparations may be made, similar to the "acetone yeast." The process is much cheaper than the acetone and the ether-alcohol methods. With the fluorides the results are not satisfactory. Rapid treatment is not necessary. For instance, using sulphuric acid, it is advisable to leave the yeast in contact with a 0·1 per cent. solution for several hours, in order to make sure of killing all the cells.[1]

Zymin can be deprived of its fermenting power by washing with water, but addition of boiled yeast juice restores this power. Harden[2] has shown that a similar restoration of fermenting activity is brought about by adding potassium or ammonium phosphate, together with either potassium pyruvate or acetaldehyde. By itself, the phosphate has no such effect. Thes experiments suggest that possibly acetaldehyde may be the "co-enzyme" of yeast juice. They also indicate that potassium and ammonium ions have some specific function in fermentation which is not possessed by the sodium ion, since *sodium* phosphate gave negative results with acetaldehyde.

Moulds (Hyphomycetes, Zygomycetes).—These are fungi forms without chlorophyll, in which sexual reproduction takes place by conjugation, so that the moulds are somewhat higher than the yeasts in the vegetable kingdom. The mould spore develops a much branched mycelium, which spreads over or through the nutrient matter in which the fungus grows. The mycelium sends up branches (hyphæ) into the air, which develop rounded and enlarged ends: these are the spore-cases, or sporangia, containing new spores.

Certain of the moulds (*Mucor*, spp.) have in recent years become of considerable importance in the alcohol industry, owing to the fact that during the growth of the mycelium they secrete amylase (diastase), and also fermentation enzymes. Thus they can both saccharify starch and convert the sugar so formed into alcohol. Chiefly, however, they have been used as sources of diastase-activity in the saccharification of starchy materials, effecting in this way a considerable economy in malt. The fermentation is then completed by adding yeast.

Amylomyces Rouxii is a mucor which was isolat[illegible] by Calmette

[1] *Allgem. Brau.-Hopf. Zeit.*, 1916, **56**, 1547; *J. Soc. C*[illegible]*. Ind.* (Abst.), 1917, **36**, 300.
[2] *Biochem. J.*, 1917, **1**[illegible]

in the year 1892 from Chinese rice-ferment. Calmette studied more especially its starch-saccharifying properties, but a few years later it was found (Boidin: Sanguinetti) that this organism could also convert sugars and dextrins into alcohol; and in 1898 it was used industrially for this purpose. It is from the **A. Rouxii** that the "amylo"-process of alcohol making took its name. The organism, however, was replaced later on by others which produced less acid.

Aspergillus oryzæ, another of the moulds, was separated from the Japanese "koji" ferments used in making "saki"; and was applied practically by Takamine to the saccharification of rice. Its action, however, is too energetic.

Rhizopus oligosporus, R. Japonicus, and **R. Delemar** are other moulds which have been employed for saccharifying starch: their action resembles that of **A. Rouxii.**

Other mucors, *viz.* **Mucor-**β obtained from koji, and **Mucor-**γ from Tonkin rice, were subsequently isolated (Boidin, Collette, and Mousain), and having been found to produce less acid than **A. Rouxii,** have supplanted the latter. **Mucor Boulard** No. 5, introduced in 1912 by the *Soc. Française des Distilleries de l'Indo-Chine,* is claimed to be as strong a saccharifying agent as the mucors previously used industrially, and, in addition, to do its work in media containing active bacteria, so that there is no necessity to work under aseptic conditions.[1]

III.—CONVERSION OF STARCH AND SUGAR INTO ALCOHOL: MASHING AND FERMENTATION

Mashing.—The object of "mashing" is to bring the starchy material into a condition favourable for its conversion into sugar and other products by the enzymes present, and eventually to effect this conversion.

In Continental practice the starchy substances—potatoes, maize, rice—are generally steamed under pressure to gelatinise the starch, as a preliminary to the mashing operation. Any other cereals used may be similarly treated for convenience of obtaining a concentrated mash, although with malt, barley, wheat, and oats actual gelatinisation is not necessary for attack of the starch by diastase.

The steaming is usually effected in a conical iron vessel known as a "converter," which is commonly of a size to take a charge of two or three tons of potatoes. In this vessel the potatoes are

[1] F.P. 459634 and 459815, Sept., 1912.

subjected to the action of steam at a pressure of three atmospheres during forty-five minutes or so, the temperature rising to about 135°. On opening the discharge valve at the bottom of the converter when the steaming is finished, the softened mass of potatoes is forced out by the pressure, and passes through a grid or cutting arrangement which helps to complete the pulping of the mass. The latter goes then to a mash-tun fitted with rotating stirrers, where the gelatinisation finishes as the mass cools down. The cooling is effected by water flowing through "attemperator" coils in the tun, or, in some forms, by means of an external water-jacket.

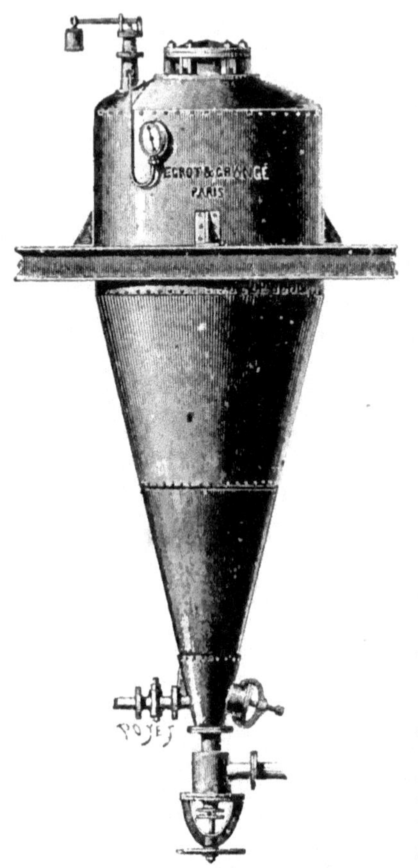

Fig. 17.—"Converter."
For steaming potatoes, maize, etc., under pressure (Egrot and Grangé).

Maize, rice, and other cereals, since they contain less water than potatoes do, are mixed with one or two parts of water before steaming. If very dry, maize may be first steeped in water for a day; and if the steam pressure for the converter is limited, the grain may be coarsely ground before treatment with water. Moreover, the product obtained by steaming maize is liable to form a stiff, unworkable paste on cooling down, and to obviate this a little malt (0·5 to 1 per cent.) is added in order to effect a partial saccharification. Alternatively, a small quantity of hydrochloric acid, equivalent to about 0·2 per cent. of HCl calculated on the weight of the maize, may be used instead of malt. The effect of the acid is to convert the basic phosphates of the grain, which are said to be chiefly responsible for the partial solidification of the pulp or paste, into acid salts. The coarsely-crushed maize is mixed with the requisite quantity of water, to which the hydrochloric acid has been added, at a temperature of 50–60°, kept stirred by means of an air jet for an hour, and then run into the converter. During the steaming operation the maize is kept in motion by jets of steam or air entering at the bottom of the converter, a small valve at the top serving as outlet for the air; this prevents the softened grain settling down and blocking the discharge tube. The steaming takes about two hours. Sometimes the operation is divided into two stages, the charge being passed into an intermediate converter for completion of the gelatinisation before being blown into the mash-tun. Here it is stirred and cooled as above described, until the proper temperature for saccharification is attained.

The temperatures at which various kinds of starch are gelatinised are given by Lintner[1] as follows :—

Starch.	Gelatinisation temperature. C.	F.
Barley	80°	176°
Maize	75	167
Malt, green	85	185
Malt, kilned	80	176
Oat	85	185
Potato	65	149
Rice	80	176
Rye	80	176
Wheat	80	176

Dox and Roark, however, using an electrically heated chamber on a microscope slide, and taking the loss of optical anisotropy as indicating the point at which gelatinisation occurs, found that different varieties of maize have different temperatures of gelatinisation.[2] The range found was from 64·1° to 71·1°. Probably therefore the temperatures in the above table are approximations only.

Saccharification.—As already indicated, the starch does not itself undergo alcoholic fermentation; it is first converted into maltose and other products by the action of the enzyme diastase (amylase). This diastase is usually supplied by malt—or, in the "amylo"-process (described further on) by certain moulds.

The proper quantity of malt, amounting to 1½–3 per cent. of the weight of potato used, is ground finely and added to the mash-tun, where the starchy mass from the converter has been cooled down to a temperature of 50–55°. The mash has usually a specific gravity of about 1·110, or, in the amylo-process, about 1·070. The temperature mentioned is the one most favourable for diastatic action, and the mass soon becomes more fluid by reason of the liquefaction of the starch. When a portion of the liquid, tested with iodine solution, no longer gives the blue colour of starch iodide, the process of conversion is complete. The time required for this may vary from one to three hours or more, according to circumstances.

[1] *Brauer und Mälzer Kalendar*, 1880.

[2] *J. Amer. Chem. Soc.*, 1917, **39**, 742.

Usually the mash at this stage is heated to a temperature of 70–75° for a few minutes in order to destroy injurious bacteria with which the wort may have become infected during the course of saccharification. This is accomplished by reserving a part of the hot, gelatinised, starchy material in the converter, and allowing it to pass into the main bulk as soon as the conversion of the latter is completed. By the time the temperature of the whole has been raised sufficiently to destroy the micro-organisms, the starch of the fresh portion is saccharified.

Whilst this raising of the temperature destroys harmful bacteria, it is liable greatly to impair the diastase. This is a disadvantage, because as long as diastase is present there is a further slow conversion of dextrins into maltose during the subsequent period of fermentation, and therefore to that extent a better yield of alcohol. To allow of this further conversion, one device is to raise the temperature, but not beyond 68°. Diastase in solutions containing much sugar can withstand this temperature without its activity being greatly impaired, although in water alone it is much weakened even at 63°. Another plan, now frequently adopted, is not to heat the mash to these high temperatures at all, but to add a small quantity of hydrofluoric acid or of ammonium fluoride during the fermentation. This antiseptic, in proportion up to about 0·2 per cent., is not toxic to the enzymes of yeast which has been "acclimatised" to it, whereas bacteria are destroyed at a far smaller concentration. Hence if this procedure is adopted, the saccharification can be effected at the most favourable temperature (50–55°), and the diastase retained in full vigour to play its further part in the secondary fermentation.

Whichever process is used, the mash, after saccharification is complete, is cooled down to about 20°, and passed through a centrifugal or other form of de-husking apparatus to remove solid matters. It is then ready to be "pitched" with yeast for the fermentation.

In this country potatoes are rarely used for making alcohol. Malt alone is employed in many distilleries, chiefly pot-still distilleries which make whisky; but a mixture of malt and unmalted grain is usual in distilleries using patent stills. (Molasses is largely employed in the manufacture of industrial alcohol.)

The unmalted grain used is chiefly maize, with a relatively large proportion of malt, ranging from 10 to 25 per cent. A part of the maize may be replaced by barley, oats, rice, rye, sago, or wheat, in various proportions up to 40 per cent. of the whole.

A preliminary partial conversion of the raw maize or rice is generally effected by treating the ground material (grist) with either a small quantity of green malt, or with sulphuric (or hydrochloric) acid. In the former case, the grist is mixed with three or four times its weight of warm water in the converter or "maize tun," and steam is passed in until the liquid is nearly at the boiling point in order to gelatinise the starch. The temperature is then reduced to 40°, and a quantity of green malt, about 4 per cent. of the grist by weight, is suspended in water and mixed with the starchy materials in the maize tun. After the action of the diastase has proceeded for an hour or so, the maize or rice mash is run into the mash-tun, in which malt and water have already been placed,

FIG. 18.—MASH TUN, WITH STEEL'S MASHING MACHINE.
For effecting a preliminary mashing of the grist between hopper and tun (Haslam Foundry Co., Ltd., Derby).

together with any barley or oats that may be required. To facilitate drainage, oat-husks are often included in the mash.

Matters are so arranged that when the mixture is made the temperature is about the optimum for diastatic action (50–55°), and not above 57° or 58° in any case. By means of stirrers fitted in the tun the mash is kept well mixed, and saccharification proceeds apace. Warmer water is then admitted until the temperature has risen to 63–65°, for the purpose of inhibiting bacterial development. After settling, the wort is run off, and the residual grains are extracted again with hot water ; in some cases a third or even a fourth extraction is made. The weaker worts thus obtained are, after separation from the grains, used for mashing the next charge.

The saccharified mash is then cooled down and passed to the "wash-backs" for fermentation. In this country distillers usually arrange the materials of the wort so that the specific gravity of the latter before fermentation is about 1·030 to 1·040, or else 1·045 to 1·055. If too much saccharine matter is present, the large proportion of alcohol formed tends to check fermentation before all the sugar is decomposed, thus causing a loss of material. (Special races of yeast, however, can be "acclimatised" to withstand relatively high concentrations of alcohol, and these are used on the Continent, where the "thick mash" system is

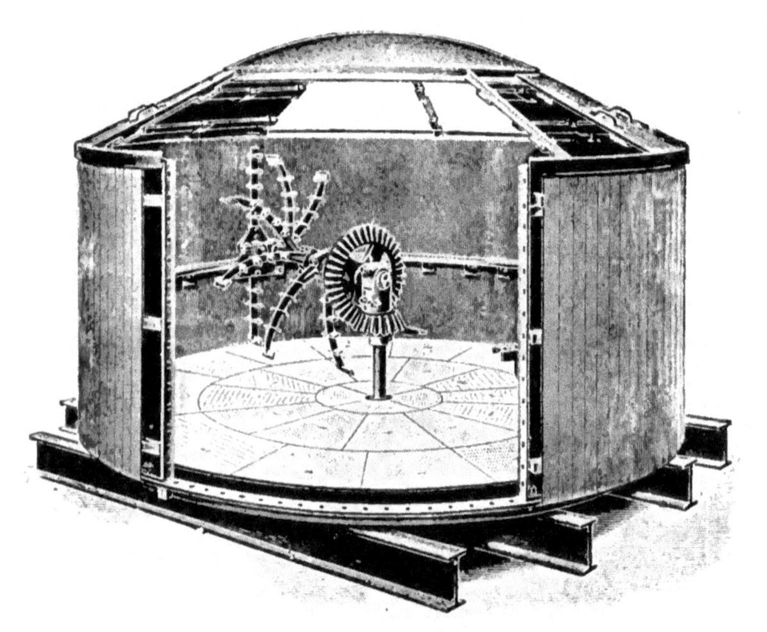

FIG. 19.—MASH TUN WITH RAKE STIRRING GEAR (Blair, Campbell, and McLean).

practised.) On the other hand, too small a proportion of alcohol is uneconomical, by reason of the comparatively large expenditure of time and fuel required for the distillation. In distilleries where yeast is made, a low specific gravity of the wort is the rule.

Thick potato-mashes are common in Germany, because there is a tax levied which depends upon the capacity of the mash-tun, and the inducement therefore is to obtain the largest yield from a given tun. Towards the end of the fermentation, when the effervescence has moderated, water is added to dilute the mash. This lowers the alcoholic concentration, and also that of the carbon dioxide, thus allowing the yeast to complete the fermentation better.

Saccharification of grain mashes with a small proportion of malt.—A. Vasseux describes the following procedure, which has given good results, and is recommended to distillers who wish to abandon saccharification by acid in order to produce spent grains suitable for feeding purposes.[1]

The raw grain is "cooked" as usual, and transferred hot into small closed vats similar to those used in the "amylo"-process (p. 79). When full, the vats are cooled, sterilised air being introduced meanwhile. When the temperature has fallen to 55°, a mash of green or dried malt, representing 3 to 5 per cent. of the charge of grain, is added, and the charge is kept in motion, without further cooling, for an hour, within which period the saccharification is complete. There is little risk of infection, but antiseptics may be used if necessary.

Cooling is then resumed, and the yeast is introduced when the temperature has fallen to 35°. At 24° cooling is stopped. After the fermentation has become vigorous, the charge is transferred to open vats, in which the fermentation is completed as usual.

Saccharification without malt or acid.—In certain small Continental distilleries spirit is made entirely from raw rye. No malt or acid is used: the starch is saccharified by the diastase present in the raw grain.

Thirty kilos. of rye grist are added all at once to 54 litres of water at 64°. The mash in covered up and steeped for half an hour, by which time the temperature falls to 44°. Boiling water (60 litres) is then added, in order to raise the temperature again to 65–66°. After the mash has stood for a further two hours, cold water is stirred in until the temperature falls to 31°. At this stage pressed yeast (¾ lb.), worked up with water, is added, the mash cooled by a coil to 19°, and passed to the fermenting-vat. The fermentation is started at 16°, and goes on for five days.

Investigating the yields given by this process with rye and other materials—wheat, barley, oats, maize, buckwheat, rice, millet, potatoes, and artichokes—Windisch and Jetter found that rye was the only grain that contained sufficient diastase to yield as much alcohol without malt as with malt.[2] Wheat contains a good proportion of diastase, but not enough to give the full yield of alcohol unless some malt is added. Buckwheat approximates to wheat; barley and oats give lower results. Maize contains only a little diastase, and the raw starch is much less readily saccharified by malt than the steamed material; rice and millet are similar to

[1] *Bull. Assoc. Chim. Sucr.*, 1917, **35**, 237; *J. Soc. Chem. Ind.* (Abst.), 1917, **36**, 1284.

[2] *Zeitsch. Spiritusind.*, 1907, **30**, 541, 552.

maize. Potatoes contain only traces of diastase, and the raw starch is only partially saccharified by malt. With artichokes, the whole of the inulin is saccharified, whether malt is used or not, and whether the material is steamed or not.

"Brewing extract."—This is a term commonly used by distillers in this country to denote the weight, expressed in lb., of the dissolved material present in the wort. It may be calculated from the specific gravity of the wort thus:—

Let the sp. gr. be, for example, 1047 (water = 1000; it is always taken thus in practice).

Weight of a gallon of water = 10 lb.
∴ ,, ,, ,, wort = 10 × 1·047 lb.,
= 10·47 lb.

∴ dissolved extractive matter = weight of wort *minus* weight of water = 10·47 — 10 = 0·47 lb.

This is the brewing extract per gallon of wort.

Hence to find the brewing extract for any given quantity of wort, multiply the number of gallons of wort by the expression

$$\frac{\text{sp. gr. of wort} - 1000}{100}.$$

Example:—Given 7000 gallons of wort, sp. gr. 1045. The brewing extract is $7000 \times \frac{45}{100} = 3150$ lb. If this has been produced from 300 bushels of malt, the brewing extract *per bushel* is 3150 ÷ 300 = 10·5 lb. per bushel. This would be a fair average yield from unscreened malt. From screened malt, the average yield would be higher—about 11 lb. extract per bushel.

Changes during saccharification.—The action of diastase upon starch is one of hydrolysis, whereby the starch is converted into dextrins, maltose, and intermediate products. The changes involved are very complex. Much study has been devoted to them, and much discussion has ensued, but it cannot be said that there is even yet general agreement as to the exact transformations which take place. Nevertheless, the main outlines of the changes are established definitely.

The hypothesis most generally favoured as to the reactions which occur is one due to Brown and Morris.[1] These investigators explain the action of diastase upon soluble starch, at mashing temperatures, as a progressive degradation proceeding as follows:—

The starch molecule is regarded as being composed of five "amylin" groups, each having the formula $(C_{12}H_{20}O_{10})_{20}$. Four of these groups are arranged about the fifth.

[1] *Trans. Laboratory Club*, 1890, **3**, 83.

When attacked by diastase, the starch molecule first breaks up into its five component groups. One of these is very markedly resistant to further attack ("stable dextrin"); the four others ("amylin" groups) are more readily hydrolysable:—

$$\{(C_{12}H_{20}O_{10})_{20}\}_5 = (C_{12}H_{20}O_{10})_{20} + 4(C_{12}H_{20}O_{10})_{20}.$$

Starch molecule. Stable dextrin. Amylin groups.

The amylin groups are then progressively hydrolysed into "amyloin" or "maltodextrin" complexes. Each $C_{12}H_{20}O_{10}$ group in its turn takes up a molecule of water, forming a maltose group, $C_{12}H_{22}O_{11}$, which, however, remains for the time attached to its amyloin complex. Thus this first stage would be:—

$$(C_{12}H_{20}O_{10})_{20} + H_2O = \begin{cases} C_{12}H_{22}O_{11} \\ (C_{12}H_{20}O_{10})_{19} \end{cases}$$

Amylin group. Water. Maltodextrin (amyloin).

An intermediate stage, when more maltose groups have been formed, would give a different maltodextrin, *e.g.*,

$$\begin{cases} (C_{12}H_{22}O_{11})_{10} \\ (C_{12}H_{20}O_{10})_{10} \end{cases},$$

in which the change has proceeded half-way. The final maltodextrin would be

$$\begin{cases} (C_{12}H_{22}O_{11})_{19} \\ C_{12}H_{20}O_{10} \end{cases}.$$

As the hydrolysis proceeds, the complex maltodextrins break down into smaller molecular aggregations, which, however, retain all the characteristics of the maltodextrins. This goes on until the maltose stage is reached—that is, until all the $C_{12}H_{20}O_{10}$ groups of a maltodextrin have been hydrolysed to $C_{12}H_{22}O_{11}$ groups. Thus, for example, the particular maltodextrin last formulated above would, on taking up another molecule of water, give 20 molecules of maltose:—

$$\begin{cases} (C_{12}H_{22}O_{11})_{19} \\ C_{12}H_{20}O_{10} \end{cases} + H_2O = 20C_{12}H_{22}O_{11}$$

Maltodextrin. Water. Maltose.

It follows, therefore, according to Brown and Morris's views, that if diastase is allowed to act for a sufficiently long time on starch under proper conditions of temperature, the products will eventually be maltose and "stable dextrin," the latter being only very slowly attacked.

As already indicated, however, the reactions are complex, and other products than those mentioned have been found. Thus Ling and Davis[1] have shown that dextrose also is formed by the

[1] *Trans. Chem. Soc.*, 1904, **85**, 16.

prolonged action of diastase on starch; and the production of an "isomaltose" (Lintner), or "dextrinose" (Syniewski) has also been noted. Baker and Hulton[1] have found that when diastase acts on barley starch *granules* the products are maltose, dextrose, dextrins, and a dextrin-like carbohydrate having the same molecular weight as maltose.

Under the ordinary mashing conditions for brewing, where the action of the diastase is stopped by boiling the wort, there will be a considerable proportion of the intermediate maltodextrins present, as well as the maltose and stable dextrin. These maltodextrins are important to the brewer of beer, because they are less readily fermented than the maltose in the main fermentation, but are gradually broken down, and undergo a slow "secondary" fermentation whilst the beer is stored in casks, and thus prevent it becoming "flat." The distiller's interest, however, lies in having as much as possible of the wort directly fermentable, in order to get the best yield of alcohol. Hence the wort is not boiled, but the diastase is allowed to act as fully as possible, and this not only during the mashing, but during the subsequent fermentation also, when, under the combined action of diastase and yeast, the remaining maltodextrins and even the "stable" dextrin are largely converted into fermentable sugars. Since the distiller's wort is not boiled, it is, as already mentioned, more liable to bacterial contamination than the brewery wort is, and hence arises the necessity for heating to a high temperature (68° or 75°) after saccharification; or, alternatively, for the use of hydrofluoric acid or other antiseptic.

Saccharification of starch by acid.—It has been mentioned above that the preliminary conversion of maize or rice may be made with acid, as an alternative to using green malt. For this purpose, the ground grain is mixed with three to four times its weight of hot water, and dilute sulphuric acid added. The quantity of acid used is equivalent to 1 or $1\frac{1}{4}$ per cent. of strong sulphuric acid, calculated on the weight of the grist; or a corresponding amount of hydrochloric acid may be used. Steam is passed in until gelatinisation is effected, the mash being kept stirred during the process. The acid is then largely neutralised with milk of lime, and the liquid brought to the actual neutral point, or near it, by means of calcium carbonate. After being cooled down to about 63° with water, the gelatinised starchy product is run off into the mash tun, and the process finished as already described.

[1] *Trans. Chem. Soc.*, 1914, **105**, 1529.

In some Continental distilleries an essentially similar process is used, but the grain is heated under pressure, so as to give a more complete conversion, and in a shorter time. The maize is mixed with two and a half times its weight of hot water and steamed under a pressure of three atmospheres for two to three hours to effect gelatinisation. Strong hydrochloric acid is then added, in proportion equivalent to $2\frac{1}{2}$ per cent. of the weight of maize. After completion of the saccharification, which takes about half-an-hour, the wort is neutralised, cooled, strained, and run into the fermenting vats.

The main chemical reaction occurring in this process of acid saccharification is the hydrolysis of the starch, first to dextrins and maltose, and then to dextrose as the final product. It may be summarised in the equation :—

$$\underset{\text{Starch.}}{C_{12}H_{20}O_{10}} + 2H_2O = \underset{\text{Dextrose.}}{2C_6H_{12}O_6}$$

In practice, however, more or less of unchanged dextrins and maltose remain with the dextrose produced.

FIG. 20.—DIGESTER.
For saccharifying grain with acid under pressure (Egrot and Grangé, Paris).

Solid "glucose" and glucose-syrups intended for fermentation purposes are also manufactured in a similar manner, namely, by converting the starch of maize, rice, etc., into sugar through the action of acids. The cereal substances are heated with water under a pressure of about three atmospheres, until the starchy material is converted into a paste. This is then mixed with the requisite quantity of sulphuric acid (about 3 per cent. of the weight of grain treated), and the heating continued until the conversion is complete. The acid is neutralised with chalk, and after settling, the clear liquid is removed from the precipitated calcium sulphate. The liquid, after being filtered through animal charcoal to decolorise it, is concentrated *in vacuo,* either far enough to solidify on cooling, or only sufficiently to yield a thick syrup, according to whether solid glucose or a glucose-syrup is required.

There is a good deal of variation in the composition of the

FIG. 21.—BATTERY OF FOUR DIFFUSION VESSELS FOR EXTRACTION OF SUGAR. BEETS
(Egrot and Grangé, Paris).

products. Solid glucose generally contains about 60 to 80 per cent. of dextrose, a little maltose, and dextrins up to 10 per cent. or more; the syrups may contain about 50 to 60 per cent. of dextrose.

Worts from Sugar-containing Materials.

Sugar-beets.—In France, the juice of beets for alcohol-making is obtained in a manner quite similar to that adopted in the sugar factory for extracting the juice to be used as a source of sugar. After being washed and sliced, the beets are extracted with water by a process of diffusion, which takes place in a battery of vessels set in series. These vessels, charged with the slices of beet, are so arranged that the water issuing from the bottom of one vessel passes into the top of the next, percolates downwards through the packing of beet slices, and extracts their sugar as it goes. The same thing occurs in the next vessel, and thus by the time the end vessel of the series is reached, the juice has become sufficiently rich in sugar to be ready for fermentation. To minimise the action of harmful bacteria during fermentation, the juice is slightly acidified with sulphuric acid, and frequently small quantities of antiseptics such as fluorides are added.

In Austria-Hungary, also, sugar-beets have in recent years been extensively used as a source of alcohol.[1] Many of the distilleries use the diffusion process described above; but others utilise the plant formerly employed for mashing potatoes, and extract the beets by heating with steam under pressure in a conical (" Hentze ") converter. The beets are freed from leaves and then topped, the roots and tops being stored separately and the tops worked off first, as they are more prone to lose sugar during storage. For the steaming operation a pressure of two atmospheres, maintained for one and a quarter to one and a half hours, is sufficient, all the sugar being then dissolved, and the beet tissues reduced to a pulp. Both potatoes and beets are sometimes steamed together, the lower half of the converter being filled with potatoes and the upper half with beets. When the steaming of the potatoes is completed, they are blown out into the fermenting vessel. The beets require longer treatment, and are given another half-hour's steaming before the pulped mass is in its turn blown out to be fermented. Economically, the use of beets is said to compare favourably with that of potatoes.

Molasses.—In preparing beet molasses for fermentation, it is

[1] K. Antal, *Zeitsch. Spiritusind.*, 1911, **34**, 239, 252.

usual to sterilise them by slightly acidifying the diluted molasses, and boiling the solution. A portion is withdrawn after cooling, partly fermented with yeast, and returned to the bulk with the now-increased amount of yeast to complete the main fermentation. As the molasses themselves are poor in yeast-food, it is the practice to add a little maltopeptone or saccharified maize, or other nutrient substance.

Cane-sugar molasses as used in this country are simply dissolved in water to make a wort of specific gravity about 1·030 to 1·040. In general, no preliminary inversion of the cane-sugar present is considered necessary, the action of the invertase of the yeast during fermentation being sufficient to invert the cane-sugar and render it fermentable. When a preliminary inversion is required, it is carried out by treatment of the diluted molasses with acid at boiling temperature for an hour, the acid being subsequently nearly neutralised before the fermentation is started. Alternatively, a special inversion operation with yeast may be carried out, at a temperature of about 50°.

In the tropics, juice expressed from the sugar-cane, and containing about 14 per cent. of sugar, is fermented directly. A wild yeast is found on the surface of the cane, and this sets up an active spontaneous fermentation when the juice is kept at a temperature of 30–35°. Nipa-palm juice is liable to contain a peroxydase, sometimes in sufficient quantity to destroy an appreciable proportion of the sugar, and the juice is therefore treated with a sulphite to reduce the peroxydase before fermentation. A wild yeast is also present in nipa-juice, and is used for the direct fermentation of the sap. In distilleries which employ both nipa juice and molasses, it is the practice to inoculate a portion of the diluted molasses with nipa juice to produce a ferment, which is then used for the fermentation of the main bulk.

Fermentation.—When the saccharified wort obtained in the manner described has been cooled to about 15–20° and run into the fermenting vessels or "wash-backs," it is "pitched" with yeast to start the fermentation. Brewery yeast (top fermentation) is often used, but the best results are given with special distillery yeasts—that is, selected culture-yeasts adapted to distillery conditions. If pressed yeast is added, about 2 lb. are employed for every 100 gallons of wort. The usual practice, however, is to make what in this country is called "bub"—a small-scale preliminary fermentation in a good malt or malt and grain wort. This is "seeded" with the yeast and set to ferment a few hours before the main wort is ready for pitching; it provides a culture of vigorous young yeast-cells, and is added to the main wort in the proportion of 4 to 5 per cent.

It is important to check the growth of harmful bacteria in the early stages, as these organisms, by the subsidiary fermentations which they set up, both diminish the yield of alcohol and lower its quality. Generally, in the past, lactic acid has been used for this purpose, since a slightly acid wort tends to inhibit the bacterial development, whilst favouring the growth of the distillery yeast. The acid is produced in the separate small mash or "bub" by inoculating this, before adding yeast, with a pure culture of the lactic acid bacillus at a temperature of 50°. The acid itself eventually checks the growth and activity of the bacilli which produce it. The growing organism, however, should not be introduced into the main wort, there to rejuvenate itself and produce unnecessary acid. Hence its destruction is usually made certain by heating the bub to about 74°, after a sufficient acidity has been produced. When cooled, the mixture is seeded with yeast and fermented as already described.

Latterly, however, the method most in favour for eliminating undesirable micro-organisms is the employment of antiseptics to which the selected yeast has been acclimatised. Thus small proportions of bismuth nitrate or calcium bisulphite have been used, but hydrofluoric acid or ammonium fluoride is now almost always chosen. The proportion of the acid employed is in general such as to give 0·005 per cent. of HF in the wort. This is reasonably effective against harmful bacteria, whereas yeasts can be accustomed to withstand forty times the amount. When such acclimatised yeasts and the fluorides are used, the previous saccharification of the starch by diastase can be carried out at the temperature, 55°, most favourable for the production of maltose (Effront's method).

In the early stage of the fermentation process there is a rapid development of the yeast, for which the best temperature is about 17–21°. The temperature rises as the operation proceeds, and the main fermentation occurs, in which the maltose and dextrose are transformed into alcohol; this goes on best at 26–30°. A secondary fermentation also ensues as the wort becomes warm, the diastase acting on any dextrins which remain, and gradually converting them more or less completely into fermentable sugars, to be promptly attacked by the yeast. During the early hours of the process, the "wash" (as it is now termed) is roused to aerate it and expel the carbon dioxide formed, and the temperature of the wash is preferably not allowed to rise above 30°, at any stage. After about forty to forty-eight hours, the chief fermentation is over, and the wash has become "attenuated" down to a specific gravity approximating to that of water. It is kept for another day at 25–26°, by the end of which time the process is complete. The wash, when ready for distillation, contains usually about 12 per cent. or more of alcohol where the system of using concentrated worts is in practice, or from $4\frac{1}{2}$ to $7\frac{1}{2}$ per cent. where, as in most distilleries in this country, the wort before fermentation has a specific gravity of 1·030 to 1·055.

The fermentation of beet mashes, or of mixed beet and potato mashes, is carried out in Austria-Hungary as follows.[1] With beet-mashes alone, beer yeast is sometimes used, the proportion being 15 to 20 litres of fresh yeast to each 1000 litres of the mash. After twenty-four hours, during which time about two-thirds of the sugar is fermented, a further quantity of fresh beet-mash is added, and fermentation continued to completion in another twenty-four hours. Culture-yeasts are, however, preferable to beer-yeasts, and the best results have been obtained with a pure culture wine-yeast capable of fermenting both sucrose and raffinose sugars. This yeast is grown for twenty-four hours in a portion of the beet-mash which has been acidified with sulphuric acid, sufficient to bring its total acidity to 0·7°, the temperature being kept below 30°. The partially fermented product is then mixed with fresh beet-mash, a portion of the latter, however, being reserved for growing the yeast to be used in the next day's mash. The temperature of the main mash is maintained at 29° for eight to ten hours, after which the temperature shows no tendency to rise. Fermentation is complete in twenty-four hours after mixing. It is immaterial whether the fermenting vats are closed or open, since there is little danger of infection. Working with the culture-yeast, the quantity of alcohol produced per 100 kilos. of sugar present is about 60·4 litres, whereas when beer-yeast is employed the yield is only 54 to 55 litres.

When both beets and potatoes (or maize) are used, the potato- (or maize-) mash is first fermented for twenty-four hours at a temperature not above 25°. At the end of this period, the beet-mash is well stirred in, and the fermentation allowed to proceed for another twenty-four hours, by which time it is complete.

Changes during fermentation.—When yeast acts upon the saccharified starch of the wort, it converts the maltose at first into dextrose :—

$$C_{12}H_{22}O_{11} + H_2O = 2C_6H_{12}O_6$$

Maltose. Dextrose.

[1] K. Antal, *Zeitsch. Spiritusind.*, 1911, **34**, 239, 252.

This conversion is brought about through the agency of the enzyme, *maltase*, contained in ordinary yeast.

The dextrose is then decomposed by the action of another yeast enzyme, namely, *zymase*, chiefly into alcohol and carbon dioxide. In the main, the change proceeds according to the following equation :—

$$\underset{\text{Dextrose.}}{C_6H_{12}O_6} = \underset{\text{Alcohol.}}{2C_2H_5{\cdot}OH} + \underset{\text{Carbon dioxide.}}{2CO_2}$$

This, however, is very far from representing all the products of the complex series of changes included under the name of alcoholic fermentation. Many by-products result, the nature and proportion of which depend upon the conditions—*e.g.*, the character of the wort and yeast. Chief among these by-products as regards quantity are glycerol, fusel oil, and succinic acid ; in smaller proportions are other fatty acids (formic, acetic, propionic, butyric, and lactic) with aldehydes and various esters (ethyl acetate, butyrate, caproate, etc.).

Pasteur first observed (1858) the constant occurrence of glycerol in the fermentation of sugar solutions ; the production of succinic acid had been noted by Schmidt eleven years previously. The quantity of glycerol found by Pasteur was 3·16 per cent., and of succinic acid 0·67 per cent., of the weight of cane-sugar taken ; but, as already indicated, these amounts vary somewhat with the particular conditions. Probably the glycerol is derived from the sugar. The fusel oils and the succinic acid, however, have a different origin. In the fermenting wort, and also in the yeast, there are proteid substances which become hydrolysed to amino-acids ; these, in their turn, take up the elements of water, and are decomposed with the elimination of ammonia and carbon dioxide and the production of higher alcohols (Ehrlich) :—

$$\underset{\text{Amino-acid.}}{R{\cdot}CH(NH_2){\cdot}COOH} + H_2O = \underset{\text{Higher alcohol.}}{R{\cdot}CH_2{\cdot}OH} + NH_3 + CO_2$$

These higher alcohols constitute the "fusel oil" (*q.v.*, Chap. X).

The succinic acid is formed in a somewhat similar manner from glutamic acid, but oxidation is also involved. The ammonia eliminated is apparently assimilated by the yeast.

Cane-sugar solutions are not directly fermentable by yeast. The sugar is first hydrolysed to "invert"-sugar, a mixture of dextrose and lævulose, by the enzyme *invertase* contained in brewers' yeast :—

$$\underset{\text{Cane-sugar.}}{C_{12}H_{22}O_{11}} + H_2O = \underbrace{\underset{\text{Dextrose}}{C_6H_{12}O_6} + \underset{\text{Lævulose.}}{C_6H_{12}O_6}}_{\text{Invert-sugar.}}$$

Both the dextrose and the lævulose are then, like the dextrose obtained from maltose, converted into alcohol and carbon dioxide by the instrumentality of the zymase. The production of invert-sugar, however, is more rapid than its fermentation, so that the invert-sugar accumulates in the solution until the cane-sugar is all inverted.

When a soluble phosphate is added to a mixture containing yeast juice and undergoing alcoholic fermentation, the rate of fermentation is much increased, though the increase is not permanent. There is evidence to show that hexosephosphates,

$$C_6H_{10}O_4(PO_4R_2)_2,$$

are formed during the fermentation of sugars, and they play an important part as intermediate compounds in the production of alcohol.[1]

This increased rate of fermentation on addition of phosphates does not, however, occur with fermentation by living yeast-cells, as distinct from fermentation by yeast-juice. The difference is perhaps due to the fact that with living yeast the process takes place within the cell, which already contains a sufficient supply of phosphate. Moreover, the cell-membrane may not be sufficiently permeable to phosphate to allow of an additional quantity being utilised.

It seems probable that when the sugar diffuses into the cell a compound of sugar and enzyme is formed, which reacts with the phosphate present to form a hexosephosphate and, simultaneously, alcohol and carbon dioxide. Harden suggests that two molecules of sugar take part in the reaction, according to the following equation :—

$$2C_6H_{12}O_6+2PO_4HR_2=2CO_2+2C_2H_6O+2H_2O+C_6H_{10}O_4(PO_4R_2)_2.$$

The hexosephosphate is then decomposed, and the liberated phosphate again enters into the reaction with more sugar.

The hexose present in the phosphate appears to be lævulose. Free hexosediphosphoric acid itself is dextrorotatory,

$$([\alpha]_{D15^{\circ}} = +3{\cdot}55)\ ;$$

but when the acid is hydrolysed the rotation changes, and lævulose is produced. According to C. Neuberg and his collaborators,[2] neither the free acid nor its soluble or insoluble salts with alkalis or alkaline earths can be fermented by living yeast, even if co-ferment is added, or artificial activators.

Another view of the process of fermentation has been much

[1] A. Harden, "Alcoholic Fermentation," Chap. III.

[2] *Biochem. Zeitsch.*, 1917, **83**, 244.

discussed. According to this, the sugar itself is converted into some intermediate compound with three carbon atoms, before being finally transformed into alcohol and carbon dioxide. Lactic acid, methyl glyoxal, polymers of formaldehyde, glyceraldehyde, and dihydroxyacetone are some of the compounds which have been suggested; but there is little positive evidence in favour of the actual occurrence of these compounds as stages of alcoholic fermentation. On the contrary, there is good evidence against the probability of some, at least, of these compounds being the necessary precursors of alcohol in the transposition of sugar. Thus lactic acid, $C_3H_6O_3$, might conceivably be split up into alcohol and carbon dioxide, as shown in the simple equation :—

$$C_3H_6O_3 = C_2H_6O + CO_2.$$

As an experimental fact, however, lactic acid is found not to be fermented by living yeast. Hence the lactic acid hypothesis is not accepted, although there is evidence (see below) that a small quantity of this acid is, in fact, produced during fermentation. There is somewhat better reason to think that dihydroxyacetone is actually an intermediate product in alcoholic fermentation; but with our present knowledge no final conclusion can be drawn as to the precise chemical changes which occur.

Fernbach, however, has shown that pyruvic acid is formed in relatively large proportion during alcoholic fermentation, and it is produced at the expense of the sugar. By fermenting glucose in the presence of calcium carbonate, the pyruvic acid was neutralised as it was formed; and the calcium salts separated, which in some experiments amounted to one-fourth the weight of sugar fermented, were mainly composed of calcium pyruvate.[1] Some calcium lactate was also produced, the lactic acid being presumably formed by the reduction of pyruvic acid. The latter is readily fermentable by yeast, the products being carbon dioxide and acetaldehyde; and Fernbach suggests that the aldehyde is further converted into alcohol by the reducing action of the yeast. Also a possible source of the succinic acid produced in fermentations is suggested by the fact that pyruvic acid readily condenses to a lactone, which with elimination of CO_2 is transformed into methyl succinic acid.

Some further evidence in support of the acetaldehyde–pyruvic acid theory of fermentation has recently been obtained by Neuberg and Reinfurth.[2] According to the theory as set forth by these authors, when 1 molecule of sugar is decomposed a part of the molecule forms 1 molecule of aldehyde, the other part acting as

[1] *J. Inst. Brewing*, 1916, **22**, 354. [2] *Biochem. Zeitsch.*, 1918, **89**, 365.

"acceptor" for hydrogen. By fermenting sugar in the presence of disodium sulphite to "fix" the aldehyde formed, it has been found possible to isolate aldehyde to the extent of about three-fourths of the amount required by the theory.

E. F. Armstrong has suggested that the enolic form of the hexose-sugars is the substance actually entering into fermentation.[1] This view is based upon the facts (i) that, according to this investigator, all yeasts which ferment dextrose also ferment lævulose and mannose; and (ii) that these three sugars have a common enolic form.

Rate of fermentation.—Slator[2] has shown that the rate of fermentation of dextrose by yeast is proportional to the concentration of the *yeast*, over a wide range of concentration. The rate is almost independent of the concentration of the *sugar*, except in very dilute solutions. The diffusion of sugar into the yeast-cell is sufficiently rapid to supply more sugar than can be fermented by the cell, even in dilute solutions.[3] Lævulose is fermented at the same rate as dextrose by different yeasts; and maltose at almost the same rate, by those yeasts which contain maltase. Malt wort, during the first part of the fermentation, is also fermented at the same rate as dextrose; the temperature and the concentration of the yeast are the chief factors which determine the rate. Temperature, in fact, has a considerable influence upon the activity of yeast. At 35°, for instance, the quantity of sugar fermented per unit of time in an experiment was nearly double the quantity at 25°, and this again was about six times as much as at 10°.

Autofermentation.—It may be mentioned that yeast itself undergoes fermentation. Nearly all samples of yeast contain glycogen, the amount varying according to the age of the yeast. Glycogen is the reserve carbohydrate of the yeast-cell, and it is readily fermented within the cell, this "autofermentation" producing alcohol and carbon dioxide as in the fermentation of the ordinary sugars. It has been suggested, indeed, that the formation of glycerol also is due to a similar autolytic destruction of the yeast itself, and not to the decomposition of sugar by yeast. Such an autolysis, it is considered, might occur through the action of an enzyme on the protein material of the yeast-cells.[4] This view is supported by the statement that when egg-albumin is added to sugar solutions which are undergoing fermentation by yeast, the proportion of glycerol produced is greatly increased. No further evidence, however, appears to have been adduced in favour of this

[1] *Proc. Roy. Soc.*, 1904, **73**, 516–26. [2] *Trans. Chem. Soc.*, 1906, **89**, 128.
[3] Slator and Sand, *ibid.*, 1910, **97**, 922–927.
[4] J. R. Carracido, *Revista Acad. Sci.*, Madrid, 1904, **1**, 217.

suggestion, and the sugar is generally regarded as the most probable source of the glycerol.

Yield of alcohol.—To obtain a complete conversion of the starch into sugar and alcohol is impracticable. Even under the best conditions the yield of alcohol is, from various causes, appreciably lower than the quantity theoretically obtainable if the starch could be all converted into alcohol and carbon dioxide only. This theoretical quantity would be :—

From the $C_6H_{12}O_6$ sugars (dextrose, etc.)	. . . .	51·1 per cent.
,, $C_{12}H_{22}O_{11}$,, (maltose, sucrose, etc.)	.	53·8 ,,
From starch $(C_6H_{10}O_5)_n$	. . . .	56·8 ,,

About six-sevenths of the theoretical yield is obtained. Taking starch as the starting-point, it is estimated that from 12 to 20 per cent. is generally lost in one way or other by the time the fermentation is finished. From 6 to 10 per cent. of the starch and dextrin remains unfermented. During the fermentation, 2 to 3 per cent. of glycerol is formed ; a part of the sugar is used up in providing nutriment for the yeast ; and a little alcohol is lost by evaporation. Any side-fermentations that occur through the agency of bacteria or other non-yeast organisms will still further diminish the yield of alcohol. In a badly-conducted operation the alcohol produced may represent not more than about 72 per cent. of the original starch. A good yield is 6 gallons of absolute aclohol per 100 lb. of starch, as compared with a theoretical yield of 7·16 gallons if the starch could be all transformed into alcohol and carbon dioxide alone. This 6 gallons represents 83·8 per cent. of the theoretical yield, showing therefore a loss of 16·2 per cent. A yield of $6\frac{1}{3}$ gallons, corresponding with a loss of 11·3 per cent., would be a high yield, obtainable under the best conditions ; $5\frac{3}{4}$ gallons would represent a medium result, and $5\frac{1}{2}$ would point to the conditions being unsatisfactory somewhere.

In British practice, the average yield of alcohol obtained in ordinary good working with kiln-dried malt and grain may be put at about $65\frac{1}{2}$ gallons of absolute alcohol or 115 gallons of proof spirit per ton of materials.

"Attenuation" yield. — For revenue purposes, in this country a presumptive yield of alcohol is calculated from the quantity of wort, and its specific gravity before and after fermentation. If, for example, 7000 gallons of wort at sp. gr. 1045° (water = 1000) are fermented down until the sp. gr. is 998°, the amount of "attenuation," or "degrees of gravity lost," is 1045 — 998 = 47°. It is presumed that for every 5 degrees of gravity lost there is produced alcohol equivalent to 1 per cent. of proof spirit; the quantity of proof spirit thus calculated is the "attenuation charge." Thus in the example taken, the charge is :—

$$\frac{7000 \times 47}{100 \times 5} = 658 \text{ proof gallons.}$$

In practice, the yield of alcohol obtained is about 13 to 15 per cent. more than this. The calculation, however, serves as a rough check upon the quantity of alcohol actually obtained, and in special circumstances the charge of duty may be based upon it.

The table given below, calculated from data given by Ullmann,[1] shows the average yield said to be obtained in Continental practice :

Material.	Alcohol produced. Gallons per ton.
Barley	72
Buckwheat	74
Dari (sorghum grain)	85
Maize	79
Manioc	88
Molasses, beet	64
,, cane	76
Oats	65
Potatoes	26
,, , dried	83
Rice	85
Rye	75
Sugar-beets	11 to 24
,, -cane	18 to 25
,, , raw	139
Wheat	78

The following table, showing the yield which may be obtained practically from various materials, is due to T. H. P. Heriot [2] :—

PRACTICAL YIELD OF ALCOHOL FROM DIFFERENT RAW MATERIALS.

Material.	Assumed content of starch or sugar.	Gallons of absolute alcohol produced per ton.	Percentage of theoretical yield.
Cane molasses	57·7% total sugars (as dextrose).	69	83
Beet molasses	50% sucrose.	63	83
Potatoes	20% starch.	30*	77*
Beet roots	15·4 sucrose.	20	87
Maize	60% starch and sugar with 8% of malt.	84	87
Rice	75% starch.	80 to 90	—
Wood sawdust	—	28 to 45	—
Nipa-palm sap	14–16% sucrose.	5–6% by volume.	74

* Given thus in the original, but one or other of the numbers is incorrect.

[1] *Enzyklop. der Techn. Chemie*, I, 752.

[2] *J. Soc. Chem. Ind.*, 1915, **34**, 338.

H. Ost[1] gives the following scheme showing the operations in a distillery using potatoes :—

Potatoes (100 kilos., 20 per cent. starch). Steamed in converter and blown out.

Barley (2·5 kilos.) malted.
↓
Green malt ("Long" malt) 3 kilos.
↓
Green malt (1·5 kilos.) mashed at 65°. (Yeast-mash or "bub").
↓
Soured at 50°.
↓
Cooled to 20°, and pitched with mother-yeast.
↓
One-eighth of the yeast reserved for next batch.

Potato mash, with green malt (1·5 kilos.) saccharified at 60°.
↓
Main wort.
↓
Pitched with yeast (seven-eighths).
↓
Fermented wash. | Carbon dioxide, about 9 kilos. = 4·6 cm.
↓
Distillation.
↓
Spirit (12·5 litres, 100 per cent.). | Spent wash (150 litres) ; 9 kilos. dry substance.

The "Amylo"-process of fermentation.—It has already been mentioned under "Yeast" (p. 56) that certain of the moulds secrete amylase (diastase) and also fermentation-enzymes. This property has been utilised in a process of combined saccharification and fermentation, whereby the use of malt is dispensed with in obtaining alcohol from starchy materials. The method in question is employed on a large scale in Belgium, France, Hungary, Italy, and Spain.

The mould originally employed was the mucor *Amylomyces Rouxii*, from which the "amylo"-process took its name. This organism, however, was later on supplanted by other moulds,

[1] *Lehrb. Chem. Technologie*, 1914, p. 528.

Mucor-β, *Mucor-γ*, and *Rhizopus Delemar*, which were found to produce less acid than *A. Rouxii.*

In addition to obviating the use of malt, another feature of the process is the adoption of pure-culture principles for the operations. The mash is sterilised, and the conversion and fermentation are carried out in closed vessels. As regards this, however, it may be noted that a special culture mould (*Mucor Boulard* No. 5) has recently been introduced, which is stated to act so vigorously that there is no longer any necessity for the adherence to aseptic conditions : bacterial development is suppressed when this organism is used.

Calmette isolated *A. Rouxii* in 1892 from Chinese rice-ferment, and he, with M. Boidin, worked out the industrial process, which was first tried at a distillery near Lille in 1898.

Although the moulds employed can not only convert gelatinised starch into dextrose, but can ferment this sugar into alcohol, the fermentation stage is a slow one. Hence, in practice, yeast is added in order to hasten and complete the fermentation. The yeast generally employed is *Saccharomyces anamensis* (" Annamite " yeast), which acts best at the same temperature as that at which the moulds develop, namely, 35–38°.

The chief materials used for mashing are maize, rice, potatoes, manioc, dari, and millet. A mash of sp. gr. about 1·060 is prepared by steaming the material under pressure, in essentially the same manner as already described under " Mashing."

The fermenting vessel is a vertical iron cylinder with dome-shaped ends, closed, and of capacity about 22,000 gallons, or more. An outlet is provided at the bottom for the fermented mash. This outlet serves also for passing in a current of aseptic air during the early stages of the fermentation. Near the top is an inlet for the steamed mash, a vent for escape of air and carbon dioxide, and tubules which allow of the introduction of the mould-culture and the yeast, as also of the withdrawal of samples to observe the progress of the operations.

The hot mash having been passed from the steamer or " cooker " into the fermenting vessel, a current of air, filtered through sterilised cotton wool to free it from micro-organisms, is injected into the mash whilst the latter cools, since the mould requires a certain amount of oxygen for its proper development. The cooling is done by running water down the outside of the vessel from a perforated tube passing round the top : it requires ten or twelve hours with a vessel of the size mentioned. When the temperature is down to 40°, the mash is inoculated with the mould, of which a culture has been prepared by growing the organism on sterilised rice until a copious production of spores is obtained. The spores are distributed in sterilised water and the mixture added to the mash, precautions against bacterial infection being taken during the addition.

The current of air keeps the mash in motion, and the spores are soon distributed throughout the starchy material. They develop very rapidly, and in the course of twenty to twenty-four hours the mash is permeated by the growing mycelium. No saccharification goes on during this first stage, whilst the mould is developing. After about twenty-one hours, however, the conversion of starch into sugar begins; and at the end of another eight hours or so, when the saccharification is well under way, the requisite quantity of yeast is added.

About twenty-four hours are required for the yeast to develop sufficiently to set up a vigorous fermentation. The current of air is then stopped, and the operation proceeds until the fermentation is complete and the wash ready for distillation. In this later stage, the two processes of saccharification and fermentation go on side by side, the mould finishing the transformation of the starch into sugar, and the yeast converting the sugar into alcohol. About four days are required for the saccharifying and fermenting operation, but this time can be shortened by employing a "bub" of the mould.[1]

Advantages claimed for the amylo-process are a better yield of alcohol, a purer product, and economy of malt, as compared with the ordinary method. Since the conditions of working exclude bacterial contamination, there are no bacterial side-fermentations, and the spirit contains fewer impurities--less foreshots and tailings, and less fusel oil. As regards the malt, a single gram of the mould suffices to convert 25 tons of maize. Compared with operations where 10 or 12 per cent. of malt is used, when this 1 gram of mould is employed there is a saving of about 3 tons of malt, and, in addition, of another ton of starch which is used up and lost in making that quantity of malt.

Some published figures show a yield in the amylo-process of 40·5 litres of alcohol per 100 kilos. of maize, and 42·3 litres per 100 kilos of rice, equivalent, respectively, to 7·92 and 8·27 gallons of proof spirit per cwt.[2]

There is a legal obstacle to the use of the amylo-process in this country. It is a statutory requirement that the specific gravity of distillers' wort before fermentation shall be ascertained by means

[1] O. Grove, *J. Inst. Brewing*, 1914, **20**, 248. [2] Grove, *loc. cit.*, p. 259.

of the saccharometer, and this, as will be gathered from the description given, is impracticable in the amylo-process. That such an obstacle exists is unfortunate. It prevents advantage being taken of any benefits which the process may offer, or of any developments to which it may give rise. In short, it impedes progress.

Use of bacterial enzymes.—Another interesting application of micro-organisms to the purposes of the distilling industry has been worked out by Boidin and Effront.

In the saccharification of starch by means of malt, the malt is an expensive ingredient, and much of it is used up in liquefying the starch. In both the malt conversion and the amylo-process there is a considerable loss of the nitrogenous constituents of the grain, over and above what is necessary for nutrition of the yeast, by reason of the conversion of proteins into soluble nitrogenous compounds which pass away in the residual liquid after the alcohol has been distilled off.

Boidin and Effront seek to avoid or minimise this loss, to economise malt, and also to obviate the need for "cooking" or steaming the grain under pressure in the preliminary stages of mashing. This they do by the use of bacterial enzymes capable of liquefying starch but having little or no action on the proteins.[1] The organism employed is a certain species of *Bacillus mesentericus*, "acclimatised" by cultivation under the special conditions to produce a maximum amount of enzyme. The bacillus is grown in an alkaline medium, strongly aerated; the culture liquid thus obtained has an activity such that it will liquefy 1000 times its weight of grain, and by concentration *in vacuo* products six times as strong can be prepared.

In using these enzymes, the grain is first soaked in an alkaline solution, then coarsely ground, mixed with two volumes of water, and heated to 75–80°. The solution of the enzymes is added at this temperature, and allowed to act for a period of thirty to sixty minutes, by the end of which time the starch is all liquefied. Then the mash is heated for some time at 110–120°, and subsequently cooled to 60° in open vats. Malt is now added, in the proportion of 1 to 2 per cent. of the grain, and the saccharifying action allowed to proceed for an hour. By reason of the previous liquefaction, this small amount of malt suffices for complete saccharification, and it also supplies sufficient yeast nutriment.

After cooling, the wort is "pitched" with yeast acclimatised to hydrofluoric acid, and the fermentation completed as usual.

In this way a larger amount of nitrogenous substance remains

[1] Effront, "Biochemical Catalysts in Life and Industry," p. 615. (Wiley, 1917.)

undissolved in the "grains" or residue from the mash, and is available as a foodstuff for cattle, instead of being rendered soluble and run to waste in the spent lees, as in the ordinary process.

IV.—DISTILLATION AND RECTIFICATION

The fermented wash contains as chief volatile constituents alcohol, water, and fusel oil, with small quantities of acetic acid, aldehyde, and esters. Its non-volatile ingredients include solid particles of husks, yeast, proteins, glycerol, succinic, lactic, and other fatty acids; and mineral salts. To separate the alcohol from this mixture recourse is had to the process of distillation.

Pot stills.—At the smaller distilleries where malt whiskies

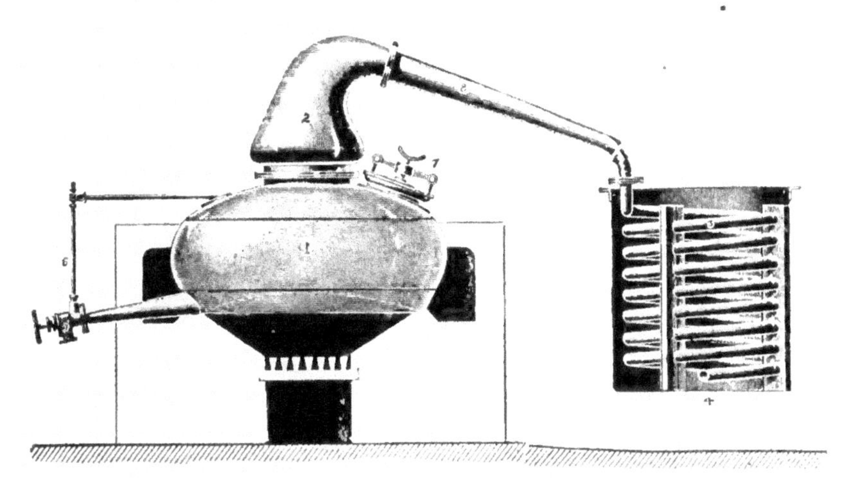

FIG. 22.—SIMPLE POT-STILL, FIRE-HEATED, WITH CONDENSER.
(1) Boiling vessel; (2) still-head; (3) condenser worm (Haslam Foundry Co., Ltd., Derby).

are produced, and where it is the object of the distiller to retain in the product some of the esters, higher alcohols, and other bodies which give the spirit its characteristic flavour, the apparatus employed is the relatively simple "pot" still. This may consist merely of a boiling vessel, with a retort head and a worm condenser. Or the head may be attached to one or more fractionating vessels similar to Woulfe's bottles, through which the alcoholic vapours pass before reaching the condenser. Or, again, the simple retort head may be replaced by a rectifying still-head, consisting of a series of water-jacketed vessels arranged one above the other, the vapour rising through each of these successively.

Usually the pot still is heated by the direct flame of a furnace, though steam is now frequently used as the heating agent. The steam is applied either as a "jacket" outside the still, or by means of coils inside the vessel. When a furnace is employed, a stirring apparatus is often fitted into the still to remove the sediment of vegetable matter which is prone to settle on the bottom, and which, if not displaced, is decomposed by the heat and communicates an empyreumatic flavour to the spirit.

With a pot still, the spirit produced by the first distillation is always very impure, and has a disagreeable odour and taste. It is called **"low wines."** On redistillation of the low wines, the first portion of the distillate ("foreshots") is contaminated with oily matters, including apparently esters of fatty acids deposited in the

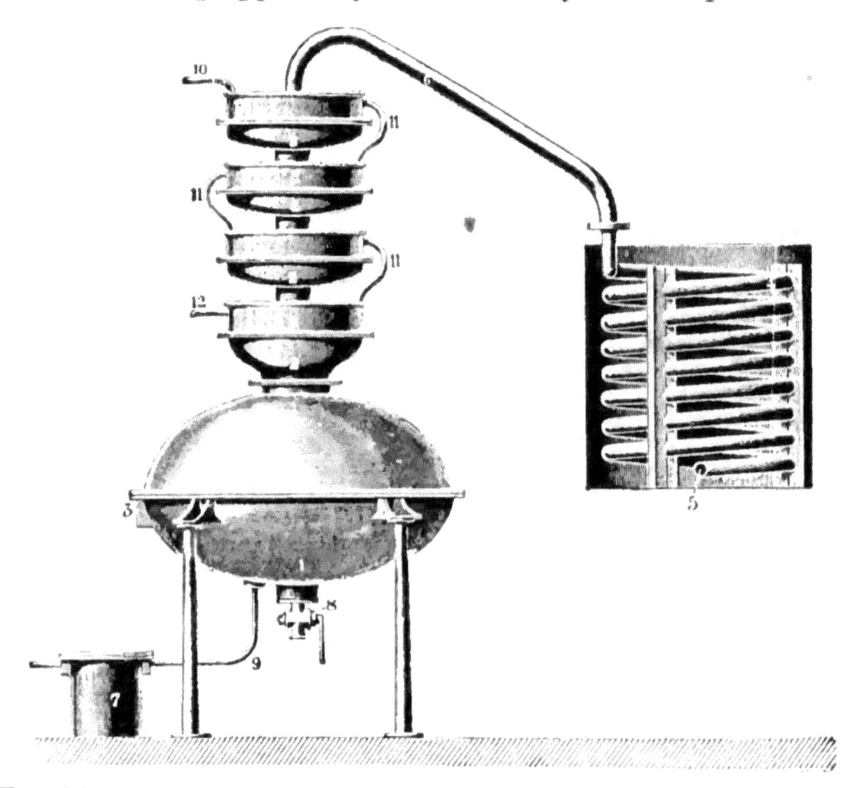

FIG. 23.—STEAM-HEATED POT-STILL, WITH RECTIFYING HEAD (Corty's). (2) Rectifying-baths (Haslam Foundry Co., Ltd., Derby).

condenser towards the end of the previous distillation and now redissolved by the strong spirit. As the distillation proceeds the proportion of oily matters diminishes until the distillate no longer becomes turbid on dilution with water, when the spirit is considered sufficiently pure to be collected as potable alcohol. Towards the close of the process the spirit again becomes oily ("tailings"). The impure portions of the distillate obtained in this second distillation are termed "**feints**"; they are redistilled with the succeeding "low wines" to recover the alcohol from them. It is usual to have separate stills for the two distillations, one for the "wash" only ("wash still") and a smaller one for the low wines ("low wines still "); though occasionally one still serves for both operations The low wines still is generally of about one-half the capacity of the wash still; the latter is of any size up to 10,000 gallons, or even more, occasionally 20,000. Not infrequently, a second low wines still (" spirit still ") is used to obtain the final product from the low wines, or for the re-distillation of the strong feints.

The residue from the distillation of the wash is termed " pot ale "; that from the low wines is called " spent lees." Both are run to waste, as a rule, though the pot ale is sometimes evaporated and the product used as a fertiliser.

In the following table[1] are shown the approximate boiling points of wash or feints containing various proportions of alcohol, and also the percentage of alcohol in the distillate, as obtained from a simple still :—

Wash or feints.		Distillate.	Wash or feints.		Distillate.
Temperature.	Alcohol, per cent.	Alcohol, per cent.	Temperature.	Alcohol, per cent.	Alcohol, per cent.
83°	50	85	94°	7	50
83·5	40	82	95	5	42
86	30	78	96	3	36
88	20	71	97	2	28
90·5	15	66	99	1	13
92	10	55	100	0	0

As an example of the effect of successive distillations in a simple still upon the proportion of alcohol in the distillate, the following series of experiments may be quoted.[2]

A fermented wash containing, by weight, 11·3 per cent. of alcohol, was distilled until practically free from spirit. The distillate was then treated in the same way, the operation being repeated five times :—

Liquid distilled.	Alcohol, per cent. by weight.
Wash	11·3
1st distillate	32·3
2nd ,,	55·0
3rd ,,	70·3
4th ,,	78·5
5th ,,	83·0

Simple pot stills are also used to some considerable extent for the distillation of wine in the making of brandy. Often, however, a rectifying still of more effective type is employed, which at the same time is not effective enough to give a " neutral " spirit by removing all the characteristic esters, higher alcohols, and aldehydes. The use of a high still-head, or the insertion of a perforated

[1] Gröning (adapted from). Maercker-Delbrück, " Handbuch der Spiritus-fabrikation," 1908, p. 771.

[2] Maercker-Delbrück, *loc. cit.*

plate in the upper part of the still, tends to increase the rectifying effect and to give a purer distillate. With the simpler forms of

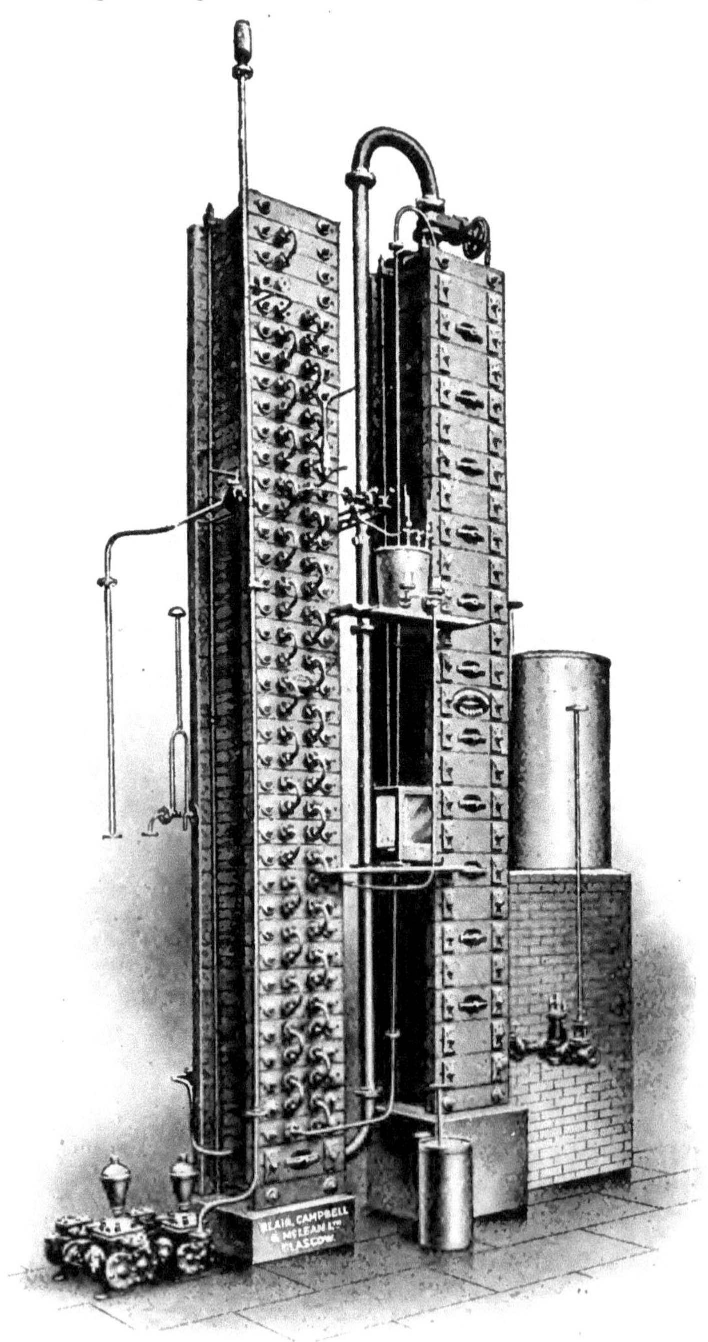

FIG. 24.—COFFEY'S PATENT CONTINUOUS-WORKING STEAM-STILL (Blair, Campbell, and McLean, Ltd., Glasgow). Exterior.

still, two distillations are necessary, as described above for ordinary alcohol, but "continuous" stills are also in use, giving potable spirit from wine by a single distillation.

Patent stills.—By far the greater quantity of ordinary alcohol, however, is distilled in highly-effective apparatus which produces a nearly pure "silent" or "neutral" spirit of from 94 to 96 per cent. strength in one continuous operation. The "Coffey" or "patent" still, which is largely used in this country, may be taken as example; though other stills used abroad and differing in detail claim to be of at least equal efficacy, especially for dealing with thick washes.

In this still the alcohol is expelled by blowing steam through the wash, which is spread in layers over a considerable surface. The wash enters at the top of the still, and passes downwards over a series of perforated diaphragms of copper plate, trickling over small orifices which serve as so many traps where the liquid is met by the uprising steam. The latter, bubbling through the perforations, heats the wash, and carries off the alcohol vapour, so that by the time the wash reaches the lowest plate it has been deprived of all its alcohol, and passes out with its dissolved and suspended solids, whilst the alcohol, steam, and volatile impurities pass to the top of the apparatus. The higher these vapours get, the richer they become in alcohol; their boiling point becomes lower; and more and more of the steam is condensed. The part of the still in which this operation takes place is termed the "analyser."

The escaping vapours are now led into the *bottom* of a similar column of perforated plates, termed the "rectifier." From top to bottom of this column there passes a zig-zag tube full of cold liquid to serve as a condenser. To economise heat this liquid is, in fact, the cold wash on its way to the analyser. The alcoholic vapours passing upwards through the plates into one cool chamber after another become cooled, and deposit more and more of their water as they near the top, finally condensing as strong alcohol on an unperforated copper sheet (the "spirit plate"), and passing out. The strength of the spirit thus continuously obtained is about 94 to 96 per cent. by volume, whereas with a simple still the strongest alcohol obtainable, even by repeated distillations, is only about 90 to 92 per cent., and at this strength is produced only in small quantities from each operation.

A mixture of weak, impure alcohol and oils ("hot feints") collects in the bottom of the "rectifier"; this is pumped into the "analyser" again to recover the alcohol. But towards the end of a distilling process, instead of completing the purification of all the alcohol, it is found more economical to raise the temperature of the apparatus and distil off the whole residue of impure spirit:

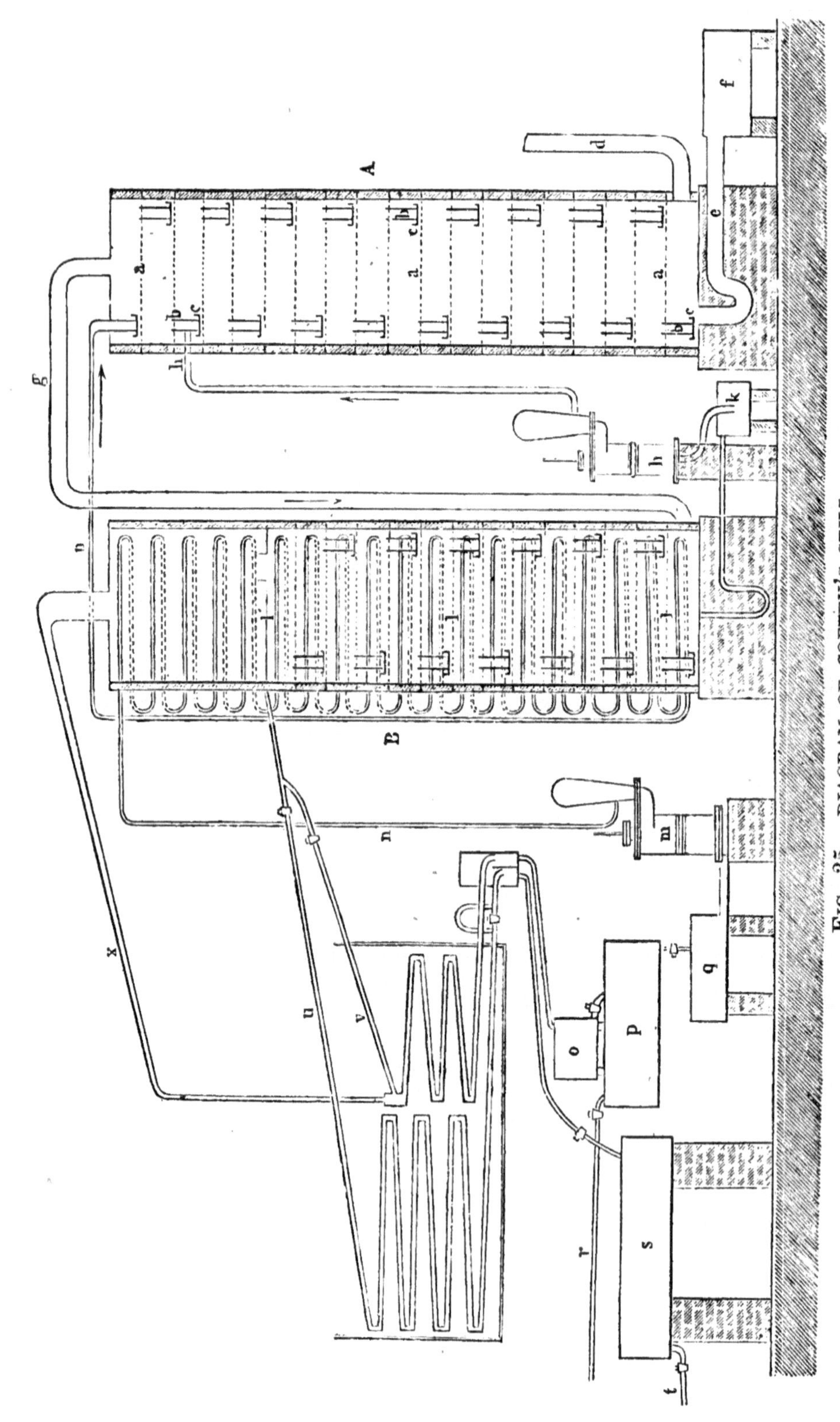

FIG. 25.—DIAGRAM OF COFFEY'S STILL.

A, analyser; *B*, rectifier; *a*, perforated copper diaphragms; *m*, pump, forcing wash through zig-zag tube *n* to top of *A*: *g*, pipe leading spirit-vapour to bottom of rectifier.

this is condensed and collected as "feints" in a separate receiver.

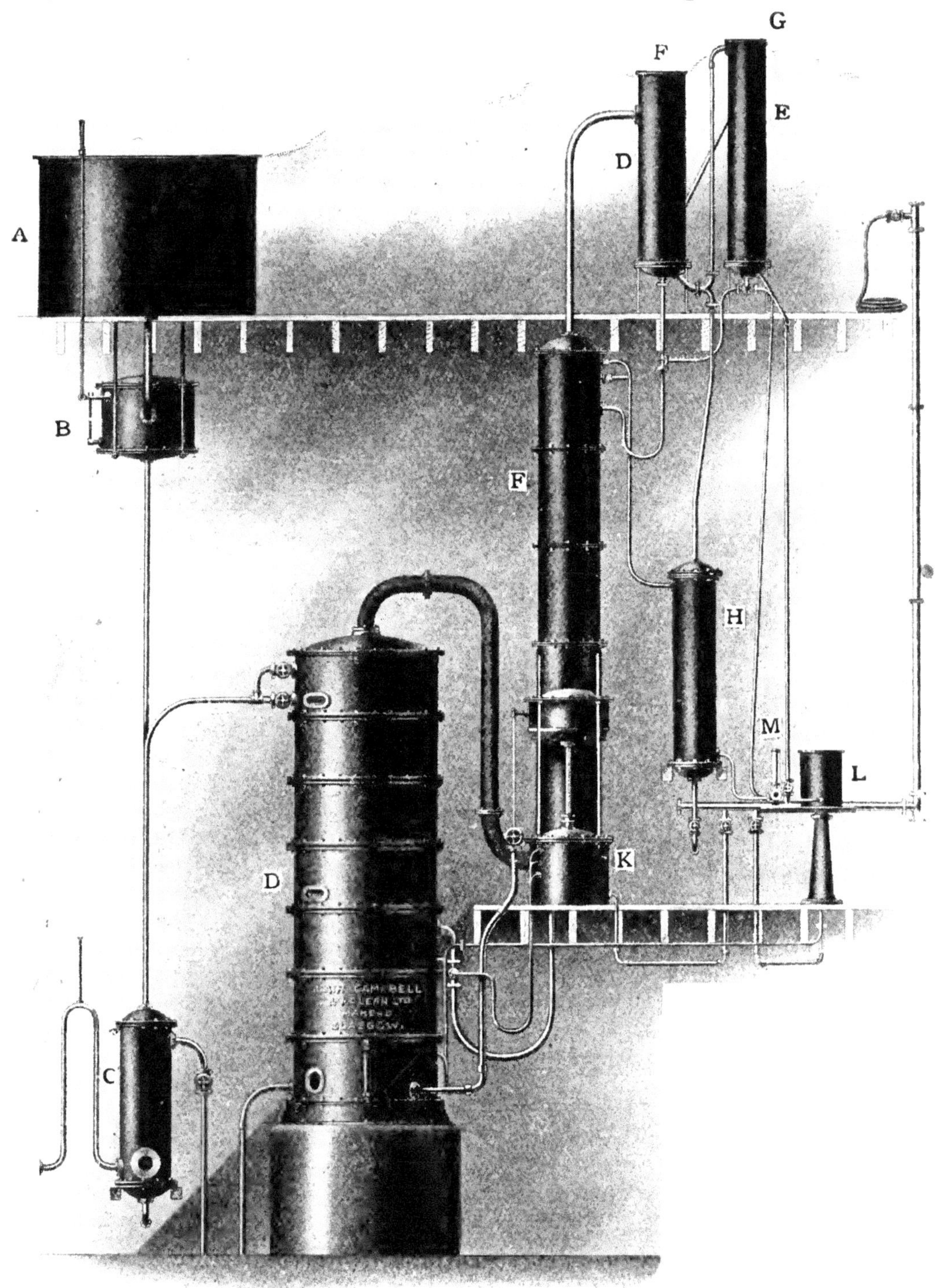

FIG. 26.—DOUBLE COLUMN CONTINUOUS STILL.

A, Supply tank; *B*, liquor regulator; *C*, preheater; *D*, boiling column; *E*, rectifying column; *F*, rectifying column rectifier; *G*, rectifying column condenser; *H*, rectifying column cooler; *K*, steam regulator; *L*, oils cooling tank; *M*, run-off tester (Blair, Campbell, and McLean, Ltd., Glasgow).

Here the fusel oil which has accumulated during the process separates to a large extent from the weak spirit and is skimmed off, the remaining " feints " being redistilled with the wash of the succeeding operation to recover the ethyl alcohol from them.

The " Coffey " still was patented in 1832. Various other " continuous " alcohol stills are employed, especially on the Continent and in America: their essential principle is similar to that of Coffey's apparatus. Barbet's stills have a considerable reputation in France and abroad, as have also those of Messrs. Egrot and Grangé. Guillaume's system includes a sloping, instead of vertical, distilling column, to obviate risk of obstruction when thick washes are being distilled. Of the others, it will suffice to mention the Ilges " automatic " still, which is said to yield a pure spirit of 96 to 96·5 per cent. strength, and to recover all the fusel oil and low wines at strengths of 80 and 97 per cent. respectively.

The alcohol of high strength distilled in apparatus of the Coffey or allied types is a nearly pure product, and is known as " silent," " neutral," or " patent-still " spirit. Large quantities are employed without further purification, as, for instance, in making acetic acid, explosives, and varnishes; in the production of methylated spirit or other forms of industrial alcohol; in extracting drugs, preparing spirituous medicines, and so on.

Rectification.—When, however, special purity is required, or when the alcohol obtained is of cruder character, it is further purified by special rectification. This is usually accomplished by diluting the spirit with water to a strength of about 45–50 per cent., and re-distilling it. Various kinds of stills are used for the purpose. Some are " intermittent " stills which fractionate the distillate, the impurities being eliminated in the first and last runnings; others are " continuous action " rectifying stills. Purification by treatment with wood charcoal is also employed, the alcohol, suitably diluted, being passed through a battery of cylindrical filters containing the charcoal. The purifying effect is mainly a chemical one, due to oxidation. According to circumstances, the filtration through charcoal may either precede or follow a rectification by distillation.

V.—CONVERSION OF CELLULOSIC SUBSTANCES INTO ALCOHOL

Alcohol from wood.—In obtaining alcohol from sawdust or other waste-wood material, the so-called " cellulose " of the wood is hydrolysed by treatment with acids under pressure. By this means it is in part converted into dextrose and other fermentable sugars. The acid is then neutralised, or nearly so, with lime or alkali, and the resulting liquid is fermented and distilled.

There is some doubt as to what is the "cellulose" actually hydrolysed. The cellulose of cotton does not respond to the treatment. Also the material left by sawdust which has been once treated still contains cellulose, but a repetition of the process

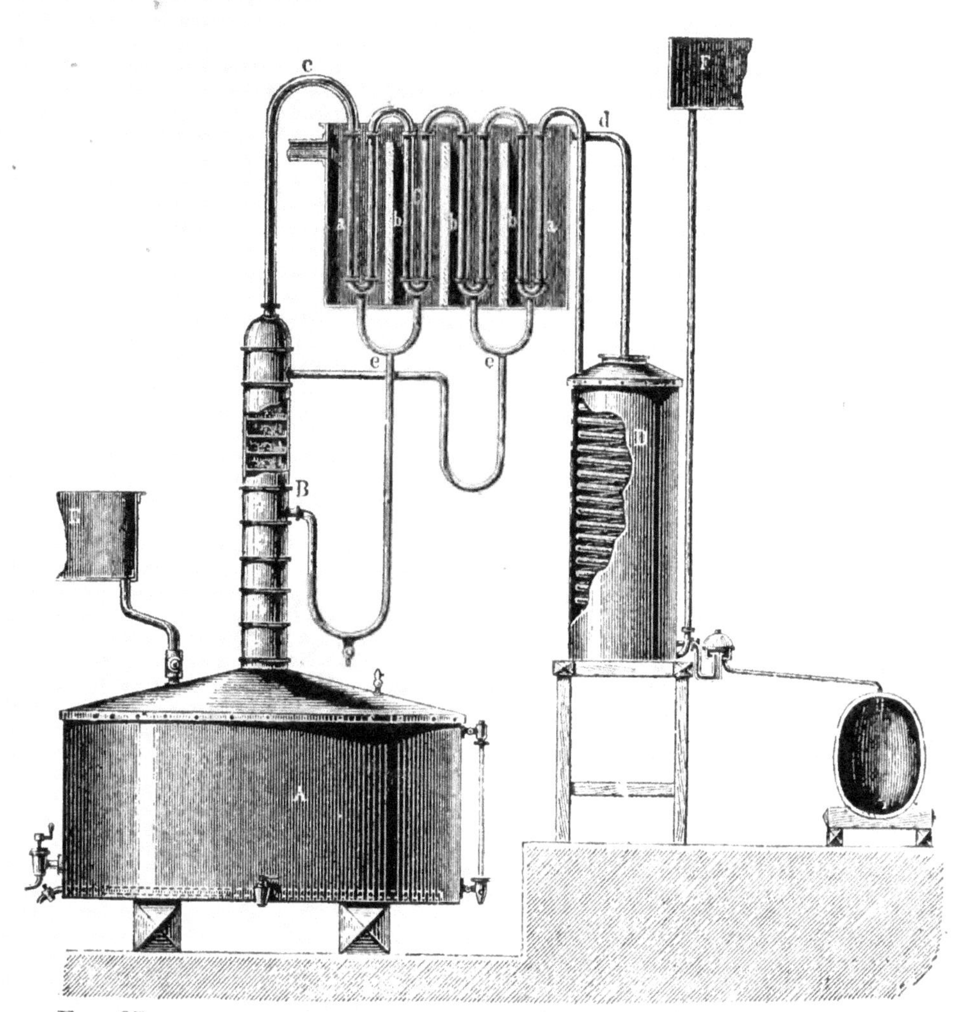

Fig. 27.—French column apparatus for rectification of alcohol.

Formerly much used abroad. *A*, boiling vessel, heated by steam; *B*, rectifier; *C*, condenser; *D*, refrigerator.

yields very little more fermentable sugar. The portion which is transformed is sometimes distinguished as the "easily-attacked" cellulose. It probably consists of polysaccharides of pentoses and hexoses.

According to Willstätter and Zechmeister,[1] cellulose can be completely converted into dextrose at the ordinary temperature by treatment with a strong solution of hydrochloric acid (40 to

[1] *Ber.*, 1913, **46**, 2401.

41 per cent. of HCl), which dissolves it in a few seconds, and gives complete hydrolysis in twenty-four to forty-eight hours. Their

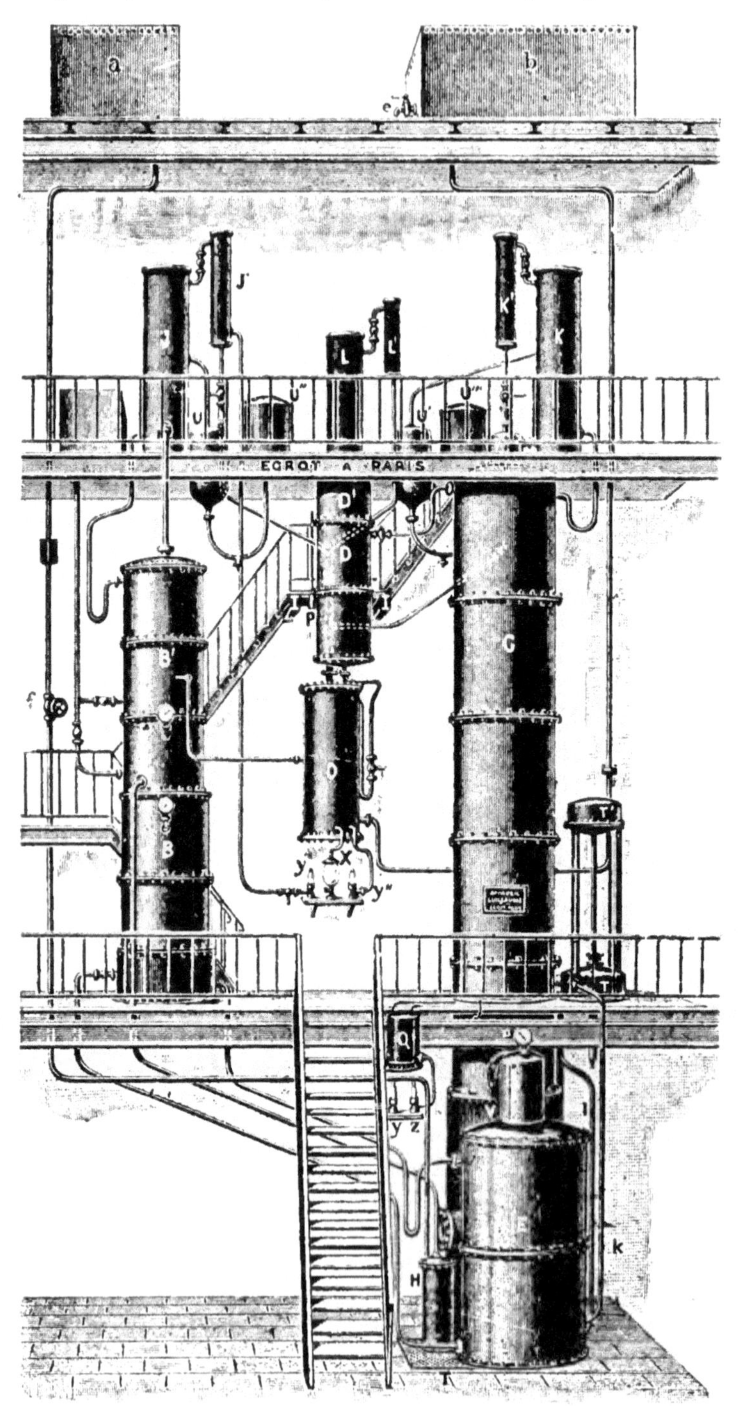

Fig. 28.—Modern still, for continuous rectification.

a, back for crude spirit; *b*, back for water. *B*, *B'*, purifying and concentrating columns for foreshots; *C*, rectifying column; *D*, *D'*, final purifying columns; *J*, *K*, *L*, condensers; *J'*, *K'*, *L'*, *O*, refrigerators (Egrot and Grangé, Paris).

statement, however, appears to be erroneous.[1] In any case,

[1] M. Cunningham, *Trans. Chem. Soc.*, 1918, **113**, 173.

their observation does not seem to have been utilised industrially.

As far back as 1819, Braconot showed that when wood waste was heated with sulphuric acid a product was obtained which contained sugar. Simonsen, however, some eighty years later, appears to have been the first to attempt the manufacture of sugar from sawdust on any large scale.[1] He used diluted sulphuric or hydrochloric acid, at a strength of 0·3 to 0·7 per cent., and heated the mixture of sawdust and acid under a pressure of 7 to 8 atmospheres. Ekström attempted to solve the same problem by using strong sulphuric acid.[2]

Classen, in 1900, showed that aqueous sulphurous acid converted wood celluloses into dextrose when the mixture was heated under pressure to a temperature of 120–140°. There is an advantage in using a volatile acid, such as sulphurous or hydrochloric, instead of sulphuric, inasmuch as a better penetration of the wood is obtained.

After laboratory experiments at Aachen, the method was tried in an experimental plant near Chicago, and afterwards an installation on a commercial scale was erected at Hattiesburg, Missouri. It consisted of an apparatus for preparing the sulphur dioxide; a converter in which the wood was treated with the acid; an extraction battery; neutralisation vats; fermentation vessels, and distillation apparatus. The sawdust was treated in the converter with a saturated aqueous solution of sulphur dioxide, the temperature being gradually raised to 143–149° and the action allowed to proceed during from four to six hours. Then the sulphur dioxide was blown off by steam and collected for re-use, the woody residue treated with water in the extraction-vessels to remove the sugar, and the solution thus obtained neutralised, fermented, and distilled. One hundred kilos. of sawdust gave from 7½ to 8½ litres of alcohol.

As thus worked, the process fell just short of success. The reasons given for the failure were: (1) Length of time required for the conversion (four to six hours for two tons); (2) production of gummy matters and caramelisation due to the prolonged action; (3) the large quantity of acid required; and (4) difficulties due to the action of the acid on the lead lining of the converter—a cylinder 30 ft. long, and 3 ft. in diameter.

Two chemical engineers, Messrs. Ewen and Tomlinson, improved the process by using a much shorter and wider converter (12 ft. by

[1] W. P. Cohoe, *J. Soc. Chem. Ind.*, 1912, **31**, 513.
[2] D. R.-P., 193112.

8 ft.), and lining it with firebrick instead of with lead.[1] Sulphur dioxide gas to the extent of 1 per cent. of the weight of wood treated is introduced into the converter, and steam passed in until a pressure of 100 lb. is obtained. The steam is then turned off and the cylindrical converter slowly revolved for forty–forty-five minutes, the temperature and pressure being kept constant: the total time required for conversion is about an hour. The temperature is raised as quickly as possible to the "critical" point, between 135° and 163°, above which there is an excessive destruction of sugars and production of unfermentable substances.

When the extraction is completed, the solution obtained has a total acidity of 0·64 per cent. (calculated as H_2SO_4), and contains about 5½ per cent. of reducing sugars, with small amounts of phenols, tannins, and furfural. It is neutralised, fermented, and distilled as usual, and gives about 38½ gallons (U.S.) of alcohol per ton of dry wood, or between 75 and 80 per cent. of the theoretical yield.[2]

More recent particulars have been given by G. H. Tomlinson.[3] The digesters or converters now employed are standard 14 ft. globular rotatory bleaching boilers, protected on the inside with an acid-proof tile lining. This type allows of easy filling and emptying. Separation of the sugar from the woody residue is effected in a standard beet-sugar diffusion battery provided with a similar lining to that of the digester. From 80 to 100 tons of material per day can be treated in this apparatus. Per ton of dry wood, the maximum yield is 35 gallons of alcohol (95 per cent.), but on a large scale the actual average yields have hardly exceeded half of this amount.

According to R. von Demuth,[4] dilute sulphuric acid has replaced sulphur dioxide as hydrolysing agent in some of the American factories. To obviate destruction of the sugars formed, the process is accelerated as much as possible. The steaming lasts only long enough to hydrolyse a certain proportion of cellulose and produce a condition of equilibrium (between sugar destroyed and sugar produced); this takes about an hour. The hydrolysed wood is then extracted in a diffusion battery, pressed, dried, and used as fuel.

The extract, after being nearly neutralised with lime, is fermented with yeast that has been cultivated in a rye and malt mash; cooked malt combings are used as yeast nutriment. About 7·3 to 9·5 litres of alcohol (100 per cent.) are obtained per 100 kilos. of dry wood: this corresponds with 16 to 21 imperial gallons per ton. In addition,

[1] U.S. P. 938308 of 1909. [2] A. Hirsch, *J. Ind. Eng. Chem.*, 1912, **4**, 479.
[3] *Chem. Tr. J.*, 1918, **63**, 103. [4] *Zeitsch. angew. Chem.*, 1913, **26**, 786.

a small quantity of turpentine oil, about 0·03 per cent., is recovered as a by-product. Only traces of fusel oil and esters are present in the alcohol produced.

According to E. Hägglund,[1] only very dilute acid is likely to be commercially successful for the hydrolysis of wood in the making of alcohol. Dilute sulphuric acid of strength 0·25 to 1 per cent. can be employed, and the best temperature is 175°. The proportion of wood to acid may be as high as 1 to 3. Under these conditions the yield of alcohol was found to be from 75 to 85 litres per ton of wood (pine or fir). The use of sulphurous acid or calcium bisulphite decreased the yield to about 40 litres and 60 litres per ton respectively. Comparison experiments carried out with much stronger sulphuric acid (70 per cent.) indicated that under the most favourable conditions as much as 158 litres of alcohol per ton could be obtained, but the greater cost of the acid more than offset the increased yield of alcohol.

Some lengthy and careful investigations have also been carried out by F. W. Kressman.[2] He concludes that for commercial working the most satisfactory conditions for the digestion of the wood are: Pressure, 7½ atmospheres; duration of the digestion, twenty minutes from the time the working pressure is attained; ratio of water to dry wood, 125 to 100; ratio of acid to dry wood, 2½ to 100. Under these conditions, white spruce yielded 23·6 per cent. of total sugars, calculated on the dry wood, and 71·4 per cent. of the sugar was fermentable. The yield of alcohol was 8·54 per cent. of the weight of dry wood. Larch was found to yield much galactose, which is not fermentable with ordinary yeast.

Reviewing the present position of this industry, Tomlinson regards it as one of relative stagnation, due partly to the fact that operations have been started prematurely, with little regard to the commercial conditions involved.[3] The fact, however, that several million gallons of alcohol have actually been produced from wood waste, and that at least two plants have been operating more or less continuously over a period of years, justifies the belief that ultimate success is assured.

It was originally assumed that almost every sawmill represented a possible location for the establishment of an alcohol plant. There were large numbers of sawmills at which the disposal of the wood-waste was a problem, and even an element of expense. Hence it was assumed that this waste could be purchased at a purely nominal figure, and so an almost endless chain of alcohol-producing

[1] *J. pr. Chem.*, 1915, **91**, 358. [2] *J. Ind. Eng. Chem.*, 1915, **7**, 920.
[3] *Chem. and Metall. Eng.*, 1918, **19**, 552.

plants might be established. It was soon found, however, that while there was no question regarding the number of sawmills or the quantity of waste wood produced, nevertheless there were very few mills at which the conditions were altogether favourable for setting up the extensive plant which the manufacture of alcohol requires. The "life" of the lumbering operations may be uncertain, the water supply deficient, labour or transportation facilities unfavourable, and so on. Moreover, the lumberman who has a suitable "location" soon recognises his advantage and exacts his price. The alcohol maker must pay it, for the plant when once established has no other source of supply. Sawdust and other waste wood is bulky and difficult to handle and transport; so that, in practice, it must be treated at the place where it is produced.

For these various reasons, the authority quoted considers that if the industry is to be greatly extended, a modification of procedure will be necessary. In general, the sawmills should produce the sugar solution from the waste wood, but should not ferment and distil it. They should evaporate it to a syrup or molasses, which could then be conveyed to suitable distilleries working on a large scale, where it would be fermented and distilled under the most favourable conditions.

This would mean that only a molasses plant would need to be installed at the sawmill, instead of the complete distillery outfit. Smaller units could be worked economically; less skilled labour would be required; and the plant would be free from revenue regulations. Further, if the molasses product is sold to those already engaged in the distilling industry, many market and other trade difficulties are removed. Complete installations for the production of alcohol would, of course, still be erected in localities where the conditions were specially suitable.

Naturally, the important factor in the development of the industry, as thus outlined, would be the cost of the syrup obtained, as compared with that of cane-sugar molasses. The following particulars of actual working costs are given.

Working for twenty-two days in 1913, at three-fourths of the full capacity, the Fullerton plant, previously mentioned, dealt with 6125 tons of green waste wood containing 48 per cent. of moisture, and yielded 1,688,600 gallons (U.S.) of sugar solution at about 10·3 per cent. strength. The total cost was 31·8 cents per 100 gallons. The molasses obtained by concentrating 100 gallons of the sugar solution down to 12½ gallons cost about 3 cents per gallon, including cost of evaporation. This is much lower than the cost of cane molasses. But whereas one gallon of the wood molasses yields only about 0·39 gallon of proof spirit (U.S. proof), cane molasses yields about one gallon. Proper chemical control, however, might result in obtaining a product equal to cane molasses. "There is thus within reach an almost unlimited supply of wood molasses which the distiller can readily convert into alcohol, with little or no modification in the ordinary distillery equipment."[1]

In W. P. Cohoe's process, the conversion is done in two stages, First, steam is used alone; this produces some acetic acid, which is collected. Then a mixture of steam and gaseous hydrochloric acid is introduced to complete the conversion.[2]

Gazagne and de Demuth have described the following procedure.[3]

Peat, or sawdust, or other wood waste, is saccharified by heating under pressure with a mineral acid. The product is then systematically extracted with hot water, or with vinasse liquor from beet-sugar manufacture, in a battery of extraction-vessels, as in the extracting of sugar from beets. The solution thus obtained is neutralised with ammonia or alkali hydroxide, and fermented. To improve the fermentation, yeast is used which has been specially acclimatised to liquors from cellulose materials containing tannins; and yeast nutriment is added in the form of saccharifiable substances relatively rich in nitrogen and phosphorus. These substances may either be included with the charge in the autoclave, or saccharified separately and added to the liquor after the extraction is completed.

Mention may be made here of lævoglucosan, obtained by Pictet and Sarasin on distilling cellulose or starch under reduced pressure. This product is hydrolysed by dilute sulphuric acid to glucose, which could be used as a source of alcohol.[4] As the lævoglucosan could be obtained in quantity, the authors suggest that it may prove to be utilisable for the industrial production of alcohol.

Alcohol from sulphite-waste liquor.—Waste sulphite liquor is a by-product of the wood pulp industry, and very large quantities are available in the countries where this industry is carried on. For every ton of cellulose about 10 tons of the liquor are produced. Among the substances present in it are dextrose and other sugars; xylose; acetic, sulphurous, and tannic acids; methyl alcohol; and nitrogenous and resinous bodies, together with calcium lignin-sulphonate, the chief by-product of the reaction involved in the production of the pulp.

The amount of fermentable sugars in the liquor varies rather considerably, but is usually between 1·5 and 2 per cent. An analysis by Klason gave dextrose 1·65, mannose 0·53, and galactose

[1] *Chem. and Metall. Eng.*, 1918, **19**, 555. [2] U.S. P. 985725 and 985726.
[3] F.P. 477077, 1914. [4] *Helv. Chim. Acta*, 1918, **1**, 87.

0·27 per cent. Of these sugars, galactose ferments more slowly than the others, and the highest yields of alcohol obtained, namely, 1·4 per cent. of the volume of the liquor, corresponds approximately with the dextrose and mannose content.

Various processes are in use for utilising the waste liquor as a source of alcohol (" sulphite spirit "), but all are based upon the same principle. The free sulphurous acid, which is strongly toxic to yeast, is partly removed by evaporation and partly by neutralisation to a point of acidity favourable for fermentation. The hot liquor is neutralised in large vats, then cooled in towers, and aerated. A yeast nutriment, such as malt extract, or dead yeast, is added to the cooled, neutralised liquor, which is then fermented. After the fermentation is finished, which takes three days or more, the yeast is separated and the liquid distilled in a continuous-action still. The alcohol obtained is already partly denatured, since it usually contains a little methyl alcohol derived from the original liquor, with some aldehydes and furfural, and sometimes acetone.

Ekström's process[1] has been in operation for several years at Skutskär (Sweden), and that of Wallin at Forss, whilst others employed industrially are Landmark's and Marchand's. The difference in the various processes lies mainly in the method of neutralisation. It is not advisable to neutralise with lime alone, as a large excess is required, causing destruction of some of the sugar. In the Swedish plants which are operating under Ekström's and Wallin's patents, the neutralisation is partly effected with lime, and then finished with calcium carbonate. In Landmark's process, calcium carbonate only is employed, and in Marchand's, barium carbonate. The waste liquor does not contain sufficient nitrogen and phosphate for normal fermentation, and these must be supplied in a suitable form, with the yeast extract or otherwise. In Ekström's method, a yeast specially acclimatised to sulphite liquor is used. In Landmark's process, milk or whey is heated with acid, the precipitate separated, and the liquid portion added to the sulphite liquor, which can then be fermented directly with ordinary brewers' yeast. The cost of the milk is said to be covered by the " lignocasein " obtained, which can be used for sizing paper.[2] A. V. Jernberg[3] adds to the liquor a neutralising agent and a sufficient quantity of calcium cyanamide, previously treated with water or steam, to supply the deficiency in nitrogen.

The yield of alcohol is about 1 per cent. of the waste liquor, on

[1] B.P., 6741, 1910. [2] Bjarne Johnsen, *J. Soc. Chem. Ind.*, 1918, **37**, 131T.
[3] U.S. P. 1221058, 1917.

an average, though rather greater yields are claimed for some of the methods.

VI.—SYNTHETIC ALCOHOL FROM ACETYLENE AND CALCIUM CARBIDE

In the introductory chapter it was pointed out that Hennell, as long ago as 1828, had effected a synthesis of alcohol from ethylene. This gas was dissolved in sulphuric acid, forming ethyl hydrogen sulphate, from which alcohol was obtained by diluting the acid solution and distilling it.

This method of obtaining alcohol has remained a purely laboratory operation for the greater part of a century. Indeed, instead of ethylene being used as a source of alcohol, the latter substance has been the most convenient material from which to obtain ethylene. With the coming of the electric furnace, however, matters have altered. By its aid calcium carbide is produced, and serves as a cheap source of acetylene. Hence it has become practicable, by converting acetylene into ethylene, to utilise Hennell's synthesis, and thus obtain alcohol on a commercial scale from acetylene or from calcium carbide. The ultimate raw materials of the carbide, of course, are coal and chalk.

The waste gas from coke ovens contains from 1 to 4 per cent. of ethylene. If a practicable means of utilising this by the sulphuric acid process were found, coke oven gas might prove to be an economical source of alcohol.

A drawback to this method appears to be the relatively considerable volume of strong sulphuric acid that would be necessary for operations on a large scale. Another possibility, however, is the conversion of acetylene into acetaldehyde, and the reduction of the latter to alcohol.

Various patents have been taken out for methods of obtaining ethylene and aldehyde from acetylene.

Thus Traube[1] converts acetylene into ethylene by the aid of chromous salts in acid solution, under pressure. The chromous salt can be regenerated from the resulting chromic compound by reduction with zinc, or by electrolytic methods. For example, 4 parts of crystallised chromium chloride, 20 parts of hydrochloric acid (25 per cent. strength), and 4 parts of zinc are shaken with 0·4 part by weight of acetylene under pressure. Ethylene and hydrogen are produced, and can be separated by ordinary methods.

In a process described by Freeman,[2] ethylene is said to be pro-

[1] D.R.-P., 287565, 1913; 295976, 1914. [2] B.P., 20893, 1913.

duced by injecting a current of hydrogen into an electric arc between carbons in a chamber from which air is excluded. The ethylene thus obtained is led through a tower, where it is absorbed by sulphuric acid. The alcohol is distilled off, and purified by rectification.

In another process,[1] ozonised oxygen (540 litres) is made to act upon a mixture of acetylene (45·6 litres) and hydrogen (173 litres) at a low temperature. The product other than the escaping gas (oxygen) is neutralised with sodium carbonate and fractionally distilled ; it gives first aldehyde and then alcohol. The yield of alcohol is said to be about one-fourth of the theoretical.

Hibbert and Morton[2] obtain aldehyde (*a*) by passing acetylene into dilute sulphuric acid containing a salt of mercury and a salt of a relatively weak acid, such as a borate, which is not reduced under the working conditions ; or (*b*), by passing acetylene into a solution containing a salt of mercury and an acid salt of a strong acid, *e.g.*, a bisulphate, but practically no hydrogen ions. A salt of a weak acid may also be present in process (*b*). The acetaldehyde produced is distilled off simultaneously.

Dreyfus[3] obtains aldehyde by the combination of water with acetylene in the presence of a mercury salt. The nitrate, the acetate, and the chloride are the most active. A liquid medium is employed in which the mercury compound is soluble, such as, for example, acetic acid ; so that the catalyst acts in a nearly homogeneous system. Or acetone may be used as medium ; it has a greater solvent action on acetylene than water has. The acetic acid is employed at a concentration of 80 per cent., and this is maintained by adding water as required to replace that taken up by the acetylene. From 8 to 10 per cent. of the catalyst is used in the mixture. In Dreyfus's process, the aldehyde produced may, if required, be oxidised forthwith to acetic acid by including an oxidising agent in the mixture ; the oxidiser may be a peroxide, or oxygen, with a catalyser such as cerium oxide or manganese acetate. The temperature is kept between 50° and 100°.

Dilute sulphuric acid (15 to 30 per cent)., with mercuric oxide as catalyst, has also been used to effect the hydration of the acetylene.

A German process,[4] based on a similar principle to that of Dreyfus's method, is thus described :—Acetylene is led into a well-stirred mixture of glacial acetic acid (1000 grams), strong sulphuric acid (22·5 grams), and mercuric oxide (100 grams), at a temperature

[1] D.R.-P., 149893, 1902, Jay & Co.

[2] U.S. P., (*a*) 1213486, (*b*) 1213487, 1917.

[3] F.P., 479656, 1914.

[4] B.P., 5132, 1915, *Consortium f. Elektroch.*, Nürnberg.

of 80–85°. The excess of gas passing out is conducted successively through a fractionating apparatus, a condenser cooled by a freezing mixture, an absorption vessel charged with water in which the aldehyde is absorbed, and then back to the reaction-vessel again. Absorption takes place at the rate of 100 to 200 litres per hour, and water is added to replace that used up ($C_2H_2 + H_2O = CH_3{\cdot}CHO$).

Aldehyde produced in this and other processes may then be either reduced to alcohol or oxidised to acetic acid, according to circumstances.

The reduction is effected by passing a mixture of aldehyde vapour and pure hydrogen in excess over a column of reduced nickel at a temperature of 140°.[1] At a higher temperature (180°), the aldehyde is decomposed into methane and carbon monoxide; and in any case the reaction tends to be reversed by the dehydrogenation of the alcohol formed. At 140°, however, about 80 per cent. of the aldehyde passing once over the nickel is converted into alcohol. The catalyst is prepared by reducing nickel oxide with hydrogen at a temperature not higher than 350°. On a large scale, the main process is carried out in metal tubes, preferably of nickel heated electrically, in order to regulate the temperature most easily.

The outgoing vapours are strongly cooled in order to condense the alcohol and unchanged aldehyde, which are then separated by fractional distillation.

In order to avoid "poisoning" the catalyst, it is necessary to use well-purified hydrogen and aldehyde.

According to the claim of A. G. Bloxam (for the Electrizitätswerk Lonza),[2] a large excess of hydrogen is advisable, in order to reduce the proportion of unchanged aldehyde in the product, and also to keep the reaction-chamber at the proper temperature by conducting away the excess of heat developed in the reaction, which is a strongly exothermic one (nearly 300 Cal. per kilo. of alcohol produced).

With a six-fold excess of hydrogen above the theoretical, the alcohol obtained is free from malodorous by-products, and contains but little aldehyde. If the hydrogen and aldehyde-vapour are passed at a temperature of 90° into the reaction-chamber containing the nickel, a thirty-fold excess of hydrogen keeps the temperature of the chamber at 150°. The excess of hydrogen can be returned again to the chamber through an external circulation system.

The foregoing process, or some modification of it, is understood to

[1] Sabatier and Senderens, *Compt. rend.*, 1903, **137**, 301.
[2] B.P. 120163, 1918.

be actually in use in Germany (1918) for producing both alcohol and acetic acid.

It was reported in 1917 that the leading Swiss hydro-electric company, working with the Lonza aluminium company, had completed researches upon the production of alcohol from calcium carbide, and that the Swiss Federal Government jointly with the Lonza firm would introduce the new industry into Switzerland. Presumably the process is based upon either the ethylene or the aldehyde synthesis, but the actual details do not appear to have been published. It was computed that an output of 7,500 to 10,000 metric tons would be reached, leaving a surplus for export above the country's requirements. In 1918, a large plant, capable of producing 28 millions of gallons per annum, was stated to be in course of erection at Visp.

In Germany, it may be mentioned, the production of alcohol from cellulose and from calcium carbide is to be reserved to the State (Imperial Spirit Monopoly Bill, 1918). This is done in the interests of the farming community, "in order to guard against a development which, under a system of free competition, would be dangerous to agriculture." The manufacture of alcohol from calcium carbide is said to have been carried out very successfully for some time past, especially by the Höchst Farbwerken.

VII.—STATISTICS AND MISCELLANEOUS NOTES

Materials used in distilleries (United Kingdom). Year ended September 30th, 1913.*

Country.	Malt. Quarters.	Unmalted grain. Quarters.	Molasses. Cwts.	Rice. Cwts.	Other materials. Cwts.
England . . .	91,157	247,047	1,204,223	3,780	20,713
Scotland . . .	781,862	606,251	—	—	—
Ireland . . .	180,589	345,432	—	—	—
United Kingdom.	1,053,608	1,198,730	1,204,223	3,780	20,713

* Later figures are available, but on account of war conditions they are less representative of normal production.

The making of yeast is now a very important operation in many of the larger distilleries, in addition to spirit production. About two-fifths of the total alcohol distilled in the United Kingdom is made at distilleries where the production of yeast is also carried on.

Normally, there are about 150 to 160 alcohol-producing distilleries in the kingdom. The following table shows the number working, and the number of those making yeast, in the year ended

September 30th, 1913. The fifteen yeast-producing distilleries contributed 20·6 millions of proof gallons of alcohol towards a total production of 49·6 millions from all the distilleries.

DISTILLERIES IN THE UNITED KINGDOM. YEAR 1912–13.

Kind.	England.	Scotland.	Ireland.	United Kingdom.
I. *Making yeast*— Using patent-stills, with or without pot-stills ..	3	7	5	15
II. *Not making yeast*— (*a*). Using patent-stills, with or without pot-stills	5	6	2	13
(*b*). Using pot-stills only	—	114	17	131
Totals	8	127	24	159

Thus as regards the number of distilleries Scotland comes easily first. The quantity of alcohol distilled in Scotland, however, is only about twice as much as in England, and two and a-half times as much as in Ireland. Small pot-still distilleries are a notable feature of the Scotch alcohol industry. The 114 pot-stills noted in the table produced barely one-third of the total amount of spirit distilled north of the Tweed. Of course, the number of distilleries working may vary a little from year to year. In 1914 it had risen from 159 to 163 ; and in 1915 it had fallen to 142, probably by reason of war conditions.

Spirits distilled in the United Kingdom : quantities.—During the ten years from 1907 to 1916 the annual production of distilled alcohol in Scotland ranged from 20 to 28 millions of *proof* gallons, in England from 10·7 to 13·9 millions, and in Ireland from 9·7 to 12·2 millions. In gallons of absolute alcohol (100 per cent. alcohol) these figures are approximately equivalent to :—

For Scotland, 11·4 to 16·0 millions ;
,, England, 6·1 ,, 7·9 ,,
,, Ireland, 5·5 ,, 7·0 ,,

The actual total production of spirits distilled in the United Kingdom in each of the five years 1912–1916 is shown below :—

Year ended March 31st.	Proof gallons.	Equivalent gallons of absolute alcohol.
1912	45,717,249	26,071,994
1913	46,692,764	26,628,319
1914	51,802,468	29,542,321
1915	50,139,557	28,593,983
1916	49,135,199	28,021,210

An idea of the relative proportions in which pot-still and patent-still spirits are produced in Scotch and Irish distilleries may be gathered from the following figures :—[1]

Year 1907.	From malt only.	From malt and grain.
	Proof gallons.	
Scotland :		
Pot-still	10,487,685	—
Patent-still	399,547	14,339,836
Ireland :		
Pot-still	279,728	3,313,446
Patent-still	—	8,372,607

The table shows also the proportion produced from malt only compared with the quantity obtained from a mixture of malt and unmalted grain. These are practically the only materials which at the date of the report quoted (1909) had been recently used in Scotland or Ireland for the production of distilled alcohol, though molasses, sugar, and potatoes were used to a small extent in years gone by.

In England at the present time a considerable quantity of alcohol is produced from molasses, as well as from malt and unmalted grain. Rice and other materials are also employed, but to a relatively small extent, as will be seen from the table previously given (p. 102).

The total quantity of *spirits retained for home consumption* in the United Kingdom during the year 1913–14 was 32,596,426 proof gallons, equivalent to 18,589,348 gallons of absolute alcohol. This does not include alcohol intended for making into methylated spirit, nor that for use duty-free in arts and manufactures.

For the separate countries, and per head of the population, the quantities were as follows :—

	Total quantity. Proof gallons.	Quantity per head of the population. Proof gallons.
England	22,559,759	0·61
Scotland	6,850,419	1·45
Ireland	3,186,248	0·72
United Kingdom	32,596,426	0·71

The quantity of spirits received by methylators during the same period, for conversion into methylated spirit, was 7,719,308 proof gallons, equivalent to 4,402,228 gallons of absolute alcohol. For

[1] Royal Commission on Whisky, Report, pp. 7, 8.

use duty-free, either in a pure state by colleges, hospitals, etc., or with special denaturants in various arts and manufactures, the quantity was 791,228 proof gallons, equivalent to 451,227 gallons of absolute alcohol. This includes 63,179 proof gallons of methyl alcohol, imported from abroad.

Alcohol exported and imported : United Kingdom.—The exports of home-made spirits (other than methylated spirit) amount approximately to 10 million proof gallons per annum.

In normal times "plain" spirits—*i.e.*, alcohol not sweetened or flavoured—are imported to the extent of about half a million to three-quarters of a million proof gallons, chiefly from Germany and Russia.

Revenue from Spirits : United Kingdom.—The net receipts of revenue from home-made and imported spirits in the five years 1911–15 were as follows :—

Year.	Home-made.	Imported.	Total.
	£	£	£
1911	18,751,206	4,298,484	23,049,690
1912	18,511,392	4,215,745	22,727,137
1913	18,432,492	4,166,795	22,599,287
1914	19,539,777	4,435,500	23,975,277
1915	20,302,500	4,972,005	25,274,505

Rates of Duty, 1918 (United Kingdom).

Excise :—

	£	*s.*	*d.*	
Beer, of original specific gravity 1055°	2	10	0	per 36 gallons.
Cider or perry	0	0	4	,, gallon.
Spirits :—				
Warehoused for 3 years or more	1	10	0	the proof gallon.
,, 2 ,, and less than 3 years	1	11	0	,, ,,
Not warehoused, or warehoused for less than 2 years	1	11	6	,, ,,

Customs :—

Spirits : The Customs duties on plain spirits, and also on Geneva and imitation rum, are 5*d.* per proof gallon more than those shown above. On brandy and rum, the excess above the Excise rate is 4*d.* per gallon. For sweetened spirits and perfumed spirits, the rate varies according to whether the spirits are imported in cask or in bottle.

	£	*s.*	*d.*	
Chloral hydrate	0	1	9	per lb.
Chloroform	0	4	4	,, ,,
Collodion	1	14	11	,, gallon.
Ether, acetic	0	2	7	,, lb.
,, butyric	1	1	10	,, gallon.
,, sulphuric	1	16	6	,, ,,
Ethyl bromide	0	1	5	,, lb.
,, chloride	1	1	10	,, gallon.
,, iodide	0	19	0	,, ,,

Imports, into the United Kingdom, of methyl alcohol not purified sufficiently to be potable :—

Country.	1913. Gallons.	1914. Gallons.
Canada	162,631	82,755
United States	297,702	355,881
Germany	93,500	32,326
Other countries	64,210	26,281
	618,043	497,243
Value	£70,175	£53,264

Annual production of alcohol.—The following table summarises the approximate annual quantities of alcohol produced by the larger countries, with the principal raw materials employed.

AVERAGE FOR THE FIVE YEARS 1909–1913.

Country.	Million gallons (Imp.) of 100 per cent. alcohol.			Chief materials employed.
	Total produc-tion.	Used in beverages, etc.	Used for technical purposes.	
Austria-Hungary .	60·6	42·7	10·4	Maize ; beet molasses.
France	59·3	42·3	14·7	Beet ; molasses ; fruit ; potatoes.
Germany . . .	82·9	46·7	34·9	Potatoes ; grain ; molasses ; fruit.
Italy	9·4	6·1	2·3	
Russia	125·9	97·3	8·8	Potatoes ; grain.
United Kingdom .	26·0	18·2	3·9	Grain ; molasses.
United States . .	72·2	56·4	5·8*	Grain ; molasses.

* 3 years' average.

Belgium and Holland each produce about 7½ million gallons.

In France, approximately one-half of the total quantity is obtained from sugar-beets, and one-sixth from molasses. About one-sixth also is produced from wine and fruits. The remainder is supplied by potatoes and other starch-bearing materials. In the year 1912 about 12½ million gallons were used for heating and lighting, and 4 millions for making explosives.

In the United States, the bulk of the alcohol produced was derived from grain, chiefly maize, but an appreciable proportion is obtained from molasses. According to A. M. Breckler,[1] the total molasses available in the States and Cuba would suffice to produce about 67 million gallons (Imp.) of alcohol. At the price of 5 cents per U.S. gallon for molasses, alcohol could be produced from this

[1] *J. Ind. Eng. Chem.*, 1917, **9**, 612.

material at about 10 cents per U.S. proof gallon, equivalent to 1*s.* per Imperial gallon at 100 per cent. strength. The average price of alcohol from maize during the five years prior to 1917 was 17·5 cents per U.S. proof gallon. From the point of view of the use of alcohol as a motor fuel, maize spirit is too expensive, and the total amount obtainable from molasses would represent only about 5 per cent. of the country's requirements of motor fuel.

Germany, it will be noticed, is, after Russia, the largest producer of alcohol, with more than three times the quantity made in this country. A large proportion, however, roughly one-fourth of the whole, is used in heating and lighting, for which purposes in the United Kingdom cheaper petroleum and gas are available. In Germany, the alcohol-distilling industry, instead of being concentrated into a few hands as in this country, is a very widespread one. In fact, the distillery is often an appanage of the farm or the small holding. The total number of distilleries is more than 70,000. Five-sixths of the number, however, are very small "farm" distilleries producing alcohol from fruit, and with an average output of only about 10 to 20 gallons yearly. There are more than 6,000 larger farm distilleries with an average yearly output of rather less than 1000 gallons each, producing alcohol from grain. The great bulk of the German alcohol, about four-fifths of it, is, however, obtained from potatoes. Most of the distilleries employed in this branch of the industry—approximately 6,000—are also agricultural distilleries.

The German distilleries are divided into three classes, which are accorded certain differences of treatment in the matter of taxation. There are first, "industrial distilleries" (*gewerbliche Brennereien*), carried on by individuals or companies solely for manufacturing purposes. Secondly, there are "agricultural distilleries" (*landwirthschaftliche Brennereien*); these use as raw materials potatoes or grain grown on the owners' farms, or on the farms of one or more of the owners if the distillery belongs to a co-operative organisation. "Material distilleries" (*material-Brennereien*) form the third class; they are the very small concerns which use fruits, berries, wine lees, and the marcs of grapes for their raw materials. By far the greater proportion of the spirit made in Germany is produced by the second group—the "agricultural" distilleries.

In the interests of agriculture, the production of alcohol from potatoes has all along been fostered by the State. The residual product from the distillation is valuable as a feeding stuff and fertiliser, and the agrarian interests have urged that without the distilling industry as ancillary to their agricultural operations large tracts of light soils in the eastern provinces could not profitably be cultivated. The situation is now, however, becoming complicated by the threatened competition of alcohol from calcium carbide, wood waste, and sulphite liquors.

The subjoined abstract of a United States publication gives a useful *résumé* of the steps taken to foster the industry.

Abstract of U.S.A. Department of Agriculture. Bulletin No. 182. Professional Paper.—"Agricultural Alcohol: Studies of its Manufacture in Germany"

By E. Kremers, Washington, Government Printing Office, 1915.

1. *Introduction.*—Up to 1840, the alcohol industry in Germany was based on the use of cereals, and was developed mainly in the towns. With the expansion of the cultivation of potatoes—which give a larger yield of starch per acre than cereals—the distillation of alcohol became largely an agricultural industry. The agricultural significance of this development is as follows:—

(*a*) All the ingredients taken by the potatoes from the soil are returned to the soil.

(*b*) The spent mash is an important feed for cattle.

(*c*) The introduction of potatoes into the rotation of crops has made possible larger yields of cereals.

(*d*) The farmer has been able to convert the unstable potato crop into a stable product which may be held as a surplus stock for several years.

2. *Mash capacity taxes,* 1820 *and* 1868.—Up to 1820, the tax was levied on the still; this was replaced in Prussia and other North German States by a mash-capacity tax. In 1868 this tax was extended to all States in the North German Federation.

3. *Taxes on the finished products,* 1887.—In 1887, a tax was levied on the finished product, when disposed of, in addition to the mash-capacity tax. The second tax was higher than the first, and was graduated according to the quantity of spirit produced. A certain amount (*Kontingent*) supposed to equal the consumption for beverage purposes was taxed at the rate of 2*s.* 1*d.* per gallon. The surplus (*Ueberkontingent*) was taxed at the rate of 2*s.* 11*d.* per gallon. Alcohol used for industrial purposes was not affected by this legislation, since the tax paid was refunded (see below). After this Act came into force denatured alcohol became as free as any other commercial commodity, and its price

was lowered. The result was that the quantity of industrial alcohol used was about doubled in one year.

4. *Increase in technical utilisation of alcohol.*—After 1887, there was a constant increase in the consumption of alcohol for technical purposes. It was recognised that the most important field in which this consumption could be looked for was in its application to the production of heat, light, and power. Alcohol burners and cooking apparatus had been used for a long time. Its application for illumination and the generation of power were, however, new. But in order to accomplish anything of real importance, the price of alcohol had to be reduced to such a point that it could compete with petroleum.

5. *Distillation tax,* 1895, *and bonus on industrial alcohol.*—Freedom from taxation did not suffice for the purpose desired. The distillation tax was accordingly brought into force in 1895. The revenues from this source were used for paying a refund or bonus on the alcohol used in Germany for other than beverage purposes. In other words, the money necessary to lower the price of industrial alcohol was raised within the distilling industry itself. The result was that from 1895 to 1896 the quantity of alcohol used industrially increased from less than 19 million to more than 21 million gallons.

6. *Increase in potato culture.*—From 1897 the production of alcohol in Germany made enormous strides, and, as a result of progress in the cultivation of potatoes, harvests increased to an extraordinary degree. The increased production of alcohol was due not only to the larger yields, but also to the cultivation of potatoes richer in starch and to improvements in technology.

In several years after 1887, the financial success of the distilleries was not great. The price fell by about 5*d.* per gallon, while the *Kontingent* did not afford a sufficient substitute for the reduction in price. Moreover, the prices of alcohol were regulated by the Berlin Chamber of Commerce in such a way that they were relatively low during months in which the alcohol was in the hands of the distiller, but they were raised as soon as the producers had disposed of the spirit. The result was that the dealers and not the manufacturers enjoyed the greatest part of the profits.

7. *Co-operation in marketing.*—It was soon recognised that relief would come only from the co-operative disposal of the alcohol produced. Various attempts in this direction were made, and a number of provincial sale associations were organised. It was, however, only with the third attempt that these efforts were crowned with success.

8. *Organisation of the Central Association.*—In 1899 the "Society of German Distillers for the Disposal of Alcohol" was established. This included practically all the distilleries. This organisation made a contract for nine years, since renewed for a further period of nine years, with the "Central Organisation for the Disposal of Alcohol," which was also a new organisation including nearly all the rectifiers of alcohol. The Distillers' Society agreed to turn over to the Central Association all their alcohol, and the Central Association undertook to dispose of the alcohol on the best terms possible for a certain compensation primarily for the rectification of the spirit. The essential feature of this arrangement was that the distillers were no longer at the disadvantage of low prices at the time they wanted to dispose of their product.

The Central Association from the outset regarded the increase in demand as its prime object, and for this purpose the Technical Section of the Central Association was created. The main objects of this section were as follow, viz. :—

(*a*) To test and develop apparatus for heat, light, and power.
(*b*) To establish stores for the sale of such apparatus.
(*c*) To start a literary campaign for the application of alcohol to household needs.
(*d*) To send exhibits to various centres.
(*e*) To organise a retail trade in denatured alcohol of the required strength and at a stable price.

9. *Success of the Central Association.*—In 1899, the consumption of industrial alcohol was 23½ million gallons, and by 1906 it had increased to 39 million gallons. The increase would have been greater had it not been for the fact that in 1901–2 the development of industrial alcohol had to overcome the serious obstacle of the removal of the distillation tax of 1895. In spite of the increased use of industrial alcohol, it became difficult to establish an equilibrium between production and consumption because of the enormous increase in the production of potatoes. The surplus of alcohol was increasing from year to year.

10. *Voluntary regulation of production.*—In 1902, the surplus exceeded 26 million gallons, with the result that some means had to be found for the regulation of production. A successful appeal was made to the agricultural distillers, about 90 per cent. of whom agreed voluntarily to reduce their output by about 18 per cent. The result was that the surplus carried over in the following year fell to about 8 million gallons. The regulation of output henceforth became a standard feature of the distilling industry.

11. *The potato the principal source of alcohol.*—Of 64,860,000

acres of arable land in Germany, 8,150,000, or 12·5 per cent., were planted with potatoes in 1901, while only 3,090,000 acres, or 4·75 per cent., were devoted to cereals. The yield of potatoes in bushels of 60 lb. per acre rose from 157·5 in 1896 to 205 in 1907. Potato-growing forms one of the best supports for rational methods of agriculture, especially where circumstances are unfavourable—as in a large part of Germany—to the cultivation of the sugar-beet. In fact, thousands of agricultural undertakings in Germany owe their existence to the distilleries.

In 1908 about 6,400 agricultural potato distilleries were in operation in Germany, the production of spirits from other sources in that country being insignificant.

Alcohol from sulphite liquor.—Bjarne Johnsen,[1] who has considered this question from the point of view of Canadian industry, gives some calculations of the cost of manufacturing alcohol from sulphite waste liquor. They rest upon data obtained by Hagglund on the basis of operations at three large pulp factories in Scandinavia, 800 gallons being taken as the quantity of liquor recovered per ton of pulp. Assuming for Canadian conditions that the costs of plant, labour, salaries, and repairs are 50 per cent. higher than in Scandinavia, and allowing 15 per cent. for depreciation and interest, the total cost of one Imperial gallon of alcohol (100 per cent.) works out at 0·22 dollar (11*d.*) for a factory turning out 30,000 tons of pulp, and 0·32 dollar (1*s.* 4*d.*) for a smaller factory with one-third of this output. By another calculation, based upon manufacturing expenses as estimated by Landmark, the cost of production works out to somewhat less than the first figure—namely, to 0·19 dollar (9½*d.*) per Imperial gallon.

A. M. Breckler discusses this question from the American point of view, and adds some general information also, in an article on the cheap production of alcohol.[2] The chief points are :—

Fuel and water-supply are important considerations. Waste sulphite liquor as concentrated for fermentation contains 4 per cent. of hexose sugars, corresponding, in practice, with a yield of about 2·2 per cent. of alcohol. The heat of distillation per (U.S.) gallon of 80 per cent. alcohol (vol.) from such a liquid would be 126,000 B.Th.U. under the best conditions, and would probably in practice approach 180,000 B.Th.U. On this basis, 10 to 14 lb. of a good coal would be required. At a price of 3 dollars per ton for coal, the cost of the distillation would be from 1·5 to 2·1 cents per gallon.

In like manner, the cost of distilling 80 per cent. alcohol from

[1] *J. Soc. Chem. Ind.*, 1918, **37**, 131.
[2] *J. Ind. Eng. Chem.*, 1917, **9**, 612.

sorghum juice, containing 15 per cent. of hexose sugars, would be from 0·4 to 0·6 cent per gallon with coal at the same price.

With starch-containing materials, where the mash requires preliminary "cooking," the number of B.Th.U. as calculated for the distillation may be multiplied by the factor 2·5. In a grain distillery the fuel required for grinding, pumping, etc., is about 50 per cent. of the total quantity used. To condense 100 gallons of 80 per cent. alcohol and cool it down to 85° F. (29° C.), the quantity of water required will range from 900 gallons at 55° F. (13° C.) to 1250 gallons at 80° F. (27° C.).

In general, assuming a liquid as prepared for fermentation to contain 10 per cent. of fermentable matter, the following table shows the maximum permissible cost per pound of fermentable matter for the production of alcohol at any given cost per proof gallon, allowing a yield of 85 per cent. (N.B.—U.S. "proof" = 50 per cent. alcohol by volume, and U.S. gallon = 0·833 Imperial gallon).

Maximum cost per lb. of hexose; cents.	Minimum cost per proof gallon of alcohol; cents.	Maximum cost per lb. of hexose; cents.	Minimum cost per proof gallon of alcohol; cents.
1·0	9·6	2·2	18·7
1·2	11·2	2·4	20·2
1·4	12·6	2·6	21·8
1·6	14·2	2·8	23·3
1·8	15·7	3·0	24·4
2·0	17·2		

Thus in examining whether alcohol from potatoes could compete with gasoline (petrol) as a motor fuel, suppose the price of the gasoline to be 30 cents per gallon. Assuming that absolute alcohol and gasoline give the same amount of power per gallon, the cost of the alcohol must be taken as 15 cents per *proof* gallon. Then from the table, the raw material must cost not more than 1·7 cents per lb. of fermentable material. Potatoes for alcohol contain 20 per cent. of starch = 22·2 per cent. of dextrose; so that the maximum allowable cost per lb. of potatoes is 0·222 × 1·7 = 0·38 cent if the residue is not utilised as a feeding-stuff. Or, reckoning 0·1 cent per lb. of potatoes for the value of the residue as a feeding-stuff, the maximum that could be paid for potatoes in this case would be 0·48 cent per lb., or 28·8 cents per bushel. The average farm value of potatoes, however, was 61·4 cents per bushel during the nine years 1907–1915, and the price of gasoline per gallon in 1917 was 20 cents, not 30; so that according to these calculations potatoes in the United States, just as in this country, do not promise to be a sufficiently cheap raw material of alcohol to compete with petrol as a fuel under present conditions.

CHAPTER III

THE GENERAL CHEMISTRY OF THE ALCOHOLS

FOR a complete account of the important class of bodies termed "alcohols," including the proofs of their chemical constitution, reference must be made to text-books of organic chemistry. It would be beyond the scope of the present work to set out fully the reasons which have led chemists to group together as "alcohols" substances so dissimilar in appearance as light, mobile wood spirit; viscid, heavy glycerol; and solid, wax-like cerotin. None the less, it will be useful and convenient to have here a summary of the chief chemical facts which are common to the alcohols as a whole.

In this chapter, therefore, it is proposed briefly to describe the chemical characters which distinguish the alcohols as a class, and more particularly the aliphatic, monohydric alcohols. The special properties of ethyl alcohol, as also of its congeners methyl, propyl, butyl, and amyl alcohols, will be dealt with in subsequent chapters.

Ordinary alcohol (ethyl alcohol, $C_2H_5{\cdot}OH$) is the best-known member of a series of neutral substances, some liquid, others solid, which can be looked upon chemically as derived from hydrocarbons by the replacement of one hydrogen atom by a hydroxyl group.

Thus corresponding with :—

Methane,	CH_4,	we have	$CH_3{\cdot}OH$,	methyl alcohol,
Ethane,	C_2H_6,	,,	$C_2H_5{\cdot}OH$,	ethyl ,,
Propane,	C_3H_8,	,,	$C_3H_7{\cdot}OH$,	propyl ,,
Butane,	C_4H_{10},	,,	$C_4H_9{\cdot}OH$,	butyl ,,
Pentane,	C_5H_{12},	,,	$C_5H_{11}{\cdot}OH$,	amyl ,,

And so on; the further members of this series of alcohols being designated hexyl, heptyl, octyl, etc., alcohols, according to the number of carbon atoms which they contain.

Classification.—Alcohols are classified as **monohydric, dihydric, trihydric,** and **polyhydric,** according to whether one, two, three, or more hydroxyl groups are present in them. Thus those of the series represented above are all monohydric alcohols. Glycol, the formula of which is $C_2H_4(OH)_2$, is an example of a dihydric alcohol; and glycerol, $C_3H_5(OH)_3$, is a trihydric alcohol. In this work, we are concerned almost exclusively with the monohydric series.

A further distinction into **primary, secondary,** and **tertiary** alcohols is based upon differences of structure. When a carbon atom is linked to only one other carbon atom, it is termed *primary*. If linked to two others, it is a *secondary*, and if to three, a *tertiary*, carbon atom. Now a primary alcohol is one in which the hydroxyl group is attached to a primary carbon atom; whilst in a secondary or a tertiary alcohol the hydroxyl group is attached to a secondary or a tertiary carbon atom respectively. Whence it follows that:—

1. **Primary** alcohols contain the group $-CH_2{\cdot}OH$. Example: $CH_3{\cdot}CH_2{\cdot}CH_2{\cdot}OH$, *propyl alcohol.*

2. **Secondary** alcohols contain the group $>CH{\cdot}OH$. Example: $CH_3{\cdot}CH(OH){\cdot}CH_3$, *isopropyl alcohol.*

3. **Tertiary** alcohols contain the group $\rangle C{\cdot}OH$. Example:

$$\begin{matrix} H_3C \diagdown \\ H_3C - C{\cdot}OH, \\ H_3C \diagup \end{matrix}$$ *tertiary isobutyl alcohol.*

Methyl alcohol, $CH_3{\cdot}OH$, is a primary alcohol containing only one carbon atom. The group $-CH_2{\cdot}OH$ is in this case attached to a hydrogen atom.

Formulation.—The alcohols can be looked upon as derived from methyl alcohol, the simplest member of the series, by replacing hydrogen of the CH_3-group with various alkyl groups, thus:—

$$C\begin{cases} H \\ H \\ H \\ OH \end{cases} \longrightarrow C\begin{cases} CH_3 \\ H \\ H \\ OH \end{cases} \longrightarrow C\begin{cases} C_2H_5 \\ H \\ H \\ OH \end{cases}$$

$CH_3{\cdot}OH$	$CH_3{\cdot}CH_2{\cdot}OH$	$C_2H_5{\cdot}CH_2{\cdot}OH$
Methyl alcohol.	Ethyl alcohol.	Propyl alcohol.

The name "carbinol" was proposed for methyl alcohol by Kolbe. As shown by the formulæ above, ethyl alcohol can be described as "methyl carbinol," propyl alcohol as "ethyl carbinol," and so on.

If a *second* hydrogen atom is replaced, we get a **secondary** alcohol:—

$$C\begin{cases} CH_3 \\ CH_3 \\ H \\ OH \end{cases}$$

Isopropyl alcohol. (Dimethyl carbinol.)

Similarly, if all three hydrogen atoms are replaced by alkyl groups, **tertiary** alcohols result. This method of formulation and this nomenclature are often convenient.

The systematic names, "methanol," "ethanol," "propanol," and so on, have also been proposed for the methyl, ethyl, propyl, etc., alcohols. They indicate the relationships with the corresponding hydrocarbons, methane, ethane, propane, etc.; whilst the termination "ol" signifies that the substances are alcohols. The position of the OH-group is indicated when necessary by a numeral; thus isopropyl alcohol, $CH_3{\cdot}CH(OH){\cdot}CH_3$, would be 2-propanol.

Isomerism in the alcohols.—Whilst only one methyl alcohol is possible, and only one ethyl alcohol, the formulæ show that two propyl alcohols, four butyl, and eight amyl alcohols can exist. In the last three classes, isomerism may be produced (1) by the OH-group taking up different positions in the molecule; (2) by the branching of the carbon chain; and (3) by both these causes acting together.

Consider, for example, butyl alcohol, $C_4H_9{\cdot}OH$. The **normal primary** formula is :—

$$\overset{4}{C}H_3{\cdot}\overset{3}{C}H_2{\cdot}\overset{2}{C}H_2{\cdot}\overset{1}{C}H_2{\cdot}OH \quad . \quad . \quad . \quad . \quad . \quad . \quad . \quad \text{(i)}$$

where the carbon atoms are marked 1, 2, 3, and 4 for convenience of reference. Instead of being attached to a terminal carbon atom $\overset{1}{C}$, as shown, the OH group might be united to one of the intermediate carbon atoms $\overset{2}{C}$ or $\overset{3}{C}$, giving in either case the **normal secondary** alcohol,

$$CH_3{\cdot}CH_2{\cdot}CH(OH){\cdot}CH_3 \quad . \quad . \quad . \quad . \quad . \quad . \quad \text{(ii)}$$

Or, the group $\overset{1}{C}H_2{\cdot}OH$ remaining as shown in (i), the straight carbon chain, $\overset{4}{C}H_3{\cdot}\overset{3}{C}H_2{\cdot}\overset{2}{C}H_2-$ may be replaced by the branching system $\begin{matrix}CH_3\diagdown\\CH_3\diagup\end{matrix}CH-$, giving **isobutyl alcohol,**

$$(CH_3)_2{\cdot}CH{\cdot}CH_2{\cdot}OH \quad . \quad . \quad . \quad . \quad . \quad . \quad . \quad \text{(iii)}$$

Finally, the straight chain shown in formula (ii), $CH_3{\cdot}CH_2{\cdot}CH\langle$, can be likewise replaced by the branching system $\begin{matrix}CH_3\diagdown\\CH_3\diagup\end{matrix}C\langle$, giving the tertiary butyl alcohol, **trimethyl carbinol,**

$$(CH_3)_3{\cdot}C{\cdot}OH \quad . \quad . \quad . \quad . \quad . \quad . \quad . \quad . \quad \text{(iv)}$$

These, then, are the formulæ of the four possible butyl alcohols.

In the same way, it can be shown that eight different amyl alcohols are theoretically possible, and all are known. The following table gives particulars of the alcohols above referred to, and further descriptions of the higher members are included in a subsequent chapter :—

Name.	Formula.	B.p.	Sp. gr. at 20°/4°.
Methyl alcohol . . .	$CH_3 \cdot OH$.	66°	0·796
Ethyl alcohol . . .	$CH_3 \cdot CH_2 \cdot OH$.	78·3	0·78945
Propyl alcohols, $C_3H_7 \cdot OH$:—			
Normal propyl . .	$CH_3 \cdot CH_2 \cdot CH_2 \cdot OH$.	97·4	0·8044
Isopropyl	$CH_3 \cdot CH(OH) \cdot CH_3$.	82·7	0·7887
Butyl alcohols, $C_4H_9 \cdot OH$:—			
Normal primary . .	$CH_3(CH_2)_2 \cdot CH_2 \cdot OH$.	116·8	0·8099
„ secondary .	$CH_3CH_2 \cdot CH(OH) \cdot CH_3$.	99	0·827
Isobutyl	$(CH_3)_2 \cdot CH \cdot CH_2 \cdot OH$.	108·4	0·8020
Trimethyl carbinol .	$(CH_3)_3 \cdot C \cdot OH$.	83·5 (m.p. 25·5)	0·7788 at 30°
Amyl alcohols, $C_5H_{11} \cdot OH$:—			
Normal primary . .	$CH_3(CH_2)_3 \cdot CH_2 \cdot OH$.	137	0·8168
Isobutyl carbinol. .	$(CH_3)_2 \cdot CH \cdot CH_2 \cdot CH_2 \cdot OH$	131·4	0·8104
Secondary butyl carbinol	$CH_3 \cdot CH(C_2H_5) \cdot CH_2 \cdot OH$	128·7	0·816
Methyl propyl carbinol	$CH_3(CH_2)_2 \cdot CH(OH) \cdot CH_3$	118·5	0·824 at 0°
Methylisopropylcarbinol	$(CH_3)_2 \cdot CH \cdot CH(OH) \cdot CH_3$	112·5	0·833 „
Diethyl carbinol . .	$C_2H_5 \cdot CH(OH) \cdot C_2H_5$.	116·5	0·832 „
Dimethyl ethyl carbinol	$(CH_3)_2 \cdot C(OH) \cdot C_2H_5$.	102·5	0·827 „
Tertiary butyl carbinol	$(CH_3)_3C \cdot CH_2 \cdot OH$.	112 (m.p. 48-50)	0·812

General methods for preparing alcohols.

Alcohols are produced in various chemical reactions, the chief of which are described below. It will, of course, be understood that these methods are adduced, primarily, as exemplifying the chemical attributes of alcohols generally, not as processes for the commercial preparation of the particular alcohol employed as illustration.

(1) When an alkyl iodide (*e.g.*, ethyl iodide) is brought into contact with freshly-precipitated, moist silver oxide, the substances react, producing an alcohol and silver iodide :—

$$C_2H_5I + AgOH = C_2H_5 \cdot OH + AgI.$$

Here the silver oxide and the water present together react like silver hydroxide, as shown in the equation.

A similar conversion is effected by heating the alkyl iodide with lead oxide or zinc oxide and water, and even with excess of water alone at 100°. Or the iodide may first be converted into the corresponding acetate (ethyl acetate in the example given) by heating it with potassium acetate :—

$$C_2H_5I + CH_3{\cdot}CO_2K = CH_3{\cdot}CO_2{\cdot}C_2H_5 + KI.$$

Ethyl acetate
(Ethyl acetic ester).

On then hydrolysing the ester by boiling it with a solution of sodium hydroxide, it is transformed into the alcohol and sodium acetate :—

$$CH_3{\cdot}CO_2{\cdot}C_2H_5 + NaOH = CH_3{\cdot}CO_2{\cdot}Na + C_2H_5{\cdot}OH.$$

To effect this hydrolysis, the ethyl acetate is boiled with an excess of sodium hydroxide solution in a flask connected with a reflux condenser until the conversion is complete, as shown by the eventual disappearance of the undissolved portion of the acetate. The condenser is then reversed, and the resulting alcohol distilled off.

(2) An essentially similar reaction to the foregoing is one by which ethyl alcohol can be obtained from ethyl sulphuric acid, $C_2H_5{\cdot}HSO_4$. On distilling this acid with water, it yields alcohol and sulphuric acid :—

$$SO_2\left\langle\begin{matrix}O{\cdot}C_2H_5\\OH\end{matrix}\right. + H_2O = SO_2\left\langle\begin{matrix}OH\\OH\end{matrix}\right. + C_2H_5{\cdot}OH.$$

This reaction is of both theoretical importance and historical interest. Ethyl sulphuric acid (sulphovinic acid, hydrogen ethyl sulphate) can be obtained by the interaction of ethylene with sulphuric acid, and ethylene itself is obtainable from acetylene, which in turn can be synthesised from its elements carbon and hydrogen. Thus the series of reactions forms a method whereby alcohol itself can be synthesised. This method, in fact, was the one by which, starting with ethylene, alcohol was first synthetically produced (Hennell, 1828 ; and later, by Berthelot, 1854).

Other unsaturated hydrocarbons besides ethylene (*e.g.*, propylene) furnish the corresponding sulphates and alcohols in a similar manner. Some (*e.g.*, isobutylene) are even dissolved by dilute nitric acid, and yield the corresponding alcohols on absorbing the elements of water.

(3). Primary amines, when treated with nitrous acid, yield alcohols, with elimination of nitrogen :—

$$C_2H_5{\cdot}NH_2 + HNO_2 = C_2H_5{\cdot}OH + N_2 + H_2O.$$

Ethylamine. Ethyl alcohol.

A convenient method of showing this reaction is to distil a solution of ethylamine hydrochloride with potassium nitrite, which supplies the nitrous acid by interaction with the HCl of the ethylamine salt.

(4). Aldehydes, acid chlorides, and acid anhydrides may be reduced by sodium, sodium amalgam, iron filings, or zinc dust, employed with dilute sulphuric acid or acetic acid, and yield the corresponding alcohols :—

(*a*) $C_2H_5 \cdot CHO + H_2 = CH_3 \cdot CH_2 \cdot CH_2 \cdot OH.$
Propyl aldehyde. Propyl alcohol.

(*b*) $CH_3 \cdot COCl + 2H_2 = CH_3 \cdot CH_2 \cdot OH + HCl.$
Acetyl chloride. Ethyl alcohol.

(*c*) $(C_2H_3O)_2O + 2H_2 = C_2H_5 \cdot OH + CH_3 \cdot COOH.$
Acetic anhydride. Ethyl alcohol. Acetic acid.

Theoretically, this reaction is important as one of the steps by which we can "ascend the series" of alcohols, passing from one alcohol to another containing more carbon atoms.

Thus starting with methyl alcohol, by acting upon it with phosphorus and iodine we obtain methyl iodide. This treated with potassium cyanide gives methyl cyanide, which on hydrolysis yields acetic acid. By means of phosphorus chloride or oxychloride, acetic acid can be converted into acetyl chloride, which, reduced as shown in equation (*b*) above, gives ethyl alcohol.

Similarly, ethyl alcohol itself can be transformed into propyl alcohol, and so on. The foregoing series of reactions may be summarised thus :—

$$CH_3 \cdot OH \xrightarrow{HI} CH_3I \xrightarrow{KCN} CH_3 \cdot CN \xrightarrow{KOH} CH_3 \cdot COOH \xrightarrow{PCl_3}$$
Methyl alcohol. Methyl iodide. Methyl cyanide. Acetic acid.

$$CH_3 \cdot COCl \xrightarrow{H_2} CH_3 \cdot CH_2 \cdot OH.$$
Acetyl chloride. Ethyl alcohol.

Whilst the aldehydes, acid chlorides, and anhydrides give *primary* alcohols when reduced as above, the reduction of ketones yields *secondary* alcohols, together with *di-tertiary* alcohols or "pinacones." Thus when acetone is reduced with sodium amalgam the chief product is isopropyl alcohol, but pinacone is also produced :—

$$\begin{matrix} CH_3 \\ CH_3 \end{matrix} \Big> CO + H_2 = \begin{matrix} CH_3 \\ CH_3 \end{matrix} \Big> CH \cdot OH$$
Acetone. Isopropyl alcohol.

$$2(CH_3)_2 \cdot CO + H_2 = \begin{matrix} CH_3 \\ CH_3 \end{matrix} \Big> C(OH) - (OH)C \Big< \begin{matrix} CH_3 \\ CH_3 \end{matrix}$$
Pinacone.

The pinacone is a solid (m. p. 42°, as the crystallised hydrate).

(5). Secondary alcohols are also obtained by converting polyhydric alcohols (*e.g.*, glycerol) into the iodides with phosphorus and iodine, the iodide being then transformed into the alcohol as in reaction (1), *ante* :—

$$\begin{array}{ccccc} CH_2{\cdot}OH & & CH_3 & & CH_3 \\ | & & | & & | \\ CH{\cdot}OH & \xrightarrow{+HI} & CHI & \xrightarrow{+AgOH} & CH{\cdot}OH \\ | & & | & & | \\ CH_2{\cdot}OH & & CH_3 & & CH_3 \\ \text{Glycerol.} & & \text{Isopropyl iodide.} & & \text{Isopropyl alcohol.} \end{array}$$

For preparing the iodide, amorphous phosphorus in the proportion of 25 grams, and iodine 140 grams, are used for 100 grams of anhydrous glycerol, the phosphorus being added gradually to the other ingredients, and the mixture distilled in a slow current of carbon dioxide gas. With half the weight of iodine and using yellow phosphorus, the same operation yields allyl iodide as the main product. Alternatively, the glycerol may be diluted with an equal volume of water and distilled with 150 grams of iodine and 28 grams of yellow phosphorus, added gradually. The first portion of the distillate is returned to the retort and re-distilled. Admixed allyl iodide may be removed from the isopropyl iodide by treating the mixed iodides with hydriodic acid.

(6) Two notable synthetic methods of obtaining secondary and tertiary alcohols are available, depending upon the use of alkyl compounds of zinc and magnesium respectively. The first was originally described by Butlerow (1864). By means of zinc methyl and zinc ethyl, acting on the acid chlorides, **tertiary** alcohols are produced; with aldehydes or with esters of formic acid instead of acid chlorides, **secondary** alcohols result.

Take, for example, the synthesis of tertiary butyl alcohol by Butlerow's method. Acetyl chloride, $CH_3{\cdot}COCl$, is dropped slowly into well-cooled zinc methyl. The mixture is allowed to stand two or three days in the cold, until the whole has become crystalline, when it is decomposed by adding water, yielding the required alcohol. There are three stages in the reaction. First, one molecule of the zinc methyl combines with one molecule of the chloride to form an additive product:—

$$CH_3{\cdot}COCl + Zn(CH_3)_2 = CH_3{\cdot}C\begin{cases} CH_3 \\ O{\cdot}ZnCH_3. \\ Cl \end{cases}$$

If this product is decomposed by adding water at this stage, it yields acetone, not an alcohol. But if a second molecule of zinc methyl is allowed to react with the new compound, it gradually replaces the Cl atom with a CH_3-group, giving the crystalline compound $CH_3{\cdot}C\begin{cases}CH_3\\O{\cdot}ZnCH_3\\CH_3\end{cases}$.

On now treating the product with water, it is decomposed, the tertiary alcohol being produced, together with zinc hydroxide and methane :—

$$CH_3{\cdot}C\begin{cases}CH_3\\O{\cdot}ZnCH_3\\CH_3\end{cases} + 2H_2O = \underset{\text{Tertiary butyl alcohol.}}{CH_3{\cdot}C\begin{cases}CH_3\\OH\\CH_3\end{cases}} + Zn(OH)_2 + CH_4$$

At the second stage it is possible to employ a different zinc alkyl—for example, zinc ethyl instead of zinc methyl. The Cl atom would then be replaced by a C_2H_5-group, and the final product would be the tertiary *amyl* alcohol, $(CH_3)_2{\cdot}C(OH){\cdot}C_2H_5$—*i.e.*, dimethyl ethyl carbinol.

If, however, aldehydes are used instead of acid chlorides, *secondary* alcohols result :—

$$CH_3{\cdot}CHO + Zn(C_2H_5)_2 = \underset{\text{Additive product.}}{CH_3{\cdot}CH\begin{cases}C_2H_5\\O{\cdot}ZnC_2H_5\end{cases}}$$

Decomposed with water, this product yields secondary butyl alcohol, $CH_3{\cdot}CH\begin{cases}C_2H_5\\OH\end{cases}$, together with zinc hydroxide and ethylene.

As already mentioned, secondary alcohols are also obtained by using formic acid esters with zinc alkyls. The reactions are quite similar to the foregoing, an additive product of the zinc alkyl with the ester being formed, which yields the alcohol on decomposition with water. When zinc methyl, for instance, reacts with ethyl formate, two methyl groups are eventually introduced, and isopropyl alcohol obtained :—

$$\underset{\text{Ethyl formate.}}{HC\begin{cases}O\\O{\cdot}C_2H_5\end{cases}} \longrightarrow \underset{\text{1st additive product.}}{HC\begin{cases}O{\cdot}ZnCH_3\\CH_3\\O{\cdot}C_2H_5\end{cases}} \longrightarrow$$

$$\underset{\text{2nd additive product.}}{HC\begin{cases}O{\cdot}ZnCH_3\\CH_3\\CH_3\end{cases}} \longrightarrow \underset{\text{Isopropyl alcohol.}}{HC\begin{cases}OH\\CH_3\\CH_3\end{cases}}.$$

Instead of the zinc alkyl, a mixture of alkyl iodide and metallic zinc can be employed. By using different alkyl iodides or different zinc alkyls in the first and second stages, different alkyl groups can be introduced, and different alcohols obtained as the resulting products.

It will be seen that all these syntheses by means of zinc alkyls depend upon the fact that the doubly-linked oxygen atom in the acid chloride, aldehyde, and ester, respectively, becomes singly-linked, with eventual formation of the alcoholic hydroxyl group.

(7) **Secondary** and **tertiary** alcohols are, however, more conveniently obtained in many instances by the use of Grignard's reagent. This is prepared by adding magnesium-turnings to an ethereal solution of an alkyl iodide or bromide, one molecule of the alkyl compound being used for each atom of magnesium. The metal forms a combination with the alkyl halide and dissolves in the ether. Thus with ethyl iodide we obtain an ethereal solution of C_2H_5MgI, ethyl magnesium iodide.

This reacts with aldehydes and ketones to form additive products, which are decomposed on treatment with water, yielding secondary and tertiary alcohols respectively. Thus with acetaldehyde :—

$$\underset{\text{Aldehyde.}}{CH_3{\cdot}CHO} + C_2H_5MgI = \underset{\text{Additive product.}}{CH_3{\cdot}CH\Big\langle{}^{OMgI}_{C_2H_5}}.$$

And on decomposing with water :—

$$2CH_3{\cdot}CH\Big\langle{}^{OMgI}_{C_2H_5} + 2H_2O = \underset{\text{Secondary alcohol.}}{2CH_3{\cdot}CH(OH){\cdot}C_2H_5} + MgI_2 + Mg(OH)_2.$$

In practice, acidified water is used : this dissolves the magnesium hydroxide produced.

Similarly, by using methyl magnesium iodide and acetone we can obtain the tertiary butyl alcohol, trimethyl carbinol :—

$$\underset{\text{Acetone.}}{(CH_3)_2{\cdot}CO} + CH_3MgI = \underset{\text{Additive product.}}{(CH_3)_2{\cdot}C\Big\langle{}^{OMgI}_{CH_3}}.$$

And with water :—

$$2(CH_3)_2{:}C\Big\langle{}^{OMgI}_{CH_3} + 2H_2O = \underset{\text{Trimethyl carbinol.}}{2(CH_3)_3{\cdot}C(OH)} + MgI_2 + Mg(OH)_2.$$

In an analogous manner, esters react with *two* molecules of the magnesium alkyl halide to form, in general, tertiary alcohols. Formic acid esters, however, yield secondary alcohols.

Conversion of primary alcohols into secondary and tertiary alcohols.—On distillation with dehydrating agents, *e.g.*, sulphuric acid or zinc chloride, primary alcohols have the elements of water removed and yield unsaturated hydrocarbons :—

$$CH_3{\cdot}CH_2{\cdot}CH_2{\cdot}OH - H_2O = CH_3{\cdot}CH{:}CH_2.$$

Propyl alcohol. Propylene.

On treating the hydrocarbon with concentrated hydriodic acid, the iodine atom attaches itself to the carbon having least hydrogen, forming a secondary iodide :—

$$CH_3{\cdot}CH{:}CH_2 + HI = CH_3{\cdot}CHI{\cdot}CH_3$$

Propylene. Isopropyl iodide.

When the iodide is treated with moist silver oxide, the iodine atom is replaced by a hydroxyl group according to the general method (1), above, thus yielding a **secondary alcohol** :—

$$CH_3{\cdot}CHI{\cdot}CH_3 + AgOH = CH_3{\cdot}CH(OH){\cdot}CH_3 + AgI.$$

Isopropyl alcohol.

If, instead of starting with propyl alcohol, we had taken isobutyl alcohol, which contains the primary group $-CH_2{\cdot}OH$ united to a secondary radical $\begin{matrix}CH_3\\CH_3\end{matrix}\!\!>\!CH-$, the resulting product would have been a **tertiary** alcohol :—

$$\begin{matrix}CH_3\\CH_3\end{matrix}\!\!>\!CH{\cdot}CH_2{\cdot}OH \longrightarrow \begin{matrix}CH_3\\CH_3\end{matrix}\!\!>\!C = CH_2 \longrightarrow$$

Isobutyl alcohol. Isobutylene.

$$\begin{matrix}CH_3\\CH_3\end{matrix}\!\!>\!CI{-}CH_3 \longrightarrow \begin{matrix}CH_3\\CH_3\end{matrix}\!\!>\!C(OH){\cdot}CH_3.$$

Tertiary butyl iodide. Tertiary butyl alcohol.

Distinction of primary, secondary, and tertiary alcohols from one another.—(1) If the alcohols are distilled with phosphorus and iodine, the corresponding iodides are formed :—

$$3C_2H_5{\cdot}OH + P + I_3 = 3C_2H_5I + H_3PO_3.$$

Ethyl iodide.

The iodides, on heating with silver nitrite, are converted into the nitroso-derivatives :—

$$C_2H_5I + AgNO_2 = C_2H_5NO_2 + AgI,$$

Nitroethane.

Now the *primary* nitro-compounds, when mixed with potassium nitrite in strong potassium hydrate solution, give a deep red colour on the addition of strong sulphuric acid. The *secondary* nitro-compounds give a dark blue colour, and the *tertiary* yield no colour. Hence these reactions serve to distinguish the three classes of alcohols.

(2) When the vapour of the alcohols is passed over finely-divided copper heated to 300°, *primary* alcohols are decomposed into hydrogen and aldehydes, *secondary* alcohols give hydrogen and ketones, and *tertiary* alcohols yield water and unsaturated hydrocarbons.[1]

The apparatus employed for this reaction consists of a hard glass tube about 28 inches long and ½ an inch in diameter, containing a layer of finely divided copper 24 inches long. The copper is prepared from powdered copper oxide by reduction in a current of dry hydrogen at 300°. To one end of the tube is attached a bent capillary, to the vertical part of which is fixed by means of a cork a piece of glass tubing about 3 inches long and ½ an inch in diameter. The other end of the hard glass tube is connected with a receiver, which is cooled by a mixture of ice and salt. A space of 4 or 5 inches next the capillary is kept free from copper, so that the alcohol may be vaporised before coming into contact with the finely-divided metal. To regulate the temperature, it is found convenient to use a cylindrical air-bath about 26 inches in length, with two small holes on the top about 12 inches apart, carrying two thermometers.

When the tube has attained a temperature of 300°, a small quantity (2 or 3 c.c.) of the alcohol to be examined is poured into the short, wide tube connected with the capillary, through which the liquid slowly flows into the heated tube and is vaporised. The vapour, which contains some unaltered alcohol, condenses in the cooled receiver. To a few drops of this distillate a solution of magenta, decolorised by sulphur dioxide, is added, when a red coloration indicates the presence of an aldehyde and shows that the alcohol is a primary one. If no red colour appears, a solution, containing 1 gram of semicarbazide and 1 gram of potassium acetate to 6 c.c. of water, is added to a second portion of the distillate. A white precipitate, formed at once, or only after some time, shows the presence of a ketone. Finally, an unsaturated hydrocarbon can be detected by its power of decolorising bromine.

(3) Another general method for distinguishing between the three

[1] Sabatier and Senderens, *Bull. Soc. chim.*, 1905, **33**, 263; and G. B. Neave, *Analyst*, 1909, **34**, 346.

classes of alcohols is afforded by oxidation. *Primary* alcohols when oxidised yield first the corresponding *aldehyde*, two atoms of hydrogen being removed from the group $-CH_2{\cdot}OH$, leaving the characteristic aldehyde group $-CHO$; then by further oxidation this is converted into the carboxyl group, $-C\begin{matrix}{/\!\!/O}\\{\backslash OH}\end{matrix}$, the characteristic group of organic acids. *Secondary* alcohols give *ketones* on oxidation, two hydrogen atoms being removed from the group $=C\begin{matrix}{/H}\\{\backslash OH}\end{matrix}$ with formation of the ketone group $=CO$. *Tertiary* alcohols when oxidised do not give the corresponding acids, aldehydes, or ketones, but are decomposed, with the production of acids having a smaller number of carbon atoms than were present in the original alcohols.

As oxidising agents, potassium chromate or dichromate with sulphuric acid are employed; or potassium permanganate in acid or in alkaline solution; or hydrogen peroxide in acid solution, according to circumstances.

(4) According to an observation of L. Wacker,[1] primary alcohols may be distinguished from secondary and tertiary alcohols by the strong red coloration which the primary compounds give with phenylhydrazine sulphonic acid.

Centinormal solutions of the alcohols are prepared, and 10 or 20 c.c. of each are diluted to 100 c.c. with water in a cylinder. A solution of phenylhydrazine sulphonic acid in dilute sodium hydroxide is prepared, containing 0·4 gram of the acid per c.c.; this solution should be used quite fresh. One c.c. is added to each cylinder, followed immediately by 25 c.c. of sodium hydroxide solution (33 per cent.), and the cylinders are shaken every fifteen minutes during the first two to three hours to develop the coloration. The colours are best compared after seven to eight hours. A "blank" test with water is made at the same time. Only the primary alcohols show intense colorations, the others will be found to differ but little from the "blank."

General properties of the alcohols.—Whilst the alcohols, as already stated, are neutral bodies, they have some resemblance to bases on the one hand, and to acids on the other. Thus they react with acids to form **esters,** or ethereal salts, *e.g.*, $C_2H_5{\cdot}O{\cdot}NO_2$, ethyl nitrate; also the alkali metals react with the alcohols, giving the **alcoholates,** for example $C_2H_5{\cdot}ONa$, sodium alcoholate or ethylate. In the first case, the hydrogen atom of

[1] *Ber.*, 1909, **42**, 2675; Abst. *Analyst*, 1909, **34**, 410.

the OH-group has been replaced by an acid radical, in the second by a metal.

The OH-group itself can be replaced by halogens, most readily by using the halogen compounds of phosphorus :—

$$C_2H_5 \cdot OH + PCl_5 = C_2H_5Cl + POCl_3 + HCl.$$

In the case of the iodides, phosphorus and iodine can be used instead of the phosphorus iodide, as already shown in connection with the distinction of the primary, secondary, and tertiary alcohols from one another.

The boiling points of the normal alcohols increase regularly with the increase of the molecular weights ; the difference for each increment of CH_2 in the formula being about 20° as we pass from ethyl alcohol upwards :—

Name.	Formula.	B.p.
Methyl alcohol	$CH_3 \cdot OH$	66°
Ethyl ,, ...	$C_2H_5 \cdot OH$	78
Propyl ,, ...	$C_3H_7 \cdot OH$	97
Butyl ,, ...	$C_4H_9 \cdot OH$	117
Amyl ,, ...	$C_5H_{11} \cdot OH$	137
Hexyl ,, ...	$C_6H_{13} \cdot OH$	157

The primary alcohols boil at a higher temperature than the secondary alcohols that are isomeric with them. Similarly, the latter have higher boiling points than their tertiary isomerides. (Ex., primary butyl alcohol, b.p. 117° ; secondary butyl alcohol, b.p. 100° ; tertiary butyl alcohol, b.p. 83°.)

As regards obvious properties, the lower alcohols, from methyl to butyl, are mobile liquids ; the intermediate members are of a more viscous, oily character (fusel " oil ") ; and the higher alcohols, containing twelve carbon atoms and upwards, are solids at the ordinary temperature (dodecatyl alcohol, $C_{12}H_{25} \cdot OH$, melts at 24°). Up to and including the propyl alcohols, they are miscible with water in all proportions. The butyl alcohols are only partly miscible with water, and from the amyl members upwards the solubility diminishes rapidly. All the alcohols are colourless or slightly yellow ; the lower members have a characteristic spirituous smell, the intermediate ones are unpleasant, and the solid alcohols are odourless and tasteless. They are all lighter than water The higher alcohols decompose, on distillation, into water and hydrocarbons.

CHAPTER IV

METHYL ALCOHOL: ITS PRODUCTION AND PROPERTIES

Methyl alcohol (Methanol), $CH_3{\cdot}OH$. **Molecular Weight** 32·03.—The liquid obtained by distilling wood was shown by Boyle in the *Sceptical Chymist*, as far back as the seventeenth century, to contain both an acid constituent and a neutral, inflammable body. This neutral liquid could be separated from the pyroligneous acid by distillation over burnt corals. From its neutral or "indifferent" character, Boyle termed it "*adiaphorous spirit.*" In the early part of the nineteenth century various chemists investigated this spirit, and showed that it differed from ordinary alcohol, inasmuch as it did not yield "sulphuric" ether (ethyl ether) when heated with sulphuric acid. (Taylor, 1812; Macaire and Marcet, 1824; Gmelin, 1829; Liebig, 1832.) The name "methyl alcohol" was given to the compound by Dumas and Péligot, who in 1834 made the first careful study of it, and pointed out the analogy existing between it and ordinary alcohol.[1]

Occurrence in nature.—Methyl alcohol is found in a large number of plants, chiefly as methyl esters, *e.g.*, methyl salicylate, anthranilate, and cinnamate, which are constituents of various essential oils. Notably, methyl salicylate occurs as the glucoside gaultherin in oil of wintergreen from *Gaultheria procumbens*, and in the bark of the sweet birch, *Betula lenta*. Methyl anthranilate is present in oil of neroli, oil of orange, oil of jasmine, oil of gardenia, and oil of bergamot. Methyl cinnamate is found in the oil obtained from *Alpinia malaccensis*, and in wartara oil, probably from the seeds of species of *Xanthoxylum*; whilst methyl benzoate occurs in oil of cloves and in ylang-ylang oil.

Production.—For commercial purposes methyl alcohol is obtained chiefly from the products of wood which has been submitted to dry distillation, or treated with hot producer-gas. Almost any hard wood may be employed for the distillation. The species generally used are beech, birch, maple, oak, and thorn: in this

[1] *Ann. Chym. Phys.*, 1835, **58**, 5; 1836, **61**, 193.

country, the thorn is regarded as one of the best for the purpose, though it is not always obtainable in sufficient quantity. Vinasse, a by-product of beet-sugar manufacture, is also a source of methyl alcohol.

A wood-distilling industry of considerable magnitude has been developed in the United States. In Canada, and Australia also, the industry is a growing one; and an important quantity of wood spirit, amounting in 1907–8 to about 6½ million kilos., is produced in Austria-Hungary and Germany. In this country the industry is on a smaller scale.

In the United States, the wood used is thoroughly seasoned for one or two years. Usually it is divested of its bark, and cut into 50-inch lengths. The destructive distillation is carried out in large iron retorts at a temperature of 400° to 500° F. (204° to 260° C.). These retorts are usually made of steel, and are provided with outlet tubes about 15 inches in diameter. The retorts are set in pairs in brickwork, and batteries of from 2 to 20 pairs are common. The wood is fed through the door, and carefully stacked so as completely to fill the retort; or in some cases the wood is loaded into steel cars and these run into the retort. In the larger works, the retorts are constructed of brick, and are of 50 cords capacity. They are provided with heavy iron doors, which are tightly closed after the charging is completed, and the retorts are then heated from below with burning wood, coal, or charcoal, supplemented by tar, oil, and gas obtained as by-products of the industry. Natural gas is also used as the fuel in some cases.

The gaseous products of the distillation are passed through condensers. Any gases not condensed are returned and burned under the retorts.

The condensed products are run into tanks, in which the tar settles out; whilst the "pyroligneous acid," containing acetic acid, methyl alcohol, acetone, allyl alcohol, etc., forms the upper layer. The pyroligneous acid is a dark red-brown liquid with a peculiar empyreumatic odour; it is used to a limited extent in making an impure acetate of iron ("black iron liquor"), but is usually treated to separate the methyl alcohol, acetone, and acetic acid. It contains about 4 per cent. of methyl alcohol.[1]

The separation is effected by fractional distillation. To recover the acetic acid, the vapours are passed into milk of lime, whereby "grey acetate of lime" is produced. Alternatively, the pyroligneous acid may be neutralised with lime before distilling off the methyl alcohol. Usually three stills of about 2,500 gallons capacity each

[1] Baskerville, *J. Ind. Eng. Chem.*, 1913, **5**, 768.

are employed, and from them are obtained distillates containing 15, 42, and 82 per cent. of wood alcohol respectively. The last product—82 per cent. wood spirit—still contains acetone, in varying amount, as well as other substances.

The processes may be shown diagrammatically as follows :—

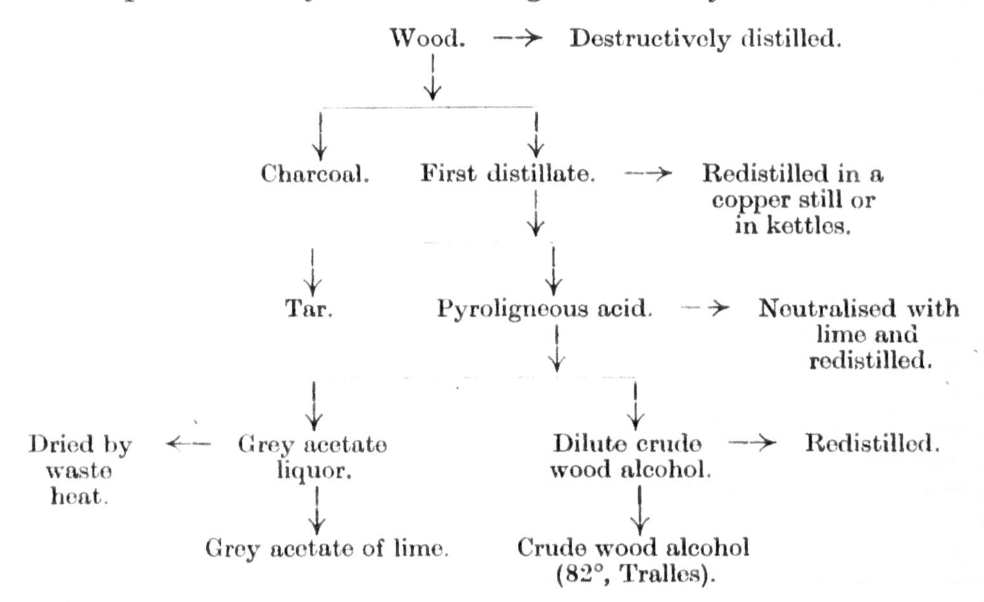

No decomposition occurs below 160° during the distillation. Between 160° and 275°, the pyroligneous acid is formed ; about 275°, the yield of gaseous products becomes well marked ; between 350° and 450°, liquid and solid hydrocarbons are formed ; and above 450° little change occurs.

The crude wood alcohol obtained is generally sent to a centrally-located refinery in tank-cars, iron drums, or barrels, for purification and rectification. This is accomplished by further distillation from lime or caustic soda, with special methods for removing acetone, as described below. The final product ordinarily obtained is commercial wood alcohol (wood spirit, wood naphtha), which is usually sold at 95 per cent. strength (Tralles), but which may contain from 10 to 20 per cent. of acetone and varying proportions of other impurities. A more highly-rectified and refined product containing 97 to 98 per cent. of actual methyl alcohol is also obtained ; this is sold under various trade names, such as "Columbian Spirits," "Colonial Spirits," "Manhattan Spirits." In Canada, a similar product is known as "Green Wood Spirits" and "Standard Wood Spirits."

During the year 1909 there were distilled in the United States 1,150,000 cords of hard woods such as beech, birch, and maple ; and 116,000 cords of yellow pine, fir, and other soft woods. From the hard woods, the chief products obtained were, per cord of wood :—

Charcoal	46·1 bushels.
Crude wood alcohol	7·4 gallons.
Grey and brown acetates	131·2 lb.

(Mainly grey acetate of lime.)

The soft woods yielded, besides charcoal, chiefly turpentine and wood tar. They are of more value for the production of these than as a source of wood alcohol and acetic acid.

Figures for the relative yields obtained from different kinds of wood in laboratory tests have been given by Hawley and Palmer.[1] For the three hard woods commonly used on a large scale for distillation in the United States the average results were as follows.

(1). Expressed as percentage of the dry weight of wood.

	Wood alcohol (100 per cent.).	Acetic acid (100 per cent.).
Beech	1·87	5·55
Birch	1·50	6·50
Maple	1·93	4·95

(2). Expressed in terms of commercial products and referred to the basis of a cord (90 cb. ft.) of air-dried wood (15 per cent. of moisture) :—

	Gallons of 82 per cent. wood alcohol.	Lb. of calcium acetate, 80 per cent.
Beech	11·4	299
Birch	8·6	334
Maple	11·7	275

Methyl alcohol is also obtained as a by-product in the manufacture of wood pulp. In the sulphate process for "easy bleaching" pulp, about 13 kilos. of methyl alcohol are formed per 1,000 kilos. of cellulose, and a part of this alcohol is recovered by condensing the vapours discharged from the digesters at pressures between 10 and 4 atmospheres. This is a fairly pure alcohol, containing only about 0·5 per cent. of acetone. A further quantity, of less pure spirit, is obtained from the vapours passing at pressures below 4 atmospheres, and from the evaporation of the lye. In the Ritter-Kellner sulphite process, 8 to 10 kilos. of methyl alcohol are formed per ton of cellulose.[2]

Methyl alcohol can also be obtained from the "black liquor" yielded in the digestion of wood by the "soda-pulp" process,[3] and from waste esparto liquors.[4]

[1] *Eighth Int. Cong. Appl. Chem.*, 1912; (Abst.) *J. Soc. Chem. Ind.*, 1912, **31**, 865.

[2] Bergström, *Papierfabrikant*, 1912, **10**, 677.

[3] White and Rue (Abst.), *J. Soc. Chem. Ind.*, 1917, **36**, 383.

[4] Lawrence, *ibid.*

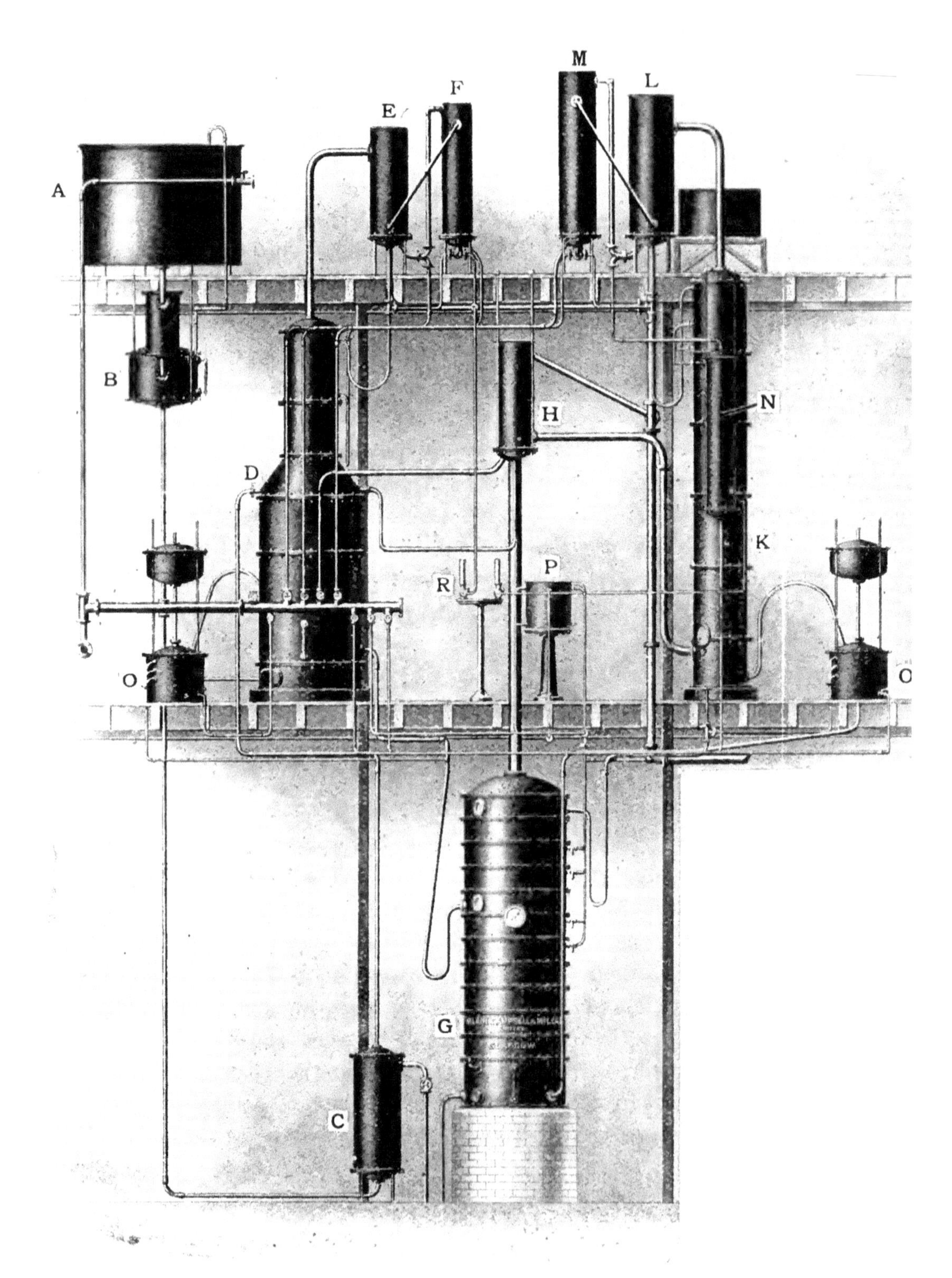

FIG. 29.—TRIPLE-COLUMN CONTINUOUS STILL.

For wood alcohol, ether, etc. *a*, supply tank; *b*, liquor regulator; *c*, preheater; *d*, separating column; *e*, separating column rectifier; *f*, separating column condenser; *g*, boiling column; *h*, boiling column rectifier; *k*, rectifying column; *l*, rectifying column rectifier; *m*, rectifying column condenser; *n*, rectifying column cooler; *o*, steam regulators; *p*, oils condensing tank *r*, run-off testers (Blair, Campbell & McLean, Ltd., Glasgow).

Rectification.—In general, we may say that from 100 parts of air-dried wood are obtained by distillation 25 to 27 parts of charcoal, and 45 to 50 parts of pyroligneous liquor, or "crude wood vinegar." This last contains about 6 to 8 per cent. of acetic acid and 3 to 4 per cent. of methyl alcohol, with a little acetone and about 7 per cent. of tarry matter. In small proportions, there are present also esters (mainly methyl acetate), higher ketones, allyl alcohol, pyridine, and amines.

Various methods of obtaining purified methyl alcohol from the liquor are employed, one process being to distil it and pass the distillate through vessels containing hot milk of lime, which retains the acetic acid, the vapours of methyl alcohol and acetone passing on to be fractionated and condensed. The distillate is again rectified, then diluted, mixed with 2 or 3 per cent. of milk of lime, and very slowly distilled. The first runnings now contain much acetone, and the "tailings" include ketones of higher boiling point, whilst the middle fractions are approximately pure methyl alcohol and water.

Further purification is effected by re-distillation from lime or caustic soda, and finally from a little sulphuric acid to remove organic bases.

Oxidising agents and filtration through charcoal are other means sometimes employed in the purification. Any small quantity of acetone still remaining may be removed by passing dry chlorine into the boiling alcohol, which is then separated by fractionation from the higher-boiling chlorinated acetone, and purified from chlorine by re-distillation over lime. Bleaching powder is also used for the removal of acetone; it converts the latter into chloroform.

On a smaller scale, purification of methyl alcohol may be effected by mixing it with anhydrous calcium chloride, with which it forms a crystalline compound. This can be separated, freed from acetone by heating, and then decomposed by distillation with water.

Chemically-pure methyl alcohol is obtained by decomposing the oxalate, acetate, formate, or other methyl ester with alkalis, or with water alone. For example: The impure alcohol is digested with solid sodium hydroxide in the proportion of 150 grams of the latter to 100 c.c. of the former, and then distilled. Five hundred grams of oxalic acid are mixed with 200 c.c. of sulphuric acid, and 400 c.c. of the distilled alcohol added; the mixture is then heated on the water-bath, and the crystals of methyl oxalate which form are separated, dried by pressure between filter-paper, and hydrolysed by heating with water at 70°. The alcohol is then distilled off and dehydrated with barium oxide, calcium oxide, and anhydrous copper sulphate.[1]

"Absolute" methyl alcohol is best obtained by treating the strong pure spirit successively with freshly ignited lime and recently-heated potassium carbonate, leaving it in contact with the latter for some weeks, and then distilling it several times from metallic calcium.

Properties.—Pure methyl alcohol is a mobile, colourless liquid which has a faint spirituous odour, and burns with a pale blue flame. It is miscible with water in all proportions, and also with ethyl alcohol, and with ether. The *boiling point* has been variously given; some of the discrepancies are probably due to the presence of acetone in the spirit. The value that has been most generally accepted is 66° at normal pressure; but according to J. Gyr[2] the b.p. is 64·56° at 760 mm., and Fuchs[3] gives it as 65·06° at 710 mm., ranging up to 68·00° at 790 mm. The *melting point* of the solidified alcohol is −94·9° (Ladenburg and Krugel). The *specific gravity* of methyl alcohol is 0·8100 at 0°/4°, and 0·79647 at 15°/15°.

Mixtures of methyl alcohol and water have nearly, but not quite, the same specific gravities as corresponding mixtures of ethyl alcohol and water. For certain proportions the difference is substantial, as will be seen from the following table:—

Sp. gr. at 15·6°/15·6°	Percentage by volume.	
	Methyl alcohol.	Ethyl alcohol.
0·9743	20	21·7
0·9621	30	32·7
0·9487	40	41·9
0·9335	50	50·4
0·9147	60	59·4
0·8931	70	68·7
0·8670	80	78·8

The greatest difference is shown by mixtures the specific gravities of which are about 0·962 to 0·963. Ethyl alcohol mixtures at these specific gravities contain 2·7 per cent. more alcohol than methyl alcohol mixtures at the same specific gravities.

Hence, although for approximate purposes the ordinary tables of (ethyl) alcoholic strength can be used with methyl alcohol mixtures, for exact work the special methyl alcohol tables should be employed. The following are published by the Bureau of Standards, Washington (Circular No. 19).

[1] Dittmar and Fawsitt, *Trans. Roy. Soc. Edin.*, 1888, **33**, 509.
[2] *Ber.*, 1908, **41**, 4322.
[3] *Zeitsch. angew. Chem.*, 1898, 871.

I.—Density at 15° of mixtures (by weight) of methyl alcohol and water.

[Calculated from the specific gravity determinations of Doroschewsky and Roschdestvensky at 15°/15°[1].]

Per cent. methyl alcohol by weight.	D 15°/4°.	Differences.	Per cent. methyl alcohol by weight.	D 15°/4°.	Differences.
0	0·99913	0·00186	40	0·93720	0·00177
1	0.99727	184	41	0·93543	178
2	0·99543	173	42	0·93365	180
3	0·99370	172	43	0·93185	184
4	0·99198	169	44	0·93001	186
5	0·99029	165	45	0·92815	188
6	0·98864	163	46	0·92627	191
7	0·98701	154	47	0·92436	194
8	0·98547	153	48	0·92242	194
9	0·98394	153	49	0·92048	196
10	0·98241	148	50	0·91852	199
11	0·98093	148	51	0·91653	202
12	0·97945	143	52	0·91451	203
13	0·97802	142	53	0·91248	204
14	0·97660	142	54	0·91044	205
15	0·97518	141	55	0·90839	208
16	0·97377	140	56	0·90631	210
17	0·97237	141	57	0·90421	211
18	0·97096	141	58	0·90210	214
19	0·96955	141	59	0·89996	215
20	0·96814	141	60	0·89781	218
21	0·96673	140	61	0·89563	222
22	0·96533	141	62	0·89341	224
23	0·96392	141	63	0·89117	227
24	0·96251	143	64	0·88890	228
25	0·96108	145	65	0·88662	229
26	0·95963	146	66	0·88433	230
27	0·95817	149	67	0·88203	232
28	0·95668	150	68	0·87971	232
29	0·95518	152	69	0·87739	232
30	0·95366	153	70	0·87507	236
31	0·95213	157	71	0·87271	238
32	0·95056	160	72	0·87033	241
33	0·94896	162	73	0·86792	246
34	0·94734	164	74	0·86546	246
35	0·94570	166	75	0·86300	249
36	0·94404	167	76	0·86051	250
37	0·94237	170	77	0·85801	250
38	0·94067	173	78	0·85551	251
39	0·93894	174	79	0·85300	252
40	0·93720		80	0·85048	

[1] *J. Russ. Phys. Chem. Soc.*, 1909, **41**, 977–996.

I.—Density at 15° of mixtures (by weight) of methyl alcohol and water—*contd.*

[Calculated from the specific gravity determinations of Doroschewsky and Roschdestvensky at 15°/15°.]

Per cent. methyl alcohol by weight.	D 15°/4°.	Differences.
80	0·85048	0·00254
81	0·84794	258
82	0·84536	262
83	0·84274	265
84	0·84009	267
85	0·83742	267
86	0·83475	268
87	0·83207	270
88	0·82937	270
89	0·82667	271
90	0·82396	0·00272
91	0·82124	275
92	0·81849	281
93	0·81568	283
94	0·81285	286
95	0·80999	286
96	0·80713	285
97	0·80428	285
98	0·80143	284
99	0·79859	282
100	0·79577	

II.—Specific gravity at 15°/15° of mixtures (by volume) of methyl alcohol and water.

[Calculated from the same data as the preceding Table.]

Per cent. methyl alcohol by volume at 15°.	D 15°/15°.	Differences.
0	1·00000	0·00149
1	0·99851	148
2	0·99703	143
3	0·99560	138
4	0·99422	139
5	0·99283	137
6	0·99146	135
7	0·99011	134
8	0·98877	131
9	0·98746	125
10	0·98621	125
11	0·98496	126
12	0·98370	123
13	0·98247	122
14	0·98125	122
15	0·98003	119
16	0·97884	118
17	0·97766	118
18	0·97648	118
19	0·97530	117
20	0·97413	0·00118
21	0·97295	118
22	0·97177	119
23	0·97058	119
24	0·96939	119
25	0·96820	120
26	0·96700	120
27	0·96580	121
28	0·96459	121
29	0·96338	122
30	0·96216	125
31	0·96091	125
32	0·95966	128
33	0·95838	130
34	0·95708	132
35	0·95576	133
36	0·95443	135
37	0·95308	138
38	0·95170	141
39	0·95029	143
40	0·94886	

II.—Specific gravity at 15°/15° of mixtures (by volume) of methyl alcohol and water—*contd.*

[Calculated from the same data as the preceding Table.]

Per cent. methyl alcohol by volume at 15°.	D 15°/15°.	Differences.	Per cent. methyl alcohol by volume at 15°.	D 15°/15°.	Differences.
40	0·94886	0·00145	70	0·89327	0·00239
41	0·94741	148	71	0·89088	244
42	0·94593	150	72	0·88844	248
43	0·94443	152	73	0·88596	250
44	0·94291	155	74	0·88346	254
45	0·94136	157	75	0·88092	256
46	0·93979	159	76	0·87836	258
47	0·93820	163	77	0·87578	266
48	0·93657	164	78	0·87312	272
49	0·93493	167	79	0·87040	280
50	0·93326	171	80	0·86760	286
51	0·93155	173	81	0·86474	294
52	0·92982	176	82	0·86180	297
53	0·92806	180	83	0·85883	301
54	0·92626	183	84	0·85582	306
55	0·92443	187	85	0·85276	309
56	0·92256	189	86	0·84967	321
57	0·92067	190	87	0·84646	332
58	0·91877	195	88	0·84314	343
59	0·91682	199	89	0·83971	348
60	0·91483	201	90	0·83623	354
61	0·91282	203	91	0·83269	362
62	0·91079	206	92	0·82907	369
63	0·90873	210	93	0·82538	375
64	0·90663	213	94	0·82163	391
65	0·90450	216	95	0·81772	409
66	0·90234	220	96	0·81363	421
67	0·90014	224	97	0·80942	428
68	0·89790	229	98	0·80514	432
69	0·89561	234	99	0·80082	435
70	0·89327		100	0·79647	

III.—Percentages by volume at 15°, corresponding with various percentages by weight in mixtures of methyl alcohol and water.

Per cent. by weight.	Per cent. by volume at 15°.	Differences.	Per cent. by weight.	Per cent. by volume at 15°.	Differences.
0	0·000	1·253	5	6·222	1·232
1	1·253	1·249	6	7·454	1·228
2	2·502	1·244	7	8·682	1·225
3	3·746	1·240	8	9·907	1·221
4	4·986	1·236	9	11·128	1·217
5	6·222		10	12·345	

III.—Percentages by volume at 15°, corresponding with various percentages by weight in mixtures of methyl alcohol and water—*contd.*

Per cent. by weight.	Per cent. by volume at 15°.	Differences.	Per cent. by weight.	Per cent. by volume at 15°.	Differences.
10	12·345	1·214	55	62·783	0·995
11	13·559	1·211	56	63·778	0·989
12	14·770	1·207	57	64·767	0·983
13	15·977	1·204	58	65·750	0·975
14	17·181	1·201	59	66·725	0·968
15	18·382	1·197	60	67·693	0·961
16	19·579	1·194	61	68·654	0·953
17	20·773	1·190	62	69·607	0·945
18	21·963	1·186	63	70·552	0·938
19	23·149	1·183	64	71·490	0·930
20	24·332	1·180	65	72·420	0·924
21	25·512	1·176	66	73·344	0·918
22	26·688	1·172	67	74·262	0·910
23	27·860	1·169	68	75·172	0·905
24	29·029	1·164	69	76·077	0·899
25	30·193	1·161	70	76·976	0·888
26	31·354	1·156	71	77·864	0·882
27	32·510	1·152	72	78·746	0·872
28	33·662	1·147	73	79·618	0·862
29	34·809	1·143	74	80·480	0·856
30	35·952	1·139	75	81·336	0·846
31	37·091	1·133	76	82·182	0·840
32	38·224	1·128	77	83·022	0·833
33	39·352	1·124	78	83·855	0·825
34	40·476	1·118	79	84·680	0·819
35	41·594	1·114	80	85·499	0·811
36	42·708	1·108	81	86·310	0·800
37	43·816	1·103	82	87·110	0·789
38	44·919	1·097	83	87·899	0·778
39	46·016	1·093	84	88·677	0·771
40	47·109	1·086	85	89·448	0·764
41	48·195	1·082	86	90·212	0·756
42	49·277	1·076	87	90·968	0·748
43	50·353	1·069	88	91·716	0·740
44	51·422	1·064	89	92·456	0·732
45	52·486	1·058	90	93·188	0·724
46	53·544	1·051	91	93·912	0·715
47	54·595	1·044	92	94·627	0·699
48	55·639	1·039	93	95·326	0·691
49	56·678	1·034	94	96·017	0·680
50	57·712	1·027	95	96·697	0·673
51	58·739	1·020	96	97·370	0·666
52	59·759	1·014	97	98·036	0·660
53	60·773	1·008	98	98·696	0·655
54	61·781	1·002	99	99·351	0·649
55	62·783		100	100·000	

BOILING POINTS OF MIXTURES OF METHYL ALCOHOL AND WATER.*

Methyl alcohol. Per cent. by weight.	B.p. at 700 mm.	B.p. at 760 mm.	B.p. at 800 mm.
0	97·72°	100°	101·44°
10	89·51	91·72	93·14
20	83·97	86·16	87·57
30	80·00	82·17	83·56
40	76·97	79·10	80·48
50	74·44	76·54	77·91
60	72·17	74·29	75·65
70	69·98	72·08	73·44
80	67·77	69·87	71·22
90	65·32	67·40	68·75
100	62·53	64·57	65·92

* Doroschewsky and Poljansky, *J. Russ. Phys. Chem. Ges.*, 1910, **42**, 109—134.

The **vapour pressure** and **heat of vaporisation** of methyl alcohol at various temperatures up to the critical point are shown in the following table (slightly abbreviated) due to S. Young.[1]

METHYL ALCOHOL.

Temp.	Vapour pressure, mm.	Heat of vaporisation, calories.
0°	29·6	289·17
10	54·7	287·36
20	96·0	284·54
30	160·0	282·07
40	260·5	277·78
50	406·0	274·14
60	625·0	269·41
70	—	264·51
80	1341	258·96
90	1897	252·76
100	2621	246·01
120	4751	232·00
140	8071	216·12
160	13027	198·34
180	20089	177·16
200	29787	151·84
220	42573	112·53
230	50414	84·47
232	52202	77·73
234	53939	70·15
236	55624	61·66
238	57576	50·22
238·5	58329	44·23
239	58741	—
239·5	59145	—
240 Critical temp.	59660	0

The **specific heat** of methyl alcohol at temperatures from 18° to 100° is 0·6581 (Doroschewsky). This investigator has also deter-

[1] *Scient. Proc. Roy. Dublin Soc.* [N.S.], 1910, **12**, 440.

mined the specific heats of mixtures of methyl alcohol and water over the range 18° to 100°,[1] the results being as follows :—

Per cent. of methyl alcohol by weight.	Specific heat.
90·01	0·7200
80·00	0·7744
69·99	0·8287
60·03	0·8689
49·98	0·9162
40·00	0·9542
30·02	0·9871
24·98	1·0001
20·00	1·0021
15·01	1·0065
10·01	1·0114
5·00	1·0085
0·00 (water)	1·0060

The **viscosity** of methyl alcohol at 20° is 0·005972 ; at 25°, 0·00564 ; and at 45°, 0·00424. The **molecular magnetic rotation** is 1·640.[2]

Oxidising agents convert methyl alcohol into formaldehyde and then into formic acid, and ultimately under certain conditions into carbon dioxide and water. Examples of each of these reactions are described in Chap. VI in connection with the estimation of methyl alcohol.

When heated with soda-lime, methyl alcohol yields sodium formate :—

$$CH_3{\cdot}OH + NaOH = H{\cdot}COONa + 2H_2.$$

In certain crystalline compounds, methyl alcohol functions as alcohol of crystallisation. The most noteworthy is the combination with calcium chloride, $CaCl_2,4CH_4O$, which crystallises in hexagonal plates, and is obtained by the direct union of the alcohol and the calcium salt. Lithium chloride and magnesium chloride supply other examples of such combinations. Magnesium itself dissolves in warm methyl alcohol, giving the methoxide in crystals which contain 3 molecules of the alcohol. Barium oxide is dissolved by methyl alcohol to give the crystalline compound $BaO,2CH_4O,2H_2O$.

Electrolysis.—On electrolysing methyl alcohol in aqueous sulphuric acid, hydrogen is evolved, and oxidation products are formed. These consist of methyl formate, methylal, methyl acetate, acetic acid, and methyl sulphuric acid, with a little carbon dioxide and carbon monoxide. Under special conditions, formaldehyde is produced.

[1] *J. Russ. Phys. Chem. Ges.*, 1909, **41**, 958 ; *Chem. Zentr.*, 1910, **1**, 156.
[2] Perkin, *Trans. Chem. Soc.*, 1902, **81**, 178.

In aqueous solution, on addition of potassium acetate, methane and potassium methyl carbonate are produced, as well as the carbon oxides.

Electrolysed without a solvent, either alone or with the addition of a little alkali, methyl alcohol yields chiefly carbon dioxide, together with monoxide, oxygen, and hydrogen. In presence of alkali, carbonate of the latter is formed.

Catalytic decomposition.—When methyl alcohol vapour is passed over reduced copper at a temperature of about 200–240°, it is decomposed into formaldehyde and hydrogen (Sabatier and Senderens). At higher temperatures, the formaldehyde is partly destroyed, carbon monoxide being produced. Thus, according to Mannich and Geilmann,[1] at 240–260° the evolved gas contains 10 to 12 per cent. of carbon monoxide, corresponding with the decomposition of about one-seventh of the primarily formed formaldehyde. A large proportion of the latter is polymerised to methyl formate.

With reduced nickel as catalyst in the place of copper, Sabatier and Senderens found that the action is more violent and takes place at a lower temperature, but partial decomposition of the aldehyde cannot be avoided. Reduced cobalt acts similarly to nickel. Platinum sponge also effects the decomposition of the alcohol, but at a higher temperature.[2]

The catalytic decomposition of methyl alcohol is of considerable technical importance in the production of formaldehyde. Reduced copper, platinised asbestos, and silvered gauze or pumice are commonly used as the catalysts. Formaldehyde itself is largely used in the dyeing industry, in making certain medicinal products (hexamine), and in the manufacture of synthetic resins (bakelite).

If methyl alcohol is heated in absence of air, in a vessel provided with a reflux condenser, by means of a platinum or nickel wire electrically heated to about 700°, hydrogen and carbon monoxide with traces of dioxide are given off, and formaldehyde is found in the reaction vessel. If ammonia is dissolved in the methyl alcohol, the formaldehyde is converted into hexamethylenetetramine.[3] A mixture of methyl alcohol vapour and air yields formaldehyde when exposed to sunlight, though not when kept in the dark at the ordinary temperature, and only traces at 100°.[4]

Applications.—Methyl alcohol finds important applications in the manufacture of medicinal and photographic chemicals and of

[1] *Ber.*, 1916, **49**, 585
[2] *Compt. rend.*, 1903, **136**, 921.
[3] Löb, *Zeitsch. Elektrochem.*, 1912, **18**, 847.
[4] H. D. Gibbs, *Phil. J. Sci.*, 1912, **7**, 57.

dyestuffs. It is employed both as a solvent—as, for example, in the preparation of "Salvarsan"—and as a means of introducing methyl groups into a compound. For this latter purpose, it is usually employed in the form of a salt or ester, *e.g.*, methyl sulphate, chloride, iodide, or picrate. Methyl anilines are largely used in the preparation of certain dyestuffs. Methyl salicylate, or synthetic oil of wintergreen, is of some importance in medicine, and is also employed as a constituent of flavourings. Various methyl esters are used in perfumery, as, for instance, methyl benzoate (Niobe essence), methyl anthranilate, methyl cinnamate, and methyl beta-naphtholate (nerolin).

In its less pure forms as wood spirit or wood naphtha, methyl alcohol is largely used as a solvent for resins in the varnish industry, and it finds an important application in the denaturing of ethyl alcohol used in manufactures.

Wood naphtha.—("Wood Spirit").—This is crude methyl alcohol, containing water and various impurities, chiefly acetone and esters. The amount of these impurities allowed to remain in the various grades of wood spirit depends upon the purpose for which the spirit is required. For example, in the making of formaldehyde, and also in the colour industry, it is important to have the methyl alcohol nearly free from acetone; whereas there is no objection to a moderate proportion of acetone in wood naphtha used as a denaturant of ethyl alcohol, and its presence is even advantageous in wood naphtha employed as a solvent for resins in making varnishes, polishes, and lacquers.

For a description of the analytical methods used in examining wood naphtha, and for typical analyses, see Chap. VIII.

Toxic character of methyl alcohol.—A number of observations have been recorded tending to show that methyl alcohol is distinctly more poisonous than its ethyl homologue. This toxic character has been ascribed to the oxidation of the methyl alcohol in the tissues to formaldehyde, which, as is well known, has a strong chemical action on nitrogenous organic substances. Or again, it has been attributed also to the further oxidation-product formic acid, which appears in the urine in cases of methyl alcohol poisoning, and has been found in the cadaver after death: this acid is said to cause fatty degeneration of the blood-vessels in the sheaths of the optic nerve and choroid membrane, leading to serious affection of the eyesight.[1]

As regards instances of actual poisoning through drinking methyl alcohol in quantity, the best known is perhaps the Berlin case which

[1] Kasass, *Zentr. Biochem. Biophys.*, **15**, 205.

occurred in 1911. A factitious "brandy" or "schnapps" had been concocted with methyl and ethyl alcohols in the proportion of about 4 parts of the former to 1 part of the latter, and drunk by a large number of people, with the result that there were 95 cases of illness and 70 deaths.[1] Another instance is recorded, with the symptoms, by Dr. C. A. Wood as occurring in Indiana during 1911.

Five men made a mixture of one gallon of wood alcohol and three gallons of grain (ethyl) alcohol, and all drank freely of it, with fatal results. Blindness came on about six to eight hours before death.[2]

According to observations made by Nicloux and Placet,[3] *large* intravenous doses of methyl alcohol are relatively less toxic than ethyl alcohol; but in repeated small doses every twenty-four hours the reverse is the case. This appears to be due to the cumulative effect obtained, since methyl alcohol is eliminated more slowly, and is less readily destroyed in the tissues, than is ethyl alcohol.

The latter phenomenon is illustrated by some experiments on dogs carried out by Voltz and Dietrich.[4] It was found that after administration of methyl alcohol (2 c c. per kilo. of body weight), only 39 per cent. was oxidised in the tissues during forty-eight hours. On the other hand, when ethyl alcohol was given under similar conditions, about 90 per cent. of the alcohol was oxidised and destroyed in the tissues during a much shorter time, namely, fifteen hours.

Numerous references to papers on the toxicology of methyl alcohol are given by E. Merck.[5] The conclusions summarised "show that methyl alcohol itself, when habitually used, or when taken in a single large dose, may act as a poison, and that "the toxicity is not due to the presence of impurities in the preparation." Some persons are able to take large doses of methyl alcohol without apparent harm. It is, however, impossible to say beforehand how large a dose will show an injurious effect. According to one investigator (Ruhle), the lethal dose varies between 50 and 100 grams. "but the toxic dose is much less, and blindness may ensue after doses of only 7 or 8 grams."

Olivari[6] found that with pure methyl alcohol the minimal lethal dose for small animals (guinea-pigs, mice, frogs) was about 10 grams per kilogram of body weight, the dose ranging from 9·5 to 11·5 in the three animals mentioned.

[1] *Zeitsch. Nahr. und Genussm.*, 1912, **24**, 7.
[2] *Blindness from Wood Alcohol*, pub. American Med. Assoc.
[3] *J. Physiol. Path.*, **14**, 916.
[4] *Biochem. Zeitsch*, 1912,. **40**, 15.
[5] "*Annual Report*," 1912.
[6] *Chem. Zentr.*, 1913, **1**, 1780.

CHAPTER V

ETHYL ALCOHOL: ITS OCCURRENCE AND PHYSICAL PROPERTIES

Ethyl alcohol (Ethanol), $C_2H_6{\cdot}OH$. Mol. wt. 46·05.

Occurrence of alcohol in natural products.—Ethyl alcohol is present in a number of plants, chiefly combined with organic acids to form the ethyl esters of these acids. Thus ethyl acetate is contained in the flowers of *Magnolia fuscata*; ethyl butyrate in the oil from the fruits of *Heracleum giganteum* and *H. sphondylium*; ethyl valerate probably occurs in Algerian oil of rue; and ethyl cinnamate is present in liquid storax from *Liquidambar orientalis* and in the oil from *Kaempferia galanga*. This last oil contains also the ethyl ester of *p*-methoxycinnamic acid; whilst ethyl esters of hexoic, octoic, decoic, lauric, palmitic, and oleic acids are present in the juice from the fruits of the saw palmetto (*Sabal serrulata*).

Certain lichens also contain the ethyl esters of various acids: for these and others mentioned, see the references compiled by the late Prof. Meldola.[1]

The alcohol itself is found in many distillates obtained by distilling plants or parts of plants with water; but in most cases it is probably produced partly or wholly from the esters by hydrolysis during the distillation. Thus the aqueous distillates from the fruits of *Heracleum* sp., of *Pastinacca sativa*, and of *Anthriscus cerefolium* contain ethyl alcohol, as also do those from the oil of the leaves of *Indigofera galegoides*, from oil of storax, and from grass and leaves which have been macerated in very dilute sulphuric acid. The forerunnings obtained in the distillation of oil of *Eucalyptus globulus* likewise contain ethyl alcohol.

In the distillate from rose leaves alcohol is found, but is perhaps due to fermentation of carbohydrates, not to its production by the living petals.

According to Berthelot, however, alcohol is formed in the tissues of certain growing plants, *e.g.*, wheat and hazel. It is produced in the cells of plants from carbohydrates by what has been called

[1] "The Chemical Synthesis of Vital Products," p. 45.

"intracellular respiration" when the cells have an insufficient supply of oxygen.

Besides the true yeasts (*Saccharomyces* sp.), other related micro-fungi, and certain moulds and bacteria, are capable of producing alcohol from sugars and other carbohydrates. Species of *Torula, Mycoderma, Aspergillus, Mucor, Monilia,* and *Penicillium*; *Bacillus acidi lactici, B. ethaceticus, B. coli communis, B. typhosus, Saccharobacillus pastorianus,* and *Amylobacter butylicum* are among the chief of these alcohol-producing organisms. A long list of the yeasts and these other ferments is given by Meldola.[1]

According to investigations carried out by A. R. Minenkoff,[2] alcoholic fermentation can take place in the higher plants, both under aerobic and anaerobic conditions, and is directly related to the vital activity of the plant organism, particularly to its growth. In the presence of oxygen, the formation of alcohol is increased when growth is retarded either by high or low temperatures, or by changes in osmotic pressure due to dissolved organic or inorganic substances. Formation of acid diminishes with increasing production of alcohol, and ceases completely before the plant dies. When the retardation of growth is at a maximum, the ratio of carbon dioxide to alcohol approaches that observed in pure alcoholic fermentation. Absence of oxygen promotes the fermentation, owing to the growth of the plant being inhibited.

Properties of ethyl alcohol.—Anhydrous ethyl alcohol is a mobile, colourless liquid, possessing a slight but agreeable spirituous odour and a pungent taste, and burning with a pale-blue, non-luminous flame.

Boiling point.—This was found by Kopp[3] to be 78·4°, and by Mendeléeff 78·3°, at 760 mm. pressure. Fuchs[4] gives it as ranging from 76·36° at 710 mm. to 79·31° at 790 mm.

R. W. Merriman[5] gives the following as the boiling points of ethyl alcohol at pressures from 50 to 2000 mm.:—

Pressure in mm.	B.p.	Pressure in mm.	B.p.
50	22·20°	350	59·84°
100	34·35	400	62·87
150	42·06	450	65·59
200	47·83	500	68·06
250	52·47	550	70·33
300	56·41	600	72·43

[1] *Loc. cit.*, pp. 45–53.
[2] *Bull. Agric. Intell.*, 1915, **6**, 1464; see *J. Soc. Chem. Ind.*, 1916, **35**, 135.
[3] *Annalen*, 1854, **92**, 9.
[4] *Zeitsch. angew. Chem.*, 1898, 870.
[5] *Trans. Chem. Soc.*, 1913, **103**, 632.

Pressure in mm.	B.p.	Pressure in mm.	B.p.
650	74·39°	1,300	92·52°
700	76·24	1,400	94·58
760	78·30	1,500	96·53
800	79·61	1,600	98·37
900	82·65	1,700	100·12
1,000	85·42	1,800	101·78
1,100	87·96	1,900	103·37
1,200	90·32	2,000	104·89

According to Wroblewski and Olsewski,[1] the **solidifying point** of ethyl alcohol is −130·5° ; but a later determination by Ladenburg and Krugel[2] gives the value −112·3°.

Vapour pressure.—Merriman gives the vapour pressures at various temperatures up to 25° and between 0° and 105° as follows :—

VAPOUR PRESSURE OF ETHYL ALCOHOL.

I. *Temperatures from 0° to 25°.*

Temp.	Pressure in mm.	Temp.	Pressure in mm.
0°	12·0	13°	28·4
1	12·9	14	30·3
2	13·9	15	32·2
3	14·9	16	34·3
4	15·9	17	36·4
5	17·0	18	38·7
6	18·2	19	41·2
7	19·4	20	43·8
8	20·7	21	46·5
9	22·1	22	49·4
10	23·5	23	52·4
11	25·1	24	55·6
12	26·7	25	59·0

II. *Temperatures from 0° to 105°.*

Temp.	Pressure in mm.	Temp.	Pressure in mm.
0°	12·0	55°	281·2
5	17·0	60	352·7
10	23·5	65	438·9
15	32·2	70	542·5
20	43·8	75	666·0
25	59·0	80	812·7
30	78·6	85	985·2
35	103·6	90	1187·0
40	134·9	95	1422·0
45	174·0	100	1694·0
50	222·2	105	2007·0

The following data, giving **vapour pressure** and **heat of vaporisation** at various temperatures up to the critical temperature, are due to Young.[3]

[1] *Compt. rend.*, 1883, **96**, 1140, 1225. [2] *Ber.*, 1899, **32**, 1818.
[3] *Scient. Proc. Roy. Dublin Soc.*, [N.S.], 1910, **12**, 441.

Temperature.	Vap. pressure, mm.	Heat of vaporisation. Calories.
0°	12·24	220·9
10	23·77	221·2
20	44·00	220·6
30	78·06	220·1
40	—	218·7
50	—	216·0
60	—	213·4
70	—	209·9
80	—	206·4
90	1,194	201·6
100	—	197·1
110	2,356	190·3
120	—	184·2
130	4,320	177·6
140	5,666	171·1
150	7,326	164·7
160	9,366	156·9
170	11,856	148·4
180	14,763	139·2
190	18,178	128·4
200	22,164	116·6
210	26,821	103·2
220	32,097	88·2
230	38,176	70·6
240	45,504	40·3
241	46,210	35·0
242	46,917	28·4
242·5	47,206	22·1
243·1 Critical temp.	47,850	0

The **specific heat** at temperatures from 16° to 40·5° is 0·612 (Schüller); and the **critical temperature** 243·6° at 48·9 m., 1 gram at this point occupying a volume of 3·5 c.c. (Ramsay and Young).[1]

Doroschewsky and Rakowsky[2] found the specific heat of ethyl alcohol at 20° to be 0·618. For mixtures of alcohol and water, the specific heats over the range 22° to 99° were found to be as follows:—

Percentage of alcohol by weight.	Specific heat.	Percentage of alcohol by weight.	Specific heat.
100·00	0·6597	44·95	0·9702
94·43	0·7089	39·93	0·9924
90·02	0·7390	34·98	1·0116
85·05	0·7732	29·94	1·0277
80·00	0·8030	24·97	1·0411
74·99	0·8309	20·09	1·0440
69·96	0·8603	15·00	1·0422
64·96	0·8859	10·04	1·0300
59·95	0·9079	5·02	1·0169
54·93	0·9296	0·00	1·0067
50·00	0·9489		

[1] *Proc. Roy. Soc.*, 1885, **38**, 329.

[2] *J. Russ. Phys. Chem. Soc.*, 1908, **40**, 860; *Chem. Zentr.*, 1908, **2**, 1568.

Specific gravity.—Owing to its fiscal as well as to its scientific importance, the specific gravity of ethyl alcohol has been the subject of numerous investigations. In this country, the value obtained by Fownes,[1] namely, 0·7938 at 15·6/15·6°, and the practically identical number found by Drinkwater,[2] 0·79381, have been largely used. In Germany, the value 0·7946 at 15·6°/15·6° was adopted by Tralles,[3] and employed for many years, but has been replaced for fiscal purposes by data based on the work of Mendeléeff.[4] This investigator, whose determinations are probably the most accurate of all, obtained the following results :—

At 0°/3·9°, 0·80625 ;
,, 15°/3·9°; 0·79367 ;
,, 30°/3·9°, 0·78096.

Referred to the temperature 15·6°, and compared with water at the same temperature, these values correspond with 0·79384 *in vacuo*, or to 0·79359 in air.

More recent workers (Young,[5] 1902 ; Klason and Norlin,[6] 1906) have found values somewhat higher than those of Fownes and Drinkwater—namely, 0·79395 and 0·79394 respectively. On the other hand, lower results even than Mendeléeff's have been published ; thus Squibb[7] found the specific gravity 0·7935. Since there is difficulty in eliminating the last traces of water, the lowest value ought to represent the purest alcohol, provided there is no other source of error. Squibb's result, however, has not been confirmed, and it has been suggested that perhaps the presence of a little ether may have caused the value obtained to be a little lower than the truth.

A careful review of the most trustworthy determinations indicates Mendeléeff's result, which corresponds with 0·79359 at 15·6°/15·6° (in air), as probably the most accurate value of the specific gravity of ethyl alcohol.

Thermal expansion and specific gravity of aqueous solutions of alcohol.—The ordinary tables of alcoholic strengths at 15·56° are given in the section on "Alcoholometry." The following data, due to Osborne, McKelvy, and Bearce,[8] allow of the specific gravity of aqueous alcohol mixtures being calculated for any temperature between 10° and 40°.

[1] *Phil. Trans.*, 1847, 249.
[2] *Phil. Mag.*, 1848, **22**, 123.
[3] *Gilb. Annal.*, 1811.
[4] *Pogg. Ann.*, 1869, **138**, 230.
[5] *Trans. Chem. Soc.*, 1902, **81**, 717.
[6] *Arkiv Kem. Min. Geol.*, 1906, **2**, No. 24.
[7] Ephemeris, 1884–5 ; *Pharm. J.*, [iii], 1884, **15**, 44, and 1885, **16**, 147–8.
[8] *Bull. U.S. Bureau of Standards.* Scientific Paper No. 197.

The specific gravity of alcohol at 25° was found to be 0·78506 gram per c.c.

The specific gravity of various mixtures of alcohol and water was determined at 10°, at 40°, and at each interval of 5° between these temperatures. From the results, the values of the coefficients in the following equation were calculated :—

$$D_t = D_{25} + \alpha(t-25) + \beta(t-25)^2 + \gamma(t-25)^3.$$

Here D_t is the specific gravity at any temperature $t°$ between 10° and 40°, and D_{25} is the specific gravity at 25°. The values of the coefficients α, β, and γ are given in the following table.

Alcohol per cent. by weight.	Sp. gr. at 25°. Gram per c.c.	$\alpha \times 10^7$.	$\beta \times 10^8$.	$\gamma \times 10^{10}$.
0·000 (water).	0·997077	− 2565	− 484	+ 319
4·907	0·988317	− 2684	− 502	+ 311
9·984	0·980461	− 3119	− 484	+ 258
19·122	0·967648	− 4526	− 393	+ 180
22·918	0·962133	− 5224	− 331	+ 100
30·086	0·950529	− 6431	− 226	+ 47
39·988	0·931507	− 7488	− 145	− 4
49·961	0·909937	− 8033	− 128	− 24
59·976	0·887051	− 8358	− 121	− 24
70·012	0·863380	− 8581	− 117	− 9
80·036	0·839031	− 8714	− 108	− 69
90·037	0·813516	− 8746	− 93	− 51
99·913	0·785337	− 8593	− 57	− 62

With the aid of this table and the following one giving an extended range of alcohol percentages, the specific gravity of any mixture of ethyl alcohol and water, at any temperature between 10° and 40°, can be calculated from the foregoing equation.

Alcohol per cent. by weight.	Sp. gr. at 25°. Gram per c.c.	Alcohol per cent. by weight.	Sp. gr. at 25°. Gram per c.c.
0	0·997077	55	0·898502
2	0·993359	60	0·886990
5	0·988166	65	0·875269
6	0·986563	70	0·863399
10	0·980434	75	0·851336
15	0·973345	80	0·839114
20	0·966392	85	0·826596
25	0·958946	90	0·813622
30	0·950672	95	0·799912
35	0·941459	98	0·791170
40	0·931483	99	0·788135
45	0·920850	100	0·785058
50	0·909852		

Contraction.—Alcohol is hygroscopic, though not remarkably so. It is miscible with water in all proportions. On mixing the two liquids, a rise in temperature occurs, and on cooling the mixture to the original temperature there is found to be a contraction of the total volume, the extent of the decrease depending upon the relative proportions of the constituents. The maximum contraction, when calculated as a percentage on the sum of the initial volumes, is given by a mixture containing one molecule of alcohol and three molecules of water,[1] the amount of contraction being 3·64 per cent. at 15·56°. Expressed in another way, the maximum contraction is obtained by mixing 52 volumes of alcohol with 48 volumes of water, and the volume of the resulting mixture (measured at 20° in this case) is 96·3 instead of 100.

J. Holmes[2] has given a table showing the actual contraction, measured in cubic centimetres at 15·56°, which occurs when 100 c.c. of alcohol are mixed with increasing quantities of water. From this table, it appears that a maximum amount of contraction, 9·08 c.c., is reached when the mixture corresponds with one molecule of alcohol to eight molecules of water. This is to be distinguished from the maximum *percentage* contraction, which, as stated above, occurs with the proportions $C_2H_6O,3H_2O$. A part of the table is given here by way of illustration :—

	Volumes at temperature 15·56°.	
Mixture.	Actual contraction; initial vol. of alcohol 100 c.c.	Percentage contraction, calculated on sum of initial volumes.
$C_2H_6O,\frac{1}{6}H_2O$	1·21 c.c.	0·99
C_2H_6O,H_2O	3·79 ,,	2·89
$C_2H_6O,3H_2O$	7·03 ,,	3·64
$C_2H_6O,6H_2O$	8·87 ,,	3·09
$C_2H_6O,8H_2O$	9·08 ,,	2·61
$C_2H_6O,12H_2O$	8·78 ,,	1·86
$C_2H_6O,20H_2O$	7·88 ,,	1·09

Holmes deduces from his experiments that the "true molecular volume" of ethyl alcohol is 3·22, that of water at the same temperature being taken as unity. For methyl alcohol, the "true molecular volume" deduced is 2·23, and for *n*-propyl alcohol 4·07.

Apparent specific volume of alcohol in aqueous mixtures.— Dr. H. T. Brown deduces from the following considerations that with very dilute mixtures of alcohol and water there is an expansion of volume instead of a contraction.[3]

The apparent specific volume, *i.e.*, the volume occupied by unit weight of alcohol, may be expressed by the formula

$$1-(D-W)/W,$$

[1] Graham, *Phil. Trans.*, 1861, **151**, 373.
[2] *Trans. Chem. Soc.*, 1906, **89**, 1775.
[3] *Analyst*, 1915, **40**, 379.

where D is the specific gravity of the mixture at 15·6°/15·6°, and W the weight of alcohol, expressed in grams, in 1 c.c. of the mixture. The values of the specific volume for mixtures of comparatively low alcoholic concentration are given in the following table:—

Sp. gr. of mixture.	Sp. vol. of alcohol in mixture.
0·988	1·1713
9	1·1732
0·990	1·1750
1	1·1770
2	1·1788
3	1·1807
4	1·1818
5	1·1834
6	1·1850
7	1·1862
8	1·1874
0·999	1·1890

These values represent the volume in c.c. occupied by 1 gram of alcohol at the different concentrations when the volume-changes are all thrown on the alcohol.

The apparent specific volume of the contained alcohol increases steadily with the dilution. It follows that on progressive dilution within these limits the volume of the mixture must exceed the sum of the initial volumes of the constituents, so that an actual increase of volume must occur instead of the contraction which is observed at higher concentrations of alcohol. The critical point at which dilution ceases to produce contraction and begins to give rise to expansion occurs at a concentration corresponding very nearly with the specific gravity 0·9652. This point would seem to mark the completed formation of a definite alcohol hydrate, during the formation of which continuous contraction takes place; and the expansion which occurs on still further dilution may be regarded as an expression of progressive dissociation of this hydrate.

A hydrate having the composition $C_2H_5 \cdot OH,8H_2O$, would contain 24·21 per cent. of alcohol, and dilute alcohol of specific gravity 0·9652 contains 24·82 per cent. (by weight).

Surface tension.—At 20°, and for alcohol of 99·54 per cent. strength, the surface tension is 20·90 dynes per centimetre.

Refraction.—The **refractive index** of ethyl alcohol for the line H_β is 1·3667 (Brühl).

Holmes[1] has determined the indices of refraction (N_D) at 15·5° for various mixtures of alcohol and water, and shows that a maximum value is given by a mixture containing 79·2 per cent. of alcohol by weight. An abridgment of his table of results is as follows:—

[1] *Trans. Chem. Soc.*, 1913, **103**, 2165.

Molecular mixture.	Value of (N_D) at 15·5°.
C_2H_6O	1·36316
$4C_2H_6O,H_2O$	1·36574
$2C_2H_6O,H_2O$	1·36651
C_2H_6O,H_2O	1·36630
$C_2H_6O,2H_2O$	1·36408
$C_2H_6O,3H_2O$	1·36152
$C_2H_6O,4H_2O$	1·35883

The maximum value, corresponding with the proportion of alcohol stated above, is 1·36661.

Browning and Symons[1] found a maximum value of the refractive index, at 30°, with a mixture containing about 78·25 per cent. of alcohol by weight.

L. W. Andrews[2] gives the refractive index (μ) of alcohol against air as 1·35941 ± 0·00001 at 25°, and the refractive constant $(N_D - 1)/d$ as 0·45833, whilst $(\mu_D - 1)/d = 0·45779$. With the Zeiss immersion refractometer, the reading obtained was 85·30° ± 0·02°. The maximum value of the refractive index was given by a mixture of 20·7 per cent. of water and 79·3 per cent. of alcohol, corresponding with $3C_2H_6O,2H_2O$. This maximum value is 1·363315 at 25°.

The indices of refraction for various mixtures of ethyl alcohol and water at temperatures between 15° and 55°, and for the sodium rays, have also been determined by Doroschewsky and Dvorschantschik.[3] Some of the principal results are as follows :—

Alcohol per cent. by weight.	$N_D^{15°}$.	$N_D^{30°}$.	$N_D^{40°}$.	$N_D^{50°}$.	$N_D^{55°}$.
0	1·33345	1·3318	1·3306	1·3290	1·3281
10	1·34020	1·3384	1·3368	1·3349	1·3339
20	1·34778	1·3450	1·3429	1·3406	1·3393
30	1·35470	1·3510	1·3481	1·3452	1·3435
40	1·35948	1·3550	1·3518	1·3484	1·3468
50	1·36290	1·3578	1·3543	1·3506	1·3488
60	1·36505	1·3597	1·3560	1·3522	1·3501
70	1·36645	1·3608	1·3570	1·3528	1·3505
80	1·36690	1·3611	1·3569	1·3525	1·3502
90	1·36626	1·3603	1·3561	1·3515	1·3491
100	1·36332	1·3573	1·3531	1·3487	1·3465

These authors found that the influence of temperature upon the index of refraction of the mixtures could be expressed by the equation $N_t = N_0/(1 + kt)$, where k is a constant and $t°$, $0°$ denote the temperatures.

[1] *J. Soc. Chem. Ind.*, 1914, **33**, 819–21.

[2] *J. Amer. Chem. Soc.*, 1908, **30**, 353.

[3] *J. Russ. Phys. Chem. Soc.*, 1908, **40**, 908–931 ; *Chem. Zentr.*, 1908, **2**, 1569–71.

Dispersion of ultra-violet rays.—The refractive indices of methyl, ethyl, and propyl alcohols for rays of wave-length $\lambda = 4200 - 2150$ have been measured by V. Henri.[1] The molecular refractive power can be accurately represented by the formula :—

$$\frac{M}{d} \cdot \frac{n^2-1}{n^2+2} = \frac{a+\beta\lambda^2_0}{\lambda^2-\lambda^2_0}.$$

The values of the constants a, β, and λ_0, which hold good from $\lambda = 6563$ to $\cdot 2150$, are :—

	a.	β.	λ_0.
Methyl alcohol	8·0195	5·1132	1063
Ethyl "	12·707	7·1734	1239
Propyl "	17·112	10·148	1114

Electric conductivity.—The electric conductivity of ethyl alcohol, and of various mixtures of alcohol and water, has been determined by Doroschewsky and Roschdestvensky.[2] They purified the alcohol by repeated distillation over quicklime, and the water by distillation from barium hydroxide, potassium permanganate, and phosphoric acid. The results obtained at 15° were as follows :—

Alcohol. Per cent. by weight.	Conductivity. ($\lambda \times 10^6$).	Alcohol. Per cent. by weight.	Conductivity. ($\lambda \times 10^6$).
0·0	1·097	60·4	0·223
2·6	0·949	71·4	0·235
13·6	0·540	74·6	0·238
20·1	0·414	80·6	0·248
28·2	0·313	86·3	0·235
37·4	0·256	91·1	0·215
44·2	0·237	94·9	0·196
50·4	0·234	98·5	0·133
56·0	0·219	100·0	0·097

The relation between the specific conductivity, λ, and the concentration, C, of the alcohol in the mixtures can be represented by the equation $\lambda C^{\frac{3}{4}} =$ a constant, the value of the constant depending, however, upon the temperature, and upon the degree of purity of the alcohol and the water.

For mixtures containing 10 to 50 per cent. of alcohol, the relation between the viscosity N, the conductivity λ, and the dielectric constant D, can be represented by the equation $N\lambda/D =$ a constant.

Electrolysis of alcohol.—According to Löb and Lorenz,[3] when ethyl alcohol is electrolysed in sulphuric acid solution the

[1] *Compt. rend.*, 1914, **158**, 1892.

[2] *J. Russ. Phys. Chem. Soc.*, 1908, **40**, 887–908; *Chem. Zentr.*, 1908, **2**, 1568; *J. Soc. Chem. Ind.*, 1909, **28**, 853.

[3] "Electrochemistry of Organic Compounds," 1906, p. 60.

final products are aldehyde, acetic ester, formic ester, ethyl sulphuric acid, and ethylidene oxy-ethyl ether [$CH_3 \cdot CH(OH) \cdot O \cdot C_2H_5$].

In nitric acid solution, in addition to these oxidation products, carbon derivatives of ammonia have been observed at the negative pole.

In hydrochloric acid solutions, chloro-acetic acids occur, as well as oxidation products, whilst in alkaline solution an aldehyde resin is obtained. Finally, with alcohol in aqueous solution, after addition of potassium acetate, the products were ethane, carbon dioxide, acetic ester, and potassium ethyl carbonate.

Dielectric constant.—Walden[1] has found the following values of this constant for ethyl alcohol :—

Temperature	Diel. const. *K*.
1·5°	28·8
18·5°	25·4
49·2°	20·8

Electric absorption.—The following data are due to P. Beaulard.[2] For convenience, the figures relating to methyl and propyl alcohols are also included.

	Length of wave. Metres.	True specific inductive power.	Apparent spec. induct. power.
Methyl alcohol	12	33·28	2·567
	35	33·31	4·303
Ethyl alcohol	12	25	3·701
	35	25	4·565
Propyl alcohol	12	13·32	3·347
	35	13·39	4·959

Specific inductive powers of mixtures of ethyl alcohol and water (Beaulard and Maury).[3]

Alcohol, per cent.	Apparent spec. induct. power. $\lambda = 35$ *m.*	$\lambda = 12$ *m.*
99	4·876	3·684
97	4·775	3·825
95	4·648	4·969
90	4·531	3·700
85	4·312	3·486
80	4·152	3·505
70	6·120	3·892
60	5·761	3·903
50	5·144	3·162
40	4·562	3·629
30	4·501	3·588
15	4·956	3·456
0	4·418	3·592

[1] *Zeitsch. physikal. Chem.*, 1910, **70**, 573. [2] *Compt. rend.*, 1910, **151**, 56.
[3] *Journ. de Phys.*, 1910, [iv], **9**, 43.

The **molecular magnetic rotation** of ethyl alcohol was found by Perkin[1] to be 2·780.

Solubility of alcohol in water.—As already stated, alcohol is miscible with water in all proportions, but Wroth and Reid[2] have devised an ingenious method of estimating the "ideal" solubility, based upon the value of the partition-coefficient of alcohol between water and cotton-seed oil.

If S_a and S_b represent respectively the solubilities of alcohol in water and in the oil, C_a and C_b the concentrations in the same two solvents at equilibrium, and k the partition-coefficient, then $S_a/S_b = k = C_a/C_b$.

By determining experimentally the proportion of alcohol in the aqueous layer and in the oily layer after the mixture has been shaken up and allowed to separate, the values of C_a and C_b are found, and therefore the value of k is known. It was found to be 28·3 at 25°. Then, by determining the value of S_b experimentally, the value of S_a can be calculated. Thus ethyl alcohol was found to dissolve in the oil to the extent of 21·2 grams per 100 c.c., whence $S_a = kS_b = 28{\cdot}3 \times 21{\cdot}2 = 600$ grams per 100 c.c.

This represents the "ideal" solubility of ethyl alcohol in water at 25°, which could be realised if water and alcohol were separated by a semi-permeable membrane through which only the alcohol molecules could pass. For methyl alcohol, the corresponding number is 501,[3] the value of k being 103·6 and the solubility in cotton-seed oil 4·84 grams per 100 c.c.

In the foregoing experiments, the mixtures were shaken for an hour in a bath kept at a constant temperature of 25°. About three weeks' standing, or six hours' centrifuging, were required before the layers became clear.

Viscosity of ethyl alcohol and its aqueous mixtures.—Ethyl alcohol and its aqueous solutions form useful standard liquids for testing viscometers, within the range of viscosities obtainable. A mixture of 45 per cent. by volume of ethyl alcohol and water has a viscosity which is almost exactly four times that of water at 0°. Since the viscosity of alcohol–water mixtures passes through a maximum at this concentration, the viscosity does not change rapidly with the concentration, which is a marked advantage.

The following table is abridged from one compiled by Bingham

[1] *Trans. Chem. Soc.*, 1902, **81**, 179.

[2] *J. Amer. Chem. Soc.*, 1916, **38**, 2316.

[3] The value 505 is given by the authors, but this appears to be an arithmetical error.

VISCOSITY, IN CENTIPOISES, OF ALCOHOL, AND OF ALCOHOL–WATER MIXTURES.

Temp.	Percentage of alcohol by weight.										
	0.	10.	20.	30.	40.	50.	60.	70.	80.	90.	100.
0°	1·792	3·311	5·319	6·94	7·14	6·58	5·75	4·762	3·690	2·732	1·773
10	1·308	2·179	3·165	4·05	4·39	4·18	3·77	3·268	2·710	2·101	1·466
20	1·005	1·538	2·183	2·71	2·91	2·87	2·67	2·370	2·008	1·610	1·200
30	0·801	1·160	1·553	1·87	2·02	2·02	1·93	1·767	1·531	1·279	1·003
40	0·656	0·907	1·160	1·368	1·482	1·499	1·447	1·344	1·203	1·035	0·834
50	0·549	0·734	0·907	1·050	1·132	1·155	1·127	1·062	0·968	0·848	0·702
60	0·469	0·609	0·736	0·834	0·893	0·913	0·902	0·856	0·789	0·704	0·592
70	0·406	0·514	0·608	0·683	0·727	0·740	0·729	0·695	0·650	0·589	0·504
80	0·356	0·430	0·505	0·567	0·601	0·612	0·604	—	—	—	—

and Jackson from the most trustworthy data available.[1] The unit is the "centipoise," one-hundredth of the absolute C.G.S. unit of viscosity ("poise," from Poiseuille).

For some purposes, it is convenient to use the "fluidity" instead of the viscosity; this is the reciprocal of the viscosity expressed in *poises*. Thus the fluidity of 100 per cent. alcohol at 0° is 1/0·01773 = 56·4, and at 40°, 1/0·00834 = 119·9.

FREEZING POINTS OF AQUEOUS ALCOHOL MIXTURES.*

Freezing point.	Grams EtOH to 100 grams of water.	Freezing point.	Grams EtOH to 100 grams of water.
− 1·0°	2·65	− 12·0°	27·6
− 2	5·5	− 14	31·3
− 3	7·95	− 16	35·1
− 4	10·6	− 18	39·0
− 5	13·0	− 20	42·8
− 6	15·3	− 22	46·6
− 7	17·8	− 24	50·6
− 8	19·8	− 26	54·8
− 9	21·9	− 28	59·2
− 10	23·6	− 30	64·6
		− 32·0	70·0

* Raoult, *Ann. Chim. Phys.* [v], 1880, **20**, 221.

In a series of experiments made with a view to ascertain how far the depression of the freezing point could be used as a method of determining alcohol in dilute solutions, R. Gaunt obtained the following results.[2] Beckmann's apparatus was used, and the freezing mixture of ice-water and salt kept at about −8°.

Alcohol in 100 grams of solution Grams.	Lowering of freezing point, compared with that of water.	Calculated decrease for each 1 per cent. of alcohol.
1·0	0·424°	0·424°
2·0	0·849	0·424
3·0	1·269	0·423
4·0	1·691	0·423
5·0	2·128	0·425
6·0	2·562	0·427
7·0	3·015	0·430
8·0	3·515	0·440
10·0	4·528	0·453
12·0	5·595	0·467

Thus with the lower percentages the lowering of the freezing point is proportional to the quantity of alcohol, but at about 7 per cent. and beyond it becomes sensibly greater.

[1] "Standard Substances for the Calibration of Viscometers," Scientific Paper No. 298, *U.S. Bureau of Standards*, p. 77.

[2] *Zeitsch. anal. Chem.*, 1905, **45**, 106.

BOILING POINTS OF AQUEOUS ALCOHOL MIXTURES.*

Alcohol per cent. by weight.	(i) At 700 mm.	(ii) At 760 mm.	(iii) At 800 mm.
0	97·72°	100°	101·44°
10	89·28	91·47	92·86
20	84·89	87·05	88·43
30	82·42	84·58	85·94
40	81·00	83·13	84·49
50	79·78	81·91	83·26
60	78·92	81·04	82·38
70	78·03	80·14	81·47
80	77·22	79·32	80·64
90	76·46	78·54	79·86
100	76·26	78·35	79·66
95·57	76·16	78·23	79·54

* Doroschewsky and Poliansky, *J. Russ. Phys. Chem. Soc.*, 1910, **42**, 109–134.

Noyes and Warfel[1] found that alcohol containing 8 to 9 per cent. of water boils at 78·26° to 78·27°.

Azeotropic mixtures.—Alcohol forms azeotropic mixtures with water—*i.e.*, mixtures which distil at a constant temperature, when the pressure is kept constant, without change of composition. At the standard pressure, 760 mm., the "mixture of constant boiling point" distils at 78·15°, and contains 4·43 per cent. of water (by weight).[2] Since this temperature is lower than the boiling point of either of the two components, it is impossible at ordinary pressures to obtain pure alcohol from a dilute aqueous solution by fractional distillation only; some dehydrating agent is necessary.

The composition of the azeotropic mixture, as well as the boiling point, depends upon the pressure employed. The following values were found by R. W. Merriman:—[3]

Pressure in mm.	B.p. of mixture.	Water, per cent.	B.p. of ethyl alcohol.
1451·3	95·35°	4·75	95·58°
1075·4	87·12	4·65	87·34
760·0	78·15	4·4	78·30
404·6	63·04	3·75	63·13
198·4	47·63	2·7	47·66
129·7	39·20	1·3	39·24
94·9	33·35	0·5	33·38
70·0	—	0·0	27·96

The ratio of water to alcohol is thus diminished as the pressure is lowered. Eventually a point is reached below which an azeotropic mixture (binary mixture) is not formed; this occurs at pressures below about 80 mm. Under these conditions, anhydrous alcohol is the more volatile phase present; and it is then possible

[1] *J. Amer. Chem. Soc.*, 1901, **23**, 467.
[2] Young, *Trans. Chem. Soc.*, 1902, **81**, 710.
[3] *Ibid.*, 1913, **103**, 635.

to separate absolute alcohol from the water in ordinary strong spirit by systematic fractional distillation, as shown in the last line of the table.[1]

For the same reason, although alcohol, contrary to the general belief, is not specially hygroscopic, the percentage of water in moist alcohol is slowly increased by exposing it to air, or even by passing dry air through it.

M. Wrewski[2] finds that the azeotropic mixture of alcohol and water has the following composition at the temperatures shown :—

Temp.	Alcohol, per cent.
39·76°	97·6
54·81°	96·5
74·79°	95·7

Ethyl alcohol forms with benzene also a mixture of constant boiling point, 68·25°, at normal pressure, and with water these two liquids give a ternary azeotropic mixture boiling at a still lower temperature (64·85°). Based on these properties, an ingenious method of dehydrating alcohol has been described by Young.[3] If benzene be added to a mixture of alcohol and water, and the whole distilled, the ternary mixture of all three liquids will come over first, since it has the lowest boiling point (64·85°). If there is more than sufficient benzene to carry over the whole of the water, and if the alcohol is present in excess, the ternary mixture will be followed by the binary mixture of alcohol and benzene boiling at 68·25°, and the last substance to come over will be the alcohol, which should now, theoretically, be free from water. In practice, however, a single operation does not suffice completely to eliminate the water even when a dephlegmating column is used; but by redistilling the partly dehydrated alcohol once or twice with a further quantity of benzene, the water can be finally removed, and "absolute" alcohol obtained. Equal weights of benzene and alcohol of 93 per cent. strength (by weight) may be employed, and the distillate collected in fractions corresponding with the points 67·5°, 73°, and 78·3° for the recovery of weak alcohol and benzene; the remainder in the still is the more or less completely dehydrated alcohol.

W. R. G. Atkins [4] points out that this method can be applied to the dehydration of organic tissues, thus avoiding risk of oxidation; and also to the preparation of solid chemical compounds in the anhydrous state for analysis. The substance is placed

[1] Wade and Merriman, *Trans. Chem. Soc.*, 1911, **99**, 997.
[2] *J. Russ. Phys. Chem. Soc.*, 1910, **42**, 1–35.
[3] *Loc. cit.*
[4] *Nature*, 1915, **95**, 118; *Trans. Chem. Soc.*, 1915, **107**, 916.

in the distillation flask with alcohol and a suitable quantity of benzene. When all the turbid ternary mixture of constant boiling point has been removed by distillation from a water-bath, the remaining mixture of alcohol and benzene may be rapidly distilled away, and the last traces can be eliminated in a vacuum desiccator. By adjusting the quantities, either alcohol or benzene can be obtained as the final liquid.

The two isomeric acetylene dichlorides also form binary mixtures with alcohol, and ternary mixtures with water and alcohol, boiling at low temperatures. They can therefore be used in the same way as benzene to obtain absolute alcohol. For the isomer of b.p. 48·35°, the binary mixture boils at 46·5° and the ternary at 44·4°; for the other isomer, boiling at 60·25°, the corresponding mixtures have the boiling points 57·7° and 53·8° respectively.[1]

With chloroform, alcohol forms a binary mixture distilling at 59·4°, the composition of the mixture being 93 per cent. of chloroform and 7 per cent. of alcohol. A ternary mixture boiling at 55·5° has the composition: chloroform, 92·5, alcohol 4·0, and water 3·5 per cent.[2]

As noted by Atkins,[3] azeotropic mixtures may sometimes serve to identify an unknown liquid. The identification of a liquid by its boiling point is possible only when the liquid can be purified previously, and in dealing with small quantities such purification is often a difficult matter. It may happen, however, that another liquid can be added, with which the unknown substance will form a mixture of constant boiling point, so that the unknown liquid may be identified in this way. For example, benzene was added to a liquid smelling of alcohol, and the mixture was distilled. The temperature remained constant for a short time at 58·35° (the boiling point of the binary mixture of methyl alcohol and benzene), thus indicating the presence of methyl alcohol, and there were other halts at 64·8°, 68·25°, and 78·3°, these being respectively the boiling points of the mixtures ethyl alcohol–water–benzene, alcohol–benzene, and of alcohol. Hence the liquid consisted of a mixture of methyl alcohol, ethyl alcohol, and a trace of water.

Alcohol as solvent.—Alcohol is one of the most useful of solvents, both for organic and inorganic substances, but especially the former. It dissolves balsams, essential oils, esters, fatty acids, hydrocarbons, resins, soaps, sugars, most vegetable alkaloids, and a large number of pharmaceutical drugs such as acetanilide, camphor,

[1] G. Chavanne, *Bull. Soc. chim. Belg.*, 1913, **27**, 205.
[2] Wade and Finnemore, *Trans. Chem. Soc.*, 1904, **85**, 946.
[3] *Analyst*, 1916, **41**, 334.

chloralamide, phenacetin, and phenazone. The fixed oils and fats are but sparingly soluble in alcohol, a notable exception, however, being castor oil, which is readily dissolved. As regards inorganic substances, alcohol dissolves the hydroxides of the alkali metals, but not the carbonates. Ammonium chloride, and indeed most of the chlorides which are readily soluble in water, are dissolved by alcohol. The following table of the solubility of various alkali halides in methyl and ethyl alcohols is due to Turner and Bissett :—[1]

GRAMS OF ANHYDROUS SALT DISSOLVED BY 100 GRAMS OF THE ALCOHOLS AT 25°.

	Methyl alcohol.	Ethyl alcohol.
Lithium chloride	42·36	25·83
,, iodide	343·40	250·80
Sodium chloride	1·31	0·065
,, iodide	90·35	46·02
Potassium chloride	0·53	0·022
,, bromide	2·17	0·142
,, iodide	18·04	2·16
Rubidium chloride	1·41	0·078

Some of the metallic nitrates are dissolved by alcohol; the sulphates are generally insoluble. Deliquescent salts are usually soluble in alcohol, potassium carbonate being a notable exception to this rule, while salts which effloresce are mostly insoluble. Sulphur and phosphorus are dissolved to a small extent, and iodine freely. Many gases are more soluble in alcohol than in water; thus 100 volumes of alcohol dissolve 7 volumes of hydrogen, 25 of oxygen, and 13 of nitrogen.

Aqueous alcohol gives a turbid mixture with chloroform unless the proportion reaches a certain value, depending on the strength of the alcohol. According to K. Enz,[2] the following proportions of alcohol at different concentrations are necessary for giving a clear mixture with 10 parts of chloroform :—

Sp. gr. of alcohol.	Parts of alcohol for 10 parts of chloroform.
0·834	3·0
0·830	2·2
0·820	0·93
0·818	0·87
0·814	0·43
0·812	0·32

The alkali-metals dissolve in alcohol to form ethylates (so-called "alcoholates"), *e.g.*, sodium ethylate, $C_2H_5{\cdot}ONa$.

Alcohol forms crystalline compounds with certain salts, *e.g.*,

[1] *Trans. Chem. Soc.*, **103**, 1913, 1904.
[2] *J. Soc. Chem. Ind.*, 1913, **32**, 1169 (Abst.).

calcium chloride, magnesium chloride, appearing as "alcohol of crystallisation" in these compounds—$CaCl_2,4C_2H_6O$, for example.

Photolysis of alcohol.—According to Berthelot and Gaudechon,[1] ethyl alcohol in absence of air is not decomposed by sunlight (of wave-length greater than $0{\cdot}3\mu$). It is, however, photolysed by the direct rays of a mercury vapour lamp, used without any interposed screen. The decomposition is primarily into acetaldehyde and hydrogen, but usually there is some further photolysis of the aldehyde into carbon monoxide and ethane. When water is present, the reactions are substantially the same, but with a tendency to form acid products.

Of the gases produced when a 110-volt lamp is used and the temperature allowed to rise to 80–90°, 60–70 per cent. is hydrogen, 10–20 per cent. carbon monoxide, and 15–20 per cent. ethane. Methyl and propyl alcohols are also decomposed in a similar manner.

Oxidation of alcohol.—Speaking broadly, oxidising agents convert ethyl alcohol into aldehyde and acetic acid:—

$$C_2H_5{\cdot}OH + O = CH_3{\cdot}CHO + H_2O;$$
$$C_2H_5{\cdot}OH + O_2 = CH_3{\cdot}COOH + H_2O.$$

The character and quantity of the products vary, however, according to the conditions of the oxidation. When this is carried out with potassium dichromate or permanganate in aqueous-acid solution, the foregoing are the products; with permanganate in neutral solution, acetic acid, or acetic acid and a little carbonic acid, are given; and with *alkaline* permanganate solution, oxalic, acetic, and carbonic acids are produced.

A nearly quantitative conversion of ethyl alcohol into acetic acid can be obtained by treating an aqueous solution of the alcohol with potassium dichromate and sulphuric acid. Various proportions of the reagents have been used for this purpose. In oxidising a mixture of ethyl and methyl alcohols, Thorpe and Holmes[2] employ 7·5 grams of dichromate and 30 grams of sulphuric acid per gram of alcohol, in a total volume of about 57 c.c. The dichromate and acid are added in two stages, and the mixture is finally boiled (see p. 188). A small quantity of carbonic acid is also produced from the ethyl alcohol at the same time—about 0·01 gram for each gram of alcohol.

Dox and Lamb,[3] for oxidising small quantities of alcohol ranging from 0·2 to 2·0 grams, use an oxidising mixture composed of

[1] *Compt. rend.*, 1913, **156**, 68–71; 1910, **151**, 478.
[2] *Trans. Chem. Soc.*, 1904, **85**, 1.
[3] *J. Amer. Chem. Soc.*, 1916, **38**, 2563.

potassium dichromate, sulphuric acid, and water in the proportions of 1 : 2 : 7 by weight. About 150 c.c. of this mixture are used for the quantity of alcohol mentioned.

Evans and Day[1] have studied the action of neutral and alkaline solutions of potassium permanganate on ethyl alcohol. Using about 30 grams of this salt in a litre of water at 50°, and 3 to 6 grams of alcohol, they found that with no potassium hydroxide added the product was almost wholly acetic acid, with a very small proportion of carbonic acid. When, however, the solution was made alkaline with potassium hydroxide, oxalic acid was also one of the products, and the proportion of carbonic acid was much increased. The concentration of the alkali ranged from 5·3 to 340·8 grams per litre; and at the higher strengths (85 grams and upwards) the amount of oxalic acid produced was almost as much as that of the acetic acid. One experiment may be quoted to illustrate the whole:—Permanganate used, 30 grams; alkali, 170·4; alcohol, 3·34; oxalic acid obtained, 2·0 grams; acetic acid, 2·11; carbonic acid, 1·18. To reduce completely 30 grams of permanganate in a litre of water at 50°, 6 grams of alcohol were required when no alkali was added; but 3·5 grams sufficed for the reduction when potassium hydroxide was present in the proportion of 105 grams per litre.

Ethyl alcohol (and also methyl, propyl, butyl, and iso-amyl alcohols) are oxidised by potassium permanganate or hydrogen peroxide in the presence of ferrous salts, which act as catalysts.[2] Ferric and manganous salts are without catalytic effect on the oxidation. When ferrous sulphate is present, permanganate oxidises ethyl alcohol, in dilute solution, almost exclusively to the aldehyde; but in presence of ferrous oxalate the oxidation proceeds further, part of the aldehyde being transformed into acetic acid. These oxidations proceed so regularly that the course of the reaction may be investigated quantitatively. Hydrogen peroxide acts still more energetically on ethyl alcohol, which, in presence of ferrous sulphate or oxalate, is oxidised to a mixture of acetaldehyde and acetic acid, the aldehyde predominating with the former, and the acid with the latter, catalyst. These oxidations serve as striking lecture experiments, decolorised magenta solution being used as indicator.

Charcoal acts as an oxidiser of alcohol by reason of its adsorbed oxygen, and ferrous salts increase the oxidising power. The addition

[1] *J. Amer. Chem. Soc.*, 1916, **38**, 375.

[2] Doroschewsky and Bardt, *J. Russ. Phys. Chem. Soc.*, 1914, **46**, 754–85; *J. Chem. Soc.*, 1915, **108** (Abst.), ii, 331.

of a ferrous salt to a solution of alcohol containing charcoal results in considerable increase of the amount of aldehyde formed. Ferric salts produce no such increase.

Electrolytic oxidation of alcohol.—P. Askenasy and coadjutors have investigated the conditions necessary for obtaining the best yield of acetic acid when alcohol is oxidised electrolytically.[1] No diaphragm was used in the experimental cell employed, the electrodes being placed only 3 mm. apart. A little sulphuric acid was added to the diluted alcohol. Using rectified spirit, the best yield (80·6 per cent.) was obtained with current density 21 amperes per sq. dcm., potential 4 volts, and temperature 35°. Some aldehyde and ethyl acetate was formed during the process of electrolysis: the ethyl acetate becomes hydrolysed as the alcohol is used up, and towards the end of the oxidation some of the acetic acid is decomposed with evolution of carbon dioxide. On neutralising the electrolysed liquid with soda and evaporating down, sodium acetate is obtained, contaminated with sodium sulphate only. For economical working, fermented beetroot juice was used instead of rectified alcohol, and the best results were obtained when about 2 grams of chromium sulphate per litre of electrolyte were added as an oxygen-carrier. Under these conditions, at temperature 30–35°, with current density 12 amperes per sq. dcm. and potential 3·7 volts, a yield of about 93 per cent. was obtained. The authors consider that, given cheap power, and using the fermented beetroot juice as the source of alcohol, the electrolytic process might compete with existing methods of manufacturing acetic acid.

Chlorination of alcohol.—If dry chlorine is passed into strong alcohol to saturation, the mixture being at first cooled and afterwards heated slowly to 100°, the alcohol is chlorinated, the final product being a crystalline mixture of chloral hydrate, chloral alcoholate, and trichloroacetal. On distilling the crystalline product with sulphuric acid, chloral is obtained. With bromine, the corresponding product, bromal, is given. Alcohol distilled from bleaching powder yields chloroform. This reaction is usually explained as one in which both oxidation and chlorination proceed simultaneously, aldehyde being first produced by oxidation, and then ultimately converted into trichloroaldehyde or chloral, $CCl_3{\cdot}CHO$. The latter substance reacts with the calcium hydroxide present, yielding chloroform and calcium formate:—

$$2CCl_3{\cdot}CHO + Ca(OH)_2 = 2CHCl_3 + CaH_2(CO_2)_2.$$

[1] *Zeitsch. Elektrochem.*, 1909, **15**, 846.

Fixation of nitrogen by alcohol.—Under the influence of the electric spark discharge in an atmosphere of nitrogen for a lengthened period, ethyl alcohol and its homologues combine with nitrogen, yielding bodies of an amido- or basic nature (Berthelot).[1] Hydrogen is evolved, methyl alcohol yielding 1 atom per molecule, and ethyl alcohol 2 atoms. One atom of nitrogen is fixed for every 2 atoms of hydrogen evolved.

W. Löb has also investigated the fixation of nitrogen by alcohol.[2] Under the influence of the silent electric discharge, the nitrogen is not fixed as such, but first forms ammonia with the hydrogen produced. The alcohol is decomposed into acetaldehyde and hydrogen, and the acetaldehyde further changed into methane and carbon dioxide. Eventually, formaldehyde also is produced, together with formic acid; these combine with the ammonia to form hexamine and ammonium formate. Ethyl butyrate and ammonium butyrate are also among the products.[3]

Catalytic decomposition of ethyl alcohol.—According to Berthelot,[4] ethyl alcohol vapour when heated begins to decompose at 500°, yielding on the one hand ethylene and water, and on the other aldehyde and hydrogen; but secondary reactions also take place, with the formation of acetylene, ethane, benzene, naphthalene, carbon monoxide, and carbon dioxide.

Jahn[5] found that in the presence of zinc dust ethyl alcohol decomposes into ethylene and water at 300–350°.

Ipatieff[6] has shown that at 600°, in the presence of zinc and litharge, aldehyde and hydrogen are formed from ethyl alcohol, and at 580–680°, when the alcohol is distilled over aluminium powder, divinyl is yielded, in addition to the products of the decomposition of aldehyde and ethylene.

Ehrenfeld[7] passed the vapour of ethyl alcohol over carbon heated to dull redness, and found that the alcohol is decomposed into equal volumes of methane, carbon monoxide, and hydrogen, according to the equation:—

$$C_2H_6O = CH_4 + CO + H_2.$$

At a lower temperature, large quantities of ethane are formed, probably as a primary reduction product. When distilled over aluminium below a dull red heat, the products are ethylene and water, the latter being to a large extent further reduced to hydrogen.

[1] *Compt. rend.*, 1898, **126**, 616. [2] *Biochem. Zeitsch.*, 1909, **20**, 136.
[3] *Ibid.*, 126. [4] *Traité de Chimie organique*, 1872, 164.
[5] *J. Chem. Soc.*, 1880, **38** (Abst.), 794.
[6] *Ibid.*, 1902, **82**, i, 4, 335; and 1903, **84**, i, 453.
[7] *J. pr. Chem.*, 1903, [ii], **67**, 49.

At a dull red heat, decomposition into methane, carbon monoxide, and hydrogen also takes place, and, at a bright red heat, is predominant.

Sabatier and Senderens[1] have studied the action of reduced copper, nickel, cobalt, and spongy platinum as catalysts in the decomposition of alcohols generally by heat. When ethyl alcohol is passed over reduced copper, a reaction begins at 200° and is very vigorous at 250°, the alcohol being decomposed exclusively into aldehyde and hydrogen. Up to a temperature of 300°, the same change occurs, and at this temperature as much as half the alcohol is decomposed. At 420°, the gas evolved consists of equal volumes of methane (12·5 per cent.) and carbon monoxide (12·5 per cent.), together with hydrogen (75 per cent.). The two gases first-mentioned are formed at the expense of the aldehyde, which, in the presence of reduced copper, begins to decompose at 400°.

When reduced nickel is used as the catalyst, decomposition of the alcohol begins at 150°, and is rapid at 170°. At 178°, some aldehyde is formed, but nearly half is destroyed again; the evolved gases at this temperature consist almost wholly of carbon monoxide, methane, and hydrogen. Decomposition of the carbon monoxide into carbon dioxide and carbon begins at 230°, and is very rapid at 300°; at 330°, the gas consists of carbon dioxide, methane, and hydrogen. Reduced cobalt acts in the same manner as nickel.

Spongy platinum begins to decompose ethyl alcohol at 270°—a much higher temperature than is required with copper or nickel. The action increases regularly with the temperature; at 310°, the gas evolved consists of carbon monoxide, methane, and hydrogen. Only a small quantity of aldehyde is obtained, most of it being destroyed, with the production of carbon monoxide and methane.

J. B. Senderens[2] finds that the oxidation of ethyl alcohol occurs at temperatures of 405° to 450° by simple heating, without the aid of a catalyst. If a current of dry air is passed through ethyl alcohol at the rate of 100 c.c. per minute, and the mixture of alcohol vapour and air then led through a heated glass tube, oxidation is found to commence at about 405°, and at 450° all the oxygen is used up. The main products are carbon monoxide, carbon dioxide, and water, with much smaller quantities of aldehyde and acid. Magnesium, zinc, and aluminium are therefore regarded as having no great value as catalysts in this reaction, since the oxidation takes place almost as readily without them as with them.

[1] *Compt. rend.*, 1903, **136**, 738, 921, 983.
[2] *Ibid.*, 1913, **156**, 1909–1912.

Catalytic dehydration by means of metallic oxides.—Various oxides, such as thoria, alumina, and the blue oxide of tungsten, exert a dehydrating action on ethyl and other alcohols at a temperature of 300–350°, the products being ethylene hydrocarbons, almost exclusively. In some cases, the dehydration may be restricted at lower temperatures, and the ethers formed. Sabatier and Mailhe[1] have pointed out that the mechanism of this reaction is strictly analogous to the dehydration of alcohol which is effected by sulphuric acid. The analogy is further illustrated by the fact that the oxides in question act as esterifying catalysts: thus if a mixture of the vapours of ethyl alcohol and acetic acid is passed over titanium dioxide at 300°, a good quantity of ethyl acetate is produced.

Similarly, alcohols and ammonia passed over heated thorium oxide yield the corresponding amines; and alcohols with hydrogen sulphide give thiols.

Absolute alcohol.—In preparing anhydrous alcohol, the usual procedure is to digest 95 per cent. spirit with quicklime for some days, and then to distil off the alcohol slowly from a water-bath and treat the product in the same way. The first and last portions of the distillate are rejected. A sufficient excess of lime must be used, otherwise too large a proportion of calcium hydroxide is formed, and towards the end of the distillation this yields up water and thus dilutes the alcohol again. About one-fourth or one-fifth the weight of the alcohol is a suitable quantity of lime for the distillation.

If strong spirit is not available to start with, it may readily be obtained, of about 94 or 95 per cent. strength, by distilling weak alcohol from potassium carbonate. The strength may be raised to about 97 per cent. by distilling the product over fused calcium chloride, and the distillate may then be treated with quicklime to obtain the absolute alcohol.

Barium oxide may also be used as a dehydrating agent, and powdered calcium carbide has been employed.[2] Simple percolation of strong alcohol through a column of quicklime, after digestion with the latter for several days, yields a nearly anhydrous product —containing, however, a small quantity of lime, which may be removed by distillation. Metallic sodium and metallic calcium have been used for removing the last traces of water, but quicklime appears to be, on the whole, the best dehydrating agent of all. Its action may be accelerated by heating the mixture under a reflux condenser, and by using a larger proportion of the lime—up to one-half the weight of the alcohol—in the first treatment.

[1] *Compt. rend.*, 1910, **150**, 823. [2] Yvon, *Chem. News*, 1898, 52.

The following details of an actual experiment are given by R. W. Merriman.[1]

(*a*) Ten litres of 95 per cent. alcohol were boiled in a copper drum for twenty-four hours with 4 kilos. of quicklime made from marble. On distilling the product, spirit containing about 0·5 per cent. of water was obtained. This formed the stock, which was further dehydrated as required in batches of 700 grams.

(*b*) Seven hundred grams of the 99·5 per cent. alcohol were boiled on the water-bath, under a reflux condenser, with 150 grams of quicklime, taking the usual precautions for preventing the absorption of atmospheric moisture. After six hours, the product was distilled from the water-bath, a double spray trap being fixed on to the flask. The first 50 grams were rejected; the distillate obtained by boiling almost to dryness (about 600 grams) had a density of 0·80630 at 0°/4°, and thus contained 0·006 per cent. of water.

(*c*) The alcohol of sp. gr. 0·80630 was again treated with lime, and the density of the main fraction was 0·80628 at 0°/4°. Another treatment with lime, and also with metallic calcium, left the density unchanged.

The density of the product, it may be remarked, is slightly higher than that of Mendeléeff's alcohol; but the experiment shows, at all events, that a very nearly anhydrous alcohol is given by the treatment described.

Young's method of dehydrating alcohol by distillation with benzene has already been referred to (p. 157).

Anhydrous potassium fluoride is a good preliminary dehydrant for alcohol. It acts rapidly on account of its solubility, and is somewhat more effective than potassium carbonate, as the saturated solution has a lower vapour pressure. It absorbs a large proportion of water (62 per cent.), forming the hydrate $KF,2H_2O$, the vapour pressure of which is 3·5 mm., and the limit of dehydration of ethyl alcohol is reached at 97·5 per cent., when the vapour pressure corresponds with that of the above hydrate.[2]

According to L. W. Winkler,[3] alcohol can be completely dehydrated by distilling it over filings of metallic calcium. The latter may contain some nitride, which will yield ammonia by the action of water in the alcohol; but this ammonia can be eliminated afterwards. The filings are sifted in a coarse sieve to free them from any powdered nitride, and traces of oil and more nitride are removed

[1] *Trans. Chem. Soc.*, 1913, **103**, 629.

[2] G. B. Frankforter and F. C. Frary, *J. Phys. Chem.*, 1913, **17**, 402.

[3] *Zeitsch. angew. Chem.*, 1916, **29**, 18.

by shaking the filings vigorously with dry carbon tetrachloride in a glass-stoppered flask, transferring them to a loosely-stoppered funnel, washing them again with the same solvent, and then drying in carbon dioxide. The alcohol is distilled with the purified metal in the proportion of 20 grams to the litre. Ammonia is removed from the distillate by dissolving in the latter a little alizarin (a few centigrams per litre) and then adding a solution of about 0·5 gram of tartaric acid in 10 c.c. of the distilled alcohol until the reddish-blue colour has turned to a pure yellow. After the addition of a few more drops of the acid solution when this point has been reached, the alcohol is re-distilled, care being taken to exclude atmospheric moisture during the operation.

Perkin and Pratt have found that when metallic calcium is allowed to remain in contact with ethyl (or methyl) alcohol for a period of 30 to 60 minutes, a reaction occurs between the metal and the alcohol.[1] Once started, the reaction, which may become very vigorous, continues to completion, with formation of calcium ethoxide (or methoxide) according to the equation :—

$$2C_2H_5 \cdot OH + Ca = (C_2H_5 \cdot O)_2Ca + H_2.$$

If the mixture is heated to the boiling point of the alcohol, the reaction proceeds much more rapidly.

L. W. Andrews[2] found that absolute alcohol, dehydrated by means of lime freshly prepared from marble, and freed from aldehyde, had the same specific gravity, the same refractive index, and the same critical temperature of solution, as alcohol had which was dehydrated with magnesium amalgam[3] or metallic calcium. The specific gravity found was, at 25°/4°, 0·78510 ± 0·00001.

Winkler, in 1905, obtained the value 0·78509 at 25°/4° for the specific gravity of absolute alcohol dehydrated by means of metallic calcium. A. Kailan[4] later found a somewhat higher value, namely, 0·78513 at 25°/4°, using the same method of dehydration. Mendeléeff's absolute alcohol was dehydrated by means of quicklime: its specific gravity referred to the above temperatures (25°/4°) was 0·78522. Referred to the temperature 15·6°/15·6° the value is 0·79359, and as already stated, this is regarded as probably the most accurate result.

According to a German patent,[5] alcohol of 90 per cent. strength or more can be dehydrated completely in a short time by means of anhydrous sodium sulphide. This compound is indifferent towards ethyl alcohol, and can be entirely recovered by heating after use.

[1] *Proc. Chem. Soc.*, 1907, **23**, 304.
[2] *J. Amer. Chem. Soc.*, 1908, **30**, 353.
[3] *Ibid.*, 1904, **26**, 1158.
[4] *Ber.*, 1911, **44**, 2881.
[5] D.R.-P. 256591 (1909).

Commercial "absolute" alcohol usually contains water in quantity ranging from about 0·5 to 1·5 per cent. The "absolute alcohol" of the British Pharmacopœia is defined as "ethyl hydroxide, $C_2H_5 \cdot OH$, with not more than 1 per cent. by weight of water. Specific gravity (at 15·5°/15·5°) from 0·794 (equivalent to 99·95 per cent. of ethyl hydroxide by volume and by weight) to 0·7969 (equivalent to 99·4 per cent. of ethyl hydroxide by volume or 99 per cent. by weight)." More accurate values for the specific gravity would be 0·7938 and 0·7967 respectively. The test prescribed to exclude excess of water is as follows. "Anhydrous copper sulphate shaken occasionally during two or three hours with about fifty times its weight of absolute alcohol does not assume a decidedly blue colour."

Other tests for water in alcohol are given in Chap. VI, and also methods for the examination of alcohol as regards the presence of impurities.

According to the French Pharmacopœia, commercial "absolute" alcohol should have a specific gravity not higher than 0·79683 at 15°/15°.

For the benefit of microscopists and other private workers who have no chemical balance or hydrometer, H. Garnett mentions that pure oil of cedarwood (*Juniperus virginiana*) may be employed for testing the strength of absolute alcohol.[1] (The so-called "thickened" oil used for immersion lenses will not serve.) With absolute alcohol, the oil mixes clear in all proportions at the ordinary temperature. An alcohol of 98·2 per cent. strength by volume mixes without turbidity with cedarwood oil at 15·5°, but turbidity is produced if the temperature is lowered even 1°. An alcohol of this strength will suffice for microscopical work.

Calcium carbide can be used to increase the strength of an alcohol. Thus alcohol of 98·9 per cent. strength (by volume) was digested with a small quantity of powdered carbide for three days in a warm place. Some acetylene was evolved, and the strength was raised to 99·94 per cent. Any disagreeable odour left may be removed by shaking the alcohol with a minute trace of potassium permanganate.

Rectified spirit.—The "Spiritus Rectificatus" or "Alcohol (90 per cent.)" of the British Pharmacopœia is defined as "a mixture of ethyl hydroxide and water, containing in 100 parts by volume 90 parts by volume of ethyl hydroxide, $C_2H_5 \cdot OH$. Specific gravity 0·8337. Contains 85·68 per cent. by weight of ethyl hydroxide,

[1] *Pharm. J.*, 1918, **100**, [iv], 127.

and 14·32 per cent. by weight of water." The analytical tests of purity are given in Chap. VI.

It should be noted that on account of the contraction which occurs, "Alcohol (90 per cent.)" would *not* be given by mixing 90 volumes of (true) absolute alcohol and 10 volumes of water.

There are four official "Diluted Alcohols" in the Pharmacopœia, containing respectively 70, 60, 45, and 20 per cent. of ethyl hydroxide by volume. They are obtained by diluting the 90 per cent. alcohol of sp. gr. 0·8337 with water as shown in the following table, either (1) or (2) being used, as may be the more convenient :—

Alcohol required.	Sp. gr.	(1). Volume of water to be *mixed with* 1 litre of 90 per cent. alcohol.	(2). Vol. of 90 per cent. alcohol to be *diluted to* 1 litre at 15·5°.
70 per cent.	0·8899	310·5 c.c.	777·8 c.c.
60 ,,	0·9134	536·5 ,,	666·7 ,,
45 ,,	0·9435	1053·4 ,,	500·0 ,,
20 ,,	0·9760	3558·0 ,,	222·2 ,,

CHAPTER VI

THE ANALYTICAL CHEMISTRY OF METHYL AND ETHYL ALCOHOLS

I. Separation of the alcohols from other substances.—Before the alcohol in a mixture can be examined as to its character, or its quantity accurately determined, it must, as a rule, be obtained practically free from all other substances except water.

Simple distillation suffices for this where the admixed or dissolved ingredients are not volatile with steam. When volatile bodies are present, however, it is necessary either to render them incapable of distillation, or to remove them. Solutions containing ammonia or amines, for instance, may be made acid with sulphuric acid; volatile acids may be fixed by the addition of sodium or potassium hydroxide; free iodine may be converted into sodium iodide by treatment with sodium thiosulphate. Neutral organic volatile substances in general are best removed by a preliminary extraction with an immiscible solvent, or else by distillation, extraction of the distillate, and re-distillation.

For such articles as spirituous medicines, tinctures, essences, and perfumes, the method most generally applicable is that described by Thorpe and Holmes.[1] By this process essential oils, camphor, ether, chloroform, ethyl acetate, and most other volatile constituents which would vitiate the subsequent examination of the distillate, are removed, either entirely or with sufficient completeness for the purpose. It is devised especially for the accurate determination of the *proportion* of alcohol; if this is already known or not required, some of the directions may obviously be modified.

Twenty-five c.c. of the sample, measured at 15·5°, are mixed with water in a separator to a bulk of 100 to 150 c.c., and common salt is added in sufficient quantity to saturate the liquid. The mixture is now shaken vigorously for five minutes with from 50 to 80 c.c. of light petroleum, boiling below 60°, and after standing

[1] *Trans. Chem. Soc.*, 1903, **83**, 314.

for about half an hour, the lower layer is drawn off into another separator, extracted if necessary a second time with petroleum and then drawn off into a distillation flask. Meanwhile, the petroleum layers are washed successively with 25 c.c. of saturated common salt solution, and the washings added to the main bulk, which is neutralised if necessary, and then distilled and the distillate made up to 100 c.c.

In this description the article examined is assumed to be strongly spirituous, which is why it is diluted, and distilled to four times the volume taken. A weakly alcoholic liquid would not, of course, need to be diluted; 100 or 150 c.c. would be taken in the first instance.

Discussing the quantitative aspect of the process, the authors make the following comments.

On account of the high vapour pressure of ethyl alcohol and its avidity for water, the distillation of a strong spirituous liquid into its own volume of water so as to obtain an accurate determination of the amount of alcohol present is practically impossible with the apparatus and the methods of distillation commonly used. It is practicable to distil a strong spirituous liquid into twice its own volume with the requisite degree of accuracy, whilst distillation into four times the initial volume is quite easy, and the results are uniformly accurate. There is practically no error due to distillation, and as regards extent of dilution, it was found that the alcohol in 25 c.c. of strong spirit when diluted with water even to the extent of 500 c.c. and the solution saturated with salt, could be entirely recovered in the first 100 c.c. of the distillate.

The method, as described, is applicable to preparations containing chloroform, ether, benzaldehyde, and esters. In the greater number of other cases—for example, essences of lemon, juniper, peppermint, and santal oil preparations—a single extraction with petroleum ether is sufficient. For camphor preparations, 25 c.c. of normal sulphuric acid solution are used instead of common salt, and a single extraction with light petroleum is made, the acid being neutralised with caustic soda solution before the alcohol is distilled off.

Special devices are occasionally necessary to eliminate volatile foreign bodies from alcoholic liquids. Chloral, for instance, may be removed by heating the solution with caustic soda under a reflux condenser, the chloroform thus produced being afterwards extracted with light petroleum as usual. Coumarin, again, which distils to some extent with alcohol, is converted into the sodium salts of coumaric and coumarinic acids by the same treatment, and can thus be eliminated. Sometimes, too, extraction of a substance can advantageously be made with chloroform, carbon tetrachloride, ether or other solvent, the residue of which in its turn may have to be extracted with petroleum ether.

Another method of eliminating volatile oils and some similar substances is to dilute the sample until it contains about 20–25 per cent. of alcohol by volume, shake it well with powdered magnesium carbonate, and filter. The following example of a combination of this treatment with subsequent chemical removal of acetone is given by Leach and Lythgoe,[1] for the case of a denatured alcohol containing light petroleum and acetone.

Take 25 c.c. of the sample and dilute it to 100 c.c. with water. Add about 5 grams of powdered magnesium carbonate, shake well, and filter. The filtrate will be free from petroleum, but will still contain the acetone and alcohols.

A measured portion of the filtrate, 55 c.c., is washed into a distilling flask and treated with 10 grams of powdered potassium bisulphite, and after standing an hour is distilled, 55 c.c. of distillate being collected. This is free from acetone, but contains some sulphurous acid, and in order to remove this it is distilled with sodium hydroxide, the final distillate being made up to 55 c.c. (for the determination of specific gravity and refraction).

II. Concentrating the alcohol.—For certain of the reactions described further on, the alcohol is required to be of about 90 per cent. strength, or more. Where the iodides are prepared, for example, as in the nitromethane test for methyl alcohol or in the Riche and Bardy process (p. 192), 10 c.c. of strong alcohol are used.

A ready means of obtaining this from a weak distillate, without using a fractionating column, is to take such a quantity of the liquid as will give 11 or 12 c.c. of the required strong alcohol, saturate it with common salt, and distil off about one-third. A liberal quantity of dry potassium carbonate is then added to the distillate, the mixture re-distilled, and the requisite quantity of distillate collected. The potassium carbonate forms with the water present a heavy layer under the separated alcohol, and the latter can be distilled off at high strength.

Suppose, for example, that a strong tincture or essence containing about 90 per cent. of alcohol has been purified by the Thorpe and Holmes method as described in the previous section, and it is now required to apply one of the above-mentioned tests to the distillate. Since 25 c.c. of the sample have been diluted to 100 c.c.

[1] *J. Amer. Chem. Soc.*, 1905, **27**, No. 8.

the alcoholic strength of the distillate will be about 22·5 per cent. One-half of the 100 c.c. will yield more than sufficient spirit for one of the experiments in question. Hence 50 c.c. are taken, placed in a flask, saturated with salt, and 16 or 17 c.c. distilled off; the quantity thus obtained is redistilled from potassium carbonate and 10–11 c.c. collected. This will be of suitable strength for conversion into iodide.

For concentrating very dilute solutions—containing, say, a few tenths per cent. of alcohol—the liquid may be partly saturated with either calcium chloride or sodium chloride, one-sixth to one-third distilled off, and the operation repeated if necessary on the distillate. Thus R. F. Bacon found that 500 c.c. of a 0·2 per cent. solution, after addition of 200 grams of calcium chloride, gave on distillation 96·8 per cent. of its alcohol in the first 100 c.c. of distillate, and the whole in the first 150. A similar solution, about three-fourths saturated with sodium chloride, also gave up 96·8 per cent. in the first 100 c.c.; and on similarly salting the latter quantity and redistilling, the alcohol was obtained without further loss in the first 50 c.c. of distillate.

Of a still weaker solution, containing only 0·1 per cent. of alcohol, 1 litre was taken, and distilled after being about three-fourths saturated with sodium chloride. The first 150 c.c. of distillate were similarly salted and redistilled, with the result that 96 per cent. of the alcohol originally present was recovered in the first 25 c.c. of the second distillate.[1]

By one or more of the operations indicated above, ethyl and methyl alcohols are separated from the other constituents of mixtures in a condition of sufficient purity and strength for further examination. The final distillate obtained may of course contain either or both of these two alcohols.

III. Identification of methyl alcohol.—A useful review of the chief reactions which had been used for the detection of methyl alcohol previously to the year 1905 has been given by H. Scudder.[2] Some of the main points are mentioned in the section which follows.

The tests for methyl alcohol are principally used for the detection of this substance in ethyl alcohol. Hence their value is dependent first upon the sharpness with which they distinguish between the two alcohols, and then on their delicacy and rapidity. Occasionally, however, it is merely a question of identifying methyl alcohol alone, mixed with more or less water, in which case readier

[1] *Circular* 74, 1911, *U.S. Dept. Agr. Bureau of Chemistry.*
[2] *J. Amer. Chem. Soc.*, 1905, **27**, 892–906.

methods of no great degree of delicacy are called for. The first three methods given below will generally meet such cases.

Methyl formate reaction.—Dissolve a little sodium formate in about 2 c.c. of water, add 1 or 2 c.c. of the liquid to be tested, then pour into the mixture an equal volume of strong sulphuric acid. On mixing the contents of the tube, warming a little more if necessary, an odour of methyl formate is developed if methyl alcohol is present. The odour recalls that of chloroform.

Boric acid flame reaction.—Powder some borax finely, and mix it in a porcelain basin with a few c.c. of the alcoholic liquid, which for this test should be free from acid, and strong enough to burn. Allow the mixture to stand for a minute or two and then ignite the vapour. A green coloration is imparted to the flame if methyl alcohol is present in sufficient quantity, whereas ethyl alcohol gives the coloration only after sulphuric acid is added. About 5 per cent. of methyl alcohol in ethyl alcohol can be thus detected (E. Pieszczek).[1]

Formic acid reaction.—The liquid to be tested is mixed with an equal volume of 50 per cent. sulphuric acid, and introduced into a small flask in which has been placed 3 or 4 grams of powdered potassium dichromate and about 5 c.c. of water. After mixing and allowing to stand a few minutes, the contents of the flask are diluted with an equal volume of water and distilled. Formic acid is produced by the oxidation :—

$$CH_3{\cdot}OH + O_2 = H{\cdot}COOH + H_2O.$$

The distillate is neutralised with sodium carbonate and evaporated to expel any formaldehyde or acetaldehyde that may have been formed during the oxidation. A portion is then tested with ferric chloride solution ; if a formate is present this gives a red coloration, destroyed by hydrochloric acid. But as a similar red colour is also given by acetic acid (which will be present if the original liquid contained ethyl alcohol) the result must be confirmed. To do this add solution of silver nitrate to another portion of the evaporated liquid ; on warming, a black or brownish-black deposit of reduced silver is produced.

Or a portion of the evaporated liquid may be heated after adding to it a little mercuric chloride solution ; a white precipitate of mercurous chloride is given if a formate is present.

For a quantitative method of estimating methyl alcohol by conversion into formic acid, see p. 194.

Conversion into formaldehyde.—Many of the tests which have

[1] *Pharm. Zeit.*, 1913, **58**, 850.

been proposed for detecting the presence of methyl alcohol depend upon the oxidation of the alcohol to formaldehyde, and the recogniton of the latter by a colour reaction of some kind. Thus Denigès employs the well-known Schiff or Gayon reaction with decolorised fuchsine solution to show the presence of the formaldehyde, Bono (p. 176) uses an alkaline solution of phenylhydrazine and sodium nitroprusside; Mulliken recommends the resorcinol–sulphuric acid test, and Hinkel uses the reaction with morphine and sulphuric acid. Gallic acid and phloroglucinol have also been employed.

By far the most generally useful process is that devised by Denigès,[1] which is carried out as follows: Into a test-tube, chosen of rather wide diameter to facilitate admixture of the various liquids, 0·1 c.c. of the strong alcohol is introduced, followed by 5 c.c. of a 1 per cent. solution of potassium permanganate, and 0·2 c.c. of strong sulphuric acid. The liquids are mixed and allowed to stand two or three minutes; then 1 c.c. of an 8 per cent. solution of oxalic acid is added and the tube again shaken. Rapid decolorisation of the liquid ensues. When the solution has become of a sherry-yellow colour, 1 c.c. of strong sulphuric acid is added and the whole well mixed; the decolorisation now becomes complete. Five c.c. of decolorised solution of fuchsine are next added to the contents of the tube. In the course of a few minutes a violet colour appears, the depth of which depends upon the proportion of methyl alcohol in the liquid under examination. Except in considerable dilutions, the colour generally attains its maximum intensity by the end of fifteen minutes. With 10 per cent. of methyl alcohol it is extremely intense, with 1 per cent. very strong, and appreciable even at a dilution of 0·1 per cent. The test is not conclusive unless the alcoholic liquid has been properly purified, as glycerol and several other substances give a similar reaction.

The decolorised solution of fuchsine (Schiff's reagent, Gayon's reagent) employed by Denigès is prepared as follows:—To a litre of 0·1 per cent. solution of fuchsine add 20 c.c. of solution of sodium bisulphite at 36° Bé., and after five to ten minutes pour into the mixture 20 c.c. of pure hydrochloric acid (D = 1·18). At the end of an hour or two the reagent becomes colourless, and is then ready for use.

A modified form of this method, adapted for the quantitative determination of methyl alcohol, is described a little further on (p. 183).

According to A. Bono,[2] about 1 per cent. of methyl alcohol in ethyl alcohol can be detected by the following process.

[1] *Compt. rend.*, 1910, **150**, 530, 831. [2] *Chem. Zeit.*, 1912, **36**, 1171.

Seventy-five c.c. of the sample, containing alcohol equivalent to 10 c.c. of strong alcohol, are distilled, and the vapour passed direct into a flask containing 50 c.c. of oxidising solution. The latter is a solution of potassium bichromate, saturated in the cold, and containing 60 c.c. of sulphuric acid per litre. The delivery-tube dips to the bottom of the solution, and the vapour after passing through the oxidising mixture is led into a condenser and collected. No formaldehyde is found, as a rule, in the first 25 c.c. of the distillate, which may be rejected. The next 10 c.c. are collected apart, and 2 c.c. of it are tested for formaldehyde by adding to it 10 drops of 0·5 per cent. solution of phenylhydrazine hydrochloride, 1 drop of 0·5 per cent. solution of sodium nitroprusside, and 10 drops of 10 per cent. solution of sodium hydroxide. If any formaldehyde is present, a blue coloration is obtained, changing to green and afterwards to a yellowish-red.

A more summary process is thus described by Mulliken.[1]

Dissolve one drop of the alcohol in 3 c.c. of water in a 6-inch test-tube. Wind a piece of rather light copper wire round a lead pencil, so that the closely-coiled spiral shall form a cylinder 2 cm. in length, while 20 cm. is left unbent to serve as a handle. Oxidise the spiral superficially by holding it in the upper part of the flame of a Bunsen burner; and then, while still at a red heat, plunge it into the alcoholic solution. (This treatment oxidises a portion of the methyl alcohol to formaldehyde.) Withdraw the spiral immediately and cool the test-tube with running water. Repeat the oxidation of the solution twice by the method given. Add one or two drops of 0·5 per cent. aqueous solution of resorcinol. Pour the mixture slowly into a second inclined test-tube containing 3–5 c.c. of pure concentrated sulphuric acid. If formaldehyde is present, a contact ring is formed, and on very gentle shaking, flocks of a characteristic red colour appear. A contact ring is also given by acetaldehyde, but the flocks are of a colour varying from yellow to brown. In this form, the test will show about 8 to 10 per cent. of methyl alcohol in ethyl alcohol.

A modified and more delicate form is due to Mulliken and Scudder.[2] The oxidation is carried out in the same way, but the acetaldehyde is removed by boiling the solution down to about one-half its volume. Some of the formaldehyde is always lost in doing this; the best results are therefore obtained by evaporating down under diminished pressure at 25° to 30°. With very little formaldehyde, the formation of the characteristic flocks is slow;

[1] "Identification of Pure Organic Compounds," Vol. I, p. 160.

[2] *Amer. Chem. J.*, 1900, **24**, 444.

hence after addition of sulphuric acid the solution is allowed to stand for three minutes, and then shaken very gently for one minute, so as to cause the two liquid surfaces to mix, but slowly and not excessively. The formation of the red flocks is a necessary part of the test, as red contact rings are given by other substances, *e.g.*, acetone and dimethyl ethyl carbinol. Methyl esters, methyl ethers, and secondary and tertiary butyl alcohols give the same reaction as methyl alcohol. This form of the test will detect about 2 to 3 per cent. of methyl alcohol in ethyl alcohol.

The method of oxidation proposed by Hinkel[1] is somewhat less sensitive than the foregoing. About 5 per cent. of methyl alcohol in ethyl alcohol can be detected by it. Ammonium persulphate is used as the oxidising agent.

Add 0·8 gram of this salt to 1 c.c. of the alcohol, followed by 3 c.c. of sulphuric acid (20 per cent.); dilute the mixture with water to a bulk of 20 c.c. and distil it. Collect the distillate in fractions measuring 2 c.c. each, until five are obtained. The first two are rejected, as they contain acetaldehyde; the others are tested by adding a few drops of solution of morphine hydrochloride (1 in 200) to the liquid, and then carefully pouring a layer of strong sulphuric acid down the side of the tube. If formaldehyde is present, a violet ring is produced at the surface of contact of the acid and upper liquid. A blank experiment on pure ethyl alcohol should be done at the same time. Acetaldehyde gives a deep orange colour. Hinkel found that traces of formaldehyde, enough to give a faint violet ring with the morphine test, were always produced in oxidising ethyl alcohol, whether with persulphate, permanganate, or bichromate.

Phloroglucinol may also be used as a test for formaldehyde. It gives a colour varying from yellowish-red to violet-red, according to the relative concentrations of the formaldehyde and phloroglucinol. Acetaldehyde, however, unless in very small quantity, also gives a colour; and, moreover, ethyl alcohol may under certain conditions of oxidation yield traces of formaldehyde, as noted by Hinkel. Hence the acetaldehyde must be removed, and a comparative experiment should be made with ethyl alcohol. The acetaldehyde may be eliminated by distillation as described by Hinkel; or by boiling the liquid down to about one-half its bulk; or by oxidising with hydrogen peroxide, excess of the latter being removed with a little sodium thiosulphate solution.

Gallic acid also gives a delicate reaction with formaldehyde. The liquid to be tested is mixed with 0·2 c.c. of a saturated alcoholic

[1] *Analyst*, 1908, **33**, 417.

solution of gallic acid, and poured carefully on the top of some strong sulphuric acid contained in a test-tube. A ring of blue colour, or green and blue, is produced at the surface of contact if formaldehyde is present.

Sanglé-Ferrière and Cuniasse have applied both the phloroglucinol and the gallic acid reactions for the detection of methyl alcohol in absinthe.[1] Fifty c.c. of the distillate are mixed with 1 c.c. of pure sulphuric acid and then treated with 5 c.c. of a saturated solution of potassium permanganate. After a few minutes the liquid should have a brown colour, and if any excess of permanganate has been used, one or two drops of a concentrated solution of tannin are to be added. Sodium carbonate solution is then added until a slight alkaline reaction is obtained, the liquid filtered, and a part of the clear filtrate treated with 2 c.c. of a 0·1 per cent. solution of phloroglucinol and 1 c.c. of a strong solution of potassium hydroxide. A bright red colour is given if the absinthe contained methyl alcohol; any yellowish-rose or violet colour is disregarded. Then to confirm the result another part of the alkaline filtrate is acidified with dilute sulphuric acid, and shaken with a few centigrams of powdered gallic acid until the latter has dissolved, when a little strong sulphuric acid is cautiously poured down the side of the tube. After a few seconds a blue coloration appears at the zone of contact if formaldehyde is present.

H. Scudder considers the confirmatory part of the test (with gallic acid) as of no value, because the reaction is too delicate, and may be produced with traces of formaldehyde yielded in the oxidation of ethyl alcohol.

Two other processes depending upon colour reactions given by formaldehyde may be briefly mentioned.

G. Franceschi detects methyl alcohol in beverages and tinctures by distilling 20 c.c. and collecting 15 c.c. of distillate, which is again distilled and 8 c.c. collected. This is oxidised with a glowing copper spiral, and the solution is divided into two portions. One of these is treated with 1 drop of 10 per cent. solution of sodium nitroprusside and 1 drop of piperidine; a blue coloration indicates the presence of ethyl alcohol. The other portion is boiled for one minute, a drop of phenol is added, and the solution poured on the surface of strong sulphuric acid; a red zone develops if the sample contained methyl alcohol.[2]

U. Pazienti proceeds as follows: Five c.c. of the alcohol, diluted to 50 c.c., are distilled with 3 grams of sodium persulphate and

[1] *Ann. Chim. anal.*, 1903, **8**, 82–3; *Analyst*, 1903, **28**, 148.
[2] *J. Chem. Soc.* (Abst.), 1915, **108**, ii, 588.

10 c.c. of 20 per cent. sulphuric acid from a 250 c.c. flask. The distillate is collected in fractions, each of about 2 c.c., and the fifth such fraction is tested with Schryver's reagent. This reagent consists of 2 c.c. of a freshly-prepared and filtered solution (1 per cent.) of phenylhydrazine hydrochloride, 1 c.c. of freshly-prepared potassium ferricyanide solution, and 5 c.c. of concentrated hydrochloric acid: it gives a red coloration with formaldehyde. It is claimed that 1 part of methyl alcohol in 1000 parts of ethyl alcohol may be detected in this manner. Too much formaldehyde diminishes the sensitiveness; hence if the colour is not very distinct the distillate should be diluted and again tested.[1]

Trillat's method,[2] as improved by Wolff.[3]—The principle of this method consists in the transformation of methyl alcohol into formaldehyde and methylal, followed by the condensation of these products with dimethylaniline. Tetramethyldiamino-diphenylmethane is obtained:—

$$CH_2 \begin{matrix} \diagup C_6H_4N(CH_3)_2 \\ \diagdown C_6H_4N(CH_3)_2 \end{matrix} .$$

By oxidation of this with lead dioxide, in a solution slightly acid with acetic acid, a fine blue coloration is produced, intensified by heating.

Procedure.—In a round-bottomed, short-necked flask of 300 c.c. capacity place 200 c.c. of a mixture containing, per litre, 90 grams of potassium dichromate and 85 c.c. of sulphuric acid (D = 1·845). Add 10 c.c. of the alcohol to be tested, at 90 per cent. strength, or else such a quantity as will contain this amount of alcohol. Side by side with the main experiment carry out also control experiments with (1) pure ethyl alcohol and (2) ethyl alcohol containing 0·2 per cent. of methyl alcohol.

Mix the alcohol thoroughly with the dichromate solution, let the mixture stand thirty minutes, and then distil it slowly. Reject the first 20 c.c. of distillate, as this portion contains acetaldehyde and ethers which mask the final reaction. Collect the next 50 c.c., distilled slowly, in a small stoppered flask of 51–52 c.c. capacity, and add 1 c.c. of pure dimethylaniline (b.p. 192°). Close the flask, which should now be quite full, hermetically; and keep it during eighteen to twenty hours at a temperature of 15–18° to effect the condensation.

Pour the contents into a round-bottomed distillation flask (120–125 c.c.), add 3 granules of pumice and 4 or 5 drops of phenol-

[1] *J. Chem. Soc.* (Abst.), 1915, **108**, ii, 588. [2] *Compt. rend.*, 1898, **127**, 232.
[3] *Ann. Inst. Pasteur*, 1902, **16**, 8.

phthalein solution (1 gram per litre); then from a burette run in sodium hydroxide solution (160 grams per litre) until a permanent rose coloration is just obtained. Now distil off 30 c.c. to eliminate the excess of dimethylaniline, cool the residue in the flask, and add to it 30 c.c. of water and 1 c.c. of glacial acetic acid. Shake well, and remove 10 c.c. of the mixture to a small test-tube. Make a suspension of lead dioxide in water (4 grams per litre), and add a few drops (the same number in the controls as in the main experiment) to the contents of the test-tube, which then clo.e with the thumb and invert a time or two. If methyl alcohol was present a fine blue colour is produced. The pure ethyl alcohol should show no blue tint; or in any case, if a slight coloration should appear, too much importance must not be attributed to it. After the tubes have been compared they may be heated to the boiling point of the liquids and again examined at the end of five minutes; the differences of colour are thus much accentuated.

H. Scudder[1] remarks that this method is delicate and fairly rapid (time required, about five hours). But it must be used with care, as the test may be spoiled by slight variations in procedure, or even sometimes by causes of unknown origin when the process has been strictly carried out. The chief objection is that all the acetaldehyde must be removed, otherwise an interfering colour will result. But some *methylal* distils over with the acetaldehyde, and hence, since the test depends upon the methylal, if only a small quantity is present the result may be vitiated.

J. Wolff[2] has found that spirits containing caramel or sucrose, when treated with chromic acid and distilled in a current of steam, yield polymerisation products of formaldehyde which give the strong blue colour as above described on treatment with dimethylaniline and lead peroxide. It was found that lævulose, whether added directly or arising from the hydrolysis of cane-sugar, was the only sugar giving this reaction. Hence spirits containing cane-sugar, invert-sugar, or caramel should always be re-distilled before they are examined by the foregoing process. (Distillation is, of course, a general precaution which should be taken whatever process is used.)

Catalytic dehydrogenation of methyl alcohol to formaldehyde.— Methyl alcohol passed over heated copper is decomposed into formaldehyde and hydrogen (Sabatier and Senderens). This reaction has been used by Mannich and Geilmann[3] for the detec-

[1] *Loc. cit.*
[2] *Bull. Assoc. Chim. Sucr.*, 1907, **24**, 1623; (Abst.) *Analyst*, 1907, **32**, 333.
[3] *Arch. Pharm.*, 1916, **254**, 50.

tion of methyl alcohol in various liquids. The vapour of the liquid under examination is passed over pumice impregnated with reduced copper and heated to 280–300°. In the condensed product, the formaldehyde which results is detected by the violet coloration developed on treatment with morphine and strong sulphuric acid as already described.

An aqueous solution containing 0·1 per cent. of methyl alcohol gives a condensate which develops the coloration very faintly after one hour. In twenty-four hours the colour becomes more distinct, though still faint. The method is stated to be useful for detecting methyl alcohol in blood or urine, a positive result being obtained from as little as 0·01 gram of the alcohol in 100 c.c. of either of these liquids. The blood or urine, however, must be fractionated to concentrate the methyl alcohol, and the fraction containing the latter must be boiled for some time with freshly ignited animal charcoal before being passed over the catalyst. Even with these precautions the catalyst gradually becomes poisoned.

In order to detect methyl alcohol in the presence of ethyl alcohol, the mixture is diluted, if necessary, to contain about 50 per cent. of water, and passed over the catalyst. Acetaldehyde is removed from the condensate by heating it in a vacuum, and the residual liquid tested for formaldehyde with morphine and sulphuric acid as before. If the original mixture contains less than 1 per cent. of methyl alcohol, the diluted solution should be repeatedly fractionated before the test is applied to the fraction in which the methyl alcohol has been concentrated. 0·5 Per cent. of methyl alcohol in brandy can be detected by this process.

The foregoing method is included here because it introduces a new principle, the dehydrogenation of methyl alcohol by heat instead of conversion of the alcohol into formaldehyde by the ordinary oxidation processes. It may be useful in special cases, but appears to be less sensitive, and is certainly more troublesome, than some of the other processes.

Conversion into nitromethane (P. N. Raikow [1]).—Two hundred c.c. or other suitable quantity of the sample are acidified with phosphoric acid, and 10 c.c. distilled off. To this, contained in a small flask, 25 grams of powdered iodine are added, and then 4 grams of amorphous phosphorus; the flask is at once connected with a reflux condenser and the action allowed to proceed for twenty minutes. The condenser is then reversed, and 5 c.c. distilled off; this is mixed in a small flask with from 2 to 3 grams of silver nitrite and gently distilled, the distillate being collected in fractions of

[1] *Eighth Intern. Cong. Applied Chemistry*, 1912, **25**, 417.

three or four drops in small test-tubes. A little strong ammonia solution is added to each fraction, followed by a small quantity of a strong solution of sodium nitroprusside.

If methyl alcohol is present, nitromethane is formed from it according to the well-known reactions :—

$$3CH_3{\cdot}OH + P + I_3 = 3CH_3I + H_3PO_3$$
$$CH_3I + AgNO_2 = CH_3NO_2 + AgI.$$

The nitromethane, when treated with ammonia and sodium nitroprusside as described, yields a blue colour, changing to green and finally to yellow. The test is not vitiated by acetone, which under similar conditions gives a colour similar to Hofmann's violet.

Instead of sodium nitroprusside, C. D. Manzoff employs vanillin in this test. To the first five drops of the distillate from the silver nitrite, five drops of ammonia solution and 0·01 gram of vanillin are added, and the mixture heated. A red colour, which disappears on cooling, shows the presence of nitromethane, and hence of methyl alcohol in the original liquid. Nitroethane under similar conditions gives only a slight yellow colour. It is claimed that this test will detect one part of nitromethane in 100,000 parts of nitroethane.[1]

Conversion into methyl 3 : 5-dinitrobenzoate (Mulliken).—See the corresponding process for ethyl alcohol, p. 201. The directions given by Mulliken are :—

"Convert 4 drops of the alcohol into its 3 : 5-dinitrobenzoate," as described in the case of ethyl alcohol.

"Boil the reaction-product with 12 c.c. of dilute ethyl alcohol (3 : 1). Cool, shake, allow to stand for a minute or two, and filter. Wash with 2 c.c. of strong cold alcohol. Recrystallise from 12 c.c. of boiling dilute alcohol (3 : 1). Cool, shake, allow to stand for a minute or two, and filter. Wash the crystals with 2 c.c. of cold strong alcohol. Dry at a temperature not above 100° and determine the melting point.

"The crystalline methyl dinitrobenzoate obtained in this reaction melts at 107·5° (uncorr.)."

Conversion into 2 : 4-dinitroanisole (Blanksma).—This reaction corresponds with the one noted on p. 202 for ethyl alcohol. The sodium derivative of methyl alcohol is formed, and by its action on 1-chloro-2 : 4-dinitrobenzene the compound $C_6H_3(NO_2)_2{\cdot}O{\cdot}CH_3$ is obtained, and identified by its melting-point, 86·9°.

IV.—**Determination of methyl alcohol in the presence of ethyl alcohol.**—In the following pages are

[1] *Zeitsch. Nahr. Genussm.*, 1914, 27, 469.

described methods which can be used for the estimation of methyl alcohol when present in mixture with ethyl alcohol. Certain processes are included here which are essentially qualitative, but which can nevertheless be made to yield fairly good approximate results by comparison with "control" experiments made on known mixtures. For example, the time-honoured method of Riche and Bardy, tedious but trustworthy, can be employed in this way.

As regards the best method to use in any particular case, much will depend upon the probable proportion of methyl alcohol in the mixture. No one method will suit every case. The refractometric process, for instance, would be useless in examining wood naphtha, on account of the acetone present; the iodide method used for wood naphtha would be inapplicable (without modification) when ethyl alcohol is also a constituent of the mixture examined; the oxidation process of Thorpe and Holmes is not suitable for very small quantities; and so on. Moreover, apart from the question of proportion, it may happen that in particular circumstances one process will be advantageous as compared with another, though the latter may be usually the better. But so far as a general indication can be given, the following comments will serve as a useful guide.

For very small quantities, ranging up to 3 or 4 per cent., Denigès's process as modified by the writer (p. 184) will be found, in general, by far the best to use. Even when the proportion is as much as 5 to 10 per cent. of the total alcohols, the method can often be used to advantage, though of course any error in matching the colours is then multiplied rather largely, since only about 0·002 to 0·004 gram of methyl alcohol is employed in the actual comparison.

With moderately large proportions of methyl alcohol—say from 5 to 15 per cent.—the process proposed by Thorpe and Holmes (p. 188) gives quite satisfactory results. With still larger proportions fair estimations may be made by means of the immersion refractometer (see Chap. VII). But in ordinary practice the cases are few which cannot be treated by one or other of the two methods first mentioned, confirmed if necessary by the shortened form of the Riche and Bardy process, or by such of the remaining methods as may best suit the circumstances. (For the determination of methyl alcohol when no ethyl is present, see under "Wood naphtha" and "Alcoholometry").

Denigès's method,[1] modified by the author.[2]—The principle of this very convenient method is the oxidation of

[1] *Compt. rend.*, 1910, **150**, 832. [2] *The Analyst*, 1912, **37**, 16.

the methyl alcohol to formaldehyde, and the detection of the latter by means of Schiff's reagent in the presence of sufficient sulphuric acid to prevent the development of colour with any acetaldehyde formed from the ethyl alcohol during the oxidation.

The following solutions are required :—

Potassium permanganate.—2·0 Grams of $KMnO_4$ per 100 c.c.

Oxalic acid.—9·5 Grams of the crystallised acid per 100 c.c.

Schiff's reagent.—Dissolve 1 gram of pure fuchsine (rosaniline hydrochloride) in about half a litre of hot water ; then add, little by little and shaking well after each addition, 20 c.c. of a saturated aqueous solution of sodium bisulphite, followed by 10 c.c. of strong hydrochloric acid. Cool, and make the bulk up to 1 litre with distilled water. The reagent should give no colour with pure ethyl alcohol when this is treated as described below.

Methyl alcohol.—1 Gram per litre, in 10 per cent. ethyl alcohol.

The alcoholic mixture, purified by extraction with petroleum ether as already described (p. 170), is diluted with water or mixed with ethyl alcohol, as the case may require, until it contains 10 per cent. of total alcohols.

To 5 c.c. of this prepared liquid contained in a wide test-tube are added 2·5 c.c. of the permanganate solution, and then 0·2 c.c. of strong sulphuric acid, and the liquids mixed. When the reaction has proceeded about three minutes, 0·5 c.c. of the oxalic acid solution is added, to dissolve the precipitated manganese oxide. On shaking, the liquid becomes clear and nearly colourless. 1·0 C.c. of strong sulphuric acid is now run in and well mixed with the solution, which is finally treated with 5 c.c. of the Schiff's reagent. A violet colour is developed in the course of a few minutes if methyl alcohol was present, unless in mere traces, when twenty or thirty minutes may be required.

A preliminary experiment carried out as described serves to detect the presence of methyl alcohol (if this is not already known) and to give some idea of the quantity. According to the indications thus obtained, another part of the prepared liquid is further diluted, if necessary, with ethyl alcohol of 10 per cent. strength until it contains from 0·001 to 0·004 gram of methyl alcohol in 5 c.c. ; and the experiment is repeated, side by side with two or more standards for comparison. These contain 0·001, 0·002, 0·003, etc., gram of methyl alcohol in 5 c.c. of 10 per cent. ethyl alcohol. The colours produced are compared in small Nessler-tubes (25 c.c.), or in a suitable colorimeter.

With properly sensitive Schiff's reagent, as little as 0·0003 gram of methyl alcohol in the 5 c.c. of liquid taken is readily detected.

The best depths of colour for comparison, however, are those given by the formaldehyde produced in the manner described from quantities of 0·001 to 0·004 gram of methyl alcohol.

It is convenient to keep a standard solution (1 gram per litre) of methyl alcohol in 10 per cent. ethyl alcohol. This is diluted as required with 10 per cent. ethyl alcohol to form the standards for comparison. The strength of the alcoholic mixture for oxidation is chosen at 10 per cent. for convenience, as the distillates ordinarily obtained are of higher alcoholic strength, and can thus be diluted down to the required degree instead of having to be concentrated or mixed with stronger alcohol.

The process has the advantages of (1) being rapidly executed, (2) requiring only a small quantity of material, and (3) being directly applicable to relatively weak distillates. It is especially suitable for the estimation of small quantities of methyl alcohol—say from 0·1 up to 1 per cent.—in ethyl alcohol.

Formaldehyde, of course, must be absent from the unoxidised solution of alcohols, or else its effect must be determined and allowed for. Glycerol must also be absent.

Notes.—The quantities of reagents mentioned should be measured accurately, especially in respect of the permanganate solution and the sulphuric acid. Within limits, the former governs the quantity of formaldehyde produced and therefore, primarily, the intensity of colour obtained. Too little total sulphuric acid would allow of colour developing from the acetaldehyde, as well as from the formaldehyde; whilst too much lessens the intensity of the colour from the latter. A considerable excess of sulphuric acid at the oxidising stage may result in some formaldehyde being produced even from ethyl alcohol itself. Again, if the final volume of the liquid is increased considerably—as by the addition of 10 c.c. of Schiff's reagent instead of 5 c.c.—the concentration of the sulphuric acid may be so much reduced as to allow of colour developing from the acetaldehyde. But provided the directions given are adhered to with reasonable exactness there is no risk of any such errors arising. A useful criticism of the method has been written by G. Cecil Jones.[1]

To obtain the greatest degree of accuracy, it is necessary to treat the sample and the standards quite alike as regards quantities of reagents. The second quantity of sulphuric acid added, for example, may not be exactly 1·0 c.c.—it may be 0·9 c.c. or 1·1 c.c.; but so long as the *same* volume is added to sample and to standard this small variation will make no difference to the results. Provided

[1] *Analyst*, 1915, **40**, 221.

all the other conditions are rigidly adhered to, the best way of increasing the sensitiveness of the test is, in the opinion of the writer quoted, to use 5 c.c. of permanganate solution instead of 2·5, and as a consequence, 1 c.c. of oxalic acid solution instead of 0·5 c.c.

The purification of the distillate by extraction with petroleum ether as indicated should never be omitted, unless it is known that interfering substances are absent. According to E. Salkowski,[1] many different alcoholic liquids yield a distillate which gives a reaction indicating the presence of methyl alcohol when tested by Denigès's method. These should therefore be purified as indicated.

Some three years or more after the foregoing process was published T. von Fellenberg described the same method with some slight modifications.[2] He adapts it, for use with a distillate which may contain only aqueous methyl alcohol, by adding a mixture of ethyl alcohol and dilute sulphuric acid before oxidation. See his subsequent application of the method to the determination of pectin in spices, given a little later on.

Elias Elvove has applied the process to the detection and estimation of methyl alcohol vapour in air.[3] He finds that the sensitiveness is increased for this purpose by reducing the proportion of ethyl alcohol present from 10 per cent. to 0·5 per cent., the quantity of oxalic acid being increased to 0·7 c.c. on account of the decreased amount of ethyl alcohol. In these circumstances, as little as 0·1 mg. of methyl alcohol showed a coloration on standing for 40 minutes.

(This is, of course, a different problem from the detection and estimation of methyl alcohol occurring in ethyl alcohol, as the methyl alcohol vapour is absorbed in *water*.) A definite volume of air containing the vapour is suitably passed through water, and to estimate the methyl alcohol in this or any similar aqueous solution proceed as follows:

Ascertain by a preliminary experiment the approximate amount of methyl alcohol in the solution. If this shows that 5 c.c. of it contain more than 1 mg. of methyl alcohol, dilute so as to bring it within this limit. Mix 4·5 c.c. of this diluted solution with 0·5 c.c. of 4 per cent. ethyl alcohol. Similarly, prepare several 5 c.c. portions of standard methyl alcohol solutions by diluting the proper amounts of a 0·1 per cent. (0·1 gram per 100 c.c.) aqueous

[1] *Zeitsch. Nahr. Genussm.*, 1914, **28**, 225.

[2] In *Mitt. Lebensmittelunters. Hyg.*, 1915, **6**, i; *J. Chem. Soc.* (Abst.), 1915, **108**, ii, 587.

[3] *J. Ind. Eng. Chem.*, 1917, **9**, 295.

solution of methyl alcohol to 4·5 c.c. with water and then adding 0·5 c.c. of 5 per cent. ethyl alcohol to each. These standards are made to vary by 0·1 mg. of methyl alcohol, and the limits are chosen so as to bring the unknown solution for estimation within their range. The liquids are then treated with permanganate, etc., as already described, but using 0·7 c.c. of the oxalic acid instead of 0·5 c.c. Before adding the Schiff's reagent, the solutions are allowed to cool to the ordinary temperature for the sake of uniformity in treatment; and after the addition, they are allowed to stand forty minutes before being compared.

The directions given by Elvove for preparing the Schiff's reagent are substantially similar to those already noted, but a weighed quantity of *anhydrous* sodium sulphite is used instead of a saturated solution of the bisulphite. 0·2 Gram of finely powdered fuchsine is dissolved in about 120 c.c. of hot water and cooled to the ordinary temperature; 2·0 grams of anhydrous sodium sulphite are dissolved in about 20 c.c. of water and added to the fuchsine solution; then 2·0 c.c. of hydrochloric acid (sp. gr. 1·19) are added, and the whole diluted to 200 c.c. with water. After standing for about an hour the solution is ready for use.

Another interesting application of the method has been made by T. von Fellenberg, who has used it for the determination of pectin in spices by estimating the methyl alcohol derived from the pectin.[1] From 1 to 2 grams of the sample are placed on a filter and treated with small quantities of boiling 95 per cent. alcohol until the filtrate measures about 40 c.c. After a similar treatment with light petroleum, the contents of the filter are dried, transferred to a flask, and distilled with 40 c.c. of water, 20 c.c. of distillate being collected. The mixture in the flask is now treated, while hot, with 5 c.c. of 10 per cent. sodium hydroxide solution. After five minutes, 2·5 c.c. of dilute sulphuric acid (1 : 4) are added, and 16·2 c.c. are distilled over. This distillate is mixed with 5 drops of 10 per cent. silver nitrate solution and again distilled, 10 c.c. of distillate being collected and again distilled. The final distillate, measuring exactly 6 c.c., is weighed. Three c.c. of it are then treated with 1 c.c. of an alcohol–sulphuric acid solution (21 c.c. of 95 per cent. alcohol and 40 c.c. of conc. sulphuric acid diluted with water to 200 c.c.), and 1 c.c. of 5 per cent. permanganate solution. Comparison solutions containing 5 mg., 1 mg., and 0·3 mg. of methyl alcohol, respectively, are similarly treated at the same time. After two minutes, the mixtures are each treated with 1 c.c. of 8 per cent. oxalic acid solution, 1 c.c. of conc. sulphuric acid,

[1] *Chem. Zentr.*, 1916, i, 530.

and 5 c.c. of magenta–sulphurous acid solution (Schiff's or Gayon's reagent), and the colorations obtained are compared after the lapse of one hour. The pectin content of the sample is ten times the content of methyl alcohol.

Method of Thorpe and Holmes.[1]—This process is based upon the fact that, under the conditions described, methyl alcohol is completely oxidised to carbon dioxide and water by treatment with potassium dichromate and sulphuric acid, whereas ethyl alcohol in the same circumstances gives acetic acid. The carbon dioxide produced is then weighed.

The liquid to be analysed is mixed with water in such proportion that 50 c.c. of the mixture shall contain not more than 1 gram of methyl alcohol, and in the presence of ethyl alcohol not more than 4 grams of the mixed alcohols.

Fifty c.c. of the diluted liquid are then introduced into a flask of about 300 c.c. capacity, 20 grams of potassium dichromate and 80 c.c. of dilute sulphuric acid (1 : 4) added, and the mixture allowed to remain for eighteen hours. A further quantity of 10 grams of potassium dichromate and 50 c.c. of strong sulphuric acid mixed with an equal volume of water are now added, and the contents of the flask heated to the boiling point for about ten minutes, the evolved carbon dioxide being swept out of the apparatus by a current of air, and after drying with sulphuric acid, collected in weighed soda-lime tubes. From the weight of CO_2 thus obtained a deduction of 0·01 gram is made for each gram of ethyl elcohol present, as it has been found that the process of oxidising ethyl alcohol in the manner described is always accompanied by the production of carbon dioxide in the proportion stated. The remainder, multiplied by 32/44, gives the equivalent weight of methyl alcohol.

The apparatus used for carrying out this process is as follows. The flask in which the oxidation is performed is fitted with a ground-in stopper carrying (1) a funnel tube with stop-cock, and (2) an exit-tube also fitted with a stop-cock. In the absence of a ground-in stopper a two-holed rubber stopper can be employed. The funnel tube passes nearly to the bottom of the flask. Its upper end is fitted with a rubber stopper and tube to make connection with a soda-lime receptacle for freeing incoming air from carbon dioxide.

The exit-tube is attached to a small **U**-tube containing a little soap solution, in order to retain the bulk of the water and any small quantity of acetic acid which may distil over during the boiling. At its other end this **U**-tube is connected with the absorption

[1] *Trans. Chem. Soc.*, 1904, **85**, 1.

train. This consists of, first, two **U**-tubes containing pumice moistened with sulphuric acid to dry the gases expelled; next, two weighed **U**-tubes containing soda-lime to absorb the carbon dioxide; and finally, a guard **U**-tube containing soda-lime in the near limb and calcium chloride in the further limb, which is attached to a suitable aspirator. The tared soda-lime tubes contain, as usual, a little recently-heated calcium chloride at the top of each limb, covered with a layer of glass wool or cotton wool to keep fine particles out of the exits. The arrangement is, of course, tested with a

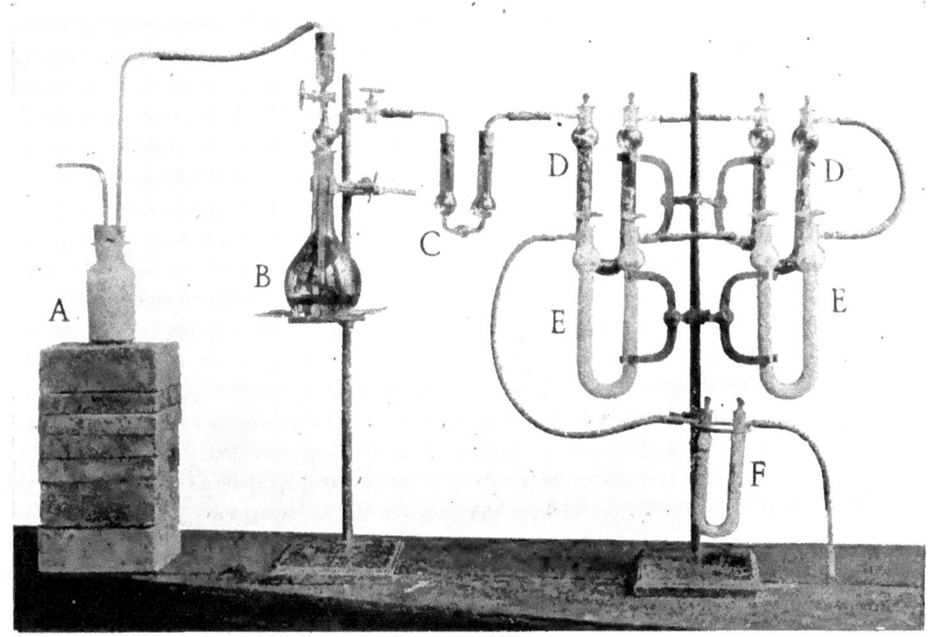

FIG. 30.—APPARATUS FOR ESTIMATION OF METHYL ALCOHOL BY THORPE AND HOLMES'S METHOD.

A, soda-lime bottle for purifying air-current; *B*, oxidation flask; *C*, **U**-tube with soap solution; *D*, *D*, tubes with pumice and sulphuric acid; *E*, *E*, soda-lime tubes for absorbing CO_2; *F*, guard tube.

current of air free from CO_2 to ascertain that the weight of the tared tubes remains constant.

In performing the experiment, the oxidation flask is kept cooled in an ice-bath during the addition of the first quantity of dichromate and sulphuric acid. It is then connected up with the absorption train, and allowed to stand at the ordinary temperature all night. In the morning the second quantity of dichromate and acid is run in through the tap-funnel; the latter is then connected with the air-purifying vessel, and a gentle current of air freed from carbon dioxide is aspirated through the apparatus. Heat is then applied, and the liquid kept boiling gently for about ten minutes, when the flame is withdrawn and the apparatus allowed to cool down, the current of air being maintained long enough to ensure that all the carbon dioxide evolved is carried into the absorption-tubes. The latter are then removed and weighed.

Details of an actual experiment are as follows.

Twenty-five c.c. of a mixture containing ethyl and methyl alcohols were purified by Thorpe and Holmes's method (p. 170), the distillate being made up to 250 c.c.

Specific gravity of distillate = 0·9873, = 9·39 per cent. of total alcohol by volume, = 7·452 grams per 100 c.c.

Fifty c.c. of the distillate (= 5 of the original sample) therefore contained 3·726 grams of total alcohols. This on oxidation yielded 0·2524 gram of CO_2.

Let x = grams of ethyl alcohol,
and y = ,, methyl ,,

in the 50 c.c. taken for oxidation.

$$\text{Then } x + y = 3{\cdot}726 \quad . \quad . \quad . \quad \text{(i).}$$

Also, since 1 gram of ethyl alcohol gives 0·01 gram of CO_2,
and 1 gram of methyl alcohol gives 44/32 gram of CO_2,
and the total CO_2 produced is 0·2524 gram, we have

$$0{\cdot}01x + 44y/32 = 0{\cdot}2524. \quad . \quad . \quad \text{(ii).}$$

Solving the two simultaneous equations (i) and (ii), we find $x = 3{\cdot}5684$ and $y = 0{\cdot}1576$. Whence the proportion of methyl alcohol in the original sample = 0·1576 × 100/5 = 3·15 grams per 100 c.c. Dividing this result by the specific gravity of methyl alcohol, 0·7964, we get 3·95 as the percentage of methyl alcohol by volume in the original sample.

For practical purposes, it suffices to deduct from the weight of CO_2 found a quantity = 1 per cent. of the *total* alcohol—therefore in this case 0·0372 gram—and calculate the remainder to methyl alcohol, though this gives a result slightly lower than the truth. Thus 0·2524 − 0·0372 = 0·2152 net CO_2; and 0·2152 × 32/44 = 0·1565 gram methyl alcohol in the 50 c.c. of distillate oxidised. Whence the proportion in the original sample, calculated as before, is found to be 3·93 per cent. by volume.

W. Koenig[1] modifies Thorpe and Holmes's method slightly, and gives the following details. A flask of 1 litre capacity is used for the oxidation operation. It is fitted with a two-holed rubber stopper through which passes (1) a dropping funnel closed at the top with a soda-lime tube, and (2) a reflux condenser connected at the upper end with the absorption train for the carbon dioxide.

[1] *Chem. Zeit.*, 1912, **36**, 1025–1028.

This train consists of, first, two drying-tubes, one containing calcium chloride, the other sulphuric acid and pumice-stone; next, two tared **U**-tubes containing soda-lime; and finally, two guard-tubes containing soda-lime and calcium chloride.

Air freed from CO_2 is drawn through the apparatus, and the mixture of methyl and ethyl alcohols passed into the flask. From 5 to 10 c.c. of the mixed alcohols are used, according to circumstances. The oxidising mixture, consisting of 30 grams of potassium bichromate in 500 c.c. of water with 50 c.c. of sulphuric acid (sp. gr. 1·84), which has been boiled for fifteen minutes and then cooled to 5°, is then run into the flask from the dropping-funnel. The contents of the flask are mixed and allowed to stand four hours, after which they are heated slowly to the boiling-point and boiled for an hour. To sweep out the carbon dioxide from the flask, air is aspirated through the apparatus, at first gently, and then more rapidly, during about forty-five minutes, after which the absorption-tubes are weighed. The weight of carbon dioxide obtained, multiplied by the factor 0·728, gives the amount of methyl alcohol in the quantity of alcohols taken.

Pure ethyl alcohol in the conditions described yielded carbon dioxide equivalent on an average to 0·5 per cent. of methyl alcohol.

Mixtures made up to contain from 4 to 15 per cent. of methyl alcohol gave results agreeing with the theoretical quantities within ± 0·19 per cent.

W. A. R. Wilks[1] has also published the results of an investigation upon Thorpe and Holmes's method, and describes a modified procedure which reduces the correction for oxidised ethyl alcohol to 0·004 gram of carbon dioxide instead of the 0·01 gram indicated in the original process. Less sulphuric acid is used, and the temperature is kept low during the initial stages.

A solution of 30 grams of potassium dichromate in 150 c.c. of water is first run into the distilling flask, which is well cooled with a freezing mixture. When the contents are thoroughly cold (a large proportion of the dichromate crystallises out), 50 c.c. of the suitably diluted sample are added, and finally, in small quantities at a time, a mixture of 20 c.c. of sulphuric acid and 20 c.c. of water previously cooled in a mixture of ice and salt. The flask, connected to the absorption apparatus, is allowed to stand overnight, and then heated to boiling and the experiment concluded as in the original process. Under these conditions the subtractive correction is 0·004 gram of CO_2 for each gram of ethyl alcohol present.

[1] Bulletin No. 1, 1914, Wellcome Tropical Research Laboratories, Chemical Section. Pub. by the Sudan Government.

Riche and Bardy's method.—One of the oldest and most trustworthy processes for the detection of methyl alcohol in the presence of ethyl alcohol is that described by Riche and Bardy.[1] It is based upon the conversion of the two alcohols first into the corresponding iodides and then into the alkyl anilines, by the oxidation of which a violet dyestuff is produced from the dimethylaniline, but not from the ethyl compound. As given by M. Louis Calvet,[2] the process is as follows :—

(1) **Conversion into the iodides.**—Place 10 c.c. of the alcohol to be tested in a flat-bottomed flask of 90 c.c. capacity containing 10 grams of iodine, add 2 grams of red phosphorus, attach the flask to a condenser, and warm gently to distil the iodides. Receive the latter in a vessel containing 20 c.c. of water.

(2) **Combining the iodides with aniline.**—Pour the iodides and the water into a separating funnel, and draw off the iodides into a flask similar to that used in (1); add 10 grams of pure aniline, and heat under a reflux condenser.

(3) **Conversion of the hydriodides of the ethyl- and methyl-anilines into the free bases.**—When the above-mentioned reaction is complete, dissolve the resulting crystalline mass in about 50 c.c. of hot water, and decompose the hydriodides with an excess of sodium hydroxide solution (D = 1·33). The free bases separate as an oily layer which is allowed to collect in the neck of the flask.

(4) **Oxidation of the methyl- and ethyl-anilines.**—Take 1 c.c. of the liberated bases and mix it intimately with 10 grams of oxidising powder composed of :—Sand, 100 grams, copper nitrate 3 grams, and sodium chloride, 3 grams. Place the mixture loosely in a test-tube, and heat it during six hours in a water-bath kept at a temperature of 90°. Then fill the tube with alcohol, pour the whole contents into a nickel or porcelain basin of about a litre capacity; add 300 c.c. of water, boil to expel the alcohol and to precipitate resinous matters formed during the oxidation, filter, and make up the volume of the filtrate to 500 c.c. with water.

(5) **Dyeing.**—Measure out 20 c.c. of this filtrate into 350 c.c. of water, contained in a porcelain basin of 500 c.c. capacity and heated on a water-bath, and place in it a square of cashmere of 1 dcm. side. Heat till the dye is completely extracted from the bath, stirring the fabric from time to time with a glass rod. Compare the colour thus obtained with that given by a control experiment on ethyl alcohol containing a known quantity of methyl alcohol.

The process has the advantage of yielding dyed material which can be preserved and produced as evidence of the presence of methyl

[1] *Compt. rend.*, 1875, **80**, 1076. [2] "Alcools," p. 109.

alcohol. In the form just described, however, it is stated (Calvet, *loc. cit.*) not to be capable of detecting methyl alcohol unless the latter is present to the extent of $1\frac{1}{2}$ to 2 per cent. of the mixture of alcohols. Moreover, it is somewhat lengthy.

Much smaller proportions can be detected by the following modification of the method used in the Government Laboratory, London. The process is also much shortened.

Ten c.c. of the alcohol, of strength not less than 85 per cent., are placed in a flask of about 75 c.c. capacity, containing 10 grams of powdered iodine. 1·5 Grams of red phosphorus are then added, and the flask connected at once with a reflux condenser. The reaction commences almost immediately. When it has ceased, and after reversing the condenser, the mixture is slowly distilled, and 0·5 c.c. of the mixed iodides collected under water in a very small separating funnel marked to show this volume (0·5 c.c.). A Cribb's condenser about 6 inches long is convenient for the distillation. With small proportions of methyl alcohol such as the method is specially devised for detecting, most of the methyl iodide will be present in this 0·5 c.c. fraction.

The mixed iodides thus obtained are then run into a small wide-necked flask (50 c.c. capacity) containing 0·5 c.c. of recently distilled aniline. The flask is loosely corked, and allowed to stand for thirty minutes or so on a sand-bath at a temperature of about 60°.

The crystalline mass of alkylaniline hydriodides thus obtained is dissolved in 30 to 50 c.c. of warm water, and decanted from any small globule of unchanged aniline into a separator of about 100 to 150 c.c. capacity. Two c.c. of sodium hydroxide solution (D = 1·3) are now added, and 20 c.c. of petroleum ether. After shaking the mixture and allowing it to separate, the lower layer is run off and discarded, and the ethereal solution washed twice with a little water. It is then poured into a wide-necked flask (100 c.c.) containing 5 grams of oxidising mixture (sand, 100 grams, copper nitrate, 3 grams, sodium chloride, 2 grams). The petroleum ether is evaporated off, and the flask heated in a steam oven at approximately 100° for $1\frac{1}{2}$ hours.

The dye thus formed is extracted by digestion with 50 c.c. of boiling alcohol for two or three minutes under a reflux condenser. When cold, 5 c.c. of the alcoholic extract are filtered off and made up to 100 c.c. with water.

Of this diluted dye 5 c.c. are added to 400 c.c. of hot water, and a piece of clean Berlin wool, 18 inches long, is immersed in the solution. The latter is then kept at about 60° for twenty minutes or so, with occasional stirring, in order to fix the dye on the wool.

After rinsing the wool in water and allowing it to dry, it may be coiled into a flat coil and attached to gummed paper for comparison of its depth of violet colour with that given by control experiments, carried out in the same way with pure ethyl alcohol and known mixtures of the two alcohols.

As little as 0·1 per cent. of methyl alcohol in mixture with ethyl alcohol can be thus detected. With much larger proportions, the whole of the dyestuff will not be extracted by the wool, in which case a smaller quantity than 5 c.c. of the diluted dye—say 1 or 2 c.c.—should be taken to make the dye-bath.

With a little practice the method can be made approximately quantitative for small proportions of methyl alcohol. It is a useful confirmatory process in specially-important cases.

Conversion into trimethylsulphine iodide.—When we have obtained a mixture of ethyl iodide and methyl iodide from the alcohols by treatment with phosphorus and iodine, the quantity of methyl iodide can be estimated by a method described by G. Reif.[1] This depends upon the fact that methyl iodide reacts in the cold with methyl sulphide to form trimethylsulphine iodide, whilst ethyl iodide does not form a similar compound. The trimethylsulphine iodide behaves as a salt of hydriodic acid, and may be estimated volumetrically by titration with standard silver nitrate solution.

Formic acid method.[2]—This process is based upon the oxidation of the methyl alcohol to formic acid by means of hydrogen peroxide, and the estimation of the formic acid by the mercurous chloride reaction.

The sample is cooled to 5°, made alkaline with sodium hydroxide solution, and treated with successive portions of 3 to 5 c.c. of a 1 per cent. solution of hydrogen peroxide. This reagent is added first at intervals of thirty minutes, and afterwards at intervals of forty-five to sixty minutes, until no more gas is evolved. The oxidised liquid is then allowed to stand for eight hours.

At the end of this period the excess of hydrogen peroxide is destroyed by means of sodium thiosulphate, the solution being then acidified and distilled with steam. The distillate is collected in a receiver containing a suspension of calcium carbonate in boiling water. About 700 c.c. of the distillate having been obtained, it is filtered hot, the filtrate evaporated to dryness, and the residue of calcium formate, etc., heated for an hour at 125° to 130°. It is

[1] *Arbeit. Kais. Gesund.*, 1915, **50**, 50–56; in *Zeitsch. angew. Chem.*, 1916, **29**, Ref. 82.

[2] R. Schmiedel, *Pharm. Zentr.-h.*, 1913, **54**, 709–716; *Analyst*, 1913, **38**, 508.

then dissolved in 100 c.c. of water, and the solution extracted twice with 25 c.c. of ether. The aqueous layer is mixed with 2 grams of crystallised sodium acetate, slightly acidified with hydrochloric acid, and heated with 100 c.c. of a 5 per cent. solution of mercuric chloride for two hours in a boiling water-bath. The precipitated mercurous chloride is washed by decantation with hot water, filtered on a Gooch crucible, washed again with hot water and then with alcohol and with ether, and dried to constant weight.

Each gram of Hg_2Cl_2 thus obtained = 0·0875 gram of $H{\cdot}COOH$ = 0·0678 gram of $CH_3{\cdot}OH$.

Permanganate method.—For the determination of small quantities of methyl and ethyl alcohols in aqueous solution, J. Hetper[1] proposes a method based upon two oxidations of the liquid with permanganate. One oxidation is carried out with acid permanganate, the other with an alkaline solution of this reagent.

Solutions required :—

(1). *Acid* $N/2$-$KMnO_4$: 16 grams of $KMnO_4$ + 40 grams of crystallised phosphoric acid in 1 litre of water.

(2). *Alkaline* $KMnO_4$: 16 grams $KMnO_4$ + 40 grams NaOH per litre.

These two solutions are standardised against $N/2$-oxalic acid.

The liquid to be examined must not contain other substances which reduce permanganate. Previous to the estimation it must be diluted or concentrated until it contains from 0·1 to 0·25 per cent. by weight of total alcohols.

A preliminary experiment is made to determine the alcoholic strength of the liquid. Twenty-five c.c. of the solution (2) are diluted with 50 c.c. of water, heated on a steam-bath, and the alcoholic liquid added in small quantities until the colour of the permanganate is changed to green. The mixture is then heated for a period of twenty minutes, when 25 c.c. of $N/2$-oxalic acid solution are added, and the excess of oxalic acid titrated with $N/2$ permanganate. Each c.c. of $N/2$-permanganate required is equivalent to 0·0025 gram of alcohol. The sample is then diluted or concentrated accordingly.

For the **alkaline oxidation,** 25 c.c. of the solution (2) are diluted, heated to 40°, and 10 c.c. of the alcoholic liquid added. The mixture is at once heated on the water-bath, and kept at 94° for fifteen to twenty minutes. It is then treated hot with 25 c.c. of $N/2$-oxalic acid, and titrated with the solution (1). The

[1] *Zeitsch. Nahr. Genussm.*, 1913, **26**, 342.

quantity of (1) reduced should not be less than 7 c.c. nor more than 12 c.c.

For the **acid oxidation,** 30 c.c. of the solution (1) are diluted with water, from 10 to 20 c.c. of the alcoholic liquid added, and the mixture heated under a reflux condenser to 94° for two hours. Thirty c.c. of $N/2$-oxalic acid solution are then added, and the excess titrated with $N/2$-$KMnO_4$. The volume of permanganate reduced should be from 8 to 14 c.c., and 0·1 c.c. is deducted from the quantity used up.

The calculation is made as follows :

Let p = grams of total alcohols in 100 c.c. of the liquid ;
x = ,, MeOH in 100 grams of total alcohols ;
y = ,, ,, ,, c.c. of the liquid ;
z = ,, EtOH ,, ,, ,,
n_1 = c.c. of the alcoholic liquid, and v_1 = c.c. of the $N/2$-$KMnO_4$, used in the *alkaline* oxidation,
n_2 and v_2 = the corresponding volumes used in the *acid* oxidation ;

then
$$p = \frac{0{\cdot}2667 v_1}{n_1}; \quad x = \frac{50 v_2}{p n_2} - 87;$$

$$y = \frac{px}{100}; \text{ and } z = p - \frac{px}{100} \text{ or } \frac{\dfrac{v_1}{n_1} - \dfrac{v_2}{n_2}}{2{\cdot}01}.$$

Example :—30 c.c. of sample required 9 c.c. of permanganate in the preliminary test.

$9 \times 0{\cdot}0025 \times \frac{100}{30} = 0{\cdot}075$ gram of total alcohols per 100 c.c., = approximately 0·078 per cent. by weight. Therefore 100 c.c. of the sample were distilled to 75 c.c. in order to bring the strength within the required limits.

In the oxidation :—

(1) 20 c.c. of the distillate = 7·6 c.c. alkaline $KMnO_4$;
(2) 40 ,, ,, ,, ,, = 8·9 − 0·1 = 8·8 c.c. acid $KMnO_4$.

$$\text{Hence } p = \frac{0{\cdot}2667 \times 7{\cdot}6}{20} = 0{\cdot}1014;$$

$$x = \frac{50 \times 8{\cdot}8}{0{\cdot}1014 \times 40} - 87 = 21{\cdot}47;$$

$$y = \frac{50 \times 8{\cdot}8}{0{\cdot}1014 \times 40} = 0{\cdot}0218;$$

$$\text{and } z = 0{\cdot}1014 - \frac{0{\cdot}1014 \times 21{\cdot}47}{100} = 0{\cdot}0796$$

Multiplying these values of *p*, *y*, and *z* by 75/100 to correct for the preliminary concentration, we have: total alcohols, 0·0760; methyl alcohol, 0·0163; and ethyl alcohol, 0·0597 gram per 100 c.c. of the original sample.

Other processes.—Various other methods of detecting and estimating methyl alcohol in mixture with ethyl alcohol have been proposed. They are mostly of specialised application, and a brief reference to one or two will suffice here. Thus W. G. Toplis dries the alcohol over potassium carbonate, and then measures the volume of hydrogen evolved from a given quantity by treatment with a fragment of metallic sodium.[1] The presence of methyl alcohol increases the quantity of hydrogen obtainable.

F. Wirthle detects and estimates the methyl alcohol in a mixture of the two alcohols by means of the boiling point, amount, and saponification value of the mixed iodides obtained from the sample.[2]

In the alcohol poisoning cases which occurred in Berlin during 1911, the proportion of methyl alcohol in the beverage taken was determined from the results of combustion analyses.[3]

E. Aweng confirms the presence of formaldehyde, resulting from the oxidation of methyl alcohol with permanganate, by converting it into hexamethylenetetramine with ammonia, and identifying microscopically the characteristic crystals formed by the tetramine with mercuric chloride or potassio-mercuric iodide.[4]

It may be noted that according to Voisenet[5] minute traces of formaldehyde, detectible by the sulphuric acid and protein reaction, are formed when ethyl alcohol is oxidised by *Mycoderma aceti* or *M. vini*, or by electrolysis, as well as by oxidation with ozone, hydrogen peroxide, etc.

A scheme for the examination of liquids, animal organs, etc., in forensic cases where wood spirit is suspected has been given by Olivari.[6] It is based upon the usual analytical procedure of separating bases and acids by means of their non-volatile salts, so as to obtain the neutral alcohols, etc., in the distillate.

The liquid is acidified with phosphoric acid, and the volatile acids, alcohols, etc., distilled off, leaving amines, pyridines, and other bases in the residue.

The distillate is neutralised and again distilled, the salts of the acids remaining behind, whilst neutral bodies, including alcohols, acetone, and aldehydes, distil over.

[1] *Amer. J. Pharm.*, 1918, **90**, 636.
[2] *Chem. Zeit.*, 1912, **36**, 700.
[3] *Zeitsch. Nahr. Genussm.*, 1912, **24**, 7.
[4] *Apoth. Zeit.*, 1912, **27**, 159.
[5] *Compt. rend.*, 1910, **29**, 169.
[6] *Arch. Farmacol. Sperim.*, 1913, **15**, 83; *Chem. Zentr.*, 1913, i, 1780.

Aldehydes are "fixed" by treatment with metaphenylene-diamine hydrochloride (see Chap. XI, Girard and Cuniasse's method for estimation of higher alcohols). On again distilling, the methyl alcohol is obtained in the distillate, together with any acetone present in the wood spirit, and the two can now be estimated by any convenient process.

V. Methyl alcohol and formaldehyde.—When these two substances occur together in aqueous solution they may be estimated by one or other of the following methods :—

(1). If only very small quantities of the two are in question, the solution is mixed with ethyl alcohol in such proportion as to give 10 per cent. of alcohol, as described for Denigès's method of estimating methyl alcohol (p. 183).

(*a*). In one quantity of 5 c.c. the formaldehyde is determined by colorimetric comparison with a standard solution of formaldehyde, proceeding just as described for methyl alcohol, but omitting the oxidation with permanganate, and using 3 c.c. of water instead of the same volume of permanganate and oxalic acid.

(*b*). At the same time, the colour produced is matched by comparison with a standard solution of methyl alcohol, oxidised precisely as required in the estimation of this alcohol.

(*c*). In another 5 c.c. of the prepared sample the alcohol is oxidised and the resulting total colour with Schiff's reagent estimated in terms of methyl alcohol, as described on p. 184. Deducting the result of (*b*) from that of (*c*) gives the proportion of methyl alcohol.

(2). With larger proportions of formaldehyde the quantity of this ingredient may be determined by one of the well-known methods —*e.g.*, by oxidation with iodine in alkaline solution, and determining the excess of iodine, after acidifying, with sodium thiosulphate. The methyl alcohol is estimated by Denigès's or other convenient method after removing the formaldehyde by distillation with potassium cyanide, twice repeated.

(3). When still larger proportions of formaldehyde are present, as in the commercial product "formalin," the process described by Lockemann and Croner[1] may be used. On adding hydroxylamine hydrochloride to formaldehyde, hydrochloric acid is liberated according to the equation :—

$$CH_2O + NH_2 \cdot OH \cdot HCl = CH_2 \cdot NOH + H_2O + HCl.$$

The acid can be titrated, and the formaldehyde thus estimated. Methyl orange is used as the indicator.

Alternatively, by adding sodium sulphite to the formaldehyde

[1] *Zeitsch. anal. Chem.*, 1915, **54**, 11.

solution free alkali is produced, and the estimation may be made by titrating this :—

$$CH_2O + Na_2SO_3 + H_2O = CH_2(OH)SO_3Na + NaOH.$$

In this case rosolic acid is used as the indicator.

The methyl alcohol is determined by oxidising the mixture with alkaline permanganate and calculating the alcohol from the quantity of permanganate reduced, after deducting the quantity used up by the formaldehyde. The 40 per cent. solution (formalin) of formaldehyde is diluted to 100 times its bulk with water, and 5 c.c. of this solution are mixed in a flask with 75 c.c. of water and 25 c.c. of *N*/2-permanganate, containing 15·82 grams of $KMnO_4$ and 40 grams of NaOH per litre. After being heated on the steam bath for 20 minutes, the mixture is treated with an excess of *N*/2-oxalic acid solution (31·51 grams of the crystallised acid with 75 c.c. of strong sulphuric acid, per litre). The excess of oxalic acid is then determined by titration with acid permanganate solution of *N*/2-strength, containing 40 grams of crystallised phosphoric acid per litre. Each c.c. of the alkaline *N*/2-permanganate used up oxidises 0·00375 gram of formaldehyde or 0·00267 gram of methyl alcohol, and the quantity of formaldehyde having been already determined the corresponding amount of permanganate can be calculated and deducted, the remainder being then calculated to methyl alcohol.

Determination of methyl alcohol in the blood and in the body-tissues.—According to Nicloux,[1] small quantities of methyl alcohol in blood may be estimated by adding to the blood six or seven times its volume of a saturated solution of picric acid, and distilling the mixture. If a fractionating apparatus of suitable type is employed, all the methyl alcohol is obtained in the first portion of the distillate measuring one-fifth of the original volume. In this distillate, the methyl alcohol is determined by oxidation with potassium dichromate, as described later on for ethyl alcohol (p. 209). With urine or any other liquid of the organism except blood, it suffices to use an equal volume of the picric acid solution.

When dealing with body-tissues, a quantity of 10 to 20 grams is taken, placed in about 40 c.c. of the picric acid solution, and cut into small pieces under the liquid. The mixture is then distilled and the distillate oxidised as above described.

Methyl alcohol in the air.—Methyl alcohol vapour in air is estimated by Nicloux by passing the air through a series of six or

[1] *Compt. rend. Soc. Biol.*, 1910, **73**, 59.

seven wash-bottles containing water at the ordinary temperature. The solution thus obtained is distilled and oxidised with dichromate in the same way as before.

In order to differentiate between methyl alcohol and other substances oxidisable by dichromate, the ratio of the carbon dioxide produced to the oxygen used up in the reaction is determined. The volume of dichromate reduced gives the quantity of oxygen in question by a simple calculation. To obtain the amount of carbon dioxide, a specially-designed sealed tube is employed in which the distillate is oxidised; the resulting carbon dioxide is then withdrawn by a mercury pump and its volume ascertained by absorption in potassium hydroxide solution, as in ordinary gas analysis.

(NOTE.—It would be simpler to estimate the methyl alcohol in any of the foregoing distillates by the author's modification of Denigès's process already described; or, for the air, by Elvove's adaptation of the same method.)

VI. Identification of ethyl alcohol.—As a rule, the detection of ethyl alcohol presents no difficulty, though occasionally, where minute quantities are being dealt with, or interfering substances are present, a definite proof may demand both skill and care. The first two tests described below will often suffice, but should be supplemented by one or more of the others if the circumstances require it.

Ethyl acetate reaction.—Mix a little sodium acetate, or 2 or 3 drops of acetic acid, with 2 or 3 c.c. of the liquid to be tested, then add about an equal volume of concentrated sulphuric acid, and heat the mixture. The characteristic fruity odour of ethyl acetate is developed if ethyl alcohol is present.

Iodoform reaction.—A few drops of solution of iodine are added to about 2 c.c. of the alcoholic liquid, which is then heated to about 60°, and solution of sodium hydroxide or carbonate added drop by drop until the colour of the iodine is discharged. The characteristic odour of iodoform is produced even with very dilute solutions of alcohol; with stronger solutions a turbidity, or a definite yellowish, crystalline precipitate of iodoform, appears when the liquid cools.

The iodoform is produced in accordance with the equation:—

$$C_2H_5{\cdot}OH + 5I_2 + 7NaOH = CHI_3 + CO_2 + 7NaI + 6H_2O.$$

A similar reaction is given by acetone, hence the result should be confirmed by one or more of the other tests described.

Iodoform is also produced from acetone in the cold, but not by ethyl alcohol, except to a slight extent and on standing some time.

Ethyl benzoate reaction.—Shake a few c.c. of the liquid with a little benzoyl chloride, allow to settle, pipette off the lower layer, and warm it with solution of potassium hydroxide. If ethyl alcohol is present, the odour of ethyl benzoate will be detected (Berthelot).

Guaiacum reaction.—Place a fragment or two of guaiacum resin, newly broken from a lump, in a test-tube, add the liquid to be tested, shake well, and filter into a Nessler glass. Do a similar experiment with distilled water, and then add to each glass a little dilute solution of hydrocyanic acid and one or two drops of a dilute solution of copper sulphate. If the sample contains alcohol a blue colour will be produced, much deeper than that given by the distilled water.

Aldehyde reaction.—Mix 5–10 c.c. of the alcoholic liquid with an equal volume of 50 per cent. sulphuric acid, and introduce it into a small flask containing 3 or 4 grams of powdered potassium dichromate and about 5 c.c. of water. Allow the mixture to stand a few minutes, and then distil off the aldehyde formed, collecting it in a little water. The acetaldehyde may be recognised :—

(1). By its odour.

(2). By the production of reddish-violet colour, either immediately or after a few minutes, when treated with Schiff's reagent.

(3). By the formation of aldehyde-resin, showing a yellow colour, on being allowed to stand some time in contact with a piece of caustic potash.

(4). By the production of a silver mirror when heated with an ammoniacal solution of silver nitrate.

Conversion into ethyl-*m*-dinitrobenzoate.—In special cases the following test described by Mulliken[1] has been found useful by the writer. It is applicable only to a nearly pure alcohol containing not more than about 10 per cent. of water :—

Heat together gently in a 3-inch test-tube held over a small flame 0·15 gram of 3–5 dinitrobenzoic acid and 0·20 gram of phosphorus pentachloride. When signs of chemical action are seen, remove the heat for a few seconds. Then heat again, boiling the liquefied mixture *very gently* for one minute. Pour out on a very small watch glass and allow to solidify. As soon as solidification occurs remove the liquid phosphorus oxychloride with which the crystalline mass is impregnated by rubbing the latter between

[1] "Identification of Pure Organic Compounds," I, 161.

two small pieces of porous tile. Place the powder in a dry 5- or 6-inch test-tube. Allow 4 drops of the alcohol to fall upon it, and then stopper the tube tightly without delay. Immerse the lower part of the test-tube in water having a temperature of 75–85°. Shake gently, and continue the heating for ten minutes.

To purify the ester produced in the reaction crush any hard lumps that may form when the mixture cools with a stirring-rod, and boil gently with 15 c.c. of methyl alcohol (2 : 1) until all is dissolved, or for a minute or two. Filter boiling hot if the solution is not clear. Cool. Shake and filter. Wash with 3 c.c. of cold methyl alcohol (2 : 1). Recrystallise from 9 c.c. of boiling methyl alcohol (2 : 1). Wash with 2 c.c. of the same solvent. Spread out the product on a piece of tile. Allow to become air-dry, and determine the melting point.

Ethyl 3 : 5-dinitrobenzoate, the product in this test, crystallises in white needles melting at 92–93° (uncorr.).

This method is given by Winter Blyth[1] for the definite proof of the presence of ethyl alcohol in toxicological cases.

Conversion into dinitrophenetole.—A somewhat similar reaction to the foregoing has been used by Blanksma.[2] By the action of sodium ethylate on 1-chloro-2 : 4-dinitrobenzene the compound 2 : 4-dinitrophenetole is obtained :—

$$C_6H_3(NO_2)_2Cl + C_2H_5{\cdot}ONa = C_6H_3(NO_2)_2{\cdot}O{\cdot}C_2H_5 + NaCl.$$

The alcohol is concentrated to a strength of 90–95 per cent., and 0·5 gram taken. In this is dissolved 0·012 gram of sodium, and 0·1 gram of the powdered chlorodinitrobenzene added. On warming the mixture, needles of the dinitrophenetole are obtained, which may be recrystallised from dilute alcohol or benzene, and the identity of the compound established by its melting point (85·2°). Methyl alcohol similarly treated yields 2 : 4-dinitroanisole, melting at 86·9°. As the difference between these melting-points is small, the process must evidently be used with circumspection. Mixtures of the two products, containing respectively 20·5, 46·2, and 80·5 per cent. of the phenetole, have the melting points 76°, 53°, and 75°.

Conversion into phthalic ester.—A more general application of the same principle has been described by E. E. Reid.[3]

Alcohols when heated with phthalic anhydride yield phthalic esters ; and the sodium salts of these, heated with para-nitrobenzyl bromide, give mixed phthalic esters which have definite melting

[1] "Poisons," p. 147. [2] *Chem. Weekblad.*, 1914, **11**, 26.
[3] *J. Amer. Chem. Soc.*, 1917, **39**, 1249.

points. These reactions may be used for the identification of many different alcohols.

A moderate excess of the alcohol to be tested is heated for one hour with 1 gram of phthalic anhydride. For a primary alcohol, the temperature employed is 100°, for a secondary, 140°. In the case of the lower alcohols, the mixture is sealed up in a tube and heated in a boiling water-bath, whilst with the less volatile alcohols the mixture may be heated in an open tube. The product is then mixed with 10 c.c. of water and shaken with 15 c.c. of ether and 5 c.c. of normal sodium hydroxide solution; the aqueous layer drawn off, and evaporated to dryness. The residue thus obtained is heated for one hour under a reflux condenser with 5 c.c. of water, 10 c.c. of 95 per cent. alcohol, and 1 gram of *p*-nitrobenzyl bromide, and the product is recrystallised from 63 per cent. alcohol, and its melting point determined.

Ethyl-*p*-nitrobenzyl phthalate melts at 80°. The corresponding methyl compound has the melting point 105·7°, the propyl compound 53°, the isopropyl 74°, the normal butyl 62°, and the allyl 61·5°.

The method may be used for the detection of ethyl alcohol in admixture with ethyl benzoate or menthol, and also of borneol in camphor.

Another general reaction for the lower alcohols of the aliphatic series has been described by E. de Stoecklin.[1] Iron tannate, prepared by the interaction of tannin and a ferric salt, acts as a peroxydase; and in the presence of hydrogen peroxide it serves as a convenient means of oxidising the lower alcohols. The aldehyde produced is then detected by the violet colour given with rosaniline bisulphite solution (Gayon or Schiff's reagent). Glycerol, if present, is also oxidised, and yields a colour. Some other iron combinations act in a similar manner as oxygen carriers.

One c.c. or less of the liquid to be tested is made faintly acid with acetic acid; or, if already acid, is made almost neutral to phenolphthalein. Two drops of an iron solution (made by adding a ferric salt to a saturated solution of hydroquinone and diluting it to contain 1 mg. of iron per c.c.) are then added, followed immediately by 4 drops of hydrogen peroxide solution. After shaking for a few seconds, the liquid is treated with a little of the rosaniline bisulphite solution. If alcohols were originally present, a violet colour is produced. The test is repeated with an iron tannin solution containing 1 mg. of iron per c.c., made by adding a ferric salt to a 3 per cent. aqueous solution of tannin.

A positive result indicates the presence of methyl, ethyl, propyl,

[1] *Compt. rend.*, 1908, **147**, 1489; 1910, **150**, 43.

or butyl alcohols in the original liquid. If the latter has not been distilled, glycerol may also be a cause of the colour produced; and hence if the volatile alcohols are expelled by boiling, and the liquid still shows the reaction, the presence of glycerol is indicated.

Specific reaction for ethyl alcohol.—The presence of aldehyde or acetone, which are difficult to remove, interferes with some of the ordinary tests for ethyl alcohol. According to A. Toninelli,[1] the following reaction is not affected by the presence of these impurities, and when carried out as described is quite characteristic of ethyl alcohol.

The reagents required are (1) 1·5 grams of pure crystallised dinitrotoluene (m.p. 70·5°) dissolved in 200 c.c. of a mixture of 1 part of carbon disulphide and 2 parts of ether; (2) 12 grams of iodine dissolved in 100 c.c. of ether; and (3) 40 grams of potassium hydroxide dissolved in 100 c.c. of water.

In a 10 c.c. graduated stoppered tube are placed 2 c.c. of the liquid to be tested, and 2 c.c. of the iodine solution. After shaking and allowing to stand for two minutes, 4 c.c. of the potash solution are added, and the mixture shaken until it is decolorised. Finally, 2 c.c. of the dinitrotoluene reagent are added with vigorous shaking, after which the graduated tube is placed upon a white surface and the upper layer closely observed. If ethyl alcohol is present in quantity sufficient to react, an orange yellow colour is developed which passes through various shades, terminating in an intense garnet red. With as little as 3 per cent. of alcohol, the colour is a light rose.

Neither methyl alcohol nor pure acetone gives this reaction, and aldehyde diminishes the sensitiveness of the test only when present in large amount.

Some of the higher alcohols, however, give similar results to those obtained with ethyl alcohol. When it is necessary to eliminate them, 25 to 100 c.c. of the sample, according to its presumed content of ethyl alcohol, are placed in a separator, and treated with two volumes of a 5 per cent. solution of alum in water, shaking up several times after addition of a little benzene or petroleum ether. The aqueous layer, which contains nearly all the ethyl alcohol present, is drawn off and distilled, fractions of 2 c.c. being collected of the distillate passing over between 60° and 80°. The test is then applied to these.

Pasteur's method for small quantities.—This is of some historical interest, as having been used by Pasteur in showing, for example,

[1] *Ann. Chim. anal.*, 1914, **19**, 169; *Pharm. J.*, 1914, **39**, 47.

that certain *torulæ* produce no alcohol in the course of their development.[1]

Minute traces of alcohol were detected by distilling the liquid under examination from a long-necked retort connected with a Liebig's condenser. "A certain sign of the presence of alcohol is contained in the first few drops distilled; these always assume the form of little drops or striæ, or, better still, oily tears, when alcohol is present in the distillate." In this way, taking 100 c.c. of the liquid, the presence of 0·1 per cent. of alcohol can be detected, and with care and practice even 0·01 per cent. Distilling one-third of the liquid, and redistilling, much smaller proportions can be detected.

Klöcker has modified this process, so that it is possible to detect as little as 0·002 or 0·001 per cent. of alcohol in liquids such as yeast-water or wort.[2] Five c.c. of the liquid are placed in a test-tube, 18 cm. long by 2·4 cm. diameter, fitted with a cork through which passes a glass tube of length 80 cm. and external diameter 3 mm. The lower end of the tube extends only to the bottom of the cork. The test-tube is fixed vertically over a piece of wire gauze, and is heated by a small flame. To promote regular ebullition, a small spiral of thin copper wire may be placed in the test-tube. Frothing may be minimised by adding 3 drops of strong nitric acid.

The presence of alcohol in the liquid is shown by the formation of drops having a characteristic oily appearance ("tears") in the long tube. The higher these drops appear in the tube, the smaller is the quantity of alcohol present.

This reaction is not shown by any substance, except alcohol, likely to be present in fermenting liquids.

VII. Examination of commercial alcohol.—Specimens of "plain" spirit are frequently required to be tested as regards general purity and suitability for use in pharmacy, perfumery, or other arts. Defects due to imperfect rectification are not often met with in ordinary "patent-still" spirit of good quality; but even with such spirit impurities may have been introduced through careless storage or accidental admixture.

The nature of the general examination will of course depend to some extent upon the particular purpose for which the spirit is required. Usually, however, it will include at least a determination of the alcoholic strength of the sample, and proof of the absence of solid matters, dissolved oily substances, excessive acidity, and

[1] "Studies on Fermentation" (Eng. trans., 1879), p. 78.

[2] *Compt. rend. trav. Lab. Carlsberg*, 1911, **10**, 99.

methyl alcohol. In the case of "absolute" alcohol, it may be necessary to prove also that excess of water is not present.

The "rectified spirit" of the Pharmacopœia is required to pass the following tests :—

"Specific gravity 0·8337. Burns with a blue smokeless flame. Leaves no residue on evaporation (absence of non-volatile matter). Remains clear when mixed with water (absence of oily or resinous substances). A little exposed on clean white filter paper leaves no unpleasant smell after the alcohol has evaporated (absence of fusel oil and allied impurities)."

"One hundred c.c., with 2 c.c. of *N*/10 solution of silver nitrate, exposed for twenty-four hours to bright light and then decanted from the black powder which has formed, undergo no further change when again exposed to light with more *N*/10 solution of silver nitrate (absence of more than traces of amyl alcohol and of other organic impurities). When mixed with half its volume of an aqueous solution (1 in 5) of sodium hydroxide, the mixture does not immediately darken in colour (absence of more than traces of aldehyde). No immediate darkening in colour is caused by the addition of solution of ammonia (absence of tannin, excess of aldehyde, and other organic impurities)."

The French Pharmacopœia prescribes the following tests for alcohol :—It should be colourless, and show no acid reaction when diluted with two volumes of water. It should leave no residue on evaporation.

Heated on a water-bath in a porcelain capsule, no foreign odour should be perceptible either during evaporation of the alcohol or subsequently. When diluted with two volumes of water, it should remain clear, and the odour and flavour should be those of ethyl alcohol, without extraneous admixture.

Distil 100 c.c. from a water-bath until 60 to 70 c.c. of distillate are collected. With this distillate and with the residue carry out the two following series of tests.

(1). **Distillate** (for "foreshot" impurities).

(*a*). Ten c.c. of the distillate in a test-tube are mixed with 5 c.c. of ammoniacal solution of silver nitrate (10 per cent. of $AgNO_3$) and heated in the water-bath : the mixture should remain clear and colourless. If the alcohol is impure (*aldehydes*), a brown colour or a precipitate of metallic silver will be given.

(*b*). In a stoppered flask of 100 c.c. capacity place 50 c.c. of the distillate and 2 c.c. of solution of potassium permanganate (0·2 gram of $KMnO_4$ per litre). Maintain the temperature at 15° to 18°. If the alcohol is pure, the rose-violet tint of the solution should persist during twenty minutes, before passing to a salmon-pink shade. (Absence of acetone, aldehydes, commercial methyl alcohol.)

(2). **Residue from distillation** (for "taillings" impurities).

(*c*). In a flat-bottomed flask cooled in a cold water-bath, pour 10 c.c. of the residue, and add, little by little, with shaking, 10 c.c. of pure sulphuric acid, in such manner as to prevent rise of temperature. With pure alcohol, the mixture remains colourless; if impure, it acquires a colour varying from yellow or light rose to granite red, violet, or even dark brown. (*Higher alcohols*, etc.)

(*d*). Introduce into a test-glass 2 c.c. of an acid and colourless solution of aniline acetate, made by mixing equal volumes of redistilled aniline and glacial acetic acid. On the surface of this pour carefully about 10 c.c. of the residual liquid from the distillation; the mixture should remain colourless. If a bright red colour is produced at the surface of contact, gradually penetrating into the bulk, *furfural* is present.

A third series of tests, carried out on the alcohol itself, has for its object the detection of nitrogen compounds.

To 50 c.c. of the sample add 1 or 2 drops of dilute sulphuric acid to give an acid reaction, and then 10 c.c. of distilled water. Evaporate the mixture on the water-bath down to a bulk of 10 or 12 c.c., and apply the following tests:—

(*e*). Make 5 c.c. of the liquid, in a test-tube, alkaline with a few drops of a 10 per cent. solution of potassium hydroxide, and pour in one or two drops of Nessler's reagent (alkaline solution of mercuric potassium iodide). If ammonia is present a yellow colour, or a reddish-brown precipitate, is produced.

(*f*). To 5 c.c. of the same residue add 5 c.c. of dilute sulphuric acid, and pour the liquid little by little, with shaking, into 5 c.c. of solution of bismuth–potassium iodide (10 grams of KI dissolved in 80 c.c. of water, and this solution divided into two equal parts. In one part 12 grams of sublimed BiI_3 are dissolved, then the remaining part of the KI solution added, and the mixture filtered. Kept protected from the light). Pure alcohol remains clear; if **pyridine bases** are present an orange-red precipitate forms, which is crystalline if amyl alcohol is absent.

The ordinary (95 per cent.) alcohol is usually transported in metal drums or other vessels, and often contains sensible traces of the common metals. These are tested for as follows.

To 100 c.c. of the alcohol add 10 c.c. of dilute acetic acid and an equal volume of water; and evaporate on the bath till reduced to 20 c.c. The residue thus obtained should give no precipitate or coloration with hydrogen sulphide or ammonia.

An objectionable, pungent odour which is sometimes present in both crude and refined alcohol appears to be due to an aldehydic constituent, which, according to E. Bauer,[1] is probably acrolein. The presence of this body is, in general, attributable to the decomposition of the fermentation-glycerol during distillation. Traces of ammonia may also have a deleterious effect upon the quality of the spirit. A leek-like odour and flavour are traceable to sulphur compounds; these may be present as free hydrogen sulphide and as sulphur in organic combination. As the latter is chiefly responsible for the objectionable odour, it is usually sufficient in analysing the spirit to determine the total sulphur, which may be done in the following manner. Not less than a litre of the alcohol is treated with an excess of bromine-water, then diluted with 300 c.c. of water, the alcohol distilled off, and the residue concentrated to a conveniently small bulk—say about 50 c.c. The sulphuric acid present is then precipitated with barium chloride solution in the usual manner, and the resulting barium sulphate weighed. Sulphur to the extent of 0·005 to 0·007 gram per litre was found by Bauer in crude molasses spirit.

The same author recommends that, in determining the acidity of alcohol, the spirit should first be heated to 63° to expel carbon dioxide. Cochineal and hæmatoxylin are preferable to phenolphthalein as indicators; Congo red and rosolic acid are useless.

An opalescence shown by a rectified spirit on dilution with water may be due to the presence of caoutchouc or other substances extracted from rubber, if the alcohol has been in contact with rubber tubing or washers.

Detection of water in "absolute" alcohol.—If the alcohol is shaken with anhydrous copper sulphate, the latter will become blue if the liquid contains water to the extent of about 0·8 per cent.

This test is applied to the "Absolute Alcohol" of the Pharmacopœia in the following form: "Anhydrous copper sulphate shaken occasionally during two or three hours in a well-closed vessel with about fifty times its weight of absolute alcohol does not assume a decidedly blue colour (absence of excess of water)." The limit of water allowed in the B.P. absolute alcohol is 1 per cent. by weight.

A still more delicate test is to shake the alcohol with a crystal or two of potassium permanganate. This salt is insoluble in absolute alcohol, but dissolves sufficiently to give the liquid a pink tinge if as little as 0·4 or 0·5 per cent. of water is present.

Calcium carbide may also be used to detect the presence of water

[1] *Proc. Seventh Int. Cong. Appl. Chem.*, London, 1909. Sec. VIB, 77–81.

in alcohol. Acetylene gas is liberated by the action of the water, and calcium hydroxide formed, rendering the liquid turbid.

For methods of estimating small quantities of water in alcohol *v. post* (p. 219.)

VIII. Determination of ethyl alcohol.—The ordinary methods of estimating ethyl alcohol when mixed with water only are dealt with in the chapter on Alcoholometry. In the following pages various special processes are given, including methods for the determination of ethyl alcohol in mixture with ether, chloroform, acetone, and other substances.

Chemical methods for the estimation of ethyl alcohol.—For the estimation of small quantities of alcohol chemically, oxidation with potassium dichromate and sulphuric acid may be employed.

Nicloux's method.—A series of six mixtures of dilute alcohol is prepared, containing respectively 0·2, 0·15, 0·1, 0·066, 0·05, and 0·033 per cent. of alcohol by volume. Of each of these mixtures, 5 c.c. are placed in test-tubes, 2 to 3 c.c. of strong sulphuric acid added, and then a solution of potassium dichromate (2·0 grams per 100 c.c.) is run in from a burette. Into the strongest alcoholic solution (0·2 per cent.) 2·0 c.c. of the dichromate are run, into the next 1·5 c.c., into the third 1·0 c.c., and so on. The dichromate is reduced, and the colour of the solution in each tube, after mixing its contents, becomes yellowish-green.

Six other tubes are prepared similarly, but adding now 0·1 c.c. of dichromate less than before in each case—*i.e.*, 1·9 c.c., 1·4 c.c., 0·9 c.c., and so on. These twelve tubes serve as standards.

The dilute solution of alcohol to be estimated is now treated in the same way, namely, to 5 c.c. of the alcohol sulphuric acid and dichromate solution are added. If 2 c.c. of the latter make the liquid yellow, the dichromate is in excess, and a smaller quantity is used in a repetition until the yellowish-green tint is obtained, after which the tube is compared with the standard most nearly approaching it in depth of colour. If the 2 c.c. of dichromate make the liquid green, the alcohol is in excess, and must be diluted accordingly before repeating the experiment.

Pozzi-Escot[1] found with Nicloux's method that it was essential to maintain absolutely identical conditions in the comparative experiments, and even then somewhat discordant results might be obtained in duplicate experiments. It is obvious that no substances other than alcohol which would reduce dichromate may be present.

Bordas and Raczkowski shortened the foregoing procedure by omitting the standards. They added 2·5 c.c. of strong sulphuric

[1] *Ann. Chim. Anal.*, 1902, 7, 11.

acid to 5 c.c. of the liquid to be tested, then 1·0 c.c. of the dichromate solution, and boiled the mixture. From what precedes, 1 c.c. of dichromate indicates 0·1 per cent. of alcohol when the transition-tint is obtained, and the experiment is repeated with more or with less of the dichromate, or with the sample further diluted, until the proper colour is given.

Blank and Finkenbeiner describe a modification of the dichromate oxidation process, which they apply to the estimation of small quantities of methyl alcohol, but which can equally be used for determining ethyl alcohol.[1] A very dilute aqueous solution of the alcohol is prepared, and mixed with an excess of decinormal dichromate acidified with sulphuric acid. After standing for some hours at the ordinary temperature, potassium iodide is added, and the mixture titrated back with decinormal thiosulphate solution. Each c.c. of dichromate used up represents 0·004 gram of methyl alcohol or 0·00575 gram of ethyl alcohol, as calculated from the equation :—

$$CH_3{\cdot}CH_2{\cdot}OH + O_2 = CH_3{\cdot}COOH + H_2O$$

for ethyl and the corresponding equation for methyl alcohol.

"Aeration" process.—Dox and Lamb[2] describe an "aeration" method of expelling alcohol from fermentation mixtures, absorbing it in sulphuric acid, and determining its amount by oxidation with dichromate. The acetic acid produced is distilled off and titrated.

The alcoholic liquid is saturated with neutral ammonium sulphate (80 grams in 100 c.c.), and is contained in a gas-washing bottle. This is connected at one end with a guard-flask of oxidising solution, and at the other with two cylinders containing concentrated sulphuric acid—the first about 18 c.c. and the second 8 to 10 c.c. Air is drawn through the apparatus at the rate of about 25 litres per hour ; this removes the alcohol from the solution, and the vapour of the alcohol is absorbed by the acid. The aeration is generally complete in eight to ten hours, but slightly higher results are obtained by aeration at a slower rate for twenty-four hours.

After the aeration is finished, the sulphuric acid is mixed with 10 to 15 grams of potassium dichromate in water in a distilling flask, and the cylinders well rinsed with water (free from carbon dioxide). The mixture is allowed to stand for about fifteen minutes, and then distilled carefully over a free flame, using asbestos board with a small circular opening for the bottom of the flask. To prevent bumping and foaming, a glass bead and two small pieces

[1] *J. Soc. Chem. Ind.*, 1906, **25**, 500.
[2] *J. Amer. Chem. Soc.*, 1916, **38**, 2565.

of pumice-stone are placed in the liquid. The volume of liquid in the flask should not become so low as to allow sulphuric acid to distil over. The distillate is titrated with decinormal alkali, and the distillation repeated with additions of water freed from carbon dioxide until the last titration shows less than 0·5 c.c. of decinormal alkali; this is generally reached after four or five distillations. Each c.c. of alkali = 0·004606 gram of alcohol.

Amounts of alcohol up to 2 grams can be determined accurately by this method, according to the authors' statements. In the presence of 0·5 gram or more, the sulphuric acid and dichromate solutions must be mixed carefully and cooled. The process has been used for the determination of alcohol in various kinds of silage, with very satisfactory results. The oxidising solution in the guard-flask is composed of dichromate, sulphuric acid, and water in the proportions of 1 : 2 : 7 by weight.

Estimation by conversion into iodoform.—The following method is described by Villedieu and Hébert[1] for the estimation of ethyl alcohol in dilute solutions containing 0·1 to 1 per cent., and is applied to the estimation of alcohol in urine. It depends upon the fact that, at a definite dilution, the quantity of alcohol converted into iodoform is constant. The iodoform is transformed into potassium iodide and the amount of this estimated volumetrically with silver nitrate.

Solutions are prepared containing quantities of alcohol varying from 0·1 to 1 per cent., and these solutions are treated as follows in order to obtain the value of the silver nitrate solution in terms of the different quantities of alcohol.

One hundred c.c. of the alcoholic solution are treated with 10 c.c. of 16 per cent. sodium hydroxide solution, and about 30 c.c. of 10·5 per cent. iodine solution are then added drop by drop. After three hours, a further small quantity of iodine solution is added, so that the mixture exhibits a yellow coloration. At the end of twenty-four hours the precipitated iodoform is collected on a filter and washed with cold water. With the smaller quantities of alcohol it is necessary to "seed" the mixture with a trace of iodoform in order to promote precipitation.

The filter and precipitate are now transferred to a flask, and boiled for twenty minutes under a reflux apparatus with 30 c.c. of saturated alcoholic potassium hydroxide solution. The contents of the flask are then acidified with nitric acid, 20 c.c. of $N/100$-silver nitrate solution are added, and the excess of silver nitrate titrated with $N/100$-thiocyanate solution. The number of c.c. of

[1] *J. Pharm. Chim.*, 1917 (vii), **15**, 41.

the silver nitrate solution required to precipitate the potassium iodide formed from the iodoform is thus obtained for the respective alcoholic solutions, and the numbers correspond with the quantities of alcohol present in the solutions.

Any dilute alcoholic solution of unknown strength is treated similarly, and the alcohol content ascertained from the volume of silver nitrate required to precipitate the resulting iodide.

To estimate alcohol in urine by this method, 200 c.c. of the sample, which must be free from acetone and aldehydes, are distilled after the addition of 1 c.c. of phosphoric acid, and 100 c.c. of distillate collected. This is treated as above described.

Oxidation with permanganate.—When only a small quantity of a very dilute solution of alcohol is available, an accurate estimation may be made by means of alkaline permanganate. In the following process, described by Barendrecht,[1] the alcohol is completely oxidised to carbon dioxide and water, and the quantity calculated from the volume of permanganate used up. Other oxidisable (non-volatile) substances such as sugar or extractive matters may be present; but if the proportion of these is considerable in relation to the alcohol-content, the liquid may be distilled and the determination carried out on the distillate. Ten c.c. of a solution containing about 0·2 per cent. of alcohol will suffice for the experiment.

In a hard glass flask of about 700 c.c. capacity are placed 100 c.c. of potassium permanganate solution (9·75 grams per litre) and 40 c.c. of sodium hydroxide solution (150 grams per litre), and the mixture is heated to boiling. Five c.c. of the alcoholic liquid, diluted if necessary to contain about 0·2 per cent. of alcohol, are then rapidly run in, and boiled for one minute. The flame is then removed. One hundred c.c. of oxalic acid solution (20 grams per litre) are now added, followed by 40 c.c. of sulphuric acid (2 vols. of acid, sp. gr. 1·84, mixed with 5 vols. of water) and the liquid shaken; after which the excess of oxalic acid is forthwith titrated with permanganate solution of strength 3·182 grams per litre.

Another 5 c.c. of the dilute alcohol solution are evaporated in a hard glass dish on the water-bath to expel the alcohol, and 5 c.c. of a sucrose solution (1 gram in 250 c.c. of water) are added to the residue. The foregoing operations are then repeated on this mixture.

The sucrose added (0·02 gram) corresponds with 28·05 c.c. of the $KMnO_4$ solution used in the titration. If A and B are the volumes in c.c. of permanganate used in the respective titrations, the weight

[1] *Zeitsch. anal. Chem.*, 1913, **32**, 304.

of alcohol present is obtained (in mg.) by multiplying the expression $A - (B - 28{\cdot}05)$ by the factor 0·384. Alternatively, by using the factor 0·483, the volume of the alcohol is given in c.mm.

Physical methods of estimating alcohol.—Apart from the usual method of estimation by means of the specific gravity and appropriate tables, which is dealt with at length in the chapter on "Alcoholometry," there are various other physical processes whereby the proportion of alcohol in an aqueous solution can be deduced. Some of the more interesting of these are described below. A passing reference will suffice for several of them, as they have no practical application—except possibly in occasional special circumstances.

Brewster's "**staktometer**" or drop-measurer is in the form of a bulbed pipette with a finely-tapering delivery tube. Filled with water, and then allowed to empty itself, it does so in a certain number of drops, which are counted. Filled with alcohol, and allowed to discharge similarly, the number of drops is much greater; it varies, in fact, according to the strength of the alcohol. Thus with a particular instrument distilled water gave 734 drops, and aqueous-alcohol of specific gravity 0·920 gave 2,117 drops. By constructing a table of the number of drops required for different proportions of alcohol, the instrument can therefore be used to ascertain alcoholic strengths.

Geissler's **vaporimeter** is designed to give the percentage of alcohol in a liquid by measuring the vapour pressure of the liquid. The lower end of a barometer tube is bent twice at right angles. At the extremity, which now points upwards, is fitted a stopcock, and also a detachable bulb. In this bulb the spirit is placed. The tube being charged with mercury, the bulb containing the alcohol is re-attached, the stopcock opened, and the alcohol vaporised by heating the bulb with hot water. A graduated scale on the tube shows the height to which the mercury is forced by pressure of the alcohol vapour, and the corresponding alcoholic strength is given by tables constructed for the instrument.

Dilatometers have also been devised for measuring percentages of alcohol by means of the expansion shown when a definite volume of the liquid is raised from one fixed temperature to another. The amount of expansion varies with the proportion of alcohol in the liquid (Silbermann).

Potassium carbonate, added in sufficient quantity to aqueous solutions of alcohol, absorbs the water and causes the alcohol to separate out. If the liquid is contained in a long glass tube fitted with a graduated scale, the volume of the alcohol layer can be read off. The scale is calibrated by experiments with alcohol solutions of known strength (Brande). For rough purposes, an ordinary stoppered glass graduated cylinder can be used.

Ebullioscope.—Obviously the foregoing methods will give results of only an approximate character. The following, however, is a tolerably accurate process for estimating alcohol in such articles as wine or beer, and is expeditious, especially where a number of determinations are required. It depends upon the principle that the boiling point of an alcoholic liquid is lower than that of water in proportion to the quantity of alcohol present. The special instrument devised for taking the boiling point is known as the *ebullioscope.* It was originally used for the purpose by the Abbé Broussard-Vidal, of Toulon, and later was improved by Malligand and Mlle. E. Broussard-Vidal.[1] Field in 1847 patented an "alcoholmeter" based on the same principle, and Ure subsequently made some improvements in Field's apparatus.

Essentially, Malligand's form of the ebullioscope consists of a boiling vessel fitted with a condenser and a special thermometer, and heated by a spirit lamp. The thermometer is graduated, not in temperature degrees, but in figures showing directly the percentage of alcohol by volume. A few years ago J. C. Cain tested Malligand's ebullioscope by the determination of alcohol in beer, comparing the results with those obtained by the distillation process; he found a satisfactory agreement.[2] Cain's description is essentially as follows:—

In making an experiment, distilled water is first placed in the lower part of the vessel (up to the mark inside), the lid screwed on, the thermometer inserted, the condenser filled with cold water and screwed in, and the water heated to boiling. The spirit lamp should be protected from draughts. When the water has boiled steadily for a short time, the mercury thread of the thermometer remains at one point, and the scale of the thermometer is then moved by means of the controlling screw until the zero point is coincident with the position of the end of the mercury thread. The water may be boiled until the steam begins to escape through the condenser, by which time the zero point will have been accurately ascertained.

This "setting" of the instrument renders unnecessary any other correction for barometric pressure. It is required on each day when the instrument is to be used.

After the zero point has been fixed and the vessel emptied of the water, the beer (at any ordinary temperature) is filled up to the

[1] *Compt. rend.*, 1874, **78**, 1470. [2] *Chem. News*, 1914, **109**, 37.

mark and boiled as described in the case of the water. Readings of the mercury are conveniently taken at fifteen seconds intervals, beginning when the regular boiling commences. The true boiling point is not reached until the beer has been boiling steadily for some time, when the mercury remains stationary for a period. The steady boiling is easily recognised by placing the ear near the top of the condenser, when a continuous bubbling is heard. If the boiling is continued, the mercury advances again after a time, and vapour escapes from the top of the condenser. The following readings, taken at fifteen seconds intervals, show the course of an experiment :—

5·95
5·9
5·85
5·8 ⎫
5·8 ⎬ True boiling point (in terms of alcohol percentage).
5·8 ⎪
5·8 ⎭
5·7
5·6
5·65
5·6—Alcohol escaping.

The result was therefore 5·8 per cent. of alcohol (by volume). Distillation gave the same result.

The solids present in beers and wines exert no practical influence on the boiling point, as their molecular weights are so great. Abbé Vidal had originally found that there was no sensible effect produced on the temperature of ebullition by such ingredients as sugar, if not present in greater amount than 15 per cent.

An adaptation of the instrument for use in determining the "original gravity" of beer has been described by T. H. Pope.[1]

Another form of ebullioscope for estimating alcohol in wines has been described by Ph. Malvezin[2], which claims to obviate certain sources of error, notably those arising from the presence of a high proportion of extract. The wine is contained in a conical vessel immersed in a conical water-bath, and there are two thermometers, one giving the temperature of the wine and the other that of the water-bath. The readings are referred to tables constructed from actual determinations. A figure of the instrument, but not the tables, is given in the *J. Soc. Chem. Ind.* for 1915, p. 846.

Using the following table, which is due to P. N. Evans,[3] it is possible to estimate approximately the percentage of alcohol in mixtures of alcohol and water by a simple determination of the boiling point. The table was constructed from observations made

[1] *Brewers' J.*, 1914, **50**, 239. [2] *Bull. Assoc. Chim. Sucr.*, 1915, **32**, 104.
[3] *J. Ind. Eng. Chem.*, 1916, **8**, 260–262.

when 500 c.c. of alcohol was distilled at a uniform rate of 1 drop per second. The temperature was noted when 7·5 c.c. had distilled over, and the distillation continued until 15 c.c. was collected. The mean of the percentages of alcohol in the liquid in the flask before and after distillation, as ascertained from the density, was taken to represent the composition of the liquid, and the percentage of alcohol in the distillate was taken to represent the composition of the vapour at the temperature observed when 7·5 c.c. of distillate had been collected. The temperatures given are corrected for barometric pressure and for the exposed mercury column of the thermometer.

Boiling points and condensing points of aqueous alcohol.

B.p.	Alcohol, per cent. by weight in		B.p.	Alcohol, per cent. by weight in		B.p.	Alcohol, per cent. by weight in	
	Liquid.	Vapour.		Liquid.	Vapour.		Liquid.	Vapour.
78·2°	91	92	82·0°	41	79	91·5°	8	55
78·4	85	89	82·5	36	78	92·0	8	53
78·6	82	88	83·0	33	78	92·5	7	51
78·8	80	87	83·5	30	77	93·0	6	49
79·0	78	86	84·0	27	76	93·5	6	46
79·2	76	85	84·5	25	75	94·0	5	44
79·4	74	85	85·0	23	74	94·5	5	42
79·6	72	84	85·5	21	73	95·0	4	39
79·8	69	84	86·0	20	72	95·5	4	36
80·0	67	83	86·5	18	71	96·0	3	33
80·2	64	83	87·0	17	70	96·5	3	30
80·4	62	82	87·5	16	69	97·0	2	27
80·6	59	82	88·0	15	68	97·5	2	23
80·8	56	81	88·5	13	67	98·0	1	19
81·0	53	81	89·0	12	65	98·5	1	15
81·2	50	80	89·5	11	63	99·0	—	10
81·4	47	80	90·0	10	61	99·5	—	5
81·6	45	80	90·5	10	59	100·0	0	0
81·8	43	79	91·0	9	57			

Rapid estimation.—A rapid process for determining the proportion of alcohol in a liquid has been described by D. Sidersky.[1] It depends upon the miscibility of ether with strong alcohol.

Twenty c.c. of the alcoholic liquid under examination and 10 c.c. of ether, sp. gr. 0·724, are shaken in a closed vessel. On standing, the liquids separate into two layers. Successive quantities of alcohol (98 per cent.) are now added from a special burette, the mixture being shaken between each addition. The volume of the ether–alcohol layer decreases as the proportion of alcohol increases, until it finally disappears on addition of a further drop of alcohol.

[1] *Bull. Assoc. Chim. Sucr.*, 1909, **27**, 562.

The total amount of alcohol which will cause the solution of the ether under these conditions is determined once for all by preliminary experiments. Deducting the amount run in from the burette gives the quantity in the 20 c.c. of liquid dealt with.

The burette used is so graduated as to show the percentage of alcohol in the sample directly. The vessel used for the mixing has a narrow neck, to facilitate observation of the two layers. (Patented; H. Rapeller.)

Solubility-curve method.—Anhydrous potassium fluoride dehydrates alcohol somewhat more effectively than potassium carbonate, and like the latter, when added in certain proportions it causes an aqueous solution of the alcohol to separate into two layers. If more water is added, separation no longer occurs, and at the point where this just happens the liquid contains, for a given temperature, definite proportions of fluoride and alcohol. Frankforter and Frary[1] have constructed a solubility curve of potassium fluoride in alcohol-water mixtures, and by means of it have devised a method of estimating alcohol based on the foregoing principle.

A weighed quantity of freshly-ignited potassium fluoride is introduced into a weighed stoppered flask, then a weighed quantity of the alcoholic solution is added, and the fluoride dissolved. The proportions of solution and fluoride are so chosen that the resulting liquid separates into two layers. Water is then added drop by drop from a burette, with frequent shaking, until the solution is just homogeneous again at 25°; the whole is then weighed again. Thus the total quantity of liquid and of fluoride is known; and by reference to the following table (or a curve plotted from it) the quantity of alcohol in the homogeneous liquid, and therefore in the original solution, can be calculated.

The method is not applicable to solutions, such as beer, containing a large quantity of dissolved solids. Moreover it will, of course, be understood that the process is not given as one for use in the ordinary estimations of alcohol, but as one based upon a different principle from those of the usual methods, and of theoretical interest.

A modification of the method, whereby it can be used for estimating alcohol in tinctures, etc., has been described by Haines and Marden.[2] Weighing is dispensed with, the volume of the separated alcohol being read off in centrifuge tubes. These are of 15 c.c. capacity, graduated to 0·1 c.c., and carefully calibrated so that readings can be estimated to 0·01 c.c. Ten c.c. of the sample are taken, unless the alcoholic strength is 50 per cent. or more,

[1] *Eighth Int. Cong. App. Chem.*, 1912; *J. Phys. Chem.*, 1913, **17**, 402.
[2] *J. Ind. Eng. Chem.*, 1917, **9**, 1126.

in which case 5 c.c. are diluted with water to 10 c.c. in the tube. Dry potassium fluoride is then added until the volume in the tube reads about 13 c.c., and a small crystal of malachite green is dropped in to colour the alcohol layer. The tube is then closed with a well-fitting stopper, shaken vigorously for two minutes, and centrifuged for two or three minutes. The alcohol separates in an upper layer. Its volume is then read off. If its temperature is not 15·6°, a correction can be applied, based on the consideration that the variation in volume per 1° is approximately 0·001 c.c. for each c.c. of alcohol. Further, since traces of alcohol are still

TERNARY SYSTEM WATER, ALCOHOL, AND POTASSIUM FLUORIDE. (FRANKFORTER AND FRARY.)

Grams per 100 c.c. of solvent.					
Fluoride.	Alcohol.	Fluoride.	Alcohol.	Fluoride.	Alcohol.
60	2·82	40	6·32	20	23·4
59	2·92	39	6·65	19	25·1
58	3·02	38	7·01	18	26·9
57	3·13	37	7·40	17	28·8
56	3·24	36	7·83	16	30·8
55	3·36	35	8·30	15	32·9
54	3·48	34	8·81	14	35·0
53	3·61	33	9·37	13	37·2
52	3·75	32	9·98	12	39·4
51	3·90	31	10·64	11	41·7
50	4·06	30	11·36	10	44·0
49	4·23	29	12·14	9	46·4
48	4·41	28	12·99	8	49·0
47	4·60	27	13·92	7	51·9
46	4·80	26	14·94	6	55·1
45	5·01	25	16·07	5	58·7
44	5·24	24	17·33	4	62·8
43	5·48	23	18·74	3	67·5
42	5·74	22	20·26	2	78·6
41	6·02	21	21·80	—	—

retained in the fluoride layer, an addition of 0·15 c.c. should be made to the observed reading, taken from the bottom of the meniscus. With careful readings fairly accurate results can be obtained, namely, to within about ± 0·4 per cent. A solution containing 1 per cent. of alcohol just shows the presence of the latter by this method. Liquids such as acetone, essential oils, etc., must be absent; and if the addition of the fluoride produces a precipitate, the sample should be distilled before applying the test. Whisky, however, can be analysed without distillation if it is first clarified with alumina cream.

MM. Duboux and Dutoit[1] consider that the determination of the **critical temperature of solution** as described below affords a more rapid and sensitive method of estimating alcohol than the determination of the specific gravity. The liquids found to give the best results as solvents were: (*A*), a mixture of 5 volumes of aniline with 3 volumes of 95 per cent. alcohol; and (*B*), a mixture of 1 volume of nitrobenzene with 9 volumes of 95 per cent. alcohol. On mixing 15 c.c. of liquid *A* with 10 c.c. of an aqueous solution of alcohol, and heating the mixture, the critical temperature of solution varied proportionately with the amount of alcohol in the aqueous solution, at the rate of 2·35° for each 1 per cent. Similarly, in the case of liquid *B*, each 1 per cent. of alcohol caused the critical temperature of solution to vary by 1·2°.

The apparatus required consists of a test-tube 3·5 cm. in diameter and about 15 cm. long, closed by a cork, through which is passed a thermometer graduated in tenths of a degree, and a glass stirring-rod (bent to a circle at the end) which can move freely through another opening. Fifteen c.c. of the liquid *A* and 10 c.c. of the alcoholic distillate (*e.g.*, from wine) are gently heated and stirred in the tube until the turbidity suddenly disappears. On now cooling the liquid the turbidity should reappear at the same temperature, and this is noted as the critical temperature of solution. The result may then be checked with liquid *B* in the place of *A*.

To establish the relationship between the critical temperature of solution and the proportion of alcohol, three solutions are prepared, containing approximately 8, 10, and 12 per cent. of alcohol, the exact quantities being found by determinations of the specific gravities. Then, by plotting a curve in which the percentages of alcohol form the ordinates and the respective critical temperatures of solution the abscissæ, the percentage of alcohol corresponding with a given critical temperature of solution may be found.

Applied to the distillates from wines, the method gave results rather higher (0·1 per cent.) than those obtained from the specific gravity. This is attributed to the presence of traces of substances other than alcohol and water, and affecting the critical temperature more than the specific gravity.

Estimation of traces of water in alcohol.—According to Nussbaum,[2] a mixture of equal volumes of absolute alcohol and light petroleum is homogeneous when heated slightly, but becomes turbid when cooled. The point at which the turbidity

[1] *Ann. Chim. Anal.*, 1908, **13**, 4.

[2] *J. Pharm. Chim.*, 1917, **15**, 230; *J. Chem. Soc.* (Abst.), 1917, **112**, ii, 215.

appears is sharply defined, but is raised by about 16° when the alcohol contains 1 per cent. of water.

The presence of water in alcohol may therefore be ascertained, and its quantity estimated, by determining the temperature at which the alcohol gives a turbidity when mixed with an equal volume of light petroleum. It is necessary, however, to make preliminary tests with light petroleum and quantities of alcohol containing definite amounts of water, because the point at which the turbidity is observed depends on the kind of light petroleum used.

The same principle—determining the critical temperature of solution—has also been applied by V. Rodt for the estimation of **very small quantities of water** in alcohol.[1] The solvent employed is a mixture of transformer oil and commercial paraffin oil. To standardise it, perfectly anhydrous alcohol must be prepared, which is done as follows. About 2 litres of 99 per cent. alcohol are placed in a large flask with 300 grams of quicklime, and the flask is suspended in a water-bath which can be quickly removed. The alcohol is gently boiled for some days under a reflux condenser protected by a phosphorus pentoxide guard-tube. The condenser is then reversed and arranged to deliver the distillate into a wide, corked burette, also guarded with moisture-absorption tubes. Successive portions of alcohol are distilled over into the burette and tested as follows with the solvent until a constant minimum value is obtained.

For the test, all the apparatus must be dried in an oven at 150°, and every precaution taken against access of atmospheric moisture.

An Erlenmeyer flask of about 50 c.c. capacity fitted with a rubber stopper is accurately tared, a few drops of water are introduced rapidly from a pipette, and the weight noted. Then 15 to 25 c.c. of alcohol are drawn from the distillation burette and the flask is weighed again, so that the gravimetric composition of the aqueous alcohol is accurately known. The rubber stopper is replaced by another, which has also been dried in the oven, and has two holes ; through one of these passes a standardised thermometer, reading to 0·2°, and through the other a short glass rod. The glass rod is withdrawn, the point of a burette being inserted through the hole, and a measured volume of the solvent is run in, calculated from its specific gravity to amount to 12/13 by weight of the alcohol employed. The measurement should be accurate to 0·1 c.c. The rod is then replaced ; the contents of the flask are warmed with gentle rotation until the liquid is perfectly clear, and rotation is continued while cooling, until a sudden sharp clouding of the solution

[1] *Mitt. K. Materialprüf.*, 1915, **33**, 426 ; *Analyst*, 1916, **41**, 316.

appears. The temperature at which this occurs is the critical temperature. It may be noted with an accuracy of 0·2°, which corresponds with 0·01 per cent. of water in the alcohol.

For a given oil, a standardisation curve is plotted, using different proportions of water to alcohol. This curve may be used subsequently for rapid and simple estimations of water in strong alcohol according to the foregoing procedure, *mutatis mutandis.* The rise of critical temperature is almost a straight line function of the percentage of water within the limits of 0 to 2·5 per cent.

M. Jones and A. Lapworth have used α-bromonaphthalene for the determination of water in moist alcohol.[1] Weighed quantities of the alcohol and bromonaphthalene are mixed, and the solution is cooled down slowly until clouding appears. An opalescence occurs just above the critical point, but this is easily distinguished from the true critical point, when the liquid suddenly becomes opaque. The temperature at which this occurs is noted : it varies with the percentage of water in the alcohol if the concentration of the bromonaphthalene is constant, and also with the concentration when this varies. A table of values has been constructed, showing the percentage of water corresponding with various concentrations and temperatures : for this and details of manipulation, the original paper should be consulted.

Ethyl alcohol in the presence of methyl alcohol. —Where a considerable proportion of ethyl alcohol is mixed with methyl alcohol, the refractometer, as already explained, will both show the presence and indicate approximately the proportion of the ethyl alcohol. Or the proportions of the two may be deduced from the density of the mixed iodides (Bardy and Meker's method) ; or the methyl alcohol may be estimated separately by one of the methods described earlier, and the ethyl alcohol taken by difference.

But when only a small quantity of ethyl alcohol is contained in a large volume of methyl alcohol, the problem of its detection and estimation becomes more difficult. With such proportions as one or two per cent. of ethyl alcohol probably Berthelot's well-known method is the best. It depends upon the conversion of the ethyl alcohol into ethylene by means of sulphuric acid, and the absorption of the ethylene in bromine with the formation of ethylene dibromide, which can be separated and measured. The details of this process as used officially in France are given by M. Louis Calvet[2] as follows.

Into a flask of about 2 litres capacity fitted with a safety-funnel and connected with a wash bottle containing water, are poured

[1] *Trans. Chem. Soc.*, 1914, **105**, 1086. [2] "Alcools," p. 154.

350 c.c. of sulphuric acid at 66° Bé. To this is added carefully 50 c.c. of the methyl alcohol, avoiding too much rise of temperature. The reaction is allowed to proceed during half an hour, after which the flask is heated, at first gently, and then more rapidly and strongly. The vapours given off are passed through the wash bottle to remove sulphur dioxide, and collected in a bell-jar of 2 litres capacity, over water. When the jar is full, which will be in the course of about an hour and a half, the gases are passed through another wash-bottle containing a solution of potassium hydroxide, and then through an absorption bulb containing bromine covered with a little water. To the outlet of the bulb a washing jar containing caustic potash solution is attached to absorb any bromine vapour carried over.

When the operation is finished, the contents of the absorption bulb are poured into dilute alkali solution, which absorbs the excess of bromine, leaving the ethylene dibromide undissolved, in the form of oily droplets. The volume of the dibromide is measured; each 0·1 c.c. corresponds with about 1 per cent. of ethyl alcohol in the liquid taken for analysis.

Denigès has described a method for detecting ethyl alcohol in the presence of methyl alcohol, which can also be used for estimating the proportion. The process is based upon the fact that ethyl alcohol is readily oxidised to acetaldehyde by means of bromine water, whereas methyl alcohol under similar conditions is not appreciably affected.[1]

A mixture of 0·2 c.c. of the alcohol to be tested and 5 c.c. of bromine water (0·3 c.c. of Br in 50 c.c. of water) is heated in a boiling water-bath for a period of five to six minutes, unless the colour is discharged sooner. The mixture is then cooled, and if still coloured, a solution of sodium sulphite (commercial, 36 to 40° Bé., diluted to one-fifth strength) is added drop by drop until the colour just disappears. Then 5 c.c. of fuchsin-bisulphite solution are added, and the mixture allowed to stand for five to eight minutes. In the presence of ethyl alcohol a red or reddish-violet colour is developed, the intensity of which is proportional to the amount of ethyl alcohol present. One per cent. of ethyl alcohol can thus be detected, and the method can be made quantitative by comparing the colour with that obtained from standard solutions containing known quantities of ethyl and methyl alcohols.

The fuchsin-bisulphite solution is best prepared by adding 10 c.c. of sodium bisulphite solution (30° Bé.) to 1 litre of an aqueous solution of fuchsin (0·1 per cent.), and when the colour has become

[1] *Bull. Soc. chim.*, 1910, **7**, 951.

faint, mixing in 10 c.c. of concentrated hydrochloric acid solution. With very small quantities a blank experiment on pure methyl alcohol is made, for comparison.

In the absence of methyl alcohol, or if only a small proportion is present, ethyl alcohol is detected by adding an equal volume of methyl alcohol to the sample under examination, and applying the test as described. In examining very dilute solutions (0·5 to 3·0 per cent.), the mixture to be heated is made by adding 0·2 c.c. of methyl alcohol and 0·03 c.c. of bromine to 5 c.c. of the alcohol for testing.

Determination of alcohol in chloroform.—Small quantities of alcohol are often added to chloroform as a preservative, especially to chloroform intended for pharmaceutical purposes. The British Pharmacopœia requires 2 per cent. of absolute alcohol to be added. For quantities of this order the following method is satisfactory.

Fifty c.c. of the sample are extracted in a separator with strong sulphuric acid, first with 20 c.c., again with 20 c.c., and finally with 10 c.c. The acid extracts are run into 200 c.c. of water, and distilled gently until 100 c.c. have been collected. The distillate is saturated with salt and extracted with petroleum ether to remove any traces of chloroform, and then distilled again, the distillate made up to 100 c.c. with water, and the proportion of alcohol determined from the specific gravity in the usual manner.

For the *detection* of alcohol in chloroform the same method may be used for the extraction, except that 10 c.c. will usually suffice, with proportionately smaller quantities of acid and water, and the treatment with petroleum ether is not necessary. To the distillate from the acid the iodoform test is applied, supplemented if desired by any others of the qualitative tests already described. Take 10 c.c. of the distillate, add 6 drops of a 10 per cent. solution of potassium hydroxide, and warm the liquid to about 50°. A solution of potassium iodide saturated with free iodine is next added drop by drop with agitation, until the liquid becomes permanently yellowish-brown in colour, when it is carefully decolorised with potassium hydroxide solution If ethyl alcohol is present, iodoform is gradually deposited at the bottom of the tube in yellow crystals.[1]

Nicloux's method for estimating alcohol in chloroform is given in some foreign pharmacopœias, and is often useful, though not very accurate as described. Five c.c. of the sample are shaken with 20 c.c. of water to extract the alcohol; 5 c.c. of the aqueous-alcoholic extract (which should contain not more than 0·2 per cent.

[1] Hager, as quoted by Baskerville and Hamor, *J. Ind. Eng. Chem.*, 1912, **4**, 502.

of alcohol) are mixed in a test-tube with 0·1 to 0·2 c.c. of a solution of potassium bichromate (19 grams per litre), and then with pure sulphuric acid (D = 1·84), added cautiously. When the acid is in sufficient quantity (4·5 to 6 c.c.) the solution is decolorised, and the liquid is now gradually titrated with the bichromate solution, being shaken and gently warmed after each addition, until the colour changes from greenish-blue to a permanent greenish colour. This change is most readily recognised in solutions containing less than 0·2 per cent. of alcohol.

It is advisable to make a second experiment in which the amount of dichromate used in the first determination, less 0·1 c.c., is run in at once, the sulphuric acid added, and the liquid heated to boiling. The contents of the tube should remain greenish-blue, whilst in another determination in which 0·1 c.c. of dichromate *more* than the first reading is added, the colour should change to greenish-yellow. The number of c.c. consumed, divided by 1,000, gives the amount of absolute alcohol in c.c. per c.c. of solution. When the proportion of alcohol is less than 0·1 per cent., the strength of the dichromate solution should be doubled.

As mentioned above, this method does not give very accurate results, the reason being that all the alcohol is not removed by the treatment described. This can be done, however, by shaking the chloroform with twice its volume of water, separating the aqueous extract, and repeating the operation at least ten times. The combined extracts are then made up to a definite volume, and a suitable quantity taken for the oxidation.

Another useful method for the detection of alcohol in chloroform is one proposed by Thresh.[1] The sample of chloroform is shaken with an equal volume of water, the aqueous extract distilled with sulphuric acid and potassium dichromate, and the distillate tested for acetaldehyde by passing it into a tube containing a few c.c. of a strong (syrupy) solution of caustic soda. The liquid in the tube is boiled for a few seconds, and then set aside for a couple of hours. A yellow colour and a characteristic odour are developed, and if the proportion of aldehyde is sufficient, flocks of the aldehyde-resin are deposited. The general directions given by Thresh for the oxidation of dilute alcohol solutions are to use 100 c.c., 2 c.c. of saturated solution of potassium dichromate, and 8 c.c. of a dilute sulphuric acid (equal quantities of B.P. acid and water), distilling 20 c.c. of the mixture. As applied to the detection of alcohol in chloroform, one-fourth of these quantities, or less, can be taken. Thresh made the method approximately quantitative by colori-

[1] *Chem. News*, 1878, **38**, 251.

metric estimation of the resin produced (dissolved in warm alcohol and diluted to match standard solutions), but the method already given is preferable when quantitative results are required.

Estimation of ethyl alcohol in mixture with acetone.—Where the proportion is not too small, an approximate determination of the alcohol can be made by converting it into ethyl iodide and measuring the volume of this. The following process can be used for mixtures of alcohol and acetone containing 10 per cent. and upwards of alcohol. If more than a small proportion of water is present—about 5 per cent., say—the mixture should first be dehydrated with lime or potassium carbonate.

Where the proportion of alcohol is likely to be low—not more than 20 to 40 per cent. by volume, say—20 c.c. of the mixture are taken, and added to 20 grams of iodine in a small flask, together with 5 c.c. of water: the latter helps to regulate the reaction. Two grams of amorphous phosphorus are then added, the flask attached to a small reflux condenser, and the action allowed to proceed for about ten minutes. If the action becomes too violent, the flask must be cooled a little.

When the reaction is over and the flask has cooled down, the condenser is reversed and the mixture distilled. The ethyl iodide is collected under 15 c.c. of water contained in a graduated 25 c.c. cylinder, surrounded by a bath of cold water; and the distillation is continued as far as practicable in order to obtain the whole of the ethyl iodide. The delivery-tube should dip under the surface of the water in the cylinder; and it should preferably be a bulbed tube, to guard against liability to back-suction due to absorption of hydriodic acid gas by the water. When the iodide is all collected it should be allowed to settle for some hours, and the volume read off. Each c.c. of iodide = 0·573 gram of ethyl alcohol.

With higher proportions of alcohol 15 c.c. or 10 c.c. of the acetone–alcohol mixture should be taken, and treated in the same manner, but using 30 grams of iodine and 3 grams of amorphous phosphorus, instead of the preceding quantities. Where nothing is known as to the probable proportion of alcohol, or indicated by the specific gravity and refraction of the dehydrated sample, a preliminary experiment should be made, using 10 c.c., and the larger quantities of iodine and phosphorus, and the experiment repeated with any necessary modification.

Detection of alcohol (and aldehyde) in presence of acetone.—According to H. Agulhon,[1] a reagent prepared by dissolving 0·5 gram

[1] *Ann. Chim. Anal.*, 1912, **17**, 50.

of potassium dichromate in 100 c.c. of pure nitric acid, sp. gr. 1·310, gives a blue colour at once, in the cold, with alcohols and aldehydes, but does not react with ketones until after some hours' contact. One c.c. of pure acetone with 3 c.c. of the reagent develops an olive-green colour only after three hours ; a solution of acetone (1 : 5) requires twenty-four hours to form the colour. With solutions of alcohol, and of formaldehyde, a blue colour appears in one or two minutes at a dilution of 1 in 200 ; with double this dilution no colour appears. Approximate determinations of the alcohol or aldehyde can be made colorimetrically by means of the reagent.

Estimation of acetone in presence of ethyl alcohol.—J. Rakshit modifies Messinger's method by substituting lime water or baryta water for caustic potash solution, with the view of diminishing the error due to formation of iodoform from the ethyl alcohol.[1]

The sample to be examined, containing about 0·05 gram of acetone, is placed in a 750 c.c. flask, and 300 c.c. of freshly-prepared lime-water added ; the flask is loosely closed with a rubber cork, and heated to about 35°. Drop by drop 5 c.c. of *N*/5-iodine solution are added, and the mixture shaken for five minutes, then another 5 c.c. of iodine are similarly added with shaking, and so on until 40 c.c. of iodine have been run in. If during the addition the colour of the iodine persists after thorough shaking, more lime-water should be added. Ten minutes after the final addition of iodine, a few drops of starch solution are added, the contents of the flask shaken and cooled, 15 c.c. of *N*/1-sulphuric acid run in, and the excess of iodine titrated with *N*/10-thiosulphate. The number of c.c. of *N*/5-iodine used up, multiplied by 0·00193, gives the quantity of acetone present.

Each c.c. of ethyl alcohol present was found to use up 0·8 c.c. of *N*/5-iodine, and this correction should be applied. Accurate results are given with 1 part of acetone to 10 of alcohol ; with 1 to 100 parts of alcohol the results are less satisfactory, as the correction is then relatively great.

Estimation of ethyl alcohol in ethyl ether.—When the proportion of alcohol is not too small, the following table, due to Meker,[2] may be used to ascertain the proportion from the density of the mixture. The latter, if not anhydrous, should be dehydrated by treatment with potassium carbonate.

[1] *Analyst*, 1916, **41**, 245.
[2] Calvet, "Alcools," p. 343.

ABSOLUTE ALCOHOL AND ETHER; PROPORTIONS BY VOLUME.

Alcohol, D_{15} = 0·795; Ether, D_{15} = 0·720.

Ether.	Alcohol.	Density at 15°.	Ether.	Alcohol.	Density at 15°.
100	0	0·720	50	50	0·7635
95	5	0·726	40	60	0·771
90	10	0·731	30	70	0·7775
85	15	0·7355	20	80	0·784
80	20	0·740	10	90	0·790
70	30	0·748	0	100	0·795
60	40	C·756			

For alcohol of 95 per cent. strength the densities are as follows :—

Ether.	Alcohol, 95 per cent.	Density at 15°.	Ether.	Alcohol, 95 per cent.	Density at 15°.
95	5	0·727	80	20	0·744
90	10	0·733	70	30	0·755
85	15	0·739	60	40	0·7655

When the amount of alcohol is too small to be determined by means of the density the following process, due to P. Szeberényi[1] may be adopted. It is based upon the fact that alcohol is readily oxidised by a moderately acid solution of potassium dichromate, whilst ether is but slightly affected.

Five c.c. of the sample are diluted with water to 100 c.c. Thirty c.c. of this are placed in a 500 c.c. flask, into which have already been introduced 10 c.c. of *N*/2-dichromate, 20 c.c. of dilute sulphuric acid (1 : 1), and 40 c.c. of water. After boiling for fifteen minutes under a vertical condenser, and cooling, the excess of dichromate is titrated iodometrically. Anything above 0·9 c.c. of dichromate used represents 0·64 mg. of alcohol for each c.c. The exact quantity of dichromate used up by ether must be determined by experiment.

For somewhat larger amounts of alcohol, 5 c.c. of the aqueous solution are taken with 20 c.c. of the dichromate, 55 c.c. of water, and 20 c.c. of the dilute sulphuric acid. In such cases, no correction need be made for the dichromate used up by the ether.

If the ether is also to be estimated, a 2 per cent. aqueous solution is prepared, and 10 c.c. are treated for alcohol, as described. Another 10 c.c. are then placed in a stoppered 500 c.c. flask with addition of 40 c.c. of *N*/2-dichromate and 40 c.c. of sulphuric acid previously mixed with 10 c.c. of water, and cooled. After waiting for twelve hours, the contents of the flask are diluted with 400–500 c.c. of water, and the excess of dichromate is titrated as before.

After deducting from the result the dichromate used up by the alcohol (multiplied by 1·1), the proportion of ether is found by multiplying the number of c.c. reduced by the factor 4·6.

[1] *Zeitsch. anal. Chem.*, 1915, **54**, 409–11.

The following approximate method for the determination of alcohol and ether in a mixture of the two is described by J. Fleischer and H. Frank.[1]

When 10 c.c. of a mixture of alcohol and ether are treated with 5 c.c. each of benzene and water, separation takes place, the alcohol going into the aqueous layer and the ether into the benzene layer. The proportions of alcohol and ether can then be determined approximately by the increase in volume of the two layers.

If the alcohol–ether mixture already contains water, the specific gravity of the mixture must first be ascertained. The volume of the ether is then determined in the foregoing manner. The specific gravity D of the aqueous alcohol in the original mixture is calculated from the formula

$$D = \frac{10d - 0{\cdot}729a}{10 - a},$$

where d = the specific gravity of the original mixture, a = the number of c.c. of ether found in the 10 c.c., and 0·729 = the sp. gr. of ether. From the value of D the percentage of alcohol is obtained from the tables as usual.

For determining small amounts of water and alcohol in "anæsthetic" ether a process has been worked out by Mallinckrodt and Alt.[2] It depends upon the removal of the water by means of a weighed quantity of potassium carbonate, any alcohol remaining with the carbonate being eliminated by washing with absolute ether. The operations are carried out in a Regnault pyknometer as used for estimating the specific gravity of solids, and the increase in weight of the potassium carbonate gives the quantity of water in the ether treated.

To determine the alcohol, another portion (100 grams) of the sample is dehydrated by treating it in a stoppered flask for fourteen hours with freshly-dried potassium carbonate (40 grams). The specific gravity of the anhydrous mixture of ether and alcohol is then ascertained, and the proportion of alcohol read off from a curve which has been constructed with data given by mixtures of ether and alcohol in known amounts. For these data and the details of manipulation the original paper should be consulted.

A simpler procedure has been described by R. L. Perkins, who determines both alcohol and water from the specific gravity of the sample, taken before and after dehydration with potassium carbonate.[3]

[1] *Chem. Zeit.*, 1907, **31**, 665. [2] *J. Ind. Eng. Chem.*, 1916, **8**, 807.
[3] *Ibid.* 1917, **9**, 521.

The specific gravity of the ether is taken at 25°/25°. From 100 to 200 c.c. are then placed in a flask, 30–50 grams of (dry) potassium carbonate added, and the mixture allowed to stand for twenty-four hours, with occasional shaking. The specific gravity of the treated ether is then again determined. By reference to a graph constructed from the undermentioned data the percentages of both alcohol and water are obtained.

Pure anhydrous ether has the sp. gr. 0·70968 at 25°/25°. Mixtures of this with known quantities of "absolute" alcohol (0 to 4 per cent.) and water (0 to 1 per cent.) were made, and gave the specific gravities shown in the table below. The alcohol contained 0·8 per cent. of water by weight, thus introducing the small quantities of water (0·006, 0·012, etc.) shown in the second column. The percentages are by volume.

ETHER, ALCOHOL, AND WATER MIXTURES (PERKIN).

Alcohol per cent. by vol.	Water, per cent. by volume.					
	0·00		0·25	0·50	0·75	1·00
	Water in alcohol.	Specific gravity at 25°/25°.				
0	0·000	0·70968	0·71100	0·71240	0·71370	—
1	0·006	0·71092	0·71219	0·71358	0·71490	0·71622
2	0·012	0·71205	0·71333	0·71474	0·71612	0·71742
3	0·018	0·71322	0·71447	0·71581	0·71720	0·71850
4	0·025	0·71429	0·71556	0·71691	0·71828	0·71957

The value of the specific gravity obtained for the dehydrated ether is referred to the lowest curve in the accompanying diagram. This gives the percentage of alcohol in the dehydrated ether, which is practically that in the original sample. (A correction could be made on account of the water removed, but it would always be less than 0·05 per cent.)

The intersection of a vertical line through the point thus found with the horizontal line representing the specific gravity of the *original* sample indicates the quantity of water in the sample. If the point of intersection falls on one of the curves, the percentage of water is shown by that curve. If it falls between two curves, the percentage is obtained by interpolation of the vertical distance between them.

Estimation of small amounts of benzene in alcohol.—The following method is due to Holde and Winterfeld.[1]

[1] *Chem. Zeit.*, 1908, **32**, 313; (Abst.) *Analyst*, **33**, 242.

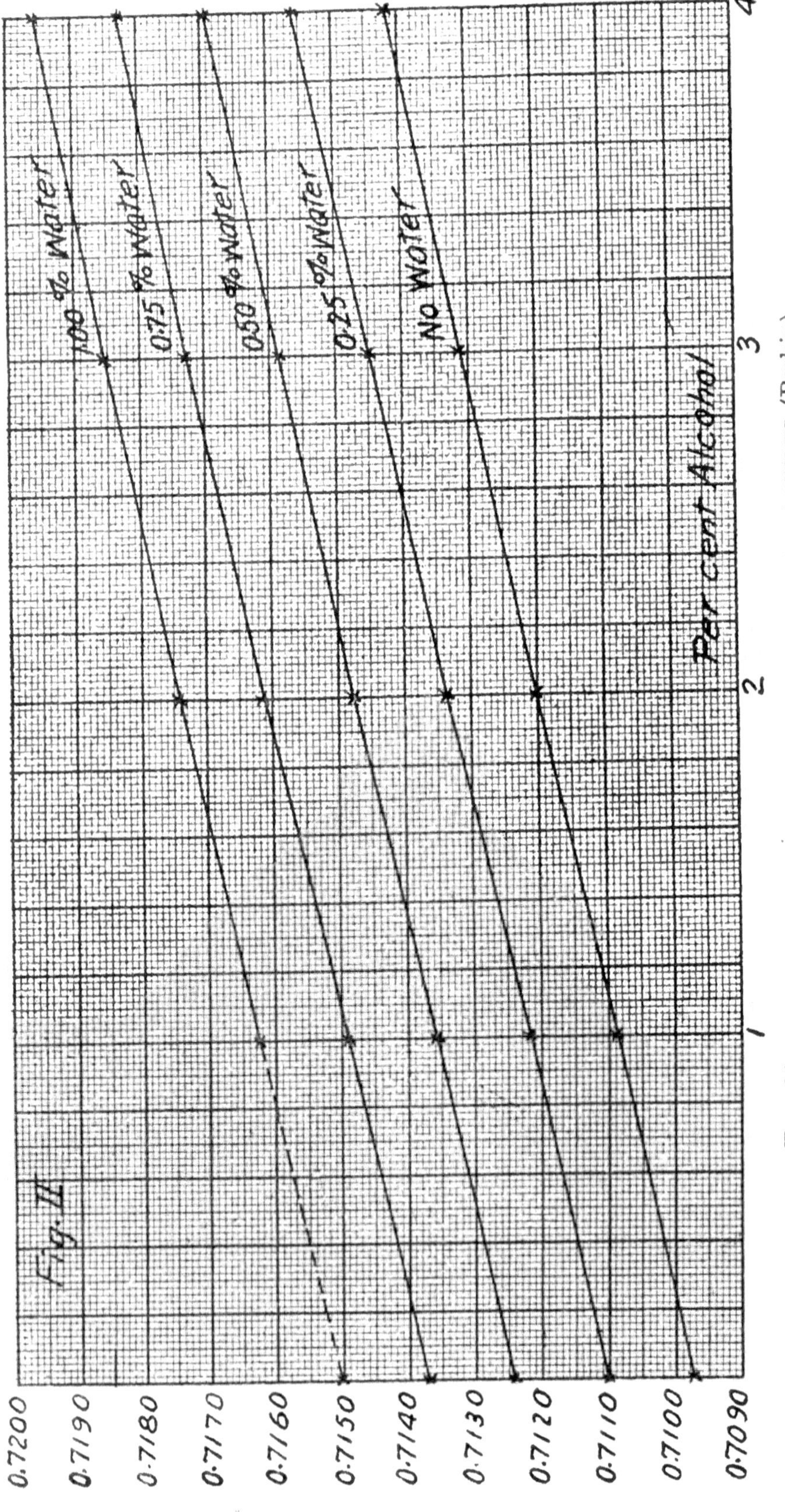

Fig. 31.—Graph for Ether, Alcohol, and Water Mixtures (Perkin).

It is based upon the fact that on distillation the whole of the benzene passes over in the first 10 per cent. of the distillate, and appears as an oily layer floating on the surface.

One hundred c.c. of the alcohol under examination, diluted with sufficient water to bring the alcoholic strength to 24·7 per cent. by weight, are distilled, and the first 10 c.c. of the distillate collected in a flask cooled with ice-cold water. On diluting this distillate with 10 to 20 c.c. of water and transferring it to a measuring cylinder or a burette, the proportion of separated benzene may be read directly. The benzene remaining dissolved in the turbid lower layer amounts to about 0·3 per cent. by volume, and is practically constant whether the original quantity of benzene be 0·5 or 5 per cent.

A modification of this method, due to Wolff,[1] can be used for the determination of ether in alcohol, as well as benzene.

One hundred c.c. of the sample are diluted until the specific gravity is 0·96, and distilled into a graduated cylinder (100 c.c. capacity) until 20 c.c. have been collected. The delivery-tube of the condenser should dip at least 3 cm. into the cylinder.

To the distillate 80 c.c. of a concentrated sodium chloride solution are added, the mixture shaken vigorously twenty times, and allowed to stand. The volume of the upper layer gives the proportion of ether (or benzene) in the sample.

Bubbles of ether entrained by the sodium chloride are easily freed by turning or tapping the cylinder. The error of experiment is usually less than 0·5 per cent. If the alcohol contains more than about 12 to 13 per cent. of ether, 50 or 25 c.c. are taken for distillation, instead of 100 c.c.

Mixtures of ethyl iodide and ethyl alcohol.—The boiling points of various mixtures of ethyl iodide and ethyl alcohol have been determined by S. C. Jana and J. N. S. Gupta.[2] At normal pressure, the results were as follows :—

Per cent. of ethyl iodide in mixture.	B.p.	Per cent. of ethyl iodide in mixture.	B.p.
26·69	70·2°	78·36	61·9
35·69	68·8	84·87	61·4
41·38	67·0	88·35	61·3
52·86	64·8	90·50	61·5
57·28	64·0	94·50	62·0
62·70	63·3	97·63	64·0
69·42	62·2		

A mixture containing 87 per cent. of ethyl iodide and 13 per cent. of alcohol distilled as a homogeneous liquid at 61·2°.

Determination of alcohol in the presence of phenol.—If alcohol is separated from phenol by distilling a

[1] *Chem. Zeit.*, 1910, **34**, 1193. [2] *J. Amer. Chem. Soc.*, 1914, **36**, 115.

strongly alkaline solution of the two substances, the distillate will contain some phenol, due to dissociation of the alkali phenate. According to J. Ehrlich,[1] a complete separation is obtained if the phenol is converted into tribromophenol before distilling. A preliminary separation by distillation from alkali is, however, desirable unless the quantity of phenol is small.

Fifty c.c. of the sample are measured into a 300 c.c. flask containing 30 c.c. of water, and made strongly alkaline with about 20 c.c. of sodium hydroxide solution. The liquid is then distilled into a 50 c.c. flask containing 1 or 2 c.c. of water, the end of the condenser being extended so that it almost touches the level of the liquid in the receiver. When nearly 50 c.c. of distillate have been collected, the contents of the receiver are made up to the mark, shaken, and 25 c.c. measured out into another 300 c.c. flask containing 30 c.c. of water. The phenol is precipitated by adding bromine water drop by drop in slight excess, and the liquid at once decolorised with a few drops of normal solution of sodium thiosulphate. Sufficient strong sodium hydroxide solution is then added to dissolve the tribromophenol and leave a decided excess of alkali, but the total volume should be less than 100 c.c. The liquid is distilled as before, the contents of the receiver are made up to 50 c.c., and the specific gravity taken. The percentage of alcohol corresponding with this specific gravity, multiplied by 2, gives the percentage in the original sample. The action of the small excess of bromine on the ethyl alcohol is inappreciable in a short time at the ordinary temperature, and introduces no error.

Acetone, Alcohol, and Benzene.—A method of determining small quantities of acetone, alcohol, and benzene present in air has been described by Elliott and Dalton.[2] A measured volume of the air is aspirated through the undermentioned liquids, which absorb the respective vapours. An alkaline iodine solution is used for absorbing the acetone, and the excess of iodine titrated with standard thiosulphate. The alcohol vapours are oxidised to acetic acid by means of a dilute solution of chromic acid, excess of the latter being then titrated with iodide and thiosulphate. For absorbing the benzene vapour a mixture of strong sulphuric acid and fuming nitric acid is employed. With the benzene this yields dinitrobenzene, which can then be extracted with ether, and estimated by reduction with a known quantity of stannous chloride, the excess of the latter being titrated with solution of iodine.

[1] *J. Ind. Eng. Chem.*, 1916, **8**, 240. [2] *Analyst*, 1919, **44**, 132.

CHAPTER VII

ALCOHOLOMETRY

In a broad, general sense, the term "alcoholometry" signifies the determination of the proportion of alcohol contained in a liquid, whatever the nature of the liquid and whatever the method used. It is usually, however, employed in a somewhat narrower sense; thus chemical processes, such as the determination of alcohol by oxidation to acetic acid and finding the amount of this acid produced, would not generally be considered as coming under the head of "alcoholometry." Neither would such operations as the preliminary extraction, purification, and distillation, which many liquids must undergo in the determination of their alcoholic content, be regarded as operations of alcoholometry in the narrower and more usual sense. "The determination by physical methods of the proportion of alcohol in mixtures of alcohol and water" indicates fairly well what the term generally connotes.

The method almost invariably employed for the purpose is to determine the specific gravity of the mixture. This is done either directly, by means of a specific gravity bottle, a Sprengel tube, or other form of pyknometer; or else indirectly with a hydrometer or some form of hydrostatic balance. Next in importance to these means is the refractometer, which in certain cases can be usefully employed for estimating alcohol. Other physical methods are sometimes made use of, such as those depending, for example, upon the temperature of ebullition of the mixture, or on its vapour pressure; for these see Chapter VI.

Specific gravity.—In the laboratory the specific gravity bottle is generally the most convenient instrument to use for ordinary miscellaneous work; but if a large number of routine determinations have to be made, it is a common practice to use a hydrometer. A particular form of the latter instrument is alone used by revenue officers in assaying spirits for fiscal purposes, as is described later on (see "Hydrometry").

The specific gravity bottle is made in various sizes, 50 c.c., 100 c.c., or 1,000 grains being the most generally convenient. The form mostly used is fitted with a perforated stopper, which when pushed home allows the excess of liquid to escape through the perforation; and the bottles are carefully adjusted to hold the required weight of water at the proper temperature when the exuded excess of liquid has been removed.

In this country the temperature 60° F. (= 15·56° C.) is the one usually adopted as the standard temperature in alcoholometry, and it is the practice in trade circles to refer specific gravities of alcoholic liquids to water at this temperature taken as 1,000. Thus beer of sp. gr. 1·055 (water = 1) is said to have the sp. gr. 1,055; and dilute alcohol of sp. gr. 0·9842 is referred to as of sp. gr. 984·2. This has the practical advantage of making the chief figures integers, and reducing the decimals to one, or at most two.

FIG. 32.—ORDINARY PYKNOMETER.
With perforated stopper, as used for alcohol determinations.

For this reason also, in dealing with spirituous liquors for trade or fiscal purposes in this country, if many samples are examined it is convenient to use a 1,000-grain specific gravity bottle and take the weights in grains. This gives the sp. gr. without calculation. It also economises time in distillation, compared with what is required by the use of a 100 c.c. bottle, since in the former case it is only necessary to distil 75 c.c., whilst at least 110 c.c. must be distilled if the larger bottle is used. For occasional requirements, however, an ordinary 100 c.c. or 50 c.c. bottle with gram weights is perfectly satisfactory.

In using the bottle form of pyknometer, the liquid to be tested is first brought as nearly as practicable to the standard temperature, and the bottle filled nearly to the neck with it. A sensitive thermometer is then inserted, and the liquid brought exactly to the standard temperature by placing the bottle in an ice-bath, or by warming with the hand, as may be required; the liquid being stirred frequently with the thermometer. The latter is then removed, the bottle filled up to the top, the stopper inserted, excess of liquid at once wiped off the top of the stopper, the bottle carefully dried externally with the balance-cloth, and weighed.

The specific gravity having thus been determined, the corresponding percentage of alcohol is obtained by reference to a suitable

table. The one appended (p. 237) is abridged from official tables published for the Board of Customs and Excise in 1912, and is reproduced here by permission of the Controller of H.M. Stationery Office. It is based upon a careful revision of the results obtained by Mendeléeff, the Kaiserliche Normal Eichungs Kommission, Blagden and Gilpin, and Drinkwater; it is believed to be one of the most accurate and trustworthy alcohol tables in existence. The revision was carried out at the Government Laboratory, London, under the auspices of Sir Edward Thorpe, who was at that time the principal chemist of the laboratory.

Temperature-corrections.—If for any reason the specific gravity of the alcohol is not taken at the standard temperature, it is necessary to include a correction to compensate for the deviation. The correction is greater at higher strengths than at lower, as will be seen from the table given below, which is used in the following manner:—

The difference between the standard temperature and the actual temperature of the observation is multiplied by the appropriate factor, taken from the table. If the actual temperature is higher than the standard, the product is added to the observed specific gravity; if it is lower, the product is subtracted. The unit throughout is water at the *standard* temperature (60° F.).

TABLE OF TEMPERATURE CORRECTIONS.

Sp. grav.	Correction for		Sp. grav.	Correction for	
	1° F.	1° C.		1° F.	1° C.
0·794	0·00046	0·00083	0·966	0·00025	0·00045
0·864	45	81	0·967	24	43
0·889	44	79	0·968	23	41
0·902	43	77	0·969	22	40
0·912	42	76	0·970	21	38
0·921	41	74	0·971	20	36
0·928	40	72	0·973	19	34
0·935	39	70	0·974	18	32
0·940	38	68	0·975	17	31
0·943	37	67	0·976	16	29
0·946	36	65	0·977	15	27
0·949	35	63	0·978	14	25
0·951	34	61	0·980	13	23
0·953	33	59	0·981	12	22
0·955	32	58	0·983	11	20
0·957	31	56	0·985	10	18
0·959	30	54	0·987	0·00009	16
0·961	29	52	0·990	8	14
0·962	28	50	0·995	7	13
0·963	27	49	1·000		
0·965	0·00026	0·00047			

Example :—At the temperature 65° F., the sp. gr. of a specimen of diluted alcohol is 0·9475, referred to water at 60° F. as unity. As this lies between 0·946 and 0·949, the appropriate factor is 0·00036, and the correction is 5 × 0·00036 = 0·0018. Hence the sp. gr. of the sample at the standard temperature, 60° F., is 0·9475 + 0·0018 = 0·9493.

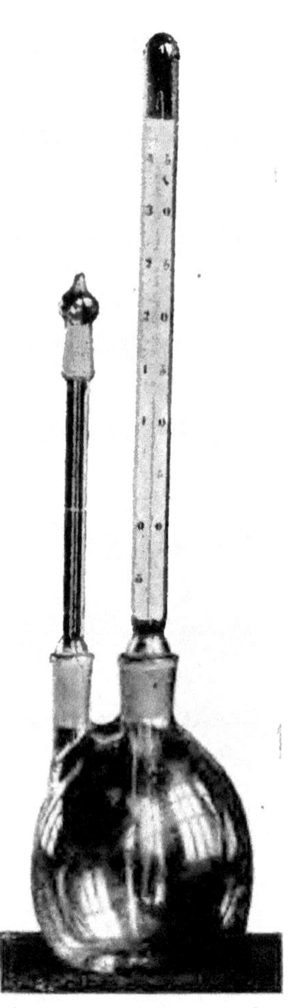

FIG. 33.—GEISSLER'S FORM OF PYKNOMETER. With ground-in thermometer and capped side-tube.

Had the temperature of observation been 55° F. instead of 65° F., the product 0·0018 would have been *subtracted*, and the sp. gr. at 60° would then have been 0·9475 — 0·0018 = 0·9457.

It may be pointed out that where the greatest accuracy is required the temperature of the spirit must be very carefully adjusted in taking the specific gravity. For ordinary purposes it suffices if the sp. gr. is correct to one unit in the fourth place of decimals, which corresponds with about 0·1 per cent. of proof spirit. To obtain a result correct to one unit in the fifth place of decimals it is necessary to adjust the temperature to 0·01° C. or 0·02° F.; and in general for fairly accurate work the temperature of the alcohol should be correctly adjusted to within 0·1° F. This is requisite for a result accurate within five units in the fifth decimal place of the specific gravity, corresponding with about 0·05 per cent. of proof spirit at medium and lower strengths. When special accuracy is required, the desired temperature should be obtained by

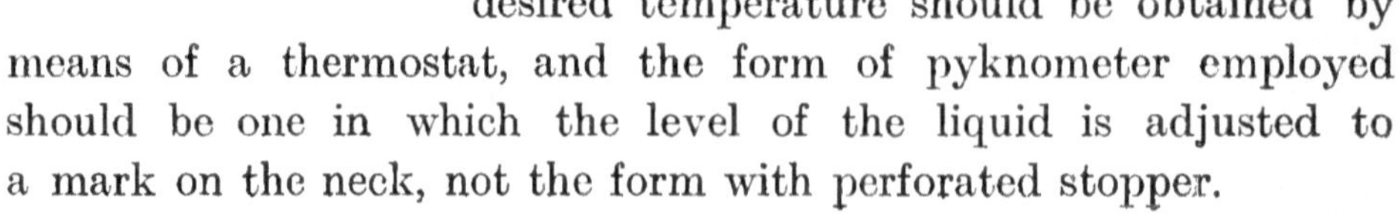

means of a thermostat, and the form of pyknometer employed should be one in which the level of the liquid is adjusted to a mark on the neck, not the form with perforated stopper.

ALCOHOL TABLE. SPECIFIC GRAVITY AT 60°/60° F. (15·56°/15·56° C.).

Specific gravity in air at 60/60° F.	Percentage of proof spirit.	Percentage of alcohol.		Specific gravity in air at 60/60° F.	Percentage of proof spirit.	Percentage of alcohol.	
		By weight.	By volume at 60° F.			By weight.	By volume at 60° F.
0·7936	175·35	100·00	100·00				
7	·31	99·97	99·98				
8	·28	·93	·96				
9	·24	·90	·94				
0·7940	175·21	99·87	99·92	0·7980	173·80	98·57	99·12
1	·18	·84	·90	1	·76	·54	·10
2	·14	·81	·88	2	·73	·51	·08
3	·11	·77	·86	3	·69	·47	·06
4	·07	·74	·84	4	·66	·44	·04
5	·04	·71	·82	5	·62	·41	·02
6	·01	·68	·80	6	·58	·38	·00
7	174·97	·65	·78	7	·55	·34	98·98
8	·94	·61	·76	8	·51	·31	·95
9	·90	·58	·74	9	·48	·27	·93
0·7950	174·87	99·55	99·72	0·7990	173·44	98·24	98·91
1	·84	·52	·70	1	·40	·21	·89
2	·80	·49	·68	2	·37	·18	·87
3	·77	·45	·66	3	·33	·14	·85
4	·73	·42	·64	4	·30	·11	·83
5	·70	·39	·62	5	·26	·08	·81
6	·66	·36	·60	6	·22	·05	·79
7	·63	·32	·58	7	·18	·01	·77
8	·59	·29	·56	8	·15	97·98	·74
9	·56	·25	·54	9	·11	·94	·72
0·7960	174·52	99·22	99·52	0·8000	173·07	97·91	98·70
1	·48	·19	·50	1	·03	·88	·68
2	·45	·16	·48	2	·00	·85	·66
3	·41	·12	·46	3	172·96	·81	·64
4	·38	·09	·44	4	·93	·78	·62
5	·34	·06	·42	5	·89	·75	·60
6	·30	·03	·40	6	·85	·72	·58
7	·27	·00	·38	7	·82	·68	·56
8	·23	98·96	·36	8	·78	·65	·53
9	·20	·93	·34	9	·75	·61	·51
0·7970	174·16	98·90	99·32	0·8010	172·71	97·58	98·49
1	·12	·87	·30	1	·67	·55	·47
2	·09	·84	·28	2	·63	·52	·45
3	·05	·80	·26	3	·60	·48	·43
4	·02	·77	·24	4	·56	·45	·41
5	173·98	·74	·22	5	·52	·42	·39
6	·94	·71	·20	6	·48	·39	·37
7	·91	·67	·18	7	·44	·35	·35
8	·87	·64	·16	8	·41	·32	·32
9	·84	·60	·14	9	·37	·28	·30

ALCOHOL TABLE. SPECIFIC GRAVITY AT 60°/60° F. (15·56°/15·56° C.)—*cont.*

Specific gravity in air at 60/60° F.	Percentage of proof spirit.	Percentage of alcohol.		Specific gravity in air at 60/60° F.	Percentage of proof spirit.	Percentage of alcohol.	
		By weight.	By volume at 60° F.			By weight.	By volume at 60° F.
0·8020	172·33	97·25	98·28	0·8070	170·37	95·55	97·16
1	·29	·22	·26	1	·33	·52	·14
2	·25	·18	·24	2	·29	·48	·12
3	·22	·15	·21	3	·24	·45	·09
4	·18	·11	·19	4	·20	·41	·07
5	·14	·08	·17	5	·16	·38	·05
6	·10	·05	·15	6	·12	·34	·03
7	·06	·01	·13	7	·08	·31	·00
8	·02	96·98	·10	8	·04	·27	96·98
9	171·98	·94	·08	9	·00	·24	·95
0·8030	171·94	96·91	98·06	0·8080	169·96	95·20	96·93
1	·90	·88	·04	1	·92	·17	·91
2	·86	·84	·02	2	·88	·13	·88
3	·83	·81	97·99	3	·83	·10	·86
4	·79	·77	·97	4	·79	·06	·83
5	·75	·74	·95	5	·75	·03	·81
6	·71	·71	·93	6	·71	94·99	·79
7	·67	·67	·91	7	·67	·96	·76
8	·64	·64	·88	8	·62	·92	·74
9	·60	·60	·86	9	·58	·89	·71
0·8040	171·56	96·57	97·84	0·8090	169·54	94·85	96·69
1	·52	·54	·82	1	·50	·82	·67
2	·48	·50	·80	2	·46	·78	·64
3	·44	·47	·77	3	·42	·75	·62
4	·40	·43	·75	4	·38	·71	·59
5	·36	·40	·73	5	·34	·68	·57
6	·32	·37	·71	6	·30	·64	·55
7	·28	·33	·68	7	·26	·61	·52
8	·24	·30	·66	8	·21	·57	·50
9	·20	·26	·63	9	·17	·54	·47
0·8050	171·16	96·23	97·61	0·8100	169·13	94·50	96·45
1	·12	·20	·59	1	·09	·47	·43
2	·08	·16	·57	2	·05	·43	·40
3	·04	·13	·54	3	·00	·40	·38
4	·00	·09	·52	4	168·96	·36	·35
5	170·96	·06	·50	5	·92	·33	·33
6	·92	·03	·48	6	·88	·29	·31
7	·88	95·99	·46	7	·83	·26	·28
8	·85	·96	·43	8	·79	·22	·26
9	·81	·92	·41	9	·74	·19	·23
0·8060	170·77	95·89	97·39	0·8110	168·70	94·15	96·21
1	·73	·86	·37	1	·66	·12	·19
2	·69	·82	·35	2	·62	·08	·16
3	·65	·79	·32	3	·57	·05	·14
4	·61	·75	·30	4	·53	·01	·11
5	·57	·72	·28	5	·49	93·98	·09
6	·53	·69	·26	6	·45	·94	·07
7	·49	·65	·23	7	·41	·91	·04
8	·45	·62	·21	8	·36	·87	·02
9	·41	·58	·18	9	·32	·84	95·99

ALCOHOL TABLE. SPECIFIC GRAVITY AT 60°/60° F. (15·56°/15·56° C.)—*cont.*

Specific gravity in air at 60/60° F.	Percentage of proof spirit.	Percentage of alcohol. By weight.	Percentage of alcohol. By volume at 60° F.	Specific gravity. in air at 60/60° F.	Percentage of proof spirit.	Percentage of alcohol. By weight.	Percentage of alcohol. By volume at 60° F.
0·8120	168·28	93·80	95·97	0·8170	166·06	92·00	94·71
1	·24	·76	·95	1	·01	91·96	·68
2	·19	·73	·92	2	165·97	·93	·66
3	·15	·69	·90	3	·92	·89	·63
4	·10	·66	·87	4	·88	·86	·61
5	·06	·62	·85	5	·83	·82	·58
6	·02	·58	·82	6	·78	·78	·55
7	167·97	·55	·80	7	·74	·74	·53
8	·93	·51	·77	8	·69	·71	·50
9	·88	·48	·75	9	·65	·67	·48
0·8130	167·84	93·44	95·72	0·8180	165·60	91·63	94·45
1	·80	·40	·70	1	·55	·59	·42
2	·76	·37	·67	2	·51	·56	·40
3	·71	·33	·65	3	·46	·52	·37
4	·67	·30	·62	4	·42	·49	·35
5	·63	·26	·60	5	·37	·45	·32
6	·59	·22	·57	6	·32	·41	·29
7	·54	·19	·55	7	·28	·38	·27
8	·50	·15	·52	8	·23	·34	·24
9	·45	·12	·50	9	·19	·31	·22
0·8140	167·41	93·08	95·47	0·8190	165·14	91·27	94·19
1	·37	·04	·45	1	·09	·23	·16
2	·32	·01	·42	2	·04	·20	·14
3	·28	92·97	·40	3	·00	·16	·11
4	·23	·94	·37	4	164·95	·13	·09
5	·19	·90	·35	5	·90	·09	·06
6	·14	·86	·32	6	·85	·05	·03
7	·10	·83	·30	7	·81	·01	·00
8	·05	·79	·27	8	·76	90·98	93·98
9	·01	·76	·25	9	·72	·94	·95
0·8150	166·96	92·72	95·22	0·8200	164·67	90·90	93·92
1	·92	·68	·20	1	·62	·86	·89
2	·87	·65	·17	2	·57	·83	·87
3	·83	·61	·15	3	·53	·79	·84
4	·78	·58	·12	4	·48	·76	·82
5	·74	·54	·10	5	·43	·72	·79
6	·69	·50	·07	6	·38	·68	·76
7	·65	·47	·05	7	·34	·64	·73
8	·60	·43	·02	8	·29	·61	·71
9	·56	·40	·00	9	·25	·57	·68
0·8160	166·51	92·36	94·97	0·8210	164·20	90·53	93·65
1	·46	·32	·94	1	·15	·49	·62
2	·42	·29	·92	2	·10	·46	·60
3	·37	·25	·89	3	·06	·42	·57
4	·33	·22	·87	4	·01	·39	·55
5	·28	·18	·84	5	163·96	·35	·52
6	·24	·14	·81	6	·91	·31	·49
7	·19	·11	·79	7	·86	·27	·46
8	·15	·07	·76	8	·82	·24	·44
9	·10	·04	·74	9	·77	·20	·41

ALCOHOL TABLE. SPECIFIC GRAVITY AT 60°/60° F. (15·56°/15·56° C.)—*cont.*

Specific gravity in air at 60/60° F.	Per-centage of proof spirit.	Percentage of alcohol.		Specific gravity in air at 60/60° F.	Per-centage of proof spirit.	Percentage of alcohol.	
		By weight.	By volume at 60° F.			By weight.	By volume at 60° F.
0·8220	163·72	90·16	93·38	0·8270	161·26	88·27	91·98
1	·67	·12	·35	1	·21	·23	·95
2	·62	·09	·32	2	·16	·19	·92
3	·58	·05	·30	3	·11	·16	·90
4	·53	·02	·27	4	·06	·12	·87
5	·48	89·98	·24	5	·01	·08	·84
6	·43	·94	·21	6	160·96	·04	·81
7	·38	·90	·18	7	·91	·00	·78
8	·33	·87	·16	8	·85	87·96	·75
9	·28	·83	·13	9	·80	·92	·72
0·8230	163·23	89·79	93·10	0·8280	160·75	87·88	91·69
1	·18	·75	·07	1	·70	·84	·66
2	·13	·71	·05	2	·65	·80	·63
3	·09	·68	·02	3	·60	·77	·61
4	·04	·64	·00	4	·55	·73	·58
5	162·99	·60	92·97	5	·50	·69	·55
6	·94	·56	·94	6	·45	·65	·52
7	·89	·52	·91	7	·40	·61	·49
8	·85	·49	·89	8	·34	·58	·46
9	·80	·45	·86	9	·29	·54	·43
0·8240	162·75	89·41	92·83	0·8290	160·24	87·50	91·40
1	·70	·37	·80	1	·19	·46	·37
2	·65	·33	·77	2	·14	·42	·34
3	·60	·30	·75	3	·09	·39	·32
4	·55	·26	·72	4	·04	·35	·29
5	·50	·22	·69	5	159·99	·31	·26
6	·45	·18	·66	6	·94	·27	·23
7	·40	·14	·63	7	·89	·23	·20
8	·36	·11	·61	8	·83	·19	·17
9	·31	·07	·58	9	·78	·15	·14
0·8250	162·26	89·03	92·55	0·8300	159·73	87·11	91·11
1	·21	88·99	·52	1	·68	·07	·08
2	·16	·95	·49	2	·63	·03	·05
3	·11	·92	·47	3	·57	·00	·02
4	·06	·88	·44	4	·52	86·96	90·99
5	·01	·84	·41	5	·47	·92	·96
6	161·96	·80	·38	6	·42	·88	·93
7	·91	·76	·35	7	·37	·84	·90
8	·86	·73	·32	8	·31	·81	·87
9	·81	·69	·29	9	·26	·77	·84
0·8260	161·76	88·65	92·26	0·8310	159·21	86·73	90·81
1	·71	·61	·23	1	·16	·69	·78
2	·66	·57	·20	2	·11	·65	·75
3	·61	·54	·18	3	·05	·62	·73
4	·56	·50	·15	4	·00	·58	·70
5	·51	·46	·12	5	158·95	·54	·67
6	·46	·42	·09	6	·90	·50	·64
7	·41	·38	·06	7	·85	·46	·61
8	·36	·35	·04	8	·79	·42	·58
9	·31	·31	·01	9	·74	·38	·55

ALCOHOL TABLE. SPECIFIC GRAVITY AT 60°/60° F. (15·56°/15·56° C.)—*cont.*

Specific gravity in air at 60/60° F.	Percentage of proof spirit.	Percentage of alcohol.		Specific gravity in air at 60/60° F.	Percentage of proof spirit.	Percentage of alcohol.	
		By weight.	By volume at 60° F.			By weight.	By volume at 60° F.
0·8320	158·69	86·34	90·52	0·8370	156·02	84·38	88·99
1	·64	·30	·49	1	155·96	·34	·96
2	·59	·26	·46	2	·91	·30	·93
3	·53	·23	·43	3	·85	·27	·90
4	·48	·19	·40	4	·80	·23	·87
5	·43	·15	·37	5	·74	·19	·84
6	·38	·11	·34	6	·69	·15	·81
7	·32	·07	·31	7	·63	·11	·78
8	·27	·03	·28	8	·58	·07	·74
9	·21	85·99	·25	9	·52	·03	·71
0·8330	158·16	85·95	90·22	0·8380	155·47	83·99	88·68
1	·11	·91	·19	1	·42	·95	·65
2	·06	·87	·16	2	·36	·91	·62
3	·00	·84	·13	3	·31	·87	·59
4	157·95	·80	·10	4	·25	·83	·56
5	·90	·76	·07	5	·20	·79	·53
6	·85	·72	·04	6	·14	·75	·50
7	·79	·68	·01	7	·09	·71	·47
8	·74	·64	89·97	8	·03	·67	·43
9	·68	·60	·94	9	154·98	·63	·40
0·8340	157·63	85·56	89·91	0·8390	154·92	83·59	88·37
1	·58	·52	·88	1	·86	·55	·34
2	·52	·48	·85	2	·81	·51	·31
3	·47	·45	·82	3	·75	·48	·28
4	·41	·41	·79	4	·70	·44	·25
5	·36	·37	·76	5	·64	·40	·22
6	·31	·33	·73	6	·59	·36	·19
7	·25	·29	·70	7	·53	·32	·16
8	·20	·25	·67	8	·48	·28	·12
9	·14	·21	·64	9	·42	·24	·09
0·8350	157·09	85·17	89·61	0·8400	154·37	83·20	88·06
1	·04	·13	·58	1	·31	·16	·03
2	156·99	·09	·55	2	·26	·12	·00
3	·93	·06	·52	3	·20	·08	87·96
4	·88	·02	·49	4	·15	·04	·93
5	·83	84·98	·46	5	·09	·00	·90
6	·78	·94	·43	6	·03	82·96	·87
7	·72	·90	·40	7	153·98	·92	·84
8	·67	·86	·36	8	·92	·88	·80
9	·61	·82	·33	9	·87	·84	·77
0·8360	156·56	84·78	89·30	0·8410	153·81	82·80	87·74
1	·51	·74	·27	1	·75	·76	·71
2	·45	·70	·24	2	·70	·72	·68
3	·40	·66	·21	3	·64	·68	·64
4	·34	·62	·18	4	·59	·64	·61
5	·29	·58	·15	5	·53	·60	·58
6	·24	·54	·12	6	·47	·56	·55
7	·18	·50	·09	7	·42	·52	·52
8	·13	·46	·05	8	·36	·48	·48
9	·07	·42	·02	9	·31	·44	·45

ALCOHOL TABLE SPECIFIC GRAVITY AT 60°/60° F. (15·56°/15·56° C.)—*cont.*

Specific gravity in air at 60/60° F.	Per-centage of proof spirit.	Percentage of alcohol.		Specific gravity in air at 60/60° F.	Per-centage of proof spirit.	Percentage of alcohol.	
		By weight.	By volume at 60° F.			By weight.	By volume at 60° F.
0·8420	153·25	82·40	87·42	0·8470	150·39	80·39	85·79
1	·19	·36	·39	1	·33	·35	·76
2	·14	·32	·36	2	·27	·31	·73
3	·08	·28	·32	3	·22	·27	·69
4	·03	·24	·29	4	·16	·23	·66
5	152·97	·20	·26	5	·10	·19	·63
6	·91	·16	·23	6	·04	·15	·60
7	·86	·12	·20	7	149·98	·11	·56
8	·80	·08	·16	8	·92	·06	·53
9	·75	·04	·13	9	·86	·02	·49
0·8430	152·69	82·00	87·10	0·8480	149·80	79·98	85·46
1	·63	81·96	·07	1	·74	·94	·43
2	·57	·92	·04	2	·68	·90	·39
3	·52	·88	·00	3	·63	·86	·36
4	·46	·84	86·97	4	·57	·82	·32
5	·40	·80	·94	5	·51	·78	·29
6	·34	·76	·91	6	·45	·74	·26
7	·29	·72	·87	7	·39	·70	·22
8	·23	·68	·84	8	·33	·65	·19
9	·18	·64	·80	9	·27	·61	·15
0·8440	152·12	81·60	86·77	0·8490	149·21	79·57	85·12
1	·06	·56	·74	1	·15	·53	·09
2	·01	·52	·71	2	·09	·49	·05
3	151·95	·48	·67	3	·04	·45	·02
4	·90	·44	·64	4	148·98	·41	84·98
5	·84	·40	·61	5	·92	·37	·95
6	·78	·36	·58	6	·86	·33	·92
7	·72	·32	·55	7	·80	·29	·88
8	·67	·28	·51	8	·74	·25	·85
9	·61	·24	·48	9	·68	·21	·81
0·8450	151·55	81·20	86·45	0·8500	148·62	79·17	84·78
1	·49	·16	·42	1	·56	·13	·75
2	·43	·12	·39	2	·50	·09	·71
3	·38	·08	·35	3	·45	·05	·68
4	·32	·04	·32	4	·39	·01	·64
5	·26	·00	·29	5	·33	78·97	·61
6	·20	80·96	·26	6	·27	·93	·58
7	·14	·92	·22	7	·21	·89	·54
8	·09	·87	·19	8	·15	·84	·51
9	·03	·83	·15	9	·09	·80	·47
0·8460	150·97	80·79	86·12	0·8510	148·03	78·76	84·44
1	·91	·75	·09	1	147·97	·72	·41
2	·85	·71	·05	2	·91	·68	·38
3	·80	·67	·02	3	·85	·64	·34
4	·74	·63	85·98	4	·79	·60	·31
5	·68	·59	·95	5	·73	·56	·28
6	·62	·55	·92	6	·67	·52	·25
7	·56	·51	·89	7	·61	·48	·21
8	·51	·47	·85	8	·55	·43	·18
9	·45	·43	·82	9	·49	·39	·14

ALCOHOL TABLE. SPECIFIC GRAVITY AT 60°/60° F. (15·56°/15·56° C.)—*cont.*

Specific gravity in air at 60/60° F.	Percentage of proof spirit.	Percentage of alcohol. By weight.	Percentage of alcohol. By volume at 60° F.	Specific gravity in air at 60/60° F.	Percentage of proof spirit.	Percentage of alcohol. By weight.	Percentage of alcohol. By volume at 60° F.
0·8520	147·43	78·35	84·11	0·8570	144·39	76·29	82·38
1	·37	·31	·08	1	·33	·25	·35
2	·31	·27	·04	2	·27	·21	·31
3	·25	·23	·01	3	·20	·17	·28
4	·19	·19	83·97	4	·14	·13	·24
5	·13	·15	·94	5	·08	·09	·21
6	·07	·11	·91	6	·02	·05	·17
7	·01	·07	·87	7	143·96	·01	·14
8	146·95	·02	·84	8	·90	75·96	·10
9	·89	77·98	·80	9	·84	·92	·07
0·8530	146·83	77·94	83·77	0·8580	143·78	75·88	82·03
1	·77	·90	·74	1	·72	·84	·00
2	·71	·86	·70	2	·66	·80	81·96
3	·65	·82	·67	3	·59	·76	·93
4	·59	·78	·63	4	·53	·72	·89
5	·53	·74	·60	5	·47	·68	·86
6	·47	·70	·56	6	·41	·64	·82
7	·41	·66	·53	7	·35	·60	·79
8	·35	·61	·49	8	·28	·55	·75
9	·29	·57	·46	9	·22	·51	·72
0·8540	146·23	77·53	83·42	0·8590	143·16	75·47	81·68
1	·17	·49	·39	1	·10	·43	·64
2	·11	·45	·35	2	·04	·39	·61
3	·05	·41	·32	3	142·97	·34	·57
4	145·99	·37	·28	4	·91	·30	·54
5	·93	·33	·25	5	·85	·26	·50
6	·87	·29	·22	6	·79	·22	·46
7	·81	·25	·18	7	·73	·18	·43
8	·74	·20	·15	8	·66	·13	·39
9	·68	·16	·11	9	·60	·09	·36
0·8550	145·62	77·12	83·08	0·8600	142·54	75·05	81·32
1	·56	·08	·05	1	·48	·01	·29
2	·50	·04	·01	2	·41	74·97	·25
3	·44	·00	82·98	3	·35	·93	·22
4	·38	76·96	·94	4	·28	·89	·18
5	·32	·92	·91	5	·22	·85	·15
6	·26	·88	·87	6	·16	·81	·11
7	·20	·84	·84	7	·10	·77	·08
8	·13	·79	·80	8	·03	·72	·04
9	·07	·75	·77	9	141·97	·68	·01
0·8560	145·01	76·71	82·73	0·8610	141·91	74·64	80·97
1	144·95	·67	·70	1	·85	·60	·93
2	·89	·63	·66	2	·78	·56	·90
3	·82	·58	·63	3	·72	·51	·86
4	·76	·54	·59	4	·65	·47	·83
5	·70	·50	·56	5	·59	·43	·79
6	·64	·46	·52	6	·53	·39	·75
7	·58	·42	·49	7	·47	·35	·72
8	·51	·37	·45	8	·40	·30	·68
9	·45	·33	·42	9	·34	·26	·65

ALCOHOL TABLE. SPECIFIC GRAVITY AT 60°/60° F. (15·56°/15·56° C.)—*cont.*

Specific gravity in air at 60/60° F.	Percentage of proof spirit.	Percentage of alcohol. By weight.	Percentage of alcohol. By volume at 60° F.	Specific gravity in air at 60/60° F.	Percentage of proof spirit.	Percentage of alcohol. By weight.	Percentage of alcohol. By volume at 60° F.
0·8620	141·28	74·22	80·61	0·8670	138·10	72·14	78·80
1	·22	·18	·57	1	·04	·10	·76
2	·16	·14	·54	2	137·97	·06	·73
3	·09	·09	·50	3	·91	·01	·69
4	·03	·05	·47	4	·84	71·97	·66
5	140·97	·01	·43	5	·78	·93	·62
6	·91	73·97	·39	6	·72	·89	·58
7	·84	·93	·36	7	·65	·85	·54
8	·78	·88	·32	8	·59	·80	·51
9	·71	·84	·29	9	·52	·76	·47
0·8630	140·65	73·80	80·25	0·8680	137·46	71·72	78·43
1	·59	·76	·21	1	·39	·68	·39
2	·52	·72	·18	2	·33	·64	·36
3	·46	·67	·14	3	·26	·59	·32
4	·39	·63	·11	4	·20	·55	·29
5	·33	·59	·07	5	·13	·51	·25
6	·27	·55	·03	6	·07	·47	·21
7	·21	·51	·00	7	·00	·43	·17
8	·14	·47	79·96	8	136·94	·38	·14
9	·08	·43	·93	9	·87	·34	·10
0·8640	140·02	73·39	79·89	0·8690	136·81	71·30	78·06
1	139·96	·35	·85	1	·74	·26	·02
2	·89	·31	·82	2	·68	·22	77·99
3	·83	·26	·78	3	·61	·17	·95
4	·76	·22	·75	4	·55	·13	·92
5	·70	·18	·71	5	·48	·09	·88
6	·64	·14	·67	6	·42	·05	·84
7	·57	·10	·64	7	·35	·01	·80
8	·51	·05	·60	8	·29	70·96	·77
9	·44	·01	·57	9	·22	·92	·73
0·8650	139·38	72·97	79·53	0·8700	136·16	70·88	77·69
1	·32	·93	·49	1	·09	·84	·65
2	·25	·89	·46	2	·03	·80	·62
3	·19	·84	·42	3	135·96	·75	·58
4	·12	·80	·39	4	·90	·71	·55
5	·06	·76	·35	5	·83	·67	·51
6	·00	·72	·31	6	·76	·63	·47
7	138·93	·68	·27	7	·70	·59	·43
8	·87	·63	·24	8	·63	·54	·40
9	·80	·59	·20	9	·57	·50	·36
0·8660	138·74	72·55	79·16	0·8710	135·50	70·46	77·32
1	·68	·51	·12	1	·43	·42	·28
2	·61	·47	·09	2	·37	·38	·24
3	·55	·42	·05	3	·30	·33	·21
4	·48	·38	·02	4	·24	·29	·17
5	·42	·34	78·98	5	·17	·25	·13
6	·36	·30	·94	6	·10	·21	·09
7	·29	·26	·91	7	·04	·17	·05
8	·23	·22	·87	8	134·97	·12	·02
9	·16	·18	·84	9	·91	·08	76·98

ALCOHOL TABLE. SPECIFIC GRAVITY AT 60°/60° F. (15·56°/15·56° C.)—*cont.*

Specific gravity in air at 60/60° F.	Percentage of proof spirit.	Percentage of alcohol. By weight.	Percentage of alcohol. By volume at 60° F.	Specific gravity in air at 60/60° F.	Percentage of proof spirit.	Percentage of alcohol. By weight.	Percentage of alcohol. By volume at 60° F.
0·8720	134·84	70·04	76·94	0·8770	131·53	67·93	75·06
1	·78	·00	·90	1	·46	·89	·02
2	·71	69·96	·87	2	·39	·85	74·98
3	·65	·91	·83	3	·33	·80	·95
4	·58	·87	·80	4	·26	·76	·91
5	·52	·83	·76	5	·19	·72	·87
6	·45	·79	·72	6	·12	·68	·83
7	·39	·74	·68	7	·06	·64	·79
8	·32	·70	·65	8	130·99	·59	·76
9	·26	·65	·61	9	·93	·55	·72
0·8730	134·19	69·61	76·57	0·8780	130·86	67·51	74·68
1	·12	·57	·53	1	·79	·47	·64
2	·06	·53	·49	2	·72	·43	·60
3	133·99	·48	·46	3	·66	·38	·57
4	·93	·44	·42	4	·59	·34	·53
5	·86	·40	·38	5	·52	·30	·49
6	·79	·36	·34	6	·45	·26	·45
7	·73	·32	·30	7	·38	·22	·41
8	·66	·27	·27	8	·32	·17	·37
9	·60	·23	·23	9	·25	·13	·33
0·8740	133·53	69·19	76·19	0·8790	130·18	67·09	74·29
1	·46	·15	·15	1	·11	·05	·25
2	·40	·11	·12	2	·04	·01	·21
3	·33	·06	·08	3	129·98	66·96	·18
4	·27	·02	·05	4	·91	·92	·14
5	·20	68·98	·01	5	·84	·88	·10
6	·13	·94	75·97	6	·77	·84	·06
7	·07	·90	·93	7	·70	·79	·02
8	·00	·85	·90	8	·64	·75	73·99
9	132·94	·81	·86	9	·57	·70	·95
0·8750	132·87	68·77	75·82	0·8800	129·50	66·66	73·91
1	·80	·73	·78	1	·43	·62	·87
2	·73	·69	·74	2	·36	·58	·83
3	·67	·64	·71	3	·30	·53	·80
4	·60	·60	·67	4	·23	·49	·76
5	·53	·56	·63	5	·16	·45	·72
6	·46	·52	·59	6	·09	·41	·68
7	·39	·48	·55	7	·02	·36	·64
8	·33	·43	·52	8	128·96	·32	·60
9	·26	·39	·48	9	·89	·27	·56
0·8760	132·19	68·35	75·44	0·8810	128·82	66·23	73·52
1	·12	·31	·40	1	·75	·19	·48
2	·06	·27	·36	2	·68	·15	·44
3	131·99	·22	·33	3	·62	·10	·41
4	·93	·18	·29	4	·55	·06	·37
5	·86	·14	·25	5	·48	·02	·33
6	·79	·10	·21	6	·41	65·98	·29
7	·73	·06	·17	7	·34	·94	·25
8	·66	·01	·14	8	·28	·89	·21
9	·60	67·97	·10	9	·21	·85	·17

ALCOHOL TABLE. SPECIFIC GRAVITY AT 60°/60° F. (15·56°/15·56° C.)—*cont.*

Specific gravity. in air at 60/60° F.	Per-centage of proof spirit.	Percentage of alcohol.		Specific gravity. in air at 60/60° F.	Per-centage of proof spirit.	Percentage of alcohol.	
		By weight.	By volume at 60° F.			By weight.	By volume at 60° F.
0·8820	128·14	65·81	73·13	0·8870	124·67	63·67	71·15
1	·07	·77	·09	1	·60	·63	·11
2	·00	·73	·05	2	·53	·59	·07
3	127·94	·68	·02	3	·46	·54	·03
4	·87	·64	72·98	4	·39	·50	70·99
5	·80	·60	·94	5	·32	·46	·95
6	·73	·56	·90	6	·25	·42	·91
7	·66	·51	·86	7	·18	·37	·87
8	·59	·47	·82	8	·11	·33	·83
9	·52	·42	·78	9	·04	·28	·79
0·8830	127·45	65·38	72·74	0·8880	123·97	63·24	70·75
1	·38	·34	·70	1	·90	·20	·71
2	·31	·30	·66	2	·83	·16	·67
3	·25	·25	·62	3	·76	·11	·63
4	·18	·21	·58	4	·69	·07	·59
5	·11	·17	·54	5	·62	·03	·55
6	·04	·13	·50	6	·55	62·99	·51
7	126·97	·09	·46	7	·48	·94	·47
8	·91	·04	·42	8	·41	·90	·43
9	·84	·00	·38	9	·34	·85	·39
0·8840	126·77	64·96	72·34	0·8890	123·27	62·81	70·35
1	·70	·92	·30	1	·20	·77	·31
2	·63	·88	·26	2	·13	·73	·27
3	·56	·83	·23	3	·05	·68	·23
4	·49	·79	·19	4	122·98	·64	·19
5	·42	·75	·15	5	·91	·60	·15
6	·35	·71	·11	6	·84	·56	·11
7	·28	·66	·07	7	·77	·51	·07
8	·21	·62	·03	8	·70	·47	·03
9	·14	·57	71·99	9	·63	·42	69·99
0·8850	126·07	64·53	71·95	0·8900	122·56	62·38	69·95
1	·00	·49	·91	1	·49	·34	·91
2	125·93	·45	·87	2	·42	·30	·87
3	·86	·40	·83	3	·34	·25	·83
4	·79	·36	·79	4	·27	·21	·79
5	·72	·32	·75	5	·20	·17	·75
6	·65	·28	·71	6	·13	·13	·71
7	·58	·23	·67	7	·06	·08	·67
8	·51	·19	·63	8	121·99	·04	·63
9	·44	·14	·59	9	·92	61·99	·59
0·8860	125·37	64·10	71·55	0·8910	121·85	61·95	69·55
1	·30	·06	·51	1	·78	·91	·51
2	·23	·02	·47	2	·71	·87	·47
3	·16	63·97	·43	3	·63	·82	·43
4	·09	·93	·39	4	·56	·78	·39
5	·02	·89	·35	5	·49	·74	·35
6	124·95	·85	·31	6	·42	·70	·31
7	·88	·80	·27	7	·35	·65	·27
8	·81	·76	·23	8	·28	·61	·22
9	·74	·71	·19	9	·21	·56	·18

ALCOHOL TABLE. SPECIFIC GRAVITY AT 60°/60° F. (15·56°/15·56° C.)—*cont.*

Specific gravity in air at 60/60° F.	Percentage of proof spirit.	Percentage of alcohol.		Specific gravity in air at 60/60° F.	Percentage of proof spirit.	Percentage of alcohol.	
		By weight.	By volume at 60° F.			By weight.	By volume at 60° F.
0·8920	121·14	61·52	69·14	0·8970	117·54	59·37	67·09
1	·07	·48	·10	1	·47	·33	·05
2	·00	·44	·06	2	·39	·28	·01
3	120·92	·39	·02	3	·32	·24	66·96
4	·85	·35	68·98	4	·24	·19	·92
5	·78	·31	·94	5	·17	·15	·88
6	·71	·27	·90	6	·10	·11	·84
7	·64	·22	·86	7	·03	·06	·80
8	·56	·18	·81	8	116·95	·02	·75
9	·49	·13	·77	9	·88	58·97	·71
0·8930	120·42	61·09	68·73	0·8980	116·81	58·93	66·67
1	·35	·05	·69	1	·74	·89	·63
2	·28	·01	·65	2	·66	·85	·59
3	·20	60·96	·61	3	·59	·80	·54
4	·13	·92	·57	4	·51	·76	·50
5	·06	·88	·53	5	·44	·72	·46
6	119·99	·84	·49	6	·37	·68	·42
7	·92	·79	·45	7	·29	·63	·38
8	·84	·75	·41	8	·22	·59	·33
9	·77	·70	·37	9	·14	·54	·29
0·8940	119·70	60·66	68·33	0·8990	116·07	58·50	66·25
1	·63	·62	·29	1	·00	·46	·21
2	·56	·58	·25	2	115·92	·41	·17
3	·48	·53	·21	3	·85	·37	·12
4	·41	·49	·17	4	·77	·32	·08
5	·34	·45	·13	5	·70	·28	·04
6	·27	·41	·09	6	·63	·24	·00
7	·20	·36	·05	7	·55	·19	65·96
8	·12	·32	·00	8	·48	·15	·91
9	·05	·27	67·96	9	·40	·10	·87
0·8950	118·98	60·23	67·92	0·9000	115·33	58·06	65·83
1	·91	·19	·88	1	·26	·02	·79
2	·84	·15	·84	2	·18	57·97	·75
3	·76	·10	·79	3	·11	·93	·70
4	·69	·06	·75	4	·03	·88	·66
5	·62	·02	·71	5	114·96	·84	·62
6	·55	59·98	·67	6	·89	·80	·58
7	·48	·93	·63	7	·81	·75	·54
8	·40	·89	·58	8	·74	·71	·49
9	·33	·84	·54	9	·66	·66	·45
0·8960	118·26	59·80	67·50	0·9010	114·59	57·62	65·41
1	·19	·76	·46	1	·52	·58	·37
2	·12	·72	·42	2	·44	·53	·33
3	·04	·67	·37	3	·37	·49	·28
4	117·97	·63	·33	4	·29	·44	·24
5	·90	·59	·29	5	·22	·40	·20
6	·83	·55	·25	6	·14	·36	·16
7	·76	·50	·21	7	·07	·31	·11
8	·68	·46	·17	8	113·99	·27	·07
9	·61	·41	·13	9	·92	·22	·02

Alcohol table. Specific gravity at 60°/60° F. (15·56°/15·56° C.)—*cont.*

Specific gravity in air at 60/60° F.	Per-centage of proof spirit.	Percentage of alcohol.		Specific gravity. in air at 60/60° F.	Per-centage of proof spirit.	Percentage of alcohol.	
		By weight.	By volume at 60° F.			By weight.	By volume at 60° F.
0·9020	113·84	57·18	64·98	0·9070	110·06	54·98	2·83
1	·77	·14	·94	1	109·98	·94	·79
2	·69	·10	·90	2	·90	·89	·74
3	·62	·05	·85	3	·83	·85	·70
4	·54	·01	·81	4	·75	·80	·65
5	·47	56·97	·77	5	·67	·76	·61
6	·40	·93	·73	6	·59	·72	·57
7	·32	·88	·69	7	·52	·67	·52
8	·25	·84	·64	8	·44	·63	·48
9	·17	·79	·60	9	·37	·58	·43
0·9030	113·10	56·75	64·56	0·9080	109·29	54·54	62·39
1	·02	·71	·52	1	·21	·50	·35
2	112·95	·66	·48	2	·13	·45	·30
3	·87	·62	·43	3	·06	·41	·26
4	·80	·57	·39	4	108·98	·36	·21
5	·72	·53	·35	5	·90	·32	·17
6	·65	·49	·31	6	·82	·28	·13
7	·57	·44	·26	7	·74	·23	·08
8	·50	·40	·22	8	·67	·19	·04
9	·42	·35	·17	9	·59	·14	61·99
0·9040	112·35	56·31	64·13	0·9090	108·51	54·10	61·95
1	·27	·27	·09	1	·43	·06	·91
2	·20	·22	·05	2	·36	·01	·86
3	·12	·18	·00	3	·28	53·97	·82
4	·05	·13	63·96	4	·21	·92	·77
5	111·97	·09	·92	5	·13	·88	·73
6	·89	·04	·88	6	·05	·83	·69
7	·81	·00	·83	7	107·97	·79	·64
8	·74	55·95	·79	8	·90	·74	·60
9	·66	·91	·74	9	·82	·70	·55
0·9050	111·58	55·86	63·70	0·9100	107·74	53·65	61·51
1	·50	·82	·66	1	·66	·61	·47
2	·43	·77	·61	2	·59	·56	·42
3	·35	·73	·57	3	·51	·52	·38
4	·28	·68	·52	4	·44	·47	·33
5	·20	·64	·48	5	·36	·43	·29
6	·12	·60	·44	6	·28	·39	·25
7	·05	·55	·39	7	·20	·34	·20
8	110·97	·51	·35	8	·13	·30	·16
9	·90	·46	·30	9	·05	·25	·11
0·9060	110·82	55·42	63·26	0·9110	106·97	53·21	61·07
1	·74	·38	·22	1	·89	·17	·03
2	·67	·33	·18	2	·81	·12	60·98
3	·59	·29	·13	3	·74	·08	·94
4	·52	·24	·09	4	·66	·03	·89
5	·44	·20	·05	5	·58	52·99	·85
6	·36	·16	·01	6	·50	·95	·81
7	·29	·11	62·96	7	·43	·90	·76
8	·21	·07	·92	8	·35	·86	·72
9	·14	·02	·87	9	·28	·81	·67

Alcohol table. Specific gravity at 60°/60° F. (15·56°/15·56° C.)—*cont.*

Specific gravity in air at 60/60° F.	Percentage of proof spirit.	Percentage of alcohol. By weight.	Percentage of alcohol. By volume at 60° F.	Specific gravity in air at 60/60° F.	Percentage of proof spirit.	Percentage of alcohol. By weight.	Percentage of alcohol. By volume at 60° F.
0·9120	106·20	52·77	60·63	0·9170	102·24	50·53	58·38
1	·12	·73	·59	1	·16	·49	·33
2	·04	·68	·54	2	·08	·44	·29
3	105·97	·64	·50	3	·00	·40	·24
4	·89	·59	·45	4	101·92	·35	·20
5	·81	·55	·41	5	·84	·31	·15
6	·73	·51	·37	6	·76	·26	·10
7	·65	·46	·32	7	·68	·22	·06
8	·57	·42	·28	8	·59	·17	·01
9	·49	·37	·23	9	·51	·13	57·97
0·9130	105·41	52·33	60·19	0·9180	101·43	50·08	57·92
1	·33	·29	·15	1	·35	·03	·87
2	·25	·24	·10	2	·27	49·99	·83
3	·18	·20	·06	3	·19	·94	·78
4	·10	·15	·01	4	·11	·90	·74
5	·02	·11	59·97	5	·03	·85	·69
6	104·94	·06	·92	6	100·95	·80	·64
7	·86	·02	·88	7	·87	·76	·59
8	·79	51·97	·83	8	·78	·71	·55
9	·71	·93	·79	9	·70	·67	·50
0·9140	104·63	51·88	59·74	0·9190	100·62	49·62	57·45
1	·55	·84	·70	1	·54	·57	·40
2	·47	·79	·65	2	·46	·53	·36
3	·39	·75	·61	3	·37	·48	·31
4	·31	·70	·56	4	·29	·44	·27
5	·23	·66	·52	5	·21	·39	·22
6	·15	·61	·47	6	·13	·35	·17
7	·07	·57	·43	7	·05	·30	·13
8	·00	·52	·38	8	99·96	·26	·08
9	103·92	·48	·34	9	·88	·21	·04
0·9150	103·84	51·43	59·29	0·9200	99·80	49·17	56·99
1	·76	·39	·24	1	·72	·12	·94
2	·68	·34	·20	2	·64	·08	·90
3	·60	·30	·15	3	·55	·03	·85
4	·52	·25	·11	4	·47	48·99	·81
5	·44	·21	·06	5	·39	·94	·76
6	·36	·16	·01	6	·31	·89	·71
7	·28	·12	58·97	7	·23	·85	·66
8	·21	·07	·92	8	·14	·80	·62
9	·13	·03	·88	9	·06	·76	·57
0·9160	103·05	50·98	58·83	0·9210	98·98	48·71	56·52
1	102·97	·94	·79	1	·90	·66	·47
2	·89	·89	·74	2	·82	·62	·43
3	·81	·85	·70	3	·73	·57	·38
4	·73	·80	·65	4	·65	·53	·34
5	·65	·76	·61	5	·57	·48	·29
6	·57	·71	·56	6	·49	·43	·24
7	·49	·67	·52	7	·41	·39	·19
8	·40	·62	·47	8	·32	·34	·15
9	·32	·58	·43	9	·24	·30	·10

ALCOHOL TABLE. SPECIFIC GRAVITY AT 60°/60° F. (15·56°/15·56° C.)—*cont.*

Specific gravity in air at 60/60° F.	Per-centage of proof spirit.	Percentage of alcohol.		Specific gravity in air at 60/60° F.	Per-centage of proof spirit.	Percentage of alcohol.	
		By weight.	By volume at 60° F.			By weight.	By volume at 60° F.
0·9220	98·16	48·25	56·05	0·9270	93·95	45·94	53·65
1	·08	·20	·00	1	·86	·89	·60
2	97·99	·16	55·95	2	·78	·85	·55
3	·91	·11	·91	3	·69	·80	·51
4	·82	·07	·86	4	·61	·76	·46
5	·74	·02	·81	5	·52	·71	·41
6	·66	47·97	·76	6	·43	·66	·36
7	·58	·93	·71	7	·35	·61	·31
8	·49	·88	·67	8	·26	·57	·26
9	·41	·84	·62	9	·18	·52	·21
0·9230	97·33	47·79	55·57	0·9280	93·09	45·47	53·16
1	·25	·74	·52	1	·00	·42	·11
2	·16	·70	·47	2	92·92	·38	·06
3	·08	·65	·43	3	·83	·33	·02
4	96·99	·61	·38	4	·75	·29	52·97
5	·91	·56	·33	5	·66	·24	·92
6	·83	·51	·28	6	·57	·19	·87
7	·74	·47	·24	7	·49	·14	·82
8	·66	·42	·19	8	·40	·10	·77
9	·57	·38	·15	9	·32	·05	·72
0·9240	96·49	47·33	55·10	0·9290	92·23	45·00	52·67
1	·40	·28	·05	1	·14	44·95	·62
2	·32	·24	·00	2	·06	·91	·57
3	·23	·19	54·96	3	91·97	·86	·53
4	·15	·15	·91	4	·89	·82	·48
5	·06	·10	·86	5	·80	·77	·43
6	95·98	·05	·81	6	·71	·72	·38
7	·89	·01	·76	7	·62	·67	·33
8	·81	46·96	·72	8	·54	·63	·28
9	·72	·92	·67	9	·45	·58	·23
0·9250	95·64	46·87	54·62	0·9300	91·36	44·53	52·18
1	·56	·82	·57	1	·27	·48	·13
2	·47	·78	·52	2	·19	·44	·08
3	·39	·73	·48	3	·10	·39	·03
4	·30	·69	·43	4	·02	·35	51·98
5	·22	·64	·38	5	90·93	·30	·93
6	·14	·59	·33	6	·84	·25	·88
7	·05	·54	·28	7	·76	·21	·83
8	94·97	·50	·24	8	·67	·16	·78
9	·88	·45	·19	9	·59	·12	·73
0·9260	94·80	46·40	54·14	0·9310	90·50	44·07	51·68
1	·72	·35	·09	1	·41	·02	·63
2	·63	·31	·04	2	·32	43·97	·58
3	·55	·26	·00	3	·24	·93	·53
4	·46	·22	53·95	4	·15	·88	·48
5	·38	·17	·90	5	·06	·83	·43
6	·29	·12	·85	6	89·97	·78	·38
7	·21	·08	·80	7	·88	·73	·33
8	·12	·03	·75	8	·79	·69	·28
9	·04	45·99	·70	9	·70	·64	·23

ALCOHOL TABLE. SPECIFIC GRAVITY AT 60°/60° F. (15·56°/15·56° C.)—*cont.*

Specific gravity in air at 60/60° F.	Percentage of proof spirit.	Percentage of alcohol. By weight.	Percentage of alcohol. By volume at 60° F.	Specific gravity in air at 60/60° F.	Percentage of proof spirit.	Percentage of alcohol. By weight.	Percentage of alcohol. By volume at 60° F.
0·9320	89·61	43·59	51·18	0·9370	85·04	41·15	48·57
1	·52	·54	·13	1	84·95	·10	·52
2	·43	·49	·08	2	·85	·05	·47
3	·35	·45	·03	3	·76	·00	·41
4	·26	·40	50·98	4	·66	40·95	·36
5	·17	·35	·93	5	·57	·90	·31
6	·08	·30	·88	6	·48	·85	·26
7	88·99	·25	·83	7	·38	·80	·20
8	·90	·21	·77	8	·29	·75	·15
9	·81	·16	·72	9	·19	·70	·09
0·9330	88·72	43·11	50·67	0·9380	84·10	40·65	48·04
1	·63	·06	·62	1	·00	·60	47·99
2	·54	·01	·57	2	83·91	·55	·93
3	·44	42·97	·51	3	·81	·50	·88
4	·35	·92	·46	4	·72	·45	·82
5	·26	·87	·41	5	·62	·40	·77
6	·17	·82	·36	6	·53	·35	·72
7	·08	·77	·31	7	·43	·30	·66
8	87·99	·72	·25	8	·34	·25	·61
9	·90	·67	·20	9	·24	·20	·55
0·9340	87·81	42·62	50·15	0·9390	83·15	40·15	47·50
1	·72	·57	·10	1	·05	·10	·45
2	·63	·52	·05	2	82·96	·05	·39
3	·53	·48	49·99	3	·86	·00	·34
4	·44	·43	·94	4	·77	39·95	·28
5	·35	·38	·89	5	·67	·90	·23
6	·26	·33	·84	6	·57	·85	·17
7	·17	·28	·79	7	·48	·80	·12
8	·07	·23	·73	8	·38	·75	·06
9	86·98	·18	·68	9	·29	·70	·01
0·9350	86·89	42·13	49·63	0·9400	82·19	39·65	46·95
1	·80	·08	·58	1	·09	·60	·90
2	·71	·03	·53	2	·00	·55	·84
3	·61	41·99	·47	3	81·90	·50	·79
4	·52	·94	·42	4	·81	·45	·73
5	·43	·89	·37	5	·71	·40	·68
6	·34	·84	·32	6	·61	·35	·62
7	·25	·79	·26	7	·52	·30	·57
8	·15	·74	·21	8	·42	·24	·51
9	·06	·69	·15	9	·33	·19	·46
0·9360	85·97	41·64	49·10	0·9410	81·23	39·14	46·40
1	·88	·59	·05	1	·13	·09	·35
2	·78	·54	·00	2	·03	·04	·29
3	·69	·50	48·94	3	80·94	38·99	·24
4	·59	·45	·89	4	·84	·94	·18
5	·50	·40	·84	5	·74	·89	·13
6	·41	·35	·79	6	·64	·84	·07
7	·32	·30	·73	7	·55	·79	·02
8	·22	·25	·68	8	·45	·74	45·96
9	·13	·20	·62	9	·36	·69	·91

Alcohol table. Specific gravity at 60°/60° F. (15·56°/15·56° C.)—*cont.*

Specific gravity in air at 60/60° F.	Per-centage of proof spirit.	Percentage of alcohol.		Specific gravity. in air at 60/60° F.	Per-centage of proof spirit.	Percentage of alcohol.	
		By weight.	By volume at 60° F.			By weight.	By volume at 60° F.
0·9420	80·26	38·64	45·85	0·9470	75·17	36·00	42·95
1	·16	·59	·79	1	·06	35·95	·89
2	·06	·54	·74	2	74·96	·89	·83
3	79·97	·48	·68	3	·85	·84	·77
4	·87	·43	·63	4	·75	·78	·71
5	·77	·38	·57	5	·64	·73	·65
6	·67	·33	·51	6	·54	·68	·59
7	·57	·28	·45	7	·43	·62	·53
8	·47	·22	·40	8	·33	·57	·47
9	·37	·17	·34	9	·22	·51	·41
0·9430	79·27	38·12	45·28	0·9480	74·12	35·46	42·35
1	·17	·07	·22	1	·01	·41	·29
2	·07	·02	·17	2	73·91	·35	·23
3	78·97	37·96	·11	3	·80	·30	·17
4	·87	·91	·06	4	·70	·24	·11
5	·77	·86	·00	5	·59	·19	·05
6	·67	·81	44·94	6	·48	·14	41·99
7	·57	·76	·88	7	·38	·08	·93
8	·46	·70	·83	8	·27	·03	·87
9	·36	·65	·77	9	·17	34·97	·81
0·9440	78·26	37·60	44·71	0·9490	73·06	34·92	41·75
1	·16	·55	·65	1	72·95	·87	·69
2	·06	·50	·59	2	·84	·81	·63
3	77·95	·44	·54	3	·74	·76	·56
4	·85	·39	·48	4	·63	·70	·50
5	·75	·34	·42	5	·52	·65	·44
6	·65	·29	·36	6	·41	·59	·38
7	·55	·23	·30	7	·30	·54	·32
8	·44	·18	·25	8	·20	·48	·25
9	·34	·12	·19	9	·09	·43	·19
0·9450	77·24	37·07	44·13	0·9500	71·98	34·37	41·13
1	·14	·02	·07	1	·87	·31	·07
2	·04	36·97	·01	2	·76	·26	·01
3	76·93	·91	43·96	3	·65	·20	40·94
4	·83	·86	·90	4	·54	·15	·88
5	·73	·81	·84	5	·43	·09	·82
6	·63	·76	·78	6	·32	·03	·76
7	·52	·70	·72	7	·21	33·98	·69
8	·42	·65	·66	8	·09	·92	·63
9	·31	·59	·60	9	70·98	·87	·56
0·9460	76·21	36·54	43·54	0·9510	70·87	33·81	40·50
1	·11	·49	·48	1	·76	·75	·44
2	·00	·43	·42	2	·65	·70	·38
3	75·90	·38	·37	3	·54	·64	·31
4	·79	·32	·31	4	·43	·59	·25
5	·69	·27	·25	5	·32	·53	·19
6	·59	·22	·19	6	·21	·47	·13
7	·48	·16	·13	7	·10	·42	·06
8	·38	·11	·07	8	69·98	·36	·00
9	·27	·05	·01	9	·87	·31	39·93

ALCOHOL TABLE. SPECIFIC GRAVITY AT 60°/60° F. (15·56°/15·56° C.)—*cont.*

Specific gravity in air at 60/60° F.	Percentage of proof spirit.	Percentage of alcohol. By weight.	Percentage of alcohol. By volume at 60° F.	Specific gravity in air at 60/60° F.	Percentage of proof spirit.	Percentage of alcohol. By weight.	Percentage of alcohol. By volume at 60° F.
0·9520	69·76	33·25	39·87	0·9570	63·86	30·28	36·50
1	·65	·19	·81	1	·73	·22	·43
2	·54	·14	·74	2	·61	·16	·36
3	·42	·08	·68	3	·48	·09	·29
4	·31	·03	·61	4	·36	·03	·22
5	·20	32·97	·55	5	·23	29·97	·15
6	·09	·91	·49	6	·10	·91	·08
7	68·97	·85	·42	7	62·98	·85	·01
8	·86	·80	·36	8	·85	·78	35·93
9	·74	·74	·29	9	·73	·72	·86
0·9530	68·63	32·68	39·23	0·9580	62·60	29·66	35·79
1	·52	·62	·16	1	·47	·60	·72
2	·40	·56	·10	2	·35	·54	·65
3	·29	·51	·03	3	·22	·47	·57
4	·17	·45	38·97	4	·10	·41	·50
5	·06	·39	·90	5	61·97	·35	·43
6	67·94	·33	·83	6	·84	·29	·36
7	·83	·27	·77	7	·71	·22	·29
8	·71	·21	·70	8	·59	·16	·21
9	·60	·15	·64	9	·46	·09	·14
0·9540	67·48	32·09	38·57	0·9590	61·33	29·03	35·07
1	·36	·03	·50	1	·20	28·97	·00
2	·24	31·97	·43	2	·07	·90	34·92
3	·13	·92	·37	3	60·94	·84	·85
4	·01	·86	·30	4	·81	·77	·77
5	66·89	·80	·23	5	·68	·71	·70
6	·77	·74	·16	6	·55	·65	·63
7	·65	·68	·09	7	·42	·58	·55
8	·54	·62	·03	8	·29	·52	·48
9	·42	·56	37·96	9	·16	·45	·40
0·9550	66·30	31·50	37·89	0·9600	60·03	28·39	34·33
1	·18	·44	·82	1	59·90	·32	·25
2	·06	·38	·75	2	·77	·26	·18
3	65·94	·32	·69	3	·63	·19	·10
4	·82	·26	·62	4	·50	·13	·03
5	·70	·20	·55	5	·37	·06	33·95
6	·58	·14	·48	6	·24	27·99	·87
7	·46	·08	·41	7	·10	·93	·80
8	·33	·02	·34	8	58·97	·86	·72
9	·21	30·96	·27	9	·83	·80	·65
0·9560	65·09	30·90	37·20	0·9610	58·70	27·73	33·57
1	64·97	·84	·13	1	·56	·66	·49
2	·85	·78	·06	2	·43	·60	·41
3	·72	·71	36·99	3	·29	·53	·34
4	·60	·65	·92	4	·16	·47	·26
5	·48	·59	·85	5	·02	·40	·18
6	·36	·53	·78	6	57·88	·33	·10
7	·23	·47	·71	7	·74	·26	·02
8	·11	·40	·64	8	·61	·20	32·95
9	63·98	·34	·57	9	·47	·13	·87

ALCOHOL TABLE. SPECIFIC GRAVITY AT 60°/60° F. (15·56°/15·56° C.)—*cont.*

Specific gravity in air at 60/60° F.	Percentage of proof spirit.	Percentage of alcohol. By weight.	Percentage of alcohol. By volume at 60° F.	Specific gravity in air at 60/60° F.	Percentage of proof spirit.	Percentage of alcohol. By weight.	Percentage of alcohol. By volume at 60° F.
0·9620	57·33	27·06	32·79	0·9670	49·97	23·47	28·60
1	·19	26·99	·71	1	·81	·39	·51
2	·05	·92	·63	2	·65	·32	·42
3	56·92	·86	·56	3	·50	·24	·33
4	·78	·79	·48	4	·34	·17	·24
5	·64	·72	·40	5	·18	·09	·15
6	·50	·65	·32	6	·02	·01	·06
7	·36	·58	·24	7	48·86	22·94	27·97
8	·22	·51	·16	8	·70	·86	·87
9	·08	·44	·08	9	·54	·79	·78
0·9630	55·94	26·37	32·00	0·9680	48·38	22·71	27·69
1	·80	·30	31·92	1	·22	·63	·60
2	·66	·23	·84	2	·06	·55	·51
3	·51	·17	·75	3	47·90	·48	·41
4	·37	·10	·67	4	·74	·40	·32
5	·23	·03	·59	5	·58	·32	·23
6	·09	25·96	·51	6	·42	·24	·14
7	54·94	·89	·43	7	·26	·16	·05
8	·80	·82	·34	8	·09	·09	26·95
9	·65	·75	·26	9	46·93	·01	·86
0·9640	54·51	25·68	31·18	0·9690	46·77	21·93	26·77
1	·36	·61	·10	1	·61	·85	·68
2	·22	·54	·01	2	·45	·77	·58
3	·07	·46	30·93	3	·28	·70	·49
4	53·93	·39	·84	4	·12	·62	·39
5	·78	·32	·76	5	45·96	·54	·30
6	·63	·25	·68	6	·80	·46	·21
7	·48	·18	·59	7	·63	·38	·11
8	·34	·10	·51	8	·47	·30	·02
9	·19	·03	·42	9	·30	·22	25·92
0·9650	53·04	24·96	30·34	0·9700	45·14	21·14	25·83
1	52·89	·89	·25	1	44·97	·06	·74
2	·74	·82	·17	2	·81	20·98	·64
3	·59	·74	·08	3	·64	·90	·55
4	·44	·67	·00	4	·48	·82	·45
5	·29	·60	29·91	5	·31	·74	·36
6	·14	·53	·82	6	·14	·66	·26
7	51·99	·45	·74	7	43·97	·58	·17
8	·83	·38	·65	8	·81	·50	·07
9	·68	·30	·57	9	·64	·42	24·98
0·9660	51·53	24·23	29·48	0·9710	43·47	20·34	24·88
1	·37	·15	·39	1	·30	·26	·78
2	·22	·08	·30	2	·13	·18	·69
3	·06	·00	·22	3	42·96	·10	·59
4	50·91	23·93	·13	4	·79	·02	·50
5	·75	·85	·04	5	·62	19·94	·40
6	·59	·77	28·95	6	·45	·86	·30
7	·44	·70	·86	7	·28	·78	·20
8	·28	·62	·78	8	·11	·69	·11
9	·13	·55	·69	9	41·94	·61	·01

ALCOHOL TABLE. SPECIFIC GRAVITY AT 60°/60° F. (15·56°/15·56° C.)—*cont.*

Specific gravity in air at 60/60° F.	Per-centage of proof spirit.	Percentage of alcohol.		Specific gravity in air at 60/60° F.	Per-centage of proof spirit.	Percentage of alcohol.	
		By weight.	By volume at 60° F.			By weight.	By volume at 60° F.
0·9720	41·77	19·53	23·91	0·9770	33·14	15·43	18·99
1	·60	·45	·81	1	32·97	·35	·89
2	·43	·37	·72	2	·80	·27	·79
3	·26	·29	·62	3	·62	·18	·70
4	·09	·21	·53	4	·45	·10	·60
5	40·92	·13	·43	5	·28	·02	·50
6	·75	·05	·33	6	·11	14·94	·40
7	·58	18·97	·23	7	31·94	·86	·30
8	·41	·88	·14	8	·76	·77	·20
9	·24	·80	·04	9	·59	·69	·10
0·9730	40·07	18·72	22·94	0·9780	31·42	14·61	18·00
1	39·90	·64	·84	1	·25	·53	17·90
2	·73	·56	·74	2	·08	·45	·80
3	·55	·47	·65	3	30·90	·37	·71
4	·38	·39	·55	4	·73	·29	·61
5	·21	·31	·45	5	·56	·21	·51
6	·04	·23	·35	6	·39	·13	·41
7	38·87	·15	·25	7	·22	·05	·31
8	·69	·06	·16	8	·04	13·96	·21
9	·52	17·98	·06	9	29·87	·88	·11
0·9740	38·35	17·90	21·96	0·9790	29·70	13·80	17·01
1	·18	·82	·86	1	·53	·72	16·91
2	·01	·74	·76	2	·36	·64	·81
3	37·83	·65	·67	3	·18	·56	·72
4	·66	·57	·57	4	·01	·48	·62
5	·49	·49	·47	5	28·84	·40	·52
6	·32	·41	·37	6	·67	·32	·42
7	·14	·32	·27	7	·50	·24	·33
8	36·97	·24	·17	8	·33	·15	·23
9	·79	·15	·07	9	·16	·07	·14
0·9750	36·62	17·07	20·97	0·9800	27·99	12·99	16·04
1	·44	16·99	·87	1	·82	·91	15·94
2	·27	·91	·77	2	·65	·83	·85
3	·09	·82	·68	3	·49	·75	·75
4	35·92	·74	·58	4	·32	·67	·66
5	·74	·66	·48	5	·15	·59	·56
6	·57	·58	·38	6	26·98	·51	·46
7	·39	·50	·28	7	·82	·43	·37
8	·22	·41	·18	8	·65	·36	·27
9	·04	·33	·08	9	·49	·28	·18
0·9760	34·87	16·25	19·98	0·9810	26·32	12·20	15·08
1	·70	·17	·88	1	·15	·12	14·98
2	·53	·09	·78	2	25·99	·04	·89
3	·35	·00	·69	3	·82	11·97	·79
4	·18	15·92	·59	4	·66	·89	·70
5	·01	·84	·49	5	·49	·81	·60
6	33·84	·76	·39	6	·32	·73	·51
7	·66	·68	·29	7	·16	·65	·41
8	·49	·59	·19	8	24·99	·58	·32
9	·31	·51	·09	9	·83	·50	·22

Alcohol table. Specific gravity at 60°/60° F. (15·56°/15·56° C.)—*cont.*

Specific gravity in air at 60/60° F.	Percentage of proof spirit.	Percentage of alcohol.		Specific gravity in air at 60/60° F.	Percentage of proof spirit.	Percentage of alcohol.	
		By weight.	By volume at 60° F.			By weight.	By volume at 60° F.
0·9820	24·66	11·42	14·13	0·9870	16·85	7·76	9·65
1	·50	·34	·04	1	·70	·69	·56
2	·33	·27	13·94	2	·55	·62	·48
3	·17	·19	·85	3	·41	·56	·39
4	·00	·12	·75	4	·26	·49	·31
5	23·84	·04	·66	5	·11	·42	·22
6	·68	10·96	·57	6	15·96	·35	·14
7	·52	·89	·48	7	·82	·28	·05
8	·35	·81	·38	8	·67	·22	8·97
9	·19	·74	·29	9	·53	·15	·88
0·9830	23·03	10·66	13·20	0·9880	15·38	7·08	8·80
1	22·87	·58	·11	1	·24	·01	·72
2	·71	·51	·02	2	·09	6·94	·64
3	·55	·43	12·92	3	14·95	·88	·55
4	·39	·36	·83	4	·80	·81	·47
5	·23	·28	·74	5	·66	·74	·39
6	·07	·21	·65	6	·52	·67	·31
7	21·91	·13	·56	7	·37	·61	·23
8	·76	·06	·47	8	·23	·54	·14
9	·60	9·98	·38	9	·08	·48	·06
0·9840	21·44	9·91	12·29	0·9890	13·94	6·41	7·98
1	·28	·84	·20	1	·80	·34	·90
2	·12	·76	·11	2	·66	·28	·82
3	20·97	·69	·02	3	·51	·21	·74
4	·81	·61	11·93	4	·37	·15	·66
5	·65	·54	·84	5	·23	·08	·58
6	·49	·47	·75	6	·09	·02	·50
7	·34	·40	·66	7	12·95	5·95	·42
8	·18	·32	·58	8	·81	·89	·34
9	·03	·25	·49	9	·67	·82	·26
0·9850	19·87	9·18	11·40	0·9900	12·53	5·76	7·18
1	·72	·11	·31	1	·39	·70	·10
2	·56	·04	·22	2	·25	·64	·02
3	·41	8·96	·13	3	·12	·57	6·95
4	·25	·89	·04	4	11·98	·51	·87
5	·10	·82	10·95	5	·84	·45	·79
6	18·95	·75	·86	6	·70	·39	·71
7	·80	·68	·77	7	·57	·32	·63
8	·64	·60	·69	8	·43	·26	·56
9	·49	·53	·60	9	·30	·19	·48
0·9860	18·34	8·46	10·51	0·9910	11·16	5·13	6·40
1	·19	·39	·42	1	·03	·07	·32
2	·04	·32	·34	2	10·89	·01	·24
3	17·89	·25	·25	3	·76	4·94	·17
4	·74	·18	·17	4	·62	·88	·09
5	·59	·11	·08	5	·49	·82	·01
6	·44	·04	9·99	6	·36	·76	5·93
7	·29	7·97	·91	7	·22	·70	·86
8	·15	·90	·82	8	·09	·63	·78
9	·00	·83	·74	9	9·95	·57	·71

ALCOHOL TABLE. SPECIFIC GRAVITY AT 60°/60° F. (15·56°/15·56° C.)—*cont.*

Specific gravity. in air at 60/60° F.	Percentage of proof spirit.	Percentage of alcohol.		Specific gravity. in air at 60/60° F.	Percentage of proof spirit.	Percentage of alcohol.	
		By weight.	By volume at 60° F.			By weight.	By volume at 60° F.
0·9920	9·82	4·51	5·63	0·9960	4·73	2·17	2·71
1	·69	·45	·55	1	·61	·11	·64
2	·56	·39	·48	2	·49	·06	·57
3	·42	·32	·40	3	·36	·00	·50
4	·29	·26	·33	4	·24	1·95	·43
5	·16	·20	·25	5	·12	·89	·36
6	·03	·14	·18	6	·00	·83	·29
7	8·90	·08	·10	7	3·88	·78	·22
8	·77	·02	·03	8	·76	·72	·16
9	·64	3·96	4·95	9	·64	·67	·09
0·9930	8·51	3·90	4·88	0·9970	3·52	1·61	2·02
1	·38	·84	·81	1	·40	·56	1·95
2	·25	·78	·73	2	·28	·50	·88
3	·13	·72	·66	3	·16	·45	·82
4	·00	·66	·58	4	·04	·39	·75
5	7·87	·60	·51	5	·92	·34	·68
6	·74	·54	·44	6	·80	·29	·61
7	·62	·48	·36	7	·68	·23	·54
8	·49	·43	·29	8	·57	·18	·48
9	·37	·37	·21	9	·45	·12	·41
0·9940	7·24	3·31	4·14	0·9980	2·33	1·07	1·34
1	·11	·25	·07	1	·21	·02	·27
2	6·99	·19	·00	2	·09	0·96	·20
3	·86	·14	3·92	3	1·98	·91	·14
4	·74	·08	·85	4	·86	·85	·07
5	·61	·02	·78	5	·74	·80	·00
6	·48	2·96	·71	6	·62	·75	0·93
7	·36	·90	·64	7	·51	·69	·86
8	·23	·85	·56	8	·39	·64	·80
9	·11	·79	·49	9	·28	·58	·73
0·9950	5·98	2·73	3·42	0·9990	1·16	0·53	0·66
1	·85	·67	·35	1	·04	·48	·59
2	·73	·62	·28	2	0·93	·42	·53
3	·60	·56	·20	3	·81	·37	·46
4	·48	·51	·13	4	·70	·31	·40
5	·35	·45	·06	5	·58	·26	·33
6	·23	·39	2·99	6	·46	·21	·26
7	·10	·34	·92	7	·35	·16	·20
8	4·98	·28	·85	8	·23	·10	·13
9	·85	·23	·78	9	·12	·05	·07
				1·0000	0·00	0·00	0·00

For use at a series of temperatures between 10° and 40°, the following table may be found useful (Circular No. 19, Bureau of Standards, Washington).

DENSITY[1] (IN GRAMS PER C.C.) OF MIXTURES OF ETHYL ALCOHOL AND WATER.

Per cent. alcohol by weight.	Temperature.						
	10°	15°	20°	25°	30°	35°	40°
0	0·99973	0·99913	0·99823	0·99708	0·99568	0·99406	0·99225
1	785	725	636	520	379	217	034
2	602	542	453	336	194	031	0·98846
3	426	365	275	157	014	0·98849	663
4	258	195	103	0·98984	0·98839	672	485
5	098	032	0·98938	817	670	501	311
6	0·98946	0·98877	780	656	507	335	142
7	801	729	627	500	347	172	0·97975
8	660	584	478	346	189	009	808
9	524	442	331	193	031	0·97846	641
10	393	304	187	043	0·97875	685	475
11	267	171	047	0·97897	723	527	312
12	145	041	0·97910	753	573	371	150
13	026	0·97914	775	611	424	216	0·96989
14	0·97911	790	643	472	278	063	829
15	800	669	514	334	133	0·96911	670
16	692	552	387	199	0·96990	760	512
17	583	433	259	062	844	607	352
18	473	313	129	0·96923	697	452	189
19	363	191	0·96997	782	547	294	023
20	252	068	864	639	395	134	0·95856
21	139	0·96944	729	495	242	0·95973	687
22	024	818	592	348	087	809	516
23	0·96907	689	453	199	0·95929	643	343
24	787	558	312	048	769	476	168
25	665	424	168	0·95895	607	306	0·94991
26	539	287	020	738	442	133	810
27	406	144	0·95867	576	272	0·94955	625
28	268	0·95996	710	410	098	774	438
29	125	844	548	241	0·94922	590	248
30	0·95977	686	382	067	741	403	055
31	823	524	212	0·94890	557	214	0·93860
32	665	357	038	709	370	021	662
33	502	186	0·94860	525	180	0·93825	461
34	334	011	679	337	0·93986	626	257
35	162	0·94832	494	146	790	425	051
36	0·94986	650	306	0·93952	591	221	0·92843
37	805	464	114	756	390	016	634
38	620	273	0·93919	556	186	0·92808	422
39	431	079	720	353	0·92979	597	208
40	238	0·93882	518	148	770	385	0·91992
41	042	682	314	0·92940	558	170	774
42	0·93842	478	107	729	344	0·91952	554
43	639	271	0·92897	516	128	733	332
44	433	062	685	301	0·91910	513	108

[1] The density values given in this table are numerically the same as specific gravities at the various temperatures in terms of water at 4° as unity.

DENSITY (IN GRAMS PER C.C.) OF MIXTURES OF ETHYL ALCOHOL AND WATER.—*cont.*

Per cent. alcohol by weight.	Temperature.						
	10°	15°	20°	25°	30°	35°	40°
45	0·93226	0·92852	0·92472	0·92085	0·91692	0·91291	0·90884
46	017	640	257	0·91868	472	069	660
47	0·92806	426	041	649	250	0·90845	434
48	593	211	0·91823	429	028	621	207
49	379	0·91995	604	208	0·90805	396	0·89979
50	0·92162	0·91776	0·91384	0·90985	0·90580	0·90168	0·89750
51	0·91943	555	160	760	353	0·89940	519
52	723	333	0·90936	534	125	710	288
53	502	110	711	307	0·89896	479	056
54	279	0·90885	485	079	667	248	0·88823
55	055	659	258	0·89850	437	016	589
56	0·90831	433	031	621	206	0·88784	356
57	607	207	0·89803	392	0·88975	552	122
58	381	0·89980	574	162	744	319	0·87888
59	154	752	344	0·88931	512	085	653
60	0·89927	523	113	699	278	0·87851	417
61	698	293	0·88882	466	044	615	180
62	468	062	650	233	0·87809	379	0·86943
63	237	0·88830	417	0·87998	574	142	705
64	006	597	183	763	337	0·86905	466
65	0·88774	364	0·87948	527	100	667	227
66	541	130	713	291	0·86863	429	0·85987
67	308	0·87895	477	054	625	190	747
68	074	660	241	0·86817	387	0·85950	507
69	0·87839	424	004	579	148	710	266
70	602	187	0·86766	340	0·85908	470	025
71	365	0·86949	527	100	667	228	0·84783
72	127	710	287	0·85859	426	0·84986	540
73	0·86888	470	047	618	184	743	297
74	648	229	0·85806	376	0·84941	500	053
75	408	0·85988	564	134	698	257	0·83809
76	168	747	322	0·84891	455	013	564
77	0·85927	505	079	647	211	0·83768	319
78	685	262	0·84835	403	0·83965	523	074
79	442	018	590	158	720	277	0·82827
80	197	0·84772	344	0·83911	473	029	578
81	0·84950	525	096	664	224	0·82780	329
82	702	277	0·83848	415	0·82974	530	079
83	453	028	599	164	724	279	0·81828
84	203	0·83777	348	0·82913	473	027	576
85	0·83951	525	095	660	220	0·81774	322
86	697	271	0·82840	405	0·81965	519	067
87	441	014	583	148	708	262	0·80811
88	181	0·82754	323	0·81888	448	003	552
89	0·82919	492	062	626	186	0·80742	291

DENSITY (IN GRAMS PER C.C.) OF MIXTURES OF ETHYL ALCOHOL AND WATER.—*cont.*

Per cent. alcohol by weight.	Temperature.						
	10°	15°	20°	25°	30°	35°	40°
90	0·82654	0·82227	0·81797	0·81362	0·80922	0·80478	0·80028
91	386	0·81959	529	094	655	211	0·79761
92	114	688	257	0·80823	384	0·79941	491
93	0·81839	413	0·80983	549	111	669	220
94	561	134	705	272	0·79835	393	0·78947
95	278	0·80852	424	0·79991	555	114	670
96	0·80991	566	138	706	271	0·78831	388
97	698	274	0·79846	415	0·78981	542	100
98	399	0·79975	547	117	684	247	0·77806
99	094	670	243	0·78814	382	0·77946	507
100	0·79784	360	0·78934	506	075	641	203

For examining very dilute alcohol solutions in the tropics, the following table of the "density" at 32·5° C. (= 90·5° F.) of solutions containing 0 to 1·6 per cent. of alcohol by weight, may be found useful. It is due to A. F. Joseph and W. N. Rae.[1]

Alcohol per cent. by weight.	"Density"; gram per c.c. at 32·5°.	Difference for 0·2 per cent.
0·0	0·99489	38
0·2	0·99451	40
0·4	0·99411	38
0·6	0·99373	36
0·8	0·99337	38
1·0	0·99299	38
1·2	0·99261	37
1·4	0·99224	38
1·6	0·99186	

There are three methods in general use for expressing the percentage of alcohol in a liquid—(1) percentage of alcohol by weight, (2) percentage of alcohol by volume, and (3) percentage of *proof spirit* by volume. The first method is the best for scientific purposes, and in general for miscellaneous analytical work, where often alcohol is only one of several ingredients of a mixture the composition of which is required. But the second method is by far the most convenient when alcoholic beverages or spirituous medicines are concerned, and both in this country and on the Continent, when "percentage of alcohol" is stated in connection with wines, spirits, etc., percentage *by volume* is generally understood, unless the contrary is stated or obviously implied. To obtain percentage by

[1] *J. Soc. Chem. Ind.*, 1914, **33**, 991.

weight it is necessary to take the specific gravity of the liquid examined, or to weigh the liquid out; and when obtained, the percentage by weight may be misleading unless used carefully. For example, two specimens of wine may contain identical amounts of alcohol per litre, but expressed as percentage by *weight* the quantities may be appreciably different one from the other, because one wine may be sweetened and the other not. The sweetened wine being heavier than the other, contains a smaller percentage of alcohol *by weight*, though a litre of each contains the same amount.

Beverages and spirituous medicines being almost invariably used, measured, compared, and referred to in terms of their volumes, and being of widely different densities, a truer idea of their relative alcoholic contents is given by expressing the latter as percentage by volume rather than by weight.

For commercial and fiscal purposes in this country, however, "proof spirit" is the unit of volume for alcohol. That this is so is, from some points of view, a pity. The use of the term, and of its adjuncts "over proof" and "under proof," is confusing and cumbersome. But it has been so long in employment, and is so much interwoven with trade practices, that a change to the simpler method of expressing alcoholic strength by means of alcohol percentage would undoubtedly cause serious inconvenience. It must be carefully borne in mind, however, that although "proof spirit" terminology is cumbersome, there is no loss of scientific precision in adopting a diluted alcohol as unit, instead of absolute alcohol, so long as the unit is properly defined. On the contrary, there is more accuracy, because the diluted alcohol can be defined by means of its specific gravity to any degree of precision required, whilst the exact specific gravity of absolute alcohol is a matter of some doubt. In this connection it is of interest to quote from a report made in 1833 by a Committee of the Royal Society, who had been asked by the Treasury to advise them on the subject of spirit valuation for fiscal purposes:—

"With regard to the substance alcohol, upon which the excise duty is to be levied, there appears to be no reason, either philosophical or practical, why it should be considered as absolute. A definite mixture of alcohol and water is as invariable in its value as absolute alcohol can be. It is also invariable in its nature, and can be more readily and with equal accuracy identified by that only quality or condition to which recourse can be had in practice, namely, specific gravity. A diluted alcohol is, therefore, that which is recommended by us as the only excisable substance."

The legal definition of "proof spirit" is given a little later on.

Hydrometry.—Various rough-and-ready methods for trying the strength of "*aqua vitae*" were practised in bygone times. The property of inflammability was early made use of for this purpose. A piece of cloth was moistened with the spirit, and a lighted taper applied; if the cloth ignited the spirit was *aqua vitae rectificata*, or strong spirit. Another test was made by pouring oil into the spirit; if the latter were strong it formed a layer on the surface of the oil; if weak, it rested beneath the oil. Basil Valentine, in the fifteenth century, judged the strength of *aqua vitae* by igniting a certain volume of it; if the whole burned away, it was pure spirit; if more than half burned off, the spirit was strong; if less than half, it was weak. The well-known gunpowder "proof" test was applied by moistening a little gunpowder with the spirit and applying a light; rapid combustion implied "high proof" spirit; failure to burn, or burning only with difficulty, indicated weak or under proof spirit. The formation of bubbles or "beads" when the spirit was shaken in a glass vessel, and the length of time during which the bubbles persisted, gave to a practised observer a rough idea of the strength of a spirit, and is a test sometimes used for this purpose even at the present time.

With the increasing importance of spirit taxation, however, the need for more satisfactory methods of evaluation became more and more apparent. Towards the close of the seventeenth century a good deal of attention was given to the question of obtaining a form of "areometer" or hydrometer suitable for testing spirits, as the use of this instrument appeared to promise a method easy of application and accurate in results. Robert Boyle, in his studies upon the properties of fluids, appears to have been the first to apply the principle of the hydrometer to the testing of distilled liquors, and a description of his instrument ("Boyle's Bubble") appears in the *Philosophical Transactions* of the Royal Society for 1675. Pepys, however, mentions having seen the instrument, "a glass bubble to try the strength of spirits with," some eight years earlier.

Boyle's hydrometer, like all hydrometers, was an application of the famous principle of Archimedes—a body immersed in a liquid loses a part of its weight equal to the weight of the displaced liquid. It was composed of two glass bulbs surmounted by a glass stem; the lower and smaller bulb contained mercury, the larger contained water; these liquids served as ballast to maintain the instrument erect when in use. Placed in water, it sank only so far as to cover the bulbs, leaving the whole of the stem exposed. Placed in strong spirit, it sank till only the top of the stem was uncovered. Placed in mixtures of spirit and water, it sank to intermediate positions depending on the proportions of the two ingredients. The larger the proportion of spirit, the deeper the " bubble " sank.

Later, the stem of the areometer was roughly graduated by means of " small bits of glass, of different colours, stuck on the outside " (*Phil. Trans.*, 1730), or it was marked off into degrees by lines ; also forms of the instrument were introduced with an attachment at the base on which different weights could be hung or screwed. These weights gave the hydrometer a greater range in use, since they allowed of the total mass of the instrument being varied. One form of hydrometer—Clarke's—used in the Excise about the year 1761, was provided with special " weather weights " for use when the weather was " hot," " warm," " cold," and so on, thus introducing a rough correction for variations of specific gravity due to changes in temperature. This hydrometer, moreover, was made of copper, instead of glass, wood, or ivory as in the earlier forms. There were three marks on the stem, one showing " proof " strength, the others one-tenth under proof and one-tenth over proof respectively (*i.e.*, 10 per cent. over or under proof). Clarke's methods, however, eventually became very cumbersome with their unwieldy notation and their multiplicity of weights to meet different requirements, and in 1816–18 they were superseded by the Sikes's system, which is still employed for fiscal purposes in the United Kingdom. On account of the importance of Sikes's method of assaying spirits it must be described at a little length.

For some years previously there had been dissatisfaction with the processes in use for determining the amount of duty payable on spirits, and the Government of the day had applied to the Royal Society for assistance in the matter. The Secretary of the Society, Dr. Chas. Blagden, assisted in arranging experiments for the elucidation of the question, and in 1790 presented a first " Report on the best method of proportioning the Excise on Spirituous Liquors."[1] It was recognised that " no method can be accurate except one based upon specific gravities," and the experiments consequently took the form of determining, as accurately as possible and at a number of different temperatures, the specific gravities of a long series of mixtures containing known weights of " alcohol " and water. Dr. Dollfuss, a Swiss chemist then in London, began the experiments ; but he being called away, the work was entrusted to George Gilpin, the clerk to the Society, who in 1794 presented the results in a set of "Tables for Reducing the Quantities by Weight, in any mixture of pure Spirit and Water, to those by Measure ; and for Determining the Proportion, by Measure, of each of the two

[1] *Phil. Trans.*, 1790, **80**, 321.

Substances in such Mixtures."[1] These tables of Gilpin's were constructed with great care, and are notable as being the first alcohol tables of reasonable accuracy and comprehensiveness. The "alcohol" taken as basis had the specific gravity at 60° F./60° F. of 0·82514, which would contain 88·974 per cent. by weight of absolute alcohol.

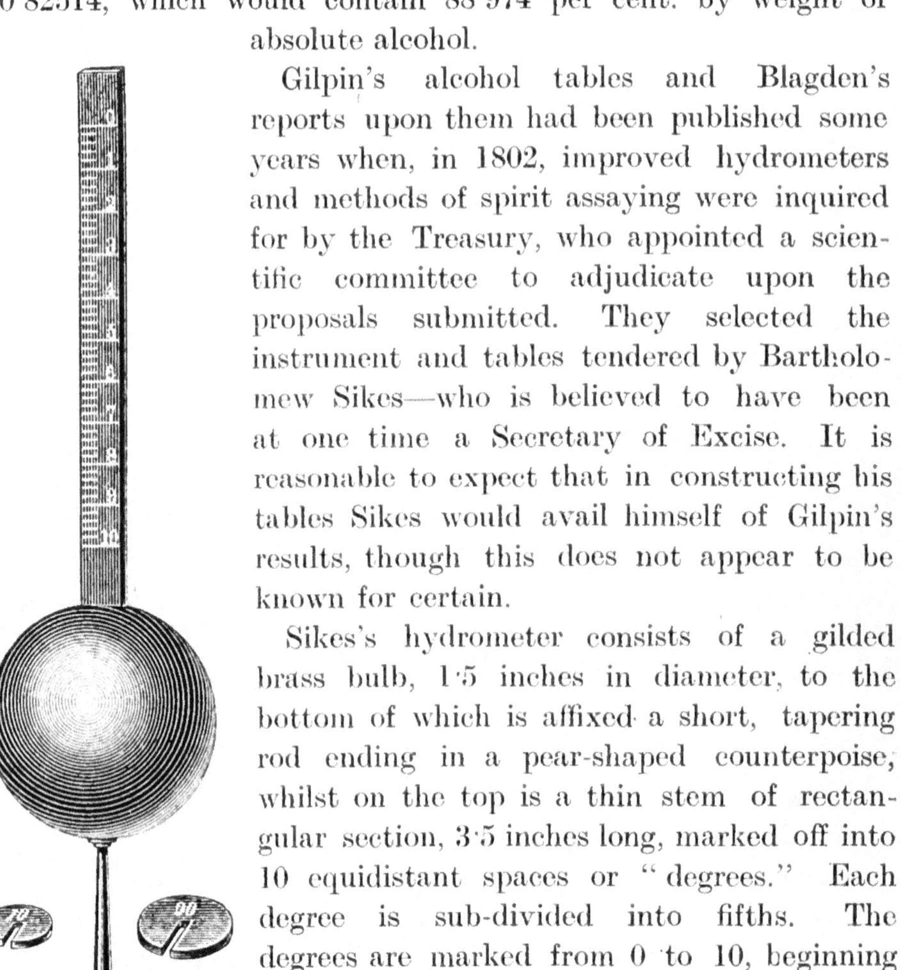

Fig. 34. — Sikes's Hydrometer. With four of the weights

Gilpin's alcohol tables and Blagden's reports upon them had been published some years when, in 1802, improved hydrometers and methods of spirit assaying were inquired for by the Treasury, who appointed a scientific committee to adjudicate upon the proposals submitted. They selected the instrument and tables tendered by Bartholomew Sikes—who is believed to have been at one time a Secretary of Excise. It is reasonable to expect that in constructing his tables Sikes would avail himself of Gilpin's results, though this does not appear to be known for certain.

Sikes's hydrometer consists of a gilded brass bulb, 1·5 inches in diameter, to the bottom of which is affixed a short, tapering rod ending in a pear-shaped counterpoise, whilst on the top is a thin stem of rectangular section, 3·5 inches long, marked off into 10 equidistant spaces or "degrees." Each degree is sub-divided into fifths. The degrees are marked from 0 to 10, beginning at the top of the stem, and are of arbitrary value—that is, they do not by themselves express the strength of the spirit or its specific gravity, but are correlated with the tables supplied with the instrument. The readings on the stem are called the "Indication," and corresponding with each indication-number the tables show the strength of the spirit tested, in terms of "proof," "over proof," or "under proof." With its 10 divisions, each having 5 sub-divisions, the instrument gives 50 indication-numbers, namely 0, 0·2, 0·4, 0·6, and so on up to 10·0. At the temperature 60° F., these indications correspond with strengths of spirit from 67·0 over proof down to

[1] *Phil. Trans.*, 1794, **84**, pt. 2, XX.

58·2 over proof. For lower strengths than these the instrument is too light: it will not sink in the weaker, and therefore heavier, alcohol. To meet this difficulty, weights are employed, which rest on the counterpoise when in use, and are therefore immersed in the liquid tested. Nine such weights are provided, numbered 10, 20, 30, and so on, up to 90. Their volumes and masses are so related to those of the hydrometer that they furnish a continuous series of indication-numbers, aggregating 500 for the whole range, and allowing of the instrument being used for the determination of alcoholic strengths ranging from 70 over proof down to *nil*.

In addition to the nine weights, a brass cap is supplied which fits on to the top of the stem of the hydrometer. The weight of this cap is exactly one-twelfth of that shown by the instrument and the weight No. 60 taken together. If this cap is placed on the instrument, together with the weight 60, it will sink the hydrometer in distilled water at 51° F. down to a certain mark on the stem at the division 0·8—that is, the "indication" shown is 60·8. This mark is called the "proof mark." If the cap is removed, and the instrument with weight 60 placed in *proof spirit* at 51° F., the indication will be found as before—viz., 60·8. As the same volume of liquid is displaced in the two experiments, but the weight supported in the second case is only $\frac{12}{13}$ths of that in the first, it follows that the density of the proof spirit at 51° F. is $\frac{12}{13}$ths of that of water at the same temperature.

The ordinary Sikes's hydrometer cannot be used with very strong spirits—*e.g.*, those of strength upwards of 70 o.p. (= 96·95 per cent. of alcohol by volume). It has therefore been supplemented by a smaller instrument of similar design, known as the "light hydrometer" or the "A" instrument. This extends the range up to 73·5 o.p. at 60° F., corresponding with 98·94 per cent. of alcohol by volume, and up to 74·0 o.p. at 30° F.

Proof spirit.—This is, legally, spirit of the strength denoted as proof by Sikes's hydrometer. Another legal definition makes proof spirit "that which at the temperature of 51° F. weighs exactly $\frac{12}{13}$th parts of an equal measure of water." This matter is dealt with more fully a little further on. Meanwhile, it is convenient to state here what has been found to be the exact composition of proof spirit, with a few brief historical notes.

In the year 1847, Drinkwater, who was then a student at University College, London, and subsequently became a Collector of Excise, published the results of a very careful investigation which he had made upon the composition of proof spirit.[1] He prepared

[1] *Phil. Mag.*, 1848, **22**, 123.

alcohol as nearly free from water as he could get it, and concluded that "the number 0·79381 expresses the specific gravity of absolute alcohol at 60° F. within a very close degree of approximation." He then prepared proof spirit according to the above definition, using this absolute alcohol, and concluded from his experiments that the proof spirit consisted of 49·24 per cent. by weight of absolute alcohol and 50·76 per cent. of water, that its specific gravity at 60° F. was 0·91984, and that the strength of the absolute alcohol was 75·25 degrees over proof.

Subsequent work has only modified Drinkwater's figures very slightly. According to a careful revision of data based upon the most trustworthy published results of several investigators, the specific gravity of proof spirit at 60° F., in air, is 0·91976, water at the same temperature being taken as the unit of reference. Proof spirit contains 49·28 per cent. of alcohol by weight, or 57·10 per cent. by volume at 60° F.

The table on p. 267 shows the percentage of proof spirit corresponding with each integral indication-degree of Sikes's hydrometer at 60° F. The complete tables, which are published in book form, are arranged for each degree of temperature from 30° F. to 100° F., and for each fifth of an integral degree of indication.

A specimen of the tables for three different temperatures is here adduced.

Specimen of Sikes's Tables. Spirits at different Temperatures.

Hydrometer indication.	Temperature. 50° F. Per cent. over proof.	60° F. Per cent. over proof.	70 F. Per cent. under proof.
58·0	4·6	1·4	1·9
·2	4·3	1·1	2·2
·4	4·0	0·8	2·5
·6	3·6	0·4	2·9
·8	3·3	0·1	3·2
		Under proof.	
59·0	3·0	0·2	3·5
·2	2·7	0·5	3·8
·4	2·4	0·8	4·1
·6	2·1	1·1	4·5
·8	1·8	1·4	4·8
60·0	1·5	1·7	5·1

All the strengths shown at the first temperature (50° F.) are "over proof" (o p.); those at the second (60° F.) are partly over and partly under proof; and those at the third are all "under proof" (u.p.).

If an *over* proof strength is added to 100, the sum represents the

PROOF SPIRIT STRENGTH CORRESPONDING WITH THE INDICATIONS OF SIKES'S HYDROMETER. Temp. 60° F.

Indication.	Strength. Over proof.	Indication.	Strength. Over proof.
Light hydrometer.		Ordinary hydrometer.	
A 0	73·5	45	19·7
1	72·9	46	18·3
2	72·2	47	17·0
3	71·6	48	15·6
4	71·0	49	14·3
5	70·3	50	12·9
6	69·6	51	11·5
7	68·9	52	10·1
8	68·2	53	8·7
9	67·5	54	7·3
Ordinary		55	5·8
hydrometer.		56	4·4
0	66·7	57	2·9
1	66·0	58	1·4
2	65·2		*Under proof.*
3	64·4	59	0·2
4	63·6	60	1·7
5	62·8	61	3·3
6	61·9	62	4·8
7	61.1	63	6·4
8	60·2	64	8·1
9	59·3	65	9·7
10	58·4	66	11·4
11	57·6	67	13·1
12	56·7	68	14·9
13	55·7	69	16·7
14	54·8	70	18·6
15	53·8	71	20·5
16	52·9	72	22·4
17	51·9	73	24·4
18	50·9	74	26·4
19	49·9	75	28·5
20	48·9	76	30·7
21	47·9	77	32·9
22	46·8	78	35·3
23	45·8	79	37·7
24	44·7	80	40·3
25	43·6	81	42·9
26	42·5	82	45·7
27	41·4	83	48·6
28	40·3	84	51·7
29	39·1	85	54·8
30	38·0	86	58·2
31	36·9	87	61·5
32	35·7	88	65·0
33	34·6	89	68·4
34	33·4	90	71·9
35	32·2	91	75·2
36	31·0	92	78·4
37	29·8	93	81·4
38	28·5	94	84·4
39	27·3	95	87·3
40	26·0	96	90·0
41	24·8	97	92·6
42	23·6	98	95·1
43	22·3	99	97·6
44	21·0	100	100·0

volume of spirit at proof strength which 100 volumes of spirit at that particular over-proof strength would make.

If an *under* proof strength is *subtracted* from 100, the remainder shows the volume of proof spirit which is contained in 100 volumes at that particular under-proof strength.

The sum and the remainder show, in fact, the percentages of alcohol, calculated as proof spirit, in the stronger and the weaker spirits, respectively. From this it is easy to find the equivalent proof quantity of any given volume of over-proof or under-proof spirit.

Suppose, for instance, that we have 120 gallons of spirit ,strength 6·5 o.p. Then the equivalent proof gallons are : 106·5 per cent. of 120 = 1·065 × 120 = 127·8 proof gallons.

If the strength had been 6·5 *under* proof, the equivalent proof gallons would have been : 93·5 per cent. of 120 = 0·935 × 120 = 112·2.

Sikes's tables are so constructed as to show, for a given spirit, the same strength at whatever temperature (within the limits of the tables) the strength is taken. A spirit, for instance, which shows 62·0 over proof at 60° F. will show the same strength at 65° F., though its *indication* will be different. This, no doubt, was often a convenience to revenue officers in identifying spirit in transit with the particulars furnished on its "permit."

There is, however, one defect of the system. It fails to take account of the change in volume due to alterations of temperature. For example, 100 gallons of proof spirit at 60° F. would become 100·5 gallons at 70° F. ; but as its *strength* is still shown as "proof," the quantity of spirit on which duty may be levied is greater than before, though the actual quantity of alcohol is the same. Conversely, at a lower temperature the quantity chargeable will be less. This error in the evaluation of spirit has never been provided against in this country, though proposals have been made to that end. The differences which may arise from this defect, and which will be sometimes in one direction and sometimes in the other, are not considered to be so great as to make the question one of much practical importance.

Sikes's table, it will be seen, expresses the indications of the hydrometer in terms of alcoholic strength, not of specific gravity. The "indications" themselves, as already noted, are constructed upon an arbitrary scale. In the year 1833, however, a Committee of the Royal Society, which had been appointed to inquire into the question of spirit valuation, reported in favour of a hydrometer with a stem graduated in terms of specific gravity at a given temperature—62° F. being recommended. The suggestion was not adopted; but, instead, a number of experiments were made to determine the specific gravities which corresponded with the indication-numbers of Sikes's hydrometer, and the results were embodied in a "Table for determining the Weight per gallon of Spirits by Sikes's Hydrometer." This table was shortly afterwards embodied in legislation authorising its use in evaluating spirits, and will be found as a schedule to the Spirits Act, 1880. It was employed by revenue officers in ascertaining the quantity of spirits in cask by the method of weighing. A revision of this original table was published in 1916, and its use is legalised by Sec. 19 (3) of the Act 5 & 6 Geo. V., cap. 89. The revised table is reproduced here for each integral indication-number: the complete table includes also the values for each fifth :—

WEIGHT OF SPIRITS PER GALLON BY SIKES'S HYDROMETER.

Ind.	Wt. per gallon, lb.	Ind.	Wt. per gallon, lb.	Ind.	Wt. per gallon, lb.	Ind.	Wt. per gallon, lb.	Ind.	Wt. per gallon, lb.
A hydrometer.		Ordinary hydrometer.		Ordinary hydrometer.		Ordinary hydrometer.		Ordinary hydrometer.	
0	7·991	10	8·326	33	8·726	56	9·145	79	9·584
1	8·007	11	·342	34	·744	57	·164	80	·604
2	·024	12	·359	35	·762	58	·183	81	·624
3	·040	13	·376	36	·780	59	·202	82	·643
4	·057	14	·394	37	·798	60	·220	83	·662
5	·073	15	·411	38	·816	61	·239	84	·682
6	·090	16	·428	39	·834	62	·257	85	·702
7	·107	17	·446	40	·852	63	·276	86	·721
8	·123	18	·463	41	·869	64	·295	87	·741
9	·140	19	·481	42	·887	65	·314	88	·761
10	·157	20	·498	43	·905	66	·333	89	·781
Ordinary		21	·514	44	·924	67	·352	90	·801
hydrometer.		22	·532	45	·942	68	·371	91	·821
0	8·157	23	·549	46	·960	69	·390	92	·840
1	·174	24	·567	47	·979	70	·410	93	·860
2	·190	25	·585	48	·997	71	·430	94	·880
3	·207	26	·602	49	9·016	72	·449	95	·900
4	·224	27	·620	50	·035	73	·468	96	·920
5	·241	28	·638	51	·052	74	·487	97	·940
6	·258	29	·656	52	·071	75	·506	98	·961
7	·275	30	·674	53	·089	76	·526	99	·981
8	·293	31	·690	54	·108	77	·545	100	10·001
9	·310	32	·708	55	·126	78	·565		

If the decimal point be moved one place to the left, the numbers showing weights per gallon will represent specific gravities.

The method of using this table is as follows. Suppose that a cask has been weighed first empty and then when filled with spirit, and the weight of the latter thus found to be 600 lb. Its indication is, say, 7·0. Then from the table, the weight of the spirit per gallon is 8·275 lb. The volume of the spirit is therefore 600 ÷ 8·275 = 72·5 gallons. These bulk gallons, of which the strength is known from the indication and the temperature, are then converted into the equivalent *proof* gallons in the manner already shown. Thus if the temperature is 60° F., the indication being 7·0, the strength is found from the table (*ante*) to be 61·1 over proof. The equivalent number of proof gallons is therefore 161·1 per cent. of 72·5, = 116·8.

In practice, the actual division (weight of spirit in lb. ÷ weight per gallon) is obviated by the use of tables (Loftus's tables) which have been worked out for the purpose.

The legal authority for the use of Sikes's hydrometer for fiscal purposes in the United Kingdom is contained in Sec. 134 of the Spirits Act, 1880:—"All spirits shall be deemed to be of the strength denoted by Sykes's hydrometer . . . in accordance with the table lodged with the Commissioners" [of Inland Revenue]. According to Sir N. Highmore,[1] the use of Sykes's hydrometer "was established by an Act of Parliament, 58 Geo. 3 c. 28," passed on 23rd May, 1818 (and known as The Hydrometer Act). It appears, however, that previously to this, in 1816, an Act had been passed sanctioning the use of this hydrometer and tables, and although it was repealed by the Act of 1818, it was nevertheless important as containing a legal definition of proof spirit. The Act in question (56 Geo. III, c. 140) recites that "an hydrometer hath with great care been completed, and hath, by proper experiments made for the purpose, been ascertained to denote as proof spirit that which at the temperature of 51° Fahrenheit weighs exactly $\frac{12}{13}$th parts of an equal measure of distilled water . . . and it is expedient to establish the same in lieu of Clarke's hydrometer. . . ."

This definition of proof spirit is not in so many words re-enacted in the Act of 1818, but this Act decrees that "all spirits shall be deemed and taken to be of the degree of strength at which the said hydrometer, called Sikes's hydrometer . . . shall denote such spirits to be" (Sec. 2). Proof spirit is therefore what is shown as such by the "said hydrometer," and the word "said" refers to the instrument described in the 1816 Act. There is perhaps room for argument as to the validity of a definition in a statute which has been repealed, so long as the definition has not been expressly re-enacted. But there is no room for doubt that proof spirit (in this country) is what is known as such by Sikes's hydrometer; and so long as this instrument is constructed to "denote as proof spirit that which at the temperature

[1] "The Excise Laws." Vol. I, p. 316.

of 51° Fahr. weighs exactly $\frac{12}{13}$th parts of an equal measure of distilled water," there is no ambiguity about the specific gravity of proof spirit. Or rather, there is only one ambiguity. The temperature of the water is not stated in the definition. It was, however, stated in the tables published for use with the instrument as being 51° F., and this removes the ambiguity.

As regards the table mentioned in Sec. 134 of the Spirits Act, 1880, the statement in the Act of 1818 is as follows (Sec. 3):—"And whereas the strengths of spirits denoted by the said hydrometer, called Sikes's hydrometer, according to the temperature thereof, have been . . . set down in a table intituled 'A Table of the Strengths of Spirits, denoted by Sikes's Hydrometer,' and which said table has been and is subscribed by the hand of the Right Honourable Nicholas Vansittart, Chancellor of the Exchequer, and lodged with the Commissioners of Excise for England . . . be it therefore enacted, that the strengths of spirits so set down in the said table, shall . . . be deemed and taken to be true and just."

It may be noted that the spelling "Sikes" used in the earlier statutes has somehow got changed to "Sykes" in the Act of 1880.

It may also be noted that, under the provisions of Section 4 of the Finance Act, 1907, the Commissioners of Customs and Excise may authorise by regulations the use of *any* means approved by them for ascertaining the strength or weight of spirit. The legalisation of the revised tables now in use is contained in Sec. 19 of the Finance (No. 2) Act, 1915, and is as follows:—

"(1). The revised and extended table, an original copy of which, marked Table I. (Spirits) has been signed by the Chairman of the Commissioners of Customs and Excise, and deposited in the office of the King's Remembrancer at the Royal Courts of Justice, shall be substituted, as the table to be used by Officers of Customs and Excise for the purpose of ascertaining the strength of spirits by means of Sikes's hydrometer, for the table of the Strengths of Spirits denoted by the said hydrometer which is required to be used for the purpose by the Spirits (Strength Ascertainment) Act, 1818.

"(2). Where by reason of the high temperature or strength of spirits the strength of the spirits cannot be ascertained by means of Sikes's hydrometer, the strength may be ascertained by means of a supplemental hydrometer (to be called Sikes's A Hydrometer), a specimen of which, marked by the Chairman of the Commissioners of Customs and Excise, has been deposited in the office of the King's Remembrancer at the Royal Courts of Justice, and by means of the use of the supplemental table applicable to that hydrometer, an original copy of which, marked Table II. (Spirits), has been signed by the Chairman of the Commissioners and deposited in the same office.

"(3). Section one hundred and fourteen of the Spirits Act, 1880 (which relates to the ascertainment by weighing of the quantity of spirits), shall be construed as if for a reference to the Table therein mentioned there were substituted a reference to the revised Tables, an original copy of which, marked Tables III. and IV., has been signed by the Chairman of the Commissioners of Customs and Excise and deposited in the Office of the King's Remembrancer at the Royal Courts of Justice, and as if any reference to casks included a reference to other receptacles."

Alcoholometry in foreign countries.—In France, the assessment of spirit duties is made with the centesimal alcoholometer and tables of Gay-Lussac, which date from the year 1824. The range of the alcoholometer (areometer, hydrometer) extends from "water" to absolute alcohol, and is divided into 100 degrees, each degree representing 1 per cent. of absolute alcohol by volume at the temperature 15°. Three separate instruments are used to cover this range. One extends from 0° to 35°, the next from 35° to 70°, and the third from 70° to 100°. If the spirit tested is at the temperature 15°, the reading of the alcoholometer shows the percentage of alcohol by volume directly: a reading of 40, for instance, indicates that the spirit contains 40 per cent. of alcohol by volume.

Raised to a temperature higher than 15°, the spirit will expand and become lighter; the alcoholometer therefore now sinks further than before. Conversely, at a temperature lower than 15° the instrument does not sink to so low a point as at 15°. The readings in such cases are termed "apparent degrees," and Gay-Lussac's chief table (*Table de la force réelle des liquides spiritueux*) gives the true percentages of alcohol corresponding with these "apparent" or "observed" readings. The table shows also the corresponding correction for the change in volume which the spirituous liquid has undergone with the variation of temperature from the standard. The true quantity of alcohol can thus be calculated.

The alcohol used as the basis for constructing Gay-Lussac's tables had the specific gravity 0·7947 at 15°, referred to water at the same temperature as unity. In 1884, however, it was decreed that the graduation of alcoholometers should be based upon a new "table of the densities of mixtures of water and absolute alcohol" drawn up by the National Bureau of Weights and Measures, in which table the specific gravity of the absolute alcohol is given as 79·433 at 15° *in vacuo*, water at the same temperature being taken as 100. The effect is to show slightly lower values than those of the original instruments, since a given percentage of the stronger alcohol (sp. gr. 0·79433) is equivalent to a higher percentage of the weaker alcohol (sp. gr. 0·7947). The maximum difference is 0·4 per cent.

With slight adaptations, Gay-Lussac's alcoholometer and tables are also used for fiscal purposes in Belgium, Norway, and Sweden. In Spain both Gay-Lussac's and an earlier French hydrometer (Cartier's) are employed.

Tralles's alcoholometer and tables were used in Germany during the greater part of the nineteenth century, and the instrument is still employed officially in Italy, and commercially in Russia. It is a glass areometer showing directly the percentage of alcohol by volume in a spirituous liquid at the standard temperature 15·6°. The alcohol taken as basis had the sp. gr. 0·7946 at 15·6°/15·6°. For use at temperatures other than the standard, tables were supplied.

Tralles's system has been superseded in Germany by the adoption of an alcoholometer graduated to show percentages of alcohol *by weight* at the standard temperature of 15°. The tables adopted are based upon the results of Mendeléeff's investigations. The official alcoholometers are made of glass, and contain a thermometer in the lower part, so that the one instrument shows both the temperature of the spirit and its alcoholic strength. Although the latter is taken *by weight*, for the purpose of charging duty the results are converted into volumes of absolute alcohol (at 15·6°) by means of tables which show the number of litres of absolute alcohol corresponding with any given number of kilograms of the spirit tested.

In what was formerly the Austrian Empire, Meisner's areometer is used for the assay of spirits. It is an instrument very similar to that of Tralles, but indicates percentages of alcohol both by weight and by volume. The alcohol on which the tables are based has the sp. gr. 0·795 at 12°/12° Réaumur (15°/15° C.).

In Holland the official hydrometer is devised upon a different plan from any of the foregoing. The stem is graduated in terms of the volume of the instrument below the zero mark, each degree being one-hundredth part of this volume. The graduation is thus not arbitrary as with Sikes's instrument, nor does it show percentages of alcohol directly, like Gay-Lussac's or Tralles's alcoholometer. Tables are supplied which convert the indications of the instrument into percentage of alcohol by volume at 15°, but the standard adopted for fiscal charges is a "proof" spirit, which at 15° contains 50 per cent. by volume of absolute alcohol.

A metal hydrometer essentially similar to that of Sikes is used officially in Russia. It is graduated, however, in the reverse manner to Sikes's instrument, water being represented by zero on the Russian hydrometer, and strong spirit by 100. The zero mark, of course, is at the bottom of the stem. Tralles's alcohol is taken as the standard, the tables used with the instrument showing percentages by volume of this alcohol at $12\frac{4}{9}$° Réaumur (15·6° C.).

In the United States, the Customs duties upon spirits were at one time levied in terms of *alcohol* percentages, but objections were made to this on the ground that it did not conform to trade usage, which was to buy and sell in terms of *proof spirit*. After inquiry, therefore, by a Committee appointed in the year 1866 to examine into the whole question of testing spirit strengths, it was decided that "the duties on all spirits shall be levied according to their equivalent in proof spirit." Tralles's alcohol was taken as the standard, and the United States proof spirit contains one-half of its volume of this alcohol at 15·6°. Gilpin's results were largely used in compiling the tables for use with the hydrometers, of which there is a series covering a range of graduations from 0 to 200. At the standard temperature 15·6° C. (60° F.), distilled water is represented by 0 on the hydrometer scale, proof spirit by 100, and Tralles's alcohol by 200.

Spirit meters.—It may be mentioned that in some countries, though not in the United Kingdom, an "Alcohol meter" or "Spirit meter" is used in distilleries for the purpose of registering automatically the quantity and strength of the alcohol produced. In one form, made by Siemens, the spirit on its way from still to receiver passes into a vessel in which its strength is recorded. For this purpose a float is employed, which, on the principle of the hydrometer, rises in weaker spirit and falls in stronger; and this motion of rise and fall is communicated to a dial indicator by means of a delicate lever mechanism. The vessel is so constructed as to provide for proper mixing of the spirit and to avoid convection effects on the float.

The spirit then passes to the measuring instrument, which consists of a cylinder or drum rotating on a horizontal axis, and divided into three equal compartments by radial planes. When one of the compartments is full, the weight causes the drum to rotate, thus allowing that compartment to discharge, and bringing another into position for filling in the meantime. The rotation is registered on an indicator dial by means of a pinion attached to the axle of the drum. Thus a continuous record of quantity and strength is obtained.

The accompanying table shows for the principal foreign countries the alcoholic strengths corresponding with various percentages of British proof spirit.

FOREIGN ALCOHOLIC STRENGTHS CORRESPONDING WITH BRITISH PROOF VALUES.

Great Britain. Proof spirit. Per cent.	France, Belgium. Alcohol by volume at 15°.	Italy, Russia, Austria (Tralles). Alcohol by volume at 15·6°.	United States. Proof spirit.	Germany. Alcohol by weight.
5	2·8	2·9	5·7	2·3
10	5·6	5·7	11·4	4·6
15	8·5	8·6	17·2	6·9
20	11·3	11·4	22·8	9·2
25	14·2	14·3	28·6	11·6
30	17·1	17·2	34·4	13·9
35	19·9	20·1	40·2	16·4
40	22·7	22·9	45·8	18·7
45	25·5	25·6	51·5	21·0
50	28·4	28·6	57·3	23·5
55	31·3	31·5	63·0	25·9
60	34·2	34·4	68·8	28·4
65	37·1	37·3	74·7	29·9
70	39·9	40·1	80·1	33·4
75	42·7	42·9	85·8	35·9
80	45·6	45·8	91·4	38·5
85	48·3	48·5	97·0	41·1
90	51·2	51·4	102·8	43·9
95	54·0	54·2	108·5	46·5
100	56·9	57·1	114·2	49·3
105	59·8	60·0	120·0	52·1
110	62·7	62·9	125·7	55·0
115	65·6	65·7	131·3	57·9
120	68·5	68·6	137·0	60·8
125	71·3	71·4	142·8	63·9
130	74·1	74·2	148·4	67·0
135	77·0	77·1	154·2	70·2
140	79·8	79·9	159·9	73·4
145	82·7	82·8	165·6	76·7
150	85·5	85·6	171·3	80·1
155	88·4	88·5	177·1	83·7
160	91·2	91·3	182·7	87·3
165	94·1	94·2	188·3	91·1
170	97·0	97·2	194·3	95·3

ALCOHOL CALCULATIONS

(1). **To convert percentage of alcohol by volume into percentage by weight.**

Multiply the volume percentage by the specific gravity of absolute alcohol (0·7936), and divide the product by the specific gravity of the liquid in question.

For let S be the specific gravity of the liquid (at 15·6°/15·6°). Then 100 c.c. weigh 100 $S\rho$ grams, where ρ is the sp. gr. of water at 15·6°/4°.

If V be the percentage of alcohol by volume, then 100 c.c. of the liquid contain V c.c. of absolute alcohol.

That is, 100 $S\rho$ grams contain V c.c.;

$$\therefore\ 100 \text{ grams contain } \frac{V}{S\rho} \text{ c.c. abs. alc.}$$

But 1 c.c. of abs. alc. weighs 0·7936 ρ gram,

$$\therefore\ \frac{V}{S\rho} \text{ c.c. weigh } \frac{V}{S\rho} \times 0{\cdot}7936\ \rho \text{ gram}; = \frac{V}{S} \times 0{\cdot}7936 \text{ gram.}$$

That is, 100 grams of the liquid contain $V \times \frac{0{\cdot}7936}{S}$ gram of alcohol,

$$i.e., \text{ percentage by weight} = \frac{\text{Per cent. by volume} \times 0{\cdot}7936}{\text{Sp. gr. of the liquid}}.$$

(2). **To convert percentage by volume into grams per 100 c.c.**

Multiply by 0·79284.

For if 100 c.c. of the liquid contain V c.c. of absolute alcohol, the weight of the V c.c. is

$$V \times 0{\cdot}7936 \times \rho \text{ grams}; = V \times 0{\cdot}7936 \times 0{\cdot}999037 = V \times 0{\cdot}79284.$$

(3). **To convert percentage of alcohol by volume into percentage of proof spirit by volume,**

Multiply by 1·7535.

For absolute alcohol is 75·35 "over proof"—that is, 100 volumes of absolute alcohol contain the same quantity of alcohol as do 175·35 volumes of proof spirit. Therefore 1 vol. of alcohol = 1·7535 vols. of proof spirit.

Or for summary calculations, multiply by 7/4 (= 1·75).

From the foregoing three examples it will be seen how any one denomination can be expressed in terms of any other. Thus from (3) a quantity of alcohol in terms of proof spirit can be expressed in terms of absolute alcohol by volume on *dividing* by 1·7535, and then either as percentage of absolute alcohol by weight, or as grams of absolute alcohol per 100 c.c., as shown in (1) and (2) respectively.

The various relations can be summarised for reference in the following "conversion equations."

Let S denote the sp. gr. of a specimen of alcohol,
P the percentage of proof spirit by volume,

V the percentage of alcohol by volume,
W " " " weight,
and G the grams per 100 c.c.

Then
$$P = 1{\cdot}7535\ V,$$
$$= 2{\cdot}2095\ WS.$$
$$V = 0{\cdot}5703\ P,$$
$$= 1{\cdot}2601\ WS:$$
$$W = \frac{1}{2{\cdot}2095} \times \frac{P}{S},$$
$$= 0{\cdot}7936 \times \frac{V}{S};$$
and
$$G = 0{\cdot}7928\ V,$$
$$= 0{\cdot}4521\ P.$$

An operation frequently required is the reduction of alcohol from a higher to a lower strength.

In the laboratory, with convenient measuring vessels at hand, the operation is simple. The volumes are inversely as the strengths. We therefore take a convenient quantity of the alcohol, measured at the standard temperature, and make it up with water to such a volume, at the same temperature, that the ratio of this volume to the first shall be the ratio of the given strength to the required strength.

Example: Given strength 90 per cent., required strength 20 per cent. Dilute 20 c.c. to 90 c.c., or 22·2 to 100, or 111·1 to 500, as may be convenient. Since the temperature of the liquid rises during the mixing, for precise work it must be adjusted before completing the volume.

It is to be carefully noted that on account of the contraction which occurs the required strength would *not* be given by adding 70 c.c. of water to 20 c.c. of the alcohol. More than 70 would be required.

For this reason, the calculation is less simple when, as in large operations, no suitable vessels may be available for accurately making up the diluted spirit to a required volume at a particular temperature. It is then necessary to calculate the actual quantity of water which must be added. This may be done as follows.

To find the volume of water which must be added to a given volume V_1 of alcohol, in order to reduce it from a given strength S_1, to a lower strength S_2, the densities D_1 and D_2, respectively corresponding with these strengths, being known.

Let x denote the weight in grams of the water required, and V_2 the resulting volume, in c.c., of the diluted spirit. Then the weight of the given volume of alcohol is V_1D_1, and that of the resulting volume is V_2D_2.

But the latter weight = the former weight + x,

$$\therefore \; V_1D_1 + x = V_2D_2, \text{ and } x = V_2D_2 - V_1D_1 \quad . \quad (1)$$

Also, since the strengths are inversely as the volumes,

$$\frac{V_2}{V_1} = \frac{S_1}{S_2}; \text{ or } V_2 = \frac{V_1S_1}{S_2} \quad . \quad . \quad . \quad . \quad . \quad . \quad (2)$$

Substituting from (2) in (1) we get :—

$$x = \frac{V_1}{S_2}(D_2S_1 - D_1S_2) \quad . \quad . \quad . \quad . \quad . \quad . \quad . \quad (3)$$

which gives the weight of water required, in terms of the known quantities, and expressed in grams.

For ordinary work this may be taken as the required *volume* of water, in c.c. The precise volume will of course depend upon the temperature of the water. At 4°, x grams = x c.c.; at 15·6°, x grams = $x \times 1{\cdot}0009$ c.c.

Example (1). How much water at 15·6° must be added to 100 c.c. of 90 per cent. alcohol in order to reduce its strength to 60 per cent.? (Strengths by volume.)

Here $V_1 = 100$, $S_1 = 90$, and $S_2 = 60$. With sufficient accuracy the values of D_1 and D_2 may be taken from the ordinary alcohol tables: $D_1 = 0{\cdot}8337$, and $D_2 = 0{\cdot}9134$.

$$\therefore x = \frac{100}{60}(0{\cdot}9134 \times 90 - 0{\cdot}8337 \times 60) \times 1{\cdot}0009 = 53{\cdot}69 \text{ c.c.},$$

or practically, 53·7 c.c.

Strictly, however, the values of D_1 and D_2 as taken from the ordinary alcohol tables are not the true densities (mass of unit volume), but the specific gravities at 15·6°, referred to water at that temperature as unity. Since the density of water at that temperature is 0·999037 (Despretz), and not 1, the values of D_1 and D_2 should be corrected accordingly. If we therefore multiply these values by 0·999037, we find the true densities D_1 and D_2 to be 0·8329 and 0·9125 respectively, and the corrected result is $x = 53{\cdot}64$ c.c.

But it is to be noted that we get the same result by simply taking the values of D_1 and D_2 from the ordinary alcohol tables and using them in equation (3), omitting the factor 1·0009 :—

$$x = \frac{100}{60}(0{\cdot}9134 \times 90 - 0{\cdot}8337 \times 60),$$
$$= 53{\cdot}64.$$

The fact is that the reciprocal of 0·999037 is 1/1·0009; and this cancels out the factor 1·0009 used in the first calculation. So that, finally, although x in equation (3) denotes the *weight* of water required, if we take the values of D_1 and D_2 as specific gravities *from the ordinary alcohol tables* the result expresses the required *volume* of water, in c.c.

This example has been elaborated a little, because the point in question is sometimes found puzzling by persons unfamiliar with alcohol calculations.

Example (2). How much water is required in order to reduce 100 gallons of spirit at 60 over proof to a strength of 20 over proof ?

From what precedes, it will be seen that equation (3) will give the answer, x, in gallons, if the specific gravities corresponding with the strengths are taken from the ordinary alcohol tables.

Here

$V_1 = 100,\ S_1 = 160,\ S_2 = 120;\quad D_1 = 0{\cdot}8295,$ and $D_2 = 0{\cdot}8936.$

Hence $$x = \frac{100}{120}(0{\cdot}8936 \times 160 - 0{\cdot}8295 \times 120)$$

$$= 36{\cdot}2 \text{ gallons.}$$

Problems of a slightly different character are set in the next two questions.

(1). What weight of water must be added to 100 grams of an alcohol (A) of given strength (percentage by *weight*) in order to produce an alcohol (B) of given lower strength ?

Let a and b be the respective given strengths (percentages by *weight*), and let x be the weight in grams of the water required.

Then the total water present is $100 - a + x$, and the weight of B produced is $100 + x$.

$\therefore$ in 100 grams of B there are $\frac{100}{100 + x}(100 - a + x)$ grams of water.

But the weight of water in 100 grams of B is also $100 - b$. Hence, equating,

$$\frac{100}{100 + x}(100 - a + x) = 100 - b.$$

Solving this equation, we get

$$x = \frac{100}{b}(a - b) \quad . \quad . \quad . \quad . \quad . \quad . \quad . \qquad \text{(i).}$$

Thus if A is alcohol of 90 per cent. strength by weight, and we require to dilute it to 70 per cent., the weight of water to be added to 100 grams of A is :—

$$\frac{100}{70}(90 - 70) = 28\tfrac{4}{7} \text{ grams.}$$

(2). If in the foregoing example we have 100 c.c. of A instead of 100 grams, what is the quantity of water required ?

Let D be the density of the alcohol A. Then 100 c.c. will weigh 100 D grams. Hence the quantity of water to be added is

$$\frac{100\,D}{100} \times \frac{100}{b}\,(a - b) \text{ grams,}$$

$$= 100\,(a - b)\,\frac{D}{b} \text{ grams} \quad . \quad . \quad . \qquad \text{(ii).}$$

Here, as explained above, the value of D, if taken from the ordinary alcohol tables, is not the true density (mass of unit volume), but the specific gravity referred to water at 15·6°. Hence 100 c.c. do not weigh exactly 100 D grams if these tables are used. In this case, as in that explained above, the quantity of water given by the expression (ii) must be taken as the *volume* in c.c., not the weight in grams. The correction for reducing the value of D to true density, and that for converting grams of water into c.c., cancel each other out.

Approximations.—In technical operations of reducing spirits from a higher to a lower strength it is common to disregard the effect of contraction when no great accuracy is required. The calculations are then much simplified. From the principle that the volume is inversely as the strength, the volume which the reduced spirit will have is calculated. The difference between this and the original volume is taken as the volume of water to be added. A few examples will make the method clear.

Example (1). Given 54·5 gallons of spirit at strength 8·5 over proof; how much water is required to reduce it to 3·5 over proof?

Here the given strength = 108·5 per cent. of proof spirit, and the required strength = 103·5. Since the volumes are inversely as the strengths, the volume of the reduced spirit will be

$$54{\cdot}5 \times \frac{108{\cdot}5}{103{\cdot}5} = 57{\cdot}1 \text{ gallons.}$$

The volume of water to be added is therefore taken as 57·1 — 54·5 = 2·6 gallons. The exact quantity should be 2·76 gallons, if contraction were allowed for, but the result is sufficiently accurate for technical purposes.

Example (2). A much greater discrepancy, however, may occur when the two strengths differ more widely. Take, for instance, the example already worked out (p. 279), *viz.*, how much water is required to reduce 100 gallons of spirit at 60 o.p. to a strength of 20 o.p.?

Here the volume of the spirit after reduction to the lower strength will be :—

$$100 \times \frac{160}{120} = 133 \cdot 3 \text{ gallons,}$$

and the quantity of water to be added would be taken as $133 \cdot 3 - 100 \cdot 0 = 33 \cdot 3$ gallons.

The accurate quantity would be 36·2 gallons, as already shown.

Example (3). Given volume 80 gallons, at strength 10 over proof; how much water must be added to reduce the spirit to 25 *under* proof ?

Here the percentage strengths are respectively $100 + 10$ and $100 - 25$, or 110 and 75 ; and the resulting volume of the reduced spirit is

$$80 \times \frac{110}{75} = 117 \cdot 3 \text{ gallons.}$$

The quantity of water to be added is therefore taken as $117 \cdot 3 - 80 \cdot 0 = 37 \cdot 3$ gallons. The correct quantity would be 38·6.

Example (4). It is sometimes convenient to calculate the equivalent *proof* gallons before proceeding to find the final volume of the reduced spirit, as in the following instance :—

Given 50 gallons of spirit at 12 over proof, and 20 gallons at 10 under proof ; how much water must be added to the mixture of these in order to reduce the strength of the whole to 25 under proof ?

First calculate each quantity to proof gallons :—

$$50 \text{ gallons at 12 o.p.} = 50 \times \frac{112}{100} = 56 \cdot 0 \text{ gallons at proof strength.}$$

$$\underline{20} \quad \text{,,} \quad 10 \text{ u.p.} = 20 \times \frac{90}{100} = 18 \cdot 0 \quad \text{,,} \quad \text{,,} \quad \text{,,}$$

70

$$\text{Total} \; . \; . = 74 \cdot 0 \quad \text{,,} \quad \text{,,} \quad \text{,,}$$

$$\text{Then } 74 \cdot 0 \text{ at proof} = 74 \cdot 0 \times \frac{100}{75} = 98 \cdot 7 \quad \text{,,} \quad 25 \text{ under proof.}$$

Hence the water to be added is taken as $98 \cdot 7 - 70 \cdot 0 = 28 \cdot 7$ gallons.

DILUTION OF ALCOHOL FROM GIVEN STRENGTH TO REQUIRED LOWER STRENGTH.

Required lower strength.	Given higher strengths, per cent. by volume								
	96.	95.	94.	93.	92.	91.	90.	85.	80.
	Volume of water in c.c. to be added to 1 litre of alcohol.								
95	12	—	—	—	—	—	—	—	—
94	25	12	—	—	—	—	—	—	—
93	38	25	12	—	—	—	—	—	—
92	50	38	25	12	—	—	—	—	—
91	64	51	38	25	12	—	—	—	—
90	77	64	50	38	25	13	—	—	—
85	147	133	119	106	92	79	66	—	—
80	224	209	195	180	166	152	138	68	—
75	310	295	279	263	249	234	219	145	72
70	408	391	374	359	342	326	310	231	153
65	520	502	484	467	449	432	415	331	246
60	650	630	613	592	573	555	536	440	354
55	800	730	759	739	719	698	678	579	480
50	981	960	936	914	892	869	847	739	631
45	1200	1175	1151	1126	1101	1077	1053	932	813
40	1472	1444	1417	1389	1362	1335	1308	1173	1040
35	1818	1787	1756	1725	1694	1663	1632	1480	1329
30	2279	2241	2205	2169	2133	2098	2062	1886	1711
25	2916	2873	2830	2788	2745	2703	2661	2451	2243
20	3872	3820	3767	3715	3662	3610	3558	3298	3040
15	5466	5397	5328	5259	5190	5121	5053	4710	4369
10	8658	8556	8453	8351	8249	8147	8045	7536	7029

Refractometric estimation of methyl alcohol.—In a mixture of methyl and ethyl alcohols which is known to be free from other substances except water, the proportions of the two alcohols can be readily ascertained by determining the refractive index of the mixture.[1] Or, what comes to the same thing, instead of the refractive index we may use the refractive value, expressed in terms of the scale degrees of the particular instrument employed. The Zeiss immersion refractometer is the most suitable apparatus. Any other form, however, may be used, so long as the index of refraction can be determined, though the immersion instrument gives the most accurate results. Leach and Lythgoe's tables give the refraction values at 20° corresponding with percentages of alcohol by weight: their *data* are used in the following description.

The refraction value of methyl alcohol is less than that of ethyl alcohol of the same strength. The greater the strength of the

[1] Leach and Lythgoe, *J. Amer. Chem. Soc.*, 1905, **27**, 964.

alcohols, the greater is the difference of refraction value. For example, at 10 per cent. strength the difference is 11·2° (Zeiss scale); at 50 per cent., 50·5°; and for the absolute alcohols, 89°.

As the strength continuously increases, the refraction-value of each alcohol first rises to a maximum, and then falls. With methyl alcohol, the maximum is reached at about 50 per cent. strength (by weight); with ethyl at about 75 per cent.

To make a determination, the specific gravity of the mixture is taken, and then the refractometer reading at 20°. From the specific gravity, the percentage of total alcohol is ascertained by means of the ordinary tables (p. 239). No appreciable error is caused by using these tables for the mixture, since the densities of ethyl and methyl alcohols are substantially the same. The refractometer reading of the mixture will lie between the values for ethyl alcohol and methyl alcohol in the refraction tables, whence the proportions of the two in the mixture are found by a simple calculation, thus :—

Suppose the total alcohol to be 30 per cent., and the refractometer reading 42·0°. From the table, the readings corresponding with 30 per cent. alcohol are 32·8 and 69·0. Then 69·0 — 32·8 = 36·2, and 69·0 — 42·0 = 27·0; so that (27/36·2) × 100 = 74·58 per cent. of the total alcohol is methyl alcohol; and as the total alcohol is 30 per cent., the methyl alcohol is 30 × 0·7458 = 22·37 per cent. of the mixture, by weight.

Apart from errors of reading the instrument, the chief source of inaccuracy to guard against is the presence of any appreciable quantity of acetone, essential oils, or other volatile substances, which may notably affect the refraction. If no such impurities are present, fairly accurate results are obtainable. An idea of the degree of accuracy may be gathered from the following results :—

Methyl alcohol, per cent.		
Present.	Found.	Difference.
5·98	6·48	+ 0·50
8·50	8·92	+ 0·42
12·21	11·77	− 0·44
22·84	23·75	+ 0·91
45·68	47·41	+ 1·73
68·52	69·88	+ 1·36

Scale readings of Zeiss immersion refractometer at 20°
(Leach and Lythgoe).

Alcohol. Per cent. by weight.	Readings. Methyl alcohol.	Readings. Ethyl alcohol.	Alcohol. Per cent. by weight.	Readings. Methyl alcohol.	Readings. Ethyl alcohol.
0	14·5	14·5	50	39·8	90·3
1	14·8	16·0	51	39·7	91·1
2	15·4	17·6	52	39·6	91·8
3	16·0	19·1	53	39·6	92·4
4	16·6	20·7	54	39·5	93·0
5	17·2	22·3	55	39·4	93·6
6	17·8	24·1	56	39·2	94·1
7	18·4	25·9	57	39·0	94·7
8	19·0	27·8	58	38·6	95·2
9	19·6	29·6	59	38·3	95·7
10	20·2	31·4	60	37·9	96·2
11	20·8	33·2	61	37·5	96·7
12	21·4	35·0	62	37·0	97·1
13	22·0	36·9	63	36·5	97·5
14	22·6	38·7	64	36·0	98·0
15	23·2	40·5	65	35·5	98·3
16	23·9	42·5	66	35·0	98·7
17	24·5	44·5	67	34·5	99·1
18	25·2	46·5	68	34·0	99·4
19	25·8	48·5	69	33·5	99·7
20	26·5	50·5	70	33·0	100·0
21	27·1	52·4	71	32·3	100·2
22	27·8	54·3	72	31·7	100·4
23	28·4	56·3	73	31·1	100·6
24	29·1	58·2	74	30·4	100·8
25	29·7	60·1	75	29·7	101·0
26	30·3	61·9	76	29·0	101·0
27	30·9	63·7	77	28·3	100·9
28	31·6	65·5	78	27·6	100·9
29	32·2	67·2	79	26·8	100·8
30	32·8	69·0	80	26·0	100·7
31	33·5	70·4	81	25·1	100·6
32	34·1	71·7	82	24·3	100·5
33	34·7	73·1	83	23·6	100·4
34	35·2	74·4	84	22·8	100·3
35	35·8	75·8	85	21·8	100·1
36	36·3	76·9	86	20·8	99·8
37	36·8	78·0	87	19·7	99·5
38	37·3	79·1	88	18·6	99·2
39	37·7	80·2	89	17·3	98·9
40	38·1	81·3	90	16·1	98·6
41	38·4	82·3	91	14·9	98·3
42	38·8	83·3	92	13·7	97·8
43	39·2	84·2	93	12·4	97·2
44	39·3	85·2	94	11·0	96·4
45	39·4	86·2	95	9·6	95·7
46	39·5	87·0	96	8·2	94·9
47	39·6	87·8	97	6·7	94·0
48	39·7	88·7	98	5·1	93·0
49	39·8	89·5	99	3·5	92·0
			100	2·0	91·0

In this country it is more usual to take the refractometer readings at 15·6° C. (= 60° F.), and the results are often wanted by volume, or at proof strength. The following tables, calculated by J. Holmes, give the required values correlated with specific gravities :—

SPECIFIC GRAVITIES, ALCOHOL PERCENTAGES, AND REFRACTION-VALUES OF AQUEOUS SOLUTIONS OF METHYL ALCOHOL AND ETHYL ALCOHOL.

Specific gravity.		Percentage of					Refractometer reading on Zeiss immersion instrument at 15·6°.	
At 15·6°/15·6°.	At 15·6°/4°.	Methyl alcohol. By volume.	Methyl alcohol. By weight.	Ethyl alcohol. By volume.	Ethyl alcohol. By weight.	Proof spirit.	Methyl alcohol.	Ethyl alcohol.
1·0000	0·9990	—	0	—	—	—	15·4	—
0·9982	0·9972	1·25	1	1·20	0·96	2·09	16·0	16·9
0·9965	0·9955	2·50	2	2·36	1·89	4·12	16·6	18·3
0·9948	0·9938	3·75	3	3·56	2·85	6·23	17·2	19·9
0·9931	0·9921	4·99	4	4·81	3·84	8·38	17·7	21·5
0·9914	0·9905	6·23	5	6·09	4·88	10·62	18·3	23·3
0·9898	0·9889	7·46	6	7·34	5·89	12·81	19·0	25·1
0·9882	0·9873	8·69	7	8·64	6·94	15·09	19·7	27·0
0·9866	0·9857	9·91	8	9·99	8·04	17·44	20·3	29·1
0·9851	0·9842	11·13	9	11·31	9·11	19·72	20·9	31·0
0·9836	0·9827	12·35	10	12·65	10·21	22·07	21·6	33·3
0·9821	0·9812	13·57	11	14·04	11·34	24·50	22·3	35·5
0·9806	0·9797	14·78	12	15·46	12·51	26·98	23·1	37·9
0·9791	0·9782	15·99	13	16·91	13·72	29·53	23·9	40·2
0·9776	0·9767	17·19	14	18·40	14·94	32·11	24·7	42·7
0·9761	0·9752	18·39	15	19·88	16·17	34·70	25·5	45·2
0·9746	0·9737	19·58	16	21·37	17·41	37·32	26·3	47·8
0·9732	0·9723	20·77	17	22·74	18·56	39·73	27·1	50·1
0·9717	0·9708	21·96	18	24·20	19·78	42·28	27·9	52·6
0·9703	0·9694	23·15	19	25·55	20·90	44·64	28·7	54·8
0·9689	0·9680	24·33	20	26·86	22·01	46·93	29·6	57·0
0·9675	0·9666	25·51	21	28·15	23·09	49·18	30·6	59·2
0·9661	0·9652	26·69	22	29·39	24·15	51·37	31·6	61·4
0·9647	0·9638	27·86	23	30·59	25·18	53·48	32·5	63·4
0·9633	0·9624	29·03	24	31·75	26·17	55·51	33·4	65·2
0·9619	0·9610	30·20	25	32·87	27·13	57·47	34·2	66·9
0·9605	0·9596	31·36	26	33·95	28·06	59·37	34·9	68·5
0·9591	0·9582	32·52	27	35·00	28·97	61·20	35·6	70·1
0·9576	0·9567	33·67	28	36·08	29·91	63·10	36·2	71·6
0·9561	0·9552	34·82	29	37·13	30·84	64·97	36·7	73·1
0·9546	0·9537	35·96	30	38·16	31·74	66·77	37·2	74·4
0·9531	0·9522	37·10	31	39·16	32·62	68·52	37·7	75·7
0·9515	0·9506	38·23	32	40·19	33·53	70·32	38·2	76·9
0·9499	0·9490	39·36	33	41·19	34·43	72·09	38·6	78·2
0·9482	0·9473	40·48	34	42·23	35·35	73·91	39·0	79·3
0·9466	0·9457	41·60	35	43·19	36·22	75·59	39·4	80·5
0·9449	0·9440	42·71	36	44·19	37·12	77·34	39·7	81·5
0·9432	0·9423	43·82	37	45·17	38·02	79·07	40·0	82·6
0·9415	0·9406	44·92	38	46·13	38·89	80·74	40·3	83·6
0·9398	0·9389	46·02	39	47·06	39·75	82·38	40·6	84·5
0·9380	0·9371	47·11	40	48·04	40·65	84·10	40·9	85·6
0·9362	0·9353	48·19	41	49·00	41·54	85·78	41·1	86·6
0·9343	0·9334	49·27	42	49·99	42·48	87·53	41·4	87·6
0·9325	0·9316	50·35	43	50·93	43·35	89·17	41·6	88·6
0·9307	0·9298	51·42	44	51·83	44·21	90·76	41·8	89·4
0·9288	0·9279	52·48	45	52·77	45·10	92·40	42·0	90·2
0·9270	0·9261	53·54	46	53·65	45·94	93·95	42·1	91·0

SPECIFIC GRAVITIES ALCOHOL PERCENTAGES, AND REFRACTION-VALUES OF AQUEOUS SOLUTIONS) OF METHYL ALCOHOL AND ETHYL ALCOHOL—*cont.*

Specific gravity.		Percentage of					Refractometer reading on Zeiss immersion instrument at 15·6°.	
At 15·6° / 15·6°.	At 15·6° / 4°.	Methyl alcohol.		Ethyl alcohol.		Proof spirit.		
		By volume.	By weight.	By volume.	By weight.		Methyl alcohol.	Ethyl alcohol.
0·9251	0·9242	54·59	47	54·57	46·82	95·56	42·2	91·7
0·9232	0·9223	55·64	48	55·47	47·70	97·16	42·3	92·4
0·9213	0·9204	56·69	49	56·38	48·57	98·73	42·4	93·1
0·9194	0·9185	57·73	50	57·27	49·44	100·29	42·5	93·8
0·9175	0·9166	58·76	51	58·15	50·31	101·84	42·5	94·4
0·9155	0·9146	59·79	52	59·06	51·21	103·44	42·5	95·1
0·9136	0·9127	60·81	53	59·92	52·06	104·94	42·5	95·7
0·9116	0·9107	61·82	54	60·81	52·95	106·50	42·5	96·3
0·9096	0·9086	62·81	55	61·69	53·83	108·05	42·4	96·9
0·9075	0·9066	63·81	56	62·61	54·76	109·67	42·3	97·6
0·9054	0·9045	64·80	57	63·52	55·68	111·28	42·2	98·2
0·9033	0·9024	65·80	58	64·43	56·62	112·87	42·1	98·8
0·9011	0·9002	66·76	59	65·37	57·58	114·52	41·9	99·2
0·8990	0·8980	67·72	60	66·25	58·50	116·07	41·7	99·7
0·8968	0·8959	68·69	61	67·17	59·46	117·68	41·5	100·2
0·8945	0·8937	69·64	62	68·13	60·45	119·34	41·2	100·7
0·8922	0·8914	70·58	63	69·06	61·44	121·00	40·9	101·2
0·8899	0·8891	71·53	64	69·99	62·42	122·63	40·5	101·7
0·8876	0·8868	72·44	65	70·91	63·42	124·25	40·1	102·1
0·8852	0·8844	73·36	66	71·87	64·45	125·93	39·6	102·6
0·8828	0·8820	74·28	67	72·82	65·47	127·59	39·2	103·0
0·8804	0·8796	75·19	68	73·76	66·49	129·23	38·8	103·4
0·8781	0·8773	76·09	69	74·64	67·47	130·79	38·3	103·7
0·8757	0·8749	76·98	70	75·55	68·48	132·39	37·8	104·0
0·8733	0·8725	77·86	71	76·46	69·48	133·99	37·3	104·2
0·8709	0·8701	78·74	72	77·36	70·50	135·57	36·7	104·4
0·8685	0·8677	79·61	73	78·25	71·51	137·13	36·1	104·6
0·8661	0·8653	80·48	74	79·12	72·51	138·68	35·5	104·9
0·8637	0·8629	81·34	75	80·00	73·51	140·21	34·9	105·0
0·8612	0·8604	82·19	76	80·90	74·56	141·78	34·2	105·2
0·8587	0·8579	83·03	77	81·79	75·60	143·35	33·5	105·3
0·8562	0·8554	83·86	78	82·66	76·63	144·89	32·8	105·4
0·8537	0·8529	84·69	79	83·53	77·66	146·41	32·1	105·5
0·8512	0·8504	85·51	80	84·38	78·68	147·91	31·3	105·6
0·8486	0·8478	86·32	81	85·26	79·74	149·45	30·4	105·6
0·8460	0·8452	87·11	82	86·12	80·79	150·97	29·5	105·5
0·8434	0·8426	87·90	83	86·97	81·84	152·46	28·5	105·4
0·8408	0·8400	88·69	84	87·80	82·88	153·92	27·6	105·4
0·8382	0·8374	89·47	85	88·62	83·91	155·36	26·6	105·3
0·8355	0·8347	90·23	86	89·46	84·98	156·83	25·6	105·1
0·8329	0·8321	90·99	87	90·25	85·99	158·21	24·6	104·8
0·8302	0·8294	91·74	88	91·05	87·03	159·63	23·5	104·5
0·8275	0·8267	92·48	89	91·84	88·08	161·01	22·4	104·2
0·8248	0·8240	93·21	90	92·61	89·11	162·36	21·3	103·9
0·8221	0·8213	93·94	91	93·35	90·12	163·67	20·1	103·5
0·8193	0·8185	94·65	92	94·11	91·16	165·00	18·9	103·1
0·8165	0·8157	95·35	93	94·84	92·18	166·28	17 6	102·6
0·8137	0·8129	96·04	94	95·55	93·19	167·54	16·3	102·0
0·8109	0·8101	96·73	95	96·23	94·19	168·74	15·0	101·3
0·8081	0·8073	97·41	96	96·91	95·17	169·92	13·7	100·5
0·8052	0·8044	98·07	97	97·57	96·16	171·08	12·3	99·7
0·8023	0·8015	98·73	98	98·21	97·15	172·22	11·0	98·8
0·7994	0·7986	99·37	99	98·83	98·11	173·30	9·6	97·8
0·7964	0·7956	100·00	100	99·44	99·09	174·38	8·2	96·8

For use in the tropics, the following table of the refraction-values of ethyl alcohol solutions at 30° C. (= 86° F.) may be found serviceable. It is due to Browning and Symons.[1] The alcoholic strengths were determined by reference to the United States' official tables.

Readings at 30°. Zeiss immersion refractometer.

Alcohol per cent. by weight.	Reading.	Alcohol per cent. by weight.	Reading.	Alcohol per cent. by weight.	Reading.
1	13·4	18	42·9	35	68·4
2	15·1	19	44·6	36	69·4
3	16·7	20	46·5	37	70·4
4	18·3	21	48·0	38	71·4
5	19·9	22	50·0	39	72·4
6	21·7	23	51·5	40	73·3
7	23·4	24	53·1	41	74·2
8	25·0	25	54·7	42	75·1
9	26·6	26	56·2	43	76·0
10	28·5	27	57·7	44	76·8
11	30·4	28	59·1	45	77·5
12	32·1	29	60·6	46	78·3
13	34·0	30	61·9	47	79·0
14	35·8	31	63·2	48	79·8
15	37·6	32	64·6	49	80·5
16	39·4	33	65·9	50	81·3
17	41·2	34	67·1	51	82·0

Refraction values of aqueous solutions of higher alcohols

Readings at 15·6°. Zeiss immersion instrument.

Per cent. by volume.	Normal propyl.	Isopropyl.	*N*-Primary butyl.	Isobutyl.	Isoamyl.
1	17·1	17·2	17·6	17·4	17·7
2	19·0	18·8	19·9	19·7	20·1
3	20·9	20·5	22·2	22·0	22·7
4	22·9	22·3	24·5	24·3	25·5
5	24·9	24·1	26·8	26·6	
6	26·9	26·0	29·1	29·0	
7	28·9	27·9	31·6	31·3	
8	31·0	29·8	34·0	33·6	
9	33·1	31·8	36·4	35·8	
10	35·3	33·8		38·0	
11	37·5	35·8		40·0	
12	39·7	37·8			
13	41·9	39·8			
14	44·1	41·9			
15	46·3	43·9			
16	48·5	46·0			
17	50·7	48·1			
18	52·9	50·2			
19	55·1	52·4			
20	57·2	54·6			

[1] *J. Soc. Chem. Ind.*, 1914, **33**, 821.

Refractive indices corresponding with scale readings of immersion refractometer (Wagner: "Tabellen").

Scale reading.	Refractive Index. N_D 1·3.			Scale reading.	Refractive Index. N_D 1·3.		
15	3320	Diff. 39.		60	5021		
16	3358			61	5058		
17	3397	1	3·9	62	5095		
18	3435	2	7·8	63	5132		
19	3474	3	11·7	64	5169		
		4	15·6				
20	3513	5	19·5	65	5205		
21	3551	6	23·4	66	5242		
22	3590	7	27·3	67	5279	Diff. 36.	
23	3628	8	31·2	68	5316		
24	3667	9	35·1	69	5352	1	3·6
						2	7·2
25	3705			70	5388	3	10·8
26	3743			71	5425	4	14·4
27	3781			72	5461	5	18·0
28	3820			73	5497	6	21·6
29	3858	Diff. 38.		74	5533	7	25·2
						8	28·8
30	3896	1	3·8	75	5569	9	32·4
31	3934	2	7·6	76	5606		
32	3972	3	11·4	77	5642		
33	4010	4	15·2	78	5678		
34	4048	5	19·0	79	5714		
		6	22·8				
35	4086	7	26·6	80	5750		
36	4124	8	30·4	81	5786		
37	4162	9	34·2	82	5822		
38	4199			83	5858		
39	4237			84	5894		
40	4275			85	5930		
41	4313			86	5966		
42	4350			87	6002		
43	4388			88	6038		
44	4426	Diff. 37.		89	6074		
45	4463	1	3·7	90	6109		
46	4500	2	7·4	91	6145	Diff. 35.	
47	4537	3	11·1	92	6181		
48	4575	4	14·8	93	6217	1	3·5
49	4612	5	18·5	94	6252	2	7·0
		6	22·2			3	10·5
50	4650	7	25·9	95	6287	4	14·0
51	4687	8	29·6	96	6323	5	17·5
52	4724	9	33·3	97	6359	6	21·0
53	4761			98	6394	7	24·5
54	4798			99	6429	8	28·0
						9	31·5
55	4836			100	6464		
56	4873			101	6500		
57	4910			102	6535		
58	4947			103	6570		
59	4984			104	6605		
				105	6640		

Example: Scale reading 23·1 = N_D 1·3 + 0·03628 + 0·000039
= 1·336319, or 1·33632 to the nearest fifth decimal.

CHAPTER VIII

INDUSTRIAL ALCOHOL

ALCOHOL suitable for use as a beverage is heavily taxed in most countries. In so far, however, as it is required for purposes other than internal consumption by human beings, there is probably no country that would wish for the imposition of a tax upon so useful an article as alcohol has proved itself to be in the arts and manufactures. To mention only a few of its industrial applications, it is largely employed as a source of heat and light, as a solvent for resins in the making of varnishes and polishes, as a reagent in the extraction of drugs and the preparation of various chemicals, and as a constituent of medicaments for external use. There may be good economic grounds for an impost upon alcohol used as a luxury; but the case is far otherwise when the spirit is employed as the raw material of, or as an adjunct to, productive industry.

For this reason it is a common practice to "denature" alcohol required in manufacturing operations, and allow it to be used free of duty. The denaturing process consists in mixing with the alcohol nauseous substances which render it unfit for drinking, but do not prevent its use for industrial purposes. Chief among these substances are wood naphtha (crude methyl alcohol), mineral naphtha, benzene, and bone oil or crude pyridine bases; though for special requirements many others are employed. The denaturing may be either "complete," the denatured alcohol being then allowed to be distributed for general industrial or domestic use with relatively few restrictions; or it may be less complete, in which case the spirit is sanctioned for manufacturing purposes only, and used under closer supervision.

I. INDUSTRIAL ALCOHOL IN THE UNITED KINGDOM

Great Britain was one of the first countries to sanction the employment of denatured alcohol free of duty for industrial uses.

The high price of duty-paid spirit was found to be interfering seriously with trade, partly by compelling manufacturers to resort to inferior substitutes, and partly, where such substitutes were not available, by making it difficult to compete with manufacturers on the Continent where the duty was inconsiderable or where, as in France, the pure alcohol was allowed to be used free of duty. The matter was brought to a head in the year 1853, when the patentee of a lubricant intended as a substitute for sperm oil applied to the Treasury for permission to receive alcohol free of duty for use in making the lubricant. This application led to an extensive series of experiments, carried out in the Inland Revenue Laboratory under the auspices of its chief, Mr. Geo. Phillips, in order to ascertain whether it would be practicable to allow the use of alcohol free of duty for manufacturing purposes, without endangering the revenue derived from potable spirits. The outcome of these experiments was the proposal to add crude wood naphtha to spirits of wine. This addition, it was considered, would suffice to prevent abuse of the privilege, if granted. The suggestion was referred to Profs. Graham, Hoffmann, and Redwood, the well-known chemists of their day, who reported in favour of a mixture of 10 per cent. of wood naphtha with spirits of wine being accepted as a denatured alcohol which could be used free of duty without serious detriment to the revenue from potable spirits.

Such a mixture, termed "methylated spirits," was legalised in 1855 by the Act 18 & 19 Vict., cap. 38. This measure was found very beneficial in its operation as regards both industry and scientific research. It also lessened the practice of illicit distillation of spirits, which has been carried on from time immemorial in various parts of the United Kingdom, and even yet, especially in Ireland, and to some extent in Scotland, is by no means extinct, in spite of the fact that exceptional legislation has been enacted for those countries.[1] Much of the alcohol formerly produced by illicit distillation was not used for drinking, but was sold to varnish makers and other manufacturers of goods in which the use of alcohol was required: this market was practically cut off by the passing of the Act above-mentioned, and the consequent production of a legal untaxed alcohol.

Down to 1861 this "methylated spirit" could be used duty free for manufacturing purposes only. From 1861 to 1891 it could be used for any purpose other than consumption as a beverage or a medicine, but if used in large quantities, as for manufacturing

[1] In the year 1914 there were 1,016 detections and seizures of illicit distilling-plant and materials in Ireland, and 2 in Scotland.

operations, it could not be purchased from a retailer of methylated spirit, but only from a methylator, and the user was subject to Excise supervision.

In 1891, however, the use of this spirit (which subsequently came to be described as " ordinary " methylated spirit) was confined to manufacturing purposes. For domestic and general requirements a " mineralised " methylated spirit was brought into use; this consisted of the above " ordinary " spirit with an addition of 0·375 per cent. of mineral naphtha (petroleum of a certain character : see p.312).

This " mineralised " methylated spirit has remained in use up to the present time, but in the year 1906 the " ordinary " spirit was modified in composition as a result of the recommendations of the Departmental Committee on Industrial Alcohol.[1] It was made cheaper and purer by the reduction of the proportion of wood-naphtha from 10 per cent. to 5 per cent., and by the granting of a rebate to compensate for the estimated enhancement of the cost of production due to Excise supervision. The amount of this rebate at the present time is 3*d*. per proof gallon of spirits methylated.

In the year 1902, however, an alternative to the use of methylated spirit was opened to manufacturers. Under the provisions of the Revenue Act, 1902, alcohol may be sanctioned for use free of duty in arts or manufactures after being subjected to some *special* process of denaturing, more appropriate to the particular industry, in cases where methylated spirit is " unsuitable or detrimental." Possibly, even, the alcohol could be used in a pure state, should the circumstances be held by the Commissioners of Customs and Excise to require it.

At the present time, therefore, the following varieties of alcohol may, so far as the provisions of the law are concerned, be used free of duty in the United Kingdom for industrial purposes :—

(1) **Mineralised methylated spirit.**
(2) **Industrial methylated spirit.**
(3) **Alcohol specially denatured.**
(4) **Alcohol not denatured.**

We proceed to describe these in some detail, adding a few notes as to the chief conditions under which each variety may be sanctioned for use.

(1) MINERALISED METHYLATED SPIRIT

This consists of a mixture of 9 volumes of ordinary " plain "

[1] Cd. 2472, 1905.

spirit and 1 volume of "wood naphtha," to which mixture has been added 0·375 per cent. of "mineral" naphtha.[1] It contains, therefore, practically 10 per cent. of wood naphtha. (For a description of these two kinds of "naphtha," see later on in this section).

The plain spirit used for methylating purposes must not be of lower strength than 50 over proof. No higher limit of strength is laid down by the regulations. Instead of plain spirit, colonial rum of strength as low as 20 over proof may be used, but in practice rum is now never methylated. Usually the strength of the spirit employed for methylating is more than 60 o.p. No duty is paid on British spirits used for making methylated spirit; and foreign and colonial spirits so used are exempt from the ordinary spirit duty, but pay a small Customs "surtax" of a few pence per gallon. The idea of this surtax is to compensate for the extra cost of alcohol manufacture in this country due to excise restrictions.

Methylated spirit may only be made by distillers, rectifiers, or licensed methylators. It is, in fact, chiefly made by methylators.

Spirits for methylation come from Customs or Excise duty-free warehouses accompanied by official permits, and are received by revenue officers who examine and check the strength and quantity, and see the spirits run into the mixing vats. To the spirit in each vat is then added one-ninth of its bulk of approved wood naphtha. The contents of the vat have to be thoroughly mixed, the total quantity and strength again measured, and the liquid then further mixed with three-eighths of one per cent. of approved mineral naphtha. The vat and its contents are then handed over to the methylator for disposal in accordance with prescribed regulations. Not less than 500 gallons of methylated spirit must be made at each mixing.

Mineralised methylated spirit is the kind which is ordinarily retailed for burning, domestic, and general purposes. It may not be purified, and it is subject to the general restriction laid down in the Spirits Act, 1880, s. 130—namely, it may not be employed in making any article capable of use as a beverage, or internally as a medicine. Any quantity up to 5 gallons may be sold by retail at one time, but the seller must be duly licensed for the sale of methylated spirit.

This mineralised spirit is very useful for a large number of purposes, but it has one marked drawback. It becomes turbid on dilution with water, by reason of the mineral naphtha being thrown out of

[1] Since June, 1918, the mineralised spirit has also been coloured with methyl violet

solution. This property interferes occasionally with its employment where a diluted spirit is required.

The alcoholic strength of mineralised methylated spirit is usually either about 61° over proof, or about 64° over proof. The general range may be taken as from 60° to 64° o.p., though, exceptionally, spirits as low as 58° or as high as 66° o.p. may be met with. Taking the average strength as 62 o.p., the general composition of the spirit may be expressed as follows :—

Mineralised methylated spirit at 62° over proof.

	Per cent. by volume
Ethyl alcohol	83·05
Methyl ,,	7·73
Ketones, calculated as acetone	1·02
Esters, ,, methyl acetate	0·13
Unsaturated compounds, as allyl alcohol	0·08
Basic compounds, as pyridine	0·02
Mineral naphtha	0·38
Water	9·21
	101·62

NOTE.—The sum of the separate percentages is greater than 100, because contraction occurs when water is mixed with alcohol.

Analysis of mineralised methylated spirits.—This ordinarily resolves itself into a determination of the alcoholic strength, and the estimation of the methyl alcohol, acetone, and mineral naphtha, with an examination as to whether any appreciable amount of residue is left on evaporation. Occasionally the proportion of esters may be required. A determination of the remaining constituents is rarely wanted except for special purposes.

Alcoholic strength.—This is given with sufficient accuracy for most requirements by the hydrometer, or by the specific gravity taken direct with the pyknometer, without distillation or preliminary purification of the sample. If it is desired to remove the mineral naphtha, together with the bulk of the acetone and the smaller impurities, the diluted sample is saturated with common salt, extracted with petroleum ether, and distilled as directed on p. 170 (Thorpe and Holmes's method).

Methyl alcohol.—This is conveniently determined by the modification of Denigès's method described on p. 183. The sample, purified if necessary, is diluted with water until it contains 10 per cent. of total alcohols by volume, and then further diluted twenty-fold with ethyl alcohol of 10 per cent. strength. Five c.c. of this diluted liquid are then oxidised with potassium permanganate as described (*loc. cit.*), employing standards for comparison which contain from 0·0015 to 0·002 gram of methyl alcohol.

Example.—Sp. gr. of sample 0·8241 = 92·8 per cent. of total alcohol. (*a*) Ten c.c. diluted to 92·8 c.c. with water give 10 per cent. of total alcohol. (*b*) Five c.c. of this were next diluted to 100 c.c. with ethyl alcohol of 10 per cent. strength. (*c*) Five c.c. of the solution obtained in (*b*) were oxidised as directed, and the colour produced was equal to that given by a standard of 0·0017 gram of methyl alcohol. Then :

$$0{\cdot}0017 \times \frac{100}{5} \times \frac{100}{5} \times \frac{92{\cdot}8}{10} \times \frac{1}{0{\cdot}7964} = 7{\cdot}97 \text{ per cent. of methyl}$$

alcohol by volume.

Alternatively, Thorpe and Holmes's method of estimating the methyl alcohol by oxidation to carbon dioxide may be employed ; see Chap. VI.

Acetone.—This is determined by Messinger's method as described under " Wood naphtha " (p. 307), 5 c.c. of the sample being used instead of 0·5, and the calculation modified accordingly. A " blank " experiment is carried out at the same time on pure alcohol of the same strength, and the result deducted from that given by the sample.

Mineral naphtha.—Five c.c. of the spirit are diluted to 50 c.c. with water in a glass cylinder of about 3 cm. internal diameter, and the opalescence produced is compared with that given by a standard mixture under the same conditions. The standard should be of approximately the same alcoholic strength as the sample, and is composed of plain spirit and wood naphtha in the proportion of 9 volumes to 1, together with known quantities of mineral naphtha. The proportion of the mineral naphtha is varied until the opalescence produced on dilution matches that of the sample under examination.

Esters.—Ten c.c. of the spirit are carefully neutralised with decinormal soda solution after addition of two drops of phenolphthalein indicator, then a further quantity of 20 c.c. of the soda solution is added, and the mixture heated for two hours in a silver pressure flask on the steam-bath—or, alternatively, boiled in a glass flask under a reflux condenser. The excess of alkali is then titrated with decinormal sulphuric acid. A " blank " experiment is made with 10 c.c. of water under the same conditions. Each cubic centimetre of $N/10$-soda used up in hydrolysing the esters in the sample represents 0·0074 gram of esters, calculated as methyl acetate.

Unsaturated compounds.—This determination is carried out in the same way as the bromine-decolorisation test for wood naphtha (p. 305). Instead of 50 c.c. of the standard bromide-bromate solution, however, only 5 c.c. are employed, and 1 c.c. of acid instead of 10 c.c. This quantity of the standard solution is equivalent to 0·05 gram of bromine, or to 0·02125 c.c. of unsaturated compounds calculated as allyl alcohol.

(2) INDUSTRIAL METHYLATED SPIRIT

This is a mixture of 19 volumes of "plain" spirit with 1 volume of wood naphtha. It differs, therefore, from the "mineralised" spirit in containing no mineral naphtha, and in having only one-half the proportion of wood naphtha—5 per cent. instead of 10 per cent. It is the variety of duty-free alcohol chiefly used in manufactures. Since it is much purer than the mineralised spirit, it is subjected to closer supervision as a check upon possible malpractices. It is not allowed to be sold by retailers; it can only be obtained from methylators, and in quantities of not less than 5 gallons at a time. Further, the user must be specifically authorised, by the Commissioners of Customs and Excise, to receive the spirit for duly approved purposes, and he cannot obtain it except upon the production of the official "requisition," which is not granted until the authority has been duly issued empowering the prospective user to receive the spirit. The chief restriction upon the purposes to which the industrial methylated spirit may be put is that it may not be used in beverages, or perfumes, or in medicines to be taken internally. It is allowed to be used, however, as a solvent in preparing medicinal extracts from crude drugs, provided all the spirit is afterwards expelled from the extracts. It is employed also for extracting and crystallising alkaloids and other solid medicinal substances, as well as for the production of ether, chloroform, chloral, and ethyl bromide, chloride, and iodide, in which the alcohol has undergone a molecular transformation, and no longer remains as alcohol in the finished product. Similarly, industrial methylated spirit may be used (under authority) in the chemical operations involved in making synthetic perfumes, but may not be present as such in perfumed spirits. Recovery of the methylated spirit by distillation from extracts, marcs, etc., is generally permitted, provided the spirit is not purified in the process. Usually the recovered alcohol is required to be used again for the same purpose as it was originally employed for.

Medicaments intended for external use, such as soap linament and also certain hair lotions, may legally be made, under authority, with industrial methylated spirit, provided always that they are not capable of internal use, or of employment as perfumes,

The average composition of industrial methylated spirit, taking the strength as 62° over proof, may be expressed as follows :—

Industrial methylated spirit at 62° o.p.

	Per cent. by volume.
Ethyl alcohol	87·92
Methyl ,, ...	3·87
Ketones, calculated as acetone	0·51
Esters, ,, methyl acetate	0·06
Unsaturated compounds, calculated as allyl alcohol ..	0·04
Basic ,, ,, pyridine ..	0·01
Water	9·21
	101·62

At a strength of 61° o.p. the proportion of ethyl alcohol is 87·35 per cent., and at 64° o.p. it is 89·06 per cent.

Analysis.—The analysis of industrial methylated spirit is carried out in the way already described for the mineralised variety—omitting, of course, the parts relating to mineral naphtha. In estimating the methyl alcohol by Denigès's process, after diluting the spirit with water to 10 per cent. alcoholic strength, it will only be necessary to dilute further *ten*-fold with 10 per cent. ethyl alcohol, since the proportion of methyl alcohol is only one-half of that in the mineralised spirit.

In order to obtain authority for the receipt of industrial methylated spirit to be used in manufactures, application should in the first instance be made to the local Surveyor of Customs and Excise, who will supply a form of application and give the applicant all necessary preliminary information. Provision must be made for the proper storage of the spirit, and certain premises are ineligible—*e.g.*, those on which spirituous liquors are distilled, or sold for consumption on the premises. Where the quantity of industrial spirit required is more than 50 gallons a year, a bond for the proper use of the spirit must usually be given. This may be done either with personal sureties or through an approved guarantee society. Where a still is kept, and in other special cases, bond may be required for smaller quantities than 50 gallons. Authority to receive the spirit is sent from headquarters after the Surveyor has forwarded the completed form of application and his report upon it. When the authority has been granted, the recipient is supplied with a book of "requisitions" enabling him to obtain the spirit from a methylator; no industrial methylated spirit is obtainable without an official requisition. Occasional inspections of the premises are made, to ascertain that the spirit is not being used in contravention of the authorisation; but on the whole the regulations are not unduly irksome. On the contrary, manufacturers testify that they work quite smoothly and easily.

NOTE.—As a temporary war measure, in order to conserve the supplies of wood-naphtha, the composition of methylated spirit was modified in June, 1918. Two kinds of "industrial" methylated spirit were issued :

(1) **"Ordinary,"** composed of :—

Wood naphtha	2·0	per cent.
Mineral ,, ...	0·5	,,
Spirits	97·5	,,
	100·0	

(2) **"Special,"** composed of :—

Wood naphtha	3·0	per cent.
Spirits	97·0	,,
	100·0	

The composition of **"mineralised"** methylated spirit was altered by reducing the proportion of wood naphtha from 10 per cent. to 5 per cent., slightly increasing the percentage of mineral naphtha, and colouring the mixture with methyl violet. The product was thus composed of :—

Wood naphtha	5·0	per cent.
Spirits	95·0	,,
	100·0	

together with an addition of 0·5 per cent. of mineral naphtha ; and to each 100 gallons of the product, 0·025 of an ounce of the aniline dye, methyl violet. Except as regards the colouring matter, these modifications were withdrawn in January, 1919.

(3) SPECIALLY-DENATURED ALCOHOL

Section 8 of the Finance Act, 1902, which forms the legal authority for allowing in certain cases denatured alcohol other than methylated spirit to be used free of duty, runs as follows :—

"(1).—Where, in the case of any art or manufacture carried on by any person in which the use of spirits is required, it shall be proved to the satisfaction of the Commissioners of Inland Revenue[1] that the use of methylated spirits is unsuitable or detrimental, they may, if they think fit, authorise that person to receive spirits without payment of duty for use in the art or manufacture upon giving security to their satisfaction that he will use the spirits in

[1] Now the Commissioners of Customs and Excise.

the art or manufacture, and for no other purpose, and the spirits so used shall be exempt from duty. . . .

"(2).—The authority shall only be granted subject to a compliance with such regulations as the Commissioners may require the applicant to observe for the security of the revenue, and upon condition that he will, to the satisfaction of the Commissioners if so required by them, render the spirits unpotable before and during use. . . ."

It will be seen that the Commissioners of Customs and Excise have absolute discretion in the matter of sanctioning the use of this variety of alcohol. A condition *sine qua non* is that methylated spirit must be "unsuitable or detrimental" for the particular purpose to which it is proposed to put the alcohol. Of course, the Commissioners must themselves be the judges of what constitutes unsuitability in the sense of the enactment. That it must be a *bona fide* unsuitability need scarcely be said. It has to be borne in mind that for the great majority of uses to which industrial alcohol is put, the methyl alcohol in methylated spirit is just as serviceable as the ethyl alcohol; and that although industrial methylated spirit, for instance, is denatured with 5 per cent. of "wood naphtha," yet four-fifths of this is methyl alcohol. In fact, as a glance at its composition (p. 296) will show, the substances other than alcohols and water in industrial methylated spirit are very small in amount, totalling to about 0·6 per cent. only. Hence there are, relatively, not a great many manufacturing requirements for which this form of industrial alcohol is in any substantial sense detrimental.

Some such requirements, however, there are. In these cases, arrangements are made for applicants to receive alcohol under bond, to be denatured at the place of use with some special denaturant suitable to the manufacture in question. The denaturant may have no particular relation to the manufacture, but may be chosen simply to render the alcohol unpotable during use—for example, bone oil in the making of fulminates. On the other hand the denaturant may be, and often is, some substance which is employed in the manufacture itself, such as aniline in the preparation of aniline dyestuffs.

Thus there is considerable latitude possible in the choice of denaturants to suit special circumstances. In fact, one of the conclusions of the Industrial Alcohol Committee[1] is that "Where spirit is used for industrial purposes, the Finance Act of 1902 provides adequate and entirely satisfactory machinery for securing

[1] Report, p. 9.

that the spirit may be used in a condition that is suitable and appropriate to each particular purpose of manufacture. The machinery is elastic—much more so than is the corresponding machinery in Germany—and it permits of every reasonable process of denaturing, or even, in the last resort, of the use of spirit in a pure state. For more than this it would be impossible to ask."

Benzene, aniline, bone oil, turpentine, petroleum-ether, and pyridine are among the most frequently used denaturants other than wood naphtha.

The general principles upon which the authorities administer the important enactment in question are explained in a minute issued by the Board of Inland Revenue in July, 1902, and quoted in an appendix to the evidence given before the Industrial Alcohol Committee. After giving the terms of the Act, the minute (slightly abridged here) proceeds :—

"It is in the first place to be observed that the privilege of using spirit duty-free, as contemplated by the section, is to be a personal privilege, entailing personal obligations on the person or persons to whom it is granted. It follows from this that there can be no question of the Board's granting any general authority under the section to classes of persons, but that each person or body of persons who desires to obtain the benefit of the section must make separate application to the Board, who will consider all the circumstances of each separate application, and form their judgment upon them.

"At the same time . . . it may be possible to indicate certain classes of cases to which the benefit of the section could not, in any circumstances, be conceded.

"Before the use of duty-free spirit can be authorised, two main conditions must be fulfilled, *viz.* :—

"(*a*) It must be proved, to the satisfaction of the Commissioners, that the use of methylated spirit is unsuitable or detrimental for the particular purpose ; and

"(*b*) The security of the revenue must be guaranteed by such means as the Commissioners may require.

"These conditions are cumulative, not alternative. Unless both can be fulfilled, there can be no question of a grant of the authority contemplated by the section. In every case, therefore, it will be necessary to scrutinise the objections that may be alleged to the use of methylated spirit, and it is only after the validity of such objections has been admitted that it will be necessary to proceed to consider whether, or by what means, the security of the revenue can be guaranteed.

"It was explicitly stated in the House of Commons . . . that the Commissioners should exercise the discretion conferred upon them with great caution and with a very strict regard to the security of the revenue ; and the Board themselves feel that no other attitude would be possible for them.

" They intend, therefore, to insist on a strict observance of the prescribed conditions in every case in which they may grant an authority under the section, and they will not hesitate to reject any application in respect of which it appears to them that the conditions are not, or cannot be, adequately complied with.

" Further, as the duty on spirit is so heavy, they consider that they may properly require that the advantage to be obtained by the use of duty-free spirit should be substantial, and that the benefit of the section should not be accorded in cases of trivial importance or in the purely personal interests of individuals.

" In accordance with these principles, the Board will refuse to entertain applications : (*a*) Where the use of methylated spirit is attended by only slight and immaterial disadvantage ; (*b*) Where the security of the revenue cannot be guaranteed with reasonable certainty, and at reasonable cost of convenience to the department.

" It is manifest that there must be many cases in which the protection of the revenue would be impossible, if the use of duty-free spirit were permitted, and of these there may be mentioned the following :—

" (i) The manufacture of articles intended for human consumption, such as medicines, tinctures, and essences.

" (ii) The manufacture of articles not intended for human consumption, but capable of being so used, if made with pure spirit or with spirit only temporarily rendered unpotable, such as perfumes or spirituous mixtures for purposes of illumination or of generation of heat or motive power.

" As regards cases to which the benefits of the section may be extended, the Board may say generally that they will be disposed to entertain favourably applications :—

" (1) From recognised bodies formed for the advancement of science, or of scientific education, and requiring the use of pure spirit in processes of research or of illustration. . . .

" (2) From persons engaged in an industrial enterprise of such magnitude and importance as to give it a character of public interest in its bearing upon national trade. In any such case the concession will commonly be made subject to an obligation to render the spirit unpotable before and during use, by such means as may be found to be most appropriate to the particular circumstances of the manufacture."

In accordance with these principles, a considerable quantity of specially-denatured spirit (about three-quarters of a million proof gallons in the year 1913–14) is authorised for use in certain manufactures. Explosives, dyestuffs, celluloid products, and various fine chemicals are the chief substances for the making of which this form of duty-free alcohol is required. Persons wishing to obtain authority to receive supplies should in the first instance refer to the local Surveyor of Customs and Excise, who will give any information that may be necessary.

Methyl alcohol, if of sufficient purity to be classed as "potable," is liable to duty at the same rate as ethyl alcohol, though it is exempted from the "surtax" on importation. Previously to July, 1918, it was allowed for use free of duty under Section 8 of the Finance Act, 1902, on similar lines to those adopted for ethyl alcohol, except that, in accordance with a recommendation of the Industrial Alcohol Committee, it was treated more leniently in the matter of denaturing.

Since the date mentioned, the use of methyl alcohol has been made still more free to manufacturers. It is now allowed with fewer restrictions, and in general without denaturing, for making fine chemicals, under regulations similar in the main to those governing the receipt and use of industrial methylated spirit. The purposes for which it is required must be duly specified to, and approved by, the Commissioners of Customs and Excise. For use in beverages or spirituous perfumes the receipt of methyl alcohol is, of course, not allowed; and the authorities must be satisfied that industrial methylated spirit is unsuitable or detrimental for the purposes in question.

(4) ALCOHOL NOT DENATURED

Although, as already remarked, the law in this country *permits* the use even of pure alcohol duty-free for industrial purposes, yet in practice such use is very limited, so far as ethyl alcohol is concerned. The fact is that the manufacturing operations requiring ethyl alcohol are practically non-existent in which either a neutral substance such as benzene, acetone, or petroleum cannot be employed as a denaturant, or else some ingredient, reagent, or product of the manufacture itself utilised to render the alcohol at least temporarily unpotable. Hence so far as manufactures are concerned the provision is almost inoperative in respect of ethyl alcohol, though a considerable quantity of methyl alcohol is used in a pure state free of duty.

The authorities, however, interpret "arts" in the statute as including teaching and scientific research carried out at public institutions, and for these purposes alcohol is allowed to be used duty-free without denaturing. A substantial quantity of pure alcohol (ethyl and methyl) is issued under this provision to universities, colleges, and other educational institutions, the number of proof gallons during the year 1913–14, for instance, being 7,849.

It may be mentioned that much misconception has existed respecting the privileges which German manufacturers have enjoyed with regard to the use of pure alcohol free of duty. This point was specially inquired into by a sub-committee for the information of the Departmental Committee on Industrial Alcohol, and they state emphatically that, with the exception of explosives, "no article can be manufactured in Germany with duty-free spirit, unless it be subjected before use to some process of denaturing." As in this country, alcohol may in Germany be used in a pure, undenatured state in public scientific institutions. It may also be used in public hospitals, and for making smokeless powder, fuses, and fulminates. "For all other purposes, without exception, duty-paid spirit must be used, *unless* the spirit be subjected to some *authorised* process of denaturing prior to use."

Possibly the misconception alluded to arose from the fact that at one time apothecaries, doctors, and others were allowed to use pure alcohol duty-free in the preparation of some eighty tinctures, spirits, and liquors made according to the formulæ of the German pharmacopœia and other authorised formulæ, and also for compounding doctors' prescriptions. Abuses, however, crept in; and the privilege was withdrawn in 1902. "All medicines have now to be prepared with duty-paid spirit."

Immature spirits.—The "Immature Spirits (Restriction) Act, 1915," provides that no British or Foreign spirits shall be delivered for home consumption unless they have been warehoused for a period of at least three years.

This restriction on delivery, however, is not to apply to spirits delivered for duty-*free* purposes, nor to mixtures, compounds, etc., prepared with duty-*paid* spirit.

Subject to payment of duty, if imposed, the following spirits are also exempted from the restriction:—

(i) Spirits delivered to rectifiers, manufacturing chemists, perfume-makers, or other duly-licensed persons.

(ii) Spirits for scientific purposes.

(iii) Imported Geneva, perfumed spirits, and foreign liqueurs.

Nothing in the section thus summarised is to interfere with the supply of rectified spirits of wine for making medicines to medical practitioners, hospitals, and persons entitled to carry on the business of a chemist and druggist.

Additional duties are imposed by the Finance Act, 1915, on Immature Spirits which have not been warehoused, or have been warehoused less than two years. But this additional duty is not to be charged on imported mixtures which are recognised by the Commissioners of Customs and Excise as being *used for medical purposes*; and *repayment* of the additional duty is to be allowed on spirits to which the restriction on delivery does not apply, if such spirits have been used for scientific purposes or for making articles recognised by the Commissioners as articles used for medical purposes.

Increased duties were imposed on spirits by the Finance Act, 1918, the excise levy being raised to 30*s.* per proof gallon, or double the previous tax. But the articles indicated in the preceding paragraph are relieved from this increase, as well as from the "additional" duty mentioned.

The effect of these enactments is that alcohol used for such purposes as making perfumes need not be kept in warehouse, but if not so kept for the statutory period it must pay the additional duty as well as the full tax; whereas alcohol used in making "recognised" medicines (or for scientific purposes) is relieved from the additional duty and pays only one-half the full tax. This rebate on immature spirit therefore lowers the cost of producing spirituous medicines, and is an important matter to manufacturing chemists.

Certain articles such as tincture of orange and spirit of peppermint are not admitted to rebate, although frequently used in medicine. The reason is that they are also largely used as perfumes or flavourings, and it is impracticable to distinguish the quantities employed in medicine from those used for other purposes.

The following statistics respecting the use of industrial alcohol in the United Kingdom may be of interest. They are taken from the annual report of the Commissioners of Customs and Excise for the year 1915.

(1) Quantity of methylated spirits sent into consumption by the makers in the year 1913–14.

Industrial methylated spirit	—	3,253,061	bulk gallons.
Mineralised ,, ,,	—	1,754,514	,,

(2) Spirits allowed to be received in a pure state for use under the provisions of the Finance Act, 1902. Year 1913–14.

For use in Arts and Manufactures — — 783,379 proof gallons.
,, scientific use (Universities, etc.) — 7,849 ,,

Wood naphtha ("*Wood Spirit*").—This is crude methyl alcohol, containing water and various impurities, chiefly acetone and methyl acetate, but often including also small quantities of higher ketones, allyl alcohol, pyridine, amines, and other bases. It is produced by the distillation of wood, as described under "Methyl alcohol."

Various qualities of wood naphtha are made, the degree of purity depending upon the purposes for which the naphtha is required. For example, in the making of formaldehyde, and also in the colour industry, it is important to have the methyl alcohol as free as practicable from acetone; whereas a considerable proportion of acetone is admissible, and even advantageous, in wood naphtha used as a solvent for resins in making varnishes, polishes, and lacquers.

When employed as a denaturant of ethyl alcohol, wood spirit may contain a substantial proportion of acetone—varying, however, with the different specifications adopted by different countries. Thus in Great Britain the maximum is 12 grams per 100 c.c., whilst in France 25 per cent. must be present. A good deal of importance attaches also to the allyl alcohol, and some to the pyridine bases, when the naphtha is required for denaturing purposes, since these compounds, though present in very small amount, help largely to make the naphtha nauseous.

In the United Kingdom the wood naphtha employed as a denaturant should conform to the following stipulations:—

(*a*) Not more than 30 c.c. of the naphtha should be required to decolorise a solution containing 0·5 gram of bromine.

(*b*) It must be neutral or only slightly alkaline to litmus, and at least 5 c.c. of decinormal acid should be required to neutralise 25 c.c. of the naphtha when methyl-orange is used as the indicator.

It should contain:—

(*c*) Not less than 72 per cent. by volume of methyl alcohol.

(*d*) Not more than 12 grams of acetone, aldehydes, and higher ketones per 100 c.c., estimated as "acetone" by the formation of iodoform according to Messinger's method.

(*e*) Not more than 3 grams of esters per 100 c.c., estimated as methyl acetate by hydrolysis.

The detailed description of the examination of wood naphtha in respect of these tests, together with some explanatory remarks, is given below.

(*a*) **Bromine decolorisation.**—A standard bromine solution is made by dissolving 12·406 grams of potassium bromide and 3·481 grams of potassium bromate in a litre of recently boiled distilled water.

Fifty c.c. of this standard solution (= 0·5 gram of bromine) are placed in a flask of about 200 c.c. capacity, having a well-ground stopper. To this are added 10 c.c. of dilute sulphuric acid (1 in 4), and the whole shaken gently. After a few minutes the wood naphtha is slowly run from a burette into the clear brown solution of bromine until the latter is completely decolorised.

This test serves as a measure of the allyl alcohol and other unsaturated compounds. The result is usually expressed in terms of the volume of naphtha required, since allyl alcohol is not, or is not known to be, the only unsaturated compound present.

(*b*) **Methyl-orange alkalinity.**—Twenty-five c.c. of the naphtha are placed in each of two beakers, and titrated with decinormal acid, using in the one case a few drops of litmus solution, and in the other a solution of methyl-orange, as indicator. With litmus usually 0·1 to 0·2 c.c. of decinormal acid is required to neutralise the naphtha. With methyl-orange the total alkalinity should be greater, at least 5 or 6 c.c. of decinormal acid being required for neutralisation.

The difference of the two results is the "methyl-orange alkalinity." It serves as a measure of the pyridine and amine bases—though of course only an approximate estimation, since there may be more than one basic substance present. It may be expressed in terms of pyridine from the knowledge that 1 c.c. of $N/10$-acid = 0·008 c.c. pyridine; but in practice is usually given as the volume of decinormal acid required, in the absence of information as to which base is actually predominant.

(*c*) **Estimation of methyl alcohol.**—Twenty-two grams of coarsely powdered iodine and 5 c.c. of distilled water are placed in a small flask and cooled by immersion in ice-cold water. Then 5 c.c. of the wood spirit (at 60 o.p. strength) are added, the flask corked, the contents gently shaken, and allowed to remain in the ice-cold bath for ten to fifteen minutes.

When well cooled, 2 grams of red phosphorus are added to the mixture of spirit and iodine in the flask, and the latter is immediately attached to a reflux condenser.

The reaction soon commences, and must be moderated by dipping the flask into a cold water-bath. (Spirit may be lost if the reaction is too violent.) After about fifteen to twenty minutes, when all action appears to have ceased, the water-bath under the flask is gradually heated to a temperature of about 75°, and the flask being occasionally shaken is allowed to remain at this temperature for fifteen to twenty minutes. The source of heat is then removed, and the apparatus left for an hour till it has cooled, when the condenser is reversed, and the methyl iodide slowly distilled off—first at a low temperature, the bath being allowed to boil towards

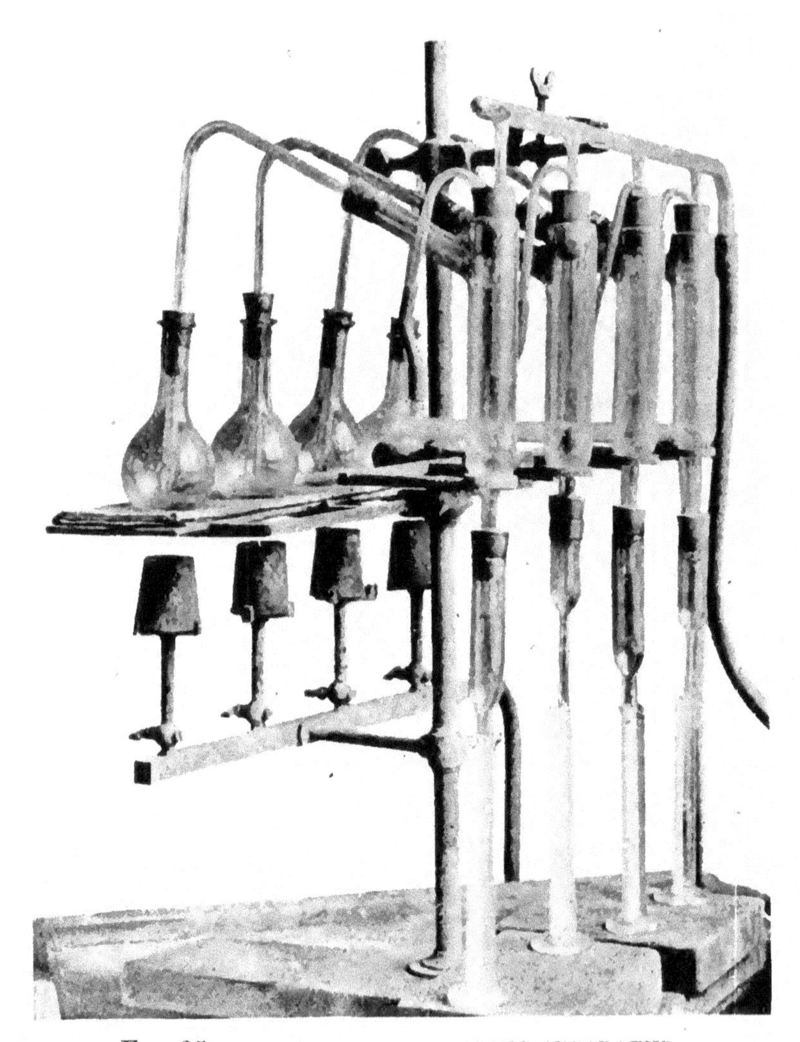

FIG. 35.—BATTERY OF DISTILLING APPARATUS.

For estimation of methyl alcohol in wood-naphtha by the methyl iodide method.

the end of the operation only. The end of the condenser dips into water in a measuring tube, and the iodide is collected under water and measured at a temperature of 15·5°.

The percentage (by volume) is found from the formula :—

$$\frac{\text{c.c. methyl iodide found} \times 0 \cdot 647 \times 100}{\text{c.c. wood spirit taken}} = \text{percentage of methyl alcohol.}$$

Or when 5 c.c. of spirit are taken:—

c.c. methyl iodide × 12·94 = percentage of methyl alcohol.

Esters and acetals also yield methyl iodide by this process, and from the percentage of methyl alcohol calculated as above, an amount equivalent to the percentage of these substances present must be deducted. Practically, however, methyl acetate is the only compound usually found in quantity sufficient materially to affect the result. The number of grams of methyl acetate per 100 c.c. of the spirit multiplied by 0·5405 gives the equivalent of methyl alcohol to be deducted from the total percentage by volume calculated from the methyl iodide found.

The method, it will be seen, depends upon the conversion of methyl alcohol into methyl iodide by the well-known phosphorus and iodine reaction :—

$$3CH_3{\cdot}OH + P + I_3 = 3CH_3I + H_3PO_3.$$

The volume of the methyl alcohol is then deduced from that of the iodide produced. There are some small errors in the process, which, however, tend to compensate one another. Thus a little of the acetone may distil over and be partly dissolved by the methyl iodide, but on the other hand traces of the iodide are dissolved by the water, and traces of vapour of methyl iodide remain in the flask ; the effects of these disturbing influences upon the volume of the iodide tend in opposite directions, and the net result is small. The degree of accuracy with which the volume of methyl iodide can be measured in an ordinary measuring tube is of more importance. Though not very great, it suffices for the purpose, and allows of the relatively simple method described being used instead of longer and more complicated processes.

A shortened form of the Zeisel process has been described by Hewitt and Jones as applicable to the determination of methyl alcohol in crude wood naphtha.[1]

(*d*) **The acetone reaction.**—Twenty-five c.c. of normal sodium hydroxide solution are placed in a flask similar to those used in the bromine test (*a*). To this is added 0·5 c.c. of the naphtha. The mixture is well shaken, and allowed to stand five to ten minutes. Into it from a burette *N*/5-iodine solution is run slowly, drop by drop, the mixture being vigorously shaken all the time till the upper portion of the solution, on standing a minute, becomes quite clear. A few c.c. more of the *N*/5-iodine solution are added, as to get concordant results an excess of at least 25 per cent. of the

[1] *Trans. Chem. Soc.*, 1919, **115**, 193.

iodine required must be present. After being shaken, the mixture is allowed to stand for ten to fifteen minutes, and then 25 c.c. of $N/1$-sulphuric acid are added. The excess of iodine is thus liberated, and is titrated with $N/10$-sodium thiosulphate solution and starch. Half the number of c.c. of thiosulphate solution used are deducted from the total number of c.c. of iodine solution added; the difference multiplied by 0·3876 = grams of acetone per 100 c.c. of the wood naphtha.

FIG. 36.—FLASK USED FOR ACETONE AND BROMINE TESTS OF WOOD-NAPHTHA.

This includes as "acetone" any aldehydes and higher ketones capable of yielding iodoform by this reaction.

If an excessive proportion of acetone is present a smaller quantity of the naphtha is taken, or the naphtha may be diluted to any convenient degree with methyl alcohol free from acetone, and the usual quantity, 0·5 c.c., taken—the result, of course, being corrected accordingly.

This estimation is based upon Lieben's well-known iodoform reaction of acetone, as adapted for volumetric determination by Messinger.[1] The reaction may be formulated thus:—

$$(CH_3)_2O + 3I_2 + 4NaOH = CH_3{\cdot}COONa + CHI_3 + 3H_2O + 3NaI.$$

The method is simple and rapid, and the results are good. They do not give the precise quantity of acetone when the naphtha contains any appreciable quantity of aldehyde or of the higher ketones (methyl ethyl ketone; methyl propyl ketone, etc.), as these are included in terms of acetone. This, however, is of no practical consequence in the case of wood naphtha to be used as a denaturant.

FIG. 37. — SILVER PRESSURE FLASK. Used for determining esters in wood-naphtha.

(*e*) **Estimation of esters.**—Five c.c. of the wood naphtha are run into a silver pressure flask of about 150 c.c. capacity, together with 20 c.c. of recently boiled distilled water and 10 c.c. of normal soda solution; the flask is then securely closed and digested for at least

[1] *Ber.*, 1888, **21**, 3366.

two hours in a water-bath at 100°. The contents are then cooled, washed into a beaker, and titrated with $N/1$-acid and phenolphthalein. Deduct the number of c.c. of acid required from 10; the difference $\times$ 1·48 = grams of esters, calculated as methyl acetate, per 100 c.c. of the naphtha.

Or more generally:—

Grams methyl acetate per 100 c.c. = c.c. of soda solution used up in the hydrolysis $\times 0{\cdot}074 \times \dfrac{100}{\text{c.c. naphtha taken}}$.

If the naphtha is not neutral to phenolphthalein, it must be neutralised before the esters are determined. Instead of using a silver pressure flask, the hydrolysis may be carried out in a hard glass flask fitted with a reflux condenser, and heated on a water-bath.

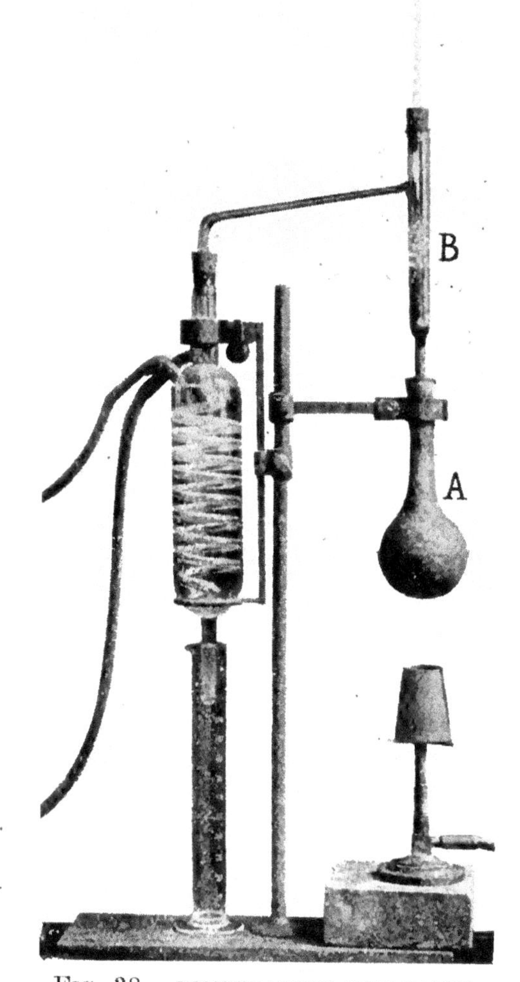

FIG. 38.—DISTILLATION APPARATUS.

Used in determining the boiling range of wood-naphtha and mineral oil. *A*, copper flask; *B*, distilling tube with glass beads.

Boiling range of wood naphtha.—No stipulations as regards this are made in the British regulations, the naphtha being judged by the results of the foregoing tests. But as a guide to makers it is stated that samples which, when fractionally distilled in the following manner, give the results indicated will as a rule be found to contain a sufficient proportion of methyl alcohol, and to be free from an excess of acetone or methyl acetate.

One hundred c.c. of the sample are to be slowly heated in a small copper flask fitted with a glass fractionating column, 7 inches high and $\frac{3}{4}$ inch in diameter, filled to the extent of 4 inches of its height with small glass beads, provided with a thermometer placed opposite the exit tube about an inch above the beads, and connected with a spiral condenser. Not more than 10 c.c. of distillate should be collected in the receiver when the thermometer marks a temperature of just under 65°. From 80 c.c. to 85 c.c. should pass over between 65° and 72·2°; and a total quantity of 97 to 98 c.c. should have distilled over before the thermometer marks 100°.

The average composition of wood naphtha submitted as suitable for denaturing purposes in the United Kingdom, and examined by the foregoing methods, may be expressed as follows :—

	Per cent. by volume.
Methyl alcohol	77·3
Ketones, in terms of acetone	10·2
Esters, calculated as methyl acetate	1·3
Unsaturated compounds, calculated as allyl alcohol	0·8
Basic ,, ,, pyridine	0·2
Water	12·2[1]
	102·0

[1] Approximate percentage. The exact change in volume occurring when water is mixed with the other ingredients is not known with certainty.

The foregoing methods, combined with obvious modifications to meet special cases—*e.g.*, determination of apparent alcoholic strength with the hydrometer or pyknometer; distillation; evaporation for non-volatile residue, and so on—will serve for the general analysis of wood spirit, whether intended for denaturing purposes or for use as a solvent, etc. Some further information, however, is added respecting the official methods of examination employed in France and Germany.

In France, methods based upon the same principles as the foregoing are employed for the determination of acetone and esters in wood naphtha intended for denaturing purposes. But since the specification for acetone is more rigid than in this country—the proportion being required to lie between 24·5 per cent. and 25·5—precautions are taken to eliminate errors of measurement due to fluctuations of temperature. This is done by keeping the samples for some hours before analysis in a place maintained as nearly as possible at 15°, and by performing a "control" experiment, at the same time and under the same conditions, upon a solution of acetone in methyl alcohol, containing 25 per cent. of pure acetone. If the analysis of this shows, for instance, only 24·7 per cent. instead of the known 25·0 per cent., a correction of +0·3 per cent. is added to the results obtained from the samples examined at the same time.

The "total impurities" of the naphtha are estimated together by an adaptation of the Röse method—namely, by shaking with chloroform and noting the amount of increase in the volume of the chloroform (see p. 417). Twenty-five c.c. of the naphtha are mixed with 60 c.c. of water and 38 c.c. of a solution of sodium bisulphite (sp. gr. = 1·35) containing no free sulphurous acid; this mixture is placed with 50 c.c. of chloroform in a suitable Röse tube and treated as in the description referred to. A "blank" experiment is made at the same time with the solution of acetone in methyl alcohol mentioned above, and any resulting correction applied. From the "total impurities" as thus ascertained (referred, of course, to 100 c.c. of the sample) is deducted the percentage of esters, calculated as methyl acetate; the result gives the "real impurities," which the French stipulations require to be not lower than 2·5 per cent.

If necessary, as when the "real impurities" exceed 5 per cent., the wood spirit is examined for the presence of ethyl alcohol (see Chap. VI, p. 221).

In Germany, the directions for testing wood naphtha are as follows:—

(1) **Colour.**—This shall not be darker than that of a solution made by dissolving 2 c.c. of $N/10$-iodine in a litre of distilled water.

(2) **Boiling point.**—One hundred c.c. of the naphtha are placed in a short-necked copper flask of about 180–200 capacity, resting on an asbestos plate in which is cut a circular hole of 3 cm. diameter. In the neck of this flask is placed a fractionating tube 12 mm. wide and 17 cm. long, with its side tube connected to a Liebig's condenser at least 40 cm. long. In the fractionating tube, which is provided with a bulb about a centimetre below the side tube, is placed a thermometer with a scale ranging from 0° to 200°, so that its mercury reservoir is in the middle of the bulb.

The flask is heated so that the distillation proceeds at about the rate of 5 c.c. per minute. The distillate is collected in a cylinder graduated in c.c., and at 75° with a normal barometric pressure of 760 mm. at least 90 c.c. shall be collected.

If the barometer is not at 760 mm. during the distillation, 1° shall be allowed for every variation of 30 mm For example, at 770 mm., 90 c.c. shall distil at 75·3°.

(3) **Miscibility with water.**—Twenty c.c. of the wood spirit mixed with 40 c.c. of water shall give a clear, or only slightly opalescent solution.

(4) **Acetone content.**

(*a*) **Separation on mixing with soda solution.**—Twenty c.c. of wood spirit are shaken with 40 c.c. of soda solution of sp. gr. 1·300. At least 5 c.c. of the spirit must have separated after the mixture has been allowed to stand for half an hour.

(*b*) **Titration.**—One c.c. of a mixture of 10 c.c. of the wood spirit with 90 c.c. of water, is mixed with 10 c.c. of 2 *N*-solution of sodium hydroxide. Then 50 c.c. of *N*/10-iodine solution are added, with continual shaking, and the mixture allowed to remain for at least three minutes. Excess of dilute sulphuric acid is then added, and the liberated iodine titrated with *N*/10-thiosulphate solution and starch. At least 22 c.c. of *N*/10-iodine solution must have been used up by the acetone. (This is equivalent to 21·3 grams of acetone per 100 c.c. of wood spirit.)

(5) **Bromine absorption.**—One hundred c.c. of a solution of potassium bromate and bromide (made up as described below) are acidified by the addition of 20 c.c. of dilute sulphuric acid (sp. gr. 1·290). To this mixture the wood spirit is added drop by drop from a burette so long as any colour remains on shaking. The rate of addition shall be so arranged that in one minute 10 c.c. of spirit shall have been added.

Not more than 30 c.c. of the wood spirit shall be required for the decolorisation, and not less than 20 c.c. This test must be made in full daylight, and at a temperature not exceeding 20°.

Bromine solution.—After at least two hours' drying at 100°, and cooling in an exsiccator, 2·447 grams of $KBrO_3$ and 8·719 grams of KBr of tested purity are dissolved in water, and the solution made up to 1 litre.

Mineral naphtha.—The mineral naphtha approved for making mineralised methylated spirit in the United Kingdom is ordinary light mineral oil having a specific gravity not lower than 0·800 at 15·5°. The sp. gr. ranges up to about 0·830, and is usually about 0·810 to 0·820. The oil, when mixed with methylated alcohol in the proper proportion (0·375 per cent.) must give a satisfactory turbidity on dilution with water.

Petroleum ether or mineral oil.—For certain special purposes some users of methylated spirit are required to employ spirit which is mixed with 3 per cent. of an approved mineral oil or petroleum ether. For this purpose the oil is required to have a specific gravity of 0·685 to 0·690 at 15·5°; or, alternatively, of 0·705 to 0·710, the latter range admitting of Eastern oils being used as well as American. In addition, when 100 c.c. of the oil, of either variety, is distilled in the apparatus described under "Wood Naphtha" (p. 309), not more than 10 c.c. should distil below 65°, at least 75 c.c. should pass over between 65° and 85°, and a total of at least 95 c.c. should distil before the thermometer marks 100°.

The cost of producing alcohol is appreciably enhanced by the restrictions necessary for safeguarding the revenue. It is calculated that the increase of cost amounts to 3*d.* per proof gallon in this country, at the present time. In order to relieve alcohol used in manufacture of this enhanced cost, an allowance of 3*d.* per proof gallon is paid on alcohol used for making industrial methylated spirit, and also on all ethyl alcohol received for use duty-free under Section 8 of the Finance Act, 1902.

The quantities of these two varieties of alcohol on which the allowance was paid are shown below for two recent years :—

	1914.	1915.	
Industrial methylated spirit	5,132,512	4,839,071	proof gallons.
Duty-free alcohol under 1902 Act ..	791,228	779,765	,, ,,

The quantities (bulk gallons) of industrial and mineralised methylated spirit actually sent into consumption by the methylators during the two years are subjoined :—

Year ended 31st March.	Industrial. Bulk gallons.	Mineralised. Bulk gallons.	Total. Bulk gallons.
1914	3,253,061	1,754,514	5,007,575
1915	3,103,362	1,771,321	4,874,683

The foregoing figures suffice to give a general idea of the quantities of methylated spirit, and of the specially-denatured alcohol, which have normally been used in the United Kingdom.

As to the particular uses to which industrial methylated spirit is put in this country, the following table indicates the chief applications of this variety of duty-free alcohol. It is taken, slightly abbreviated, from the Customs and Excise annual report issued in 1917.[1] The unit of quantity is 1,000 bulk gallons.

INDUSTRIAL METHYLATED SPIRIT. QUANTITIES USED IN THE UNITED KINGDOM. YEAR 1915–16.

Manufacture or other purpose.	Quantity, in thousands of gallons.
Finish, for sale	391·0
Varnish, polish, and lacquer, for sale	1,116·2
,, ,, ,, ,, use in makers' workshops..	303·5
Stains, paints, enamels, etc.	103·8
Felt and other hats	66·1
Celluloid, xylonite, and similar substances	23·5
Oil-cloths, leather-cloths, and similar substances	227·9
Smokeless powders, fulminates, and other explosives ..	294·3
Soap-making	202·7
Electric lamp filaments	10·7
Incandescent mantles	38·3
Ether	393·1
Chloroform	17·5
Ethyl chloride and bromide	2·6

[1] Cd. 8428.

INDUSTRIAL METHYLATED SPIRIT. QUANTITIES USED IN THE UNITED KINGDOM. YEAR 1915–16.—*cont.*

Manufacture or other purpose.	Quantity, in thousands of gallons.
Solid medicinal extracts	49·2
Alkaloids and fine chemicals	72·0
Embrocations, liniments, and lotions	32·7
Surgical dressings	15·2
Capsules and other medicinal appliances	2·5
Hair washes	47·7
Cattle medicines	3·6
Plant washes, insecticides, and sheep dips	17·6
Aniline and other dyes, solids	0·7
,, ,, ,, ,, solutions	4·6
Fireworks and matches	4·1
Photographic plates and papers, and other photographic purposes	48·9
Steel pens	2·2
Silk, crape, and embroidery	11·7
Artificial flowers, etc.	8·4
Rubber	1·0
Solidified spirit	27·0
Ships' compasses, spirit levels, etc.	1·3
Inks	0·8
Collodion	33·5
Disinfectants	2·2
Dyeing and cleaning operations	31·3
Textile printing	3·6
Electrotyping and printing	1·5
Preservation of specimens in museums and hospitals	4·5
Educational and scientific purposes in colleges and schools	4·2
Analytical and scientific purposes in laboratories of analysts, works chemists, etc.	5·6
Used in hospitals, asylums, and infirmaries	72·8
,, Admiralty dockyards and War Office arsenals and workshops	265·5
Miscellaneous uses	115·4
Total	4,082·5

That is, the total number of gallons used was 4,082,500.

II. INDUSTRIAL ALCOHOL IN FOREIGN COUNTRIES

Speaking broadly, the conditions under which denatured alcohol is allowed to be used free of duty in foreign countries are generally similar to those imposed in the United Kingdom. There is usually a heavily denatured spirit which may be sold or used with comparative freedom; and there are less nauseous kinds of spirit, or specially denatured kinds, which have to be employed under more stringent conditions of supervision than the first-mentioned variety. It may be noted that the specially denatured spirit is not of necessity less nauseous than that which is allowed to be sold and used freely. Very often it is much more nauseous. But the denaturant substance is, or may be, more easily removed, and hence the necessity for greater restrictions.

Perhaps the chief difference which strikes one in comparing the foreign regulations with those of the United Kingdom is the fact that, abroad, a number of industries are often enumerated in which "specially denatured" alcohol may be employed, and for which the special denaturants are prescribed. In this country the formulæ for special denaturing have not been published—at all events, not officially. They are regarded as confidential information. Hence two makers of the same article do not, of necessity, use the same denaturants for the alcohol employed.

Minor points of difference are that in some countries the cost of analysing the denaturants, in order to ensure that they conform to the prescribed standards, must be borne by the user of the alcohol; whilst in some cases the Administration itself furnishes the denaturants, at the expense of the users (France, Holland). In Italy, some of the denaturing substances are supplied by the person using the alcohol, whilst others are supplied by the revenue authorities at the expense of the user. In some cases, too (Russia, Switzerland), the alcohol itself is sold by the State.

The impression given by a study of the various systems is that most of the foreign countries endeavour to foster the industries which employ alcohol, by authorising the use of special denaturants suitable to the particular industry; but this necessarily involves considerable restriction and supervision.

Austria-Hungary.—The methylated spirit for ordinary use is prepared by adding 5 litres of wood naphtha and ½ a litre of pyridine bases to every 100 litres of alcohol. For some years phenolphthalein was included as a denaturant, and the wood naphtha was in smaller proportion (viz., 2 per cent.), but this has now been replaced by the formula given above.

For making varnishes and mercury fulminate the denaturing agent is 0·5 per cent. of turpentine. Specially-denatured spirit is also allowed in the making of ether, vinegar, and solutions of shellac.

Very small quantities of pure alcohol are used for scientific purposes free of duty, under certain conditions.

Belgium.—Alcohol for lighting and heating purposes is not allowed free of duty. Varnishes appear to be the only products, containing methylated spirits, that can be sold. All the other denatured spirits are for use in the factories only, and the denaturing is done under the supervision of revenue officers at the works. Accounts have to be kept of the quantity of spirit used daily. The officials frequently take stock of the spirit, and may verify the quantities of products made. No stills are allowed on the works except when specially authorised. The minimum quantity of alcohol for denaturing is two hectolitres at 50°.

Total remission of duty on the denatured spirit is allowed in a few instances only. In a number of other manufactures a proportion of the duty is remitted after the alcohol has been mixed with certain denaturing agents. In most cases, the proportion is 14/15ths; but it may range down to 114/150ths. The quantities mentioned below are those for denaturing each hectolitre of alcohol at 94° or above.

Manufacture.	Denaturing agent.
Aniline colours	10 litres of wood spirit containing 5 per cent. of acetone, and 25 grams of fuchsine or other aniline colour.
Collodion; tannin	50 litres of ether.
Pegamoids, etc.	5 litres of acetone, or 2 litres of methyl ethyl ketone, or 25 litres of ether.
Oil refining	10 litres of sulphuric acid at 66° Bé.
Smokeless powder, peptones, antiseptics, and medicaments	3 litres of methyl ethyl ketone.
Mercury fulminate	10 litres of crude distillate recovered in the process.
Quinoline yellow	3 litres of acetone oil.
Ether	10 ,, ether residues.
Acetic ether	15 ,, acetic ether residues.
Anatomical, etc., preparations, in secondary schools	500 grams of nitrobenzol, 500 grams of camphor, or 1½ litres of methyl ethyl ketone.
Artificial silk	150 litres of ether.
Vinegar	300 ,, of water and 100 litres of vinegar containing 8 per cent. of acetic acid.
Varnishes:	
(1). If for use on premises where made	8 litres of wood spirit containing 5 per cent. of acetone and 25 litres of varnish containing 30 per cent. of resin.
(2). If for sale	10 litres of wood spirit as above and 25 grams of fuchsine.
Artificial flowers	10 litres of wood spirit, 15 grams of aniline dye.
Transparent soap	5 litres essence of lavender or citronella.
Gassing fabrics	4 litres of acetone oil.
Frame-gilding	20 litres of wood spirit, 3 litres of methyl ethyl ketone.

France.—Spirits for industrial and domestic use are freed from the ordinary spirit duty on condition that they are denatured. Denatured alcohol pays a small statistical tax, and also an impost to cover the expense of examining samples and supervising the denaturing operations. The alcohol for denaturing must be of not less than 90 per cent. strength, and contain not more than 1 per cent. of fusel oil.

The denaturing may be "general" or "special." The "general" denaturant is wood spirit of not less than 90° strength, and containing 25 per cent. of acetone with 2·5 per cent. of pyroligneous impurities. Ten litres of this are used for each 100 litres of the alcohol to be denatured.

Spirit denatured by this reagent is divided into two classes :—

(1) That used for **general manufactures** such as making varnishes, extracts, soap, and so on.

(2) That used for **lighting, heating, and making "finish."**—This spirit must contain, in addition to the general denaturing reagent, 0·5 per cent. of heavy benzine, distilling between 150° and 200°, when used for lighting and heating ; and 4 per cent. of gum resin when used for "finish."

The "special" denaturing is to meet the requirements of those industries where alcohol mixed with wood spirit cannot be used. Authorised procedures[1] are :—

(1) **Ethers and esters.**—The alcohol is mixed with 10 per cent. of the residue from a previous operation, and 10 per cent. of sulphuric acid at 66° Bé., or 20 per cent. at 54° Bé. The mixture is heated to a temperature of 80° for some time.

(2) **Ethyl bromide.**—Seven and a-half litres of alcohol at 93° are mixed with 8½ litres of sulphuric acid and 15 grams of bromine.

(3) **Ethyl iodide.**—Six litres of alcohol at 96°, with 4 kilograms of iodine, and 800 grams of amorphous phosphorus.

(4) **Sodium ethylate.**—Eight litres of absolute alcohol with 500 grams of sodium.

(5) **Nitric ester.**—One part by weight of nitric acid at 36° mixed with 4 parts of alcohol at 96°.

(6) **Ethyl chloride.**—Equal weights of alcohol at 96° and hydrochloric acid at 21° Bé.

(7) **Aldehyde.**—Mix the alcohol with 10 per cent. of sulphuric acid at 66° Bé. or with 20 per cent. at 54° Bé., and heat the mixture to a temperature of 80°. After the mixture has cooled, pour it on to potassium bichromate.

(8) **Chloroform.**—The alcohol is mixed with chloride of lime in solution, as part of the process of manufacture.

(9) **Collodion.**—Mix equal volumes of alcohol and ether, and add 6 grams of gun-cotton per litre.

(10) **Chloral and chloral hydrate.**—A current of chlorine gas is passed into the alcohol. Each litre of alcohol at 95° should produce 780 grams of chloral hydrate.

Medicaments which contain alcohol after their manufacture pay the ordinary spirit duty.

Germany.—The use of denatured alcohol free of duty was first

[1] Industrial Alcohol Committee's Minutes of Evidence, Appendix IV; Calvet, "Alcools," pp. 32–40.

allowed in 1879, the system of denaturing being that followed in Great Britain at that time. In 1887, however, different regulations came into force.

The denaturing is either "*complete*"—*i.e.*, such as is deemed sufficient to make the spirit undrinkable, or "*incomplete*"—*i.e.*, such as requires the employment of other means to prevent the improper use of such spirit.

The general denaturing agent for "complete" denaturing consists of 4 parts of wood naphtha and 1 part of pyridine bases, to each litre of which mixture may be added 50 grams of lavender oil or rosemary oil to mask the odour of the pyridine bases. This general denaturant is used in the proportion of 2½ litres to each hectolitre of alcohol.

This German methylated spirit therefore contains 2 per cent. of wood naphtha, and 0·5 per cent. of pyridine bases, with optionally 0·125 per cent. of lavender oil or rosemary oil.

For use in motors, alcohol may also be completely denatured by the addition of 1¼ litres of the "general" denaturing agent and ¼ litre of a solution of methyl violet dye, together with from 2 to 20 litres of benzol to every 100 litres of alcohol.

The ordinary "completely denatured" spirit is intended for sale by retail, and is used for cleansing, burning, and general purposes, much in the same way as British "mineralised" methylated spirit is employed.

For general use on a large scale for industrial and manufacturing processes, alcohol denatured with wood naphtha only is sanctioned. This "wood-spirit-denatured" alcohol is a mixture of 5 litres of wood naphtha with 100 litres of alcohol of strength not less than 90°. It corresponds approximately with the British "industrial methylated spirit."

Where this "wood-spirit-denatured" alcohol, or the ordinary "completely denatured" alcohol, is unsuitable for any particular manufacture, special denaturing agents may be allowed for "*incomplete*" denaturing, which is carried out only at the factories where the alcohol is to be used. The following substances are used, the quantities stated being for 100 litres of spirit at 100°.

(*a*) **Industrial uses of all kinds.**—Five litres of wood spirit, or 0·5 litre of pyridine bases.

(*b*) **Brewers' varnish and similar substances.**—Twenty litres of a shellac solution (1 part by weight of shellac in 2 parts by weight of spirit at not less than 90°).

(*c*) **Celluloid and pegamoid.**—One kilo. of camphor, or 2 litres of turpentine, or ½ litre of benzol.

(*d*) **For all the following articles :—**

(1) Ether; (2) ethyl sulphates; (3) agaricin, podophyllin, scammony, guaiacum, and jalap resins, as well as other resins and gum resins; (4) aldehyde and paraldehyde; (5) white lead and acetate of lead; (6) ethyl chloride, bromide, and iodide; (7) photographic paper and dry plates, and photo-emulsions; (8) chloral hydrate; (9) electrodes for storage batteries; (10) acetic ether; (11) glucosides; (12) rubber preparations; (13) collodion, and silver bromide, chloride, and iodide emulsions of collodion; (14) pancreatin, alkaloids, santonin, tannin, salicylic acid and its salts; (15) coal tar colours, including substances used in obtaining them, and intermediate products; and (16) chemical preparations (not otherwise named) which do not retain any alcohol when finished (except formic, valerianic, and butyric esters) :—

10 litres of ether,
or 1 litre of benzol,
or 0·5 ,, turpentine,
or 0·025 ,, animal oil.

Collodion for sale must contain at least 1 per cent. of gun cotton. Ether and acetic ether are only allowed to be made from duty-free alcohol if they are to be exported, or used at home for certain specified purposes.

(*e*) **For making chloroform.**—Three hundred grams of chloroform.

(*f*) **Vinegar.**—Specified quantities of vinegar containing 3, 4, 6, 8, 10, or 12 per cent. of acetic acid, with certain proportions of water, beer, or wine.

(*g*) **Inks, sealing wax, and stamping inks.**—0·5 Litre of turpentine, or 0·025 litre of animal oil.

(*h*) **Bedstead enamels, brewers' varnish,** as well as for use in incandescent lamps, for finishing silk ribbons, and for cleansing jewellery, etc., 0·5 litre of turpentine.

(*i*) **Iodoform.**—Two hundred grams of iodoform.

(*k*) **Varnishes and polishes of all kinds.**—Two litres of wood spirit and 2 litres of petroleum benzine; *or* 0·5 litre of turpentine. If intended for sale, the varnishes and polishes must contain at least 10 per cent. of shellac or other resin.

(*l*) **Medical, botanical, and zoological preparations,** for educational purposes.—One litre of commercially pure methyl alcohol and 1 litre of petroleum benzine.

(*m*) **Soap-making.**—One kilo. of castor oil and 400 c.c. of soda lye.

(*n*) **Lanolin.**—Five litres of petroleum benzine.

The use of alcohol not denatured is only allowed in certain hospitals, asylums, and public scientific institutions and for making explosives, chiefly in Government factories. "For all other purposes, without exception, duty paid spirit must be used, unless the spirit be subjected to some *authorised* process of denaturing prior to use. The German system, while designed on liberal and comprehensive lines, is rigidly enforced, and allows of no exceptions in practice to the rules as laid down."[1]

Holland.—Two kinds of denatured alcohol are recognised, *viz.* :—

(*a*). With 7 litres of crude wood spirit ; or

(*b*). With 12 litres of colourless wood spirit,

per hectolitre of alcohol *calculated* at 50° strength. The alcohol employed must be of at least 85° strength.

The spirit (*a*) is intended for general use, and is allowed to be employed without restriction, on condition that it is not purified or used in articles of human consumption.

The spirit (*b*) is only allowed for industrial purposes and under authorisation.

Alcohol for vinegar making is denatured by the addition, to each hectolitre of spirit at 50°, of 2 hectolitres of water and 1 hectolitre of vinegar of 4 per cent. acid strength ; or 20 litres of vinegar of 4 per cent. acid strength with 20 litres of raisin juice ; or 20 litres of the vinegar alone if the revenue officials see the mixture added to the acetification vessels.

Italy.—For general purposes the denaturant employed is a mixture of wood naphtha, pyridine bases, acetone oil, benzene, and colouring matter. Of this mixture, 3 litres are added to 100 litres of alcohol, which must not be of lower strength than 90°. Spirit so denatured is used for lighting, heating, and motor purposes, and for certain kinds of varnish.

Specially-denatured alcohol is allowed for use in various industries. The denaturants used are partly furnished by the authorities, at fixed prices, and partly by the users of the denatured spirit. If any alcohol is recovered during the manufacturing operations in which the denatured spirit is employed, it may only be used again for the same purpose, and if necessary must be again denatured. The special denaturants chiefly employed are as follows, per 100 litres of alcohol.

(1). **For making ether.**—One litre of sulphuric acid at 66° Bé., 5 litres of crude ether residues, and 1 litre of crude benzol. Under permanent supervision, sulphuric acid alone may be employed.

[1] Industrial Alcohol Committee, Report, p. 13.

(2). **Varnishes.**—Four litres of a mixture of wood naphtha, acetone oil, and crude benzol, with sufficient of the particular varnish to give 10 grams of fixed residue per litre.

(3). **Mercury fulminate.**—Crude residue from previous operations, 6 litres; nitric acid, 5 litres.

(4). **Collodion, photographic paper, and artificial silk.**—Three litres of acetone, 1 litre of light acetone oil, and 20 litres of ether. The ether alone may be used for the silk if under permanent supervision. On the same condition, ether in the given proportion may be used for denaturing alcohol used in making cinematograph films.

(5). **Brewers' varnish.**—Methyl alcohol 2 litres, light acetone oil 2 litres, with 20 litres of shellac solution (50 kilos. of lac in 100 kilos. of alcohol).

(6). **Lysoform.**—0·5 Litre of acetone oil, 3 litres of acetone, and 2 litres of formalin (40 per cent. strength).

(7). **"Dermoid" varnish.**—Two litres of methyl alcohol, 2 litres of acetone, and 4 litres of "Dermoid" varnish.

(8). **Incandescent mantles.**—2·5 Litres of ether, 2·5 kilos. of camphor, 2·5 kilos. of castor oil, and 2·5 litres of collodion solution (6 per cent.).

Norway.—Alcohol is allowed free of duty if denatured either with wood naphtha or with other substances which will prevent the alcohol being used for potable purposes. The expenses of denaturing and supervision devolve upon the trader.

Portugal.—For general purposes alcohol is denatured with a mixture of wood naphtha, heavy benzine, and malachite green, in the proportions of 2 litres, 1 litre, and 2 decigrams, respectively, per 100 litres of alcohol at strength higher than 83°. For varnishes, the spirit is denatured with 2 litres of wood naphtha per 100 litres, and at least 4 per cent. of resin or gum-resin. Special processes of denaturing are also allowed, provided that they are such as to give protection against the regeneration of potable alcohol.

Russia.—The sale of alcohol is a State monopoly in Russia, and denatured alcohol for Government establishments is made less nauseous than that for private firms or individuals. In 1907, the substances and proportions used in "general" denaturing were, for 100 volumes of absolute alcohol:—

(*a*). **State establishments.**—2·5 Vols. of wood spirit, 0·5 vol. of pyridine bases, and 0·1 vol. of a solution of violet colour.

(*b*). **Private persons.**—Five vols. of wood spirit, 1 vol. of pyridine, and 0·1 vol. of violet colouring.

Subsequently, the proportion of wood spirit in each of these varieties was reduced to one-half (*i.e.*, to 1·25 per cent. and 2·5 per cent. respectively); but this was understood to be a temporary measure only. An alternative form of general denaturing for private traders' use was also authorised: per 100 vols. of absolute alcohol—2 vols. of wood spirit, 0·5 vol. of pyridine bases, 1 vol. of ketone oils, and 0·1 vol. of violet colouring.

Permission to use spirit duty free is generally limited to one year, and bond must be given.

Special denaturing processes are as follows:—

(1). **For varnishes and polishes.**—One hundred parts of spirit are mixed with 5 parts of wood naphtha and 1 part of turpentine. Or instead of turpentine, resin, shellac, or tar may be used in the proportion of ½ lb. to one vedro (2·7 gallons) of spirit.

(2). **For the preparation of wine vinegar.**—The spirit is diluted with water and vinegar, so that it shall be of strength 12° Tralles (79 under proof), and contain 1½ per cent. of acetic acid.

(3). **For making ether, chloroform, and chloral hydrate.**—The alcohol is denatured with animal oil.

(4). **For preparation of tannin, collodion, and artificial silk.** Ten parts of ether are added to 100 parts of alcohol.

(5). **Preparation of santonin.**—Fresh spirit is mixed with spirit that has already been used, in the proportion of 4 to 1; or 1 poud (36 lb.) of crude santonin is mixed with 10 vedros (27 gallons) of alcohol.

(6). **Phenacetin, salol, salipyrine, and salicitine nitro-salts.**—Five per cent. of benzene is added to the spirit.

(7). **Preparation of aniline dyes.**—Five per cent. of wood naphtha. Or, alternatively, the alcohol is denatured with animal oil.

(8). **Resinite or Kisylite.**—Seven per cent. of ether or acetone.

(9). **Smokeless powders.**—The spirit is not denatured, but its use is under strict surveillance.

(10). **Mercury fulminate.**—0·025 Per cent. of animal oil, together with 5 per cent. of the crude recovered spirit that has been used in the process.

(11). **Extraction of sugar from treacle.**—Fresh spirit is mixed with spirit that has already been used—equal volumes of each.

(12). **For preventing deposits of naphthalene in gas pipes.**—Five parts of wood naphtha and 1 part of pyridine bases are mixed with 100 of alcohol.

(13). **For street lighting.**—Twenty parts of turpentine to 100 parts of alcohol; only allowed to contractors to local authorities.

Spain.—Alcohol for lighting, heating, or motor power may be denatured with 2 per cent. of wood naphtha containing 30 per cent. of acetone; benzine may be further added in quantity to suit the trader's requirements. Alternatively, a denaturing mixture composed of one-half of benzine and one-half of wood naphtha including 30 per cent. of acetone may be employed.

Sweden.—Wood naphtha and pyridine bases are used as denaturants. Special denaturing is accorded in certain manufactures, including those of alkaloids, chloral, chloroform, fulminates, tannic acid, and varnish.

Switzerland.—The manufacture, importation, and primary sale of alcohol in Switzerland is a monopoly of the Federal Government. Farmers are permitted to distil small quantities of spirit from wine, fruits, etc., grown on their own lands ; but with this exception all the distilleries work under the supervision of the Federal Alcohol Department, and all the alcohol produced is taken over by the Administration at prices agreed upon.

The Alcohol Department is authorised to sell denatured spirit in quantities of not less than 150 litres at cost price for the following purposes :—

(*a*). For cleansing, heating, cooking, lighting, and use in motor engines.

(*b*). For industrial purposes generally, except the preparation of beverages, liquid perfumes, and cosmetics.

(*c*). For making vinegar.

(*d*). For scientific purposes.

(*e*). For preparing pharmaceutical products which do not contain alcohol in their finished condition, and are not mixed with alcohol when used.

The denaturing is either " absolute "—that is, such as is deemed sufficient to render the alcohol unpotable, or it is " relative "—that is, such as requires official supervision to prevent the spirit being used for other purposes than those for which it is allowed.

The " absolutely " denatured spirit is used for the purposes indicated at (*a*) above, and for sale by retail. Its composition is not invariable, the denaturing mixture being purposely changed two or three times a year. As an example, the following is the composition of a mixture which has been used :—Acetone oil 70 parts, pyridine bases 10, solvent naphtha 9, crude wood naphtha 11 parts. Of this mixture, 2·7 kilos. were added to every 100 kilos. of alcohol at 95°.

" Relatively " denatured spirit is allowed to be used for all manufacturing purposes. The following substances have been sanctioned :—

(*a*). **For making vinegar.**—To 100 litres of alcohol, 5 litres of absolute acetic acid dissolved in at least 200 litres of water, beer, wine, yeast pressings, etc.

(*b*). **For lacquers, varnishes, and polishes.**—To 100 litres of alcohol, either 2 litres of wood spirit and 2 litres of benzine; *or* 0·5 litre of turpentine; *or* 5 litres of wood spirit; *or* 2 kilos. of shellac; *or* 2 kilos. of copal or resin; *or* 0·5 kilo. of camphor.

(*c*). **For preparing dye substances.**—To 100 litres of alcohol, 10 litres of ether;

or 1 litre of benzene;
,, 1 ,, coal tar oil;
,, 0·5 ,, turpentine;
,, 25 grams of animal oil;
,, 25 ,, aniline blue, eosin, violet, or fluorescein;
,, 100 ,, naphthalene;
,, 2 kilos. of commercially pure methyl alcohol;
,, 0·5 kilo. of camphor.

To use other denaturants for other purposes special permission has to be obtained. The "relatively" denatured spirit must not be sold by the user, though if further denatured with wood naphtha (5 litres per hectolitre), or with acetone oils (3 litres), or with shellac (2 kilos.), it may be disposed of for use only in the purchasers' own workshops, not for re-sale.

United States.—The use of denatured alcohol duty-free for industrial and general purposes is comparatively recent in the United States. Though the principle had been recognised by Congress many years previously, it was only in 1906–7 that effect was given to the recognition.

Two varieties of **"completely denatured"** alcohol are now sanctioned:—

(1).—To 100 gallons of ethyl alcohol are added 10 gallons of wood spirit and ½ gallon of benzine.

(2).—To 100 gallons of ethyl alcohol are added 2 gallons of wood spirit and ½ gallon of pyridine bases.

The wood spirit, benzine, and pyridine bases must be of approved quality.

"Specially denatured" alcohol is sanctioned for use in certain industries according to the following list. All the quantities are referred to 100 (American) gallons of plain spirit.[1]

(1).—For preparation of lac varnish, collodion varnish, photographic plates, embalming liquids, making barometers and ther-

[1] One American gallon = 3·785 litres = 0·833 Imperial gallon.

mometers, and production of such articles as heliotropine, podophyllum resin, etc. :—

5 gallons of approved wood spirit.

(2).—For celluloid, pyralin and similar products :—

Seven pounds (American) of camphor and 5 gallons of commercially pure methyl alcohol having sp. gr. lower than 0·810 at 60° F., or alternatively, 2 gallons of wood spirit and 2 gallons of benzine.

(3).—For transparent soaps :—

6½ Gallons of the following mixture, *viz.*, 5 gallons of commercially-pure methyl alcohol as defined in (2), with 1 gallon of castor oil and ½ gallon of soda-lye at 36° Bé.

(4).—For preparation of tobacco (smoking and chewing) :—

One gallon of the following mixture, *viz.*, 2 gallons of an aqueous solution of nicotine (40 per cent.), 0·4 lb. of an acid yellow colour, 0·4 lb. of blue colour tetrazo-brilliant 2B, and water sufficient to make 100 gallons.

(5).—For photogravures :—

Sixty-five lb. of ether, 3 lb. of cadmium iodide, and 3 lb. of ammonium iodide.

(6).—Mercury fulminate :—

Five gallons of commercially-pure methyl alcohol as defined in (2) and ½ gallon of pyridine bases.

(7).—For use in watch-making :—

Five gallons of commercially-pure methyl alcohol (sp. gr. less than 0·810 at 60° F.), 1½ lb. of potassium cyanide, and ⅛ oz. of blue colour B (sodium or magnesium salt). The blue colouring matter is dissolved in the methyl alcohol, and the potassium cyanide in a small quantity of water : these two solutions are then mixed with the 100 gallons of alcohol to be denatured.

(8).—For preparation of sulphomethane :—

One gallon of pyridine bases and 1 gallon of benzol.

(9).—For purification of caoutchouc :—

Ten gallons of acetone and 2 gallons of mineral naphtha having sp. gr. between 0·650 and 0·720 at 60° F.

(10).—For pastes and varnishes with gun-cotton basis :—

Two gallons of wood spirit and 2 gallons of benzol.

(11).—For photographic collodion :—

One hundred lb. of ether and 10 lb. of cadmium iodide.

III. TECHNICAL APPLICATIONS OF INDUSTRIAL ALCOHOL

Looking at the table given on pp. 313–4, we get an idea of the numerous purposes to which industrial methylated spirit is put in the arts and manufactures.

Industrial alcohol, however, is not confined to "methylated" spirit, and still less to this particular form of it. In this section the term is used in its widest sense as embracing all forms of duty-free alcohol, ethyl or methyl. Thus in addition to industrial methylated spirit it will include, on the one hand, the "completely denatured" products such as our "mineralised" spirit, and on the other, the specially-denatured or non-denatured spirits employed for special manufactures.

Nevertheless, the table mentioned gives a good indication of the chief purposes to which alcohol is put industrially, and it will serve very well to exemplify those purposes. It is therefore taken as a basis for the following discussion.

Use of alcohol for burning, etc.—In all the countries the "completely denatured" form of spirit is mainly employed for burning, either as a motor fuel, or as a source of heat and light in domestic and public usage. This matter is dealt with at length in Chap. IX. In addition, the spirit is used as a cleanser, for making embrocations and lotions, mixing with paints, making the commoner kinds of polish, and, in general, for the coarser requirements where the odour of the denaturants or the turbidity given on dilution of the spirit is of no particular consequence.

Use as solvent.—Alcohol is very largely employed as a solvent. This, in fact, is its function in most of the manufactures indicated by the table above referred to. Where it is so used, the products may be divided into two classes: (1), those in which the spirit remains as part of the finished article; and (2), those from which the alcohol, after having served its purpose, is expelled in the subsequent stages of the manufacture.

As examples of the first class may be mentioned "finish," polish, varnish, and stains; embrocations, liniments, and lotions; hair washes; cattle medicines; plant washes, insecticides, and sheep dips; dye solutions; and collodion. Here the alcohol serves to dissolve and keep in solution some ingredient of the article which is not soluble in water, such as resin, oil, colouring matter, or organic drug. Thus "finish" (used by polishers and others) is a solution of resin or gum-resin in alcohol; liniments may contain various organic drugs such as aconite, belladonna, or camphor; collodion is a solution of gun-cotton in alcohol and ether; and so on almost *ad infinitum*.

As instances of the second group may be cited celluloid, soap, solid medicinal extracts, photographic plates, silk, artificial flowers, and textile printing.

In the preparation of celluloid, for example, alcohol is used to dissolve the camphor which is one of the ingredients of the product, the spirit being eventually dried off.

In soap-making, alcohol is employed to clarify the "transparent" varieties. Dried soap is dissolved in the spirit, and most of the latter is distilled away. The residual mass is formed into bars or cakes and stored at the ordinary temperature, when the rest of the alcohol gradually evaporates and the soap slowly becomes translucent.

To obtain medicinal extracts economically, the crude drugs (roots, barks, and other parts of plants) are extracted with industrial methylated spirit, which is then distilled from the solution so produced, and much of it recovered for future use. The residual solid extract can then be dissolved in pure (duty-paid) alcohol to form the medicinal liquid extract, which in this country cannot legally (if capable of internal use) contain methylated spirit. This procedure obviates the use, and the consequent unavoidable loss, of the expensive duty-paid alcohol in the actual extraction of the crude drug.

In photography, alcohol is employed as a solvent for the collodion used in preparing collodion-emulsions. It is also used for the drying of plates and the making of photographic varnishes, and as a solvent for colours in colour-photography.

In making artificial silk, alcohol (2 volumes) is mixed with ether (3 volumes) as a solvent for the nitro-cellulose which forms the basis of the product. The solution is essentially a kind of collodion. It is forced through tubes, of diminishing calibre, until it finally emerges as very fine filaments, which dry as they reach the air and are spun together to form the working thread. In silk dyeing, as also in the colouring of artificial flowers and in calico printing, alcohol is a solvent for the dye-stuff employed.

Another important application of the solvent properties of alcohol is in the purification of fine chemicals by crystallisation. The impure substance is usually dissolved in warm or cold alcohol of suitable strength, filtered from solid impurities if necessary, and the solution allowed to crystallise.

Alcohol as raw material.—In the foregoing cases, the

alcohol either remains as an ingredient of the finished product, or is removed at some stage; but in either event it still retains its identity *as* alcohol. In other instances, however, the ethyl (or methyl) group of the alcohol enters into the molecular composition of the product, and *quâ* alcohol the original spirit is destroyed. Thus, for instance, alcohol may be transformed into ether or chloroform. In other words, it serves as the raw material for the manufacture of these compounds.

The chief products manufactured from alcohol in this sense may be grouped as follows :—

(1). **Anæsthetics and antiseptics :** Ether; ethyl chloride and bromide; chloral, chloroform, and bromoform; iodoform.

(2). **Esters of fatty acids** : Ethyl formate, acetate, butyrate, propionate; ethyl acetoacetate, etc.

(3). **Synthetic drugs :** Phenacetin; antipyrin, etc.

(4). **Dyestuff intermediates :** Methyl and ethyl anilines, etc.

(5). **Aldehyde and formaldehyde.**

(6). **Acetic acid and vinegar.**

In the following pages the preparation of these and a few other compounds obtained from alcohol is described.

Manufacture of ether.—A mixture of 5 parts of alcohol (90 to 95 per cent.) and 9 parts of strong sulphuric acid is heated in a still to a temperature of 130–140°. Ether is formed, and distils over, together with some water. With continuous addition of alcohol in properly regulated proportion to the hot mixture, the formation of ether is maintained, and the process goes on indefinitely. The stream of alcohol is adjusted so that the volume of the mixture remains constant; and the temperature is kept between the limits stated, since below 130° much unaltered alcohol passes over, and above 140° ethylene gas is produced, with destruction of a corresponding quantity of alcohol.

The distillate of crude ether thus obtained contains sulphur dioxide, water, alcohol, and so-called "oil of ether," a decomposition product of the side reactions which occur. To purify it from the acid, it is washed with soda solution or milk of lime; and to remove the greater part of the alcohol and water the washed ether is rectified by re-distillation.

Such ether serves for most technical purposes, but always retains a small quantity of alcohol. This can be almost entirely removed by washing with water. Treatment with sulphuric acid has been proposed for the purpose, but is not used commercially. By drying the ether over fused calcium chloride and fractionating, "dehydrated" ether is obtained.

The chemical reaction involved is expressed by the well-known equations :—

$$\text{(i) } C_2H_5{\cdot}OH + H_2SO_4 = C_2H_5{\cdot}HSO_4 + H_2O \text{ ; and}$$
$$\text{(ii) } C_2H_5{\cdot}OH + C_2H_5{\cdot}HSO_4 = (C_2H_5)_2O + H_2SO_4.$$

Theoretically, therefore, 92 parts of (absolute) alcohol = 74 of ether.

The etherification vessel, constructed of lead-lined iron or other acid-resisting metal, may be heated by an external jacket of superheated steam, but in the more modern plants internal heating coils, made of lead, are employed. In one form of plant the etherifier is a cylinder of 1·8 m. diameter and 2 m. in height ; it takes a charge of 3,200 kilos. of sulphuric acid (66° Bé.) and 1,500 kilos. of 95 per cent. alcohol. Sometimes the acid and alcohol are mixed in a separate vessel, and the mixture, warmed by a steam coil, is passed into the etherifier by means of compressed air. In some installations the continuous supply of alcohol afterwards necessary is fed into the acid mixture in the etherifier through a series of vertical lead tubes, arranged in concentric circles.

The ether is freed from acid by passing the vapours through a lead-lined column, where they are washed by a solution of sodium carbonate ; or alternatively, the condensed ether may be passed into a vessel containing milk of lime to effect the removal. To separate the bulk of the alcohol and water present, the ether is then distilled in a copper rectifying-still. If desired, the vapours before condensation may be further dehydrated by passing them through a drying-column containing calcium chloride.

Unaltered alcohol remaining in the etherification vessel is recovered periodically, together with alcohol and ether remaining in the fraction retained by the rectifying apparatus.

Other apparatus for the continuous production of ether works much on the principle of the Coffey still (p. 87), though the mechanical details are, of course, different. One of the most recent is Barbet's.[1] This includes a tower divided into, say, twelve sections, each of which contains " plates " for dispersing the liquid, and is heated by a coil to a suitable temperature. Alcohol is introduced into the fourth section from the bottom, whilst sulphuric acid is fed into the top section. The alcohol meets the descending stream of hot sulphuric acid, and is partially converted into ether. Thus a mixture of ether and alcohol vapour is produced, which rises through the tower, and meets further hot acid in each successive section ; the conversion of the alcohol into ether thus becomes more and more complete. The resulting

[1] F.P. 479435, 1914 ; *v.* also B.P. 100406, 1916.

ether passes to a condenser and is collected. The three lowest sections of the tower serve to remove alcohol and ether from the diluted sulphuric acid which reaches the bottom.

This apparatus can also be used for the manufacture of ethyl acetate or other ethyl esters.

Other processes have been proposed for the manufacture of ether. The following may be mentioned, though they do not appear to have come permanently into use on a large scale.

(*a*).—Esterification by means of benzenesulphonic acid.[1] Here the ethyl ester of the acid is first formed, and reacts with more alcohol to form ether :—

(i). $C_6H_5 \cdot SO_3H + C_2H_5 \cdot OH = C_6H_5 \cdot SO_3 \cdot C_2H_5 + H_2O$; and

(ii). $C_6H_5 \cdot SO_3 \cdot C_2H_5 + C_2H_5 \cdot OH = (C_2H_5)_2O + C_6H_5 \cdot SO_3H$.

The benzenesulphonic acid is thus regenerated in the second stage. It then reacts again to form more ester ; and so on. There are said to be no side-reactions in this process.

(*b*).—Ethylene, obtained from oil gas or other convenient economical source, is treated with sulphuric acid, forming sulphovinic acid as in Hennell's synthesis of alcohol. On adding a suitable proportion of water and heating, the alcohol formed reacts with some of the remaining sulphovinic acid, and ether is produced.[2]

Ordinarily the dehydrated, " pure " ether obtained by the foregoing processes still contains traces of alcohol and water, which can be removed by distillation over metallic sodium. On a small scale this is effected by adding shavings of the metal to the ether as long as bubbles of gas are given off from the immersed sodium. When the action has ceased, the ether is distilled off, and collected in a receiver fitted with a drying tube to prevent absorption of moisture from the air during the operation.

Pure ether has the specific gravity 0·720, and boils at 35°. There are, however, several qualities of ether recognised in trade, and containing various proportions of water, alcohol, and other substances ; these admixtures modify the specific gravity and the boiling point very considerably.

In this country the bulk of the ether produced is made from industrial methylated spirit, but a certain amount is prepared with duty-paid rectified alcohol. The former product contains some methyl ether and methyl ethyl ether, due to the presence of methyl alcohol in the industrial methylated spirit. Such ether is distinguished as " Ether, Meth." Naturally the proportion of methyl compounds present will depend upon the particular fraction of the

[1] Kraft and Roos, D.R.-P., 69115.

[2] P. Fritsche, *Die Chem. Industrie*, 1912, **35**, 637.

distillate represented by the ether : some kinds of "Ether, Meth." contain but little of the methyl ethers, other kinds include a considerable quantity.

The chief varieties of ether met with in this country are the following :—

(1). **Ether pure,** sp. gr. 0·720.—This is dehydrated, nearly pure ether produced from rectified spirit.

(2). **Ether pure,** sp. gr. 0·735.—Like the above, this is made from rectified spirit, but contains approximately 10 per cent. of alcohol and water, and is less purified.

(3). **Ether, B.P.**—This has sp. gr. 0·720, and boiling range from 34° to 36°. It approximates to No. 1, but is not necessarily made from pure alcohol, and is not quite so highly purified.

(4). **Purified ether, B.P.**—This has the same sp. gr. and boiling range as No. 3, but must conform to further tests designed to exclude aldehydes, peroxides, and methyl compounds.

(5). **Ether Meth.,** sp. gr. 0·717.—Dehydrated, and practically free from water. Its low specific gravity is due to the presence of methyl ethers, which also give it a very low boiling point—about 20°. It is mainly used as a local anæsthetic.

(6). **Ether Meth.,** sp. gr. 0·720.—This contains alcohol, water, and methyl compounds in varying proportions. It is used for ordinary laboratory purposes where a dehydrated ether is not required.

(7). **Ether Meth. purif.,** sp. gr. 0·720.—This is dehydrated ether, nearly free from water and alcohol. Boiling range about 33° to 36°. Used as a laboratory solvent, and for technical purposes where a nearly pure ether is necessary.

(8). **Ether Meth.,** sp. gr. 0·730.—Contains much water and alcohol. Used as a solvent in ordinary technical operations.

(9). **Ether Meth.,** sp. gr. 0·735.—Used principally in ice-making apparatus. Rather cruder quality than No. 8.

Manufacture of ethyl chloride.—A mixture of alcohol (93 per cent.) and concentrated hydrochloric acid, in the proportion of 40 kilos. of the former to 100 kilos. of the latter, is carefully heated in a lead-lined autoclave. When the main reaction is over, the temperature is raised to 130° for about five hours, after which the vessel is allowed to cool down to 50–60° and the liquid distilled into a cooled metal receiver. The product, which contains a little hydrochloric acid, alcohol, etc., may be rectified from slightly alkaline water to remove these impurities. Alternatively, before the ethyl chloride vapour is condensed, it may be passed first through a washing vessel containing water to remove acid and alcohol, and then through a column packed with fragments of earthenware, in which higher-boiling by-products are condensed. Finally it is led through a refrigerator to a fractionating vessel. From this it is distilled by means of a water-bath, the vapour being passed through strong sulphuric acid contained in a leaden vessel, and again condensed. The finished product is filled into sealed tubes or flasks for transport and use.

In another method the use of an autoclave is dispensed with, but calcium chloride or zinc chloride is used as a catalyst. If calcium chloride (or other catalyst) is not employed, a larger proportion of hydrochloric acid must be used.

Besides being used as an anæsthetic, ethyl chloride is frequently employed as an alkylating agent, especially for amines and phenols, in the synthesis of dyestuffs and other chemical products. It is gaseous at the ordinary temperature, the boiling-point being 12·5°. Its sp. gr. at 0° is 0·921.

Methyl chloride may be prepared in a manner similar to that described for ethyl chloride, using methyl alcohol, sodium chloride, and sulphuric acid. Or Groves's process can be used. Melted zinc chloride, 1 part, is dissolved in 2 parts of methyl alcohol. Then gaseous hydrochloric acid is passed into the mixture, and the resulting methyl chloride distilled off and purified.[1]

On the large scale, however, it is obtained by the dry distillation of *vinasses*, a residue left in the manufacture of sugar from beetroot. Methylamine is evolved; this is converted into the hydrochloride, and heated to a temperature of 260–300°. Methyl chloride, mixed with methylamine and trimethylamine, is given off; the two latter can be removed by means of hydrochloric acid, and the residual methyl chloride, after being dried over calcium chloride, is condensed by pressure into steel cylinders.

A general method of obtaining the halide compounds of methyl and ethyl alcohols is described in a German patent.[2]

The alcohol is heated with an aqueous solution of the halogen acid and the corresponding calcium halide in an open vessel at a temperature not above 100°. Thus a good yield of ethyl chloride is said to be obtained by warming ethyl alcohol and aqueous hydrochloric acid (19° Bé. = sp. gr. 1·152) in the presence of anhydrous calcium chloride. Alternatively, a mixture of acid and methyl or ethyl alcohol is allowed to flow continuously into a vessel containing heated calcium chloride.

Manufacture of ethyl bromide.—For anæsthetic purposes, ethyl bromide may be prepared by distilling a mixture

[1] *Trans. Chem. Soc.*, **25**, 1874, 641. [2] D.R.-P. 280740, 1913

of sulphuric acid (1 part), strong alcohol (1 part, by weight) and sodium bromide (2 parts). The acid is first carefully run into the alcohol, the mixture being kept cooled. According to F. E. Weston,[1] the alcohol should be mixed with 5 to 10 per cent. of its weight of water. This is conveniently added in the form of ice after the mixture of acid and alcohol has cooled down. To the cold mixture the sodium bromide, coarsely powdered, is added, and the whole very gently distilled, first on a water-bath and finally on a sand-bath, the temperature being only allowed to rise as the distillation slackens. Ethyl bromide distils over. It is purified by washing with dilute sodium carbonate solution, and dried with fused calcium chloride, followed by re-distillation if necessary. To remove any ether which it may contain, the bromide can be shaken up repeatedly with a small quantity of strong sulphuric acid.[2]

A less pure product is obtained by the action of bromine and red phosphorus upon alcohol. One part of the phosphorus is mixed with 6 parts of strong alcohol and 6 parts of bromine are allowed to run slowly into the mixture, which is kept cooled and shaken during the addition. After standing for a few hours the mixture is distilled from a water-bath, the temperature of which is raised slowly. The distillate is shaken with dilute soda solution to remove alcohol and free bromine, and the ethyl bromide drawn off, further purified by washing with water, dried over calcium chloride, and re-distilled.

The chemical reaction involved may be expressed thus :—

$$\underset{\text{Alcohol.}}{5C_2H_5{\cdot}OH} + 5Br + P = \underset{\text{Ethyl bromide.}}{5C_2H_5Br} + H_3PO_4 + H_2O.$$

For medical purposes ethyl bromide prepared by the first method is preferred, as it is more free from impurities than that made by the phosphorus process.

Ethyl bromide is a colourless liquid, of boiling point 38·8°. It is used as an inhalation anæsthetic in minor medical operations, either alone or mixed with ethyl chloride or methyl chloride. It is also employed as an alkylating agent, though less frequently than ethyl chloride.

Manufacture of ethyl iodide.—This is usually prepared by the action of iodine on alcohol in the presence of red phosphorus, much as described under "ethyl bromide." Various proportions of ingredients have been recommended. Thus Wurtz indicates phosphorus 7 parts, alcohol 35, and iodine 23 ; whilst Frankland used these in the ratio of 7 : 35 : 14. According to Beilstein,

[1] *Trans. Chem. Soc.*, 1915, **107**, 1489. [2] D.R.-P. 52982.

1 part of red phosphorus is placed in a retort with 5 parts of 90 per cent. alcohol, and then 10 parts of iodine are added gradually, and the mixture allowed to stand for twenty-four hours. At the end of that period the retort is warmed, and the ethyl iodide distilled off. The crude product is purified by washing first with dilute solution of sodium hydroxide, and then with water, after which treatment it is dried over fused calcium chloride, and redistilled if necessary.

Walker[1] recommends the use of both red and yellow phosphorus, in equal quantities, and obtains about 570 grams of the iodide for 500 grams of iodine used, or 93 per cent. of the theoretical yield. As the dissolving of the iodine in the alcohol is tedious, he has devised an arrangement to shorten the time and labour. This consists essentially in an adaptation of the principle of the Soxhlet extractor to the purpose. A wide-mouthed, round-bottomed flask, of about 1 litre capacity, carries a two-holed cork into which are fitted an adapter, serving as receptacle for the iodine, and a wide side-tube, up which the alcohol vapour passes. These are connected at the top with a tube which passes to a reflux condenser. The arrangement is such that when alcohol placed in the flask is boiled, its vapour passes up the side tube, is condensed in the reflux condenser, falls back on the iodine contained in the adapter, dissolves more or less of this iodine, and carries it down into the flask, where the solution of iodine in alcohol reacts with the phosphorus present.

To obtain about 550 grams of ethyl iodide the ingredients used are 500 grams of iodine, 250 of alcohol, 30 of yellow phosphorus, and 30 of red phosphorus. The alcohol and the two kinds of phosphorus are placed in the flask, with a few fragments of porous tile to prevent bumping, and 100 grams of the iodine are packed tightly in the adapter. The flask is then connected up, and heated on a water-bath to boil the alcohol. Distillation should not be allowed to proceed too rapidly, as much heat is disengaged during the reaction. When all the iodine has been dissolved, the heating is continued until there is no longer any coloration in the liquid due to iodine. The flask is then cooled, and a fresh charge of iodine placed in the adapter, after which the heating is re-commenced, and the operations repeated until the whole 500 grams of iodine have been worked up.

When the reaction is completed, a small quantity of water is poured down the condenser to destroy any phosphonium compounds which may have been formed. The flask is then detached, and the

[1] *Trans. Chem. Soc.*, 1892, **61**, 717.

liquid distilled off by means of a water-bath. The distillate, after being washed with water, separated from the aqueous layer, and dried, is practically pure ethyl iodide.

The chief precaution to be taken is the proper regulation of the temperature when the final charge of iodine is being dealt with. Too much heat should be avoided, and the last stages conducted slowly until experience has been gained.

Methyl iodide can be prepared in a similar manner.

In Crismer's method of preparation, the iodine is dissolved in liquid paraffin. Yellow phosphorus is then added, and afterwards alcohol.[1]

Ethyl iodide has the sp. gr. 1·944 at 14°, and boils at 72·3°.

Manufacture of chloral.—Chloral is trichloroacetaldehyde, $CCl_3 \cdot CHO$, and is prepared by saturating ethyl alcohol with dry chlorine. The alcohol should be as nearly anhydrous as can conveniently be obtained—preferably commercial "absolute" alcohol. The final product of the chlorination is a crystalline mixture consisting mainly of chloral alcoholate and chloral, with some of the intermediate compounds and by-products. From this mixture chloral is obtained by distillation with strong sulphuric acid.

The reaction involved in the chlorination is a complex one. It may be explained by assuming that the alcohol is first converted into aldehyde, $CH_3 \cdot CHO$, which is then transformed into acetal, $CH_3 \cdot CH(O \cdot C_2H_5)_2$, and subsequently into the corresponding trichloroacetal, $CCl_3 \cdot CH(O \cdot C_2H_5)_2$. This, by the action of the hydrochloric acid evolved, is then converted into the chloral alcoholate, $CCl_3 \cdot CH(OH)(O \cdot C_2H_5)$.

According to another view, dichloro- and trichloro-ethyl ether are intermediate stages in the reaction, the latter compound then passing into chloral alcoholate :—

$$\underset{\text{Trichloroethyl ether.}}{CHCl_2 \cdot CHCl \cdot O\,C_2H_5} \longrightarrow CHCl_2 \cdot CH \Big\langle {OH \atop O \cdot C_2H_5} \longrightarrow \underset{\text{Chloral alcoholate.}}{CCl_3 \cdot CH \Big\langle {OH \atop O \cdot C_2H_5}}$$

Formerly the chlorination was a tedious operation. Chlorine was passed into a relatively small quantity (25 kilos.) of absolute alcohol contained in a glass balloon, first kept cold, and then gently warmed, the process extending over weeks.[2]

According to A. Trillat[3] the alcohol is placed in a large glass balloon or carboy, connected with one or more vessels containing

[1] *Ber.*, 1884, **17**, 649.

[2] Roscoe and Schorlemmer, "Treatise on Chemistry," **3**, (i), 539.

[3] *Bull. Soc. chim.*, 1897, **17**, 230.

water to absorb the gaseous hydrochloric acid evolved. The chlorine, prepared by one of the usual industrial processes and carefully dried, is introduced very gradually, to avoid possible ignition of the alcohol. Apart from this risk, unless the initial temperature is carefully controlled, the yield of chloral is diminished through the occurrence of secondary reactions. In the early stages, therefore, the vessel is cooled; but later, when the action moderates, the carboy is gently heated, at first to 60° and finally to 100°. On the completion of the reaction the liquid becomes wholly soluble in water, and acquires a specific gravity of about 1·4. In some factories the chlorination period extends over 10 to 14 days. Certain substances which act as chlorine-carriers regularise the reaction quite notably: thus iodine in the proportion of 1 per cent. of the alcohol has been recommended for this purpose (Springmühl).

The crude product is transferred to an enamelled distilling vessel (or to a lead-lined copper still) fitted with a reflux arrangement and provided with a good thermometer for fractionating purposes. An equal weight of strong sulphuric acid is added, little by little; and the mixture is then heated to the boiling-point in order to expel hydrochloric acid and other impurities, such as ethyl chloride. After the evolution of the gas has ceased, the residue is distilled until the temperature of the vapours rises above 100°. The chloral passes over at about 97°.

To remove the last traces of acid, the distillate is rectified (preferably over calcium carbonate); the fraction passing over at 94° and upwards constitutes the chloral. This is then converted into chloral hydrate by mixing it gradually with the theoretical proportion of water, namely, 12·2 per cent. of its weight. The mixture becomes warm through the reaction. It is well stirred up, and the resulting hydrate either spread out on a smooth surface and allowed to solidify, or else further purified by crystallisation from chloroform, benzine, or other solvent (see below). For example, the still warm hydrate may be mixed with one-third of its volume of chloroform, and allowed to cool in closed receptacles. After about a week the crystallisation is complete. The crystals are drained off and dried at the ordinary temperature, whilst the mother-liquor serves for crystallising further quantities.

As already indicated, the chlorination on a small scale by the older methods is a lengthy process. In recent years, however, the operations have been much shortened and cheapened by working on a larger scale and with improved methods.[1]

The chlorination vessels are of 2,000 to 5,000 litres capacity

[1] Ullmann, "Enzyklop. der Techn. Chem." **3**, 404.

(440 to 1,100 gallons), made of lead-lined iron, and fitted with coils by means of which they may be heated or cooled. They are filled two-thirds full with alcohol. The chlorine employed is purified liquid chlorine supplied in steel cylinders, or, in some cases, chlorine produced in electrolytic alkali works is used direct. It is led into the bottom of the vessel, and distributed in fine jets by means of a spreading arrangement. The supply is delivered under a gentle pressure, and any chlorine not absorbed can pass into a second chlorination vessel. In fact it is usual to instal a series of vessels, with a reflux condensing arrangement between each two, so that no chlorine is lost, and the hydrochloric acid vapours, being freed from uncombined chlorine, can be condensed and recovered as pure acid. The supply of chlorine is so regulated that the chlorination in the first vessel is finished in from two to three days.

In the early stages the temperature is kept low by means of the water coils. It is then allowed to rise, first to 50° on the second day, and finally, on the third day, to 95°. The product acquires a specific gravity of about 1·51 by the time the operation is complete, and yields at least 75 per cent. of crude chloral when a sample is tested by distillation with sulphuric acid.

The separation and purification of the chloral are carried out essentially as already described.

Chloral is an oily liquid, of characteristic penetrating odour, boiling at 97°, and of sp. gr. 1·512 at 20°. A certain quantity is used for the preparation of hypnotics, but mostly it is employed in making chloral hydrate.

Chloral hydrate.—When treated with water, chloral evolves heat and unites with the water to form a crystalline hydrate, $CCl_3 \cdot CH(OH)_2$.

The quantity of water necessary for this change is added slowly, to avoid too much development of heat. One hundred parts of chloral require 12·2 parts of water, and yield 112·2 parts of the hydrate. To obtain the purest product, the solid thus obtained is recrystallised from benzene, chloroform, carbon disulphide, or petroleum ether as already described. A mixture of ethylene chloride and ethidene chloride, obtained as a by-product in the manufacture, has also been used for recrystallising the product. In order to get the hydrate in the form of cubes or plates rather more than the calculated theoretical quantity of water is added to the chloral, slowly and with energetic shaking, which is continued until the milky, syrupy mass has quite cooled down and set; this treatment obviates the formation of lumpy masses. The product is spread on porcelain plates, cut into cubes, and dried in a drying-chamber over sulphuric acid.

Manufacture of chloroform.—Chloroform is mainly obtained commercially by the action of bleaching powder on alcohol or on acetone. Its technical preparation is described in *Chemiker-Zeitung* (1886, 10, 338), as follows.

The bleaching powder acts partly as an oxidising agent and partly as a chlorinating agent, first converting the alcohol, through various intermediate stages, into chloral, $CCl_3 \cdot CHO$. This is then decomposed by the calcium hydroxide of the bleaching powder into chloroform and calcium formate :—

$$\underset{\text{Chloral.}}{2Cl_3CHO} + Ca(OH)_2 = \underset{\text{Chloroform.}}{2CHCl_3} + \underset{\text{Calcium formate.}}{Ca(O \cdot CHO)_2}.$$

On the large scale, experience has shown that good results are obtained by taking 4 parts of bleaching powder, 3 parts of alcohol (96 per cent.), and 13 parts of water, so that there are 16 parts of liquid to 4 parts of solid. The bleaching powder is preferably of strength 32·5 to 34·5 per cent. available chlorine : a lower strength is liable to diminish the yield through paucity of hypochlorite, whilst a higher develops too much heat.

In one form of plant, designed to give a daily output of 125 kilos. of chloroform, there are four generators, in which the reaction takes place. These are cylindrical iron vessels of diameter 2 metres and height 1·4 metres, fitted with stirrers, inlet tubes for steam and water, manhole for charging, and outlet to a condenser. A water tube outside the generator allows of the latter being cooled when necessary by flushing its surface with a little water. The charge for each generator is 300 kilos. of alcohol, 400 kilos. of bleaching powder, and 1,300 litres of water.

The alcohol is first placed in the generator, and then the charge of water (or the alcoholic wash-water and distillate from a previous operation). The stirrer is then set working, the bleaching powder added, the manhole closed, and the vessel heated by steam until the temperature of the liquid reaches 40°. The steam is then shut off, whilst the stirrer is allowed to work on until the temperature, which continues to rise, attains 45°. After stopping the stirrer the mixture slowly heats up further through chemical action to 60° ; if the temperature rises above this the vessel is cooled.

The course of the reaction can be observed by means of a glass tube which is let into the connection between the generator and the condenser. A fine rain of chloroform, alcohol, and water is seen in the tube ; this lasts a few minutes, and then the chloroform begins to pass over in quantity. When about 30 kilos. have distilled, the stirrer is again set in motion until chloroform ceases to separate in the receiver, which is then changed.

The further distillate, consisting of alcohol saturated with chloroform, is collected separately. When a sample shaken with water gives no turbidity the whole of the chloroform is over, and the distillate is now collected apart until the runnings show a specific gravity of about 0·995. This last distillate consists of 500 to 600 litres of very dilute alcohol: it is used again in making up a fresh charge.

The chloroform thus obtained is purified from alcohol and ether by washing and rectification. The washing apparatus consists of a narrow vertical cylinder fitted with a screw agitator which gives a motion of the liquid from below upwards. Taps are placed in the side, to allow of the alcoholic washings being run off. After the chloroform has been well washed in this vessel, it is removed and rectified by distillation in a copper still. On an average, 98·8 kilos. of alcohol (96 per cent.) and 1,321 kilos. of bleaching powder are required to furnish 100 kilos. of chloroform.

Besson's process gives a good yield of a pure chloroform, and is a useful means of utilising waste chlorine in bleaching powder factories and electrolytic alkali works.

Chlorine is passed into strong alcohol until the density of the liquid reaches 35° Bé. (sp. gr. 1·32). Two layers are formed, the heavier of which increases gradually until the chlorination is sufficient, when the liquid becomes homogeneous. A mixture of bleaching powder, milk of lime, and water, in the respective proportions of 5 : 1 : 20 parts for 1 part of alcohol (by weight) is then added, and the whole distilled. According to K. Ukita,[1] the yield thus obtained is from 95 to 98 grams per 100 grams of alcohol.

On a large scale the process is made a continuous one, which is a great advantage. The alcohol is chlorinated in a vessel arranged somewhat on the principle of a small Coffey's still, and containing a number of perforated shallow trays placed one above the other. Entering at the top, the alcohol flows over these trays and meets a stream of dry chlorine, so that by the time it reaches the bottom the chlorination is effected. It then passes through a cooling worm into a vessel containing the bleaching powder, with which it is mixed. The mixture is next driven into a larger vessel heated by steam coils, where it is treated with the milk of lime at the proper temperature. The resulting chloroform vapours pass out and are rectified. By means of a screw worm, the mixture travels

[1] *J. Chem. Ind., Tokyo*, 1918, **21**, 219.

gradually from the entrance at one end of the larger vessel to the exit at the other end, and the feeding of the supplies is regulated so that the process can go on continuously. The yield of chloroform is said to be 95 to 105 parts per 100 parts of alcohol.[1]

F. W. Frerichs[2] gives a detailed description of experiments made with a view to improve the yield of chloroform obtained by the ordinary alcohol process. The method recommended is as follows :—

One hundred and twenty gallons of 94 per cent. alcohol are charged into a vertical still (6 ft. diameter, height 8 ft.) together with sufficient water to dilute the alcohol to 20 per cent. strength. In a vessel placed above the still, and provided with an agitator, a quantity of bleaching powder equivalent to 1,500 lb. at 35 per cent. strength is mixed with water, the amount of water used being sufficient to bring the diluted alcohol in the still down to 10 per cent. strength. After heating the alcohol to boiling by means of steam, the bleaching powder solution is introduced, in small quantities at a time, through a pipe reaching nearly to the bottom of the still. The whole charge fills the still to less than three-fourths of its total capacity.

The reaction sets in at once. The chloroform is distilled off and collected, the layer of aqueous alcohol obtained in the receiver being run off into a large vessel for use in the next charge. The average yield obtained over an extensive period corresponded with 100 lb. of chloroform from 11·22 gallons of 94 per cent. alcohol and 977 lb. of 35 per cent. bleaching powder, the consumption of steam being 2 tons at a pressure of 80 lb.

Chloroform is very largely made from acetone and bleaching powder, the process being very similar to the alcohol method.[3] Whether acetone or alcohol is used depends upon the relative costs of the two in comparison with the yields obtained. Acetone gives the better yield, and a few years ago had largely supplanted alcohol as a raw material for chloroform ; but the position afterwards became reversed, on account of scarcity of acetone.

In this country a certain amount of chloroform is made from duty-paid "rectified" spirit ; most, however, is produced from industrial methylated spirit, or from acetone, as the case may be. In particular circumstances, specially denatured duty-free spirit has been employed, the denaturants being, for example, bleaching powder and methyl alcohol. If sufficiently purified, the products obtained are almost indistinguishable one from another. Chloro-

[1] D.R.-P., 129237. [2] *J. Ind. Eng. Chem.*, 1912, **4**, 345, 406.
[3] Sadtler, *Pharm. J.*, 1889, [iii], **20**, 84.

form prepared from alcohol, however, is liable to contain a minute quantity of ethyl chloride,[1] and that from methylated spirit traces of methyl compounds.

When intended for use as an anæsthetic, the chloroform is further purified by washing with water, then with dilute sulphuric acid, and afterwards with dilute sodium hydroxide solution or lime-water, and once again with water only. Finally it is dried with fused calcium chloride and re-distilled.

Pure chloroform boils at 61°, and has a specific gravity of 1·50 at 15·5°. It is prone, however, to decompose slightly under the action of air and light, and a small quantity of alcohol is usually added as a preservative. This affects both the specific gravity and the boiling point. The British Pharmacopœia requires 2 per cent. of absolute alcohol to be added, and gives the specific gravity of the official chloroform as 1·483 to 1·487, with a boiling point not below 60°. From $\frac{1}{2}$ to 1 per cent. is often added to non-official chloroform, bringing the sp. gr. to about 1·495–1·490.

Bromoform.—This is the bromine analogue of chloroform, and has the formula $CHBr_3$. It finds some restricted application as an anæsthetic, and for other medicinal purposes. Like chloroform, it may be made from either alcohol or acetone. According to Denigès,[2] a yield of 75 per cent. may be obtained by acting upon a mixture of acetone (20) and soda lye (10) with bromine (2). After the reaction is over, more acetone is added (1 volume) to destroy the hypobromite produced. The heavy bromoform which separates (sp. gr. 2·904 at 15°) is run off and purified by washing and distillation. It boils at 151°.

From alcohol in an analogous manner bromoform may be prepared by the simultaneous action of bromine and potassium hydroxide; and also by electrolysing a solution of potassium bromide in alcohol.[3] An aqueous solution of acetone may be substituted for the alcohol in the electrolytic process: a quantitative yield is obtained.[4]

Manufacture of iodoform.—At the present day much of the iodoform produced is made by an electrolytic method, as described further on. Formerly, however, it was exclusively prepared by warming a mixture of alcohol, iodine, and sodium carbonate or hydroxide. Later, acetone often replaced the alcohol as raw material.

The earlier process, or one form of it, consisted in heating gently a mixture composed of alcohol (95 per cent.) 1 part, iodine 2 parts,

[1] Wade and Finnemore, *Trans. Chem. Soc.*, 1904, **85**, 946.
[2] *J. Pharm. Chim.*, 1891, **24**, 243.
[3] Schering, D.R.-P. 29771.
[4] *Zeitsch. Elektrochem.*, 1904, **10**, 409.

potassium carbonate 2 parts, and water 5 parts, until the liquid became colourless. The bright yellow, scaly precipitate of iodoform thus obtained was rinsed upon a filter, washed with water, and dried in the air.

The yield thus obtained, however, is only about 17 per cent. of that corresponding theoretically with the iodine used. Some five-sixths of the iodine remains unconverted into iodoform—mainly in the filtrate, though a little is lost in the form of ethyl iodide vapour.

In order to utilise as much of the iodine as possible, various methods have been devised. The filtrate contains the iodine in the form of potassium iodide and iodate. Addition of a mineral acid liberates the iodine in accordance with a well-known reaction; and, further, any excess of potassium iodide still remaining will yield its iodine on treatment with potassium bichromate and an acid, or with chlorine. On these principles R. Rother[1] based the following method.

Thirty-two parts of iodine, 32 of potassium carbonate, 16 of alcohol (95 per cent.) and 80 of water are mixed in a comparatively large flask, and warmed in a water-bath until the solution is decolorised. The clear liquid is now decanted and the precipitate rinsed, with the addition of a little water, upon a capacious filter. The decanted liquid is now treated with hydrochloric acid, added gradually at first, an excess of 16 to 24 parts being employed, together with 2 to 3 parts of potassium bichromate, to liberate the iodine. After a few moments, potassium carbonate is carefully added till the solution is neutralised, and then a further quantity, 32 parts, of the carbonate, together with 6 parts of iodine and 16 of alcohol: this mixture is again digested in the water-bath, and when effervescence has ceased in the green solution, the supernatant liquid is poured off from the precipitate, and further treated as before. The separated iodoform is rinsed into the filter with the first product, and when the operations are finally discontinued the collected crystals are well washed with water and spread out in the open air to dry.

Thus the process may be continued indefinitely, or until the accumulation of salts becomes inconveniently large.

In another method, suggested by Filhol,[2] chlorine is used to recover the combined iodine. A solution of 2 parts of soda-crystals in 10 parts of water is mixed with 1 part of alcohol, the mixture heated to 60–80°, and 1 part of iodine added gradually. The heating is continued until the solution becomes decolorised. After

[1] *Pharm. J.*, 1874, [iii], **4**, 593. [2] *J. Pharm. Chim.*, 1845, [iii], **7**, 267.

the precipitated iodoform has been filtered off, the filtrate is mixed with another charge of sodium carbonate and alcohol, heated up again to the temperature stated, and a stream of chlorine led in. This liberates more iodine, which again reacts with the alcohol to give a further precipitate of iodoform. The process is repeated until the product obtained represents approximately one-half of the original amount of iodine.

Ozone is employed in Otto's process for obtaining iodoform.[1] A mixture of 100 kilos. of water, 300 of alcohol, 10 of sodium carbonate, and 55 of potassium iodide is warmed to 50°, and ozone passed in until the whole of the iodide is decomposed.

In the electrolytic process iodoform is produced by electrolysing a solution of an iodide in the presence of alcohol. Acetone or aldehyde can also be employed. According to Elbs and Herz,[2] a solution of 13 to 15 parts of sodium carbonate, 10 of potassium iodide, 20 of alcohol, and 100 of water is suitable ; this is heated to 70° and electrolysed, using a platinum anode and a nickel cathode, and a current-density (anodic) of 1 ampere per square decimetre. The current is passed for two or three hours, and after several hours the resulting iodoform crystallises out. It is removed periodically, and the solution made up again to its original composition by the addition of sodium carbonate, potassium iodide, and alcohol. A porous cell is used as diaphragm round the anode. According to Förster and Mewes,[3] the reduction of the iodoform by the hydrogen generated in the electrolysis is insignificant. Parchment paper round the kathode can replace the usual earthenware cell with advantage : this decreases the resistance, and less electrical energy is consumed. It also helps to prevent the formation of iodate, by keeping the liberated caustic alkali from contact with the iodine set free at the anode. A stream of carbon dioxide should be passed through the solution to neutralise the caustic alkali formed, as the latter tends to prevent the formation of iodoform. A solution indicated as suitable in these circumstances is composed of 2 parts of calcined sodium carbonate, 2 of potassium iodide, 5 of alcohol, and 20 of water, the electrolysis being carried out at 50–70°. The current density at the platinum anode may be from 1 to 3 amperes per sq. dcm., and at the platinum kathode 4 to 8 amperes.

The most probable equation representing the formation of iodoform electrolytically is considered to be :—

$$C_2H_5{\cdot}OH + I_{10} + H_2O = CHI_3 + CO_2 + 7HI.$$

[1] D.R.-P. 109013, 1898.
[2] *Zeitsch. Elektrochem.*, 1897, **4**, 113.
[3] *Ibid.*, 268 ; *J. pr. Chem.*, 1897, **56**, 353.

The iodine arises from the action of nascent oxygen, liberated at the anode, upon the potassium iodide present.

Advantages claimed for the electrolytic process are that it utilises the iodine better than does the chemical process, and gives a purer product.

Iodoform is a yellow solid melting at 119°, and possessing a peculiar, characteristic odour. It is largely used in surgery as an antiseptic. In this country it is chiefly made from industrial methylated spirit.

Manufacture of ethyl acetate (Acetic ether).—A general method for obtaining the ethyl esters such as formate, acetate, butyrate, etc., is to distil a mixture of alcohol, a salt of the acid in question, and sulphuric acid. Instead of the salt, the acid itself is often used. Ethyl acetate, in fact, is usually on the large scale made from alcohol, acetic acid, and sulphuric acid; sodium acetate is less frequently employed. The sulphuric acid may be omitted if a suitable catalyst is used. When both acids are employed, a satisfactory mixture is alcohol (95 per cent.) 6 vols., acetic acid 4 vols., sulphuric acid 5 vols.[1]

The mixture of alcohol and the two acids is distilled from a vessel fitted with a fractionating column, in which a certain amount of rectification takes place. The issuing vapours, consisting of the ester, free acetic acid, alcohol, and water, pass through a vessel containing a suitable basic substance to retain the free acid, or most of it, and then into a condenser. The distillate is collected in receivers fitted with stirrers, in which it is washed with water and dilute alkaline solutions to remove alcohol and any acid that may have escaped elimination in the first vessel. It is then dried over calcium chloride and rectified by redistillation.

On a small scale the following procedure, described by Dr. Inglis Clark,[2] may be adopted.

Place 283 c.c. of rectified spirit (sp. gr. 0·838) in a copper or glass flask, and into it pour the same volume of sulphuric acid, with stirring, and keeping the flask cool. Allow the mixture to stand, and when its temperature has fallen to about 15·5°, gradually add 351 grams of dried sodium acetate, with constant agitation to ensure thorough mixture, keeping the flask as cool as possible, and connecting it with an inverted condenser to avoid loss. When all has been added, reverse the condenser, and distil the contents

[1] See, however, Senderens and Aboulenc's process, under Ethyl Formate, p. 348.

[2] *Pharm. J.*, 1883, [iii], **13**, 777. See also Wade, *Trans. Chem. Soc.*, 1905, **87**, 1656.

of the flask by means of a naked flame or a sand-bath till 400 c.c. have passed over. Digest the distillate for three days with 57 grams of freshly-dried potassium carbonate. Filter, and distil the filtrate with the aid of a water-bath, stopping the distillation before the last 30 c.c. have passed over.

Clark remarks that the excess of sulphuric acid employed secures the absence of alcohol from the distillate, whilst the action of this excess on the ethyl acetate formed is minimised by securing thorough mixture before applying heat. Alcohol being absent from the distillate, it is only necessary to neutralise and free the ester from water. For this purpose, potassium carbonate is recommended as being most convenient on a small scale, but sodium acetate is equally efficient.

Using the quantities stated above, there were distilled off 405 c.c., which contained 338·7 grams of ethyl acetate. The sp. gr. of the distillate was 0·912; after washing the ester with water and digesting with potassium carbonate, the sp. gr. was found slowly to diminish. After thirty hours, it was 0·9023, when it contained 99·36 of real acetic ether.

Pure ethyl acetate, $CH_3{\cdot}COO\,C_2H_5$, boils at 77·2°, and has the sp. gr. 0·9072 at 15°/15°. Commercial "acetic ether" often contains 25 per cent. or more of impurities, consisting mainly of water, alcohol, acetic acid, and ordinary ether. Acetic ether B.P., used in pharmacy, is required to contain not less than 90 per cent. of ethyl acetate, and to have a sp. gr. 0·900 to 0·907.

In this country pure acetic ether is required to be made from duty-paid alcohol; but a denatured product is allowed to be prepared from specially-denatured industrial alcohol. The denaturants sanctioned vary according to the circumstances—*e.g.*, according to whether the ethyl acetate is to be used, on the premises where it was made, as an intermediate product in the preparation of other compounds, or removed for sale as a solvent, etc.

Ethyl acetoacetate (Acetoacetic ether),

$$CH_3{\cdot}CO{\cdot}CH_2{\cdot}COO{\cdot}C_2H_5.$$

—This product is used in making certain synthetic chemicals, of which the most important commercially is **antipyrine,** or methylphenylpyrazolone. The ethyl acetoacetate is prepared from acetic ether by the action of metallic sodium, followed by treatment with acetic acid. On a small scale, the procedure is as follows:—

One kilogram of acetic ether, carefully dehydrated with calcium chloride, is placed in a large flask (2 to 3 litres capacity) fitted with a reflux condenser. To it are added 100 grams of sodium cut into thin pieces, the flask being cooled meanwhile. An energetic reaction commences, causing the liquid to boil. After the reaction has moderated and no more heat is evolved, the mixture is heated on a water-bath, using the reflux condenser, for about two to two and a half hours, until the sodium is all dissolved. The condenser is now reversed, the excess of acetic ether distilled off, and to the warm residual liquid 550 grams of 50 per cent. acetic acid are added, the whole being well mixed. After cooling, 500 c.c. of water are poured in, and the mixture again well agitated. On standing, the aceto-acetic ester separates out as an upper layer. It is drawn off, washed with a small quantity of water, separated from this water, and fractionally distilled. Five fractions are collected, corresponding with the temperatures 100–130–165–175–185–200°; these fractions are then refractionated twice. The final product boiling between 175–185° is nearly pure ethyl acetoacetate: the yield of this should be about 175 grams.

The production of ethyl acetoacetate on a larger scale has been described in detail by A. Cobenzl.[1]

By means of a cutting device, immersed in xylene, the sodium is obtained in very thin slices or shavings. A large surface of the clean bright metal can thus be exposed to the action of the acetic ether. Sodium encrusted with oxidation-products should not be used, as the moisture liable to be present may give rise to irregularities in the reaction.

The sodium is melted under xylene and cast into cylindrical blocks for convenience of cutting. A cog-wheel mechanism brings the block against a horizontal cutter, which removes a slice of the metal at each movement.

The acetic ether must be quite free from water and alcohol. It should boil between 78° and 79°; and bright slices of metallic sodium immersed in it should remain unattacked for at least two hours.

For the reaction operation, a hemispherical copper vessel of fully 100 litres capacity is employed. It is heated by an oil-bath, and is provided with copper coils by means of which it can either be warmed with steam or cooled with water, as may be required. To allow rapid introduction of the sodium, the vessel has a wide manhole with a lid which can be easily removed. Great care is necessary in the charging, to avoid accidental access of water.

The reaction-vessel is connected through a copper condenser with a receiver, from which the condensed acetic ether which distils over in the early stages can be passed back to the reaction-vessel as desired. This serves not only to restore the supply of acetic

[1] *Chem. Zeit.*, 1914, **38**, 665.

ether, but also to moderate the action by reducing the temperature of the mixture. Care is taken that the reaction-vessel is perfectly dry before charging, and that no water can enter in the subsequent stages.

Forty kilograms of acetic ether are placed in the cold vessel, followed by 5 kilograms of sodium shavings. By means of wooden spatulas the latter are quickly immersed and distributed. The apparatus is then closed, and the oil-bath slowly heated to 100°, but not above 105°. The temperature of the mixture in the vessel is recorded by a thermometer; it should only rise slowly. If there is a rapid rise, it indicates an irregular reaction, probably due to water or alcohol present in the ingredients, or admitted inadvertently.

When the temperature of the mixture reaches 45–50°, the heating is stopped. The reaction, however, proceeds, with increasing temperature until the boiling point of the acetic ether is attained (78–80°), when this ingredient begins to distil over. The oil-bath temperature is now kept at 55–60°. When sufficient distillate has collected in the receiver, it is run back into the reaction-vessel. The temperature in this vessel should not rise above 82–83°.

After about 30–45 minutes the distillation slackens. When this occurs, external heating is again applied, in such manner as to maintain a very slow distillation of acetic ether during the next 5–6 hours, by the end of which time the reaction is completed.

The contents of the reaction-vessel, consisting of sodium aceto-acetic ester, sodium alcoholate, alcohol, and excess of acetic ether, are now forced out into another vessel, lead-lined, and provided with a stirring-apparatus. This vessel contains 35 litres of water for every 5 kilograms of sodium employed, together with the calculated quantity of acetic acid required for combining with the sodium. After half an hour's mixing, the liquid is passed into a separator, allowed to settle out during several hours, and the lower aqueous layer then run off. The upper layer, consisting of ethyl acetoacetate mixed with alcohol and acetic ether, is distilled until the boiling point rises to 110°, thus separating most of the acetic ether and alcohol. The residue of crude ethyl acetoacetate is then rectified by distillation under reduced pressure in a strong vessel of tinned copper, heated by an oil-bath. At 10–15 mm. pressure the ethyl acetoacetate distils over between 86° and 92°. Between the condenser and the receiver a sampling device is inserted, so that the specific gravity of the distillate passing over can be ascertained; the limits 1·030 and 1·040 indicate the fraction which is collected as the final product.

For use in preparing antipyrine, a very pure acetoacetic ester is required, since the success of the reactions depends largely upon the purity of the ester. The latter should yield not more than 4 per cent. of distillate below 180°, when distilled under 750 mm. pressure, and 95 per cent. should boil between 180° and 181° at the pressure mentioned. Also the ester should contain at most 0·5 per cent. by weight of acetic acid, phenolphthalein indicator being used in the test.[1]

The recovered acetic ether, as also the alcohol produced in the reactions, are purified and concentrated for subsequent use.

The lower, light-yellow layer in the decomposition vessel consists of a solution of sodium acetate, with some alcohol and acetic ether. After distilling off the alcohol and ether, the solution is evaporated and the sodium acetate recovered by crystallisation.

Ethyl acetoacetate is a colourless liquid, with a pleasant, fruity odour. It boils at 181–182°, or at 180·6–181·2 under 754 mm. pressure; or at 71°, under 12·5 mm. Sp. gr. 1·0282 at 20°/4°. With ferric chloride, it gives a violet coloration.

Ethyl formate (Formic ether), $H{\cdot}COO{\cdot}C_2H_5$.—According to Senderens and Aboulenc,[2] a convenient procedure for the industrial production of ethyl formate is to heat together a mixture of alcohol and formic acid in molecular proportions, in the presence of a small quantity of sulphuric acid—from 1 to 2 per cent. of the volume of the mixture. Anhydrous aluminium sulphate or potassium bisulphate can also be used as catalysts, but the best results are given with the sulphuric acid.

Kopp's method is as follows.[3] A cooled mixture of 7 parts by weight of alcohol (88 per cent. strength) and 11 parts of strong sulphuric acid, is poured on to 8 parts of anhydrous sodium formate, and the whole carefully distilled from a water-bath. The yield of ester, however, is less than 80 per cent. of the theoretical quantity, and the product contains some formic acid. To remove this it is shaken with milk of lime, then dried with calcium chloride, and rectified.

By using sodium bisulphate instead of sulphuric acid, a better yield is obtained, and the ester produced is nearly free from acid.[4] The bisulphate (240 parts) is well crushed, and mixed with 46 parts (weight) of alcohol and 68 parts of sodium formate. This mixture is warmed in a closed vessel, with frequent stirring, for about ten hours at a temperature of 80°; or, alternatively, it may be gently

[1] Ullmann, "Enzyklop. der Techn. Chem.", **1**, 99.

[2] *Compt. rend.*, 1911, **152**, 1671.

[3] *Annalen*, 1845, **55**, 180.

[4] Engelskirchen, D.R.-P. 255441.

boiled in a vessel fitted with a reflux condenser. At the end of that time, the ethyl formate is distilled off.

The following process has long been used industrially for making the ethyl formate employed for fabricating "rum essence." Potato starch, 4·5 kilos., is well mixed with 14·5 kilos. of pyrolusite (containing 85 per cent. of MnO_2) and 6·7 kilos. of water. Into this is poured a cooled mixture of 10 kilos. of alcohol (80 per cent.) and 14 kilos. of strong sulphuric acid. Crude acetic acid is sometimes included : see under "imitation rum," p. 437. The vessel is connected with a condenser, and heat applied to start the reaction, but no further heating is required until towards the end of the process. From 7 to 8 kilos. of formic ester are obtained. The reaction proceeds rapidly, so that six or seven charges can be worked off in a day, and about 50 kilos. of crude ethyl formate obtained.[1]

Ethyl formate is a volatile and inflammable liquid, boiling at 54·4°, and of sp. gr. 0·948 at 0°/4°. It has some little application in medicine and in synthetic chemistry, but is chiefly used for the preparation of artificial rum.

Methyl formate, prepared in an analogous manner to that employed for the ethyl ester, is employed industrially as a solvent for acetyl-cellulose. It boils at 32·3°.

Ethyl butyrate, $C_3H_7 \cdot COO \cdot C_2H_5$.—To obtain this ester, 2 parts of butyric acid may be mixed with 2 parts of 95 per cent. alcohol, and the mixture warmed to 80° with 1 part of strong sulphuric acid. The product is then poured into water and allowed to stand : the ethyl butyrate separates out as an oil on the top of the liquid. It is drawn off, washed with sodium carbonate solution, and rectified by distillation.[2] Or, alternatively, the separated ester may be treated with calcium carbonate to neutralise acidity, dehydrated with fused calcium chloride, and distilled ; and then finally rectified by re-distillation over calcined magnesia.

A smaller proportion of alcohol and sulphuric acid is required by proceeding as follows. Ten parts of alcohol, 16 of butyric acid, and 1 of sulphuric acid are heated together to 80°, and allowed to stand for twelve hours. The product is separated, washed with water and with dilute sodium carbonate solution, and rectified.

Ethyl butyrate is a colourless, mobile liquid, of pleasant, fruity odour ; it boils at 119·9°, and has the sp. gr. 0·8978 at 18°. The cruder commercial varieties have some application as solvents ;

[1] J. Stinde, *Ding. Polyt. J.*, 1866, **181**, 402.
[2] Roscoe and Schorlemmer, "Treatise on Chemistry," **3**, [i], 595.

the purer qualities are largely used for the preparation of artificial rum and fruit essences.

Ethyl butyrate and ethyl propionate are now obtained on a considerable scale as by-products in the preparation of acetone and potassium salts from kelp. They are employed as solvents for resins, in place of amyl acetate.

Ethyl benzoate, $C_6H_5 \cdot COO\,C_2H_5$, is used to some extent in making perfumes and fruit essences, and also in the production of synthetic chemicals. It is prepared by mixing benzoic acid, 1 part, with absolute alcohol, 2 parts, and passing a current of dried hydrochloric acid gas through the liquid. The gas is conveniently obtained by dropping strong sulphuric acid into a flask containing concentrated hydrochloric acid. The dissolution of the benzoic acid in the alcohol is effected in the course of passing the gas into the mixture, by means of the heat evolved in the reaction. When the vessel cools down again it is heated on a steam-bath, and the current of gas continued until fumes of the acid come off. On pouring the liquid into water, the ethyl benzoate separates out as an oily liquid which collects at the bottom of the vessel. It is drawn off, and treated with dilute solution of sodium carbonate in order to remove free benzoic acid; then shaken with water to remove sodium carbonate; separated, dehydrated over potassium carbonate, and distilled.

Ethyl benzoate is a colourless, oily liquid boiling at 211·2°, and of sp. gr. 1·0502.

Methyl benzoate, $C_6H_5 \cdot COO \cdot CH_3$, is prepared by distilling a mixture of benzoic acid (50 parts by weight), methyl alcohol (120 parts by volume), and strong sulphuric acid (6 parts by volume). It is a colourless liquid of pleasant odour; boiling point 198·6, and sp. gr. 1·0942 at 15°/15°. The ester is used in perfumery, and is known as "Niobe oil."

Methyl salicylate, $C_6H_4(OH) \cdot COO.CH_3$, is made artificially by distilling a mixture of 2 parts of salicylic acid, 2 of methyl alcohol, and 1 of strong sulphuric acid. It boils at 222·2°, and has the sp. gr. 1·189 at 15°/15°, or 1·196 at 0°. It is used somewhat extensively in pharmacy, and also in perfumery. The naturally occurring ester is the chief constituent of oil of wintergreen (*Gaultheria*) and oil of *Betula alba*.

Manufacture of ethyl nitrite.—This product is used to some extent medicinally, two spirituous solutions containing it being described in the British Pharmacopœia. Chiefly, however, it is employed commercially for use in the preparation of various essences. For this purpose the pure nitrite itself is not prepared, but an alcoholic solution of it, which contains small quantities of acetaldehyde and ethyl acetate as well as the nitrite.

To obtain this industrial variety, 3 parts of 25 per cent. nitric acid are covered with 5 parts of alcohol, and set aside without shaking up for two days. Then 5 parts more of alcohol are added, and the mixture distilled from a steam-heated, acid-resisting retort until yellow vapours begin to appear. Calcined magnesia is then added to the distillate to neutralise the acidity, and the mixture set aside for twenty-four hours. It is then filtered, and 2 parts of alcohol added to the filtrate, which is then rectified, using gentle warming at first, until 8 parts of distillate have passed over.

Alternatively, a mixture of 3 parts of crude 40 per cent. nitric acid with 12 parts of alcohol (90 to 91 per cent.) is carefully distilled from a water-bath until red fumes appear. The distillate is then neutralised with calcined magnesia as before, and after twenty-four hours poured off clear. Three parts of alcohol are now added, and the liquid distilled until 10 parts have been collected; the whole of this is finally rectified again.

The product, as stated above, is an alcoholic solution of ethyl nitrite, but containing also aldehyde and acetic ether. It is liable to become acid on keeping, and may then be again neutralised with magnesia and redistilled.

To obtain practically pure ethyl nitrite, a process worked out by Dunstan and Dymond may be adopted.[1] In this method, no distillation is required.

Dilute sulphuric acid is made to react with sodium nitrite and alcohol at a low temperature. The quantities of the reacting compounds are calculated from the two equations:—

$$\text{(i).}\ 2NaNO_2 + H_2SO_4 = Na_2SO_4 + 2HNO_2;$$
$$\text{(ii).}\ C_2H_5{\cdot}OH + HNO_2 = C_2H_5{\cdot}NO_2 + H_2O.$$

A solution is made by dissolving (34·5) grams of sodium nitrite in water. The liquid is diluted to 120 c.c. and cooled below 0° by means of an ice- and salt-bath. Commercial sodium nitrite is of 95–98 per cent. purity, and hence a quantity corresponding with 34·5 grams of the pure salt must be taken. A slight excess does not interfere with the reaction.

13·5 C.c. of sulphuric acid are added to a cooled mixture of 32 c.c. of rectified spirit with an equal volume of water; the liquid is then diluted to 120 c.c. and cooled below 0°. This acid liquid is allowed gradually to pass through a thistle funnel, with constant stirring, to the bottom of the solution of sodium nitrite, contained

[1] *Pharm. J.*, 1888, [iii], **18**, 861.

in a long, narrow glass vessel surrounded by ice and salt. When the acid has been added, a pale yellow layer of ethyl nitrite is found, completely separated from the lower layer of solution of sodium sulphate. Melting ice alone may be used for the cooling, but the acid must then be added very slowly and carefully, to prevent rise of temperature and evolution of nitrous fumes.

The ethyl nitrite so formed contains only traces of alcohol and water. The alcohol is removed, almost completely, by shaking with cold water in a separator; the water by digestion with freshly ignited potassium carbonate.

From 30 to 35 grams of ethyl nitrite are obtained; the calculated yield is 37·5 grams. The product is almost pure, if not absolutely so.

A somewhat similar process has been described by Feldhaus,[1] but in this case the ester is separated by volatilisation and condensed. One litre of 45 per cent. alcohol is mixed with 500 grams of potassium nitrite, and the solution cooled in an ice-bath. A mixture made with 500 grams each of water, alcohol, and sulphuric acid is dropped slowly into the first solution, the vessel containing which is attached to a condenser. The heat of the reaction suffices to volatilise the ethyl nitrite, which is condensed and collected in a cooled receiver.

Pure ethyl nitrite is a mobile liquid, of boiling point 17·5°, according to Dunstan and Dymond, and sp. gr. 0·917 at 0°/0°. It is very prone to decomposition in the presence of water or traces of acid. The Pharmacopœia "solution of ethyl nitrite" is a solution of 2·5 to 3 per cent. by weight of ethyl nitrite in a mixture of 95 volumes of absolute alcohol with 5 volumes of glycerin. The glycerin acts as a preservative, presumably by reason of its affinity for water.

"Spirit of nitrous ether" (Sweet Spirit of Nitre) is an alcoholic solution containing, according to the British official requirements, from 1·52 to 2·66 per cent. by weight of ethyl nitrite, together with aldehyde and other allied substances. The Pharmacopœia directions for preparing it are to add gradually 100 c.c. of sulphuric acid to a litre of 90 per cent. alcohol, and then 125 c.c. of nitric acid, stirring constantly. The mixture is transferred to a retort or flask containing 100 grams of copper wire or turnings, and distilled gently at a temperature at first about 77°, and rising to 80°, but which does not exceed 82°. The receiver contains 1 litre of 90 per cent. alcohol, and is cooled with ice-water. When the volume of liquid in the receiver has been increased to 1,600 c.c.,

[1] *Annalen*, 1863, **126**, 71.

the retort is allowed to cool, 25 c.c. more nitric acid added, and distillation continued until the receiver contains 1,700 c.c. This is mixed with another litre of alcohol (90 per cent.), or with such a quantity as will make the product contain 2·66 per cent. by weight of ethyl nitrite.

Ethyl nitrate (Nitric ethyl ester), $C_2H_5 \cdot O \cdot NO_2$.—When alcohol is heated with nitric acid alone, there is a partial oxidation of the alcohol, which causes the formation of nitrous acid and then of ethyl nitr*ite*, instead of nitr*ate*. If, however, the nitrous acid is destroyed, as by the addition of urea, the pure ethyl nitrate can be obtained.

Distil 120–150 grams of a mixture consisting of 1 vol. of pure nitric acid (sp. gr. 1·401) and 2 vols. of alcohol (sp. gr. 0·842), to which 1–2 grams of urea have been added. Heat gently, and collect about seven-eighths. The distillate is shaken with water, and the heavier ester separated from the aqueous liquid. It is purified by washing with a dilute alkali solution, dried for a day or two over calcium chloride, and re-distilled.[1]

Alternatively, 400 grams of pure nitric acid (sp. gr. 1·40) are heated with 4 grams of urea to destroy lower oxides of nitrogen, then cooled, and mixed with 100 grams of urea nitrate and 300 grams of absolute alcohol. A similar mixture of alcohol and nitric acid is prepared without the urea. The first mixture is distilled until one-half has passed over; then the second mixture is allowed to drop into the retort, and the distillation continued. The nitric ester is separated and purified as before described. The urea nitrate can of course be recovered and used again.[2]

Ethyl nitrate is a colourless liquid with a pleasant, sweetish odour; it boils at 87·6° and has the sp. gr. 1·1123 at 15·5°. It burns with a very white flame, and will explode if suddenly exposed to a great heat. When reduced with tin and hydrochloric acid, it yields hydroxylamine.

Methyl and ethyl sulphates.—The most important of these industrially are the dimethyl sulphate and the salts of monoethyl sulphate. The former is much used as a methylating agent, especially for phenols and for amines of the aromatic series. The reaction in the latter case is expressed by the equation:—

$$(CH_3)_2SO_4 + 2R \cdot NH_2 = R \cdot NH_2 \cdot CH_3 \cdot HSO_4 + R \cdot NH(CH_3).$$

The salts of ethyl hydrogen sulphate are employed for ethylating phenols—as, for example, *p*-nitrophenol in the preparation of phenacetin; and for the making of ethyl mercaptan, etc.

These alkyl sulphates serve as a cheap raw material for use in

[1] Millon, *Ann. Chim. Phys.*, 1843, [iii], 8, 233.
[2] Lossen: *Annalen*, 1868, Suppl. 6, 220.

such operations as the foregoing. The dimethyl compound especially has been of signal service in the synthetic dye industry.

Methyl hydrogen sulphate, (Methyl sulphuric acid; monomethyl sulphate), $CH_3 \cdot HSO_4$.—A general method of obtaining methyl and ethyl sulphates is to treat the alcohols with concentrated sulphuric acid[1] or with chlorosulphonic acid.[2] The first method is convenient, but since the reaction is a reversible one it does not give the theoretical yield.

For the methyl hydrogen sulphate, 1 part by weight of methyl alcohol is mixed with 2 parts of strong sulphuric acid, and the mixture kept warm for some hours. It is then diluted with water, and barium carbonate added in excess, to neutralise the free acids. After filtration from the barium sulphate and excess of carbonate, the filtrate, which contains the barium salt of methyl hydrogen sulphate, is evaporated to a conveniently small bulk, and treated with just sufficient sulphuric acid to precipitate all the barium as sulphate, and then again filtered. An aqueous solution of the free methyl sulphuric acid is thus obtained, which can now be evaporated in a vacuum over strong sulphuric acid.

Methyl hydrogen sulphate is an oily liquid, which does not solidify on cooling to $-30°$. On distillation, it decomposes into dimethyl sulphate and sulphuric acid.

Dimethyl sulphate, $(CH_3)_2SO_4$, is made by distilling monomethyl sulphate in a vacuum. To obtain a good yield, the monomethyl compound should be free from water and other impurities. It need not, however, be separately prepared. A mixture of 25 kilos. of sulphuric anhydride with 10 kilos. of nearly absolute methyl alcohol is made, the temperature being kept below 0°, and preferably between $-5°$ and $-10°$. The mixture is then distilled *in vacuo*. An almost theoretical yield of 19 kilos. can be obtained.[3]

Alternatively, 100 parts of chlorosulphonic acid are run into 27 parts of methyl alcohol at a temperature of $-10°$ to $-15°$, care being taken that the liquids are well mixed, and moisture excluded. The mixture is then distilled in a vacuum[4] (20 mm.; the temperature being about 140°). Yield, about 80 per cent. of the theoretical.

The local overheating which easily occurs may be avoided by

[1] Dumas and Péligot, *Annalen*, 1836, **15**, 40.

[2] Claesson, *J. pr. Chem.*, 1879, **19**, 231 *et seq.*

[3] Merck, D.R.-P., 133542, 1901; Winther, "Patente," **1**, 32.

[4] Ullmann, *Annalen*, 1903, **327**, 106. For laboratory details, see Lassar-Cohn, "Arbeitsmethoden," 1907, p. 294.

diluting the methyl alcohol with carbon tetrachloride. An enamelled vessel fitted with a reflux condenser is charged with 6·4 kilos. of methyl alcohol (99 per cent. strength) and 20 kilos. of carbon tetrachloride. Into this mixture 24 kilos. of chlorosulphonic acid are slowly run, with stirring. The tetrachloride is then distilled off on a water-bath, and used again in the next charge: the residue is distilled *in vacuo* as before to obtain the dimethyl sulphate.[1] Sulphuric anhydride may replace the chlorosulphonic acid.

Haworth and Irvine have recently described a method of preparing dimethyl sulphate by the interaction of dimethyl ether and sulphur trioxide (B.P. 122498). See also p. 357.

Dimethyl sulphate finds considerable application as a methylating agent in the preparation of dyestuffs. It is a colourless, oily liquid, insoluble in water, and with a peppermint-like flavour. Boiling point 188°; sp. gr. 1·333 at 15°. It requires care in the handling, as it affects the respiratory organs strongly.[2]

Ethyl hydrogen sulphate, $C_2H_5 \cdot HSO_4$ (Monoethyl sulphate, ethyl sulphuric acid; sulphovinic acid).—The alkali or calcium salt of this acid is used for ethylating purposes in the making of phenacetin and other fine chemicals.

To obtain the salt, or the sulphovinic acid itself, the following procedure may be adopted. To 5 parts of absolute alcohol (by weight), $3\frac{3}{4}$ parts of strong sulphuric acid are slowly added, and then the whole mixed, and heated for four hours on the water-bath. After cooling, ice and water are added, in order to dilute the liquid without greatly raising the temperature. The acid is then neutralised by adding an excess of calcium carbonate mixed into a paste with water, and the liquid filtered from calcium sulphate and excess of carbonate. The solution of calcium ethyl sulphate thus obtained may be made slightly alkaline with lime-water, and concentrated for use if this salt is required. If the potassium compound is wanted, a strong solution of potassium carbonate is added to a concentrated solution of the calcium salt until the calcium is all precipitated (as calcium carbonate). The potassium ethyl sulphate thus formed is soluble; it is filtered from the precipitate, a little more potassium carbonate added, and the solution evaporated until the salt crystallises out.

If the ethyl hydrogen sulphate itself is wanted, the acid liquid after addition of ice and water is neutralised with barium carbonate or with lead carbonate, instead of with calcium carbonate, as barium or lead can be subsequently eliminated more readily than

[1] *Soc. Anon. Prod. Chim.*, D.R.-P., 193830; Friedländer, "Fortschritte der Teerfarb," 1911, **9**, 30.

[2] Lassar-Cohn, *loc. cit.*, p. 293.

calcium. The neutralised liquid is filtered from precipitated sulphate and excess of carbonate, and then evaporated. Crystals of barium or lead ethyl sulphate are thus obtained. These are separated and dissolved in water, and sulphuric acid added in quantity just sufficient to precipitate the barium or lead as sulphates. Alternatively, in the case of lead, this metal may be removed as sulphide by a current of hydrogen sulphide gas ; or the bulk may be precipitated as sulphate, filtered off, and the elimination of the lead completed by means of hydrogen sulphide. Whichever method is used, the precipitate of barium or lead sulphate or lead sulphide is filtered off, and the filtrate, which now contains the free ethyl hydrogen sulphate, is evaporated in a vacuum over sulphuric acid. It can eventually be obtained as a syrupy liquid, soluble in water and in alcohol, but not in ether.

In preparing sodium ethyl sulphate for technical use an enamelled acid-proof vessel is employed, set in a wooden vessel connected with the water supply and serving as cooler. A charge of 100 kilos. of strong sulphuric acid (96 per cent.) is placed in the former vessel, and 95 per cent. alcohol (47 kilos.) run in with stirring, and slowly, so that no excessive development of heat occurs. After the lapse of twenty-four hours, the mixture is passed into a cold emulsion of well-slaked lime, which must be always present in excess. The mixture is filtered from the calcium sulphate formed, and the latter pressed ; the filtrate is then treated with sodium carbonate to precipitate the calcium, and the resulting clear liquid removed, to be finally evaporated in a vacuum.

If the expensive ingredient, alcohol, is to be utilised more completely, it is necessary to remove the water arising from the reaction. This is most conveniently done by means of sulphuric anhydride, with which the alcohol, dissolved in strong sulphuric acid, is treated in the cold.[1]

Diethyl sulphate, $(C_2H_5)_2SO_4$.—This is somewhat more difficult to prepare, and gives a lower yield, than the corresponding dimethyl compound, but may be obtained in a similar manner. Sulphuric anhydride (17·4 kilos.) is run into 10 kilos. of absolute ethyl alcohol at a temperature of — 10° to — 20°, and the mixture distilled in a vacuum. The yield is 7 to 8 kilos., or about one-half of the theoretical quantity.[2]

Alternatively, absolute alcohol is mixed with Nordhausen sulphuric acid, the ethyl salt extracted with chloroform, and the product distilled *in vacuo*.[3]

[1] Merck, D.R.-P., 77278. [2] *Ibid.*, D.R.-P., 133542.
[3] Claesson and Lundvall, *Ber.*, 1880, **13**, 1699.

A yield of 83–90 per cent. is said to be obtained by distilling sodium ethyl sulphate *in vacuo.*[1]

Diethyl sulphate has not much technical application. It is an oily liquid, boiling at 208° (with decomposition), or at 96° under 15 mm. pressure, or 118° under 40 mm. Sp. gr. 1·1837 at 19°. The compound has toxic properties.

Irvine and Haworth[2] describe a method of obtaining methyl and ethyl sulphates by the action of sulphuryl chloride upon the alcohols. Or, instead of preparing the sulphuryl chloride first, chlorine and sulphur dioxide may be passed into the alcohol in equimolecular quantities. On distillation of the final reaction-product under reduced pressure, the alkyl hydrogen sulphate, formed together with the dialkyl compound, undergoes decomposition into sulphuric acid and dialkyl sulphate, so that the latter is obtained in good yield.

A similar process is described by Boake and Durrans.[3] Into 32 parts by weight of anhydrous methyl alcohol is passed about 35 parts by weight of chlorine, and the same weight of sulphur dioxide. This is an excess (3 parts) of the dioxide, which excess may be added at the start and maintained throughout the addition of the mixed gases. After expelling the excess of sulphur dioxide on a water-bath, the product, containing dimethyl sulphate, methyl hydrogen sulphate, methyl chloride, and some hydrochloric acid, can be used as a methylating agent ; or the methyl chloride can be distilled off at the ordinary pressure and recovered, and dimethyl sulphate obtained by distilling the residue under reduced pressure (40 mm.) and re-distilling the product at 24 mm.

Ethyl mercaptan (Ethyl hydrosulphide), $C_2H_5 \cdot SH$.—This compound is employed technically in the preparation of the hypnotics sulphonal, trional, and tetronal.

To obtain it on a small scale a solution (sp. gr. 1·3) of potassium hydroxide in water is saturated with hydrogen sulphide. The resulting solution of potassium hydrosulphide is then mixed with solution of calcium ethyl sulphate (sp. gr. 1·3) and the mixture distilled from a water-bath. The crude product is dried over calcium chloride and purified by distillation (Liebig).[4]

Klason indicates the following as a convenient procedure.[5] One litre of alcohol is poured gradually into a mixture of 500 c.c. of concentrated sulphuric acid with the same volume (500 c.c.) of

[1] Lilienfeld, Aust. P. 63526 ; *J. Chem. Soc.* (Abst.), 1914, **106**, [i], 919.
[2] B.P. 117824, 1917.
[3] B. P. 119250.
[4] Roscoe and Schorlemmer, "Treatise on Chemistry," **3**, [i], 378.
[5] *Ber.*, 1887, **20**, 3411.

fuming sulphuric acid. After cooling down, the liquid is carefully run into a solution of sodium carbonate containing 4 kilos. of the crystallised salt, ice being freely added during the operation. The mixture is then evaporated, and the greater part of the sodium sulphate which crystallises out is removed, care being taken that the reaction is alkaline during the evaporation. To the residual liquid is added a solution of potassium hydrosulphide, prepared from 800 grams of the hydroxide by passing hydrogen sulphide into its aqueous solution as before described. The mixture is then distilled from a water-bath to separate the mercaptan, About 400 grams of the crude product are obtained: it contains some ethyl sulphide, $(C_2H_5)_2S$.

To remove the latter, the crude product is either distilled, or else treated with solution of caustic alkali, which dissolves the mercaptan, but leaves the ethyl sulphide insoluble. This is separated, and the mercaptan liberated from its alkaline solution by acidifying with dilute sulphuric or hydrochloric acid.

Ethyl mercaptan is a colourless, mobile liquid, with a penetrating garlic-like odour. It boils at 36·2°, and has the sp. gr. 0·835 at 21°. It is only slightly soluble in water, but easily so in alcohol and in ether.

Preparation of esters by catalysis.—Sabatier and Mailhe have shown that various esters of fatty acids, *e.g.*, ethyl and methyl formates, acetates, propionates, and butyrates, can be prepared by passing the vapours of a mixture of the alcohol and the acid in question over heated titanium dioxide.[1] The yields obtained approximate to those given by the ordinary (Berthelot's) method of direct esterification after prolonged contact of the acid and alcohol. Thorium oxide is also effective, though less so than the titanium compound.

With titanium oxide heated to 280–300°, and using molecular proportions of alcohol and acid, the yield of methyl propionate obtained was 72·9 per cent., and of ethyl butyrate 71 per cent. The yield can be increased by using an excess of either the acid or the alcohol.

A lower temperature was used for obtaining the formic esters. Methyl, ethyl, propyl, butyl, isobutyl, and isoamyl formates were readily obtained by passing formic acid vapour, mixed with an excess of the alcohol in question, over titanium dioxide heated to 150°, or over thorium oxide at 200–220°. The catalytic effect decreases as the temperature is lowered. Thus in the case of ethyl formate, whilst equimolecular mixtures of ethyl alcohol and

[1] *Compt. rend.*, 1911, **152**, 494, 1044.

formic acid were esterified by titanium dioxide to the extent of 65 per cent. at 150°, the esterification was only 47 per cent. at 120°.

Experiments with ethyl alcohol and various acids, using equimolecular proportions of alcohol and acid in each mixture, indicated that in general the esterification was more complete the lower the molecular weight of the acid. Thus with titanium dioxide at 230°, acetic acid forms 67 per cent. of the ester, but isovaleric acid only 36 per cent. At 150°, formic acid gives 65 per cent., as noted above, but acetic acid only 20 per cent. As a catalyst, titanium oxide is more active than thorium oxide; moreover, its activity was found to persist undiminished during experiments extending over twenty days.

Primary alcohols are esterified more completely than secondary or tertiary alcohols, using the same acid for each.

Ethylene.—On an industrial scale this gas is prepared from alcohol by Ipatiew's catalytic process, for the purpose of making ethane. The alcohol is vaporised, and the vapour passed over amorphous aluminium oxide heated to 360°:—

$$C_2H_5{\cdot}OH = C_2H_4 + H_2O.$$

The ethylene thus obtained is carefully purified (to obviate "poisoning" of the catalyst in the further operation), and converted into ethane, C_2H_6, by passing it mixed with purified hydrogen over freshly-reduced nickel heated to 150–200°. The resulting ethane is used in specially constructed freezing machines.[1]

On a small scale, it may be prepared as follows. A solution of 60 c.c. of alcohol in 300 grams of strong sulphuric acid is mixed in a flask with about 200 grams of coarse sand and heated to 160–170°. A mixture of 200 c.c. of alcohol and 300 grams of sulphuric acid is dropped into the flask through a tap funnel, the rate being regulated so that a steady stream of the evolved gas is maintained. To purify the gas from ether, alcohol, sulphur dioxide, and carbonic acid, it is passed through a series of wash bottles, of which the first may be empty, and the others contain in succession sulphuric acid and dilute caustic soda solution.

The small quantity of impurity still present can be got rid of by liquefying the gas, and then vaporising it again at a temperature of — 80°. Pure ethylene, however, can be obtained by using boric anhydride to decompose the alcohol, instead of sulphuric acid.

A nearly quantitative yield of ethylene is given by Newth's method,[2] in which phosphoric acid heated to 200–220° is used.

[1] Sprent, *J. Soc. Chem. Ind.*, 1913, **32**, 171.

[2] *Trans. Chem. Soc.*, 1901, **79**, 915.

On a small scale, about 50 or 60 c.c. of syrupy phosphoric acid of sp. gr. 1·75 are placed in a small Wurtz flask of about 180 c.c. capacity. The flask is fitted with a cork carrying a thermometer and a dropping-tube, the end of the latter being drawn out to a fine tube, and reaching to the bottom of the flask. Phosphoric acid of the sp. gr. mentioned, 1·75, begins to boil at approximately 160°. It is boiled in the flask for a few minutes until the temperature reaches 200°, when alcohol is allowed to enter drop by drop. Ethylene is immediately disengaged, and by maintaining the temperature between 200° and 220° a continuous supply of the gas can be obtained. Even with so small an apparatus as that described, ethylene is produced at the rate of 10 to 15 litres per hour. It is led through a small Woulfe's bottle (100 to 150 c.c. capacity) standing in a vessel of ice, in which an aqueous liquid collects containing a small quantity of ether, alcohol, and traces of oily impurity. The gas which passes on is practically pure ethylene, free from carbon dioxide, and absorbed completely by fuming sulphuric acid.

For preparation on a larger scale, alcohol may be vaporised and the vapour bubbled through phosphoric acid kept at the temperature stated.

If *methyl* alcohol is substituted for ethyl in the foregoing process, and the temperature of the acid kept between 200° and 210°, the gas evolved is practically pure methyl ether $(CH_3)_2O$.

Synthetic drugs and fine organic chemicals.—Alcohol is not only used as a solvent in the manufacture of these articles: it frequently enters into their composition. An ethyl or a methyl group, as the case may be, is introduced into the molecule of the product.

The alcohol itself is not, in general, employed directly for this purpose. It is first converted into an intermediate compound which serves as the actual "ethylating" or "methylating" agent. Thus ethyl chloride, bromide, iodide, and sulphate are commonly employed to introduce the ethyl group into a compound. The corresponding methyl salts serve a similar purpose where a methyl group is required.

As illustrative examples the following may be mentioned.

The photographic developer known as "Metol" is obtained by methylating *para*-amidophenol, methyl sulphate being conveniently used for the purpose.

Vanillin, employed extensively as a flavouring and in perfumery, may be synthesised by methylating protocatechuic aldehyde. The latter is dissolved in a strong solution of sodium carbonate, dimethyl sulphate added, and the mixture heated to effect the required combination.

Phenacetin, of which large quantities are employed in medicine, is produced by ethylating *para*-nitrophenol, reducing the product, and acetylating it; or by alternative methods in which the ethylation follows the acetylation, instead of preceding it. Ethyl chloride, bromide, or iodide, or sodium ethyl sulphate, is commonly employed as the ethylating agent.

Antipyrin, also largely used in medicine, is an example of somewhat different character. It is obtained by the combination of ethyl acetoacetate and phenylhydrazine. Alcohol furnishes the raw material for production of the ethyl acetoacetate.

Mercury fulminate, $HgC_2N_2O_2$.—This compound is largely used in the preparation of detonators for explosives. It is made by the interaction of mercury, nitric acid, and alcohol.

Somewhat varying proportions of ingredients are given by different writers.

(i) One part of mercury is dissolved in 12 parts of nitric acid of sp. gr. 1·345; to the solution 5·5 parts of 90 per cent. alcohol are added, and the whole is well shaken. After a little time, when an energetic reaction has commenced, 6 parts more of the alcohol are gradually added. At first metallic mercury separates, but it subsequently redissolves, and deposits as mercuric fulminate in flakes.[1]

(ii) Thorpe[2] states that 1 part of mercury is dissolved in 10 parts of nitric acid (sp. gr. 1·33), and for every kilogram of acid used, 1 litre of alcohol, sp. gr. 0·833 (= 90·2 per cent. by volume) is added. The reaction begins either spontaneously or on slight warming. The operation is carried out either in a tubulated retort, the evolved gases then escaping into a flue, or else in glass balloons placed in an open wooden shed. After the alcohol has been added, the operator avoids the shed till the reaction is complete.

(iii) Marshall gives the following particulars.[3] The mercury is first cleaned by squeezing it through wash-leather. 0·5 Kilo. is weighed into a glass flask, and 5·5 kilos. of nitric acid (sp. gr. 1·36) are added. When all the mercury has dissolved, the solution is allowed to cool, and then is poured into a large glass flask containing 5 kilos. of alcohol (90 per cent. strength) which has been warmed, if necessary, to a temperature of 20° or 25°. A reaction sets in almost at once, accompanied by effervescence, and the temperature of the liquid rises rapidly to about 80°; the reaction then moderates,

[1] *Ber.*, 1876, **9**, 787. [2] "Dict. Applied Chem.," II, 631.
[3] "Explosives," 1917 edition, II, 700.

but the temperature goes on slowly rising to 83°. Crystals of fulminate form, and white fumes fill the upper part of the flask. After about ten minutes, red fumes appear, vapours are evolved more rapidly, more solid is formed, and there is a further rise of temperature to about 86°. The reaction then moderates: it lasts altogether twenty to twenty-five minutes.

The contents of the flask are then poured into water and washed by decantation until practically all the acid has been removed. The fulminate is now collected on a muslin filter, and the washing continued with distilled water until the liquid passing through is no longer acid to litmus paper. Alcohol of 82 to 85 per cent. strength is sometimes employed for the washing. The yield is generally 1·2 to 1·3 kilos. of fulminate for each kilo. of mercury.

The fumes given off are poisonous and inflammable: they should be removed by means of a good draught. They are condensed in stoneware vessels; the liquid consists of unchanged alcohol containing ethyl nitrite and nitrate, aldehyde, ether, and other by-products. It is frequently employed as a partial denaturant for fresh alcohol.

(iv) O. Hagen describes in detail the following procedure, known on the Continent as Alder's method.[1]

In each of 15 wide-necked flasks of colourless glass, 5 litres capacity, is placed 4·5 kilos. of water-clear nitric acid (40° Bé. = sp. gr. 1·38), and 35–40 grams of granulated zinc are dissolved in each quantity of acid. When the zinc has dissolved, 500 grams of pure mercury, weighed out in a 40-c.c. flask, are added, and the mercury dissolved: in winter the mixture must be heated on a water-bath. To avoid loss through spirting, the flasks are loosely stoppered; and in summer, before adding the alcohol at the next stage, the flasks are cooled with water to prevent too energetic action.

A series of 15 retorts, 50 litres capacity, is arranged with their outlets passing each into an earthenware vessel, provided with a tap at the bottom for removal of condensed fumes, and fitted at the top with earthenware condensation-tubes passing eventually to the open air. In each retort is placed 4·6 kilos. of 91 per cent. alcohol (by volume) denatured with turpentine, and 30 grams of a saturated solution of copper nitrate (56° Bé.). Then the contents of one of the large flasks are added, at a temperature of 20–25°. In a short time the temperature rises, and eventually an energetic reaction sets in, white fumes are evolved, and the fulminate begins to form. When the reaction has moderated, and the fumes have

[1] *Z. ges. Schiess- u. Sprengstoffw.*, 1911, 4, 28, 44.

become transparent, with a yellowish-red tinge, the retort is removed and set aside to cool down well.

The contents are then transferred to a large, well-glazed earthenware vessel, the retort being rinsed out with cold water. The precipitated fulminate is filtered off through a linen filter, and washed with alcohol of 82–85 per cent. strength until the washings give no turbidity when well diluted with water. Washing with water alone at this stage is not considered satisfactory, as some ethyl nitrate and nitrite may be left in; alcohol is therefore used at first. Then the washing is completed with water until the specific gravity of the washings is 1·0, and blue litmus paper is no longer reddened by them.

The fulminate may still contain extraneous impurities such as fibres, woody particles, fragments of cork, and so on. These are removed by sieving through silk gauze (100 meshes per sq. cm.) stretched over one end of a glass cylinder, 25 cm. × 20 cm., which is shaken in about 30 litres of water contained in a vessel of 80–90 cm. diameter. The foreign matters are left behind on the sieve. Before sieving, the fulminate is well stirred up in water with a wooden spatula to allow particles of metallic mercury to settle down.

Finally, the moist fulminate is rubbed down into a finely-divided state by means of a wooden pestle, in a porcelain dish. The product is collected in earthenware jars, and allowed to stand for two days, During this time the fulminate settles down, and the supernatant water can be removed, leaving the residual final product, which contains about 15 per cent. of moisture.

Condensation of the fumes by means of a cooled lead worm is adopted by Alder, but this is not recommended by Hagen. A luting for the joints of the earthenware tubes is made by grinding up dried clay to a fine powder (passing through a sieve with 25 meshes per sq. cm.), and mixing this with ordinary crude glycerin (28° Bé.) to a suitable consistency.

Intermediate products for dyestuffs: alkylanilines.—Monomethylaniline, $C_6H_5{\cdot}NH{\cdot}CH_3$, is produced by heating aniline hydrochloride or sulphate with methyl alcohol under pressure.

In an enamelled autoclave are placed 55 parts of aniline hydrochloride and 16 parts of methyl alcohol (by weight), and the mixture heated during two to three hours at a temperature of 180°. The pressure rises first to about 5 atmospheres, subsequently increasing to 25 with the progress of the reaction. After the pressure has fallen the heating is continued for a further six hours or so at 180°. An excess of milk of lime is then mixed with the products of the reaction, and the methylaniline, together with some dimethylaniline and unchanged aniline, distilled off.[1]

Alternatively, 70 parts of aniline, 42 of methyl alcohol, and 8 of sulphuric acid may be used, the mixture being heated in an autoclave to about 200°, and the free bases separated as before.[2]

In another process 140 parts of aniline, 32 of methyl alcohol, and 1 of iodine are heated together for 10 hours at 220°.[3]

Pure monomethyl aniline has not much technical application. If desired, it can be separated from the product obtained as above by treating the mixed bases with an equivalent quantity of *p*-toluene sulphochloride and dilute solution of sodium hydroxide. This converts the monomethylaniline and the aniline into the corresponding toluene-sulpho-derivatives, whereas the dimethylaniline is not attacked and can be distilled off with steam. The residue is then extracted with sodium hydroxide solution, which does not dissolve the toluene-sulpho-methylaniline. The latter can then be hydrolysed by warming for a short time at 100° with an equal weight of sulphuric acid. On pouring the product into water and adding milk of lime, the methylaniline is liberated, and can be distilled off in a current of steam.[4]

Pure monomethylaniline is a colourless liquid, boiling at 192°. Its sp. gr. is 0·976 at 15°.

Dimethylaniline, $C_6H_5 \cdot N(CH_3)_2$.—The manufacture of this has been described in detail by J. Walter.[5] It is obtained for technical purposes by heating 80 kilos. of pure aniline, 78 of methyl alcohol, and 8 of sulphuric acid (66° Bé. = sp. gr. 1·841) in an autoclave to 230–235° for nine to ten hours. The autoclave is of cast iron, enamelled inside, and the requisite temperature is obtained by means of a bath of molten alloy, in which the autoclave is immersed. The alloy is composed of lead, 71 per cent., and tin, 29 per cent. During the heating, the pressure in the autoclave rises to 30–32 atmospheres by the end of six hours, remains constant for another three hours or so, and then gradually falls.

After the reaction is completed, the vessel is allowed to cool down well, preferably during the whole of the next day, when it is opened, and the issuing vapours passed through a condenser to recover the methyl alcohol present in them. Methyl ether, formed as a by-product, is also present; it is either allowed to

[1] Cain, "Intermediate Products," p. 60.
[2] Dammer, "Chemische Technologie," **2**, 948.
[3] D.R.-P., 250236.
[4] See also a paper by Frankland, Challenger, and Nicholls, *Trans. Chem. Soc.*, 1919, **115**, 198.
[5] *Chem. Zeit.*, 1910, **34**, 641, 667, *et seq.*

escape in the gaseous form, or is recovered as dimethyl sulphate by absorbing it with fuming sulphuric acid.

The contents of the autoclave are then passed into a still, together with a quantity of caustic soda solution corresponding with the amount of sulphuric acid used. The liberated dimethylaniline is next distilled off in a current of steam, and passes into a separating vessel, from which the condensed water can be run off. The yield of the dimethyl product is about 98 kilos., or 92 per cent. of the theoretical.

The chief impurities present in commercial dimethylaniline are aniline and the monomethyl compound, with some higher boiling condensation-products arising from the use of impure methyl alcohol. When necessary, the various impurities can be removed by fractional distillation, or by freezing-out methods.

It is important to use alcohol as free as possible from acetone, as the presence of this compound diminishes the yield, and renders the product unsuitable for some purposes.

Dimethylaniline is a nearly colourless, oily liquid, which melts at 0·5°, and boils at 192·5°. Sp. gr. 0·962 at 15°/15°. It is used in the production of several dyestuffs, *e.g.*, methyl violet, methyl orange, Meldola's blue, crystal violet, and malachite green, and also for the making of nitrosodimethylaniline and dimethyl-*m*-aminophenol. It is also said to be employed in Germany for the production of "methyl rubber," in order to increase the elasticity of the product.

A catalytic process for the production of methyl anilines has recently been described. A mixture of the vapours of methyl alcohol and aniline is passed over alumina heated to a temperature of 400–430°. This gives a mixture of monomethylaniline and dimethylaniline, with only traces of aniline remaining in the mixture. On adding further methyl alcohol and repeating the operation, dimethylaniline is given (Mailhe and de Godon).[1] This process dispenses with the use of autoclaves and high pressures, and moreover, the methyl alcohol need not be specially purified from acetone, nor the aniline from water.

A similar method is said to be equally satisfactory for the preparation of the methyl toluidines. If the vapours of either *o*-, *m*-, or *p*-toluidine and methyl alcohol are passed over the aluminium oxide at 350–400° a mixture of methyl- and dimethyl-toluidines is obtained. A second treatment converts this mixture wholly into the dimethyl toluidine.[2]

Ethylaniline, $C_6H_5 \cdot NH \cdot C_2H_5$.—This is produced by heating

[1] *Compt. rend.*, 1918, **166**, 467–469. [2] *Ibid.*, 564–566.

equimolecular quantities of aniline hydrochloride and ethyl alcohol to 180° in an autoclave, as with the corresponding methyl compound. On cooling, the ethylaniline hydrochloride formed crystallises out, and can thus be separated.

Ethylaniline boils at 206°, and its sp. gr. at 15°/15° is 0·964. It has not much technical application.

Diethylaniline, $C_6H_5{\cdot}N(C_2H_5)_2$, is obtained by heating the requisite proportions of aniline hydrochloride and alcohol under pressure, but is not readily procured completely free from the monoethyl compound. It is a liquid, boiling at 216·5°, and of specific gravity 0·939 at 15°/15°.

By treatment with nitric acid it yields *p*-nitrosodiethylaniline, from which pure diethylaniline may be obtained together with nitrosophenol by heating with dilute sodium hydroxide solution. Diethylaniline is used for the production of the dyestuffs brilliant green, patent blue V, and ethyl purple 6 B.

Ethylbenzylaniline, $C_6H_5{\cdot}N(C_2H_5){\cdot}CH_2{\cdot}C_6H_5$.—This is a liquid, boiling at 285–286° under 710 mm. pressure; it is used in the preparation of the dyestuffs known as light green SF, patent blue A, and xylene blue AS. It may be prepared by boiling a mixture of ethylaniline (1 part) and benzyl chloride (2 parts) under a reflux condenser for four hours, the product being then fractionated to remove excess of benzyl chloride and ethylaniline (Stebbins).[1]

Manufacture of formaldehyde.—The principle involved is the oxidation of methyl alcohol vapour mixed with air, by means of heated "contact" substances. On passing the resulting mixture of vapours through a suitable rectifying apparatus, the water and formaldehyde are condensed, whilst unchanged methyl alcohol vapour passes on, to be itself condensed and used again.

A useful preliminary study of the process will be found in a series of papers by Orloff,[2] a short account of which may be given here. A measured quantity of air was passed through methyl alcohol of various strengths and at various temperatures, and the mixture of alcohol vapour and air was led over the various heated catalytic agents. These were copper turnings, fireclay, and coke impregnated with finely-divided copper, asbestos impregnated with freshly-reduced copper, ceric sulphate, thorium oxide, "molecular" platinum, and metallic platinum. Of these, the coppered coke at 380–420°, and the metallic platinum at 330–400°, gave the best

[1] *J. Amer. Chem. Soc.*, 1885, **7**, 42.
[2] Abstracted in *J. Soc. Chem. Ind.*, 1908, **27**, 139, 419, and 1176.

yields of formaldehyde. With the former 39·8 per cent., and with the latter 41 per cent. of the methyl alcohol could be converted into formaldehyde. The oxidation of methyl alcohol is exothermic, and under suitable conditions will proceed without the aid of external heat when once started. In other experiments, a current of air at a velocity of 2·5 litres per second was passed through methyl alcohol warmed to 53·5–55°. The air and vapour issuing were led over a layer of reduced copper gauze, 10 to 15 cm. long, in a tube of hard glass contained in a jacket of iron and asbestos, which at the beginning was heated to about 300°. No further heating was required when the reaction was once started. Under these conditions, about 49 per cent. of the methyl alcohol was converted into formaldehyde. After condensing this, the gases remaining contained up to 20 per cent. of hydrogen, together with carbon dioxide, carbon monoxide, oxygen, and nitrogen. Automatic igniters were devised, to do away with the need for heating the tube containing the catalyser at the beginning of the process. These igniters consisted of pumice impregnated with a solution of chloroplatinic acid or ammonium palladium chloride, and heated to redness, whereby finely-divided platinum or palladium is left in the pores of the pumice. In contact with this material the mixture of methyl alcohol vapour and air, previously heated to 100°, ignites, and itself heats up the copper gauze catalyser to incandescence.

As applied industrially, one form of this process is as follows. Compressed air passes at constant pressure to a "carburetting" vessel in which it is heated, and where it meets a fine rain of methyl alcohol, so that a warm mixture of air and alcohol vapour emerges. This mixture is led into the oxidising vessel containing the catalyst. Copper gauze is usually employed, sometimes coated with silver. In Calvert's patent[1] the catalysts may be copper wool, coppered asbestos, or silvered or platinised pumice, arranged between partitions of copper gauze. The methyl alcohol in this process (Calvert's) is passed with hot air on to a hot rotary fan, and the air thus "carburetted" is then led into the reaction-chamber containing the catalysts. Orloff's oxidiser consists of a large number of glass tubes containing copper gauze, each glass tube being placed in an external copper tube.

The mixed vapours issuing from the oxidising vessel pass into a rectifying or washing tower, where the water and formaldehyde are separated from the unchanged methyl alcohol, hydrogen, and other gases, and collected as a strong solution (38 to 39 per cent.) of formaldehyde, constituting the commercial "formalin." Mean-

[1] No. 814 of 1915.

while, the remaining gases and vapours pass to a condenser, where most of the methyl alcohol is recovered. The small quantity still remaining is washed out of the issuing gases by passing them through water, and the solution distilled to obtain the methyl alcohol.

Fairly pure methyl alcohol of 90 per cent. strength, and containing not more than 1 per cent. of acetone, is used for this process.

According to Birsten and others,[1] working with a vacuum distillation apparatus, even dilute solutions of methyl alcohol (16 per cent.) will with a low vacuum (690 mm.) give off vapours to an air current sufficiently rich in methyl alcohol to be used for producing formaldehyde.

Acetaldehyde.—This oxidation-product of alcohol is employed industrially in the preparation of certain aniline dyestuffs, and also in making paraldehyde, which has some application in medicine. The two chief sources of commercial aldehyde are the by-products of wood distillation, and the by-products of alcohol rectification. As the boiling point of aldehyde is only 21°, the compound is found in the first runnings of the distillates. From these it is separated by fractional distillation and rectification. The aldehyde for technical purposes obtained from wood is usually of about 95 to 96 per cent. purity.

Another method of obtaining acetaldehyde utilised in recent years is the catalytic oxidation of ethyl alcohol. A current of air is bubbled through warm alcohol, and the issuing vapours are led over a heated finely-divided metal serving as catalyst, in essentially the same manner as is described in the case of methyl alcohol. A process not involving alcohol may be briefly mentioned, namely, the decomposition of lactic acid into aldehyde and formic acid brought about by heating it with dilute sulphuric acid. The lactic acid solution employed is obtained by fermenting a "mash" of potatoes with the lactic acid bacillus.

It is quite possible that these various methods of obtaining aldehyde for industrial purposes will sooner or later be superseded by processes based upon the oxidation of acetylene. In one such process this gas is led into a hot dilute sulphuric acid solution, containing not more than about six per cent. of the acid, together with mercuric oxide. The acetylene is oxidised to acetaldehyde, which forthwith distils from the hot liquid, so that the process is a continuous one. The mercuric salt is gradually reduced to metallic mercury, which can be re-converted into the oxide electrolytically, and used again. A good yield of pure aldehyde is said to be obtained.[2]

[1] *Zeitsch. angew. Chem.*, 1911, **51**, 2429.

[2] F.P., 455370.

On a small scale aldehyde is prepared chemically as follows. Two hundred and ten grams of potassium bichromate, broken into pieces about the size of a pea, are placed in a large round-bottomed flask of about 3 litres capacity, together with 840 grams of water. The flask is fitted with a tap-funnel, and is connected with a condenser and receiver, the latter being well cooled with ice. Keeping the flask cooled, a mixture of 210 grams of alcohol (90 per cent.) and 280 grams of strong sulphuric acid, also well cooled, is slowly added through the funnel, and the mixture well shaken. Much heat is evolved, and aldehyde distils over, with more or less water, acetal, and alcohol. Towards the end of the operation the heat of a water-bath may be applied to the flask. The distillate is rectified on the water-bath at about 50°, the vapours being led through a reflux condenser, which retains water and alcohol, into receivers containing anhydrous ether. The ethereal solution of aldehyde is now saturated with gaseous ammonia (dried by passing over lime), when the aldehyde-ammonia separates out as a white, crystalline mass. This is separated, drained, washed with ether, and dried. Pure aldehyde may be obtained from it by dissolving it in an equal weight of water, and distilling the solution on a water-bath with dilute sulphuric acid (1·5 parts of conc. sulphuric acid to 2 parts of water). The distillate is collected in a cooled receiver, and dehydrated with calcium chloride.

Acetaldehyde is a colourless, mobile liquid, sp. gr. 0·7951 at 10°, and boiling point 21°. It serves for the preparation of paraldehyde as already mentioned. By the action of aluminium alcoholate it is converted into ethyl acetate.[1] Thus ethyl acetate can be produced from acetylene.

Production of vinegar from alcohol.—In this country very little alcohol is used for vinegar making. On the Continent, however, a large quantity is employed for the purpose, more than three millions of gallons being used yearly in Germany alone. The product is largely employed for ordinary domestic and preserving requirements; the quantity used industrially is mainly devoted to the making of white lead and pharmaceutical lead acetate. To some extent also it is used as a source of pure acetic acid, but it here competes with the acid derived from distillation of wood, and success or failure depends upon the price of the alcohol.

The process of manufacture is that of "acetification," or oxidation of the alcohol by means of *Bacterium aceti* and allied organisms. The most suitable of these are used as pure cultures. Pure aqueous

[1] Tischtschenko, *Chem. Zentr.*, 1906, 2, 1309, 1552.

alcohol alone, however, does not suffice as a medium in which acetic fermentation can take place, since nitrogenous substances and salts are necessary for the growth of the organisms. Cane-sugar or glucose syrup (capillaire) is usually added, in the proportion of 1 to 3 kilos. per 100 litres of pure alcohol present in the "goods" or mash, to supply the carbon requirements of the acetic bacteria; while the nitrogenous needs are met with the requisite salts. Most of the modern spirit-vinegar factories use inorganic salts, chiefly acid phosphate of ammonium, sodium, and potassium, and also ammonium and magnesium sulphates. These salts are arranged so as to correct any deficiency of mineral matter in the water supply. About 50 to 150 grams are used per 100 litres of pure alcohol. Beer and malt extracts are also employed as nutrients instead of the salts and syrups.

The acetification vessels are generally of cylindrical form, from 1 to 2 metres in diameter, and 2 to 3 metres high. They usually contain beechwood shavings, resting on a perforated false bottom, and covered with a similar perforated disc. In the sides are holes for access of air, a supply of which is necessary for the oxidation.

The alcohol is diluted to a strength of 6 to 10 per cent., mixed with the requisite nutrient materials, and delivered on the top of the shavings by means of a rotating sparger. Where the latter is not provided, the liquid is simply poured upon the upper perforated plate, and led into the interior by means of short pieces of twine passing through the holes. When starting with a newly-packed vessel, the pure culture of the bacterium is mixed with the first charge of alcohol; subsequently some of the acetified product is used for mixing with the charges.

The diluted alcohol trickles downwards through the shavings, on which the ferment secures a lodgment, and is gradually oxidised as it passes down. The temperature of the acetifying room is kept at 20–25°; and that of the vessel, in which heat is developed by the action of the ferment, is maintained at 25–35° by controlling the admission of air and of the alcoholic charge. The resulting vinegar collects in the bottom of the vessel and passes out through a swan-neck tube. It should still contain a few tenths per cent. of alcohol, since if the latter is completely converted, the acetic bacteria are liable further to attack the acid itself and diminish the yield.

Ordinarily, the product obtained by this process contains from 4 to 6 per cent. of acetic acid; a much stronger acid is liable to weaken or destroy the acetic bacteria. "Double" or "triple" strength products can, however, be produced by mixing the ordinary vinegar with fresh alcohol and treatment in other vessels containing suitable organisms. Up to 12 per cent. of acid can thus be obtained in the liquid.

Spirit vinegar naturally contains more or less extractive matter, arising from the sugar and nitrogenous substances used as nutriments. The yield is about 80 per cent. of the theoretical; much loss occurs through escape of alcoholic and acid vapours, though in some of the factories apparatus is installed to recover these.

CHAPTER IX

ALCOHOL AS A SOURCE OF LIGHT, HEAT, AND MOTIVE POWER.

Alcohol as illuminant.—The use of alcohol for lighting purposes dates from the earlier part of the nineteenth century. Its non-luminous flame was rendered luminous by an admixture of terpenes or other hydrocarbons. Turpentine was chiefly employed for the purpose, but camphor, coal-tar naphtha, and shale oil were also used. The product was variously known as camphene or camphine, gasogene, "camphorated gas," and "burning fluid"; and previously to the introduction of petroleum for lighting purposes, about the year 1860, large quantities of alcohol were employed in making these illuminating mixtures.

The names "camphene" and "camphine" were also applied to rectified turpentine, which itself was used for burning. Turpentine oil alone, however, burns with a flame which, though luminous, is very smoky. When mixed with about four parts of alcohol, turpentine gives a flame which is still luminous, whilst the smokiness is much diminished. According to R. F. Herrick[1] such a mixture was introduced by Webb into the United States in the year **1833**, but the weakness of the only alcohol obtainable by him caused some difficulties with the product. Illuminants of like character were also being produced in Great Britain and France at about the same time, or a little earlier. A patent granted to Ludersdorf of Berlin in the year 1834 describes a mixture made with 95 per cent. alcohol, of which four volumes were used with one volume of rectified spirits of turpentine. The fluid was burned in a lamp provided with a wick, and the lamp was lighted by igniting a little alcohol placed in a cup surrounding the wick tube.

Later on, the invention of the Auer incandescent mantle for gas flames afforded another means of obtaining light from alcohol, thus

[1] "Industrial Alcohol," p. 207.

dispensing with the necessity of enriching the spirit with hydrocarbons. A number of lamps have been devised for the convenient application of this principle for use with ordinary denatured alcohol. The spirit is vaporised, and the vapour mixed with air as in the Bunsen burner is ignited under such conditions that the flame impinges upon a superimposed mantle, and raises it to incandescence. Lamps of this character suitable for household use, street lighting, and the illumination of large buildings have been manufactured on the Continent for many years. Questions of price apart, the advantages claimed for alcohol as against petroleum (kerosene) for lighting are that the alcohol lamp is practically odourless and smokeless, radiates less heat, and gives a whiter and more uniform light. In addition, alcohol is safer than kerosene, inasmuch as in case of fire the flame is more readily extinguished by water, which is miscible with alcohol but not with kerosene.

Alcohol as fuel.—In addition to its employment in ordinary spirit lamps, where it is burned directly by means of an ignited wick, alcohol is used as a source of heat in various appliances for warming, cooking, and other operations. These appliances include stoves for heating small rooms; ovens, boilers, and hot plates for cooking; blowpipes for soldering and brazing work; burners for laboratory use; and heaters for flat-irons, curling-tongs, and other domestic articles. In general the principle adopted for these forms of heating apparatus is that of the Bunsen burner; the alcohol is vaporised, and the vapour mixed with air is ignited. The blowpipes are fed with alcohol, or with a mixture of alcohol and a hydrocarbon oil ("carburetted" alcohol) under pressure applied by means of a small hand-pump. Freedom from smoke, soot, and ash is an advantage of these heating appliances compared with coal fires.

"Solidified" spirit.—This product, which is used for burning, is a mixture of soap and methylated alcohol, containing usually about 5 to 7 per cent. of soap. The latter is produced within the spirit by saponifying stearin with sodium carbonate or hydroxide, the mixture being heated. On cooling, the soap forms a bulky, soft solid which occludes the spirit.

One variety is made by melting 4·5 parts of stearin, adding 0·5 part of sodium carbonate and 95 parts of methylated spirit, and heating the mixture for an hour in a closed vessel.

An American recipe is as follows: Alcohol 1,000 c.c., stearic acid 60 grams, sodium hydroxide 13·5 grams. Dissolve the stearic acid in one-half of the alcohol, and the sodium hydroxide in the other half. Warm each solution to 60°. Mix them, and pour into suitable containers which have previously been warmed to 60°, and allow to solidify.

A patented " solidified alcohol burning without soot " is composed of ethyl alcohol 60 parts, methyl alcohol 40 parts, and sodium stearate 2–3 parts.[1]

Colouring matter such as methyl violet is sometimes added to these preparations.

Instead of soap, collodion may be used; the process is rather more costly, but the product has a better appearance. In general, these spirit-soaps and collodions are used mainly as domestic luxuries such as toilet lamps or travelling spirit-lamps; they are too expensive for employment as industrial combustible substances. The soap preparations, however, put up in small tins, have been found very convenient for use as little " cookers " by troops on active service.

According to a note in the *Chemical News*,[2] the discovery of " solidified spirit " was due to an attempt to hoodwink the Paris *octroi* officials. Some years ago an unscrupulous individual, in order to deceive the officers, conceived the idea of pounding up white grated soap in a mortar and mixing it with an equal weight of alcohol. He thus obtained a sort of homogeneous paste, which he moulded into cakes, and passed through the *octroi* without difficulty. The alcohol was then recovered by simple distillation on arriving at its destination. This device presently brought its author into the police court, but the process was taken up again in an honest manner, and was the origin of the present methods of preparing " solid " alcohol. It is one of the rare services which fraud has rendered to trade.

Alcohol as motive power.—As a source of power, alcohol has been applied in a manner similar to that in which petrol is used for the driving of motor engines. The vapour of the alcohol mixed with a due proportion of air is drawn into the cylinder of the engine. It is there compressed and ignited; explosive combustion follows; and the expansion of the resulting gases propels the piston. Absence of disagreeable odours, with lower volatility and therefore less danger of fire and smaller loss by evaporation, are important advantages claimed for alcohol as compared with petrol for motors. It has a higher flash-point (about 17° C. or 65° F.) than petrol, and more of its vapour is needed to form an explosive mixture with air, so that alcohol is the less dangerous. In hot countries, where there is likely to be much waste by evaporation, the advantage of lower volatility is specially noteworthy.

[1] U.S. P., 1277149. [2] 1913, **107**, 257.

A greater "efficiency," or ratio of work done to heat expended, is also claimed for alcohol. True, its calorific value is only about five-eighths of that of petrol. Nevertheless its efficiency per brake horse power is from 28 to 31 per cent. compared with from 16 to 22 per cent. for petrol. This higher efficiency largely compensates for the lower calorific value: the product of calorific value and efficiency is approximately the same for the two fuels.

The following remarks by Prof. Lewes are instructive in connection with the question of using alcohol as a motor fuel.[1]

If alcohol and petrol be compared, it is seen that the calorific value of the former is not much more than one-half that of the latter, so that from this point of view alcohol would appear to be out of the question as a competitor with petrol :—

	Calorific values.	
	Calories per kilo.	Brit. Therm. Units per lb.
Petrol, sp. gr. 0·684	11,624	20,923
Methylated spirit	6,200	11,160

In practice, however, the difference almost disappears. A test made with these fuels in two 8-h.p. engines, designed for their use, gave the consumption as follows :—

	Per h.p. hour.
Petrol	340 grams.
Methylated spirit	373·5 ,,

The efficiency obtained with the petrol was calculated from these results to be only 16·5 per cent., as against 28 per cent. with the alcohol.

There is incomplete combustion of the petrol owing to secondary reactions. According to Sorel, in many cases as much as 82 per cent. of the hydrogen and 42 per cent. of the carbon present in petrol is wasted from this cause. Theoretically, one volume of petrol vapour requires 45·5 volumes of air for combustion, as calculated from the equation :—

$$C_6H_{14} + 19O = 6CO_2 + 7H_2O$$

(where the petrol is taken as being equivalent to hexane, C_6H_{14}). In practice, however, the volume of air admitted is generally about 1½ times the theoretical proportion, and is thus about 68 volumes of air to one of petrol vapour. Four-fifths of the air is inert nitrogen, which tends to hinder the combustion.

With alcohol there is not the same difficulty in getting approximately complete combustion, since one volume of alcohol vapour

[1] V. B. Lewes, "Liquid and Gaseous Fuels," 302.

requires theoretically only 14·3 volumes of air—or roughly about one-third of the quantity needed by petrol. Moreover, double the amount of compression possible with petrol can be employed.

Summing up, we may say that the greater efficiency of alcohol is due to several factors. The volume of air required for complete combustion is only about one-third of that required by petrol, thus reducing the waste of heat in the exhaust. This smaller dilution with air ensures more perfect admixture before the explosion, and consequently favours complete combustion. The mixture can be subjected to a pressure of 200 lb. per square inch in the cylinder without spontaneous ignition, whereas the safety limit with petrol is 80 lb. Mixtures of alcohol vapour and air, containing any proportions between 4 and 13·6 per cent. of alcohol, are all explosive, whereas the explosive range with petrol and air is only from 2 to 5 per cent., thus requiring more exact adjustment of petrol and air in the cylinder.

The exhaust from the alcohol engine is smokeless and nearly odourless, and the products of combustion do not clog the cylinder valves.

On the other hand, should the combustion be imperfect, acetic acid and other corrosive products are liable to be formed from the alcohol. These, when they condense to the liquid form on cooling, are prone to attack the metal surfaces with which they come in contact, causing deterioration of the engine. More important still, the lower volatility of alcohol has the disadvantage that it makes the engine more difficult to start, especially in cold weather. Unless the vapour tension of the fuel in the cylinder is above a certain limit, it is not possible to obtain an explosive mixture. With petrol, there is no difficulty in securing this. Using a light petrol, it has been found that an explosive mixture can be obtained at 0° and at a pressure of 40 lb. per square inch, whereas air saturated with alcohol vapour at all temperatures below 20° is incombustible even at atmospheric pressure.[1]

Nevertheless, the advantages of alcohol remain, and it is possible to remove the disadvantages. One method is to use a more volatile fuel, *e.g.*, petrol or benzol, as starter ; and when this is done, it is found that running a few revolutions with the petrol or benzol before stopping the engine will also overcome the trouble of corrosion, as acid vapours are thus swept out before they condense and attack the metal. Another method is to mix a proportion of more volatile liquid with the alcohol itself. Thus one proposed fuel (" natalite ") is stated to contain about 40 per cent. of ether, together with a

[1] Watson and others, *J. Soc. Chem. Ind.*, 1916, **34**, 266.

trace of ammonia to neutralise any tendency to acidity that may develop during the combustion. In trials of this mixed fuel the engine is described as starting easily either "from cold" or when warm, and the fuel consumption was almost identical with that of petrol. The only alteration of the engine found necessary was a slight reduction of the supply of air to the carburettor, and there was no tendency to corrosion. Other mixtures, with petrol, benzol, acetone, etc., are described later on.

A good deal of experimentation with alcohol motors for agricultural work, creameries, pumping plants, and so on, and also for locomotive purposes, has been carried out both in this country and on the Continent, but especially in Germany. In the United States an extensive investigation has been made into the question of the comparative value of alcohol as a fuel, numerous experiments on gasoline (petrol) engines and alcohol engines having been undertaken.[1] The general conclusions arrived at in these trials were :—

(1). That any petrol engine of the ordinary type can be run on alcohol without any material alteration in the construction of the engine.

(2). The chief difficulties likely to be met with are in the starting and in supplying a sufficient quantity of fuel.

(3). The maximum power is usually greater with alcohol, and the engines are more noiseless than with petrol.

(4). The fuel consumption per brake horse power with a good small stationary engine may be expected to be 1 lb. or a little more with alcohol, and 0·7 lb. with petrol (0·12 gallon and 0·10 gallon respectively).

In these United States experiments the engines were working under the best conditions, and very high efficiencies were obtained, both with alcohol engines and petrol engines, namely, 39 per cent. with the former fuel and 26 per cent. with the latter.

A special committee appointed to examine this question for the Australian Commonwealth Advisory Council on Science and Industry reports as follows.[2]

"When alcohol is used in an ordinary petrol engine the consumption of fuel per b.h.p. is about 50 per cent. greater than in the case of petrol. It appears, however, that the consumption of alcohol per b.h.p. in a specially designed alcohol engine will not exceed in volume the consumption of petrol in a petrol engine.

"The main alterations necessary in the ordinary design of petrol engines in order to fit them to work efficiently on alcohol are as

[1] *Bulletin No.* 392, U.S. Geol. Survey, 1909.

[2] Report of Executive Committee, C. 7963, 1917.

follow, *viz.*: (*a*). An increased compression from about 75 lb. per square inch, which is the average for petrol engines, to about 180 lb. per square inch, both above atmospheric pressure; (*b*) a pre-heating of either the fuel or the air or of the mixture of fuel and air; and (*c*) an increase in the area of the fuel jets and fuel supply pipes.

"Though an alcohol engine designed in the above manner will run efficiently, it cannot generally be started from cold with alcohol. In order to overcome this difficulty some special means must be provided. For example, either the carburettor must be preheated by a torch or in some other way, or an arrangement must be provided whereby a small amount of petrol can be used at the start. When a temperature sufficient to vaporise the fuel is attained, the alcohol can be gradually turned into the carburettor and the preheating of the fuel maintained by the exhaust gases."

The following is a more detailed summary of the conclusions arrived at in the American experiments already referred to.

"ABSTRACT OF U.S.A. GEOLOGICAL SURVEY BULLETIN NO. 392, 'COMMERCIAL DEDUCTIONS FROM COMPARISON OF GASOLINE AND ALCOHOL TESTS ON INTERNAL COMBUSTION ENGINES.'

"*By R. M. Strong. Washington, Government Printing Office*, 1909.

"1. *Introduction.*—The Bulletin furnishes a summary of the commercial results of 2,000 tests conducted by the U.S.A. Geological Survey at St. Louis and Norfolk in 1907 and 1908. The tests dealt primarily with gasoline and formed part of the investigation into mineral fuels. To determine the relative economy and efficiency of gasoline it was compared with denatured alcohol.

"2. *Differences in Engines.*—The only change required for the use of alcohol in a gasoline engine, if any, is in the size of the fuel passage-ways. With this change alone the consumption of alcohol will be from 1½ to 2 times as much as the consumption of gasoline for the same power.

"(i) *Special Engines for Alcohol.*—By using alcohol in an alcohol engine with a high degree of compression (about 180 lb. per square inch above atmospheric pressure) the fuel consumption rate can be reduced to practically the same as the rate of consumption of gasoline for a gasoline engine of the same size and speed.

"When alcohol is used in a gasoline engine with the maximum degree of compression for gasoline, the available h.p. of the engine is increased about 10 per cent. An alcohol engine with the maximum degree of compression for alcohol will have an available h.p. 30 per cent. greater than a gasoline engine of the same cylinder size, stroke, and speed.

"(ii) *Alteration of Gasoline Engines.*—Some gasoline engines may be so changed that a sufficiently high compression is secured to make it possible to reduce the consumption of alcohol in gallons per h.p. per hour to an equality with that for gasoline before the engine was changed. The degree of compression may be most easily changed by lengthening the connecting rod. This may often be done by putting lines between the crank pin end of the connecting rod and the crank brasses. But if the cylinder is counterbored, or if there is not sufficient room at the head of the cylinder, a new cylinder should be cast with small clearance space.

"3. *Most Economical Degree of Compression.*—A gasoline engine having a compression pressure of 70 lb., but otherwise as well suited to the economical use of denatured alcohol as gasoline, will, when using alcohol, have an available h.p. about 10 per cent. greater than when using gasoline.

"When the fuels for which they are designed are used to an equal advantage, the maximum available h.p. of an alcohol engine having a compression pressure of 180 lb. is about 30 per cent. greater than that of a gasoline engine having a compression pressure of 70 lb., but of the same size in respect to cylinder diameter, stroke, and speed.

"When denatured alcohol is used in 10 to 15 h.p. four-cycle stationary engines having a compression pressure of approximately 180 lb., and the engines are operated at their maximum loads, the pressures during explosion or combustion reach 600 to 700 lb. Stationary gasoline engines, in which the compression pressure in some cases can be raised to 180 lb., are not usually built heavy enough to withstand such explosion pressures for any length of time.

"4. *Consumption of Fuel.*—A gasoline engine having the degree of compression ordinarily used for gasoline mixtures will in general require 50 per cent. more denatured alcohol than gasoline per b.h.p.

"Gasoline and alcohol engines of similar construction having degrees of compression best suited to the fuel supplied will in general require equal volumes of gasoline and denatured alcohol respectively per b.h.p.

"When any of the usual methods of governing are used to control the speed of gasoline or alcohol engines, the rate of fuel consumption per b.h.p. per hour will ordinarily be about twice as great at one-third load as at maximum load. At the same time, an excessive rate of consumption of gasoline or denatured alcohol at any given load, if due to the incorrect adjustment of the mixture quality and time of ignition only, may be as great as, but not greater than approximately twice the minimum required before it will be noticeable from outward indications.

"5. *Thermal Efficiency of Engines.*—The thermal efficiency of alcohol and gasoline engines will in general increase with the pressure to which the charge is compressed when ignited.

"The maximum thermal efficiency of 10 to 15 h.p. four-cycle stationary engines of the usual type when operated with a minimum amount of throttling was found to increase with the compression pressure according to the formulæ $E = 1 - \left(\frac{14 \cdot 7}{P}\right)^{\cdot 17}$ for gasoline and $E = 1 - \left(\frac{14 \cdot 7}{P}\right)^{\cdot 19}$ for alcohol, where E = the thermal efficiency based on the indicated h.p. and low heating value of the fuel and P = the indicated pressure of the charge at the end of the compression stroke in lb. per square inch absolute.

"A high thermal efficiency and a rate of consumption of less than a pint per b.h.p. per hour, both for gasoline and for denatured alcohol, can often be obtained when the degree of compression, the load, the quality of the explosive mixture, and the time of ignition are carefully adjusted. A fair representation of the best economy values obtained, taken from the results of tests on 10 to 15 h.p. Nash and Otto stationary engines, and the corresponding thermal efficiencies, are given in the following table:—

"RESULTS FROM TESTS MADE ON 10 TO 15 H.P. NASH AND OTTO STATIONARY ENGINES.

Fuel.	Compression pressure (lb.).[1]	Fuel consumed per b.h.p. per hour.		Thermal efficiency (per cent.).[2]
		Lb.	Gallon.	
Gasoline . .	70	0·60	0·100	26
	90	0·58	0·097	28
Alcohol . . .	70	0·96	0·140	28
	180	0·71	0·104	39
	200	0·68	0·099	40"

[1] Per square inch above atmosphere.
[2] Based on the i.h.p. and the lower heating value of the fuel.

It must be borne in mind that by far the larger proportion of the work that has been done on internal combustion engines has been carried out with the object of perfecting them for use with petrol. It may well be that when a similar amount of research has been directed to the use of alcohol, this liquid will be found even more suitable than petrol as a motor fuel.

Possibly the question already is less one of suitability than of price. To be the more economical fuel, alcohol must be at a lower price per unit of volume than petrol. Benzol, also, which at the time of writing is being produced in large quantity for war requirements, may prove to be a serious competitor when no longer needed for munitions of war.

Whilst it is true that most of the work on internal combustion engines has been done with reference to petrol, yet, as already stated, a good deal of experimentation with alcohol-motors for agricultural work, and also for locomotive purposes, has been carried out on the Continent. This has been the case more especially in Germany, where the industry has been carefully fostered. The practicability of alcohol motors has been proved, and a good number of such engines of French and German make are in use for driving light machinery, pumping, threshing, and similar work. Alcohol-driven engines made in England have been employed for several years in Egypt and parts of South America. How far the use of such engines will be extended depends upon the relative working costs, upon questions of supply and distribution, and on the facilities obtainable in particular circumstances. For example, in a country which must import its petrol, but can produce its own alcohol, considerations of expediency might lead to preferential fiscal treatment of alcohol used for motors, in order to diminish the country's dependence upon foreign supplies of motor fuel, and also incidentally to foster its agricultural industry through the increased demand for grain, potatoes, or beet required to produce the alcohol.

In fact, though the day is not yet at hand, through the dim but perhaps not very distant future there looms the probability that when the stores of coal and petroleum at present "in sight" begin to get depleted—as some are even now—the world's industrial needs will have more and more to be met by utilising the sun's present energy through the instrumentality of alcohol employed as a source of heat and motive power, as well as his past energy stored in the form of coal and petroleum.

In this connection it may be noted that some years ago a United States official estimate indicated that the older oil-fields would probably become exhausted in about thirty-five years if the rate of increased production observed at that time were maintained. Of course any estimate of future supplies may be affected by the discovery of new oil-fields, or of new methods for utilising shale oils such as those of the Kimmeridge deposits in this country, which are at present unmarketable on account of their sulphur content; but the eventual exhaustion is only a matter of time. Meanwhile, industrial demands for liquid fuel become greater and greater. About 120 million gallons of petrol were imported into the United Kingdom in the year 1914–15, the quantity having more than doubled in four years.

Alcohol and agriculture.—Hence the question of the use of alcohol as fuel is becoming a very important one, and will be more so in the future. From the agricultural point of view, it has been urged that the alcohol equivalent to this petrol as fuel could be obtained from potatoes or sugar-beet grown in this country, with much benefit to agriculture and to the country at large. It has been estimated that alcohol equivalent to the 120 million gallons of petrol above-mentioned would be produced from about 5 million tons of potatoes, or from 4 million tons if the alcohol were "carburetted" with 20 per cent. of benzol. The average crop of potatoes is at present about 5½ tons per acre, but under the best conditions this yield could be more than doubled, with a decreasing cost of production. An average of 12 tons per acre on 600,000 acres would provide the crop necessary for food on the present basis, and the petrol substitute as well. It is urged by some agriculturists that a system could be established here similar to that existing in Germany, whereby a central distillery serves a number of farms in a certain area working on a co-operative basis, each farm devoting a guaranteed minimum acreage to potato-cultivation for supplying the distillery. In short, the organisation would be much on the same lines as with co-operative creameries. In such circumstances, the cost of carriage of the potatoes would be saved; the residual products would be returned to the farm as feeding-stuffs and fertilisers; the production of alcohol would provide a simple method of using an excessive crop of food potatoes; and the farmer would be provided with a cheap fuel for his agricultural machinery. And more than all, the country would not be dependent upon foreign supplies for its liquid fuel.

Obviously such a system as that outlined would mean a considerable modification of present revenue methods of distillery supervision.

Whether we should have the requisite amount of suitable land available for such a purpose, after providing for the great increase in food production now contemplated, is another question. The problem of cost in competition with imported materials such as maize and molasses is a further matter for consideration. Yet another is whether, unless a protective import duty is retained, the home-produced alcohol could always compete in price with possible foreign supplies. Predictions have been made that the tropical countries, when their potential resources are developed, will secure a practical monopoly of the alcohol industry, since they possess three of the cheapest sources of alcohol, namely, sugar-cane molasses, palm sap, and starch plants such as cassava and arrowroot.

"Carburetted" alcohol.—For fuel and motor purposes it is often found advantageous to mix a hydrocarbon liquid with the ordinary denatured alcohol. Petrol, benzene (benzol), and petroleum have usually been employed, the mixture being termed "carburetted" alcohol. The proportions vary. In some of the German experiments above referred to it was found that, comparing the efficiency of alcohol alone with that of alcohol carburetted with different proportions of benzol, the best results in motor power were given by the mixture containing 20 per cent. by weight of benzol. Trials of motors in Paris with French methylated spirit (which contains 10 per cent. of crude methyl alcohol) and the same spirit carburetted with 50 per cent. of a hydrocarbon fuel, showed the carburetted spirit to be superior to the other in the ratio of about 10 to 7, as judged by the consumption.

A number of comparative experiments on the use of carburetted alcohol have also been made in this country. The following may be quoted.[1]

A four-cylinder Maudslay engine running at 1,000 revolutions per minute was tested with different fuels, with the results given below. Petrol of sp. gr. 0·710 was taken as the standard, the results with the other fuels being compared with those given by the petrol reckoned as 100 :—

Fuel used.	Power obtained.	Volume of fuel used.
1. Petrol	100	100
2. Benzol	98·2	84·5
3. Methylated spirit 50 per cent., benzol 50 per cent.	99	96·3
4. " " 67 " " 33 "	92	108·9
5. " " 75 " " 25 "	91·5	124·5

Comparing experiments 3, 4, and 5 with one another, it is seen that the mixture of equal parts methylated spirit and benzol gives the best result, so far as this investigation goes. The sp. gr. of the

[1] W. R. Ormandy, *J. Gas Lighting*, 1913, **124**, 580.

methylated spirit used was 0·815, and of the benzol (two qualities) 0·885 and 0·875.

During the last few years a number of alcoholic mixtures have been recommended on the Continent as suitable for use instead of petrol. In addition to benzol and petrol, some other substances have been suggested for mixing with the alcohol, namely, acetone, naphthalene, ether, acetylene, and even a small quantity of ammonium perchlorate. Some typical mixtures are the following :—

(1). Alcohol (95 per cent.) 70 ; benzol 30.
(2). ,, (90 ,,) 50 ; ,, 30 ; acetone 20.
(3). ,, (90 ,,) 50 ; benzine 30 ; ,, 20.
(4). ,, (95 ,,) 80 ; benzol 20 ; the benzol containing naphthalene in the proportion of 200 grams per litre.

With most or all of these mixtures a preliminary heating of the carburettor is required, and a reduction of the supply of air, as compared with that necessary for petrol.[1]

Discussing this question of alcohol-substitutes for petrol, O. Mohr[2] remarks that only the simpler mixtures have proved successful. Equal parts of alcohol and benzol, or alcohol 50, benzol 25, and petrol 25, have given good results ; and the second mixture has the advantage of not giving deposits in very cold weather. Naphthalene has proved unsuitable owing to the formation of deposits.

An account of some comparative experiments with different motor fuels recently carried out abroad is given by Donath and Gröger.[3] The following results are stated to have been obtained per litre of fuel :—

Fuel used.	Distance, per litre. Kilometres.
Petrol, unmixed	5·8
Benzol, ,,	7·1
,, 1 part, alcohol 1 part	7·5
,, ,, ,, 2 parts	7·2
,, ,, ,, 3 ,,	7·0
,, ,, ,, 4 ,,	6·6
,, ,, ,, 5 ,,	6·0
Alcohol, unmixed	5·4

A mixture known as "E. H. A." in France includes ether, like the "natalite" already mentioned. The proportion of ether, however, is only about 10 per cent., instead of 40 ; and benzol or an alternative to the extent of 25 per cent. is included.

The following thermal and other particulars of the methylated

[1] K. Dietrich, *Zeitsch. angew. Chem.*, 1914, **27**, 543.
[2] *Ibid.*, 558.
[3] "*Die Treibmittel der Kraftfahrzeuge*" (Berlin, 1917).

spirit used in this country for burning are given by J. S. S. Brame.[1]

Specific gravity	0·820.
Percentage composition	C 50·7 ; H 13·0 ; O 36·3.
Coefficient of expansion per degree C ..	0·00110.
,, ,, ,, F ..	0·00062.
Calorific value, Brit. Thermal Units :—	
Per lb., gross value	11,320.
,, net ,, ...	10,350.
Air required for combustion, theoretical quantity :—	
Per gallon	930 cu. ft. at 60° F.
Calorific value of 1 cu. ft. of the theoretical mixture	97·5.
Explosive range (per cent. of vapour by vol. in the mixture)	4·0 to 13·6.
Compression limit, in lb.	About 200.

Calorific value.—It is a well-established fact that when the same weight of the same substance burns to form the same products of combustion, the quantity of heat evolved is a constant, the value of which is independent of the rate of combustion. This quantity is known as the heat of chemical combination of the substance with oxygen. In relation to substances used as fuels, it is also known as the "calorific value." Thus 1 gram of carbon burning to carbon dioxide evolves 8,080 gram-calories of heat, and 1 gram of hydrogen burning to liquid water evolves 34,462 gram-calories (Favre and Silbermann). The calorific value of carbon is therefore said to be 8,080, and of hydrogen 34,462. The gram-calorie is defined as the quantity of heat required to raise the temperature of 1 gram of water by one degree Centigrade.

When alcohol is completely burned in air or oxygen, the products of combustion are water and carbon dioxide. The heat evolved, *i.e.*, the calorific value, can be calculated theoretically from the data just given, as shown below.

The percentage composition in ethyl alcohol is : Carbon 52·13, hydrogen 13·12, and oxygen 34·75. Hence 1 gram of ethyl alcohol contains :—

Carbon	0·5213 gram.
Hydrogen	0·1312 ,,
Oxygen	0·3475 ,,

Deducting from the amount of hydrogen the quantity necessary to form water with the oxygen, *i.e.*, $\frac{0·3475}{8} = 0·0434$ gram, we have

$0·1312 - 0·0434 = 0·0878.$

Multiplying by the corresponding calorific values for the carbon and hydrogen and adding the products, we have :—

[1] "Fuel," p. 158 (1914 edition).

Carbon	0·5213 × 8,080	= 4,212·1 calories.
Hydrogen	0·0878 × 34,462	= 3,025·7 ,,
∴ Calorific value of ethyl alcohol		= 7,237·8 ,,

The calculation here shown at length may be summarised into the formula :—

$$\text{Calorific value} = 80{\cdot}8\ C + 344{\cdot}6\ (H - \frac{O}{8}),$$

where C, H, and O denote the *percentages* of carbon, hydrogen, and oxygen respectively.

A somewhat higher result is given if the values for carbon and hydrogen used in Berthelot's formula are taken—namely, 8,137 and 34,500, instead of those employed in the calculation shown. On the other hand, in summary calculations the round numbers 8,000 and 34,000 are often used.

In practice, of course, absolute alcohol is not employed as fuel; but the calculation shows the principle most simply, and the result is required in obtaining the theoretical calorific value of denatured alcohol, and of other alcohol mixtures, which are used as fuels.

In a similar manner, the theoretical calorific value of absolute methyl alcohol, the percentage composition of which is C 37·47, H 12·58, and O 49·95, is found to be 5,212·5. Acetone, C_3H_6O, has the calculated value 7,486·5: and benzene, C_6H_6, the value 10,111·4. Petrol is a variable mixture of hydrocarbons, but if taken as being substantially equivalent to octane, C_8H_{18}, its theoretical calorific value is 12,245 calories per gram.

"Gross" and "net" values.—The values here given are the "higher" or "gross" calorific values, corresponding with the formation of *liquid* water, as obtained in the calorimeter. If the water is *vaporised*, this operation absorbs some of the heat developed by the combustion. The quantity of water produced is governed by the amount of hydrogen burned. Thus in the case of ethyl alcohol the weight of hydrogen in 1 gram is 0·1312 gram, and this is equivalent to 1·1808 grams of water. Since the latent heat of vaporisation of water is 537 calories per gram, the heat absorbed in vaporising this water is 1·1808 × 537 = 634·1 calories. This quantity, therefore, is to be deducted from the result obtained above for ethyl alcohol, whenever the "lower" or "net" value is required: 7,237·8 — 634·1 = 6,603·7, the lower theoretical calorific value of absolute ethyl alcohol.

Further, if the alcohol in question is not absolute, but already contains water (as is always the case in practice), the vaporisation of this water will also absorb heat, and the corresponding number of calories must be deducted. Thus if the proportion of water be 10 per cent. by weight, 1 gram of the alcohol will contain 0·1 gram of water, and the further deduction will therefore be $0·1 \times 537 = 53·7$ calories.

Hence, finally, for 90 per cent. alcohol (by weight), when all the water already present and that produced in the combustion is vaporised, the calorific value is $6,603·7 - 53·7 = 6,550·0$ gram-calories.

Thermal units.—To express the foregoing results in terms of British thermal units (B.Th.U.) they are multiplied by 1·8. Thus for ethyl alcohol :—7,237·8 gram-calories $\times$ 1·8 = 13,028 B.Th.U.

The factor 1·8 is $= \frac{9}{5}$, the ratio of the Centigrade to the Fahrenheit degree of temperature. The British heat unit is defined as the quantity of heat required to raise the temperature of 1 lb. of water by 1° F. (from 60° F. to 61° F.). In absolute values one British heat unit = 252 gram-calories ; but for conversion purposes we need consider only the relative temperature values, since the pound, or the gram, is taken as the unit of weight for both fuel burned and water heated, and the question is only one of a smaller unit of temperature in the British system—$1°\ C. = \frac{9}{5}°\ F. = 1·8°\ F.$

The metric unit of heat adopted for technical purposes is the "large Calorie" or "K.C.U." This is the quantity of heat required to raise 1 kilogram of water through 1° in the neighbourhood of 15°. One B.Th.U.= 0·252 large Calorie, and for the reason given in the preceding paragraph, x large Calories = 1·8 x B.Th.U.

Calorific value of methylated spirit.—The alcohol used for burning purposes in the United Kingdom is mineralised methylated spirit, which, at a strength of 62° over proof,[1] may be taken as containing on an average :—

	Per cent. by volume.
Ethyl alcohol	83·1
Methyl ,,	7·7
Acetone, esters, etc.	1·2
Mineral naphtha	0·4

Without sensible error the last two items may be grouped together as acetone, 1·6 per cent., for calculating the calorific value. Expressed as percentages by *weight*, the composition of mineralised methylated spirit is then :—

[1] Somewhat stronger spirit is obtainable, up to 64° or 65° over proof (sp. gr. 0·8214 to 0·8193).

	Per cent. by weight.	In 1 gram.
Ethyl alcohol	79·9	0·799
Methyl ,, ...	7·4	0·074
Acetone, etc.	1·5	0·015
Water	11·2	0·112
	100·0	1·000

Multiplying by the corresponding higher calorific values as already given, we have :—

0·799 × 7,237·8 = 5,783·2 calories.
0·074 × 5,212·5 = 385·7 ,,
0·015 × 7,486·5 = 112·3 ,,
∴ the higher calorific value of mineralised methylated spirit = 6,281·2 ,,

This is equal to 11,306 British heat units (B.Th.U.).

To find the lower or "net" calorific value, we calculate the lower values, as already explained, for absolute ethyl and methyl alcohols and acetone : the results are 6,603·7, 4,563·7, and 6,983·0, respectively. Then :—

0·799 × 6,603·7 = 5,276·4
0·074 × 4,563·7 = 337·7
0·015 × 6,983·0 = 104·7

5,718·8

Deduct for the water present 0·112 × 537 = 60·1

∴ Lower value = 5,658·7 gram-calories, or 10,185 British thermal units

Calorific value of carburetted alcohol.—By way of example we may take a mixture of mineralised methylated spirit and benzene—containing, say, 20 per cent. of the latter, by weight. Then 1 gram of the mixture contains 0·8 gram of the mineralised methylated spirit and 0·2 gram of benzene. Taking the higher calorific values already given for the constituents, we have :—

0·8 × 6,281·2 = 5,025·0
0·2 × 10,111·4 = 2,022·3

∴ Calorific value of the mixture = 7,047·3 gram-calories.

This is the "higher" or gross value, taking the benzene as pure benzene. In practice, commercial "benzol" would be used, containing more or less toluene, xylene, etc., and giving a somewhat greater calorific value than pure benzene. The "lower" calorific value of the mixture, calculated on the principles already explained, will be found to be 6,474·8 gram-calories = 11,654·6 B.Th.U.

In general, it is better to have calorific values as determined by careful experiment rather than the calculated theoretical values, as the latter involve certain assumptions which may affect the results to some extent. The experimental values obtained for alcohol and methylated spirit by various observers show some differences, as might be expected, since the determination presents several difficulties. Lewes gives the following :—

	Calories.	B.Th.U.
Absolute alcohol	7,184	12,931
Alcohol, 90 per cent...	6,400	11,520
,, methylated	6,200	11,160

Brame gives the following as mean values from all the trustworthy determinations available. The net values have been calculated from the gross values on the assumption that in the latter the water formed was condensed to a final temperature of 15·5°.

CALORIFIC VALUES, EXPERIMENTAL.

Fuel.	Specific gravity.	British thermal units.			
		Per pound.		Per gallon.	
		Gross.	Net.	Gross.	Net.
Methyl alcohol	0·810	9,570	8,320	77,500	67,450
Ethyl alcohol	0·7946	12,790	11,480	101,000	91,100
Methylated spirit	0·820	11,320	10,350	92,820	84,900

LIMITS OF INFLAMMABILITY (THORNTON).*

	Percentage of vapour in air.	
	Upper limit.	Lower limit.
Methyl alcohol .. .	21·0	5·5
Ethyl ,, .. .	9·5	2·8
Benzene, C_6H_6 .. .	8·0	1·5
Pentane, C_5H_{12} .. .	4·5	1·35
Acetylene, C_2H_2 .. .	46·0	3·0

* *Phil. Mag.*, 1917, **33**, 190–196.

CHAPTER X

THE HIGHER HOMOLOGUES OF ETHYL ALCOHOL (PROPYL, BUTYL, AND AMYL ALCOHOLS): FUSEL OIL

Propyl alcohols (*propanols*), $C_3H_7{\cdot}OH$. Mol. wt. 60·06.

As already explained (p. 115), two isomeric propyl alcohols are possible, and are known.

(1) **Normal propyl alcohol,** $CH_3{\cdot}CH_2{\cdot}CH_2{\cdot}OH$.—Chancel[1] in 1853 showed that the normal alcohol was contained in fusel oil, and it is now obtained from this source by fractional distillation. Linnemann[2] first produced it synthetically, by reducing propionic anhydride, obtained by synthesis from ethyl alcohol.

It is a colourless liquid with an agreeable spirituous odour. Its sp. gr. is 0·8044 at 20°/4°, or 0·80765 at 15·6°/15·6°. It boils at 97·4°. Propyl alcohol is miscible with water in all proportions, but is distinguishable from ethyl alcohol by its insolubility in a cold saturated solution of calcium chloride. It forms with water a mixture of constant boiling point, 87·72°, the mixture containing 71·69 per cent. of the alcohol by weight.[3]

(2) **Isopropyl alcohol,** $CH_3{\cdot}CH(OH){\cdot}CH_3$ (Secondary propyl alcohol, dimethyl carbinol).—This alcohol does not appear to occur in fusel oil, or not in appreciable quantity. It was first obtained by Berthelot in 1855 from propylene and sulphuric acid, and somewhat later (1862) Friedel prepared it from acetone by the action of sodium amalgam and water. A modern method of using acetone for the purpose is to pass a mixture of acetone vapour and hydrogen over catalytic nickel heated to 115—125°. Chemically, the alcohol is best prepared from isopropyl iodide, itself obtained by distilling glycerine with hydriodic acid and amorphous phosphorus. These give first allyl iodide :—

$$C_3H_5(OH)_3 + 3HI = C_3H_5I + 3H_2O + I_2.$$

[1] *Compt. rend.*, 1853, **37**, 410. [2] *Ann. Chem. Pharm.*, 1868, **148**, 251.
[3] Young and Fortey, *Trans. Chem. Soc.*, 1902, **81**, 735.

With excess of hydriodic acid, this passes into isopropyl iodide :—

$$C_3H_5I + 2HI = C_3H_7I + I_2.$$

On boiling the isopropyl iodide under a reflux condenser with 10 parts of water and some freshly-prepared lead hydroxide, the isopropyl alcohol is produced, and may be distilled off and concentrated by dehydration and re-distillation. It is a colourless, mobile liquid with a spirituous odour, having the sp. gr. 0·7897 at 15·6°/15·6° (0·7887 at 20°/4°), and boiling at 82·7°. According to Erlenmeyer, it forms a hydrate, $2C_3H_8O,H_2O$, which boils constantly at 80° and has the same percentage composition as ethyl alcohol. Young and Fortey (*loc. cit.*) give the boiling point of the constant-boiling mixture as 80·37°, the percentage of alcohol being 87·90, by weight.

Isopropyl alcohol in a mixture may be determined quantitatively by oxidising it to acetone with potassium bichromate and sulphuric acid. The acetone is distilled off after neutralising the mixture, and estimated by Messinger's method, as described under "wood naphtha."

Butyl alcohols, $C_4H_9{\cdot}OH$. Mol. wt., 74·08.

Four isomers are theoretically possible, two of which are primary, one secondary, and one tertiary (see p. 115).

(1) **Normal butyl alcohol** (*n*-Propyl carbinol; 1-butanol),

$$CH_3(CH_2)_2{\cdot}CH_2{\cdot}OH,$$

has been found in the fusel oil of brandy, and is formed by the fermentation of glycerol with certain bacteria. Together with acetone, it is also formed in the fermentation of starch solutions with special cultures of micro-organisms (Fernbach's process); but is not produced in the fermentation of sugar brought about by elliptical yeast.[1] It may be obtained by adding sodium amalgam gradually to an aqueous solution of normal butyl aldehyde, kept slightly acid with dilute sulphuric acid. The alcohol is then distilled off, and concentrated as usual. Butyric acid and butyryl chloride also yield the alcohol on reduction with sodium amalgam. It is a colourless, highly refracting liquid, with a peculiar irritating odour. At 0° it has the sp. gr. 0·8233, or 0·8099 at 20°/4°. It boils at 117·2° (Brühl)[2] or at 116·8° (Richter).

Butyl alcohol burns with a luminous flame. It is soluble in 12 parts of water at 22°, and is separated from its aqueous solutions by addition of calcium chloride. Its index of refraction $\mu_a = 1{\cdot}39909$.

[1] Claudon and Morin, *J. Chem. Soc.*, 1887, **52**, 714.
[2] *Annalen*, 1880, **203**, 16.

Sabatier and Gaudion have recently shown that normal butyl alcohol can be obtained from paraldehyde, which itself may be produced synthetically from calcium carbide. (See Chap. II.) The aldehyde is "crotonised" by passing it over thorium, titanium, or uranium oxide at about 360°. On separating the product into two fractions, (1) of b. p. 90—130°, and (2) of b. p. 130—220°, and passing these separately with hydrogen over hot reduced nickel, the first fraction yields normal butyl alcohol, and the second normal hexyl alcohol. The nickel catalyst is heated to 170—180° for the first fraction, and to about 200° for the second.[1]

(2) **Secondary butyl alcohol** (Methyl-ethyl carbinol; 2-butanol), $CH_3(C_2H_5)\cdot CH\cdot OH$.—This alcohol may be obtained by the action of anhydrous aldehyde on zinc ethyl, as explained in the general methods for preparing secondary alcohols (p. 120). Alternatively, normal butyl alcohol may be taken as the starting point, and converted into the secondary alcohol by the general method described in Chapter III; namely, by first forming butylene, adding hydrogen iodide to this to give the iodide, and then hydrolysing the latter. According to Roscoe and Schorlemmer,[2] the alcohol was first obtained by De Luynes, who prepared the iodide by heating the sugar erythritol with hydriodic acid, afterwards converting the iodide into the corresponding acetic ester by the action of silver acetate, and hydrolysing the ester with caustic potash to liberate the alcohol.

Secondary butyl alcohol is a liquid boiling at 99° under 738·8 mm. pressure, and having the sp. gr. 0·827 at 0°, or 0·810 at 22°. It has a burning taste and a strong odour. Oxidising agents convert it into methyl ethyl ketone, and eventually into acetic acid.

(3) **Isobutyl alcohol** (Isopropyl carbinol, methyl 2-propanol-1), $(CH_3)_2CH\cdot CH_2\cdot OH$.—This is found in fusel oil, especially in that from potato-spirit, and is separated by fractional distillation. It may be obtained pure by first preparing the iodide from the separated alcohol, since the iodide can be more readily purified by distillation than can the alcohol itself. The iodide is then re-converted into the alcohol by the methods already described. Alternatively, isobutyric aldehyde may be reduced with sodium amalgam to give the alcohol.

Isobutyl alcohol boils at 108·4°, and has the sp. gr. 0·8020 at 20°/4°, or 0·80624 at 15·6°/15·6°. It is a colourless liquid with an odour of fusel oil, soluble in 10·5 parts of water, and mostly

[1] *Compt. rend.*, 1918, **166**, 632.

[2] "Treatise on Chemistry," III, 1881, 581.

thrown out of solution again by addition of calcium chloride or common salt. Its index of refraction $\mu_\beta = 1\cdot4007$. Its azeotropic mixture with water boils at 89·92°, and contains 66·80 per cent. of the alcohol by weight. (Young and Fortey, *loc. cit.*)

(4) **Tertiary butyl alcohol** (Trimethyl carbinol; dimethyl ethanol), $(CH_3)_3C{\cdot}OH$.—Butlerow[1] first prepared this alcohol, using the reaction between zinc methyl and carbonyl or acetyl chloride described in Chapter III. A simpler method, also due to Butlerow, is to take isobutyl alcohol as the starting point, and obtain isobutylene from it by conversion into the iodide and heating the latter with alcoholic potash; the isobutylene is absorbed by 75 per cent. sulphuric acid, and the ester thus produced is diluted with water and distilled, when it decomposes into the alcohol and sulphuric acid. According to Dobbin,[2] the alcohol can also be obtained by letting 2 parts of tertiary butyl iodide remain for two or three days in contact with 5 parts of water, the mixture being shaken occasionally.

Tertiary butyl alcohol forms a deliquescent, crystalline mass, which melts at 25·5° when anhydrous, and boils at 82·5° (81·5° to 82°, Perkin[3]). Its sp. gr. at 30° is 0·7788, and its index of refraction μ_β is 1·3924. The odour of the alcohol is described as spirituous and camphor-like. A liquid hydrate, $2C_4H_{10}O + H_2O$, boils at 80°. Young and Fortey (*loc. cit.*) found that the azeotropic mixture boiled at 79·91°, and contained 88·24 per cent. of alcohol by weight.

A study of tertiary butyl alcohol and its aqueous solutions has also been recorded by Doroschewsky,[4] who gives the sp. gr. of the alcohol at 25°/4° as 0·7806, and the index of refraction n_D^{20} as 1·38548. With aqueous solutions the index shows no maximum value.

It is noteworthy that in the oxidation of tertiary butyl alcohol some isobutyric acid is produced, as well as acetone, acetic acid, and carbon dioxide.

Amyl alcohols, $C_5H_{11}{\cdot}OH$. Mol. wt., 88·10.

The name "amyl" was given by Cahours[5] to alcohol obtained from fusel oil, as the latter had at that time been found mainly in spirit produced from substances containing starch (*amylum*). Fusel oil itself was first obtained by Scheele from the "last runnings" of rye spirit,[6] and was subsequently investigated by Dumas, who separated from it by fractional distillation a liquid

[1] *Ann. Chem. Pharm.*, 1867, **144**, 1. [2] *Trans. Chem. Soc.*, 1880, **37**, 238.
[3] *Ibid.*, 1884, **45**, 468. [4] *J. Russ. Phys. Chem. Soc.*, 1911, **43**, 66.
[5] *Ann. Chim. Phys.*, 1839, [i], **70**, 81. [6] Crell, *Annalen*, 1785, **1**, 61.

boiling at 131·5°, and having the elementary composition $C_5H_{12}O$. Cahours concluded that this body was "isomeric" with ordinary alcohol; and later Pasteur (1855) separated "amyl alcohol" itself into two isomers by means of the barium amyl sulphates.

Subsequent investigation has shown that eight isomeric amyl alcohols are theoretically possible, and all of them are known.

Of the eight, four are primary, three secondary, and one tertiary. A summary of these is given on p. 116. The formula of the third, fourth, and fifth on the list contains an asymmetric carbon atom, so that three optical modifications of each are possible—namely, a dextro-, a lævo-, and an inactive form. Including optical isomers, therefore, the possible number is fourteen.

(1) **Normal primary amyl alcohol** (Butyl carbinol),

$$CH_3(CH_2)_3 \cdot CH_2 \cdot OH.$$

—This is a liquid, of fusel-oil odour, and only slightly soluble in water. It has the boiling-point 137°, and the sp. gr. 0·8168 at 20°/4°. It may be prepared from amylamine, $C_5H_{11} \cdot NH_2$, by means of the nitrous acid reaction (p. 117). The first synthesis of the alcohol was carried out by Lieben and Rossi, starting with *n*-butyl alcohol and using the nitrile reaction.[1]

(2) **Isobutyl carbinol** (Inactive or isoamyl alcohol),

$$(CH_3)_2CH \cdot CH_2 \cdot CH_2 \cdot OH.$$

—This is the chief ingredient of the ordinary or "fermentation" amyl alcohol found in fusel oil. As a natural product it is found in Roman chamomile oil, where it occurs as the amyl ester of angelic and tiglic acids. Its constitution was first determined by Erlenmeyer, who found that the acid yielded by oxidation of the alcohol was identical with valeric acid prepared synthetically from isobutyl alcohol. This synthesis, stopping before the oxidation, can be used to prepare the pure isobutyl carbinol, the steps being conversion of isobutyl alcohol into the cyanide, the latter into the corresponding acid, this into the aldehyde, and finally into the alcohol.

Isobutyl carbinol boils at 131·6° (corr.), and has the sp. gr. 0·8248 at 0°, 0·8104 at 20°/4°, or 0·8158 at 15·6°/15·6°. Under 740·9 mm. pressure, the boiling point is 128·9° to 129·2°, and under 759·2 mm., 130·5° to 131°. The alcohol is soluble in water to the extent of 1 in 50 at 13–14°, and 1 in 39 at 16·5°. It dissolves in all proportions in acetic acid diluted with an equal bulk of water. Oxidation with platinum black converts it into isovaleric acid; distillation with sulphuric acid and potassium dichromate gives isovaleraldehyde and isovaleric acid. With water it forms an

[1] *Ann. Chem. Pharm.*, 1871, **159**, 70.

azeotropic mixture boiling at 95·15°, and containing 50·4 per cent. of alcohol by weight (Young and Fortey, *loc. cit.*).

(3) **Secondary butyl carbinol** (Active amyl alcohol),

$$CH_3{\cdot}CH(C_2H_5){\cdot}CH_2{\cdot}OH.$$

—This alcohol occurs with the inactive compound in fermentation amyl alcohol. As mentioned above, it was first separated by Pasteur. On dissolving the two alcohols in strong sulphuric acid and neutralising the solution with barium carbonate, two barium amyl sulphates are produced which differ in solubility, and can therefore be separated by repeated crystallisation. These Pasteur obtained and converted into the sodium salts, afterwards liberating the corresponding alcohols by distillation with sulphuric acid. The active modification is lævorotatory. It boils at 128·7°.

(4) **Methyl propyl carbinol,** $CH_3(CH_2)_2{\cdot}CH(OH){\cdot}CH_3$, is a liquid with fusel-oil odour, boiling at 118·5° and having the sp. gr. 0·824 at 0°. It may be prepared by the reduction of methyl propyl ketone. The alcohol is optically inactive, but the *d*-component can be destroyed by the action of *Penicillium glaucum,* thus leaving the substance lævorotatory (Le Bel).

(5) **Methyl isopropyl carbinol,** $(CH_3)_2CH{\cdot}CH(OH){\cdot}CH_3$, is a liquid boiling at 112·5°, and having the sp. gr. 0·833 at 0°. It may be obtained by reduction of the corresponding ketone.

(6) **Diethyl carbinol,** $(C_2H_5)_2CH{\cdot}OH$, is a liquid of peculiar odour, boiling at 116·5° and having the sp. gr. 0·8315 at 0°. It is formed by heating ethyl formate with zinc and ethyl iodide.

(7) **Dimethyl ethyl carbinol** (Tertiary amyl alcohol),

$$(CH_3)_2C(OH){\cdot}C_2H_5,$$

is a liquid with a camphor-like odour, boiling at 102·5°, and of sp. gr. 0·827 at 0°. It can be prepared by shaking amylene at a low temperature (—20°) with sulphuric acid mixed with one-half to an equal volume of water, and then diluting and boiling the solution. It acts as a narcotic.

(8) **Tertiary butyl carbinol,** $(CH_3)_3C{\cdot}CH_2{\cdot}OH$.—This alcohol is formed on reducing the chloride of trimethyl-acetic acid with sodium amalgam. It is a solid, melting at 48–50°, and boiling at 112°.

Fusel oil.—This is a complex mixture produced to the extent of a few tenths per cent. in ordinary alcoholic fermentation. Thus from four patent-still distilleries the following quantities of fusel oil were produced for every 100 gallons of absolute alcohol manufactured, the materials fermented being grain cereals :—[1]

[1] Appendix Q, Royal Commission on Whisky Report, 1909.

	Lb. of fusel oil.		Per cent.
A. English	4·65	=	0·58
B. Scotch	3·13	=	0·39
C. ,, ...	3·02	=	0·38
D. Irish	4·02	=	0·51

Fusel oil consists chiefly of four higher alcohols, namely, normal propyl, isobutyl, active amyl, and inactive amyl alcohols. The last is the largest constituent. Small proportions of esters and free fatty acids are also present, with more or less ethyl alcohol and water.

In addition to the foregoing, other alcohols of the butyl and amyl series, especially normal butyl, have been noted as occurring in fusel oil, and also small quantities of hexyl and heptyl alcohols, furfural, terpenes, and basic substances.

By the use of special ferments, starch mashes may be directly fermented to acetone and fusel oil, with little or no ethyl alcohol (Fernbach). The fusel oil thus obtained contains a large proportion of butyl alcohol. The acetone is separated from the oil by fractional distillation.

As regards the source of the higher alcohols in ordinary fusel oils, Ehrlich[1] has shown that they are formed by the action of yeast upon the amino-acids which result from the decomposition of proteid bodies present in the mash and also in the yeast itself. Leucine, $(CH_3)_2CH·CH_2·CH(NH_2)·COOH$, yields inactive amyl alcohol. Similarly, *iso*leucine yields the active amyl alcohol.

In order that this may take place, the nitrogenous residues of the amino-acids must be split off in the form of ammonia, but this substance cannot be detected in the liquid. Ehrlich's conclusion, therefore, is that the ammonia is assimilated as fast as it is formed, and is utilised in the production of the nitrogenous constituents of the growing yeast. The production of fusel oil depends upon whether the yeast derives its nitrogenous nutriment from amino-acids, or from other sources which yield assimilable nitrogen more readily—as, for example, ammonium salts. When these are present, the amino-acids are not attacked, and little or no fusel oil is produced. In a solution of pure sugar containing no other more readily-assimilated nitrogenous nutriment, the yield of fusel oil can be increased either by adding amino-acids or by so arranging the conditions that they are unfavourable to the growth of the yeast, and thus inducing it to excrete a part of its own nitrogen in the form of amino-acids. In the ordinary fermentation of pure sugar by yeast, the percentage of fusel oil calculated on the total

[1] *Ber.*, 1907, **40**, 1027.

yield of alcohol ranges from about 0·4 to 0·7 per cent. When leucine is added to the solution, the production of fusel oil may rise to as much as 3 per cent., the maximum yield being obtained when the proportion of yeast to sugar is one to five.[1]

In connection with Ehrlich's view that under certain conditions the yeast itself may yield up some of its nitrogen, it may be mentioned that J. R. Carracido had previously put forward a somewhat similar suggestion in discussing the mechanism of the production of glycerol during alcoholic fermentation.[2] He attributed the formation of glycerol, not to the decomposition of sugar by yeast, but to an autolytic destruction of the yeast itself, probably owing to the action of an enzyme on the protein material of the yeast-cells.[3]

Synthetic fusel oil.—It is of interest to note that proposals for the manufacture of synthetic fusel oil have been put forward. In one method gasoline is chlorinated, and the resulting chlorinated hydrocarbons heated with methyl alcohol and a formate to 140–190° under pressure. The product obtained consists of monohydric alcohols of high boiling point, which, it is claimed, can be used as a substitute for fusel oil.[4]

In another process, a petroleum distillate boiling between 25° and 75°, containing pentanes and hexanes, is treated with chlorine so as to produce chiefly monochloro-derivatives. These are then heated with an acetate to 170–250° at a pressure of 300 lb. per square inch, the product furnishing a mixture of pentyl and hexyl alcohols. A further yield of these alcohols is obtained by hydrolysing the olefines which are produced at the same time.[5]

By another method, the stearic acid ester of the higher alcohol is formed through the action of sodium stearate upon pentyl or hexyl chloride, and the alcohol obtained by hydrolysing the ester.[6] Stearic acid and solid caustic soda are heated together in a jacketed vessel at 200–240°, and when the water has been expelled, a mixture of pentyl and hexyl chlorides is introduced at the bottom of the vessel. A part of the chlorides reacts with the sodium stearate, whilst another part is converted into olefines, and some distils unchanged. After separating the volatile products, the stearic

[1] *Ber.*, 1907, **40**, 1027.

[2] *Revista Acad. Sci. Madrid*, 1904; **1**, 217; see *J. Chem. Soc.* (Abst.), 1910, **98**, [i], 350.

[3] It has recently been shown that sugar, by fermentation under special conditions, can yield as much as 21 per cent. of glycerol. (K. Schweitzer, *Helv. Chim. Acta*, 1919, **2**, 167.)

[4] Brooks and Essex, U.S.P., 1221667, 1917.

[5] U.S.P., 1214919, 1917.

[6] B.P., 119249, 1917.

ester remaining is cooled to about 150°, and decomposed by heating again with caustic soda to 200–240°. The resulting alcohol is then distilled off in the presence of a little water or steam.

Composition.—Fusel oil is of variable composition, depending upon the nature of the materials fermented, probably also on the kind of yeast, and on the method of distillation. Whilst the oil from grain spirit or potato spirit is largely composed of amyl alcohols, that from brandy-marcs contains a notable quantity of normal propyl alcohol, and sometimes normal butyl alcohol also; and much isobutyl alcohol is found in spirit distilled from beet sugar washes.

K. Windisch[1] gives the following analyses of fusel oil from potatoes and from grain; the results are calculated upon the oils freed from ethyl alcohol and water:—

	Percentage by weight.	
	Potato.	Grain (Rye).
Normal propyl alcohol	6·85	3·69
Isobutyl alcohol	24·35	15·76
Amyl ,, ...	68·76	79·85
Hexyl ,, ...	—	0·13
Heptyl ,, ...	—	Trace.
Free fatty acids	0·01	0·16
Fatty acid esters	0·02	0·30
Furfural and bases	0·005	0·02

In the grain fusel oil Windisch also found terpenes, 0·033 per cent., and terpene hydrate, 0·048 per cent. Both these, even when highly diluted, had the characteristic aroma of grain spirit. The terpene resembled phellandrene, but was not positively identified.

An old analysis of Rabuteau's[2] shows 15 per cent. of isopropyl alcohol in fusel oil from potato spirit, but this has not been confirmed.

The acids and esters shown in Windisch's analyses were found to be chiefly capric and caprylic, with smaller amounts of caproic and pelargonic, a little acetic, and traces of butyric.

Dr. J. Bell[3] gives the following as the composition of fusel oil obtained from patent-still distilleries producing (1) "grain" spirit and (2) "molasses" spirit:—

	(1) Grain spirit. Per cent.	(2) Molasses spirit. Per cent.
Ethyl alcohol	5·5	9·0
Propyl ,, ...	18·9	13·0
Butyl ,, ...	33·4	42·0
Amyl ,, ...	42·2	36·0

[1] *Arb. Kais. Gesund.*, 1892, **8**, 228.
[2] *Compt. rend.*, 1878, **87**, 500.
[3] Select Committee on Spirits, 1891, Minutes, p. 93.

Ordonneau[1] fractionated a large quantity of 25 year old cognac brandy, and obtained 344·5 grams of higher alcohols per hectolitre of brandy. This fusel oil portion had the following percentage composition :—

Normal propyl alcohol	11·6
„ butyl „	63·5
Amyl alcohol	24·3
Hexyl and heptyl alcohol	0·6

Similar treatment of commercial alcohols derived from maize, beetroot, and potatoes yielded Ordonneau no trace of *n*-butyl alcohol, but only propyl, isobutyl, and amyl alcohols. The *n*-butyl alcohol found in the brandy was attributed to the influence of elliptical yeast.

Claudon and Morin[2] subsequently examined 250 grams of the oils obtained by Ordonneau. These were dehydrated with potassium carbonate and barium oxide, and fractionated : the composition of the fraction containing the higher alcohols was as follows :—

Propyl alcohol	11·9	per cent.
Isobutyl „	4·5	„
Normal butyl alcohol	49·3	„
Amyl alcohol	34·4	„

These investigators thus confirmed Ordonneau's observation that normal butyl alcohol was a constituent of the oils. It was identified by its vapour density and by conversion into the corresponding iodide. They were inclined, however, to attribute its presence in the brandy to the development of a bacillus—perhaps *Bacillus butylicus*—in the wine from which the brandy was made, and not to the action of elliptical yeast. They adduced an experiment[3] in which sugar was fermented by elliptical yeast, obtained from wine and purified by cultivation. Foreign micro-organisms were excluded. From 100 kilos. of sugar they obtained 54·5 grams of higher alcohols, but these did not include any normal butyl alcohol. The constituents and proportions were :—

N-Propyl alcohol	2·0 grams =	3·7 per cent.
Isobutyl „	1·5 „ =	2·7 „
Amyl „	51·0 „ =	93·6 „

The proportions of propyl and isobutyl alcohols are noted as being unusually low.

Subsequently, Morin[4] distilled 92 litres of genuine cognac brandy

[1] *Compt. rend.*, 1886, **102**, 217–219.
[2] *Ibid.*, 1887, **104**, 1187.
[3] *Ibid.*, 1887, **104**, 1109.
[4] *Ibid.*, 1887, **105**, 1019.

and fractionated the products, obtaining therefrom 206 grams of higher alcohols, as follows :—

N-Propyl alcohol	..	.. 25 grams	= 12·1 per cent.
Isobutyl ,,	..	.. 6 ,,	= 29·0 ,,
Amyl ,,	..	.. 175 ,,	= 85·0 ,,

Normal butyl alcohol was absent. It would therefore appear that this alcohol is not necessarily a constituent of the fusel oil obtained from brandy. Further investigations, however, are required.

An analysis of fusel oil from potato spirit, quoted by Herrick[1] as due to Kruis and Raymann, shows 94·2 per cent. of amyl alcohol, and about 5 per cent. of ethyl alcohol, with isobutyl, propyl, and hexyl alcohols together totalling only about 0·5 per cent. This appears to be an abnormal sample ; but in any case the other examples given above show that there is considerable variation in the composition of fusel oil—as indeed would be expected from the different conditions of production and collection under which different oils are obtained.

Fusel oil is soluble in ether, chloroform, carbon tetrachloride, carbon disulphide, benzene, and petroleum ether ; but is dissolved by water to a small extent only. It absorbs chlorine with some avidity. Its chief application in the arts is for the manufacture of amyl acetate, which is employed in making flavouring essences and as a solvent for celluloid in the preparation of varnishes, leather substitutes, and similar articles. Fusel oil is also used as a source of higher alcohols, which are separated from it by fractional distillation. The special variety of fusel oil produced in Fernbach's process, which is said to contain about 65 per cent. of butyl alcohol, has been suggested for use in the manufacture of synthetic rubber.

Evaluation of fusel oil.—Ordinary fusel oil is of value chiefly on account of the amyl alcohol which it contains, and it is, or should be, appraised commercially on this basis.

An approximate method of estimating the amyl alcohol was devised by Allen. It consists in agitating the sample in a graduated tube with an equal volume of benzene (or petroleum spirit). Sufficient water is then added to cause the benzene to separate. The increase in the volume of the benzene layer gives approximately the volume of amyl alcohol in the sample.

It is obvious that this is only a rough method, which would serve fairly well if amyl alcohol were practically the only higher alcohol present, but which would include as amyl most of the butyl and propyl alcohols in the sample.

G. Heinzelman[2] has described the method used at the Institut

[1] "Industrial Alcohol," p. 176.

[2] *Zeitsch. Spiritusind.*, 1912, **35**, 612 ; *J. Soc. Chem. Ind.*, 1912, **31**, 1142.

für Gärungsgewerbe, Berlin, for determining the proportion of amyl alcohols in fusel oils. It consists in ascertaining by fractional distillation the proportion of distillate boiling at 127–131°. A special form of fractionating column is employed; a figure of this is appended.

Four fractions are collected: (*a*) up to 90°, (*b*) between 90° and 115°, (*c*) between 115° and 127°, and (*d*) between 127° and 131°.

Fraction (*a*) contains ethyl alcohol, some fusel oil, and water. It is distilled from a water-bath through the fractionating column as long as ethyl alcohol passes over. The residue is removed to a separator, saturated with common salt, and the fusel oil portion which separates is obtained by running off the saline solution.

Fraction (*b*) is also treated with salt, and the fusel oil portion separated in the same way. This is mixed with that obtained from (*a*), and re-fractionated. When the thermometer indicates 112° fraction (*c*) is added, and the distillation continued, the portion passing over at 127° and above being collected separately. Its amount, added to that of fraction (*d*), gives the total yield of amyl alcohols.

The quantity of fusel oil taken for distillation is 1,500 c.c. In an example given, fraction (*a*) amounted to 540 c.c., (*b*) to 420 c.c., (*c*) to 45 c.c., and (*d*) to 475 c.c. From the refractionation of (*a*), (*b*), and (*c*), 175 c.c. were obtained distilling above 127°. The total yield of amyl alcohols was therefore 650 c.c., or 43·3 per cent. by volume.

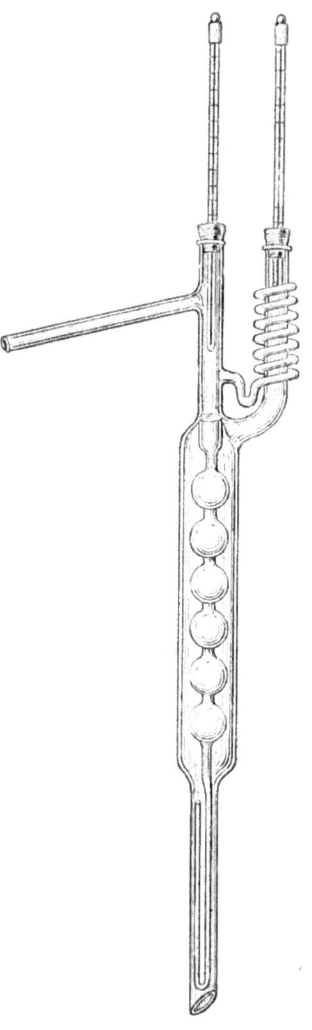

FIG. 39.—FRACTIONATING COLUMN FOR FUSEL OIL ANALYSIS.

Estimation of ethyl alcohol in fusel oil.—This is of some importance, since fusel oil containing not more than 15 per cent. of "proof spirit" is allowed to be imported into this country free of duty. As a complement to this, such fusel oil is allowed to be sent out from home distilleries also without payment of duty.

The accurate estimation of ethyl alcohol in such a complex mixture of alcohols as fusel oil is a matter of some difficulty, since the complete elimination of propyl and isobutyl alcohols is impracticable. The following method, however, due to J. Holmes, gives results which are substantially correct, and it may be used with confidence for fusel oils containing up to 20 per cent. of proof spirit. Though somewhat tedious in the detailed description, the actual operation takes only about two hours, or less if a series is being done.

Before giving the *modus operandi* it will be well to explain shortly the principles on which the process is based.

(1) The oil is extracted with a relatively large volume of water, sufficient to remove the whole of the ethyl alcohol. Some of the higher alcohols are necessarily taken out at the same time. On saturating the aqueous solution with common salt and extracting it with petroleum ether, the greater part of these higher alcohols is removed.

(2) On now distilling the spirituous salt solution, all the remaining alcohols are obtained in a relatively small volume, and a repetition of the salt-petroleum extraction removes all but a small quantity of the higher alcohols, leaving the ethyl alcohol approximately pure, but not entirely so.

(3) The disturbing effect which the small quantity of higher alcohols still present exerts upon the specific gravity of the solution can now be determined by means of the refractometer, and the necessary correction applied.

The *modus operandi* is as follows :—

I. **Extraction.**

(1).—Take 75 c.c. of the sample. Shake it vigorously in a separator (*A*) for some minutes with 150 c.c. of water. (If an emulsion forms, add a few crystals of salt.)

(2).—Draw off the aqueous layer into a second separator (*B*), saturate it with salt, and extract it with 150 c.c. of petroleum ether.

(3).—Run off the aqueous saline layer into a third separator (*C*), and extract it with a second quantity (150 c.c.) of petroleum ether. Finally draw off this saline layer into a distilling flask. Leave the two quantities of petroleum ether in the respective separators *B* and *C*.

(4).—Meanwhile, the oil in separator *A* is shaken a second time with 150 c.c. of water. The aqueous extract is run into the petroleum ether remaining in separator *B*, saturated with salt, and extracted with this petroleum ether. Run the saline liquid into the petroleum ether remaining in separator *C*, extract it with this ether, and finally add it to the first quantity in the distilling flask.

(5).—Repeat (4). Thus the sample has been extracted with three separate quantities of water, and the aqueous extracts, after addition of salt, have each been extracted twice with the same two quantities of 150 c.c. petroleum ether.

II. **Distillation and re-extraction.**

(6).—The liquid in the distilling flask (450 c.c. of spirituous salt solution) is now distilled until about 70 c.c. of distillate are collected. This is saturated with salt and again extracted with 150 c.c. of petroleum ether. Finally this purified salt solution is re-distilled, the distillate made up to 75 c.c., and the specific gravity taken.

III. **Refractometer correction.**

The refraction reading of the distillate is taken with the Zeiss immersion refractometer. This reading will be somewhat higher than that of dilute ethyl alcohol of the same specific gravity (see table at end of chapter). The difference is multiplied by the factor 1·1, and subtracted from the percentage of proof spirit corresponding with the specific gravity of the distillate. (The factor 1·1 is an experimental result.)

Example: Suppose the specific gravity to be 0·98690 and the refraction reading to be 32·0.

From the table, sp. gr. 0·98690 = 17·0 per cent. of proof spirit, the refraction value of which is 28·7.

Then (32·0 — 28·7) × 1·1 = 3·6, the subtractive correction to be applied.

Hence the percentage of proof spirit in the final distillate is 17·0 — 3·6 = 13·4.

This is also the percentage (by volume) of proof spirit in the sample, since the volume taken (75 c.c.) was the same as that of the final distillate.

In a series of mixtures, of known composition, containing from 5 to 25 per cent. of ethyl alcohol at proof strength with varying proportions of higher alcohols, the mean refractometer correction was 4·3 (lowest 3·38, highest 5·76). If, therefore, no refractometer is available, an approximation to the correct result may be obtained by deducting this mean correction from the quantity of proof spirit indicated by the specific gravity of the final distillate.

As a rough "sorting out" method, which does not pretend to estimate the ethyl alcohol, but which is useful for showing whether such alcohol in a fusel oil approaches the 15 per cent. limit or not, the following process may be employed.

Mix in a separator 100 c.c. each of the fusel oil, water, and petroleum ether. Shake vigorously for a few minutes. Let stand five minutes. Run off the aqueous layer into a graduated cylinder, and determine its volume and specific gravity. If the total quantity of proof spirit in the aqueous layer, calculated on the sample, is less than 15 per cent., it is probable that the proportion of ethyl alcohol, at proof strength, is also less than 15 per cent. But if anything more than a rough idea of the amount is wanted the longer method should be employed. A little emulsion sometimes forms; the volume of the aqueous liquid containing this can be determined separately, after the main clear portion has been run off for the specific gravity determination.

REFRACTION-VALUES OF AQUEOUS SOLUTIONS OF HIGHER ALCOHOLS, COMPARED WITH THOSE OF PROOF ETHYL ALCOHOL ("PROOF SPIRIT"). ZEISS IMMERSION REFRACTOMETER. TEMPERATURE 15·6°.

Sp. gr. 15·6°/15·6°.	Proof spirit. Per cent.	Ethyl alcohol.	Normal propyl.	Iso-propyl.	Iso-butyl.	Amyl.
0·99914	1	16·1	16·5	16·5	16·8	17·1
828	2	16·8	17·7	17·6	18·3	18·7
743	3	17·5	18·9	18·6	19·8	20·5
600	4	18·2	20·1	19·6	21·3	22·4
578	5	18·9	21·3	20·6	22·9	24·4
499	6	19·7	22·6	21·7	24·5	
419	7	20·5	23·9	22·8	26·1	
340	8	21·2	25·2	23·9	27·8	
262	9	22·0	26·6	25·0	29·4	
186	10	22·8	28·0	26·2	31·1	
112	11	23·6	29·4	27·4	32·7	
039	12	24·4	30·8	28·7	34·4	
0·98966	13	25·3	32·2	29·9	36·0	
896	14	26·1	33·6	31·2	37·7	
826	15	26·9	35·0	32·4	39·3	
757	16	27·8	36·4	33·7	41·0	
690	17	28·7	37·8	34·9		
623	18	29·5	39·3	36·2		
557	19	30·4	40·8	37·4		
492	20	31·3	42·3	38·7		
428	21	32·3	43·7	40·0		
364	22	33·2	45·1	41·3		
302	23	34·1	46·5	42·6		
240	24	35·0	47·8	43·9		
180	25	36·0	49·1	45·2		
120	26	36·9	50·4	46·5		
059	27	37·9	51·7	47·8		
000	28	38·8	52·9	49·2		
0·97940	29	39·7	54·1	50·5		
882	30	40·7	55·3	51·9		
824	31	41·7	56·5	53·2		
766	32	42·6	57·6	54·5		
708	33	43·6	58·7	55·8		
650	34	44·6	59·8	57·1		
0·97592	35	45·5	—	58·4		

Several approximate methods have been suggested for the

estimation of ethyl alcohol in fusel oil, such as that of G. L. Ulex,[1] but they are more troublesome than the foregoing short process, and do not give very accurate results. Ulex's process is as follows :—

Distil 100 c.c. of the sample until 5 c.c. have been collected. Shake this distillate with an equal volume of saturated salt solution, and let the mixture separate. If the fusel oil layer amounts to one-half the volume of the distillate or more, it may be taken that the sample contained less than 15 per cent. of spirit. If no fusel oil separates out, or if the volume is less than one-half that of the distillate, it may be assumed that there is at least 15 per cent. of spirit in the sample. To ascertain the quantity more nearly, shake 100 c.c. of the sample with an equal volume of saturated salt solution, separate the latter, and distil it. Make up the distillate to 100 c.c., take the specific gravity, and from this determine the amount of alcohol present, assuming that the distillate contains ethyl alcohol and water only.

[1] *Neu. Jahrb. Pharm.*, 1873, **39**, 333.

CHAPTER XI

SPIRITUOUS BEVERAGES

I.—THE CHEMICAL EXAMINATION OF POTABLE SPIRITS

WHAT is usually referred to as the "alcohol" of ordinary potable spirits does not consist merely of pure ethyl alcohol. Small quantities of associated by-products, especially higher alcohols, esters, aldehydes, and acids, are present with the ethyl alcohol; and upon the nature and proportion of these by-products depend the special flavour and character of the spirit. Ethyl alcohol alone would give a relatively featureless spirit, apart from its properties as an intoxicant. The differences in flavour between brandy, rum, and whisky, and also—equal alcoholic strength being postulated—any differences in physiological effects which they may show, depend upon the by-products developed during the manufacture of these spirits, in so far as these by-products are retained in the finished articles. Furthermore, the differences in character between various specimens of the same class of spirits—whisky, for example—are, other things being equal, due to variations in the character or amount of the by-products or "secondary constituents," as they are generally called. A "pot-still" whisky contains more of these than a "patent-still" spirit.

In fact, the modern patent still rectifies the spirit so thoroughly that only a small quantity of the secondary constituents may remain. Hence such spirit is known as "neutral" or "silent" spirit. It is also often referred to as "grain" spirit, from the fact that unmalted grain, as distinct from malt, is largely used to supply the wash distilled for making potable spirits in patent stills.

As it is made from cheaper materials and by more effective plant, patent-still spirit is cheaper to produce than the pot-still variety. Hence there is a temptation to substitute it for the latter kind in some cases. It is not to be assumed, however, that this is necessarily done with fraudulent intent, especially where whisky is concerned. Many people prefer a milder blend of the two kinds to the stronger-flavoured pot-still variety alone. Nevertheless, it is often necessary to know what is the character of a given specimen of spirits from this point of view—namely, as to whether it consists wholly of pot-still spirit, or of patent-still spirit, or of a mixture of the two.

The chemical analysis of potable spirits is not always sufficient to decide questions which may arise as to the genuineness of the spirits or the correctness of the designation under which they are sold. Our knowledge of some of the constituents is imperfect, our methods of determining others not very satisfactory; and, above all, the articles themselves vary, and legitimately vary, within certain limits. Notwithstanding this, chemical analysis, as remarked by the Royal Commission on Whisky,[1] "is capable of affording very important assistance in many, if not in all, cases of suspected misdescription, when the results of analysis are taken in conjunction with other evidence such as that of the expert taster." Needless to say, there are many cases in which chemical analysis is capable, not only of "affording assistance," but of showing positively whether a spirituous article is or is not what it purports to be.

The analysis usually comprises the following determinations:—

(1) **Alcoholic strength.**

(2) **Acidity,** fixed and volatile.

(3) **Total solids** and **ash,** with further examination of these when necessary as regards colouring-matters, sugars, metallic compounds, etc.

(4) **Character of the distillate,** in respect of the proportions of secondary constituents:—

(*a*). Volatile acids.
(*b*). Esters.
(*c*). Furfural.
(*d*). Aldehydes other than furfural.
(*e*). Higher alcohols.

Except as regards this last item, most analysts use substantially the same processes for making the respective determinations. Several different methods, however, are employed for estimating the higher alcohols. It will therefore be convenient to describe first of all the operations for the other constituents, leaving the higher alcohols for separate discussion. The processes adduced

[1] Final Report, Cd. 4796, p. 47.

below are those in use at the Government Laboratory, essentially as given in evidence to the Royal Commission on Whisky.[1]

Total acidity.—Fifty c.c. of the sample are titrated with decinormal soda or baryta, using phenolphthalein solution as indicator.

Fixed acidity.—Another portion of 50 c.c. is evaporated in a beaker to near dryness over a steam-bath, about 25 c.c. of distilled water added, and the solution again evaporated. The residue is then dissolved in about 25 c.c. of cold, recently boiled, distilled water and titrated with decinormal soda or baryta as before. The difference between the fixed acid so ascertained and the value obtained for the total acidity is a measure of the volatile acid. Both are expressed in terms of acetic acid.

Total solids and ash.—One hundred c.c. of the sample, or the residue left in the distilling flask from the distillation experiment mentioned below, are evaporated to dryness in a tared capsule, dried in a steam oven at 100°, and weighed after cooling in a desiccator. The residue is then ignited at a dull red heat to obtain the ash, which after weighing is examined for the presence of lead, copper, iron, etc., if required.

Distillation.—Commercial spirits are often slightly sweetened and coloured, usually with caramel, though sometimes with a coal-tar dye. Moreover, most such spirits contain colouring and other matters extracted from the cask in which they have been stored. Hence it is necessary to free the spirit from these colouring and extractive matters by distillation, before the tests described below can be applied. This practice is also advisable even when the spirit appears to be colourless.

The specific gravity and apparent strength of the sample having been ascertained, a measured quantity (120 to 150 c.c., or more, according to the strength) is placed in a distilling flask, diluted to nearly 200 c.c. with distilled water, and gently distilled to as near dryness as possible without charring the residue. The distillate is made up to 200 c.c. with water, and the alcoholic strength determined; it should be about 50 per cent. by volume (87·5 per cent. of proof spirit), and the quantity taken for distillation should have been such as to give this strength.

(*Note.*—Some analysts prefer to complete the distillation by passing a current of steam through the residual liquid when it has been distilled down to a small bulk. See below, Allen-Marquardt method.)

[1] Appendix Q, p. 17.

Examination of the Distillate.

Volatile acid.—Fifty c.c. of the distillate are titrated with decinormal soda solution, using one drop of phenolphthalein solution as indicator. The acid is calculated as acetic (c.c. $N/10$ soda used $\times$ 0·006 $\times$ 2 = acetic acid in grams per 100 c.c. of *distillate*). To express the result in the customary form as milligrams per 100 c.c. of absolute alcohol, it must be multiplied further by the factor

$$\frac{1{,}000 \times 100}{\text{per cent. of alcohol by volume in distillate}}.$$

Esters.—The 50 c.c. of neutralised distillate from the acidity determination are transferred to a screw-stoppered silver pressure flask, a few c.c. of cold, recently-boiled distilled water being used for rinsing. Twenty c.c. of decinormal soda, exactly measured, are then added, the stopper is screwed down, and the flask heated for two hours on a steam-bath. After cooling, the contents of the flask are transferred to a beaker and titrated with decinormal sulphuric acid.

If no pressure flasks are available, the solution may be boiled gently under a reflux condenser for an hour.

A " blank " experiment is made with the same quantity of alkali, using boiled distilled water in place of the alcohol. No. of c.c. $N/10$-NaOH used up in the hydrolysis $\times$ 0·0088 $\times$ 2 = grams of ester, calculated as ethyl acetate, in 100 c.c. of the *distillate*. This result is then expressed in the customary form as noted for the volatile acid.

Furfural.—A standard solution is made up containing 1 gram of colourless furfural in 100 c.c. of pure spirit of 50 per cent. strength, and from this, other standard solutions are prepared containing 0·1, 0·01, and 0·001 gram respectively of furfural per 100 c.c. of similar spirit.

Ten c.c. of the distillate to be examined are placed in a small Nessler tube (25 c.c. capacity), and similar tubes are prepared containing from 0·5 c.c. upwards of the standard 0·001 per cent. furfural solution, the volume in each case being made up to 10 c.c. with pure 50 per cent. alcohol.

To each tube is added 0·5 c.c. of freshly prepared aniline acetate (made by mixing equal volumes of pure redistilled aniline, glacial acetic acid, and water), and the contents well mixed. When furfural is present a fine pink colour is soon developed, and at the end of fifteen minutes the sample is compared with the standards ; the quantity of furfural present is thus ascertained.

Aldehydes.—For estimating the aldehydes, a standard solution of aldehyde in 50 per cent. alcohol, containing 0·01 gram of aldehyde per 100 c.c., is required; this is prepared as described later on.

Ten c.c. of the distillate under examination are placed in a small Nessler tube, and in similar tubes 10 c.c. each of 50 per cent. alcohol containing from 0·5 c.c. upwards of the 0·01 per cent. standard aldehyde solution. To each tube is added 1 c.c. of Gayon and Schiff's reagent.

After shaking, the tubes are allowed to stand for thirty minutes, when the violet colours which develop are compared.

Standard aldehyde solution.—This is prepared from purified aldehyde-ammonia, $CH_3{\cdot}CH(OH){\cdot}NH_2$. The recrystallised substance is ground in a mortar with dehydrated ether several times, the ether being decanted off after each grinding; the residue is then dried for about twenty-four hours in a desiccator over concentrated sulphuric acid.[1] 1·386 Grams, corresponding with 1 gram of aldehyde, are weighed out into a 100 c.c. flask, and dissolved in 50 c.c. of strong alcohol (96 per cent.). To the solution are added 22·7 c.c. of $N/1$-alcoholic sulphuric acid: this precipitates the ammonia as sulphate. The flask is now filled up to the 100 c.c. mark with more of the strong alcohol, and a further 0·8 c.c. of the alcohol is added to compensate for the volume of the precipitated ammonium sulphate. After being shaken and allowed to settle for twenty-four hours, the solution is filtered. It contains 1 gram of aldehyde per 100 c.c., and from it standard solutions containing 0·1 and 0·01 gram are prepared by dilution with 50 per cent. alcohol. The 0·1 per cent. solution can be used in the estimations instead of the 0·01 per cent. solution, but as the quantities required will now usually be tenths of a cubic centimetre there is less accuracy in the measurements.

Gayon and Schiff's reagent.—To prepare this, a 0·1 per cent. aqueous solution of fuchsin is made, and 150 c.c. of it are added to 100 c.c. of a saturated solution of sodium bisulphite. Fifteen c.c. of 66 per cent. sulphuric acid are added, and the whole made up to 1 litre.

The estimation of higher alcohols in spirits.—The methods used fall chiefly into three main classes.

In one class the alcohols are not separated from the spirit, but are estimated by means of the colour produced through the action of strong sulphuric acid upon them (Girard and Cuniasse; Savalle; Government Laboratory).

[1] Compare L. Ronnet, *Ann. Falsif.*, 1910, **3**, 205.

In the second class, the higher alcohols are extracted from the spirit by means of solvents (carbon tetrachloride, carbon disulphide). Their amount is then determined by conversion into the corresponding acids (Allen-Marquardt), or into the nitrites (Beckmann), or the acetates (Bardy).

In the third class, the higher alcohols are also extracted, chloroform being the solvent, but the quantity is deduced from the increase in the volume of the solvent. (The Röse process, different modifications of which are used in France and Germany.)

After describing the several methods in detail we will offer a few general remarks upon them, indicating what appear to be their relative merits or disadvantages.

Allen-Marquardt method.—The principle underlying this process is the extraction of the higher alcohols with carbon tetrachloride, and their oxidation to the corresponding acids, which are then estimated by titration. The original description[1] has been modified slightly by including suggestions made by Schidrowitz,[2] and the method as now recommended is as follows.[3]

Two hundred c.c. of the spirit are taken, 1 c.c. of strong solution of potassium hydroxide is added, and the mixture boiled for an hour under a reflux condenser to hydrolyse esters. The liquid is then distilled from a flask fitted for distillation with steam, but the steam is not passed until only about 20 c.c. of the sample remain, and thereafter the operation is so conducted that by the time 300 c.c. of distillate are collected the residue in the flask is about 10 c.c.

The distillate is then mixed with saturated salt solution (acidified slightly with a few drops of sulphuric acid), until it has a specific gravity of 1·1. It is now divided into two equal parts, so that duplicate determinations may be made, and each part is extracted with 100 c.c. of purified carbon tetrachloride, using 40, 30, 20, and 10 c.c. successively.

Some ethyl alcohol is contained in the tetrachloride extract. To remove it, the extract is shaken first with 50 c.c. of the saturated salt solution, and separated, and then with 50 c.c. of saturated solution of sodium sulphate to remove remaining chloride.

For the oxidation of the higher alcohols a mixture of 5 grams of potassium dichromate, 2 grams of strong sulphuric acid, and 10 c.c. of water is added to the carbon tetrachloride extract in a flask provided with a reflux condenser, and the liquid boiled gently

[1] Allen's "Commercial Organic Analysis," 1898, **1**, 154.
[2] *J. Soc. Chem. Ind.*, 1902, **21**, 815.
[3] Allen's "Commercial Organic Analysis," 1909, **1**, 188.

for at least eight hours on a water-bath. After the addition of 30 c.c. of water to the liquid in the flask, the contents are distilled until only about 20 c.c. remain; then this residue is steam-distilled as in the first operation until not much more than 5 c.c. remains when 300 c.c. of total distillate have been collected. The distillate is then titrated with decinormal barium hydroxide solution, shaking thoroughly after each addition, until it is neutral to methyl-orange; phenolphthalein is next added and the titration continued to the neutral point. Each c.c. of the $N/10$-solution required in the phenolphthalein stage of the titration represents 0·0088 gram of higher alcohols calculated as amyl alcohol.

The barium hydroxide used in the methyl-orange stage was formerly ignored in the calculation, as the acidity here was supposed to be due to hydrochloric acid. This, however, appears to be unjustifiable, since mere traces of chlorides may be found, whilst the methyl-orange acidity is about 10 per cent. of the total.[1] The recommendation made by Schidrowitz and Kaye is to calculate the whole of the acidity to amyl alcohol, but to estimate the chlorides gravimetrically if the methyl-orange acidity much exceeds 10 per cent. of the whole, and correct the calculation accordingly.

Beckmann's method.—As modified in 1905 from an earlier description, which had been found unsatisfactory by various observers,[2] this process is as follows.[3]

The spirit, after distillation to free it from any colouring or extractive matter, is diluted with water until it contains not more than 20 per cent. of alcohol by volume. Fifty c.c. of this diluted spirit are taken, and extracted with four successive quantities of carbon tetrachloride, using 50 c.c. of the latter each time and shaking vigorously for a few seconds. The united carbon tetrachloride extracts are washed twice with about 20 c.c. of water, and then treated in a stoppered flask with 2 grams of potassium bisulphate and 1 gram of sodium nitrite, powdered together. After shaking for a few minutes, the mixture is transferred to a separating funnel, the tetrachloride drawn off, and the residue extracted twice with a little more carbon tetrachloride. The whole of the extracts are now shaken with about 20 c.c. of a saturated solution of sodium bicarbonate to remove excess of nitrous acid; separated; and then carefully mixed with about 75 c.c. of strong sulphuric acid previously placed in a separating funnel. After being well shaken, the mixture is run on to about 150 grams of crushed ice and the resulting solution

[1] Schidrowitz and Kaye, *Analyst*, 1906, **31**, 183.

[2] Schidrowitz, *ibid.*, 1905, **30**, 192; Bedford and Jenks, *J. Soc. Chem. Ind.*, 1907, **26**, 123.

[3] *Zeitsch. Nahr. Genussm.*, 1905, **10**, 143–152.

titrated with standard permanganate solution (1 in 1,000). In order to obtain a sharp end-point, an excess of the permanganate, about 20 per cent. more than is used up, should be added, and the excess titrated back with standard solution of ferrous-ammonium sulphate. Each c.c. of the permanganate solution used up = 0·00278 gram of amyl alcohol.

Bedford and Jenks[1] have modified this process, first, by improved extraction and washing, and secondly by estimating the nitrites iodometrically. They proceed as follows.

(*a*).—To 30 c.c. of the spirit, diluted to 20 per cent. strength and contained in a separator, 25 grams of dry granular calcium chloride are added, the separator being cooled under the tap meanwhile.

(*b*).—The liquid is then shaken for seven minutes with two successive quantities of 50 c.c. of carbon tetrachloride.

(*c*).—The resulting 100 c.c. of extract is washed with two successive quantities, 30 c.c. each, of saturated calcium chloride solution (D = 1·4).

(*d*).—The washed carbon tetrachloride solution of higher alcohols is then treated with 2 grams of potassium bisulphate and 1 gram of sodium nitrite (powdered together) to convert the alcohols into the nitrites. The vessel used should be dry, not too large, and kept stoppered. A small tapped and stoppered separating funnel of about 170 c.c. capacity serves the purpose well.

(*e*).—The nitrites, after washing with solution of sodium bicarbonate and separation of the latter, as in the original process, are determined by Dunstan and Dymond's method,[2] with potassium iodide in acid solution in absence of free oxygen, the iodine thus liberated being titrated with thiosulphate solution. The reaction is based upon the following equation :—

$$2HI + 2HNO_2 = 2H_2O + 2NO + I_2.$$

Details of manipulation are given in the original paper of Dunstan and Dymond, and also in Sutton's "Volumetric Analysis" (p. 286 of the 1911 edition), but a modification of the apparatus is preferred by Bedford and Jenks, on account of the action of carbon tetrachloride on the rubber joint.

These authors use an ordinary pear-shaped separator funnel of about 350 c.c. capacity and $3\frac{1}{2}$ inches diameter, provided with a well-ground stopper and tap. The stem is about 2 in. long, is cut off obliquely, and passes through a rubber stopper to a round-bottomed flask of about 250 c.c. capacity. The whole is conveni-

[1] *J. Soc. Chem. Ind.*, 1907, **26**, 123. [2] *Pharm. J.*, 1889, [iii], **19**, 741.

ently hung on a cotton-wrapped ring on a retort stand. The tap and its socket must be perfectly clean and dry before use, and should be freely covered with vaseline.

Five c.c. of a 10 per cent. solution of potassium iodide, 5 c.c. of a 10 per cent. solution of sulphuric acid, and 40 c.c. of water are introduced into the flask, and the tap of the funnel being open, the mixture is boiled so as completely to expel the air from the flask. When the volume of the liquid has been reduced to about 10 c.c., the flame is removed with one hand, the tap is simultaneously closed with the other, and then screwed firmly into position with both hands. If the tap has been properly dried and greased at the start it will remain air-tight, and will move freely when the apparatus is cold, though it may appear to be jammed whilst cooling is taking place.

The carbon tetrachloride solution of the nitrites is passed into the cooled flask through the separator, care being taken that no air is admitted, and then 20 c.c. of alcohol (ordinary rectified spirit) are also run in. The nitrites are quantitatively decomposed, usually after vigorous shaking for a few minutes, though it is desirable to allow the flask to stand for about an hour before actual titration, and to keep it under observation for some hours longer.

The liberated iodine is titrated with decinormal thiosulphate solution, which is run from a burette into the separator, and gradually drawn into the flask by means of the tap. As soon as the iodine is decolorised any excess of thiosulphate remaining in the separator is returned to the burette; or more accurately, it may be titrated separately with standard iodine solution to ascertain its amount. From the volume of thiosulphate used up, the quantity of nitrous acid is calculated from the equation given, and thence the equivalent amount of amyl or other nitrite is obtained.

This method gave the authors very good results when tested upon known quantities of the individual higher alcohols—amyl, *n*-butyl, isobutyl, and *n*-propyl. The quantities found were generally within about 5 per cent. of the amounts added. With isopropyl alcohol, however, only about 70 per cent. of the added quantity was shown in the results. When samples of commercial spirits were examined the results obtained, as would be expected, were generally higher than those given by the Allen-Marquardt process, and sometimes considerably higher. The authors look upon the difference as a measure of the "intermediate" higher alcohols.

Government Laboratory method.—One gram of a standard mixture of higher alcohols (see below) is dissolved in 100 c.c. of pure 50 per cent. alcohol, and from this a standard solution is prepared containing 0·1 gram of the higher alcohols in 100 c.c.

To estimate the proportion of higher alcohols in a sample, 10 c.c. of the distillate, obtained as already described, are placed in a small flask of about 75 c.c. capacity, and in similar flasks are placed quantities 10 c.c. each of 50 per cent. alcohol containing from 0·5 c.c. upwards of the standard 0·1 per cent. solution. To these liquids is added 0·5 c.c. of a 1 per cent. solution of furfural in each case, and then 10 c.c. of concentrated sulphuric acid are slowly run in so that the acid forms a layer at the bottom of the flask. Each flask is placed in an ice-cold water-bath and the contents stirred by shaking gently during thirty seconds, after which it is allowed to stand for about an hour at the ordinary temperature of the room. In the presence of an appreciable quantity of higher alcohols, a reddish-violet colour develops, and the proportion of these alcohols in the sample can be estimated by comparison with the standards.

The standard mixture of higher alcohols used for comparison, and in terms of which the results of this test are expressed, contains :—

Propyl alcohol	1 part.
Isobutyl ,, ...	2 parts.
Amyl ,, ...	3 ,,
Capryl ,, ...	1 part.

This mixture is some approximation to the average composition of the "fusel oil" alcohols of pot-still spirits as determined by a number of experiments made in the Government Laboratory.

In exceptional cases it may be necessary to remove the esters and aldehydes before applying this process, but as a rule the colorations obtained with commercial spirits are very similar in tint to those given by the standard mixture, and with careful manipulation and similar conditions of working, comparable results can be obtained without much difficulty.

All the results are finally calculated to milligrams per 100 c.c. of absolute alcohol in the sample.

Girard and Cuniasse's method.—Aldehydes and furfural are first eliminated from the spirit to be tested, as they are not without effect upon the colour produced with sulphuric acid by the higher alcohols.

For this purpose, 50 c.c of the spirit at a strength of 50 per cent. are placed in a flask of about 250 c.c. content, and mixed with 1 gram of either metaphenylenediamine hydrochloride, or of aniline phosphate (equal volumes of aniline and phosphoric acid of sp. gr. 1·453). After addition of a few small pieces of pumice-stone to regularise the ebullition, the alcohol is boiled gently for an hour under a reflux condenser, and then distilled off rather rapidly, and as completely as is practicable without running risk of charring the residue. The tube connecting flask and condenser during the distillation should be of relatively large diameter, and the limb leading from the flask should be short, in order to give the minimum reflux effect.

The volume of the distillate is made up exactly to 50 c.c., mixed, and 10 c.c. are placed in a clean flask. Into this, 10 c.c. of pure, colourless sulphuric acid (monohydrated) are run from a pipette down the side of the flask so as not to disturb the alcohol appreciably. The flask is then taken in a tube-holder and agitated briskly whilst holding it in the flame of a good Bunsen burner turned full on. When ebullition commences, which should occur at the end of fifteen seconds, the flask is removed, covered with a small watch-glass, and allowed to cool.

The colour produced is then compared in a colorimeter with that given by standards containing known quantities of isobutyl alcohol, treated in the same way. (In the absence of a suitable colorimeter the comparisons may, of course, be made in small "Nessler" tubes.)

The depths of colour produced are not exactly proportional to the amounts of higher alcohols present, so that comparisons should be made with standards not differing too much from the sample. In practice, a curve is constructed for use, showing the real content of higher alcohols corresponding with the apparent content given by comparison with the standard when the latter differs from the sample: this obviates the necessity for dilutions and the corresponding calculations, and lessens the number of standards required.

Saglier makes the process more sensitive for low proportions of higher alcohols by adding 20 drops or more of a 0·1 per cent. solution of furfural (in 50 per cent. alcohol) to both sample and standard before the treatment with sulphuric acid. This intensifies the colours produced, and as both sample and standard are treated alike, no error is caused.

Rocques has introduced some modifications into the method to render it more sensitive and more precise. He distils 100 c.c. of the 50 per cent. alcohol, after refluxing with 2 grams of meta-phenylenediamine hydrochloride, to a bulk of 75 c.c., and works with the spirit at this higher strength, namely, 66·7 per cent. instead of 50 per cent. Also the mixed acid and alcohol, instead of being heated in a Bunsen burner, are heated in a bath of calcium chloride (69 per cent. solution) to 120° for an hour.

Table for converting apparent content of higher alcohols into real content, when the standard used is 0·0667 gram of isobutyl alcohol in 100 c.c. of ethyl alcohol at 66·7 per cent. strength :—

Apparent content.	Real content.	Apparent content.	Real content.
0·1125	0·1000	0·0379	0·0400
0·1009	0·0900	0·0255	0·0300
0·0886	0·0800	0·0150	0·0200
0·0760	0·0700	0·0060	0·0100
0·0640	0·0600	0·0019	0·0050
0·0500	0·0500		

The Röse process.—This method is not used in this country, but is official in France, particularly as a sorting-out procedure preliminary to the application of the longer and more exacting Bardy method, described later on. It depends upon the increase of volume produced in a given quantity of chloroform, when the alcohol in question is shaken with the chloroform under strictly defined conditions. Calvet[1] gives the following modification as used in France :—

Such a quantity of the sample is taken as will contain exactly 100 c.c. of absolute alcohol, and this is diluted to exactly 400 c.c. at 15°. Fifty c.c. of chloroform at 15° are measured into a " Röse tube." (This is a vessel of 700 c.c. capacity, the upper part of which resembles a pear-shaped separator, and the lower part is a bulb of 49 c.c. capacity, joined to the upper part by a narrow, graduated stem.) The diluted alcohol is added to the chloroform, followed by 2 c.c. of sulphuric acid (D = 1·286). After being placed in a water-bath kept at 15° for half an hour, the tube is shaken vigorously for five minutes in a mechanical shaker, and again placed in the bath. When the chloroform has all collected together its volume is read off on the graduated stem, and the increase noted.

Under these conditions, pure alcohol gives an increase of 0·45 to 0·50 c.c. in the chloroform layer. With 1 per cent. of amyl alcohol the increase is 1·9 c.c., or a net value of 1·4 c.c. on deducting 0·5 for the " blank " experiment. One per cent. of isobutyl alcohol gives a net increase of 0·6 c.c., and 1 per cent. of propyl alcohol gives 0·25 c.c. net increase ; these homologues are counted as amyl alcohol unless it is known that one or other of them is the chief alcohol present.

Bardy's method.[2]—The principle of this process is the extraction of the amyl and butyl alcohols with carbon disulphide from the sample (saturated with salt), their removal with sulphuric acid from the carbon disulphide, and their ultimate conversion into

[1] " Alcohols," p. 97. [2] *Compt. rend.*, 1892, **114**, 1201.

the acetates, the volume of which is measured. The propyl alcohol is determined by oxidation with potassium permanganate under prescribed conditions.

(1).—Mix 100 c.c. of the alcohol in a stoppered separator with 450 c.c. of saturated salt solution, and about 50 c.c. of water to prevent the salt crystallising out. Add 60–70 c.c. of pure carbon disulphide.

(2).—Shake vigorously for 1 minute; loosen the stopper a moment to equalise the pressure, then shake again for five minutes.

(3).—Run off the carbon disulphide into a 300 c.c. separator, taking care to avoid the entrance of any of the aqueous liquid.

(4).—Make two further extractions in the same way, adding the carbon disulphide extracts to that in the 300 c.c. separator. All the amyl and butyl alcohols are thus removed. Retain the saline liquid for the propyl alcohol determination (see below).

(5).—Shake the mixed carbon disulphide extracts with enough sulphuric acid (D = 1·845) to allow of the acid collecting at the bottom of the separator after shaking (about 2–3 c.c. suffice). Twirl the separator a little to assist settling, and let stand till the acid has separated.

(6).—Draw off the acid into a 125 c.c. flask. Wash the carbon disulphide twice with 1 c.c. of sulphuric acid each time, and add the washings to the first quantity of acid in the flask.

(7).—Expel any carbon disulphide from the acid extract by passing a current of air on to the surface, warming, if necessary, to about 60°.

(8).—Now add enough crystallised sodium acetate to decompose nearly all the sulphuric acid (1·5 grams for each 1 c.c. of acid will suffice), fit the flask with an air-condenser 1 metre long, and heat the flask on the water-bath during half an hour.

(9).—After cooling, add to the contents of the flask 100 c.c. of salt solution, and then remove the whole to a separator of 300 c.c. capacity, the lower part of which is drawn out and graduated into tenths of a c.c.

(10).—Allow the liquid to rest for some hours, then draw off the salt solution so as to bring the amyl and butyl acetates into the graduated stem. Place the instrument in water at 15°, and when the temperature is constant read off the volume of the acetates. The number of c.c. multiplied by 0·8, gives the quantity of amyl and butyl alcohols (together) in 100 c.c. of the spirit taken.

(11).—To determine the propyl alcohol, take the extracted liquid retained at (4), and filter it through moistened paper to remove any carbon disulphide. Then distil it until the strength of the distillate shows 50 per cent. of alcohol (at 15°). At this point all the alcohols have passed over.

Fill a burette with the distillate, and run out the alcohol drop by drop into a beaker containing 50 c.c. of water and 1·0 c.c. of $KMnO_4$ solution (1·0 gram per litre) until a copper-red tinge is obtained similar to a standard tint. The latter is given by 20 c.c. of fuchsine solution (0·1 gram per litre) mixed with 30 c.c. of K_2CrO_4 solution (0·5 gram per litre), and made up to 150 c.c. with water.

Under these conditions, the standard tint is given by approximately 2·5 c.c. of ethyl alcohol at 50 per cent. strength containing 1 per cent. of propyl alcohol; whence the percentage of propyl alcohol in the sample is deduced.

If the sample contains so much fusel oil as to give a distinct layer of supernatant oil when 100 c.c. are shaken with 500 c.c. of salt solution, the volume of this layer is read off in a suitable vessel, and the remainder of the liquid is then extracted with carbon disulphide as described above.

Komarowsky—Fellenberg method.—As a means of detecting isoamyl alcohol in spirits, A. Komarowsky in 1903 proposed treatment of the sample with salicylic aldehyde and sulphuric acid.[1] When to 10 c.c. of the spirit are added 25 to 30 drops of a 1 per cent. alcoholic solution of salicylic aldehyde and 20 c.c. of strong sulphuric acid, the mixture develops a colour which is reddish by reflected light and yellow by transmitted light if isoamyl alcohol is present to an extent not greater than 0·01 per cent. With larger quantities of isoamyl alcohol, the colour appears garnet-red, however viewed.

T. von Fellenberg[2] states that the red colour shows a yellow fluorescence, which becomes greater as the amount of salicylic reagent is increased. If, however, the mixture is diluted with 62 per cent. sulphuric acid, the yellow fluorescence disappears and a pure red is obtained. He applies the test to the colorimetric determination of the higher alcohols of cognac in the following manner. Ten c.c. of the hydrolysed distillate, diluted to a strength of 30 per cent. of alcohol by volume, are treated with 1 c.c. of a 1 per cent. alcoholic solution of salicylic aldehyde, and then carefully mixed with 20 c.c. of strong sulphuric acid. After the lapse of forty-five minutes the mixture is diluted with 50 c.c. of 62 per cent. sulphuric acid. The colour obtained is then compared with those produced in standard mixtures treated in the same manner.

Other substances than the alcohols of fusel oil give the red colour, as, for example, aromatic alcohols, phenols, and all compounds

[1] *Chem. Zeit.*, 1903, **27**, 807. [2] *Ibid.*, 1910, **34**, 791.

which contain an ethylene group in their molecule. It is not given, however, by polyhydric alcohols, or by alcohols and phenols containing a carboxyl group.

General remarks upon the determination of higher alcohols.—None of the methods for estimating higher alcohols gives results which are strictly and scientifically accurate. That is to say, none determines the exact quantity of each separate alcohol—or even of the total alcohols with certainty.

In the colorimetric processes, for example, the results are obtained in terms either of a single constituent (isobutyl or amyl alcohol) or of a standard mixture. Since the higher alcohols severally produce different intensities of colour with sulphuric acid, it follows that the results in either case are of the nature of an approximation. This objection applies, however, with less force when a mixture of higher alcohols is taken for the standard than when a single alcohol is used as the criterion.

Furthermore, some doubts have been thrown upon the trustworthiness of the standard alcohols themselves—namely, as to whether the higher alcohols, if absolutely pure, do in fact yield colorations with sulphuric acid. It has been suggested that the colorations obtained may really be due to associated and difficultly-removable impurities such as terpenes. Definite proof of this, however, is not forthcoming.

On the whole, perhaps the most precise method for the determination of higher alcohols in spirits is the Dupré–Marquardt process as improved by Allen, Schidrowitz, and others, and now generally known as the "Allen-Marquardt" method. It is, however, somewhat lengthy and troublesome, and, moreover, it cannot claim to be scientifically accurate in the sense defined above, since no determination of the separate alcohols is obtained. All are expressed in terms of amyl alcohol. Further, there is at the outset the objection that if secondary alcohols such as isopropyl alcohol or secondary butyl alcohol are present they are not, in theory, properly taken account of. Isopropyl alcohol on oxidation is converted into acetone, and would not be shown at all in the result. Secondary butyl alcohol, if oxidised beyond the ketone stage, yields eventually two molecules of acetic acid for each molecule of the alcohol, and thus would give an unduly high result. True, if both these alcohols occur together the errors tend to neutralise each other, but there is yet a further objection. It has been shown by direct experiment upon known quantities of the individual higher alcohols that whilst good results are obtainable in the case of amyl alcohol, the butyl and propyl alcohols are much under-estimated by the process. Thus Bedford and Jenks,[1] in testing the Allen–Marquardt process, obtained results of which the following is a summary :—

Alcohol.	Found. Percentage of quantity added.
Amyl	93 to 110
n-Butyl	30 ,, 70
Isobutyl	26 ,, 52
n-Propyl	13 ,, 31

A part of the losses was found to be due to the fact that when the carbon tetrachloride extract of the higher alcohols is washed with solution of sodium chloride and sodium sulphate in order to free it from ethyl alcohol, some portion of the intermediate alcohols is removed at the same time. This, indeed, is only what would be expected. If amyl alcohol were practically the only higher alcohol present, the Allen–Marquardt procedure would give excellent results.

Much the same remarks apply to the Beckmann method as to the Allen–Marquardt process, in respect of the loss in washing and the expression of the results in terms of one unit.

The nearest approach in principle to an accurate method of analysis is that due to Bardy, inasmuch as the propyl alcohol is determined separately, and it would be possible to estimate the respective proportions of amyl and butyl alcohols, if these were the only others present, by converting them into the corresponding mixed acids and finding the combining weight. The process appears, however, to be devised for the estimation of larger quantities of higher alcohols than are usually present in potable spirits, and it is undeniably lengthy and troublesome.

As regards the Röse process, it suffers in principle from the fact that the various alcohols produce different amounts of increase in the volume of the chloroform, one part of amyl alcohol being equivalent to nearly six parts of propyl alcohol in this respect. It requires very careful attention to details of temperature and manipulation. According to W. L. Dudley,[2] the results are much higher than those obtained by the Allen–Marquardt process, though a marked relationship is observable between the results given by the two methods. This author gives an account of the precautions necessary in using the Röse process. He considers the Allen–Marquardt method the better, as it is more rapid, has fewer sources of error, and gives the amyl alcohol content more accurately.

Whilst in English-speaking countries the Allen–Marquardt

[1] *J. Soc. Chem. Ind.*, 1907, **26**, 123.
[2] *J. Amer. Chem. Soc.*, 1908, **30**, 1271.

method has become the standard process, it has not been adopted universally. On the Continent, colorimetric and other methods are used, and they offer so much saving of time that they will probably remain long in favour, especially as data based on them have been accumulated which serve as standards—as, for example, in the analysis of brandy. Hence it has been necessary to describe the chief of these at some length. There is all the more reason for this since the Allen–Marquardt process, as already shown, is open to criticism in some respects, even though it may be accepted as on the whole the nearest approach to a satisfactory method. The colorimetric processes, however, should be used with discretion, and the results should not be regarded as strictly comparable with those given by the Allen–Marquardt process. A number of comparative figures obtained by this process and by colorimetric methods have been published, some of which show relatively enormous differences in the results, the colorimetric values being generally the higher. Without inquiring into the probable causes of these larger discrepancies, it may be remarked that the colorimetric method as used in the Government Laboratory has been found to give fair approximations to those obtained on the same samples by the Allen–Marquardt process, and in only a fraction of the time required for the latter (see the figures given below). Probably this is due to the facts that in the Government Laboratory process, unlike some other modifications of the colorimetric method, the action of the sulphuric acid is effected in the cold, and the standard of reference is a mixture of higher alcohols, not a single alcohol.

Where a large number of samples have to be examined, the analyst will probably find it advantageous to use one of the colorimetric processes in the first instance, employing the Allen–Marquardt method for confirmatory purposes or for special samples if desired. Wherever necessary, the method of estimation should be stated in giving the results. For brandy, if the French data are to be used for comparison, the process due to Girard and Cuniasse is obviously desirable, either with isobutyl alcohol as standard, or with amyl alcohol, and the results calculated in terms of isobutyl alcohol.

The kind of agreement which may be expected between results obtained by three of the chief methods will be seen from the following table.[1]

[1] Appendix Q, Royal Commission on Whisky.

HIGHER ALCOHOLS, ESTIMATED BY DIFFERENT METHODS.

(Parts per 100,000 of absolute alcohol.)

Allen–Marquardt.	Beckmann.	Govt. Laboratory.
250·9	320·3	228·0
221·3	304·3	245·6
310·6	278·7	350·8
313·1	276·3	266·6
260·0	288·9	317·5
291·4	288·6	317·5

It is scarcely necessary to say that very close agreement is not to be expected, in view of the admitted difficulties attending such determinations.

II.—BRANDY

"Brandy" is a potable spirit distilled from fermented grape juice.

"British brandy" is a compounded spirit prepared by a rectifier or compounder by re-distilling duty-paid spirits, made from grain, with flavouring ingredients; or by adding flavouring materials to such spirits.

There is no statutory definition of either of the above terms. The word "brandy" was used in old Acts of Parliament to denote spirits obtained from cereals—"Whereas good and wholesome brandies, *aqua vitæ*, and spirits may be drawn and made from malted corn," etc. (2 William and Mary, c. 9; 1690)—and a definition of "British brandy" as a flavoured spirit was given in the Spirits Act as late as 1860; but this has since been repealed.[1]

The French name for what is known as brandy in this country is "eau-de-vie," but this term used alone has a somewhat wide signification in France, being legally applicable to spirit made from grape marcs, cider, perry, cherries, plums, and other fruit, as well as to that from wine. More strictly, "brandy" as understood in this country corresponds with "eau-de-vie de vin," or wine spirit proper.

The most esteemed brandies are produced in the Cognac district. "Cognac," as the description of a spirit, is not expressly defined in the French law, but the name "eau-de-vie de Cognac," or "Cognac" simply, can only be applied legally to spirits made in the Cognac region from the juice of grapes grown therein. This region comprises part of the two departments of Charente and

[1] For this, and the context, see Report, Royal Commission on Whisky, p. 26.

Charente Inférieure, and is locally subdivided into the Grande or Fine Champagne, the Petite Champagne, the Borderies, and the Bois, according to the quality of the wine produced. The soil is mainly calcareous: the grape grown is small in size and white in colour; and the wine is of inferior quality for drinking purposes.

Cognac brandy is made both by the professional distiller and by the farmer who grows his own grapes. A simple pot-still is generally used, and there are two distillations, giving respectively "*brouillis*," corresponding with the "low wines" of the whisky distiller, and "*bonne chauffe*," equivalent to the "spirits." In some distilleries, however, the brandy is produced at one continuous distillation, the stills being designated "*à premier jet*."

The wines used for "Cognac" contain from 10 to 20 per cent. of proof spirit, and the product is run from the stills at a strength of about 25 over proof. The brandy is sweetened with cane-sugar, and slightly coloured, the object of colouring being merely to keep a given brand up to a given level of colour.

Next to "Cognac" in order of commercial merit come the brandies made in the Armagnac, including the Marmande district. A certain amount of brandy is made in the Nantes district; and large quantities in the Midi, in the Hérault, Gard, Aude, and Pyrénées Orientales districts, these brandies being commonly known as the "Trois-Six de Montpellier." For distilling wines with an undesirable flavour, "continuous" stills are used, giving such higher degree of rectification as may be required to eliminate the unwanted flavour.

"Marc brandies" ("eau-de-vie de marc") are spirits derived from the distillation of the skins of fresh grapes from which the greater part of the juice has been extracted.

Brandy of good quality is also produced in Algeria and in Spain. Egyptian brandies are distilled in Alexandria from grapes grown in Roumelia, parts of Greece, Cyprus, and Asia Minor. Some so-called "Egyptian" brandies are not distilled in Egypt, but are said to be probably made from currants grown in Greece.

The quantity of brandy retained for home consumption in the United Kingdom during the year 1913–14 amounted to 1,544,153 proof gallons.

Brandy is not now included in the British Pharmacopœia, but in the 1898 edition of that work it was defined as a spirituous liquid distilled from wine and matured by age, and containing not less than 36·5 per cent. of alcohol by weight, or 43·5 per cent. by volume.

As distilled, brandy is colourless; but as sold is coloured, either by direct addition of colouring matter to ensure uniformity for special brands, as already indicated, or by extraction of colouring matters from the storage casks. The total amount of solids ranges from about 0·2 to 0·8 per cent. in general, but quantities of more than 1 per cent. are often met with, and occasionally even as much as 3 per cent. The alcoholic strength of brandy when sold in this country must not be lower than 25° under proof, unless with notice to the purchaser.[1]

Ordonneau, and also Claudon and Morin, have investigated the higher alcohols of brandy, and give the composition as follows :—

	Ordonneau. Per cent.	Claudon and Morin. Per cent.
Propyl alcohol	11·9	11·7
Normal butyl alcohol	49·3	63·8
Isobutyl ,, ...	4·5	0·0
Amyl ,, ...	34·4	24·5

The characteristic flavour of brandy is considered to be due to œnanthic ester, of which Ordonneau found 4 grams in 100 litres of the alcohols obtained from a Cognac brandy twenty-five years old. The other esters discovered were ethyl acetate, 35 grams, and propionic, butyric, and caproic esters, together amounting to 3 grams.

Much discussion arose some years ago upon the proportion of esters which genuine brandy should contain. A minimum "standard" of 80 parts, calculated as ethyl acetate, per 100,000 of alcohol was advocated, and there is no doubt that most genuine brandies do contain this proportion, and more. But there is also no doubt, first, that occasional samples of genuine brandy may fall below this limit in respect of esters; and, secondly, that the adoption of such a standard based on a minimum proportion of esters alone would not afford protection against fraud, since, on the one hand, brandies of higher ester-content could be diluted down with "silent" spirit, and, on the other, esters could be added to factitious brandies to ensure the presence of the requisite quantity.

It is in every way better, in drawing conclusions from the results of analysis, to consider, not the proportion of esters alone, but the whole of the "secondary constituents," and especially the higher alcohols.

Girard and Cuniasse state that the sum of the secondary constituents, which they term the "coefficient of impurity," is rarely lower than 300 in genuine alcohol from wine.

M. Lusson (Municipal Laboratory, La Rochelle) considers that

[1] Amended during 1915 to 35° under proof for certain areas, under the Defence of the Realm Act.

the sum in question is never lower than 340 in pure *eau-de-vie* ; and that in *eaux-de-vie de Cognac* free from neutral spirit the sum of the esters and the higher alcohols is always above 300. The same author remarks that the sum of the acidity *plus* aldehydes lies normally between 10 and 36 per cent. of the total secondary constituents in *eaux-de-vie.* The lower number applies to newer spirits, the higher to products forty years old, but without being exactly proportional to age.

M. Rocques has shown that for well-made *eau-de-vie de vin* prepared in the Cognac district the ratio of the higher alcohols to the esters approximates to unity.

(In French practice, it should be remembered, the higher alcohols are determined colorimetrically and expressed in terms of an isobutyl standard. The colour produced by amyl alcohol is less than that given by isobutyl alcohol in the proportion of 3 : 5. Hence results obtained with an amyl alcohol standard require to be decreased in the same proportion for comparison with the French figures.)

If the esters in a sample of brandy fall substantially below 80, and at the same time the total secondary products are substantially below 300 when the higher alcohols are determined according to the French practice with isobutyl alcohol as standard, the inference is that the sample contains an admixture of neutral spirit. An approximate idea of the minimum amount of such admixture may be obtained by calculating from the foregoing numbers taken as standards, allowance being made for the corresponding quantities of products present in average specimens of neutral spirit.

The analysis of brandy is carried out by the methods already described for the examination of commercial spirits.

The following analyses of brandies and of neutral spirit (*alcools d'industrie*) are given by Girard and Cuniasse :—[1]

I. Eaux-de-vie of known origin. Analysed in 1896.

	Saintonge. 1880.	Saintonge. 1896.	D'Aunis. 1896.	Ile de Ré. 1896.	Armagnac. 40 years old.
Density at 15° . .	0·9157	0·8947	0·9011	0·8903	—
Alcohol, by vol. .	59·0	68·2	65·5	70·0	49·8
Extract, per 100 c.c.	—	Nil.	Nil.	Nil.	0·18
Secondary constituents :—					
Acidity	105·7	17·5	21·9	17·1	146·7
Aldehydes . . .	27·9	23·9	4·7	23·9	31·4
Furfural . . .	2·3	2·6	1·3	2·1	0·7
Esters	167·0	61·9	193·4	133·4	125·5
Higher alcohols .	159·8	259·8	190·5	219·8	203·5
Totals . .	462·7	365·7	411·8	396·3	507·8

[1] "*L'Analyse des Alcools,*" 1899, p. 287 *et seq.*

The "secondary constituents" are expressed as parts per 100,000 of absolute alcohol.

II. Eaux-de-vie de vin of known origin.

	Cozes. 1874.	Gémozac. 1893.	Gémozac. 1896.	Champagne. 15 to 20 years.
Density at 15° . .	0·9571	0·9075	0·9022	—
Alcohol, by vol. . .	37·0	64·5	66·0	59·0
Extract, per 100 c.c. .	—	—	—	0·2
Secondary constituents :—				
Acidity	201·0	100·4	29·0	111·8
Aldehydes . . .	46·0	32·3	11·5	30·0
Furfural	0·4	0·8	1·2	1·6
Esters	95·1	139·1	101·3	137·2
Higher alcohols . .	254·0	221·7	260·0	244·0
Totals . . .	596·5	494·3	403·0	524·6

III. Cognacs of normal composition.

Density at 15° . .	0·9351	0·9585	0·9415	0·8440	0·8468
Alcohol, by vol. .	51·5	89·9[1]	50·2	86·9	86·0
Extract, per 100 c.c.	1·24	1·46	2·22	0·01	0·01
Secondary constituents :—					
Acidity	149·0	210·0	148·2	11·0	16·7
Aldehydes . . .	25·5	19·2	30·0	13·5	14·3
Furfural . . .	1·6	0·7	1·2	0·2	—
Esters	133·2	92·6	148·9	338·2	261·9
Higher alcohols .	166·3	106·0	131·7	169·7	87·9
Totals . . .	475·6	428·5	460·0	532·6	380·8

[1] *Sic*, but does not agree with the density.

IV. Commercial Cognacs, deemed to be mixtures of alcohol derived from wine with "industrial" alcohol ("silent" spirit).

Density at 15° . .	0·9372	0·9433	0·9372	0·9396	0·9596
Alcohol, by vol. .	50·0	49·5	49·5	48·5	48·5
Extract, per 100 c.c.	0·956	1·760	0·568	0·648	0·668
Secondary constituents :—					
Acidity	57·6	92·1	92·1	24·7	24·7
Aldehydes . . .	18·2	24·5	22·4	18·8	21·1
Furfural . . .	0·9	1·0	1·0	1·0	1·0
Esters	66·8	71·1	69·5	65·3	61·6
Higher alcohols .	60·0	94·4	85·8	89·6	93·8
Totals . . .	203·5	283·1	270·8	199·4	202·2

V. Alcools d'industrie.

Density at 15° . .	0·8194	0·8539	0·8145	0·8164	0·8140
Alcohol, by vol. .	94·2	83·6	95·5	95·0	95·6
xtract, per 100 c.c.	0·012	0·005	0·005	0·010	—

Secondary constituents :—					
Acidity	2·5	5·7	5·1	2·5	2·5
Aldehydes	1·9	—	13·7	0·4	0·1
Furfural	—	—	—	—	—
Esters	13·0	12·3	22·1	3·7	3·6
Higher alcohols	Trace.	Trace.	Trace.	5·2	2·9
Totals	17·4	18·0	40·9	11·8	9·1

The following are analyses by the *Lancet* Commission on Brandy (November, 1904).

Secondary constituents :—				Public-house.	
	Three Star.	Two Star.	One Star.	(1).	(2).
Acidity	77·3	65·7	65·0	79·4	150·6
Aldehydes	12·6	12·2	10·0	7·4	6·6
Furfural	1·7	2·6	2·4	0·6	0·4
Esters	110·0	103·4	97·1	32·4	71·7
Higher alcohols	120·6	108·5	80·3	49·0	58·7
Totals	322·2	292·4	254·8	168·8	288·0

Of the public-house "brandies," No. 1 was considered to be a flavoured grain spirit, and No. 2 a grain spirit mixed with some rum.

Below are a few examples of brandy examined at the Government Laboratory and found to contain admixtures of neutral spirit :—

Secondary constituents :—	(1).	(2).	(3).	(4).	(5).	(6).
Acidity	41·6	38·5	26·3	25·7	51·4	5·3
Aldehydes	10·6	8·4	15·3	13·0	17·2	0·8
Furfural	3·3	0·5	0·8	0·6	1·9	Nil.
Esters	62·4	43·7	63·6	56·5	49·8	52·6
Higher alcohols	68·5	34·9	27·1	102·5	38·3	46·1
Totals	186·4	126·0	133·1	198·3	158·6	104·8

III.—GIN

Gin is a potable spirit flavoured with the volatile products of juniper berries, and often with those of other aromatic herbs as well. It may be either sweetened or unsweetened. The spirit employed is usually patent-still spirit made from cereals, of which maize, malt, and rye are the chief.

Typically, gin is grain spirit which has been rectified once or twice by the gin manufacturer, and then flavoured by actual distillation with the juniper-berries and other aromatics, if any of these are used. Hence one definition of gin which has been proposed is that the article is a spirit distilled from grain, doubly rectified, and then flavoured by distillation with juniper berries and other herbs. Sometimes, however, the flavourings are separately distilled

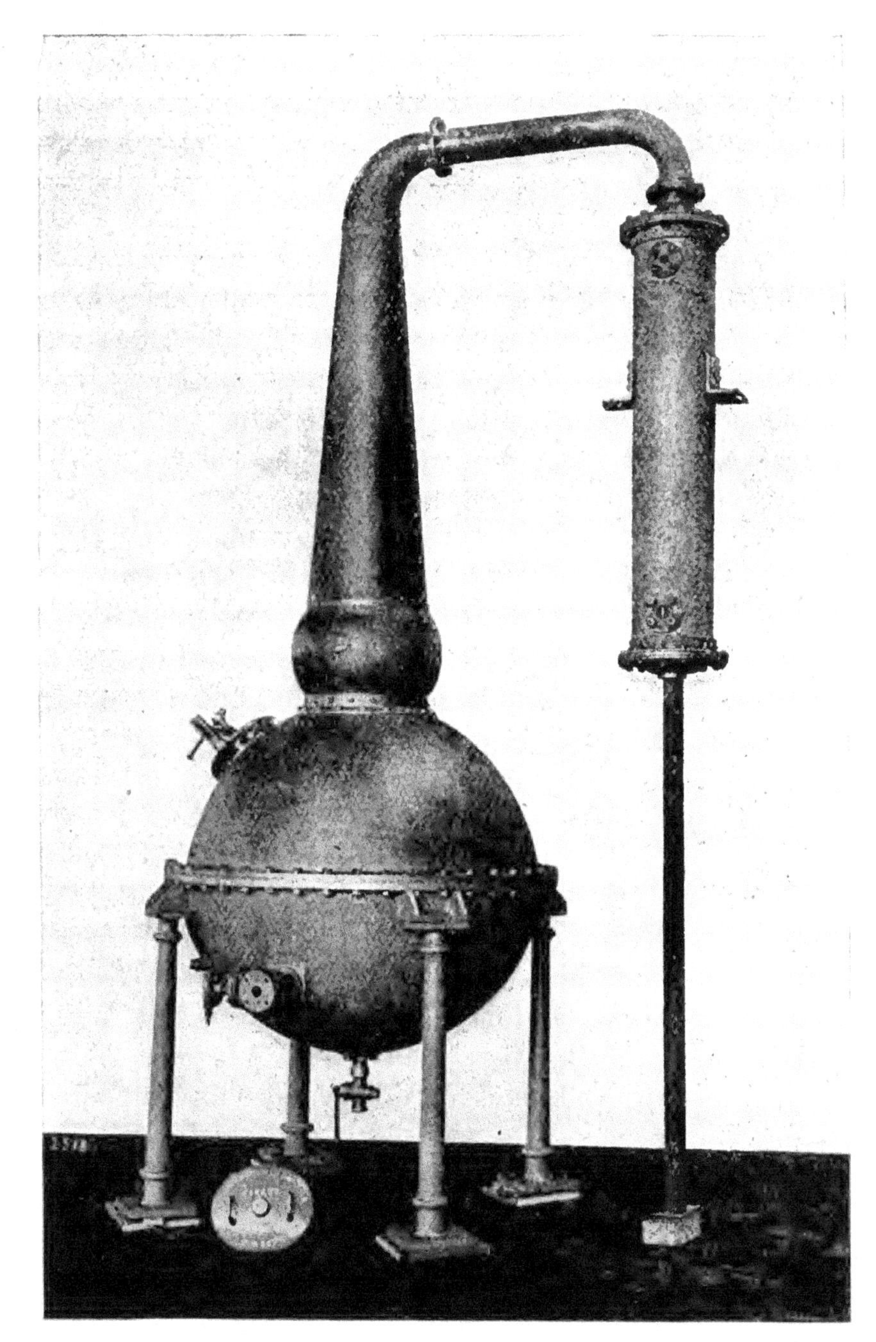

FIG. 40.—STEAM-JACKETED STILL.
Used for the manufacture of gin (Blair, Campbell & McLean, Glasgow).

with a small quantity of alcohol, and the product added afterwards to the rectified spirit.

By some it is considered that the rectification should not be so effective as to eliminate all the "grain" flavour of the spirit ; but it seems rather doubtful whether any palate except a specially-trained one would be likely to appreciate this flavour in the presence of the pronounced character of juniper oil and some of the other aromatics employed.

Ordinary patent still spirit flavoured with essential oils and not subsequently rectified is often sold as gin, though objection has been taken to this practice by what may be called the orthodox gin manufacturers.

The chief flavourings used other than juniper include angelica, almonds, calamus, cardamoms, cassia, coriander, fennel, grains of paradise, liquorice, orris, and turpentine. This last is said to be used occasionally as a substitute for the juniper. It may be mentioned that a former practice was to grind the juniper berries with the malt, so that they formed a part of the mash during fermentation and were distilled with it.

Makers of gin have their own special recipes, and the various kinds produced have differences of flavour accordingly. Thus in the West of England a favourite make is "Plymouth" gin, the particular flavour of which is said to be due to the presence of a little ether produced by adding a small quantity of sulphuric acid to the spirit before rectification. The sweetened varieties of gin, *e.g.*, "Old Tom," are made by mixing sugar syrup or "capillaire" with plain gin.

Dutch gin is known as Geneva, Hollands, and Schnapps. The name "Geneva" in this connection is probably derived, not from any association with the Swiss city, but from the Dutch word "jenever," meaning juniper. Geneva is made from a mixed mash of malted barley, rye, and maize in more or less equal proportions, the fermented wash being distilled in a pot-still to form "moutwine" or "maltwine," which is subsequently rectified and flavoured. The maltwine is made chiefly in Schiedam, and sold to the gin-makers, who rectify and flavour it.

E. J. Parry points out[1] that in the analysis of gin there is not much use in determining the "secondary constituents" of the spirit. Except for the slight "grain" character which is said to be desirable, gin is essentially "neutral" alcohol to which the characteristic flavourings are *added*, and it differs in this respect from brandy, whisky, and rum. The amount of flavouring is a matter of individual preference. Even the kind of flavouring, as well as the amount, is left to the judgment of the maker, subject, of course, to the condition that the essential character of the flavour should be that imparted by juniper.

[1] "Food and Drugs," Vol. I, p. 308.

Parry remarks that if an extract of the gin be made, proceeding as in the Allen–Marquardt method but using the lightest petroleum ether obtainable, instead of carbon tetrachloride, the taste of the residue left when the solvent is allowed to evaporate will afford considerable information as to the nature of the essential oil present. If half a litre of the gin be so treated, at least 0·5 gram of the oil can usually be obtained, and this suffices for determining the refractive index—on the Zeiss butyrometer, for instance. In ten authentic samples examined, the refractive index was never below 1·4750 (at 20°) and was usually about 1·4770. With turpentine, the value would fall to 1·4725 or lower.

Gin usually contains from 38 to 50 per cent. of alcohol by volume, or 66·5 to 87·5 per cent. of proof spirit. In this country, the legal minimum of alcoholic strength, in normal times, is 35° under proof (65 per cent. of proof spirit); and a good quality gin will approximate to 80 per cent. proof strength. In sweetened gin, the sugar may range from 1 to 6 per cent. or so, but is usually about 2 to 4 per cent.

IV.—RUM

This beverage has been defined as "a spirit distilled direct from sugar-cane products in sugar-cane growing countries," and the Royal Commission on Whisky, etc., considered that this definition "fairly represents the nature of the spirit which a purchaser would expect to obtain when he asks for rum."

Rum is a spirit which contains a somewhat high proportion of volatile acids, and owes its characteristic flavour mainly to a mixture of esters, chief among which are ethyl butyrate, formate, and acetate. Free formic acid is also present, and the flavour is no doubt affected to some extent by this and the other acids.

The rum imported into Great Britain comes chiefly from British Guiana and the British West Indian Islands, smaller quantities being obtained from the French West Indies, Dutch Guiana, and other countries.

There are two distinct types, one represented by Jamaica rum and the other by Demerara rum. The first type is the result of slow fermentation, lasting from ten to twelve days, of wash prepared at a relatively high specific gravity—namely, 1·078 to 1·096. The second is the product of a rapid fermentation, which lasts for thirty-six to forty-eight hours, of wash "set" at a low specific gravity—about 1·060.

To the Jamaica or slow-fermentation type belong the rums prepared in Grenada, St. Vincent, Antigua, Dominica, St. Kitts–

Nevis, and certain grades of Barbados and St. Lucia rums. Other varieties of Barbados and St. Lucia rum, and also Trinidad rum, are of the Demerara or quick-fermentation type. Martinique and Guadeloupe rums appear to be chiefly of the slow-fermentation kind.

Jamaica rum.—In Jamaica, the materials used in the wash are (1) molasses; (2) skimmings which accumulate during the purification of the sugar, and are allowed to "sour" during storage; and (3) "dunder," *viz.*, the residue remaining in the still after the distillation of the rum. These ingredients with water form the wash, which is fermented, and then distilled in a pot-still.

The slow fermentation allows of the development of bacterial

FIG. 41.—COPPER RUM STILL.
With double retorts and condenser, commonly used in Jamaica and West Indies (Blair, Campbell & McLean, Glasgow).

action, in addition to the alcoholic fermentation produced by the yeasts, and this appears to be an essential feature of the manufacture of Jamaica rum. This is especially the case in the production of "flavoured" or "German" rum, which, as a result of special fermentation, contains a higher proportion of esters and other secondary products than are found in the ordinary drinking variety or "common clean" rum. The "flavoured" rum is largely exported to Germany, where it is used for mixing with neutral spirit in the making of imitation rum. It may contain upwards of 2,000 parts of esters per 100,000 of alcohol. There is, however, no hard and fast line between this and the rum ordinarily used fo drinking; the two classes overlap as regards chemical composit strength, and flavour.

Demerara rum.—In British Guiana, the wash used for the making of Demerara rum is prepared by diluting molasses with water to a specific gravity of about 1·060. It is rendered slightly acid by the addition of a little sulphuric acid, in quantity sufficient to set free more or less of the combined organic acids, but not enough to leave any free sulphuric acid in the wash. The reason for making the wash acid is to guard against excessive propagation of butyric and lactic acid organisms, and to render it more suitable for active alcoholic fermentation. A little ammonium sulphate is sometimes added to serve as yeast food. Thus in rum of the Demerara type

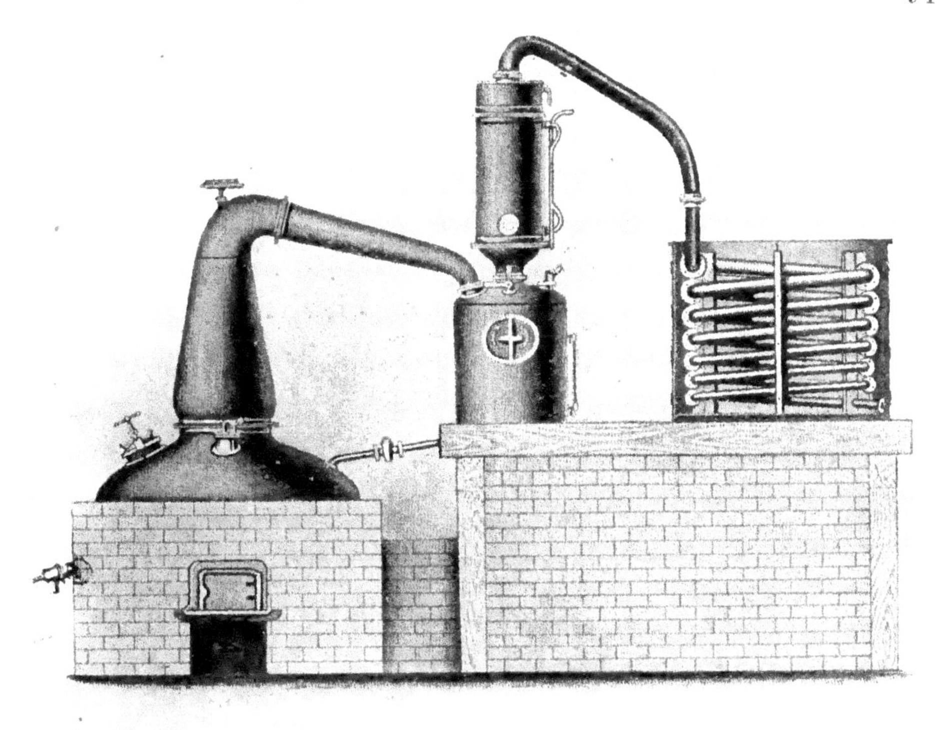

FIG. 42.—STILL FOR DIRECT FIRING.

With retort, rectifier and condenser. As commonly used in the Colonies for making rum and other strong spirits (Blair, Campbell & McLean, Glasgow).

there is a rapid fermentation, due almost solely to yeast action, and the bacterial organisms are not allowed time to develop appreciably. Both pot-stills (or "vat"-stills, a modified form of pot-still) and continuous rectifying stills are used in distilling Demerara rum. The proportion of secondary constituents in this spirit is usually very much less than in the Jamaica product.

W. Collingwood Williams[1] gives analyses of a number of authentic samples of Jamaica rum, the results being summarised below. The higher alcohols were determined by the Allen–Marquardt method, pre

[1] *J. Soc. Chem. Ind.*, 1907, 26, 499.

JAMAICA RUM.

	Alcohol. Vol. per cent.	Total solids. Grams per 100 c.c.	Total acid, as acetic.	Volatile acid.	Esters.	Higher alcohols.	Furfural.	Aldehydes.
I. Ordinary type. Twenty-one samples.								
Min. . .	68·6	0·01	30	21	88	46	1·0	5·0
Max. . .	82·1	1·16	155	146	1058	150	11·5	30·0
Average .	79·1	0·43	78·5	61	366·5	98·5	4·5	15·3
II. "Flavoured" rum. Seven samples.								
Min. . .	66·1	Nil.	45	39	391	80	2·7	13·0
Max. . .	80·6	0·61	145	137	1204	144	12·0	37·5
Average .	77·3	0·31	102·5	95·5	768·5	107	5·2	20·7

Except for the alcohol and solids, all the figures are expressed in the usual units—grams per 100 litres of alcohol.

In the following table, the analyses of a few individual samples of the above ordinary or "common clean" Jamaica rum are given as regards the secondary constituents, and also some analyses of Jamaica rum by other observers.

JAMAICA RUM.

Volatile acid.	Esters.	Higher alcohols.	Furfural.	Aldehydes.	Observer.
74	565	106	3·5	7·5	Williams.
76	372	150	4·5	18·0	,,
62	216	62	6·3	15·0	,,
61	181	46	4·6	30·0	,,
28	399	90·6	2·8	8·4	Vasey.
176	443	93·9	2·9	22·1	Girard.
48	338	84·0	3·2	11·9	Parry (mean of 10).

In Jamaica rum the esters are nearly always more than the higher alcohols as determined by the Allen–Marquardt process, and usually very much more.

As regards Demerara rum, Prof. J. B. Harrison, the official analyst, reported in 1904 that "a rum yielding 70 to 80 parts of esters (per 100,000 of alcohol) may be considered as a characteristic rum of the type known commercially as Demerara rum." He gives the following figures :—[1]

[1] *Official Gazette*, Demerara, Oct. 19th, 1904. Extract No. 2,083.

DEMERARA RUM.

Origin.	Average values. Esters.	Vol. acid.
Distilleries in Demerara county	54·7	26·5
,, Essequibo ,, ...	79·5	33·0
,, Berbice ,, ...	78·3	37·0
Continuous and Coffey-stills	44·9	18·4
Vat-stills	69·9	33·1

W. Collingwood Williams gives the following analyses of Demerara rum :—

Sample.	Total acid, as acetic.	Volatile acid.	Esters.	Furfural.
1	121	75	53	2·7
2	123	71	48	1·6
3	71	34	37	0·6
4	75	33	96	2·6

Thus it will be seen that the Demerara type of rum differs notably from the Jamaica variety, and more particularly in its low proportion of esters.

Analyses of Martinique rum are given by Bonis,[1] as follows. The first four were considered to be of superior quality, the next two of average grade, and the last three of low quality.

MARTINIQUE RUM.

	Vol. acid.	Esters.	Aldehydes.	Higher alcohols.	Furfural.
High quality . .	201	443	92	68	8·8
	201	91	59	385	5·3
	174	93	32	425	11·0
	165	62	34	339	0·9
Average quality .	173	83	20	244	0·5
	145	118	23	167	6·3
Low quality . .	197	95	16	97	3·8
	158	90	15	143	0·1
	53	51	10	280	0·7

The fixed acids ranged from 0·37 to 0·95 per cent., except in the first sample, which showed 2·2 per cent. It will be noted that in these examples the proportion of higher alcohols is usually greater than that of the esters.

As regards other varieties of rum, J. Sanarens[2] gives analyses of a number of authenticated samples, and also the results obtained from six samples of "artificial" rum. The maximum and minimum figures are summarised in the following table :—

[1] *Ann. Falsif.*, 1909, **12**, 521. [2] *Ibid.*, 1913, **6**, 488.

	Rum imported from				
	Guadeloupe.	Réunion.	Cochin China.	British Guiana.	Artificial rum.
Total acids :					
Min.	82	128	20	80	82
Max.	138	245	50	87	159
Aldehydes :					
Min.	5	4	6	10	4
Max.	36	41	17	41	14
Esters :					
Min.	31	56	12	24	127
Max.	72	101	29	46	2240
Higher alcohols :					
Min.	80	73	153	139	14
Max.	194	93	319	164	70
Furfural :					
Min.	1	1	trace.	1	1
Max.	3	4	1	2	5

The quality of rum is generally considered to depend largely upon the esters, but the other secondary constituents are also important, especially the acids. According to Williams, the proportion of esters is not an absolute measure of quality ; but, generally speaking, the higher-priced rums contain higher proportions of esters. A high proportion of aldehydes is considered by the same writer to have a deleterious effect upon the flavour, nullifying in some degree the influence of the esters.

To detect formic acid in rum, the sample should be made slightly alkaline with sodium hydroxide solution and evaporated to near dryness. The residue is then dissolved in water, transferred to a flask, acidified with phosphoric acid, and distilled. On testing the distillate with ammoniacal solution of silver nitrate, or with mercuric chloride solution, reduction is obtained if formic acid was present in the rum. To distinguish between the free and the combined acid, the sample should be carefully neutralised, the esters distilled off and hydrolysed, and the two portions evaporated and treated as above described.

H. Fincke[1] has found that Jamaica rum contains 0·0033 to 0·0050 gram of free formic acid per 100 c.c., and 0·0033 to 0·0044 gram of the acid in the form of esters. That is, there are approximately equal quantities in the two forms. In artificial rums, he found the corresponding quantities to be :—Free, 0·0027 to 0·0260 ; combined, traces to 0·0048. It is suggested that this difference may be an aid in distinguishing between genuine Jamaica rum and artificial rum.

Imitation rum or "Artificial rum" is made on the Continent, chiefly in Germany, and to a small extent in this country

[1] *Zeitsch. Nahr. Genussm.*, 1913, **25**, 589.

for exportation purposes. The Customs authorities distinguish between "rum," "rum from Jamaica," and "imitation rum"; and entries of imported spirits as "rum" are not accepted if the spirit comes from ports in countries where the sugar-cane is not grown, unless satisfactory evidence of its having been manufactured in a cane-growing country is produced.

Imitation rum may not be blended in bond with genuine rum for home consumption, but is allowed to be so mixed for exportation.

The imitation rum is made by flavouring and colouring patent-still neutral spirit, produced from grain, beet, or potatoes, with artificial essences. "Flavoured" Jamaica rum with high ester content is also employed to give some little verisimilitude to the imitation product. An essence much used is prepared by distilling a mixture of starch, alcohol, and crude acetic acid with manganese dioxide and sulphuric acid. The distillate contains formic and acetic esters, with alcohol, free acids, and probably other products of the oxidation; it is coloured with caramel if required, and mixed with silent spirit in the desired proportion.

The following analyses of factitious rum supplied to the West African Colonies were made in the Government Laboratory:—

Alcohol. Per cent. vol.	Secondary constituents.				
	Vol. acid.	Esters.	Aldehydes.	Furfural.	Higher alcohols.
32·4	31·5	52·5	8·7	Nil.	122·5
45·9	47·2	71·7	21·0	1·7	159·2
64·0	98·0	122·5	14·0	Trace.	218·7
55·5	3·5	141·7	38·5	"	140·0
42·7	5·2	126·0	59·5	Nil.	241·5
55·6	52·5	85·7	1·5	1·7	106·7

V.—WHISKY

Some years ago there was much discussion of the question, "What is whisky?" and a good deal of evidence was taken on the point before a Royal Commission, which issued its report in the year 1909.[1] One contention was that whisky muts be distilled in a pot-still, since this was the original method of distillation and at one time all whisky was made by this process. Moreover, the secondary constituents, which differentiate whisky from "neutral" or "silent" spirit, are largely eliminated by the patent-still. Against this it was argued that historically the patent-still represents an evolution from the primitive pot-still, and had long been used for the manufacture of what has been recognised both by the trade and

[1] Report, Cd. 4796.

the public as whisky; that in certain districts patent-still spirit by itself is bought and sold as whisky; and that a large proportion of the whisky of commerce is, in fact, a blend of pot- and patent-still spirit. Other questions also arose in regard to the admissible materials; whether, for example, Scotch whisky ought to be made entirely from malt; whether maize is admissible; and whether spirit distilled from potatoes could properly be regarded as whisky.

The Commission was unable to recommend that the use of the

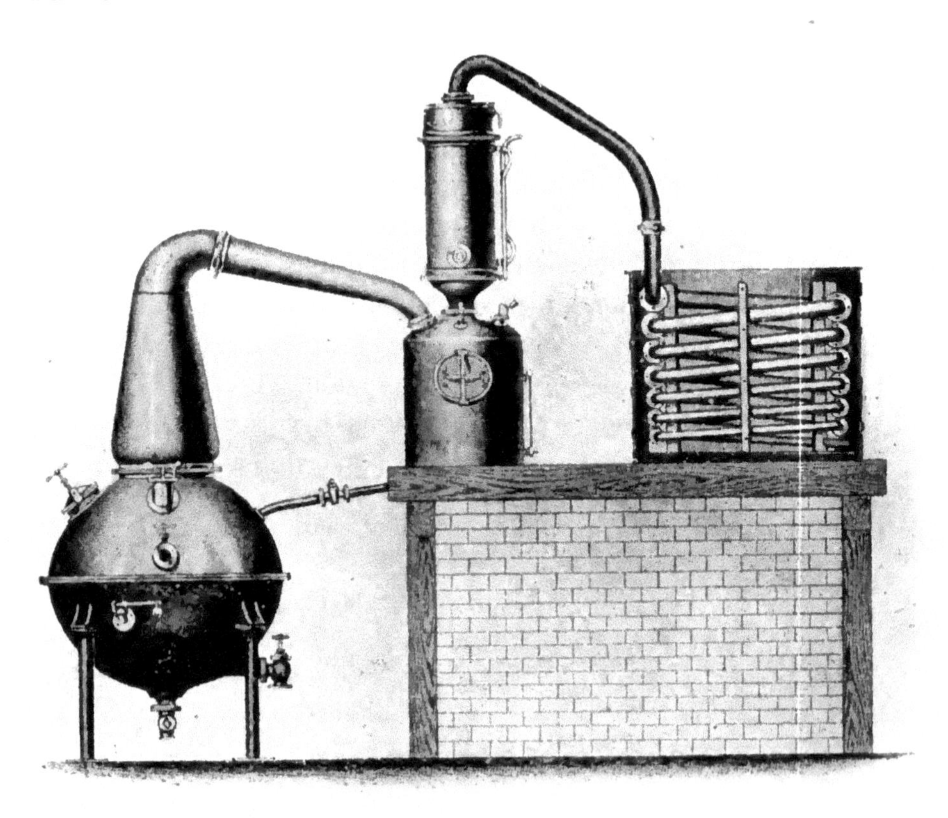

FIG. 43.—STEAM-JACKETED POT-STILL.

With retort, rectifier and condenser (Blair, Campbell & McLean, Glasgow).

word "whisky" should be restricted to spirit manufactured by the pot-still process. They give their reasons as follows:—

"The evidence which we received shows that such [patent-still] spirits have been frequently described as 'whisky' by distillers and traders since the patent-still came into use; and that for many years a section of the public, particularly in parts of Scotland and Ireland, has recognised patent-still spirit without admixture under the name of whisky, and has purchased it as whisky, no attempt being made by distillers or vendors to conceal the method of distillation. Moreover, spirit produced in the patent-still, as we have shown, has long been employed for blending with or diluting whiskies of different character and distilled in different forms of still. This has been by far its largest use, and most of the whisky now sold in the United Kingdom contains in greater or less degree spirit which has been obtained by patent-still distillation.

"Again, apart from the fact that pot-stills differ so much that a comprehensive definition would be difficult to frame without either excluding certain types of still which are now commonly regarded as pot-stills, or including other types which are not now looked upon as legitimate variations of the pot-still, there are strong objections to hampering the development of an industry by stereotyping particular forms of apparatus.

"Finally, we have received no evidence to show that the form of still has any necessary relation to the wholesomeness of the spirit produced."

As regards the materials, it appeared to the Commission that "whisky as a commercial product is regarded both by the manufacturers and by the public as a spirit made from no other materials than malt and unmalted grain; and it is as a matter of fact so made at the present time."

The general conclusion arrived at was that whisky is a "spirit obtained by distillation from a mash of cereal grains saccharified by the diastase of malt; that Scotch whisky is whisky as above defined, distilled in Scotland; and that Irish whisky is whisky, as above defined, distilled in Ireland."

An interesting outline of the history, manufacture, and technical treatment of whisky is given by the Commission in their report, which should be consulted for fuller details than can be given here. Some of the chief points, however, are included in the description given below.

History.—The early history of whisky is somewhat uncertain. The object of the original manufacturers of alcohol was in all probability to produce a stimulant only. Hence the alcoholic liquid which they obtained was named, according to the language of the different countries in which it was manufactured, "aqua vitæ," "eau de vie," "uisque-beatha," "usquebaugh," etc., all meaning the same thing, namely, "water of life."

But in course of time the advance of civilisation demanded a specially flavoured spirit rather than a mere stimulant, and it is only natural that the manufacturers in different countries, starting as they would generally with different materials, should have produced spirits of special flavours more or less peculiar to the country or district of origin. In the grape-growing countries, spirit was produced from wine; in the northern countries, where the vine is not largely cultivated, spirit was produced from grain.

The date at which "aqua vitæ" was first made in the British Isles is uncertain, but in Scotland the manufacture of spirits was a subject for legislation as early as the sixteenth century. Works on "distillation," published in the seventeenth century, show that the method of distillation in use at that period was not essentially different from that practised in the pot-still distilleries of Scotland at the present time.

Extracts from statutes seem to show that "aqua vitæ" was not the exclusive product of malted barley, but that other substances, such as unmalted grain, were also used in the early days of distillation in Scotland. The English statutes point to the same conclusion. In the year 1802 an Act of Parliament was passed, presumably owing to fear of scarcity during the continuance of the Napoleonic wars, expressly prohibiting the distillation of spirits from any kind of grain.

The term "whisky" is not used in any of these statutes, and it does not seem to have been employed until the latter part of the eighteenth century. At that time, it was undoubtedly synonymous in Scotland with "aqua vitæ." It is interesting to note that Robert Burns applies to the same subject the three terms "aqua vitæ," "usquebae," and "whisky."

Materials.—Coming to more recent times, there are excise records from the year 1827 onwards, which show that in Scotland, in the years 1827–9, when pot-stills alone were used, the quantity of spirits made from mixed malt and grain was only a little less than the quantity made from malt only. But it became much less in subsequent years, so far as the pot-stills were concerned. A small quantity of sugar and molasses was also employed, about the middle of the last century; but since then, with the exception of one year (1887), the Scotch pot-still distilleries appear to have used only malt, or malt and grain, the quantity made from malt only being always largely in excess of that made from the mixture of malt and unmalted grain. In recent years, wherever the pot-still process has been exclusively employed, malt only has been used, and practically no materials other than malt and unmalted grain have been used in either pot- or patent-stills.

A large majority of the Irish pot-stills have always produced spirit from a mixed mash of malt and unmalted grain. The quantity made by them from malt only has always been small in comparison. No other materials than malt and unmalted grain have been used to any great extent in the Irish pot-stills, or indeed in the patent-stills, during the last fifty years.

The unmalted grain employed in making whisky includes barley, maize, oats, rye, and wheat. For the manufacture of pot-still whisky in Scotland, barley malt is generally the only material employed in the mash; but in the Irish pot-still distilleries, with few exceptions a mixture of barley-malt and unmalted barley, oats, wheat, and rye is employed, maize being generally excluded. The proportions vary, with the view of obtaining particular flavours in the resulting whisky; but it may be taken that generally four-fifths of the whole mash consists of barley, malted and unmalted, and that the remaining one-fifth is made up of oats, wheat, and rye, in proportions decreasing in the order of enumeration.

For the *patent*-still process, the materials employed in the mash are much the same in both Scotland and Ireland. They are selected from malt, maize, barley, rye (malted and unmalted), and oats. The precise proportions in which they are used vary in different distilleries with the object which the distiller has in view. Thus in one Scotch distillery the mash was made up of 25 per cent. malt, 72 per cent. maize, and 3 per cent. oats; in another of 30 per cent. malt, 30 per cent. rye, and 40 per cent. maize. In one Irish distillery, it consisted of 35 per cent. malt and 65 per cent. of a mixture of barley and maize; in another, malted barley, rye, and maize were used in the proportions of 28, 36, and 36 per cent., respectively. Maize is very extensively used, both in Scotland and Ireland, in the patent-still process. Malted rye is also used in the mash in some patent-still distilleries, it being considered to improve the "body" of the whisky.

Distillation.—The general operations of distillation have already been described in Chapter II, but some further points bearing more especially upon the production of whisky may be mentioned here, or recapitulated. The simplest varieties of the pot-still are to be met with in Scotland, having long necks, but not otherwise furnished with any special means to secure rectification of the spirit. Other pot-stills, however, are in frequent use which are provided with pipes or circular vessels fitted between the neck of the still and the condenser, thus increasing the power of rectification. Such stills are, in effect, intermediate between the simple pot-still and the patent-still. As regards mode of heating, some are heated by direct fire, others by steam pipes and steam jackets. It is held by some distillers that this difference of heating is important in respect of the character of the whisky produced, in that the open fire causes a charring of the wash, and thus adds empyreumatic bodies to those already present. Others, however, contend that no difference is to be detected in the whisky obtained, whether steam or direct fire be employed.

In Scotland, two distillations are commonly required for preparing pot-still whisky from the wash. The first takes place in the "wash-still," all the alcohol being collected in one distillate, technically termed "low wines," together with secondary constituents and some water. The low wines are redistilled from a smaller still, and collected in three fractions, (1) "foreshots," (2) the clean or finished whisky, and (3) "feints." The foreshots and feints are collected together and redistilled with the next charge of low wines.

The judgment and experience of the distiller determine the

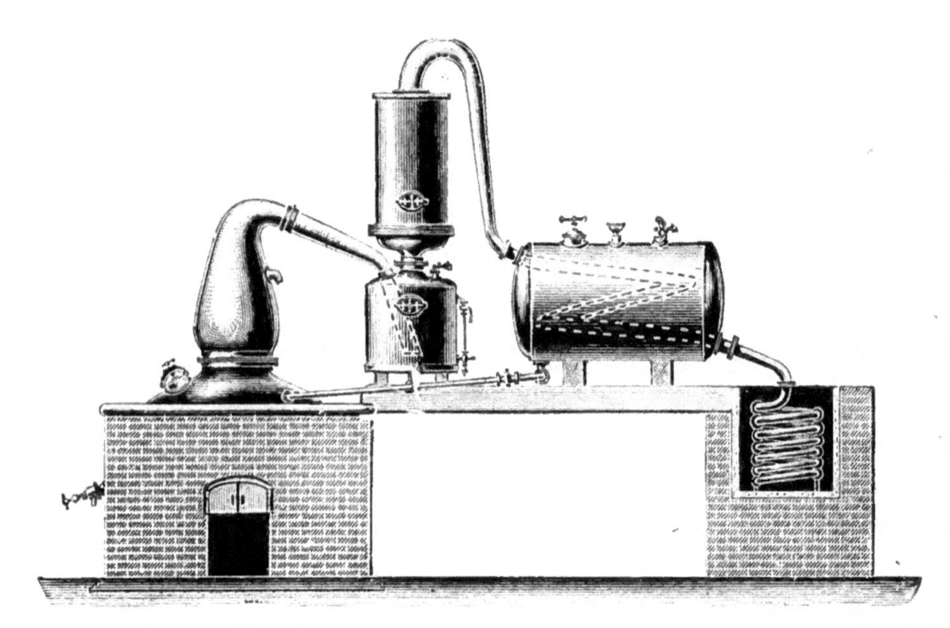

Fig. 44.—Pot-still for direct firing.

With retort, rectifier, wash heater and condenser (Blair, Campbell & McLean, Glasgow).

point at which the collection of foreshots is stopped, and that of whisky commenced; and, similarly, that at which the latter is stopped and the collection of feints begun. The strength at which the whisky fraction is run is generally about 11° to 25° over proof.

In some Scotch distilleries, however, the whisky is produced in three distillations; the spirit is then run off at 40° to 45° over proof. This practice is very general in the Lowlands.

Three distillations appear to be universally practised in Ireland for obtaining pot-still whisky; and the method of collecting fractions is somewhat more complicated than with the Scotch process. Strong low wines and weak low wines, strong feints and weak feints, are collected, and probably different practices obtain in every Irish distillery. The whisky fraction is usually run at a higher strength than in the Scotch practice, namely, from 25° to 50° over proof.

Maturing.—The flavour of newly-distilled whisky is crude and unpleasant. This is particularly the case with pot-still whisky, which contains more of the secondary constituents than the patent-still product. By storage in wooden casks certain changes are brought about in the character and amount of the secondary constituents, with the result that the flavour is improved. This process is "maturing"; it is effected more readily in the patent-still whisky than in that from pot-stills, which is often stored for many years in wood. Casks which have previously held sherry are frequently used for the purpose, and new casks sometimes receive a preliminary treatment with a sweet wine before being employed for the maturing of whisky. Much the greater quantity of the spirit, however, is matured in plain wood. The chemical changes which occur during storage will be dealt with later (p. 452).

Blending.—By this term is meant the mixing of two or more different whiskies. These may be all pot-still products, but more generally are mixtures of patent- and pot-still spirits. In the first case, the object of blending is to preserve uniformity of character; in the second, to obtain a milder, more uniform, and also a cheaper product than is furnished by pot-still spirit alone. The pronounced flavour of "self-whiskies"—the unblended products of individual distilleries—suits the taste of comparatively few consumers, whereas the blend appeals to a very much larger number. As practised in Scotland, the blending of pot-still and patent-still whisky is for the purpose of producing two distinct classes of spirits:—(1), mildly flavoured whisky of particular characters and good quality; and (2), a cheap but palatable whisky. As regards the latter, patent-still spirit costs less to manufacture than pot-still spirit, and if mixed with immature pot-still whisky—which is naturally cheaper than the fully matured article—the unpleasant taste is toned down, so that the mixture becomes more palatable. The proportion of pot-still whisky in these cheap blends depends chiefly upon the price: the cheapest may contain as little as 10 per cent., or less.

Classification.—For trade purposes Scotch whiskies are usually divided into five classes, *viz.*: (1) Highland malts; (2) Lowland malts; (3) Campbeltowns; (4) Islays, and (5) Grains, the last denoting patent-still whiskies. The first four are all whiskies made from malt only in pot-stills. Occasionally (3) and (4) are classed with (1); and (1) are sometimes subdivided into Speyside and North Country whiskies.

The Highland malt whiskies are mainly produced in the district on the mainland lying north of an imaginary line drawn from Dundee to Greenock, the Lowland malts south of this line. The Campbeltowns are distilled at the southern end of the Kintyre peninsula, and the Islays in the island of that name. The Grains are made in the district between the Firth of Forth and the Firth of Clyde. In the curing of the malt more peat is used for the Islays than for any of the other classes, and more for the Highland than for the Lowland Malts. Peat is not employed for curing the malt used in preparing the Grain whiskies. The Islays possess a notable peat flavour; the Highland malts are less strongly peaty; whilst the Lowland malts are less full-flavoured, and the Campbeltowns not so fine in character.

Irish whiskies are not classified in a similar manner. The "self" whiskies are usually sold under the name of the distiller or distillery, but the greater proportion of bottled whiskies is blended and goes either by the name of the blender or under some fanciful description. The Irish patent-still whiskies, however, as in Scotland, are sold under the name of "grains" in the wholesale trade.

Constituents.—The primary constituent of whisky is ethyl alcohol, but the characteristic flavour is due to small quantities of by-products or "secondary constituents" produced during the processes of malting, fermentation, distillation, and maturing. These secondary bodies fall into the groups of acids, aldehydes, esters, and higher alcohols which are ordinarily estimated in analyses; but, in addition, there are other substances present which quite probably affect the aroma of the spirit. Thus Schidrowitz and Kaye,[1] examining new pot-still whisky, obtained distinct evidence of the presence of pyrrol, phenolic bodies, an alkaline substance (probably an ammonium salt), hydrogen sulphide, and sulphur dioxide in different whiskies. They had also reason to suspect the presence of traces of nitriles, but did not obtain a positive identification. It was presumed that these various bodies, so far as they are products of dry distillation, were derived from the peat and coke used in malting, or from the action on the malt of the hot gases of the malt-kiln. Small quantities of volatile nitrogenous bases may also be present. Moreover, small amounts of sugars, acids, and colouring and extractive matters derived from the storage-vessels may exist in whisky, as well as added colouring matter.

As regards the nitrogenous bodies, Schidrowitz found the following proportions present in twenty samples examined by the method given below:—

[1] *J. Soc. Chem. Ind.*, 1905, **24**, 585.

NITROGEN COMPOUNDS IN WHISKY.

	Grams per 100 litres absolute alcohol. (Calculated as NH_3.)
Scotch whiskies (new).	
Highland Malts (6 samples)	0·09 to 0·19
Lowland ,, (3 ,,)	0·11 ,, 0·30
Campbeltowns (2 ,,)	0·08 ,, 0·14
Grains (6 ,,)	0·03 ,, 0·14
American rye whiskies (matured) (3 samples)	0·26 ,, 0·39

Method.—To 200 c.c. of the whisky, 0·2 gram of tartaric acid was added, and the whole evaporated to a small bulk. The residue was transferred to a small flask, made alkaline with caustic alkali, and then distilled with steam. The distillate was again rendered acid with tartaric acid, evaporated to a small bulk, transferred to a Kjeldahl apparatus, and treated in the usual manner with strong sulphuric acid and potassium sulphate. The ultimate distillate was Nesslerised.

A large number of analyses of whisky will be found in the evidence laid before the Royal Commission. Some of these are included in the selection given hereunder. The methods of analysis used in examining whisky are given in detail at the head of this section (pp. 406–423).

SPIRITS FROM PATENT-STILL DISTILLERIES.[1]

	Secondary constituents. (Mg. per 100 c.c. absolute alcohol.)					
	Volatile acid.	Aldehydes.	Esters.	Higher alcohols.	Furfural.	Total.
Scotch :—						
1. New	1·9	9·6	30·8	39·0	nil	81·3
2. ,,	1·9	4·7	41·1	97·8	,,	145·5
3. ,,	3·8	trace	22·8	14·0	,,	40·6
4. 3 months	5·2	,,	45·6	42·0	,,	92·8
5. 4½ years	15·6	14·1	46·4	81·3	,,	157·4
6. 7 ,,	19·0	10·8	35·0	21·8	0·1	86·7
7. 7 ,,	36·9	12·0	47·9	20·1	0·3	117·2
Irish :—						
8. New	3·5	trace	12·2	28·0	nil	43·7
9. 7 years	40·0	3·3	22·8	57·8	0·3	124·2

[1] Analysed in the Government Laboratory. Higher alcohols by colorimetric process.

Other particulars of these spirits may be summarised as follows.

Alcohol.—From 56·7 to 69·8 per cent. by volume, = 99·4 to 122·4 per cent. of proof spirit.

Total solids.—From 0·002 gram per 100 c.c. in No. 1 (stored in vat) to 0·029 in No. 6 (stored in plain wood cask) and 0·424 in No. 7 (stored in sherry wood cask).

Ash.—From 0·001 gram per 100 c.c. in No. 1 to 0·003 in No. 6 and 0·016 in No. 7.

Total acid.—Minimum 0·0012 gram per 100 c.c. in No. 1 (calculated as acetic acid); maximum 0·0360 in No. 7. The acid is chiefly volatile acid.

SPIRITS FROM POT-STILL DISTILLERIES.

District.	Age.	Secondary constituents. (Mg. per 100 c.c. of absolute alcohol.) Volatile acid.	Aldehydes.	Esters.	Higher alcohols.	Furfural.	Total.
Speyside	New	16·9	9·2	77·4	407·2	2·9	513·6
,,	6 yrs.	52·2	19·6	93·9	472·1	1·9	639·7
Banff	New	13·2	5·4	62·2	471·4	2·9	555·1
,,	7 yrs.	53·6	32·2	91·0	371·4	1·9	550·1
Islay	New	15·0	21·8	63·8	451·6	4·2	556·4
,,	7 yrs.	30·1	41·6	92·0	460·5	3·6	627·8
Campbeltown	New	17·0	33·6	72·9	410·9	3·5	537·9
,,	4 yrs.	37·5	34·8	81·4	453·0	3·3	610·0
Irish	New	3·3	50·2	102·8	522·6	3·1	682·0
,,	6 yrs.	32·6	55·9	86·4	771·2	2·9	949·0
,,	New	4·2	7·0	13·6	701·7	1·1	727·6
,,	6 yrs.	21·0	12·2	35·6	789·0	1·4	858·6

Other particulars of these spirits are :—

	Minimum.		Maximum.
Alcohol	59·7	per cent. by vol.	86·9
	= 104·6	,, proof spirit	152·3
Total solids	0·002	,,	0·185
Ash	0·001	,,	0·018
Acidity (calc. as acetic acid)	0·002	,,	0·046

The acidity was mainly, and in some cases entirely, due to volatile acid.

A comparison of the foregoing analyses shows very clearly the broad distinction between the "pot-still" and the "patent-still" spirits. There is always a much larger amount of the secondary constituents in the pot-still spirit.

Speaking generally, the proportion of every one of the secondary constituents usually determined is greater in the "pot" than in the "patent" spirit, but the most marked differences are in the higher alcohols and furfural. Patent-still spirit contains no furfural when new, although after storage in wooden casks it is sometimes found to contain traces of this substance, but always in much smaller amount than in pot-still spirit, from which it is never absent. The low proportion of higher alcohols and the absence of all but mere traces of furfural render it a comparatively easy matter to distinguish "patent-" from "pot-still" spirit. But the variation in the amounts of the secondary constituents in both classes of spirits makes it less easy to estimate the exact proportion of each kind of spirit present in mixtures.

Comparing the pot-still whiskies among themselves, it will be observed that there are considerable variations in both the total amount and in each constituent of the secondary bodies. The Scotch whiskies generally show a somewhat less total amount than the Irish, and the Speyside, Banffshire, and Highland samples have a rather smaller amount than the Islay and Campbeltown specimens. The latter, as well as the Irish samples, are mainly "blending," as distinguished from "self" whiskies.

The differences between new and old pot-still whiskies, so far as shown by analysis, are mainly in the increased amounts of the volatile acids and aldehydes, and to a less extent of the esters, found in the old spirit when stored in wooden casks. The higher alcohols and furfural show relatively much smaller differences.

HIGHLY RECTIFIED (PATENT-STILL) SPIRITS OF HIGH STRENGTH.

	Secondary constituents. (Mg. per 100 c.c. of absolute alcohol.)					
Description.	Volatile acid.	Alde-hydes.	Esters	Higher alcohols.	Furfural.	Total.
British, from Grain	1·2	trace	11·1	21·2	nil	33·5
" Molasses . .	1·2	3·5	7·3	63·0	"	75·0
Foreign (Hamburg) . . .	1·2	nil	5·5	10·4	"	17·1
" (Stettin)	1·2	2·2	7·2	83·7	"	94·3

Other particulars :—

Alcohol.—From 95 to 96·5 per cent. by volume, = 166·6 to 169·0 per cent. of proof spirit.

Total solids.—From 0·003 to 0·015 gram per 100 c.c.

Ash. " 0·002 " 0·010 " "

Total acid. " 0·0006 " 0·0006 " "

These spirits, it will be seen, are of much higher alcoholic strength than those in the two foregoing series, and contain in general still less of the secondary constituents than do the patent-still whiskies. They are not usually stored in wooden casks, but in metal drums or vats, and are used mainly for technical and industrial purposes. They are often of very great purity, although generally made from molasses, potatoes, and beetroot-sugar residues, or other materials not employed in making spirits intended for consumption in this country.

Ordinary public-house whisky, as sold in the working-class neighbourhoods of the principal towns in the United Kingdom, is usually either patent-still spirit, or a blend of patent- and pot-still spirits containing not more than one-third of the pot-still variety. Out of 91 samples purchased and examined officially,[1]

Sixteen were adjudged to be probably entirely patent-still spirits;

Thirty-six were considered to contain not more than 10 per cent. of pot-still spirit; and

Sixteen contained not more than one-third of the pot-still product.

Only nine of the samples were deemed to be probably pure pot-still spirit: these were all obtained from Ireland, and formed 30 per cent. of the total number (30) purchased in that country.

A few of the analyses are appended (p. 449), as regards the secondary constituents.

The *average* proportions of the chief secondary constituents in various classes of spirits were found by E. A. Mann to be as follows.[2] They are deduced from the analyses of 177 samples:—

I.—Distilled in pot-stills.

Type.	Esters.	Furfural.	Higher alcohols.
Highland malts	58·3	3·4	183
Lowland ,, ...	52·6	4·1	183
Campbeltowns	57	4·0	179
Islays	46·3	5·2	201

II.—Distilled in other stills.

Type.	Esters.	Furfural.	Higher alcohols.
Highland malts	67	2·1	179
Lowland ,, ...	46·7	1·4	189
Campbeltowns	53	2·0	169
Islays (none)	—	—	—
General average ..	56·3	3·43	184

III.—Distilled in patent-stills.

Type.	Esters.	Furfural.	Higher alcohols.
Grains	26	0·09	45·4

The higher alcohols were estimated by a slightly modified form of the Allen–Marquardt method.

[1] Sir T. E. Thorpe, Appendix Q, Report of Royal Commission.

[2] "Establishment of Standards for Whisky in Western Australia," 1915.

ORDINARY PUBLIC-HOUSE WHISKIES.

Country.	Description.	Secondary constituents. (Mg. per 100 c.c. of absolute alcohol.)					
		Volatile acid.	Aldehydes.	Esters.	Higher alcohols.	Furfural.	Total.
England	(*a*). Irish	1·4	3·5	38·0	24·0	0·1	67·0
,,	(*b*). Scotch	23·4	19·4	56·1	36·7	0·9	136·5
,,	(*c*). ,,	2·6	22·5	48·6	113·4	1·4	188·5
,,	(*d*). ,,	15·6	13·1	52·5	177·0	1·5	259·7
Scotland	(*a*). ,,	1·2	2·1	30·8	43·7	nil	77·8
,,	(*b*). ,,	7·8	11·0	42·7	66·3	0·7	128·5
,,	(*d*). Irish	18·0	17·1	51·2	172·7	1·6	260·6
Ireland	(*c*). ,,	11·0	14·0	44·9	139·8	1·5	211·2
,,	(*e*). ,,	5·9	7·3	43·5	197·9	3·8	258·4
,,	(*f*). ,,	7·7	13·6	37·8	431·6	3·3	494·0

(*a*) = probably all patent-still spirit.
(*f*) = ,, pot-still ,,
(*b*), (*c*), (*d*), (*e*) denote blends intermediate between (*a*) and (*f*).

Schidrowitz and Kaye have published a considerable number of analyses of authentic samples of whisky.[1] For the five chief classes of Scotch whisky they summarise their results as follows :—

RANGE OF SECONDARY CONSTITUENTS.

Class.	Total acid.	Non-volatile acid.	Esters.	Higher alcohols. (1) Colorimetric standard.	Higher alcohols. (2) Allen-Marquardt process.	Aldehydes.	Furfural.
Highland malts ..	10–31	0–35	33–185	328–864	112–235	4–66	1·6–6·3
Lowland malts ..	6–60	0–16	27–87	189–897	82–228	8–54	0–5·2
Campbeltowns ..	12–100	0–28	53–140	357–930	160–259	11–85	2·4–8·0
Islays	15–36	0–33	40–86	620–740	155–200	17–40	3·8–5·2
Grains	3–69	0–26	20–55	39–400	33–80	trace–17	0–0·9

[1] *J. Soc. Chem. Ind.*, 1905, **24**, 585 *et seq.*

The following analyses of Irish and American whiskies are due to Schidrowitz :—

Sample.	Age.	Alcohol, per cent. by vol.	Extract, per cent.	Total acid.	Non-vol. acid.	Esters.	Higher alcohols.	Aldehydes.	Furfural.
Irish Pot-still Whiskies :—									
1.	New	71·7	—	7	—	34	145	12	5·5
2.	13 yrs.	57·1	0·04	29	8	38	185	68	3·3
3.	New	74·1	—	6	—	28	233	8	4·1
4.	13 yrs.	60·5	0·05	32	8	47	264	21	4·4
5.	14 ,,	63·4	0·29	87	44	87	226	32	4·5
6.	Mature	46·6	0·13	67	26	59	147	16	2·6
American Whiskies :—									
Bourbon	5 yrs.	49·4	0·14	126	40	99	197	11	2·2
,,	Mature	47·8	0·56	122	30	78	129	14	3·0
Rye	7 yrs.	56·3	0·18	140	49	134	277	20	3·9
,,	Mature	49·3	0·16	160	49	141	286	18	3·4
,,	,,	46·1	0·16	135	31	125	187	21	3·9
,,	,,	46·6	0·22	82	21	71	150	13	3·6
,,	10 yrs.	44·4	0·60	70	18	79	98	11	2·7

The higher alcohols were estimated by the Allen–Marquardt process. Except in the case of the alcohol and extract, which are given in percentages, all the figures denote milligrams per 100 c.c. of absolute alcohol.

Of the Irish whiskies, Nos. 2 and 4 were stored in plain wood, and No. 5 in a sherry cask.

Changes in whisky during storage.—The most extensive examination of the changes which whisky undergoes during storage in casks is due to Crampton and Tolman, who carried out a series of experiments upon American whiskies over a period of eight years.[1] The higher temperature of storage, however, and the practice of charring the interior of the casks, make the conditions in America very different from those obtaining in this country. For the present purpose, therefore, it will be useful to consider a smaller series of experiments carried out in the Government Laboratory, London, on whisky stored in cask and in bottle over periods of $2\frac{3}{4}$ and $7\frac{1}{4}$ years.[2]

Four casks of pot-still spirits were kept in distillery warehouses, and samples were periodically drawn for examination. Two of the whiskies were of special distillation, having undergone treatment for the removal of furfural; the other two were of the ordinary character. A summary of the analytical results, sufficient to exemplify the changes, is given in tabular form on p. 453.

The corresponding samples stored in glass bottles showed practically no changes.

It will be seen that in the casks the spirit showed a gradual and quite appreciable loss of alcohol. There was during the first six months' storage a fairly well-marked increase in every one of the secondary constituents, over the amounts found in the new spirits. After nine to twelve months' storage the higher alcohols and the furfural remained practically constant, and the increases in the other constituents were very slow.

On the whole, the changes shown by these experiments to occur in the secondary constituents of whisky, though well-marked, are of comparatively limited range, even where the storage is in wooden casks; and they are practically negligible in glass bottles. This fact is of some importance in enabling spirits to be traced and identified; or, on the other hand, in showing that they are different from what they are alleged to be.

It has already been mentioned that the chief analytical difference shown between new and old pot-still whiskies stored in casks consists

[1] *J. Amer. Chem. Soc.*, 1908, **30**, 98.

[2] Appendix Q, Report of Royal Commission.

CHANGES DURING STORAGE IN WOODEN CASKS.

Cask.	Age.	Alcohol, per cent. as Proof Spirit.	Alcohol, per cent. as abs. alc.	Secondary constituents. Volatile acid.	Aldehydes.	Esters.	Higher alcohols.	Furfural.	Total.
A.	New	120·5	68·7	14·0	3·0	41·7	321·0	nil	379·7
,,	6 months	110·3	63·0	14·2	4·0	44·7	350·8	0·3	414·0
,,	$1\frac{1}{2}$ yrs.	109·5	62·5	17·5	4·0	43·9	352·6	0·3	418·3
,,	$7\frac{1}{4}$,,	103·8	59·2	18·5	6·0	47·5	375·0	0·3	447·3
B.	New	111·5	63·7	13·1	21·8	65·9	252·6	3·3	356·7
,,	2 yrs.	109·7	62·7	15·8	27·0	75·4	266·6	3·5	388·3
,,	$7\frac{1}{4}$,,	105·6	60·2	15·8	36·8	82·4	258·0	3·5	396·5
C.	New	120·2	68·6	14·0	7·5	46·3	245·6	nil	313·4
,,	9 months	111·4	63·6	15·8	21·2	47·4	350·8	0·1	435·3
,,	$2\frac{3}{4}$ yrs.	110·4	63·0	17·5	22·8	54·4	352·6	0·1	447·4
D.	New	120·0	68·5	12·2	3·1	47·5	228·0	3·5	294·3
..	9 months	110·0	62·8	13·4	5·8	50·0	350·8	3·5	423·5
..	$2\frac{3}{4}$ yrs.	108·9	62·2	15·8	5·8	45·7	352·6	3·5	423·4

in the increased amounts of acids, aldehydes, and esters. According to Thorpe,[1] much of the increase is probably due to a process of extraction of secondary products absorbed in the wood of the casks from former spirits. This absorption is to some extent selective. The ethyl alcohol slowly diffuses through the wood of the cask and passes into the air, leaving some of the esters and higher alcohols behind in the wood, which thus becomes more or less charged with these secondary constituents, according to the length of time and other circumstances attending the storage. Probably also, especially when the casks are empty, there is some production of acids and aldehydes by the slow oxidation of the alcohols in and adherent to the wood of the casks, and the increased acidity would favour the production of esters also.

Crampton and Tolman[2] found an *increase* in the alcoholic strength of spirits stored in wood, amounting to about 1 per cent. per annum. They explain this increase by the fact that water passes through the pores of the wood more readily than alcohol does. The increase in the proportion of higher alcohols is due, they consider, to the diffusion of water and ethyl alcohol through the pores, the wood being practically impervious to the higher alcohols. Furfural may be derived from the charred interior of the cask, and there is also an actual increase in the acids, aldehydes, and esters. The changes are comparatively rapid at first, but proceed very slowly after a period of three or four years.

VI.—LIQUEURS, CORDIALS, AND COMPOUNDED SPIRITS

Liqueurs and cordials.—There is no essential difference between liqueurs and cordials, but as a rule the name "liqueur" is applied to foreign products, whilst the British preparations are generally termed "cordials."

Typically they are strongly spirituous and usually sweetened compounds, flavoured with aromatic herbs, essences, or fruit extracts, and often coloured. Among the best-known foreign liqueurs are absinthe, anisette, benedictine, chartreuse, crême de menthe, curaçoa, kirsch, kümmel, maraschino, noyau, and vermouth; whilst in this country are made such preparations as cherry brandy, cherry whisky, clove cordial, ginger cordial, orange bitters, peach bitters, peppermint cordial, and sloe gin.

The flavouring of the higher class liqueurs is almost a fine art. They have been fancifully compared to musical harmonies. In a

[1] *Loc. cit.*

[2] *Loc. cit.*

scale of flavours some are concordant with others, some discordant, like the notes of a musical scale ; and the art of the expert liqueur maker consists in so choosing his flavours that they shall blend, like the notes of a chord, into a pleasing, harmonious whole. Hence in the best qualities of liqueurs care is taken to have highly-rectified, neutral alcohol and pure white sugar as the fundamentals, in order that the flavour of the final product may not be impaired. Both grape spirit and grain spirit are used, the former in the better kinds of liqueur, the latter in the commoner varieties and in cordials.

The exact recipes for the more esteemed liqueurs such as chartreuse are, of course, trade secrets ; but among the chief flavouring ingredients used in making these compounds are the following :—

Almonds, angelica (root and seeds), aniseed, balm, calamus, caraway, cardamoms, chervil, cherries, cinnamon, cloves, coriander, cubebs, curaçoa oranges, dill, fennel, gentian, ginger, hyssop, juniper, lemon peel, muskmallow, orange peel, orris root, peppermint, pineapple, raspberries, sassafras, spearmint, strawberries, wormwood, and vanilla.

In making the liqueurs three principal methods are employed for treating the flavouring ingredients.

(1). An essence is obtained by macerating the ingredients in alcohol, distilling the mixture, and rectifying the distillate.

(2). An alcoholic extract is made by digestion of the ingredients and filtration, without distilling.

(3). For inferior kinds, an essence is prepared by simple solution of essential oils (*e.g.*, oil of anise, oil of lemon) in alcohol. Whichever method is adopted, the resulting solution is mixed in the required proportions with sugar syrup and alcohol, coloured if necessary, clarified with white of egg, isinglass, or other suitable agent, and filtered. The liqueur may be " mellowed " by digestion for a short time at a gentle heat in a closed vessel.

As an illustration, the following method of making ordinary " anisette " may be cited :—

Anise seed	3 kilos.
Star anise seed	3 ,,
Coriander ,,	1 ,,
Fennel	1 ,,
Alcohol (85 per cent.)	52 litres.

(1).—The bruised seeds are digested with the alcohol for twenty-four hours, then 25 litres of water added, and the mixture distilled until 51 litres have been collected. To this distillate 25 litres of water are again added, and the mixture redistilled till 50 litres of distillate have passed over. This is the flavouring essence.

(2).—Of this essence, 5 litres are mixed with 20 litres of alcohol (80 per cent.), 12½ kilos. of sugar, and 66 litres of water. The sugar is first dissolved by heat in a part of the water, and added as a syrup. The spirituous mixture is then clarified and filtered.

In France, liqueurs are divided into four main classes as *ordinaires*, *demi-fines*, *fines*, and *surfines*; *liqueurs doubles* are also made. The *demi-fines* have more alcohol, sugar, and flavouring than the *ordinaires* of the same type; the *fines* more than the *demi-fines*; and so on. It is not merely a question of less water; the better qualities may contain additional flavouring-ingredients and be generally better prepared than the commoner kinds.

The colouring matters which have been employed for colouring liqueurs include coal tar colours such as aniline red, aniline violet, malachite green, and indigo carmine; alkanet root, brazil wood, caramel, catechu, chlorophyll, cochineal, cudbear, hæmatoxylin, indigo, orchil, saffron, sandalwood, and turmeric. With the vegetable colourings, a little alum is added to increase the permanency of the colour.

Ratafias are liqueurs prepared with the extracts of fruits, etc., not distilled. Thus raspberry ratafia *demi-fine* according to one formula is made by mixing the following :—

Extract of raspberries	20 litres.
,, wild cherries	6 ,,
Alcohol (85 per cent.)	10 ,,
Sugar	25 kilos.
Water	47 litres.

Absinthe contains oil of wormwood as its characteristic constituent, with other flavourings such as anise, fennel, coriander, and angelica. It is chiefly used in France and Switzerland.

Crême de Menthe is flavoured with essence of peppermint, and sometimes with other flavourings in addition, *e.g.*, balm, cinnamon, orris, and ginger.

Chartreuse and Benedictine are highly sweetened liqueurs. Angelica, cinnamon, hyssop, mace, lemon balm, and peppermint are some of the constituents in recipes which are said to produce good imitations of the chartreuse actually made by the Carthusian monks.

Curaçoa is flavoured with the peel of curaçoa oranges and of ordinary oranges.

Kirsch or **Kirschenwasser** is a spirit distilled from the fermented juice of wild cherries, sometimes mixed with brandy, or flavoured with almonds and apricot-seeds.

Kümmel is prepared from caraway seeds, with auxiliary flavourings such as cumin.

Maraschino is supposed to be prepared from the marasca cherry, grown in Dalmatia, but other cherries, raspberries, and auxiliary flavourings are now often used.

Noyau is flavoured with apricot or peach kernels.

Vermouth is essentially a sweetened wine of wormwood, made chiefly in Italy and France. Orange wine is often used in the cheaper qualities, and alcohol is also added. Various bitters and aromatics may be used as auxiliaries to the wormwood, such as angelica, gentian, elecampane, cinnamon, and nutmegs.

The following analyses, here slightly abbreviated, of liqueurs are given in König's work; but it should be borne in mind that liqueurs called by the same name are not always made from the same formula, and that there are sometimes different qualities of the same type.

ANALYSES OF VARIOUS LIQUEURS.

Kind.	Sp. gr.	Alcohol. Vol. per cent.	Extract.	Cane-sugar.	Ash.
Absinthe	0·9116	58·9	0·5	—	—
Angostura	0·9540	49·7	5·9	4·2	—
Anisette de Bordeaux .	1·0847	42·0	34·8	37·4	0·04
Benedictine	1·0709	52·0	36·0	32·6	0·14
Chartreuse	1·0799	43·2	36·1	34·4	—
Crême de Menthe . .	1·0447	48·0	28·3	27·6	0·04
Curaçoa	1·0300	55·0	28·6	28·5	0·06
Ginger	1·0481	47·5	27·8	25·9	0·07
Kümmel	1·0830	33·9	32·0	31·2	—

As regards the estimation of the essential oils in liqueurs, the method adopted officially in France is to distil the sample, make up the distillate to the original volume with water, and then determine the iodine absorption by Hübl's process.

One hundred c.c. of the liqueur are placed in a 250 c.c. distilling-flask, 10 c.c. of water added, and the mixture distilled till 100 c.c. have been collected. Of this, 50 c.c. are placed in a 250 c.c. glass-stoppered flask, and 25 c.c. of the following mixture added :—

Iodine, 50 grams, mercuric chloride 60 grams; separately dissolved in 1 litre each of 96 per cent. alcohol, and equal volumes of the two solutions mixed.

The distillate, after being well mixed with the 25 c.c. of iodine reagent, is set aside for three hours at a temperature of 18°. A "blank" experiment is carried out at the same time on alcohol containing no essential oils.

At the end of the three hours, 10 c.c. of a 10 per cent. solution of potassium iodide are added, and the two solutions titrated with decinormal thiosulphate solution. Let N be the number of c.c. required for the pure alcohol, and n for the liqueur. Then $(N - n) \times 0{\cdot}254$ gives the quantity of iodine absorbed per litre of liqueur.

From a knowledge of the iodine value of the oil in question, the proportion in the liqueur can be calculated. Following are the quantities of iodine absorbed by 1 gram of the various essential oils :—

Oil.	Grams of iodine absorbed.
Turpentine	3·119
Neroli	3·039
Peppermint	0·585
Orange	3·475
Bitter almonds	0·000
Absinthe* (*petite*)	0·939
,, (*grande*)	0·508
Aniseed	1·391
Star-anise	1·566
Hyssop	0·683
Fennel	1·297
Coriander	2·605
Tansy	0·109

* Absinthe petite = *Artemisia maritima*, Absinthe grande = *A. absinthium*.

For the mixture of oils used in absinthe liqueur, Sanglé-Ferrière and Cuniasse take 1·238 as the mean value of iodine absorbed per gram of the mixture.

According to A. Auguet,[1] the results are too low if the iodine solution prepared in the ordinary way is used whilst fresh : the maximum values are given with a solution which is some months old. This is attributable to the development of hydriodic acid in the Hübl's iodine solution, and the addition of this acid is therefore recommended, in order to fit the iodine solution for use at once. The proportion of hydriodic acid suggested is 7·5 to 10 grams per litre. The sample should be allowed to stand for two hours at a temperature of about 18° after mixing with the iodine solution.

Various liqueurs tested by this method gave the following results, expressed in grams of iodine absorbed per litre of the sample :—

Absinthe	2·9	Benedictine	1·0
Amer Picou	0·15	Menthe blanche	0·47
Anisette	0·3 to 1·13	Peppermint	0·39

Alcoholic solutions of various essential oils (2 parts per litre) gave the following values for iodine absorbed :—

[1] *Ann. Falsif.*, 1906, **6**, 385.

Aniseed (French) . . .	3·5	Mint	0·74
Balm-mint	4·3	Neroli (0·13 per cent.) .	3·4
Bergamot	4·7	Orange	6·3
Coriander (0·1 per cent.) .	2·2		

The Wijs method of estimating iodine absorption is not suitable for use with alcoholic solutions of essential oils.

According to X. Rocques,[1] recounting the results of an investigation carried out for the *Société des Experts-Chimistes de France*, the iodine method gives accurate determinations with aniseed and kümmel (caraway) liqueurs only. Oil of aniseed absorbs 1·45 grams of iodine by the Hübl process, and oil of caraway 2·40 grams, per gram of oil. With other liqueurs, the method recommended is to saturate the distillate with salt, extract with petroleum ether, allow the solvent to evaporate at a low temperature, and weigh the residual oil. A recent French decree fixes the maximum of total essential oils in liqueurs at 0·5 gram per litre.

C. F. Muttelet[2] points out that since menthol does not absorb iodine, it is well to use the extraction method just mentioned in examining peppermint liqueurs, otherwise added menthol is not detected. One gram of oil of peppermint will absorb 0·45 gram of iodine; hence if the iodine value of the oil extracted from peppermint liqueur by petroleum ether is determined the result will indicate whether menthol has been added. This author also remarks that liqueurs which have been coloured with caramel may yield distillates containing unsaturated (furfuraldehydic) compounds derived from the caramel. These would absorb iodine, and to that extent vitiate the results obtained by the iodine process.

Muttelet also describes the following method of carrying out the extraction process of determining the total quantity of essential oils in liqueurs. Two hundred c.c. of the sample are mixed with 75 c.c. of water and distilled, 200 c.c. of distillate being collected. Fifty grams of finely-powdered sodium chloride are then dissolved in the distillate, and the solution is extracted three times with petroleum ether (b.p. about 40°), using 10 c.c., 5 c.c., and 5 c.c. The petroleum ether solution is dried with a little anhydrous sodium sulphate, and removed to a conical weighing flask, which is fitted with a cork carrying two glass tubes. The solvent is evaporated by passing a slow current of air through the flask while the latter, in the early stages, is maintained at a temperature of about 25° to 30°. The evaporation is continued until the weight of the contents of the flask does not diminish by more than 2 mg. after continuing the air current for five minutes. Experiments with aniseed essence

[1] *Ann. Falsif.*, 1916, **9**, 127–134. [2] *Ibid.*, 70–73; 134–143.

and Chartreuse essence showed that the loss of essential oil in estimations by this method was less than one-tenth of the quantity present.[1]

"Compounded spirits" is a general term indicating spirits which have been sweetened or flavoured, or both. It includes such preparations as gin, sloe gin, British brandy, imitation rum, liqueurs, and cordials; but the term is not confined to beverages.

"British compounds" are defined in sec. 3 of the Spirits Act, 1880, as "spirits redistilled or which have had any flavour communicated thereto, or ingredient or material mixed therewith."

For certain fiscal purposes in connection with allowances on exported spirits, these are "deemed to be plain spirits or spirits in the nature of spirits of wine, unless they are proved to the satisfaction of the Commissioners [of Customs and Excise] to have been distinctly altered in character by redistillation with or by the addition of flavouring matter." (Sec. 5 (2) of Finance Act, 1902, as amended by Sec. 8 of the Revenue Act, 1906.)

There are a few other terms commonly used in dealing with spirits which it may be convenient to mention here.

"Enumerated spirits."—For the purposes of the Customs tariff, brandy, rum, imitation rum, and Geneva are classified as "enumerated" spirits. All other imported spirits are classified as "unenumerated"; they may be either sweetened or unsweetened.

Sweetened spirits are described in the revenue regulations as "spirits to which any matter has been added after distillation, which imparts to them the quality of sweetness and produces obscuration to the amount of over 0·6 per cent."

Liqueurs are not defined by statute, but official regulations describe them, solely from the revenue point of view, as "compounded spirits, the ingredients in which interfere with the correct action of the hydrometer." British liqueurs are deemed to include all sweetened or otherwise "obscured" British compounds, including essences and perfumed spirits, of which the true strength cannot be ascertained without distillation.

Tinctures, as used in pharmacy, are properly preparations obtained (1) by macerating or percolating crude drugs with alcohol (*e.g.*, Tincture of Myrrh, B.P.; Tincture of Krameria, B.P.); or (2) by dissolving definite chemical substances or proximate

[1] *Ann. Chim. Anal.*, 1916, **21**, 50–55.

principles in alcohol (Tincture of Ferric Chloride; Tincture of Cantharidin); or (3) by dissolving extracts, etc., of drugs with alcohol (Tincture of Indian Hemp). There are, however, other preparations to which the name " tinctures " has been applied with some qualification—namely, " ethereal " tinctures, and " aqueous " or " glycerin " tinctures. The **ethereal tinctures** are prepared from certain drugs by substituting ether for alcohol. The **aqueous** or **glycerin tinctures** are made by using, instead of alcohol, a mixture of glycerin, water, and acetic acid to extract or dissolve the drug.

"Tinctures," for the purposes of drawback under the British fiscal regulations, include not only medicinal articles such as those indicated above, but also flavouring essences and perfumed spirits. Moreover, spirituous toilet vinegars and waters, dentrifices, hair washes and brilliantines, are also for these special purposes deemed to be " perfumed spirits " and are therefore included as tinctures.

Essences, in British usage where spirits are concerned, are alcoholic solutions of flavourings or perfumes, and sometimes of medicinal substances. In France and some other parts of the Continent, " essence " denotes a volatile oil; in the United States spirituous flavourings, etc., are known as " extracts." Examples of essences are the essences of almonds, lemon, peppermint, and vanilla amongst the flavourings; of ambergris, bergamot, and civet in the perfumes; and of camphor, pepsin, and senna amongst the medicinal preparations. The proportion of dissolved oil or other active substance in the essences varies considerably; thus essence of lemon may contain anything between 5 and 30 per cent. of the essential oil of lemon. Many of the " essences " are quite similar to " spirits " of the same substance except as regards the proportion of dissolved ingredient; and even in this respect there is no necessary difference, though the " spirit " is generally the richer in the active ingredient. Examples are essence of cinnamon and spirit of cinnamon; essence of peppermint and spirit of peppermint. The two " spirits " are official in the Pharmacopœia, and contain, as do most of the other B.P. medicinal spirits, 10 per cent. (by volume) of the respective essential oils. The two essences may contain as little as 2 or 3 per cent. of the oils.

In the United States the Association of Official Agricultural Chemists have agreed upon certain standard strengths for extracts (essences) used in flavouring foodstuffs, as follows :—

Essence.	Essential oil. Per cent. by vol.
Sweet basil	0·1
Thyme	0·2
Celery-seed	0·3
Rose	0·4
Almond ; sweet marjoram	1·0
Cassia ; cinnamon ; clove ; nutmeg	2·0
Anise ; peppermint ; spearmint ; star-anise ; winter-green	3·0
Lemon ; orange	5·0

Ginger essence (extract) is to contain in 100 c.c. the alcohol-soluble matter of 20 grams of ginger.

Tonka essence is to contain 0·1 per cent. by weight of coumarin and a corresponding proportion of the other soluble matters of tonka beans.

Vanilla essence is to contain in 100 c.c. the soluble matter of 10 grams of vanilla beans.

The analysis of these various essences, perfumes, spirits, and tinctures, so far as the alcohol is concerned, presents no special difficulty, as a rule. The oils, etc., are extracted with petroleum ether by Thorpe and Holmes's method as described in Chap. VI, the alcohol distilled off from the saturated salt solution, and determined as usual.

For the estimation of the essential oils where the larger proportions are present, the following method can generally be employed.[1]

To 10 c.c. of the essence pipetted into an ordinary Babcock milk-testing bottle are added in the order given 25 c.c. of cold water, 1 c.c. of hydrochloric acid (sp. gr. 1·2), and 0·5 c.c. of chloroform. The mouth of the bottle is closed with the thumb, and the bottle vigorously shaken for not less than a minute. In this way all the oil is dissolved out by the chloroform. The bottle is now whirled in the centrifuge for one and a half to two minutes, and the resulting clear supernatant liquid is removed to within 3 or 4 c.c. by means of a glass tube of small bore connected with an aspirator. To the residue, 1 c.c. of ether is added, and the contents of the bottle well shaken. The bottle held at a slight angle is then placed up to the neck in a boiling water- or steam-bath, in which it is kept for exactly one minute, a gentle rotatory movement being meanwhile imparted to it. The ether present serves to sweep out all traces of the chloroform, when thus treated. Finally, the bottle is cooled, water added to bring the separated oil into the graduated neck, and the volume of the oil observed after centrifuging

[1] C. D. Howard, *J. Amer. Chem. Soc.*, 1908, **30**, 608.

for half a minute, the reading being taken at the highest part of the meniscus. With the heavier oils, such as wintergreen, diluted sulphuric acid (1 : 2) is better than water for separating the oil. In this case shaking should be avoided and the temperature kept below 25°.

The above method is inapplicable when the proportion of essential oil is very small, as in flavoured beverages and some medicines. In such cases, it is often practicable to make an approximate determination by distilling the liquid and extracting the distillate, sufficiently diluted, with chloroform or carbon tetrachloride. The iodine absorption of the oil thus extracted is then determined by adding Hübl's or Wijs's iodine solution to the chloroform or carbon tetrachloride extract, and proceeding as usual. A comparison experiment is made at the same time with a solution prepared to imitate the sample under examination, but containing a known quantity of the oil in question. This solution is distilled, and treated side by side with the sample, so that the operations are similar in all respects. From the results the approximate quantity of essential oil can be calculated. It bears the same ratio to the known quantity in the comparison sample as the corresponding iodine absorptions have to one another. (This is strictly correct only if the iodine "values" of the two specimens of oil are the same; but for the small quantities here concerned the variations are of no moment.)

Generally, 25 or 50 c.c. of the sample may be diluted and distilled till 75 or 100 c.c. have passed over, the distillate extracted three times, with 12, 8, and 5 c.c. of chloroform or carbon tetrachloride (25 altogether), and 5 or 10 c.c. of Hübl's or Wijs's iodine solution added to the separated extract. A "blank" experiment on a similar quantity (25 c.c.) of the solvent is of course made in the usual manner.

Fairly good determinations of small quantities of essential oils can also be made in many cases by saturating the distillate with sodium chloride, and extracting the oil with petroleum ether, as in Thorpe and Holmes's method for purifying alcohol. The petroleum ether is allowed to evaporate at the ordinary temperature in a tared beaker, and the residual oil weighed. (See also the methods described under "Liqueurs.")

VII.—BEER

In general terms, beer is a beverage which has been brewed, fermented, and bittered. Formerly, and typically, beer was brewed from malt, and bittered with hops; but sugars and starchy substances other than malt are now commonly employed, and bitters other than hops are used to a small extent. In the United Kingdom, beer is legally "any liquor which is made or sold as a description of beer or as a substitute for beer, and which on analysis of a sample thereof at any time is found to contain more than two per cent. of proof spirit." It "includes ale, porter, spruce beer, black beer, and any other description of beer" (10 Edw. VII, c. 8, s. 52). A later enactment excludes from the legal definition of beer any "liquor made elsewhere than upon the licensed premises of a brewer for sale which on analysis of a sample thereof is found to be of an original gravity not exceeding 1016 degrees, and to contain not more than two per cent. of proof spirit" (5 Geo. V, c. 7, s. 8).

"Ale" was at one time distinct from beer, as not being bittered with hops, but the term has long been used indiscriminately with "beer" for the lighter-coloured varieties of malt liquors as distinct from stout, porter, and black beer.

At the present day, the lighter kinds of beer drunk in this country contain about 6 or 7 per cent. of proof spirit,[1] and the original specific gravity of the wort before fermentation is usually about 1040 to 1043 (water = 1000). Ordinary dinner ale, pale ale, some makes of "porter," lager beer, and the beer generally supplied in public houses contains about 9 to 11 per cent. of proof spirit, and is of approximately 1050–1055 original gravity. Heavier beers and stout range from about 1060 to 1090 degrees of original gravity, and contain 11 to 14 per cent. of proof spirit; whilst special kinds of "strong ale" may be of more than 1100 original gravity, and contain up to 20 per cent. of proof spirit.

Chemically, beer consists of a weak spirituous solution of various sugars, acids, dextrins, proteins, flavouring and colouring matters; with a small quantity of mineral constituents, chiefly phosphates and sulphates.

On distillation, the volatile constituents are separated from the beer; these consist, apart from water, of alcohol, carbonic acid, acetic acid, and traces of minor constituents such as essential oils and higher fatty acids. The non-volatile constituents are usually referred to as the "extract"—more appropriately as the "residue."

The most frequent analytical operations required in the examination of beer are the determination of the proportion of alcohol and

[1] This refers to normal circumstances, apart from war conditions. The milder kinds of "war" beer (1918) contained about 3 per cent. of proof spirit

of the "original" specific gravity. In some cases, an estimation of the carbon dioxide, the acetic acid, the nitrogenous constituents, and the mineral ingredients, especially the chlorides, may be required; and occasionally search must be made for bitter substances other than hops, and for preservatives. The examination of the beer for saccharin is also of some importance, as the addition of this substance to beer is prohibited by law.

Original gravity. General considerations.—Beer in this country is not taxed upon the alcohol it contains; the basis of taxation is the specific gravity of the unfermented wort. Essentially, the wort of beer is a solution of maltodextrins and various sugars—maltose, dextrose, cane-sugar, and invert-sugar—either arising from the malt and grain used, or added as such. As soon as fermentation commences, the specific gravity begins to alter, and the finished beer is of lower density than the original wort, for two reasons. First, the destruction of sugar by fermentation removes solid matter from solution; and, secondly, the alcohol produced is specifically lighter than the wort. The original specific gravity of the unfermented wort can, however, be ascertained by the analysis of the partly-fermented wort, or of the finished beer, as the case may require.

As a first approximation, such an analysis might be based upon the well-known equations of Gay-Lussac denoting the conversion of sugar into alcohol. With maltose, for example:—

$$C_{12}H_{22}O_{11} + H_2O = 4C_2H_5{\cdot}OH + 4CO_2;$$

and it is readily calculable that 100 parts of this sugar yield theoretically 53·8 parts of alcohol. Hence by determining the quantity of alcohol in a given specimen of wort or beer we can find the equivalent amount of sugar destroyed; and from the known density of solutions of maltose we can thus deduce the corresponding loss of specific gravity. Also we can determine the actual specific gravity of the residual wort or beer freed from alcohol, and correcting this for the loss as above ascertained, we can, theoretically, obtain the original gravity of the wort.

In practice, however, this is not sufficiently accurate. A part of the sugar destroyed is not converted into alcohol. Moreover different sugars are present, and they do not all yield the same proportion of alcohol. Again, the introduction of yeast complicates the matter, since part of the solid matter of the wort is used up in sustaining the growth of the yeast, and a sensible quantity of alcohol may be added as such with the yeast itself. These and other disturbing factors, small individually, together influence the result sufficiently to render the figures given by the simple theoretical method as outlined above, only an approximation to what obtains in actual brewery operations.

We have, in fact, to fall back upon an empirical basis for the calculation of results sufficiently accurate to be used in practice. Starting with representative worts of known specific gravity, experimental fermentations have been carried out. From the examination of samples drawn as the operation proceeded, the actual loss of gravity consequent upon the production of known quantities of alcohol has been determined. The results have been embodied in statutory tables for use in assessing the duty on beer.

The first "original gravity" tables were constructed in the year 1847 by Messrs. Dobson and Phillips, of the Inland Revenue Department. They were drawn up with considerable care; but some discussion having arisen, the whole matter was referred a few years later to Profs. Graham, Hofmann, and Redwood, whose report was presented to the authorities in 1852, and published the same year in the *Journal of the Chemical Society*.[1] A new table was drawn up, and subsequently incorporated in the Schedule to the Inland Revenue Act, 1880. An exhaustive revision of this table was carried out during the years 1909–10 by Sir Edward Thorpe and Dr. Horace T. Brown, the work including, not only laboratory experiments, but an extensive series of observations at representative breweries, in order to obtain data which should correspond fairly with the actual working conditions met with in modern brewing practice. The revised table, of which a copy is given on p. 470, was legalised by the Finance Act, 1914, for use in determining the original specific gravity of beer in the United Kingdom.[2]

Process. (1). Distillation method.—Most of the carbon dioxide is first expelled from the beer—which is readily done by pouring it backwards and forwards from one vessel to another in such a way as to make it froth. Where many samples are examined, a small stirrer or whisk actuated by an electric motor is convenient for the purpose.

Worts or unfinished beers containing a sediment of yeast, etc., are required to be filtered.

A convenient quantity of the beer—75 c.c. will suffice—is measured out at 60° F. and placed in a distilling flask, the measuring flask being rinsed out with about 20 c.c. of water and the rinsings

[1] Vol. **5**, 229.

[2] For a fuller account of the above subject, and for a valuable study by Dr. Brown of the scientific principles involved, see the *J. Inst. Brewing*, **20**, No. 7 (Vol. **11**, new series), 1914.

added to the main quantity, which is then distilled. The distillate is received in the original 75 c.c. flask until about four-fifths (60 c.c.) has been collected; its temperature is then adjusted to 60° F. and its volume made up to 75 c.c. The specific gravity of the

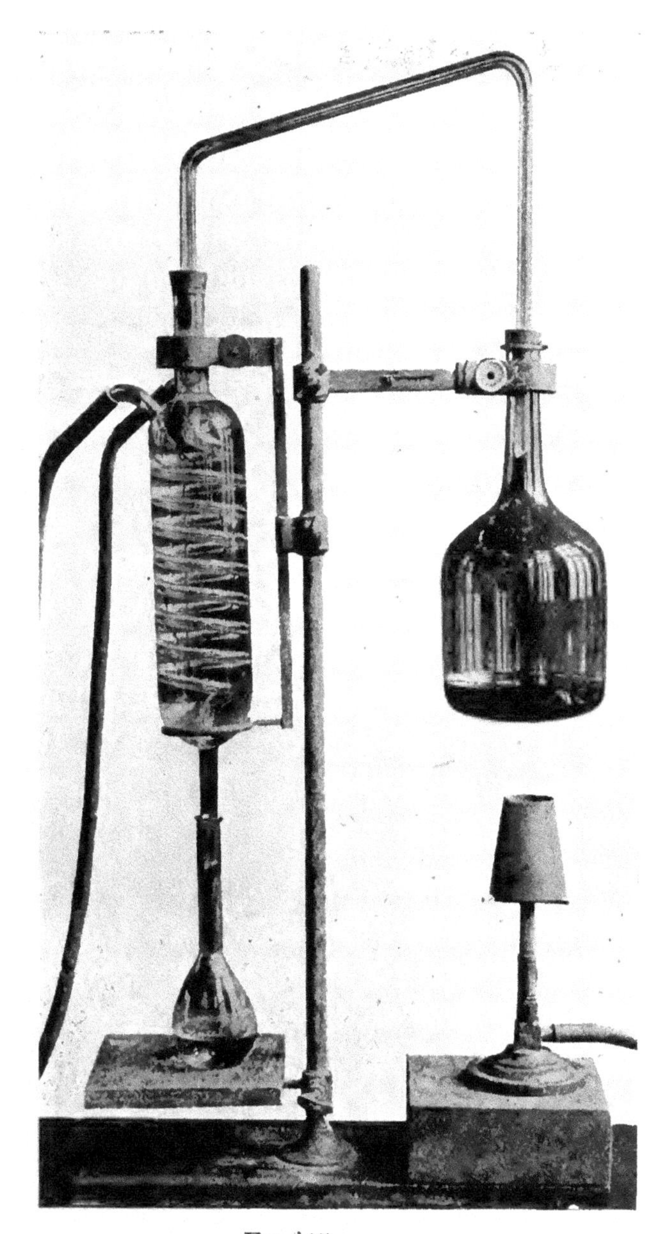

FIG. 45.—STILL.

Used for determining the original gravity of beer.

distillate, referred to water as 1000, is then determined with a 50 c.c. or (preferably) a 1000-grain pyknometer, and the result subtracted from 1000. The difference is termed the "spirit indication," and the corresponding number of "degrees of gravity lost during fermentation" is found from the accompanying table (Table I, p. 470).

Meanwhile, the residue in the distilling flask is cooled and washed into another 75 c.c. flask, the temperature adjusted to 60° F., the volume made up to 75 c.c. with water, and the specific gravity determined. This is the "extract gravity." Adding to this the "degrees of gravity lost," as above determined, we get the original specific gravity of the beer or wort.

Where, however, the acidity of the beer is greater than 0·1 per cent., calculated as acetic acid, an additive correction is required, to compensate for alcohol which has been oxidised to acetic acid. In the official method the acidity is determined with a standard solution of ammonia, using litmus paper as indicator. From the result, expressed in terms of acetic acid, and as a percentage of the sample, 0·1 is deducted, and the remainder, by reference to the annexed table (Table No. III, p. 472) gives the corresponding correction of the "spirit indication."

Example :

Specific gravity of distillate.. .. .. .. 988·45
" " extract .. .. 1022·25
Then "spirit indication" = 1000 − 988·45 = 11·55.

From Table No. I, this spirit indication = 52·60 degrees of gravity lost. Hence, if the beer contains no excess of acid,

Original gravity = 52·60 + 1022·25 = 1074·85.

If, however, the beer contains, let us say, 0·35 per cent. of acid, calculated as acetic acid, then the excess, after deducting 0·1, = 0·25, which from Table No. III = 0·33 degree of spirit indication. Adding this to the actual indication, we get 11·55 + 0·33 = 11·88, the corrected spirit indication, which = 54·25 degrees of gravity lost. Whence the original gravity = 54·25 + 1022·25 = 1076·50.

The 0·1 per cent. acidity was taken as the average acidity of unfermented wort in Profs. Graham, Hofmann, and Redwood's experiments. It may be noted that fresh wort contains practically no acetic or other volatile acid : the acidity is chiefly due to lactic acid.

When the proportion of volatile acid is very high, it affects the specific gravity of the distillate and so prevents the accurate determination of the spirit indication. In this case, the distillate should be neutralised with solution of sodium hydroxide and redistilled. The determination of the acetic acid when the proportion is high is best done by distillation in a current of steam as described for wine. Alternatively, the total acidity of 50 c.c. may be determined with standard ammonia and litmus paper as usual, and the *fixed* acidity on a similar quantity after evaporation to dryness on a steam-bath, and redissolving in water: the volatile acidity is then given by the difference.

The "standard" ammonia may be either of decinormal strength, or of sp. gr. 998·6. In the latter case, each c.c. used represents 0·1 per cent. of acetic acid when 100 c.c. of beer are taken for titration.

(2). **"Evaporation" method.**—In this process, it is not necessary actually to distil the beer. The specific gravity of the beer, freed from carbon dioxide as already explained, is determined, and then 75 c.c. or other convenient quantity, measured at 60° F., is evaporated by gentle boiling in a beaker or basin until the volume is reduced to about one-third. During the operation care must be taken not to char any of the solid matter. The alcohol being thus expelled, the residue is cooled, made up at 60° F. with distilled water to the original volume, and the specific gravity taken: this is the "extract gravity."

From this "extract gravity" deduct the specific gravity of the beer; the difference is the "spirit indication" for the evaporation method. Referring this to Table No. II we get the corresponding "degrees of gravity lost," which, added to the "extract gravity," furnishes the original gravity required. The correction for excess acidity is made in the same way as in the distillation method.

Example: Sp. gr. of the beer, 1009·25. Extract gravity, 1021·48. Total acidity, 0·26 per cent.

Then spirit indication = 1021·48 — 1009·25 = 12·23. Excess acidity = 0·26 — 0·1 = 0·16, which from the table (No. III) gives 0·22 correction of spirit indication;

∴ corrected spt. indn. = 12·45 = 58·05 degrees of gravity lost, from Table No. II.

Whence the original gravity = 1021·48 + 58·05 = 1079·53.

As compared with the distillation method, the evaporation process is somewhat the quicker, and does not require the use of a still. But the Table No. II has not received the thorough revision which Table No. I has undergone; moreover, the distillation process is the one legalised for use in this country.

It may be noted that if a sufficiently sensitive hydrometer be used for taking the specific gravities, instead of a bottle, the original gravity of beer can be determined by the evaporation process without the use of either a balance or a still.

For rough purposes, it is convenient to remember that 1 per cent. of proof spirit produced in fermentation corresponds with about 3·5 degrees of gravity lost.

TABLE NO. I.—DISTILLATION PROCESS.

Spirit indication.	0·0	0·1	0·2	0·3	0·4	0·5	0·6	0·7	0·8	0·9
	Corresponding degrees of gravity lost.									
0	0·00	0·42	0·85	1·27	1·70	2·12	2·55	2·97	3·40	3·82
1	4·25	4·67	5·10	5·52	5·95	6·37	6·80	7·22	7·65	8·07
2	8·50	8·94	9·38	9·82	10·26	10·70	11·14	11·58	12·02	12·46
3	12·90	13·34	13·78	14·22	14·66	15·10	15·54	15·98	16·42	16·86
4	17·30	17·75	18·21	18·66	19·12	19·57	20·03	20·48	20·94	21·39
5	21·85	22·30	22·76	23·21	23·67	24·12	24·58	25·03	25·49	25·94
6	26·40	26·86	27·32	27·78	28·24	28·70	29·16	29·62	30·08	30·54
7	31·00	31·46	31·93	32·39	32·86	33·32	33·79	34·25	34·72	35·18
8	35·65	36·11	36·58	37·04	37·51	37·97	38·44	38·90	39·37	39·83
9	40·30	40·77	41·24	41·71	42·18	42·65	43·12	43·59	44·06	44·53
10	45·00	45·48	45·97	46·45	46·94	47·42	47·91	48·39	48·88	49·36
11	49·85	50·35	50·85	51·35	51·85	52·35	52·85	53·35	53·85	54·35
12	54·85	55·36	55·87	56·38	56·89	57·40	57·91	58·42	58·93	59·44
13	59·95	60·46	60·97	61·48	61·99	62·51	63·01	63·52	64·03	64·54
14	65·10	65·62	66·14	66·66	67·18	67·70	68·22	68·74	69·26	69·78
15	70·30	70·83	71·36	71·89	72·42	72·95	73·48	74·01	74·54	75·07
16	75·60									

TABLE NO. II.—EVAPORATION PROCESS.

Spirit indication.	0·0	0·1	0·2	0·3	0·4	0·5	0·6	0·7	0·8	0·9
	Degrees of gravity lost.									
0	—	0·3	0·7	1·0	1·4	1·7	2·1	2·4	2·8	3·1
1	3·5	3·8	4·2	4·6	5·0	5·4	5·8	6·2	6·6	7·0
2	7·4	7·8	8·2	8·7	9·1	9·5	9·9	10·3	10·7	11·1
3	11·5	11·9	12·4	12·8	13·2	13·6	14·0	14·4	14·8	15·3
4	15·8	16·2	16·6	17·0	17·4	17·9	18·4	18·8	19·3	19·8
5	20·3	20·7	21·2	21·6	22·1	22·5	23·0	23·4	23·9	24·3
6	24·8	25·2	25·6	26·1	26·6	27·0	27·5	28·0	28·5	29·0
7	29·5	30·0	30·4	30·9	31·3	31·8	32·3	32·8	33·3	33·8
8	34·3	34·9	35·5	36·0	36·6	37·1	37·7	38·3	38·8	39·4
9	40·0	40·5	41·0	41·5	42·0	42·5	43·0	43·5	44·0	44·4
10	44·9	45·4	46·0	46·5	47·1	47·6	48·2	48·7	49·3	49·8
11	50·3	50·9	51·4	51·9	52·5	53·0	53·5	54·0	54·5	55·0
12	55·6	56·2	56·7	57·3	57·8	58·3	58·9	59·4	59·9	60·5
13	61·0	61·6	62·1	62·7	63·2	63·8	64·3	64·9	65·4	66·0
14	66·5	67·0	67·6	68·1	68·7	69·2	69·8	70·4	70·9	71·4
15	72·0	—	—	—	—	—	—	—	—	—

Table No. III.

For ascertaining the indication value of the acetic acid.

Excess per cent. of acid.	Corresponding degrees of "spirit indication."									
	0·00	0·01	0·02	0·03	0·04	0·05	0·06	0·07	0·08	0·09
0·0	—	0·02	0·04	0·06	0·07	0·08	0·09	0·11	0·12	0·13
0·1	0·14	0·15	0·17	0·18	0·19	0·21	0·22	0·23	0·24	0·26
0·2	0·27	0·28	0·29	0·31	0·32	0·33	0·34	0·35	0·37	0·38
0·3	0·39	0·40	0·42	0·43	0·44	0·46	0·47	0·48	0·49	0·51
0·4	0·52	0·53	0·55	0·56	0·57	0·59	0·60	0·61	0·62	0·64
0·5	0·65	0·66	0·67	0·69	0·70	0·71	0·72	0·73	0·75	0·76
0·6	0·77	0·78	0·80	0·81	0·82	0·84	0·85	0·86	0·87	0·89
0·7	0·90	0·91	0·93	0·94	0·95	0·97	0·98	0·99	1·00	1·02
0·8	1·03	1·04	1·05	1·07	1·08	1·09	1·10	1·11	1·13	1·14
0·9	1·15	1·16	1·18	1·19	1·21	1·22	1·23	1·25	1·26	1·28
1·0	1·29	1·31	1·33	1·35	1·36	1·37	1·38	1·40	1·41	1·42

Refractometric analysis of beer.—The percentage of alcohol and of extract in beer can be obtained, and the original gravity deduced, if the specific gravity and the refractive index are known. H. Tornöe elaborated the method at the instance of the Norwegian Government, and a description of it has been given by Ling and Pope.[1]

Addition of alcohol to water causes a diminution of the specific gravity of the latter, and an increase in its refractive index. The extractive matter of beer gives an increase of both. Let c_1 be the amount by which the *refractive index* is raised by each 1 per cent. of alcohol; c_2 the corresponding increment for each 1 per cent. of extract; c_3 the amount by which the *specific gravity* is lowered by 1 per cent. of alcohol, and c_4 the increment for 1 per cent. of extract. Let, further, S be the specific gravity of the beer, and r its refractive index, both referred to water as unity; whilst A and E respectively denote the percentages of alcohol and extract in the beer. Then we have :—

$$r = 1 + c_2E + c_1A.$$

$$\text{and } S = 1 + c_4E - c_3A.$$

From these two equations the values of A and E are readily obtained :—

$$A = \frac{c_4(r - 1) - c_2(S - 1)}{c_1c_4 + c_2c_3} \quad . \quad . \quad . \quad . \quad . \quad . \quad . \quad . \quad (1).$$

$$E = \frac{c_3(r - 1) + c_1(S - 1)}{c_1c_4 + c_2c_3} \quad . \quad . \quad . \quad . \quad . \quad . \quad . \quad . \quad (2).$$

If the values of the constants c_1, c_2, c_3, c_4, are determined once for all, these equations give A and E, the percentage of alcohol and extract in the beer, when S and r are obtained on the sample.

C_1, c_2, etc., are, however, not strictly constant, as the variations produced in the refractive index and specific gravity are not exactly proportionate to the quantity of alcohol or extract present. Hence tables are constructed, by means of which, after determining the specific gravity and the refraction of a sample, the percentage of alcohol and of extract can be read off.

Determinations of the values of c_1, c_2, c_3, and c_4 have been made by Barth.[2] The figures obtained, substituted in equations (1) and (2), give the formulæ :—

$$A = 759{\cdot}8(r - 1) - 292{\cdot}3(S - 1).$$

$$E = 336{\cdot}6(r - 1) + 130{\cdot}3(S - 1).$$

[1] *J. Inst. Brewing*, 1901, **7**, 170. [2] *Zeitsch. ges. Brauw.*, 1905, **28**, 303.

Barth's results have been checked by J. Race[1] who finds that with samples containing up to about 4·5 per cent. of alcohol the formulæ give satisfactory results, but with higher percentages the tendency

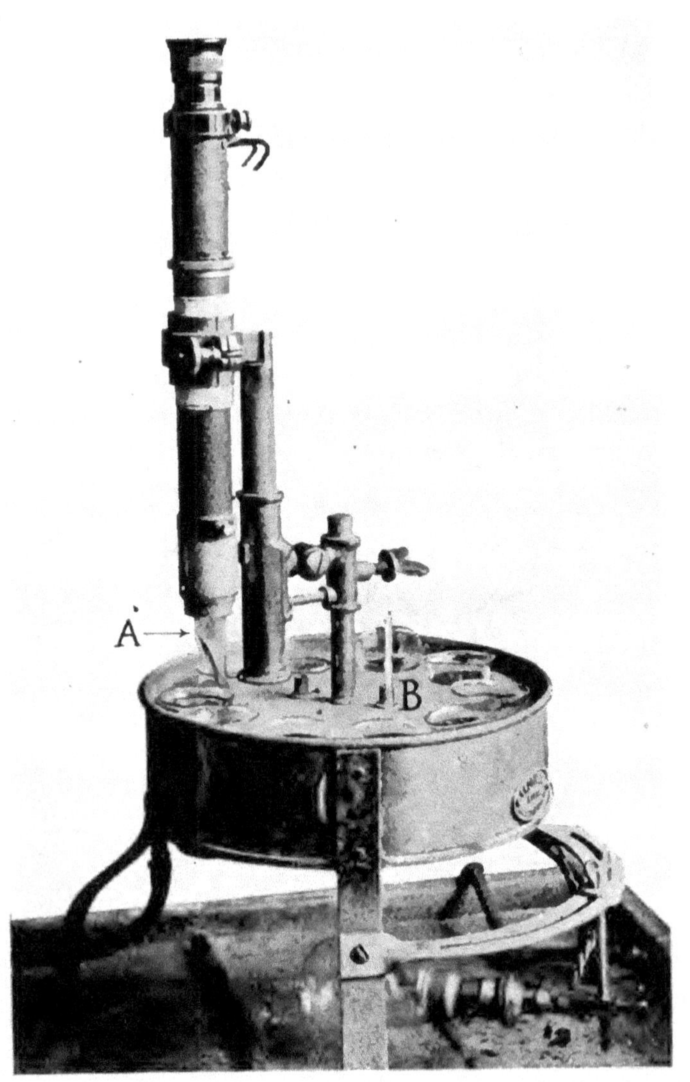

FIG. 46.—IMMERSION REFRACTOMETER, WITH ROTATING WATER-BATH.
A, prism, which dips into the liquid in the glass beneath; *B*, bath with thermometer.

is to give rather low values for *A* and *E*. For such samples Race prefers the expressions :—

$$A = 778(r - 1) - 290(S - 1).$$
$$E = 350(r - 1) + 130(S - 1).$$

Tornöe used a modification of Hallwach's prism for determining the refraction values, but the Zeiss immersion refractometer or Pulfrich's instrument is more convenient.

[1] *J. Soc. Chem. Ind.*, 1908, **27**, 544.

When the percentage of alcohol is obtained, the original gravity is readily calculated. From the former, by reference to ordinary alcohol tables, we find the specific gravity of aqueous alcohol containing the same proportion of alcohol as is present in the beer. Deducting this from 1000, the spirit indication is found, and thence the "degrees of gravity lost."

The spirit indication *plus* the specific gravity of the beer gives the extract gravity. Adding to this the degrees of gravity lost, we obtain the original gravity.

Example: Suppose we have a beer with sp. gr. 1009·5 and a refraction reading 39·0 by the Zeiss immersion refractometer at 60° F. Remembering that in the expression $r - 1$ the unit is the refractive index for *water*, 1·33335 at the above temperature, the calculation is as follows:—

Reading 39·0 = ref. index (*v.* Table, p. 288) ..	1·34237
Less ref. index of water	1·33335
$r - 1 =$	0·00902

$S - 1 = 1{\cdot}0095 - 1 = 0{\cdot}0095.$

Hence, using Barth's coefficients, the percentage of alcohol is given by:

$$A = 759{\cdot}8 \times 0{\cdot}00902 - 292{\cdot}3 \times 0{\cdot}0095,$$
$$= 4{\cdot}12 \text{ per cent. (by weight).}$$

From the ordinary alcohol tables, this corresponds with a specific gravity 992·6.

∴ spirit indication	= 7·4	= 32·86 degrees of "gravity lost."
sp. gr. of sample	= 1009·5	
∴ Extract gravity	= 1016·9	
Add gravity lost	32·86	
∴ Original gravity	= 1049·76	

In practice, lengthy calculations are obviated by the use of special tables which correlate the immersion-refractometer readings directly with the specific gravity and the original gravity.

One such table is given below. It is used as follows: Let R denote the refraction reading of the beer by the immersion instrument, and D the specific gravity *minus* 1000. Deduct D from R.

Then corresponding with the value of $R - D$ thus obtained, the table gives a number, N, which added to the specific gravity of the beer gives the original gravity of the sample.

$R - D$.	N.	$R - D$.	N.
17	4·6	30	40·1
18	7·4	31	42·7
19	10·3	32	45·2
20	13·1	33	47·7
21	15·9	34	50·1
22	18·7	35	52·6
23	21·4	36	55·1
24	24·2	37	57·6
25	26·9	38	60·1
26	29·6	39	62·6
27	32·2	40	65·0
28	34·9	41	67·5
29	37·5	42	70·0

Example :—Let the specific gravity be 1008·6, and the refraction reading 33·5.

Then $D = 8·6$, and $R - D = 24·9$. From the table, by interpolation, the value of N is found to be 26·6. Adding this to the specific gravity, we get $1008·6 + 26·6 = 1035·2$, the required original gravity. For regular use the interpolation values are, of course, calculated out and tabulated once for all.

Estimation of carbon dioxide.—The proportion of this constituent does not vary much in palatable beer, ranging from about 0·25 to 0·4 per cent. The taste alone is a good guide, as beer with less than 0·2 per cent. of carbon dioxide tastes "flat."

If the beer is in cask, a quantity of 200 to 300 grams is drawn off into a tared flask fitted with a "wash-bottle" arrangement of tubes, both closed with short pieces of rubber tubing carrying pinchcocks. By means of the cocks and an air-pump the pressure of air in the flask is reduced, to facilitate the taking of the sample. After weighing, the flask containing the drawn-off quantity is connected up with an apparatus of soda-lime tubes (or potash bulbs) for absorbing the carbon dioxide, similar to that described for the estimation of methyl alcohol by Thorpe and Holmes's method (p. 189). The pinchcock on the exit tube of the flask is opened very carefully at first to prevent too rapid escape of the carbon dioxide into the absorption tubes ; then the flask is gradually heated to gentle boiling, to expel the carbon dioxide from the beer, and finally a current of air freed from carbon dioxide is aspirated through the flask, and the absorption tubes weighed : the increase in weight shows the weight of carbon dioxide in the sample.

If the beer is in bottle, the cork may be pierced with a champagne tap, or with a cork-borer, over the blunt end of which a piece of stout rubber tubing carrying a pinchcock has been passed. The tap, or the tube, as the case may be, is then connected with the absorption train, and the bottle placed in cold water. The tap or cock is opened cautiously, and when the gas has ceased to pass, the water is warmed slowly to about 80°, and kept at this temperature for about half an hour, the bottle being shaken frequently. At the end of this period the bottle is removed, and a current of air freed from carbon dioxide passed as before.

Bottles with screw stoppers may be cooled down in ice-water, and the stopper rapidly replaced by a rubber stopper fitted with a tube and pinchcock, or with a glass tap. Some gas will often escape—but this, after all, is what would happen, and to a greater extent, if the beer were poured out for drinking.

Proportion of alcohol and "extract."—The experimental *data* furnished by the determination of the original gravity by the distillation process allow of these quantities being obtained. By referring the specific gravity of the distillate to the ordinary alcohol tables (p. 237), we get the proportion of alcohol.

Deducting 1000 from the specific gravity of the extract, and dividing the remainder by 3·86, the quotient denotes the grams of dry extract in 100 c.c. of the beer.

Further examination of the extract usually resolves itself into a determination of the reducing sugars in terms of maltose (" crude maltose," " apparent maltose "), the dextrinous matters (" apparent dextrin "), the proteids, and the ash.

Sugars.—A convenient quantity—10 to 20 c.c. according to the amount of solid matter in the extract—is diluted with water to 250 c.c., and the sugars are determined on 50 c.c. of the diluted liquid. The gravimetric Fehling process is generally adopted, and the results are expressed in terms of maltose.

Dextrins.—A quantity of extract equal to 10 c.c. of the original beer may be taken, and the dextrin hydrolysed by boiling for four hours with 40 c.c. of normal sulphuric acid. After neutralising the acidity, the total reducing sugars are determined with Fehling's solution as before. Deducting the "apparent maltose," as above determined, the remainder is calculated to dextrin.

Otherwise, the optical rotatory power of the beer is determined. From the angular value is deducted the number of grams of maltose per 100 c.c. × 1·37. The remainder, divided by 2, gives the number of grams of dextrin in 100 c.c. of the beer.

Proteids.—The total nitrogen is estimated by Kjeldahl's process on 20 or 25 c.c. of the beer, evaporated to near dryness in the long-necked flask used for the digestion with sulphuric acid. Percentage of nitrogen × 6·25 = per cent. of proteids.

Mineral constituents.—The **total ash** may be determined on 25 c.c. of the beer, first evaporating and charring the solids over a low flame, then extracting the alkali salts with water, filtering, and completing the ignition of the carbonaceous residue. The aqueous extract is then returned to the capsule, evaporated to dryness, and the whole residue cautiously ignited.

If the **chlorides** are to be determined, it is well to evaporate and ignite a separate quantity of 25 c.c. or 50 c.c. after adding a little barium carbonate (0·5 gram for 50 c.c.), and proceed as before to obtain the aqueous extract, in which the chloride may be estimated with silver nitrate, either gravimetrically or volumetrically.

The **sulphates** are also best determined on a separate quantity evaporated with addition of a little sodium hydroxide and ignited as usual. The alkali prevents loss of a little sulphuric acid, which might otherwise occur owing to the presence of acid phosphates.

Sulphites, which may be present in beer as preservatives, can be determined in terms of sulphur dioxide by distilling 250 c.c. of the sample, acidified with phosphoric acid, in a current of carbon dioxide until about 200 c.c. of distillate have passed over. The distillate containing the sulphur dioxide is allowed to drop into a flask containing a measured quantity of $N/50$-iodine solution, and the excess of iodine is determined with $N/50$-sodium thiosulphate solution, using starch as indicator. The carbon dioxide should not bubble through the iodine solution, or iodine will be lost. Alternatively, and rather more accurately, the distillate is received in a somewhat stronger solution of iodine ($N/10$ or $N/20$), and the sulphate formed is estimated gravimetrically as barium sulphate. Traces of sulphur dioxide, it should be remembered, may be given by the hops or other normal constituents of the beer.

Saccharin.—See the methods described under "Wine."

An interesting quantitative study of the nitrogenous constituents of typical British beers has been made by J. S. Sharpe.[1] The total nitrogen ranged from 0·039 to 0·112 per cent. Protein accounted for 13–37 per cent. of the nitrogen; amino-compounds for 25–46 per cent.; and purine nitrogen, present as uric acid and xanthine compounds, for 25–52 per cent. Traces (0·007 to 0·012 per cent.) of an alkaloidal oil, presumably coniine, and a small quantity of a base which was probably betaine, practically accounted for the balance of the nitrogen (2–6 per cent.).

[1] *Biochem. J.*, 1917, **11**, 101.

In the United Kingdom, the quantities of beer produced by brewers for sale in the year ended 31st March, 1914, were as follows :—

	Barrels.	Average sp. gr.
England	31,737,384	1051·69
Scotland	2,288,481	1047·67
Ireland	3,532,902	1065·93
United Kingdom .	37,558,767	1052·80

Herb beer, botanic beer.—These are beverages containing usually but a small proportion of alcohol. They are often regarded as "non-alcoholic," though this is not strictly the case. Occasionally, indeed, samples are met with containing as much alcohol as ordinary beer.

In general, the beverages of this class are fermented ; but they are sometimes made by simple dilution of a herbal extract with water, or with a weak syrup. The fermented articles are prepared by first making a decoction of the herbs, then adding sugar and yeast, and fermenting the mixture slightly. The herbs employed are principally burdock, chamomile, dandelion, ginger, horehound, liquorice, sarsaparilla, and sassafras, often with a small quantity of hops or hop-substitutes such as quassia, gentian, or chiretta ; and sometimes with quillaia to give a "heading." Instead of using the plants themselves, makers of herb beer often purchase ready-made mixtures of vegetable extracts and flavourings, which only require to be mixed with sugar and water, and fermented if desired. Sarsaparilla-beer extract, for instance, is often made from compound decoction of sarsaparilla, flavoured with oil of sassafras and a little bitter such as tincture of chiretta, sweetened with syrup and coloured with caramel. Spruce-beer extract may be made with spirit of juniper, essence of ginger, essence of pimento, and decoction of sarsaparilla, coloured with caramel. A hop-ale essence is produced by mixing tincture of hops, tincture of chiretta, and essence of pineapple ; and so on.

The proportion of sugar generally used in herb beers varies from about 3 to 10 or 12 ounces per gallon. With the smaller amounts, saccharin is sometimes added. Glucose syrup also is occasionally used for sweetening the beers, and essential oils for flavouring them ; and tartaric acid or cream of tartar may be present in small quantity. The essential oils may include cassia, cinnamon, cloves, lemon, peppermint, and wintergreen oils.

The products are sold under various names, such as Herb Beer, Herb Porter, Botanic Stout, Dandelion Stout, Hop Ale, Burdock Stout, Sarsaparilla Beer, Horehound Beer, and so on. They usually have an original specific gravity ranging from about 1005 up to about 1025, though higher values are met with ; and they contain alcohol ranging from mere traces up to about 3 per cent. of proof spirit—occasionally more, as already indicated. A fair average would be : Original gravity about 1012, proof spirit about 1·5 per cent. The solids in solution are chiefly sugars, except perhaps in the case of the low-density beers, which may be sweetened with saccharin.

The analysis of herb beers is carried out in a similar manner to that of ordinary beer. Frequently, only the percentage of proof spirit is required. A fuller analysis would include also the determination of the original gravity, the percentage of sugar, and of saccharin if present, and the nature of the extract other than sugars, so far as this can be ascertained. Liquorice, bitters, acids, saponins, and flavouring oils are often present. The preservatives chiefly used are sulphites and salicyclic acid.

Ginger beer is prepared in a similar way to the foregoing. It usually contains a higher proportion of sugar than is found in the average herb beers.

VIII.—CIDER AND PERRY

Cider is obtained by the fermentation of the juice of fresh apples. According to the definition adopted by the International Congress for the repression of food adulteration (Geneva, 1908 and 1909) a proportion of pears, not exceeding 10 per cent., may be mixed with the apples, and the juice may be extracted either with or without the addition of water. If without, the product is distinguished as "pure juice" cider. "Sparkling" cider, according to the Congress, should have been fermented in bottle, as distinguished from "aerated" cider, into which carbonic acid has been directly introduced. "Small" cider is defined as cider containing from 2 to 4 per cent. of "total" alcohol—that is, alcohol both actually existing, and potential in the sugar present ; with an extract value, when the sugar is deducted, ranging from 0·8 to 1·4 grams per 100 c.c., and ash 0·08 to 0·14 gram per 100 c.c.

In France, the regulations require that "cider" must contain at least 3·5 per cent. of alcohol, actual or potential, 1·2 grams of extract (sugar deducted), and 0·12 gram of mineral matters (ash) per 100 c.c. If any one of these constituents falls below the limits given, the product must be termed "small" cider ("*petit cidre*"). There are no special regulations for cider in this country.

In making cider, the apples are crushed in a mill, and the resulting pulp, wrapped in cloth, is pressed to force out the juice. Two or three pressings may be given, and the pulp may be moistened with water between two pressings. The richness of the juice in sugar, and therefore in the potential amount of alcohol, depends upon the variety of apple used; mediocre fruit yields juice of sp. gr. about 1·045 to 1·055 and containing 9 to 12 per cent. of sugar; while the best kinds give juice of sp. gr. 1·080 to 1·090 or above, with 16 to 18 per cent. of sugar, or more. Addition of sugar, tannin, tartaric acid, ammonium phosphate (20 grams per hectolitre), and treatment with sulphurous acid and alkali bisulphites, are regarded by the International Congress as regular operations in the process of manufacture, as are also the sweetening of the resulting cider with crystallised sugar, its pasteurisation, clarification, colouring with caramel, and treatment with citric acid. The French regulations limit the amount of added tartaric acid or citric acid to 0·05 gram per 100 c.c., and of alkali bisulphites to 0·01 gram, with the further condition that the cider shall not retain more than 0·01 gram of total sulphurous anhydride, free or combined, per 100 c.c. Colouring with cochineal, caramel, and chicory-infusion is recognised.

The sugars in the juice of ripe apples comprise saccharose, dextrose, and lævulose. These exist in varying proportions, the lævulose, however, being the largest constituent. The saccharose represents about 5 to 39 per cent. of the total sugars; and in the remainder, the proportion of lævulose to dextrose ranges from 10 to 1 down to about 3 to 1. In the progress of fermentation, the cane-sugar becomes inverted, and the original dextrose may be fermented out completely, leaving only lævulose and more or less invert-sugar, or perhaps lævulose only.

The important constituents of cider "must" other than the sugars and the small quantities of esters or essential oils to which the characteristic apple flavour is due, are the acids, pectins, and tannins. According to a table drawn up by the French "Association Pomologique," the must from eleven different varieties of apples recommended for the making of cider yielded the following data:—

Sp. gr.	1·050	to	1·133	
Total sugars	9·3	,,	26·3	grams per 100 c.c.
Acid (as H_2SO_4)	0·015	,,	0·970	,, ,,
Tannin	0·008	,,	1·055	,, ,,
Pectic substances	0·01	,,	2·10	,, ,,

Some English cider-musts analysed by A. H. Allen[1] gave the following results:—

[1] *Analyst*, 1902, **27**, 183.

Sp. gr.	1·047 to 1·055
Solids, per cent.	11·91 „ 14·63
Glucose „	8·82 „ 13·51
Sucrose „	0·38 „ 1·34
Fixed acid (as malic) per cent.	0·28 „ 0·50
Ash, per cent.	0·22 „ 0·35
Tannin „	0·22

These samples were analysed about thirty-six hours after the juice had been pressed, and contained a little alcohol, ranging up to 1·13 per cent. The "glucose" presumably represents the whole of the reducing sugars present, including any inverted saccharose.

In a report[1] upon the results of investigations into cider-making, carried out on behalf of the Bath and West and Southern Counties Society, F. J. Lloyd gives the composition of the juice from a large number of varieties of apples grown in this country. It is not stated, however, which kinds are chiefly used in cider-making. The juice from the variety known as "Kingston Black" gave the following results :—

Sp. gr.	1·050 to 1·069
Solids	11·34 to 17·30 per cent.
Grape-sugar	9·58 „ 15·06 „
Cane-sugar	0·60 „ 5·12 „
Malic acid	0·29 „ 0·64 „
Tannin	0·10 „ 0·18 „
Extractives	0·16 „ 1·90 „

The results represent apples of the variety in question grown in ten different years.

For the analysis of cider, the methods described for wine are applicable, so far as they may be required. The following processes are also useful.

Pectins.—Evaporate 100 c.c. of the cider down to about 10 c.c., and add 60 c.c. of alcohol (90 per cent.) to precipitate the pectic matters. Allow the latter to settle, decant off the liquid, redissolve the precipitate with a little water, and repeat the treatment with alcohol. Filter on a tared filter, dry carefully, raising the temperature gradually to 100°, and weigh. Incinerate the filter and its contents, and deduct the weight of the ash from the first result to obtain the weight of pectins.

Tannins.—The "apple-tannin" reaction is sometimes employed to distinguish between cider and factitious liquids containing no apple juice. About 10 c.c. of the liquid are extracted with an equal volume of ethyl acetate, the solvent is drawn off, and poured on to lime water in a test-tube. A band of yellow colour develops at the junction of the two liquids if the sample contains apple-juice. The colour is somewhat fugitive. If necessary, 100 c.c. of

[1] *Official Publication*, Cd. 1868, 1903.

the sample may be evaporated down to about 10 c.c. before applying the test.

For the estimation of tannin, Pi's method may be used. The reagents required are :—

(1) **Solution of zinc acetate.**—Dissolve 4·5 grams of crystallised zinc acetate in water, add ammonia solution until the precipitate produced is re-dissolved, and make up the volume to 200 c.c. with water.

(2) **Solution of permanganate.**—0·558 Gram of $KMnO_4$ per litre.

(3) **Solution of indigo.**—1·5 Grams of sublimed indigotin are dissolved in 15 c.c. of pure sulphuric acid, and after standing some days, the volume is made up to a litre. Each c.c. = 0·001 gram of tannin.

To standardise the permanganate, 10 c.c. of the indigo solution and 10 c.c. of strong sulphuric acid are placed in a large flask, together with sufficient water to make the volume up to 1 litre. The permanganate solution is run in from a burette until the colour of the indigo is changed to yellow, and the volume required for this is noted, say N c.c. Then N c.c. = 0·01 gram of tannin.

To make the estimation, 10 c.c. of the cider are mixed with 5 c.c. of the zinc acetate solution, and evaporated in a porcelain basin on the steam-bath. Boiling water is then added, and the precipitate of zinc tannate filtered off, washed with hot water, and dissolved in dilute sulphuric acid (1 per cent. by vol.). This solution is then titrated with the permanganate. Suppose v c.c. are required. Then since N c.c. = 0·01 gram of tannin, v c.c. will = $0·01 \times v/N$ gram of tannin, from the 10 c.c. of cider ; so that in 100 c.c. of the cider the amount of tannin will be $v/10\,N$ gram.

Boric acid is generally present in cider to a small extent, quantities of the order of 0·005 to 0·020 per cent. having been found. To estimate it, 100 c.c. of the cider are mixed with a little calcium chloride (about 5 c.c. of a 10 per cent. solution), evaporated to dryness, the residue charred, boiled with about 150 c.c. of water, and filtered. The carbonaceous matter is incinerated thoroughly, but at not too high a temperature ; then boiled with a further quantity (150 c.c.) of water, allowed to stand in the cold overnight, filtered cold, and the filtrate mixed with the first extract. (As a precaution, it is well to make a third extraction, testing this separately to show whether all the boric acid has been obtained.) The mixed liquids are then evaporated down to about 25 c.c., cooled, and exactly neutralised with $N/10$-acid, methyl-orange being used as indicator. After adding an equal volume of glycerol (or preferably a few grams of mannitol), the solution is further titrated with

$N/20$-solution of sodium hydroxide, employing phenolphthalein as indicator this time. A little more glycerol or mannitol should be added to make sure that the end-point has been reached, as indicated by the pink colour remaining permanent after the addition. Each c.c. of the $N/20$-soda used represents 0·0031 gram of H_3BO_3.

The treatment with calcium chloride is designed to eliminate the phosphates in the ash, which would affect the titration. Calcium borate is moderately soluble in water, and is dissolved out on operating as described. According to Barker and Russell,[1] the amount of phosphate present in cider ranges from 0·013 to 0·023 per cent., calculated as P_2O_5. The ash consists mainly of potassium carbonate and phosphate.

Analyses of various ciders are appended.

ANALYSES OF CIDER.

	I.	II.	III.	IV.
Sp. gr.	1·003 to 1·032	—	—	0·9977 to 1·050
Alcohol, per cent.	2·57 ,, 5·39	4·10	5·40	5·4 ,, 7·3
Extract ,,	2·12 ,, 7·93	6·40	3·03	1·923 ,, 3·023
Sugar ,,	0·94 ,, 7·24	3·75	0·65	0·1 ,, 0·3
Ash ,,	0·23 ,, 0·36	0·28	0·27	0·225 ,, 0·336
Fixed acid, as malic, per cent	0·12 ,, 0·35	0·53*	0·71*	— —
Volatile acid, as acetic ,,	0·19 ,, 0·37	—	—	— —

* Total acidity.

I = Devonshire, bottled cider (*Allen*) Alcohol by weight.
II = French, sweet ,, (*Grignon*) ,, volume.
III = ,, dry ,, ,, ,, ,,
IV = German cider (*Kulisch*) ,, ,,

Lloyd (*loc. cit.*) considers that cider should be regarded as "extra dry" if it contains not more than 2 per cent. of sugar, "dry" if the sugar is under 4 per cent. and "sweet" if above 4 per cent. The suggested "extra dry" limit strikes one as rather high.

Barker and Russell[2] give a number of analyses of pure-juice cider, each made from a single variety of apple, and also a number representing blends of pure-juice ciders, denoting more the type of cider which finds its way to the market. These latter analyses are reproduced in the following table :—

BLENDED PURE-JUICE CIDERS.

Sp. gr.	1·000	1·022	1·013	1·009	1·007	1·008
Acid, per cent.	0·48	0·59	0·32	0·33	0·34	0·45
Tannin ,,	0·264	0·260	0·212	0·248	0·180	0·270
Alcohol ,,	5·83	3·55	4·20	4·76	5·07	4·82
Solids ,,	2·412	6·878	5·740	3·920	3·880	3·614
Ash ,,	0·322	0·342	0·308	0·312	0·322	0·346
Alkalinity, per cent.	0·116	0·127	0·095	0·113	0·108	0·026
P_2O_5 per cent.	0·0153	0·0230	0·0192	0·0165	0·0191	0·0128

[1] *Analyst*, 1909, **34**, 125. [2] *Ibid.*, 130.

Dilution of cider with water will generally be indicated by deficiency in the proportions of alcohol and extract. Allen (*loc. cit.*) considers that the original solids of unwatered cider rarely fall below 12 per cent. when calculated from the analytical results as follows :—

$$\text{Sugar fermented} = \begin{cases} \text{Alcohol, per cent. by weight} \times 2{\cdot}07 \\ + \text{Acetic acid} \times 1{\cdot}5 \end{cases}$$

Adding this to the percentage of solids still remaining in the sample, the sum equals the original solids of the juice before fermentation.

Perry is produced by the fermentation of the juice of fresh pears. It resembles cider very closely, but is generally somewhat less acid. In France, a good deal of the perry produced is distilled for the fabrication of *eau-de-vie*. The following analyses of English perry are given by Allen :—

	Worcester-shire.	Devon-shire.	Gloucester-shire.
Sp. gr.	1·020	1·021	1·010
	Per cent.	Per cent.	Per cent
Alcohol, by weight	4·61	4·81	3·64
= Proof spirit	10·11	10·54	7·98
Total solids	6·51	6·49	4·50
Volatile acid (as acetic) ..	0·41	0·35	0·22
Fixed acid (as malic)	0·25	0·20	0·24
Glucose	2·71	3·60	0·36
Sucrose	None.	0·31	—
Ash	0·40	0·28	0·30
Original solids	16·61	16·92	12·33

IX.—WINES

Wine, in general terms, is the beverage produced by the fermentation of fresh grapes, or of the juice of fresh grapes. Certain additions are well recognised—*e.g.*, the "fortification" of some wines by the addition of a small proportion of distilled spirit ; "chaptalisation" of a poor "must" by the addition of sugar ; "plastering" with calcium sulphate, and the use of sulphurous acid or alkali bisulphites as preservatives. These and other additions are made under regulations as to the maximum quantities and other conditions in the chief wine-making countries.

In the United Kingdom, fermented beverages of a somewhat similar type, but made from a variety of materials which may or may not include grape juice, are known as "British Wines." "Sweets," or "made wines," are legal terms for these products, which are described more fully further on.

For fiscal purposes, all wine imported into this country, whether made from fresh grapes or not, is classed as "foreign wine," and pays a duty of customs; whereas British wine is exempt from duty so far as the alcohol is concerned.

The foreign wines usually drunk in this country may be referred to the following principal types: Burgundy, claret, champagne, hock, port, and sherry.

Burgundy and **claret** are of similar general character, both being dark red, "still" wines, nearly free from sugar, and of low alcoholic strength, ranging from about 12 to 22 per cent. of proof spirit. Burgundy, however, is of different flavour from claret, has rather more "body," and is usually somewhat stronger in alcohol. **Champagne** is a sparkling white wine containing about 16 to 23 per cent. of proof spirit, with usually a good quantity of sugar—8 to 16 per cent. or thereabouts—though the "dry" varieties may have very little. **Hock** is a white Rhine wine, either "still" or sparkling, with about the same proportions of alcohol and sugar as are found in Burgundy: **Moselle** is a similar type of wine, but produced in the Moselle district. **Port,** a product of north-east Portugal, is a sweet, strongly alcoholic red wine, containing about 26 to 38 per cent. of proof spirit; the sugar may range from about 3 up to 10 or 12 per cent. **Sherry** is a Spanish wine of characteristic flavour, yellow to brown in colour, and strong in alcohol, containing about 26 to 35 per cent. of proof spirit; **Madeira** and **Marsala** are wines of the sherry type, but with their own distinctive bouquet. Sherry may contain sugar in amount ranging from *nil* up to 5 per cent., according to whether it is dry or sweet.

Portugal sends the largest quantity of wine to the United Kingdom. France and Spain follow closely, and a long way behind come Germany, Australia and Italy. A table showing the quantities imported will be found at the end of this section.

The better-class clarets, "fine growths" and "*crus*," are named after the place of origin—*e.g.*, *St. Julien*, *Pauillac*, *Château Latour*, *Château Margaux*. The French white wines, such as *Barsac*, *Château Y'quem*, *Graves* and *Sauterne*, are produced mainly in the south-west, whilst the champagne area is in the north-east, in the neighbourhood of Rheims and Epernay. *Chablis* is a white Burgundy wine made in the department of Yonne. *Beaune*, *Mâcon*, and *Chambertin* are typical red Burgundies. *Hermitage* is a purplish-coloured wine from the Rhone valley.

Of the sherries, there are two main types—the one, *Amontillado*, being usually darker coloured and more spirituous than the other, or *Manzanilla* variety. *Alicante* and *Tarragona* are red Spanish wines approximating to the port type. *Rota tent* is a sweetened red Spanish wine, often used as a communion wine. *Malaga* is a sweetened, luscious red wine coming from the south-eastern districts of Spain.

The hocks and moselles come chiefly from vineyards in the neighbourhood of the Rhine, Moselle, and Main. Among the more noted Rhine and Moselle wines are *Steinberger*, *Johannisberger*, *Rüdesheimer*, *Rauenthaler*, *Berncasteler*, *Niersteiner*, and *Liebfraumilch*. *Assmannshauser* is a red wine produced near Bingen.

Asti, *Chianti*, *Montferrat*, and *Lacryma Christi* are Italian wines; *Tokay* is a noted sweet Hungarian wine; *Bual*, *Tinta* and *Malmsey* or *Malvoisie* are varieties of Madeira wine.

The complete analysis of wine requires a large number of determinations and tests to be made—some 20 are specified in the French regulations, and 28 in the German. A fairly full ordinary analysis would usually include determinations of: Specific gravity; alcohol; extract; acids—total, fixed, and volatile; tartaric acid; polarisation; sugars; glycerol; ash; phosphates; sulphates; and tests for artificial colouring matters, together with the organoleptic tests of taste and smell. In addition to these, the French requirements include a microscopic examination, tests for saccharin and dextrin, determination of potassium, sulphurous acid, chlorides and citric acid; and examination for free mineral acids and for antiseptics. The German regulations include, besides most of those mentioned above, tests for commercial glucose; nitric acid; barium, strontium, and copper; tannin; tartaric acid present in the free state, as cream of tartar, and as tartrates of the alkaline earths. It will, of course, be understood that certain of these data are only obtained in special cases.

Beyond a certain point, chemical analysis is only of limited value in appraising wine. The finer shades of flavour, the "bouquet" and the aroma, which so largely determine the quality and value of the more expensive wines, are matters for the expert palate, not for the analyst *quâ* analyst. In his province lie the recognition of the wine *as* wine—*i.e.*, as a product of the fermentation of fresh grape juice; the determination of its general character or type; the estimation of its main constituents; the ascertainment of its freedom from adulterants; and the formation of a judgment upon its soundness, condition, and general quality. But even if he is not an expert wine-taster, the wine-analyst will find his practised senses of taste and smell very useful to him in dealing with wines.

The chief forms of sophistication to which wine is subject may be divided into two classes: (1) those involving the addition of foreign substances such as preservatives, coal tar colours, and artificial sweetenings; and (2) those in which substances of like nature to those already present in the wine are added to the wine. The second class includes the dilution of the wine with water; the addition of ordinary alcohol; the strengthening of the must with sugar in order to augment the eventual alcoholic strength; the admixture of fermented liquors such as raisin wine, gooseberry wine, or cider, not derived from the juice of fresh grapes; and the addition of glycerine or of cream of tartar, to mask some of the other sophistications.

Since the substances in the second class are normal constituents of wine, or contain such constituents, and since some of the additions, as already mentioned, are tolerated within certain limits in wine-producing countries, it is necessary in the analysis to determine the proportions of such ingredients quantitatively, and to compare the results with recorded statistics, before conclusions can be drawn as to the probability of adulteration, so far as those ingredients are concerned. Statistics of the chemical composition of French wines have been published by Gayon and Laborde,[1] and of German and other wines there are many in König's well-known compilation. A few typical analyses are included on pp. 489–490 in illustration of the principal types.

Apart, however, from the question of general agreement of the analytical data with those of recorded analyses, each determination has its own special importance. It may be well, therefore, briefly to indicate the significance of the chief determinations before proceeding to describe them in detail.

Alcohol.—The importance of this constituent scarcely needs pointing out. It shows, in the first place, whether the sample dealt with is the ordinary type of wine, or a "non-alcoholic" product; and if the former, whether it is a normal or a "fortified" wine. It is important *per se*, as the stimulant and intoxicant constituent of the wine; its amount may help to show whether the wine agrees with an alleged description; and in conjunction with other constituents it may assist the analyst in forming a judgment as to whether the wine has been diluted with water.

Extract.—An unusually low extract may indicate that the wine has been diluted or fortified, or that it has been mixed with "marc" wine, which is poor in extract. On the other hand, a high extract is characteristic of "concentrated" sweet wines such as those of the Tokay type, which have been prepared by evaporation of the must, as distinct from wines which have been sweetened by the simple addition of sugar.

Glycerol.—This is one of the products of alcoholic fermentation,

[1] "Vins," Appendix.

Analyses of various French wines (Gayon and Laborde)

Kind	Alcohol, per cent. by volume	Extract at 100°.	Reducing sugar.	Acidity. Total.	Acidity. Volatile.	Tartaric acid.	Sulphates, as K_2SO_4.	Ash.	
		Grams per 100 c.c.							
Gironde red wines.									
Pauillac. Max.	11·9	2·78	0·24	0·383	0·068	0·363	0·048	0·375	
(5 samples). Min.	9·9	2·10	0·09	0·302	0·037	0·220	0·035	0·250	
St. Emilion. Max.	12·9	3·00	0·30	0·590	0·074	0·485	0·051	0·340	
(5 samples). Min.	10·7	2·35	0·15	0·357	0·022	0·295	0·031	0·260	
Margaux. Max.	10·9	2·78	0·19	0·404	0·082	0·410	0·055	0·350	
(4 samples). Min.	10·0	2·20	0·07	0·332	0·037	0·260	0·039	0·250	
St. Julien. Max.	13·0	2·87	0·28	0·385	0·018	0·365	—	0·295	
(2 samples). Min.	10·2	2·21	0·11	0·357	0·011	0·270	0·064	0·240	
Vins rouges ordinaires.									
(20 samples). Max.	11·5	2·91	0·55	0·574	0·123	0·528	<0·1	0·330	
Min.	8·1	1·89	<0·20	0·375	0·033	0·199	<0·1	0·165	
Vins blancs ordinaires.									
(20 samples). Max.	12·6	4·12	2·17	0·779	0·123	0·462	<0·1	0·285	
Min.	6·9	1·46	0·11	0·299	0·033	0·133	<0·1	0·115	
Sauternes.						Cream of Tartar.			Glycerol.
Grands vins blancs. Max.	15·8	19·62	14·07	0·636	0·078	0·207	0·144	0·590	2·45
(16 samples). Min.	12·8	2·32	0·55	0·245	0·042	0·075	0·030	0·250	1·18
Vins de Bourgogne.									
Rouges. Max.	14·8	3·19	0·31	0·615	0·070	—	—	0·270	
(14 samples). Min.	9·1	2·39	0·13	0·315	0·025	—	—	0·210	
Blancs. Max.	14·7	2·88	0·50	0·620	0·050	—	—	0·160	
(6 samples). Min.	10·7	1·65	<0·10	0·350	0·025	—	—	0·100	

ANALYSES OF VARIOUS TYPICAL WINES (KÖNIG).

Kind.	Alcohol by weight.	Extract.	Sugar.	Total acid, as tartaric.	Glycerol.	Ash.	Sulphates, as H_2SO_4.	Phosphates, as P_2O_5.	Potash.
French :									
Red wine	7·80	2·56	0·30	0·57	0·73	0·248	0·033	0·030	0·106
White wine	8·30	3·03	—	0·66	0·97	0·250	0·038	0·032	0·098
German :									
Moselle	7·99	2·24	0·03	0·79	0·72	0·175	0·012	0·036	0·068
Rhine wine	8·00	2·60	—	0·81	0·85	0·230	0·020	0·046	0·085
Italian	10·61	3·44	1·44	0·52	0·45	0·290	0·019	0·032	0·115
Spanish :									
Ordinary red	12·30	3·53	0·38	0·49	1·09	0·610	0·221	0·027	0·242
Sweet wine	12·78	9·69	6·55	0·59	0·63	0·740	0·212	0·039	0·296

and therefore must be present in genuine wine. The ratio of glycerol to alcohol is reduced by the addition of distilled alcohol to the wine. Also sweet wines obtained by adding alcohol to must which has been but slightly fermented are naturally poor in glycerol, whereas those which are prepared by sweetening normally fermented wines contain the normal proportion. Hence the determination of this ingredient may assist in distinguishing between these kinds of wine. Again, the ratio of glycerol to alcohol has a tendency to be high in old wines, because some of the alcohol originally present has been lost by evaporation. Unfortunately, however, there is a considerable variation in the ratio of glycerol to alcohol produced in genuine wine, so that the estimation is less helpful than it might appear to be at first sight. The usual range is from 6 to 10 grams of glycerol per 100 grams of alcohol in red wines, but in white wines the maximum may be much higher, reaching 15 or 16, and, exceptionally, even greater values. This variation is traceable to the activities of different micro-organisms in the must. Hence deductions drawn from the proportion of glycerol should be made with circumspection.

Sugar.—The estimation of the total sugar is useful in distinguishing between sweet and "dry" wines, and also in the calculation of the amount of wine extract other than sugar. Further, the separate estimation of the dextrose and lævulose is sometimes helpful in distinguishing between different kinds of sweet wine. A notable excess of lævulose over dextrose indicates a wine to which sugar has been added and then more or less fermented, since dextrose is the constituent of invert-sugar most readily destroyed during fermentation. On the other hand, if the proportions of dextrose and lævulose are substantially equal, this may indicate a fully fermented wine sweetened by maceration with raisins, or wine made from a slightly fermented must to which alcohol has been added.

Acids.—The estimation of the **tartaric acid** is of value, because this is the characteristic acid of wine, and is not present in some fruit juices which might be used as adulterants—*e.g.*, apple- and pear-juices. **Malic acid** is especially characteristic of apple juice, though wines also contain it. **Citric acid** may help to indicate the presence of gooseberry or currant wine. The **volatile acids** are of importance as showing the progress of acetous fermentation, and their proportion is used in France for calculating certain ratios employed as criteria of genuineness.

Polarisation.—This datum may often give useful information. If the wine is dextrorotatory, cane-sugar is present, or added glucose, or both. If after inversion the wine becomes lævorotatory, cane-sugar is indicated; if it still remains dextrorotatory and the polarisation value is over 2·25°, the inference is that added glucose is probably present. Should the original wine be lævorotatory, inverted cane-sugar is indicated, or lævulose, or both; and if the lævorotation is increased on inversion, some unchanged cane-sugar was present. Finally, if the original wine gave no rotation, either all the sugar has been fermented out, or a compensating mixture of dextro- and lævo-rotatory sugars is present. In this case, if inversion produces a lævorotation, the inference is that cane-sugar was present, and therefore also lævulose or other lævorotatory sugar.

Alcohol, acid, and extract ratios.—In France the relations between alcohol, acid, and extract have been much studied, with the view of detecting such falsifications of wine as the addition of water or alcohol. Certain numerical values have been deduced to which much importance is attached. With wine, however, as with other products, natural variations in the proportions of the constituents may occur, and the data obtained from the study of normal wines must therefore always be used with circumspection.

In the following description the acidity, according to the French practice, is expressed in terms of *sulphuric* acid, and the weights of the constituents other than alcohol in grams *per litre.*

(1).—**Ratio of alcohol to extract.**—This is given by dividing (*a*), the total weight of alcohol, actual and potential, per litre, by (*b*) the weight of the extract in grams per litre, determined by drying at 100°, and suitably corrected as explained below.

(*a*).—The total weight of alcohol = the actual alcohol present *plus* what would be given by any sugar in excess of 1 gram still unfermented (1 gram of sugar per litre is regarded as the average quantity remaining in normally fermented wine). It is given by the formula :—

Percentage of alcohol by volume $\times$ 8 + (wt. of sugar — 1) $\times$ 0·45.[1]

Example :—Alcohol 11·5 per cent. by vol., sugar 37·0 grams per litre. Then "total alcohol" $= 11·5 \times 8 + (37·0 - 1·0) \times 0·45$
$= 108·2$ grams per litre.

(*b*).—The "extract" or dried residue of wine will be increased in weight beyond its true value if non-volatile substances such as sugars, chlorides, and sulphates have been added to the wine. Hence to obtain the true value such additions must be deducted from the weight of the extract as actually determined. In the case of reducing sugars, chlorides, and sulphates, 1 gram per litre is regarded as normal to the wine, and only the *excess* above this

[1] The factor 8 here is the round number used instead of the true factor 7·94—*i.e.*, the specific gravity of alcohol at 15° multiplied by 10.

is deducted. Besides these ingredients, the extract may contain, for example, added citric acid, added tartaric acid, or added glycerol. Occasionally also mannitol, due to the action of special micro-organisms in the fermentation of the wine, may be present. In general, all added non-volatile matters revealed by the analysis should be deducted in calculating the corrected or "reduced" extract.

Example :—

Gross extract, as weighed .. 60·4 Grams per litre

	Found.	To be deducted.
Cane-sugar	5·0	5·0
Reducing sugars	37·0	36·0
Chlorides (NaCl)	1·5	0·5
Sulphates (K_2SO_4)	1·9	0·9
Total deductions from extract		42·4

Hence the "reduced extract" is 60·4 — 42·4 = 18·0.

Then for red wines, the quotient total alcohol ÷ reduced extract falls between 2·5 and 4·5, and for white wines between 3·5 and 6·5. It lies outside these limits in exceptional cases only.

For instance, if the examples given above refer to the same wine, the value of the quotient would be $\frac{108 \cdot 2}{18 \cdot 0} = 6 \cdot 1$, which is within the permissible limits for genuine normal white wine, but would be outside them if the wine in question were a red one. An excessive value for the quotient is considered as presumptive evidence that either sugar has been added to the must or alcohol to the wine.

The excess of alcoholic strength due to these additions can be calculated approximately from the formula

$\frac{1}{8}$ (total weight of alcohol — reduced extract × 4·5 or 6·5),

taking the factor 4·5 if it is a question of red wine, or 6·5 in the case of a white wine.

(2). **Sum of alcohol** *plus* **fixed acid** (A. Gautier).—In a broad sense, the alcohol and the acid in wine are quantitatively complementary, so that the sum of the two, within limits, is constant. This sum lies, in general, between 13 and 17 when calculated as shown below.

Divide by 8 the "total weight of alcohol" obtained as described in the preceding section (1), (*a*). To the result add the amount of fixed acid and one-tenth of the volatile acid, both expressed in terms of sulphuric acid and in grams per litre. From this total, by way of corrections, the following deductions are to be made :—

(i).—0·2 for each gram of K_2SO_4 in excess of 2 grams found in the analysis of the wine.

(ii).—The value, in terms of sulphuric acid, of the free tartaric acid in excess of 0·5 gram for red wines and 1·0 gram for white wines.

(iii).—The value, in terms of sulphuric acid, of any added foreign acids shown by the analysis.

(iv).—The proportion of alcohol presumed to be due to added sugar or added alcohol when the alcohol–extract ratio exceeds 4·5 for red wines or 6·5 for white wines, according to the calculation in (1), above.

With both red and white wines, watering is presumed when the sum " alcohol + fixed acid " falls below 12·5, or in certain special cases, 11·5 (wines of the Aramon plains, in the south of France).

Exceptionally, lower values than 11·5 are found in genuine wine. Blarez[1] gives three categories of wine, in which the minimum values of the sum " alcohol + fixed acid " are respectively 12·5, 10·8, and 10·0.

Whichever minimum value is taken, the percentage of watering is calculated from the formula

$$W = \frac{100(S - S_1)}{S},$$

where S is the value of the sum taken as standard, and S_1 is the value found. Thus if 12·5 is the standard, and 10·5 has been found,

$$W = \frac{100(12{\cdot}5 - 10{\cdot}5)}{12{\cdot}5} = 16 \text{ per cent.}$$

(3). **Ratio of acid to alcohol** (Halphen's rule).—This is another application of the fact noted in (2), that within limits the sum of the alcohol and the acid in normal wine is approximately constant. It follows that the acid varies inversely as the alcohol in quantity. In evaluating the ratio numerically, the acidity taken is the fixed acid *plus* 0·7 as the maximum for volatile acid in sound wine. The " alcohol " is the percentage of alcohol by volume. The same corrections as in (2) are required for any increase of fixed acid or alcohol by added materials.

Thus Halphen's ratio

$$R = \frac{\text{fixed acid} + 0{\cdot}7}{\text{per cent. of alcohol by vol.}}$$

Example :—Alcohol 12·75 per cent. by volume ; fixed acid 2·05 grams per litre calculated as H_2SO_4 ; corrections *nil*. Then

$$R = \frac{2{\cdot}05 + 0{\cdot}7}{12{\cdot}75} = 0{\cdot}215.$$

[1] Gayon and Laborde, " Vins," p. 214.

The value of the ratio decreases as the percentage of alcohol increases, since the acid varies inversely as the alcohol. With wines of the same kind, the value of the ratio does not vary much for the same alcoholic strength.

Now if water is added, it does not change the value of the ratio, since both acid and alcohol are diluted to the same extent. But as the alcoholic strength is reduced, this unchanged ratio is not the one which *ought* to be given, if the wine were genuine. The lower quantity of alcohol, if the wine were not watered, would mean a larger proportion of acid and therefore a greater value of the ratio. Hence a low value is presumptive evidence of the wine having been watered.

In practice, curves are constructed for different classes of wine, with ordinates showing the alcoholic strength, and abscissæ the acidity per alcoholic degree. The value obtained for Halphen's ratio is then compared with the curve for wine of the same class. By way of illustration, a few values taken from the mean curve are given here :—

Alcohol by volume.	Ratio.	Alcohol by volume.	Ratio.
6 per cent.	0·74	11 per cent.	0·38
7 ,,	0·67	12 ,,	0·32
8 ,,	0·60	13 ,,	0·24
9 ,,	0·52	14 ,,	0·17
10 ,,	0·46	15 ,,	0·10

(4). **Roos's ratio.**—This is obtained by dividing the value obtained in (2) by that given in (1), any necessary corrections being included, as already explained. In other words, the Roos ratio is :—

$$\frac{\text{alcohol} + \text{fixed acid}}{\frac{\text{alcohol}}{\text{reduced extract}}}$$

evaluated numerically as described in (2) and (1).

For red wines, the value of this ratio is ordinarily equal to or greater than 3·2, but exceptionally may be as low as 3·0. For white wines, the minimum value is 2·4. Values below these limits are presumptive evidence of watering. This ratio brings into the calculation all three of the chief elements in the composition of wine—alcohol, acid, and extract.

Examples :—

(*a*). **Red wine.**—Alcohol, 6·5 per cent. ; total acidity, 6·25 ; volatile acid, 0·50 ; reduced extract, 15·80.

Then, assuming that there are no other corrections except those included in the reduced extract, we have: alcohol + fixed acid = $6{\cdot}5 + (6{\cdot}25 - 0{\cdot}50) = 12{\cdot}25$, and alcohol/reduced extract $= \frac{6{\cdot}5 \times 8}{15{\cdot}8}$ $= 3{\cdot}28$; whence Roos's ratio $= \frac{12{\cdot}25}{3{\cdot}28} = 3{\cdot}7$.

This wine is therefore normal.

(*b*). **Red wine.**—Alcohol, 7·8 per cent.; total acidity, 4·6; volatile acidity, 0·95, reduced extract, 15·60.

As before: alcohol + fixed acid $= 7{\cdot}8 + (4{\cdot}6 - 0{\cdot}95) = 11{\cdot}45$; and alcohol extract $= \frac{7{\cdot}8 \times 8}{15{\cdot}6} = 4{\cdot}0$;

whence Roos's ratio $= \frac{11{\cdot}45}{4} = 2{\cdot}8$, and the wine is indicated as being watered.

Methods of expressing the results of analysis.—In this country, the alcohol is generally expressed in terms of proof spirit for trade purposes, or as percentage by volume for general use. The other constituents are most conveniently given in grams per 100 c.c. Following the German practice, total acid and fixed acid are usually expressed in terms of tartaric acid, and volatile acidity in terms of acetic acid. In France, the acids, total, fixed, and volatile, are all evaluated as sulphuric acid; the alcohol is given as percentage by volume (or sometimes as grams per litre); and the other constituents in grams *per litre*. The International Conference which sat at Paris in 1911 favoured the French method of expressing results, except as regards the acids, which it was recommended should be given in terms of cubic centimetres of normal alkali per litre of wine.

We proceed now to describe the analytical operations.

Alcohol.—A convenient quantity of the wine to take is 100 c.c. A little more than this is placed in a 100 c.c. flask, the temperature brought to 15·6°, and the quantity adjusted to the mark. The wine is then transferred to a distilling flask, and the measuring vessel rinsed with about 40 to 50 c.c. of water, which is added to the main quantity. About 90 c.c. are distilled over into the 100 c.c. flask, the temperature again adjusted to 15·6°, and the volume made up to the original bulk with distilled water at the same temperature. The proportion of alcohol is then obtained in the usual manner from the specific gravity of the distillate.

With ordinary sound wine, the quantity of volatile acid distilling over does not appreciably affect the specific gravity of the distillate, but if the wine is more than usually acid the distillate should be neutralised and redistilled.

Occasionally, frothing will occur during the distillation. A little tannin added to the wine will obviate this ; but the addition should not, of course, be made if the residue in the flask is required for the determination of the "extract."

Extract.—Make up the residue in the distilling-flask to the original volume at 15·6°, and determine its specific gravity (water = 1000). Deduct 1000 from this, and multiply the remainder by the corresponding factor taken from the following table. The result gives the grams of extract per 100 c.c. of the wine :—

Remainder.	Factor.	Remainder.	Factor.
1·0	0·2600	35·0	0·2586
2·0	0·2600	40·0	0·2588
3·0	0·2567	45·0	0·2589
4·0	0·2575	50·0	0·2590
5·0	0·2580	55·0	0·2591
6·0	0·2583	60·0	0·2592
7·0	0·2586	65·0	0·2594
8·0	0·2588	70·0	0·2594
9·0	0·2578	75·0	0·2596
10·0	0·2580	80·0	0·2598
15·0	0·2580	85·0	0·2599
20·0	0·2585	90·0	0·2601
25·0	0·2584	95·0	0·2602
30·0	0·2587	100·0	0·2604

Example :—Specific gravity of residue in flask = 1026·3, say. Deducting 1000, remainder = 26·3. The corresponding factor in the table is 0·2584, this being the one opposite 25, the nearest remainder to 26·3. Then the extract = 26·3 × 0·2584 = 6·80 grams, per 100 c.c., to the nearest second decimal.

The specific gravity of the residue may also be calculated from that of the original wine and that of the distillate. If S_1 and S_2 be these respective specific gravities, then :—

$$\text{Specific gravity of residue} = 1000 + S_1 - S_2.$$

When the proportion of extract is less than 4 grams per 100 c.c., it may be determined with somewhat more accuracy by direct weighing according to one of the methods described below.

In fully fermented wines, the amount of extract approximates to 2 per cent. as a mean value, the ordinary range being from about 1·3 to 2·5, though both lower and higher values are met with. The proportion varies somewhat with the district, the year, the age of the vine, the age of the wine, and the method of preparation.

On the Continent, much importance is attached to the value of the ratio $\frac{\text{alcohol}}{\text{extract}}$ as indicating added sugar or added alcohol. Consequently, a good deal of attention has been given to methods for determining the proportion of extract. In France, two processes are official ; but one of them—the determination *in vacuo*—

requiring, as it does, from four to six days for its completion, has largely fallen out of use. The other method is the direct determination by evaporation of the wine and drying the residue at 100°. By reason of the volatilisation of glycerol and the oxidation of tannins and colouring matters during the drying, it is necessary to proceed under fixed conditions if results comparable with recorded values are to be obtained. Hence the reason for the following stipulation of details.

French official process ; "extract at 100°."—Twenty c.c. of the wine are measured into a platinum capsule having a flat bottom, and with a diameter of 5·5 cm. and a depth of 2·5 cm. The capsule is placed on a steam-bath over an aperture of 5 cm. diameter, and the evaporation continued for six hours, at the end of which time the vessel is wiped, allowed to cool in a desiccator, and weighed.

German official process.—In Germany, the method of drying at 100° is also official for wines containing less than 4 per cent. of extract, but instead of being dried for six hours the sample is evaporated on the bath during about forty minutes only, until of the consistency of a stiff syrup, and then dried in the oven for two and a half hours. Fifty c.c. of the wine are taken if the percentage of extract does not exceed 3 ; if between 3 and 4 a smaller volume is employed, such that not more than 1·5 grams of extract are present. The platinum capsules employed are of 8·5 cm. diameter, 2·0 cm. depth, and 75 c.c. capacity, weighing about 20 grams ; the apertures of the steam-bath are of 6 cm. diameter.

For the preliminary calculation, in order to decide how much wine to take, it is necessary to know the specific gravity of the wine deprived of its alcohol. This may be obtained, as shown above, by deducting the specific gravity of the distillate from that of the original wine + 1000. The specific gravity 1015·5 corresponds with 4 grams, and 1011·6 with 3 grams, of extractives in 100 c.c. of the wine.

For wines with more than 4 per cent. of extract the proportion is deduced from official tables, which show the quantity of extract corresponding with the specific gravity of the de-alcoholised wine.

Total acidity.—Twenty-five c.c. of the wine are heated to the commencement of ebullition to expel carbon dioxide, and titrated whilst hot with decinormal alkali, using litmus paper as indicator. The results are usually expressed in terms of tartaric acid (in France as sulphuric acid) ; 1 c.c. $N/10$-alkali = 0·0075 gram of tartaric acid.

Volatile acidity.—Fifty c.c. of the wine, contained in a flask of about 200 c.c. capacity, are distilled in a current of steam,

The operation is so arranged as to allow the volume of the wine to be rapidly reduced to about 25 c.c., after which it is kept constant, and the distillation terminated when the volume of the distillate is about 200 c.c. This is titrated with $N/10$-alkali, using phenolphthalein as indicator, and the result expressed in terms of acetic acid. One c.c. of $N/10$-alkali = 0·006 gram of acetic acid.

Fixed acidity.—This is given by the difference between the total acidity and the volatile acidity, care being taken to express the latter for this purpose in terms of tartaric acid. Example :—

Total acidity . . . . 0·457 gram per 100 c.c., as tartaric acid.
Volatile ,, ... 0·075 ,, ,, as acetic acid.
Then fixed acidity = 0·457 — 0·075 × 1·25 = 0·363 gram per 100 c.c., expressed as tartaric acid.

In recent years a good deal of attention has been devoted to physico-chemical methods of examining wine. The acidity, for instance, has been studied from the point of view of the concentration of the hydrogen-ions, as determined by the velocity of inversion of sucrose. A given quantity of sucrose is dissolved in the wine (after any invertase present has been destroyed), and the mixture kept at a temperature of 76° by means of a bath of boiling carbon tetrachloride. From the quantity of sucrose inverted in a given time the inversion constant is obtained.[1]

A method of testing wine for free mineral acid, based upon the variation of the electrical conductivity when small quantities of alkali are added to the wine, has been described by Bosco and Belasio.[2]

For a lengthy study of the fixed organic acids of wine, with particular regard to lactic acid, see a paper by G. de Astis.[3]

Tartaric acid.—This is the most important of the fixed acids in wine. It is present partly as the free acid and partly as cream of tartar, with a small quantity of calcium tartrate. The total amount may be determined according to the French official process as follows :—

To 20 c.c. of the wine in an Erlenmeyer flask of about 250 c.c. capacity is added 1 c.c. of a 10 per cent. solution of potassium bromide and 40 c.c. of a mixture of equal volumes of ether and alcohol (90 per cent.). The flask is closed and shaken, and then set aside for three days. At the end of this time the liquid is

[1] For details, see Dutoit and Duboux, "Analyse des Vins" (Lausanne, 1912).
[2] *Annali Chim. Appl.*, 1916, **5**, 233.
[3] *Ibid.*, 1918, **9**, 155; *Chemical Abstracts*, 1918, **12**, 2224.

decanted through a small filter, and the flask and filter washed with a little of the ether–alcohol mixture. The filter is then placed in the flask, about 40 c.c. of warm water are added, and the whole digested till the precipitate is dissolved ; the solution is then titrated with $N/20$-alkali, phenolphthalein being used as indicator. If n be the number of cubic centimetres required, the total tartaric acid is given in terms of cream of tartar and in grams per 100 c.c. of the wine by the expression $n \times 0{\cdot}047 + 0{\cdot}02$. The result may be converted into terms of tartaric acid by the factor 0·7979.

With wines rich in sugar, it is well to use twice the quantities of alcohol and ether (40 c.c. of each) added separately. The alcohol is first well mixed with the wine, and the ether added afterwards : this avoids the separation of a syrupy layer of sugar.

Cream of tartar.—By omitting the potassium bromide, the same method serves for the estimation of the cream of tartar in the wine.

Free tartaric acid.—This is equal to the difference between the total tartaric acid and the cream of tartar, expressed as tartaric acid.

Alternatively, the German official process may be used. In this, the total tartaric acid is determined according to the method given below, and from this is deducted the alkalinity of the ash of the wine, calculated as tartaric acid. The ash from 50 c.c. (or 25 c.c. if rich in sugar) is dissolved in 20 c.c. of $N/4$-HCl and 20 c.c. of water, heated just to boiling over a small flame to expel carbon dioxide, and then titrated with $N/4$-NaOH, using delicate litmus paper as indicator. Each c.c. of $N/4$-HCl used up = 0·0375 gram of tartaric acid, since one molecule of potassium carbonate is produced from two molecules of cream of tartar.

A disadvantage of the foregoing process for total tartaric acid is the length of time required. If quicker results are wanted, the following method may be used :—

To 100 c.c. of the wine add 2 c.c. of glacial acetic acid, 0·5 c.c. of a 20 per cent. solution of potassium acetate, and 15 grams of powdered potassium chloride. Stir well to hasten the solution of the last ingredient. Add 15 c.c. of alcohol (95 per cent.), and rub the sides of the vessel well with a glass rod for about a minute to promote the crystallisation of the cream of tartar ; then let the whole stand for at least fifteen hours.

Decant the liquid through a thin asbestos filter in a Gooch crucible, transferring no more of the precipitate than is necessary. Wash the precipitate and filter three times with a small quantity of a mixture of potassium chloride (15 grams), alcohol (20 c.c.), and water (100 c.c.), using not more than 20 c.c. of the mixture altogether. For this purpose, a test-tube fitted with a wash-bottle arrangement of blow-off tubes is convenient. Transfer the filter and the precipitate to the beaker in which the precipitation was effected, wash out the crucible with hot water, add about 50 c.c. of hot water to dissolve the cream of tartar, heat to boiling, and titrate the solution with decinormal alkali, using delicate litmus tincture or paper as indicator. To the actual number of c.c. required add 1·5 as correction for the solubility of the precipitate, and multiply the result by 0·015 to give the total tartaric acid in grams per 100 c.c. of the wine.

Citric acid.—Denigès's process, official in France, is as follows: Ten c.c. of the wine are shaken with about 1 gram of lead dioxide, then mixed with 2 c.c. of a solution of mercurous sulphate (5 grams of HgO, 20 c.c. of H_2SO_4 conc., 100 c.c. of water), again shaken up, and filtered. Five or 6 c.c. of the filtrate are raised to ebullition in a test-tube, and one drop of a 1 per cent. solution of potassium permanganate is added. After the colour has disappeared another drop is added; and so on up to ten drops.

Normal wines give only a slight cloudiness under this treatment. With 0·01 gram of citric acid per 100 c.c. there is a distinct turbidity, and when the proportion reaches 0·04 gram and upwards, a flocculent precipitate is produced.

The presence of citric acid having been proved, comparative experiments with solutions containing known quantities of the acid serve to evaluate the proportion.

Malic and succinic acids.—The following method, due to Mestrezat, is described by Gayon and Laborde.[1]

Two hundred c.c. of the wine are neutralised with solution of barium hydroxide, then very slightly acidified with three or four drops of a 3 per cent. solution of acetic acid, and concentrated to 15 c.c. under diminished pressure.

To the residue are added 2 c.c. of a solution of barium acetate (30 per cent.), and sufficient strong alcohol to give about 80 per cent. strength in the mixture. The precipitate thus obtained is filtered and washed with 80 per cent. alcohol: it contains barium tartrate, malate, and succinate; gums, pectins, albuminoids and tannins. It is taken up with water acidified with sulphuric acid (about 3 per cent.), of which 12 to 15 c.c. suffice to liberate the acids from their combination with the barium.

Strong alcohol is now added to the mixture, bringing the total volume up to 100 c.c. The gums, pectins, and albuminoids are

[1] "Vins," p. 136.

precipitated, leaving the acids and tannins in the alcoholic solution.

To eliminate the tartaric acid, 80 c.c. of the liquid are filtered off, some potassium chloride and potassium acetate added, and the volume is made up to 100 c.c. with water. This mixture is set aside for two or three days to allow of the deposition of the tartaric acid as cream of tartar. It is then filtered, and the precipitate washed with 65 per cent. alcohol. The filtrate retains only traces of tartrate, approximately 0·01 gram per 100 c.c., for which a corrective deduction should be made eventually.

In the filtrate, the malic and succinic acids and the tannins are again precipitated by adding solution of barium hydroxide in slight excess, faintly acidifying again with acetic acid, and adding strong alcohol until the mixture is of about 80 per cent. alcoholic strength. The precipitate is filtered off, washed with alcohol, and dissolved in water slightly acidified with hydrochloric acid.

The estimation of the malic acid is made by oxidising the acid with potassium permanganate, but before this can be done it is necessary to remove the tannins. This is effected by adding a little solution of mercury and ammonium acetates made up in the following proportions :—

Mercuric acetate, 25 grams; ammonium acetate, 100 grams; water to 1 litre.

After filtering off the precipitate produced and expelling the small quantity of alcohol present, the filtrate is acidified with sulphuric acid and titrated with $N/5$-permanganate solution. Only the malic acid is oxidised; the succinic acid is unaffected. To make the end-point more distinct, a known quantity of oxalic acid may be added to the solution before titration, and the result corrected accordingly. One c.c. of $N/5$-permanganate = 0·00223 gram of malic acid.

The titrated solution is mixed with clean sand, evaporated to dryness, and then extracted with ether to recover the succinic acid. The residue left on evaporating the ether is then titrated with standard alkali. If any small quantity of sulphuric acid has been co-extracted with the succinic acid, the amount should be determined gravimetrically and deducted from the titration result.

Lactic acid.—This acid is regarded as a normal constituent of most wines, and especially of old wines. The following method of estimating it, due to Mœslinger,[1] depends upon the fact that barium lactate is soluble in strong alcohol, whereas the other barium salts present are insoluble in this medium.

[1] *Zeitsch. Nahr. Genussm.*, 1901, **4**, 1123.

Take 100 c.c. of the wine, expel the volatile acids with steam as described in the method for estimating these acids, remove the residue to a porcelain basin, and neutralise the remaining acids with barium hydroxide solution, using litmus paper as indicator. Then add 5 to 10 c.c. of a 10 per cent. solution of barium chloride, evaporate the liquid to about 25 c.c., and restore the neutrality, if necessary, with a few drops of the barium hydroxide solution. Now add carefully, with constant stirring, small quantities of pure alcohol (96 per cent.) until the liquid has a volume of 70 to 80 c.c.; transfer it to a 100 c.c. flask, and make the volume up to the mark with the alcohol. Filter off 80 c.c. through a dry folded filter, add a little water to the filtrate, and evaporate it to dryness in a platinum capsule. Ignite the residue carefully, without pushing the incineration so far as to give a white ash, and determine the alkalinity of the ash with $N/2$- or $N/4$-HCl, converting the result into terms of normal alkali per 100 c.c. of the wine. One c.c. of $N/1$ alkali = 0·09 gram of lactic acid.

Glycerol.—Though rather lengthy, the German official method of estimating the glycerol in wine is the one which, on the whole, appears best to use. The procedure varies somewhat, according as the wine is rich or poor in sugar: this will already have been determined from the amount of fixed residue or "extract," or by estimation of the sugar.

(*a*).—**Wines with less than 2 grams of sugar per 100 c.c.**—One hundred c.c. of the wine are evaporated in a porcelain basin on the water-bath till the volume is reduced to about 10 c.c. With the residue 1 gram of sand is mixed; and then sufficient milk of lime (40 per cent. strength) is added to give from 1·5 to 2 c.c. of the "milk" for each gram of extract present. The mixture is evaporated to near dryness, and 5 c.c. of 96 per cent. alcohol added. The portions adherent to the sides of the basin are detached with a spatula, and the whole macerated with a glass "crusher" to a thin cream, small quantities of the strong alcohol being added from time to time. After rinsing off the spatula with alcohol, the basin is warmed on the bath with constant agitation until ebullition commences, and the turbid alcoholic liquid poured through a funnel into a 100 c.c. flask. About 10 to 12 c.c. of the 96 per cent. alcohol are added to the pulverulent residue in the basin, the mixture is again warmed and stirred, and poured off into the flask. This is repeated until the latter contains about 95 c.c. of liquid, after which the funnel is rinsed, the flask cooled, and the volume made up to 100 c.c. at the temperature 15·6° with more of the strong alcohol. After being well mixed, the contents are filtered through a folded filter, and 90 c.c. of the filtrate evaporated gently on the water-bath. The residue is taken up with small quantities of absolute alcohol and transferred to a stoppered graduated tube, until the volume obtained is exactly 15 c.c. To this, three separate quantities of 7·5 c.c. of dehydrated ether are added, shaking well after each addition. The tube, closed, is then allowed to stand until the liquid is quite clear; the solution is poured off into a tared weighing-flask provided with a stopper, and the tube rinsed out with about 5 c.c. of mixed ether and alcohol (3 ether : 2 alcohol, both "absolute"). After expulsion of the solvents by gentle evaporation on the bath, the syrupy residue is dried in the steam oven for one hour, allowed to cool in the desiccator, and weighed. The result must, of course, be multiplied by 100/90, as only 90 c.c. of filtrate were taken for evaporating.

(*b*).—**Wines with 2 grams, or more, of sugar per 100 c.c.**—In such cases, 50 c.c. of the wine are taken in a large flask and warmed on the bath, 1 gram of sand is added, and then milk of lime in small quantities until the mixture, at first deep coloured, becomes lighter and gives off an alkaline odour. After being heated and well shaken for a time, on the water-bath, the mixture is cooled, and 100 c.c. of alcohol (96 per cent.) are added. The precipitate is allowed to settle, and is then filtered and washed with alcohol; the filtrate and washings are evaporated, and the residue is treated as in (*a*), by taking up with absolute alcohol, and so on.

A modified form of this process is proposed by M. Canónica.[1]

Sugars.—To obtain a solution in which the sugars may be determined and the polarisation value observed, place 100 c.c. of the wine in a porcelain basin, and neutralise it *exactly* with sodium hydroxide solution. Then add a drop of dilute acetic acid, to ensure that there is not even a trace of alkali in excess. The very faint acidity will not affect the sugars, whereas alkali readily acts on them when heated. Evaporate the wine down on the water-bath to about one-third or one-fourth of its bulk in order to expel the alcohol, and then wash the residue into a 200 c.c. flask. Add a slight excess of lead subacetate solution; 5 to 10 c.c. will usually suffice. If the liquid is too turbid to judge when an excess is present, withdraw a drop and test it with red litmus paper; the basic lead acetate has an alkaline reaction. Allow the precipitate to settle, and then add a saturated solution of sodium sulphate, little by little, until the excess of lead is precipitated as sulphate. Make up the bulk with water to 200 c.c., mix well, allow the precipitate to settle, and filter the liquid through a dry filter.

[1] See *J. Soc. Chem. Ind.*, 1919, **38**, 114A.

The polarimeter reading of the filtrate is taken in a 2-dcm. tube, and multiplied by 2 to correct for the dilution.

A part of the filtrate (50 c.c.) is then inverted as described below under "Saccharose," but using 5 c.c. of hydrochloric acid and making the final bulk up to 100 c.c. The polarimeter reading of this inverted liquid is taken in the 2-dcm. tube as before, but multiplied by 4 to correct for the double dilution. If this result is lower than the first, saccharose is indicated ; if the two results are sensibly equal, saccharose can be ruled out, and only the examination for reducing sugars need be proceeded with.

Saccharose is determined in the inverted liquid, and the reducing sugars in the part of the filtrate which has not been inverted. Either a gravimetric or a volumetric estimation by means of Fehling's solution may be employed, the liquids to be tested being suitably diluted, if necessary, to bring their content of sugar down to not more than 1 per cent. if the usual quantities are taken.

The foregoing process, it may be noted, takes no account of the volume of the precipitate produced by the lead acetate in the 200 c.c. flask. Hence some operators prefer to proceed as follows.

Preparation of the sample.—Deduct 2 from the extract percentage ; the remainder is approximately the percentage of sugar. If this is not greater than 1, the wine is taken without dilution for the further operations. If greater than 1, dilute a convenient quantity so as to bring the percentage of sugar down to 1 or less. In either case take 100 c.c. of the wine, diluted if necessary, neutralise it very carefully with sodium hydroxide solution, add a drop of dilute acetic acid, and evaporate it in a porcelain basin to one-fourth its original bulk in order to expel the alcohol. Cool, and make up the liquid to the original volume in a flask which will hold more than 10 c.c. above the 100 c.c. mark. Add 10 c.c. of lead subacetate solution, shake, and filter. To 66 c.c. of the filtrate add 6 c.c. of a saturated solution of sodium sulphate, shake, and again filter : this filtrate serves for the sugar estimations. By the addition of the lead acetate and sodium sulphate solutions the volume has been increased, in effect, by one-fifth ; this must, of course, be taken account of in the calculations, as well as the preliminary dilution of the wine, if any.

(1). **Reducing sugars.**—Twenty-five c.c. of the prepared wine are taken, and the reducing sugars determined gravimetrically or volumetrically by means of Fehling's solution in the usual way. The polarimetric value of the uninverted solution is also determined, using the 2-dcm. tube.

(2). **Saccharose.**—Twenty-five c.c. of the prepared filtrate are inverted by the Clerget method. The liquid is placed in a 50 c.c. flask, 2·5 c.c. of strong hydrochloric acid are added, a thermometer is placed in the liquid, and the flask heated in a beaker of water till the thermometer shows 68°. The temperature is kept between 68° and 70° for five minutes, when the flask is cooled, the solution nearly neutralised with caustic soda, and made up to 50 c.c. Of this, 40 c.c. may be taken for the gravimetric or volumetric determination of the invert-sugar by the Fehling process, and the remainder used for obtaining the polarimetric value after inversion, if this is required.

Polarisation.—When the sugars are not estimated, we may proceed as follows. In the case of white wines, take 60 c.c., neutralise carefully, evaporate on the water-bath to two-thirds the original volume, restore the volume to 60 c.c., add 3 c.c. of lead subacetate solution, and filter. To 31·5 c.c. of the filtrate add 1·5 c.c. of a saturated solution of sodium sulphate or carbonate, filter, and polarise in a 200 mm. tube. The volume is, in effect, increased by one-tenth through the additions made, and the reading of the instrument must be corrected accordingly.

With red wines, 60 c.c. are evaporated to one-third after neutralisation, filtered, made up to the original volume, treated with 6 c.c. of lead subacetate, and re-filtered. To 33 c.c. of the filtrate, 3 c.c. of sodium sulphate solution are added, the liquid again filtered, and then polarised. In this case, the volume has been increased by one-fifth.

Red wines are sometimes difficult to "clear" satisfactorily. If the treatment with lead acetate does not suffice, animal charcoal may be used, in the proportion of 5–6 grams per 100 c.c. of wine. The neutralised sample, evaporated to one-half, is digested on the bath for about a quarter of an hour, and filtered. The washing of the charcoal must be thorough: 200–250 c.c. of water may be required. The washings are kept apart from the main filtrate and evaporated to a small bulk, then added, and the whole made up with water to the original volume.

J. Laborde[1] recommends treatment with potassium permanganate for decolorising red wines. A saturated solution of this salt is added drop by drop to 100 c.c. of the wine, kept stirred, until the red colour changes completely to brown, giving in general a precipitate of oxidised tannins. The volume required is noted—it is rarely more than 4 c.c.; then 5 c.c. of lead subacetate are added and the volume completed with water to 110 c.c. After being well

[1] "Vins," p. 166.

stirred, the liquid is filtered, giving a clear and colourless, or slightly yellow, filtrate.

Ash.—If the extract has been determined by the evaporation method, the residue obtained may be used for the estimation of the ash. Otherwise take 25 c.c. of the sample for this determination. It is often convenient, with wines containing much sugar, to char and extract the mass with water, as described for Beer (p. 478).

Sulphates.—Beyond the sulphates normally present, the quantity may be increased through the oxidation of sulphites added for preservative purposes, and by sulphate used for "plastering." Up to a maximum of 2 grams per litre (calculated as potassium sulphate), the latter addition is recognised in certain countries—*e.g.* Spain and Italy; the object being the clarification of the wine. The precipitate of calcium tartrate, produced when calcium sulphate is mixed with the wine, carries down suspended solid matters as it settles, and the potassium sulphate resulting from the reaction between the calcium sulphate and the cream of tartar remains in solution. It is chiefly in connection with this question of "plastering" that the estimation of the sulphates is important in the analysis of wine. Normally, wine contains about 0·02 to 0·06 gram of sulphates per 100 c.c., calculated as potassium sulphate.

In general, the sulphates are precipitated in the wine itself, though the ash can be used in ordinary cases. Fifty c.c. are acidified with 1 c.c. of hydrochloric acid, raised to boiling, and if any sulphite is present boiled down to about 30 c.c. to expel sulphur dioxide. Then to the still boiling liquid 5 c.c. of a 10 per cent. solution of barium chloride are added drop by drop, the boiling is continued for a few minutes, the whole diluted with hot water to about double the original volume, and digested for some hours on the steam-bath. It is well to let the precipitate stand all night, and to filter through a double filter. The precipitate is washed carefully, dried, ignited, and weighed. The result is usually expressed in terms of potassium sulphate.

Phosphates.—About 1 gram of oxidising mixture (1 part KNO_3 and 3 parts Na_2CO_3) is added to 50 c.c. of the wine in a platinum capsule, the mixture evaporated to dryness, and the residue incinerated. In the resulting ash, taken up with dilute nitric acid and heated to boiling for a short time to convert any pyrophosphates into orthophosphates, the phosphoric acid is precipitated with ammonium molybdate solution in the usual manner, and either weighed as the ammonium-phosphomolybdate, or converted into the magnesium ammonium salt and weighed as magnesium pyrophosphate.

Phosphorus exists in wine both in organic combination, chiefly as lecithin, and as inorganic compounds. "Marc" wines, made by mixing a solution of sugar with the "marc" or skins of the grapes, and fermenting the mixture, are deficient in phosphates. On the other hand, sweet wines that have been made from concentrated "must" have a high phosphate content.

Sulphurous acid.—This acid may exist in wine, not merely as dissolved sulphur dioxide, but also in combination with various constituents—*e.g.*, aldehydes, sugars, colouring matters, and tannins. Hence the direct determination by means of iodine in the cold does not give accurate results; but the sulphur dioxide may be distilled off completely in a current of carbon dioxide, oxidised by iodine, and the resulting sulphuric acid precipitated as usual with barium chloride and weighed.

The French official process describes a preliminary test to ascertain whether the amount of sulphur dioxide present exceeds 0·03 gram per 100 c.c. If it does, the distillation method is used for the estimation, as follows.

A flask of about 400 c.c. capacity is fitted with a two-holed rubber stopper carrying an entrance-tube reaching to the bottom of the flask, and connected with an apparatus for generating carbon dioxide. The exit tube is attached to a large Péligot absorption tube, of which the bulbs are each of about 100 c.c. capacity. The air is first expelled from the apparatus with a current of CO_2 gas, and then 30 to 50 c.c. of iodine solution (5 grams of I + 7·5 grams of KI per litre) are introduced into the Péligot tube. The stopper of the flask is raised, and without interrupting the current of carbon dioxide, 100 c.c. of the wine are passed into the flask from a pipette, followed by 5 c.c. of phosphoric acid (sp. gr. 1·69). After re-closing, the flask, at the end of a little time, is heated until about one-half of the wine has distilled over into the bulb-tube, which it is well to immerse in cold water during the operation. The contents are then transferred to a beaker, and the sulphuric acid precipitated with barium chloride in the usual manner.

Weight of $BaSO_4$ obtained × 0·27468 = gram of SO_2 per 100 c.c.

The German official method is similar, except that a Liebig condenser is inserted between the flask and the Péligot tube.

Gayon and Laborde[1] dispense with the current of carbon dioxide and the large bulb-tube, proceeding as follows.

A flask of 250–300 c.c. capacity is filled with carbon dioxide to replace the air; 100 c.c. of the wine and 2 c.c. of syrupy phosphoric acid are introduced, and the flask is connected with a spiral con-

[1] "Vins," p. 153.

denser to which is attached a delivery tube drawn out to a very narrow bore at its lower end. This dips into a special absorption tube, the lower part of which is similar to a test-tube and the upper portion expanded into a bulb of about 80–100 c.c. capacity. 22·5 C.c. of iodine solution (of such strength that 1 c.c. = 0·002 gram of SO_2) are placed in the absorption tube, and the wine is distilled, gently at first and afterwards more rapidly, until all the alcohol has passed over. The sulphur dioxide is absorbed without loss, as the bubbles issuing from the fine delivery tube are very small, and have to traverse a column of iodine solution more than 10 cm. long. If at the end of the distillation there is still some iodine remaining, the quantity of SO_2 present is less than 0·045 gram, and the operation can be terminated if this is all that it is required to know; otherwise the liquid is removed to a beaker and precipitated with barium chloride as usual. Should the iodine show signs of becoming all used up during the distillation, a further quantity is at once added.

Salicylic acid.—It is often sufficient for qualitative purposes merely to add a drop or two of dilute, neutral solution of ferric chloride to a little of the distillate obtained from wine and contained in a porcelain dish. Any appreciable quantity of added salicylic acid will reveal itself by the violet coloration produced. Minute traces, however, are often naturally present in wine. If there is any doubt, 50 c.c. of the sample are acidified with a few drops of hydrochloric acid, and shaken gently with 50 c.c. of a mixture of ordinary ether and petroleum ether (equal volumes); the ether extract separated, passed through a dry filter, and evaporated spontaneously to dryness. On now testing with a little very dilute ferric chloride solution, a strong violet or reddish-violet colour is obtained if salicylic acid is present in sensible quantity.

To estimate the amount the following process, due to Fresenius and Grünhut,[1] may be employed.

Twenty-five or 50 c.c. of the wine are acidified with dilute sulphuric or hydrochloric acid, and extracted repeatedly in a separator with a mixture of ordinary ether and petroleum ether (equal volumes). From the mixed ethereal extracts the salicylic acid is removed by extraction with two successive quantities of 10 c.c. each of decinormal soda solution, followed by two washings with water. The combined alkaline solutions are run into a stoppered flask of about 150 c.c. capacity, and the traces of dissolved ether expelled by heating on the steam-bath. The cooled liquid is then titrated in the following manner.

[1] *Zeitsch. anal. Chem.*, 1899, **38**, 292.

The solution is first neutralised with hydrochloric acid, and a definite volume of "bromine solution" (12·408 grams of KBr + 3·481 grams of $KBrO_3$ per litre) is added, the quantity depending upon the amount of salicylic acid which is likely to be present. At least twice the quantity of bromine required for the reaction (see below) should be added. Ten c.c. of strong hydrochloric acid are now run in, the flask is at once closed, shaken gently to mix the contents, and placed in a cold bath for ten minutes.

An excess of potassium iodide solution (10 per cent. strength) is then run into the flask, and after standing for five minutes the liberated iodine is titrated with decinormal thiosulphate solution and starch in the usual manner. To standardise the "bromine solution" a blank experiment is carried out in precisely the same way on a volume of water similar to that of the neutralised extract.

The quantity of iodine liberated in the sample will be less than that in the blank experiment by the amount of halogen used up by the salicylic acid; and from the equation given below, this amounts to 6 halogen atoms for each molecule of salicylic acid. Hence the difference between the volumes of thiosulphate solution required for the two titrations, expressed in cubic centimetres and multiplied by 0·0023, gives the weight in grams of the salicylic acid present.

Reactions :—

$$(1)\ C_6H_4(OH){\cdot}COOH + 8Br = C_6H_2Br_3{\cdot}OBr + 4HBr + CO_2.$$
$$(2)\ C_6H_2Br_3{\cdot}OBr + 2KI = C_6H_2Br_3{\cdot}OK + KBr + I_2\ ;$$

so that ultimately 6 atoms of halogen are used up by one molecule of salicylic acid.

The "bromine solution" liberates bromine on acidifying, in accordance with the equation :—

$$KBrO_3 + 5KBr + 6HCl = 6KCl + 3H_2O + 6Br.$$

Its strength is about 0·01 gram of Br per c.c.

Saccharin.—For the detection of saccharin in wine and other beverages, two tests are generally relied upon—(1) the characteristic sweet taste of the substance, obtained as an ether extract from the wine, and (2) the conversion of the saccharin into salicylic acid. As regards these, it may be remarked that a sweet taste alone is not absolutely conclusive, since it might be due to dulcin, another artificial sweetening ingredient. Also, since salicylic acid may be present as such, care must be taken to remove it before applying the second test. For the quantitative determination of such small proportions of saccharin as are met with in beverages, probably the best method is the oxidation of the substance by fusion with an oxidising mixture, and estimation of the resulting sulphate.

(I.) **The wine does not contain salicylic acid.**—One hundred and fifty c.c. of the sample are mixed with sand in a porcelain basin, and evaporated on the water-bath ; 2 c.c. of syrupy phosphoric acid are added, and the mass is extracted warm with a mixture of ether and petroleum ether (equal volumes), a glass "crusher" being used to break down the solids during the extraction. The ethereal extract is poured off through an asbestos filter, and the extraction repeated until 300 c.c. of filtrate are obtained. One-third of the filtrate is taken for the qualitative tests. It is evaporated to a small bulk, and then removed to a short, wide test-tube or a porcelain crucible. A small portion is withdrawn and evaporated on a watch-glass for tasting ; if the sweet taste is detected the remainder of the solution is evaporated to dryness in the tube or crucible, then mixed with 2 c.c. of a 3 per cent. solution of *sodium* hydroxide, and again taken to dryness. The residue is next heated in an oil-bath to 250° for thirty minutes to effect the conversion of the saccharin into salicylic acid. After cooling, the substance is dissolved in a little water, acidified with sulphuric acid, removed to a separator and extracted with ether. The ethereal extract is washed with a few drops of water to remove any traces of sulphuric acid, then evaporated to dryness and tested with a drop or two of a dilute, neutral solution of ferric chloride to obtain the violet colour due to salicylic acid.

For the estimation, the remaining two-thirds of the filtrate (= 100 c.c. of the wine) are evaporated to dryness, the residue dissolved in dilute solution of sodium carbonate, and filtered into a platinum capsule. The liquid is evaporated to dryness, and mixed with four or five times its weight of dry sodium carbonate ; this mixture is then added a little at a time to an excess of potassium nitrate kept fused in a platinum crucible. After cooling, the melt is dissolved out with hot water, transferred to a beaker, covered with a watch glass to prevent loss by effervescence, then carefully acidified with hydrochloric acid, and the sulphate precipitated with barium chloride and determined in the usual manner. The weight of barium sulphate obtained × 0·7857 = weight of saccharin in the 100 c.c. of wine taken.

(II.) **The wine contains salicylic acid.**—The following procedure is described by Blarez[1] :—

Two hundred c.c. of wine are acidified with 2 grams of syrupy phosphoric acid and evaporated to a little less than half the original

[1] Gayon and Laborde, "Vins," p. 261.

volume. After the residue has cooled somewhat, 5 c.c. of a 5 per cent. solution of potassium permanganate are run in, little by little, in three portions and stirring after each addition. When the colour of the permanganate has disappeared and the reaction, which is shown by the production of bubbles, has terminated, the (cooled) solution is extracted with ether. For this purpose 70 to 75 c.c. of ether are placed in a separator of about 250 c.c. capacity, and 50 c.c. of the prepared wine poured in ; the mixture is then shaken vigorously during two or three minutes, and this shaking is repeated two or three times. After separating, the extracted wine is run off, and the rest of the prepared wine is passed into the same ether and treated in the same way. The ethereal solution is now allowed to separate completely, passed through a filter, and evaporated to dryness ; the dry residue can now be tested as before by the taste and the conversion into salicylic acid.

The presence of salicylic acid in the wine does not, of course, affect the *estimation* of the saccharin by the sulphate process described above. An approximate estimation of the saccharin, however, can also be made by noting the depth of colour given with ferric chloride in the fusion test for saccharin carried out on wine treated with permanganate as above described, compared with the colour obtained from known quantities of salicylic acid. One hundred and thirty-eight parts of the latter are given by 182 parts of saccharin.

Dulcin.—In order to detect this artificial sweetening substance, 500 c.c. of the wine are mixed with 25 grams of lead carbonate and evaporated on the water-bath to a pasty consistency. This is extracted repeatedly with alcohol, the extract evaporated to dryness, and the residue extracted with ether. On evaporating the ether, dulcin is left in the residue, and may be identified as follows :

(i).—A portion is mixed with about 5 c.c. of water in a test-tube, and 2–4 drops of a solution of mercuric nitrate are added. The tube is then heated for five to ten minutes in boiling water. If dulcin is present, a faint violet coloration is obtained, which becomes deeper on adding a little lead dioxide.[1] The mercuric nitrate solution is made by dissolving 1–2 grams of freshly precipitated mercuric oxide in nitric acid, diluting the solution, and adding caustic soda solution in sufficient quantity just to give a little permanent precipitate. The liquid is then diluted to about 15 c.c., allowed to settle, and the clear portion decanted off for use.

(ii).—Another portion of the residue is mixed with 2–3 drops of pure phenol and an equal volume of strong sulphuric acid, and the

[1] Jorissen ; *v. J. Soc. Chem. Ind.*, 1896, **15**, 620.

mixture heated to boiling for a short time. After cooling, a little of the product is poured into a test-tube, water added to about half fill the tube, and the mixture shaken up well. On carefully pouring a little ammonia or sodium hydroxide solution on to the liquid, a blue ring is obtained at the surface of contact if dulcin was present.

Tannin.—An approximate evaluation of the tannin, of the nature of a rough preliminary estimation, is given by the following German process.

Take 100 c.c. of the wine, expel the carbon dioxide, and neutralise the free acids, if necessary, with standard alkali so far as to obtain an acidity of 0·5 gram per 100 c.c., calculated as tartaric acid. (Take the total acidity, already determined on another portion of the wine, as a guide to the amount of alkali to be added.)

Add 1 c.c. of a 40 per cent. solution of sodium acetate, and then, drop by drop, a 10 per cent. solution of ferric chloride until no further precipitate is produced. Each drop of the ferric chloride solution precipitates 0·05 gram of tannin.

For the more precise determination of the tannin in wine the method (Pi's) described under "Cider" (p. 483) may be used, with the following modification.

Ten c.c. of the wine (or 5 if rich in tannin) are placed in a porcelain basin, and 5 c.c. of the ammoniacal acetate of zinc added. The mixture should be alkaline, and turn brown ; if not, a few drops of ammonia solution are added. Evaporate the liquid on the water bath until the volume is reduced to one-third or less, then add boiling water equal in amount to the original volume of liquid evaporated (15 or 10 c.c.), raise to boiling over a flame, and filter. Wash the precipitate thoroughly with hot water, and dissolve it in dilute sulphuric acid, including any traces remaining adherent to the basin.

The acid solution thus obtained is diluted to a litre, 10 c.c. of the standard indigo solution are added, and the mixture titrated with the permanganate solution. Let c be the number of c.c. of permanganate required.

If a = the number of c.c. of wine taken ; b the number of c.c. of permanganate required to oxidise 10 c.c. of indigo solution, and x the tannin content of the wine, in grams per 100 c.c.,

$$x = (c-b) \times 0{\cdot}001 \times \frac{100}{a} = \frac{c-b}{10a}.$$

The method has been found to give 93 per cent. of the tannins, and the result is therefore corrected accordingly, so that finally

$$x = \frac{100}{93} \times \frac{c-b}{10a}$$
$$= 0{\cdot}107 \times \frac{c-b}{a}.$$

Artificial colouring matters.—The French official tests for the presence or absence of foreign colours in wine are as follows :—

(*a*).—Fifty c.c. of the wine are made slightly alkaline with ammonia, and shaken with about 15 c.c. of colourless amyl alcohol. The latter should remain uncoloured. If so, it is decanted, filtered, and acidified with acetic acid ; it should still remain uncoloured.

(*b*).—Treat the wine with a 10 per cent. solution of mercury acetate until there is no further change in colour, then make the mixture alkaline with slight excess of magnesia. Boil, and filter ; the liquid made slightly acid with dilute sulphuric acid should remain uncoloured.

(*c*).—Fifty c.c. of the wine are taken in a porcelain dish (7–8 cm. diameter), one or two drops of dilute sulphuric acid added, and a tuft of white wool. Boil for exactly five minutes, adding boiling water as the liquid evaporates. Withdraw the wool, and wash it in water. It should be scarcely tinted, of dull rose colour. Placed in ammoniacal water, it should assume a dull green tinge.

These tests readily show whether or not a wine contains aniline colours. The identification of the particular colours, if found to be present, is often a troublesome task, and not usually worth while attempting. Added vegetable colours are especially difficult to detect, by reason of their similarity to those naturally present in the wine.

Detection of cider in wine.—According to Medinger and Michel,[1] when 15 c.c. of wine are shaken with a few c.c. of concentrated solution of sodium nitrite, a bright yellow or yellowish-brown coloration is obtained if the wine is pure, whereas cider or perry is coloured dark-brown or brownish-black, and a brownish-black precipitate separates. This precipitate is insoluble in water, alcohol, or ether, but dissolves to a red solution in aqueous alkali. Wines when treated with both sodium nitrite and potassium hydroxide give a yellow coloration, whilst cider and perry and mixtures of these with wine yield a pure red coloration.

[1] *Chem. Zeit.*, 1918, **42**, 230. See also Schulte, *ibid.*, 537, 557.

UNITED KINGDOM. QUANTITIES OF WINE "CLEARED" FOR CONSUMPTION IN THE YEAR 1913–14.

Country from which consigned.	Quantity. Gallons.
Portugal	3,287,128
France	2,891,447
Spain—red wine	1,799,441
,, —white wine	1,078,959
Germany	899,192
Italy	303,128
Netherlands	50,021
Madeira	20,737
Other foreign countries	246,812
Australia	766,775
Other British Possessions	332,091
Total	11,675,731
Exported	38,415
Retained for consumption	11,637,316

X.—BRITISH WINES

These are usually made by fermenting solutions of sugar with which various ingredients are mixed in order to impart the particular flavour or character required. The principal kinds are Ginger, Orange, Raisin, and Rhubarb Wines, but a number of others such as Cowslip, Elderberry, Gooseberry, and Damson wines have a certain vogue, more especially as domestic preparations. They are all included within the legal term "sweets or made wines,"[1] which are defined as "Any liquor made from fruit and sugar, or from fruit or sugar mixed with any other ingredient, and which has undergone a process of fermentation in the manufacture thereof." (Finance (1909–10) Act, c. 8, s. 52). If the wines are made for sale, the manufacturer is required to take out a maker's licence. No tax is imposed upon the alcohol produced, but the seller of British wines must be duly licensed for the sale.

Fruit juice, it will be seen, is not necessarily an ingredient of British wines. The characteristic flavour of ginger wine, for instance, is given by ginger rhizome, of orange wine by orange peel, of rhubarb wine by the rhubarb stem. This, no doubt, is why the legal definition has been made so wide. Other fruits than those mentioned above, however, are often employed. Such are, for instance, currants, prunes, and apples. Moreover, a British winemaker may, for flavouring purposes, mix with his product a proportion of foreign wine, not exceeding fifteen parts to the hundred. Imported grape "must" is fermented in this country, as also are "musts" of currants and raisins, to produce a "basis" wine,

[1] See note at the end of this section.

which can be flavoured in different ways to make various products, such as British "port" or "claret."

British wines are usually well sweetened, and mostly contain from 16 to 26 per cent. of proof spirit (9 to 15 per cent. of alcohol by volume). Occasionally somewhat higher percentages of proof spirit are found—up to 29 per cent. or so—in these cases the wine has probably been "fortified" with alcohol. Lower amounts than 16 are not infrequent. When quantities of the order of 5 or 6 per cent. of proof spirit are present they are usually due to the fermentation, through carelessness, inadvertence, or design, of so-called "non-alcoholic" beverages.

Preservatives are fairly common in British wines. *Sulphurous acid* is the most frequent; it may be derived either from direct treatment of the wine with the acid or a sulphite, or from storage in casks which had been "sulphured." The quantity ranges in general from mere traces up to 0·02 gram per 100 c.c., but larger amounts are not uncommon. **Salicylic acid** is occasionally present, though much less frequently than in the "non-alcoholic" preparations mentioned later on. **Boric acid** is also often found in small quantity, but where the proportion is less than 0·001 gram per 100 c.c. it is probably attributable to the natural juice of the grape or other fruit employed. Small quantities of **fluorides** have been found occasionally.

Artificial colouring substances are not much used in alcoholic British wines, though now and then an aniline colour such as "Fast Red" is found.

Copper in small quantity is occasionally present in British wine, as it is in foreign wine.

As there are no restrictions (other than the general prohibitions of deleterious substances) upon the ingredients which may be used in making British wines, most of the problems of analysis are simplified compared with those of foreign wines. In general it suffices to determine the specific gravity, alcohol, fixed and volatile acids, and sugars; and to examine the sample for injurious preservatives and colouring matters. The flavour characteristic of the particular variety of wine which the sample purports to be should, of course, be present: a genuine raisin wine must have the raisin flavour; a ginger wine must taste of ginger. This is a matter for the palate.

The following are typical analyses of the principal kinds of alcoholic British wines ordinarily sold in this country. With the exception of those for specific gravity and proof spirit, all the figures denote grams per 100 c.c. of the wine.

Analyses of British Wines.

Kind.	Specific gravity.	Proof spirit. Per cent.	Fixed acid (as Tartaric).	Volatile acid (as Acetic).	Extract.	Reducing sugars, as invert.	Sucrose.	Ash.	K_2O.	P_2O_5.
Black currant	1·0512	21·4	0·48	0·12	17·43	14·25	Nil.	0·48	0·20	0·02
Cowslip	1·0453	25·6	0·21	0·17	16·57	14·56	0·55	0·17	0·06	0·02
Elderberry	1·0771	21·4	0·25	0·18	24·22	19·64	0·16	0·64	0·16	0·02
Ginger	1·0088	22·4	0·30	0·12	6·56	4·50	0·28	0·16	0·06	0·01
,,	1·1189	22·4	0·33	0·07	35·42	11·83	18·09	0·25	0·09	0·02
Orange	1·0220	26·6	0·35	0·14	10·66	8·31	0·15	0·24	0·11	0·02
,,	1·0806	18·0	0·33	0·19	24·57	22·23	0·12	0·24	0·09	0·02
Raisin	1·0298	24·8	0·42	0·16	12·40	8·97	0·36	0·20	0·09	0·02
,,	1·0876	23·5	0·33	0·06	27·33	16·82	7·60	0·19	0·08	0·04
Raspberry	1·0579	19·4	0·84	0·12	18·84	10·22	3·81	0·32	0·13	0·02
British sherry	·0043	28·2	0·38	0·12	6·31	3·75	0·11	0·30	0·12	0·03

Note.—The legal term "sweets" appears on the Statute Book in 1696, "sweets or mixed liquors." In 10 and 11 Will. III., 1699, sweets are said to be "commonly used" for preparing or improving "any liquor called wine." The term "made wine" appears to be first mentioned in 1737 (10 Geo. II., c. 17). "Fermentation" as a necessary condition is first laid down in 1860.

XI.—MEDICATED WINES

These are wines containing medicinal drugs, and are typically represented by the six medicated wines of the British Pharmacopœia, namely, Antimonial Wine, Colchicum Wine, Iron Wine, Wine of Iron Citrate, Ipecacuanha Wine, and Quinine Wine. The basis may be either a foreign wine or a British wine; thus of those in the above list the preparations of iron citrate and quinine are made with orange wine, and the others with sherry.

A number of wines are sold which contain small quantities of meat extract or malt extract, or both. These are frequently referred to popularly as "medicated" wines, though they contain no medicines, but only nutriments, as the added substances. Such articles are not regarded as medicated wines by the British revenue authorities. To come within this category the wine must contain a medicinal drug, or drugs, and in such proportion that the wine is essentially a medicine. Thus a "Meat and Malt Wine" is not a medicated wine, but a "meat and malt wine with quinine" is so, provided that the proportion of quinine is equal to that in the official "Quinine Wine," namely, 2 grams in 875 c.c., or 1 grain per fluid ounce, calculated as quinine hydrochloride. Further, the wine, if necessary, is required to be made too unpalatable for use as a beverage. Thus coca wine must contain not only a certain proportion of coca alkaloids, but also a sufficient quantity of the extract of coca leaves to render the article unpalatable, if, for revenue purposes, it is to be regarded as a "medicated" wine.

The proportion of alcohol in medicated wines is, in general, substantially that in the wine used as basis, since the medicaments do not, as a rule, greatly alter the volume of the wine. Quinine wine contains about 23 to 28 per cent. of proof spirit (13 to 16 per cent. of alcohol by volume), and iron wine about 26 to 32 per cent. of proof spirit (15 to 18·3 of alcohol by volume). The more popular brands of "meat and malt" wines are usually made with fortified red wines, and contain about 29 to 34 per cent. of proof spirit (16·6 to 19·5 of alcohol by volume). Wines containing much tannin are not very suitable for medication with quinine, as a precipitate of quinine tannate is deposited during storage. In such cases it is better to use "detannated" wine—*i.e.*, wine which has been treated with gelatin to remove excess of tannin.

The analysis of medicated wines follows the lines already indicated, so far as may be necessary, supplemented by a determination of the medicaments present. It will suffice to give one or two examples of the latter estimations.

Quinine wine.—For determination of quinine alkaloids, 50 c.c. are taken—conveniently in a 100 c.c. cylinder fitted with a blow-off arrangement similar to that of an ordinary wash-bottle. The wine is made alkaline with a few drops of strong solution of ammonia, and extracted three times with about 50 c.c. of ether each time. The ethereal solutions are blown off into a tared flask, the ether is distilled off, and the residue dried and weighed. The result may be checked by dissolving the weighed alkaloid in a mixture of alcohol and ether (equal volumes), adding water and a little freshly-prepared alcoholic solution of hæmatoxylin, and titrating the liquid with decinormal acid. Each c.c. required = 0·0324 gram of alkaloids calculated as anhydrous quinine. Co-extracted colouring matter, however, sometimes masks the end-point of the reaction. If the weighed residue is obviously contaminated, it is well to purify it by dissolving in hydrochloric acid, extracting the acid solution with petroleum ether, then making alkaline again with ammonia and extracting with ether as before.

Ipecacuanha wine.—One hundred c.c. of the wine are taken, evaporated to about 50 c.c. to remove the alcohol, and transferred to a separator. The liquid is first made slightly acid with dilute sulphuric acid and extracted twice with ether, the ethereal solutions being separated, mixed, washed twice with a little water, and the washings added to the main quantity. This is now made alkaline with ammonia and extracted three times with chloroform, using about 20 c.c. of solvent each time. The chloroformic solutions are passed through a small filter into a tared beaker, the filter washed with a little chloroform, and the solution evaporated down to a bulk of about 2 c.c. To this are added 5 c.c. of ether, and the evaporation is continued to dryness at a temperature not exceeding 80°, the residual alkaloids being then weighed, after cooling in a desiccator.

XII.—"NON-ALCOHOLIC" WINES

A considerable number of beverages are sold under this designation. Some contain grape juice, unfermented, but the majority are solutions of sugar, coloured and flavoured to imitate more or less closely one or other description of wine. They are not in general strictly non-alcoholic, nor of course are they "wine," so that the designation is somewhat of a misnomer. Apart from any question of adventitious fermentation, the alcohol they contain is due to the use of spirituous flavouring ingredients. Thus a "non-alcoholic ginger wine" may be flavoured with tincture of ginger, an "orange wine" with tincture of orange, and so on. Various "wine essences" are sold ready-made, needing only to be diluted with syrup in stated proportions to produce the required beverage. One such essence, for example, is as follows: Tincture of ginger 4 dr., tincture of capsicum 3 dr., tartaric acid 6 dr., caramel 2 oz., water to 4 oz. To be added to a syrup made by boiling 4 lb. of loaf sugar in 125 oz. of water. The finer essences are spirituous solutions of various esters such as œnanthic ester, acetic ester, and nitrous ether, with flavourings of vanilla, almond, and other essential oils, tartaric or citric acids, and colourings.

So long as these "wines" contain not more than 2 per cent. of proof spirit, they are regarded by the revenue authorities in this country as non-alcoholic, and sellers of them are not required to be licensed for the sale, though the "wines" are dutiable as "table waters." They do, in fact, usually contain from 0·5 to 2 per cent. of proof spirit, though somewhat larger proportions are occasionally met with. The proportion of sugar is generally high, ranging from about 15 up to 45 grams per 100 c.c., or even more. Salicylic acid is often found as a preservative in these "non-alcoholic" preparations, as are also sulphurous acid, boric acid, and occasionally benzoates and fluorides. Artificial colouring matters are also often present; among those which have been identified are: Acid Brown Red, Acid Magenta, Fast Yellow Red, Orange, Quinoline Yellow, Resorcin Brown, Tartrazine, and Xylidene Scarlet.

XIII.—MISCELLANEOUS ALCOHOLIC BEVERAGES

Bartzsch.—Infusions of the leaf-stalks of the hogweed (*Heracleum sphondylium*), fermented with yeast, have been used as spirituous drinks from time immemorial in North America, Northern Asia, Persia, Russia, Poland, and Silesia. The name "Bartzsch" is given to the beverage in the two last-named countries.[1] In Russia it is used in the preparation of the soup "Borchtsch," as well as for drinking.

Kephir is the national beverage of the inhabitants of the

[1] Hartwich (Abst.), *Yr. Bk. Pharm.*, 1912, 126.

Caucasus, and has also been used a good deal in Europe during the last thirty years. It is a nourishing beverage produced by the fermentation of milk with "kephir grains," containing certain yeasts and lactic acid bacilli. These organisms agglomerate in the fermenting milk, forming lumps, with cauliflower-like appearance, which can easily be separated from the liquid and used for a number of successive fermentations. Kephir ferment from different sources may apparently contain different varieties of yeasts and bacilli, as several micro-organisms have been isolated.[1]

Cow's, sheep's, and goat's milk are used for the preparation of kephir, the two last especially in the Caucasus. One method of making it is to proceed as follows :—

Half a litre of milk is sterilised by boiling, cooled to about 18–20°, and then mixed with not less than 12 grams of the ferment. The mixture is allowed to stand in a covered vessel, with occasional stirring, until it curdles, which usually occurs within thirty hours. The ferment is then removed by means of a coarse sieve, and the milk allowed to undergo after-fermentation at the ordinary temperature, in a bottle with a screw stopper. From time to time the bottle is well shaken, and the fermentation allowed to continue for 12–24 hours until the desired degree of acidity and aeration with carbon dioxide has been reached, when the product is ready for consumption. It is a pleasantly-acid, creamy liquid, which is often taken medicinally.

According to König, the average composition of kephir is :—

	Per cent.
Water	90·21
Alcohol	0·75
Fat	1·44
Sugar	2·41
Lactic acid	1·02
Proteins	3·49
Ash	0·68
	100·00

Koumiss is a spirituous beverage obtained by the fermentation of mare's milk. It is the chief spirituous drink used by the Tartars and other nomadic peoples of the Russian steppes. It is made by adding one part of old koumiss to ten of fresh milk, warming for two to three hours at 20–25°, and maturing in bottles. In Switzerland, an imitation of the Russian koumiss is made from cow's milk, skimmed, which is sweetened a little and fermented with yeast. The preparation contains 3 to 4 per cent. of alcohol, with 2 per cent. of sugar and 0·2 per cent. of lactic acid.

[1] Henneberg, *Zeitsch. Spiritusind.*, 1912, **35**, 170, 177, 184.

Saké is a Japanese spirituous drink prepared by the fermentation of rice with the mould *Aspergillus oryzae*. Steamed rice is spread out on mats and mixed with a culture of the mould, which develops and partly saccharifies the starch during its growth. The mass is kept from the light, and turned each day during three or four days. The culture thus obtained (" koji ") is used to ferment a small mash of more steamed rice, and the product in its turn is employed to carry out the fermentation of a larger mash. The whole process requires about thirty days for its completion. Other methods are in use which extend over forty to fifty days.[1]

Saké contains on an average about 17 per cent. of alcohol. It is of light-yellow colour, and in flavour resembles a mixture of beer and sherry.

Toddy is an Indian beverage, obtained, like saké, by the fermentation of rice, but mostly from the sap of various palms, especially the cocoanut palm. The sap undergoes spontaneous fermentation after being collected, the process usually being rapid, and extending only over a day or so. **Arrack** is obtained by the distillation of toddy.

[1] Ikuta, *Zeitsch. anal. Chem.*, 1875, **14**, 439.

CHAPTER XII

THE PHYSIOLOGICAL EFFECTS OF ALCOHOL

NUMEROUS experiments have been made with a view to elucidate the physiological effects of alcohol. As regards the human subject, however, inherent difficulties of strict experimentation, and perhaps still more the difficulties of correctly interpreting the results, have made it desirable to exercise more than ordinary caution before accepting, as definitely established, many of the conclusions arrived at.

Particularly is this the case in regard to the effects produced by alcohol on the mental processes and the nervous functions. These processes and functions are admittedly very complex. The human subject of the experiment may himself be biassed as to the expected results, and that bias, in some experiments, may to some extent affect the results. His own estimate of his performances under the influence of alcohol is affected by that influence itself. He can scarcely be prevented from knowing when alcohol is given to him, so that it is difficult to obtain him strictly "neutral." And no doubt also preconceived ideas, in this sphere just as in others, may sometimes unconsciously affect the judgment of the experimenter, however impartial he may desire to be.

Bearing these facts in mind, a careful review of present knowledge respecting the action of alcohol on the human organism has been prepared by an influential committee of medical men for the Central Control Board (Liquor Traffic) of the United Kingdom.[1] In compiling the following account, this review has been freely drawn upon, since it is the most authoritative summary available of modern scientific views on the subject.

Absorption of alcohol into the blood.—Alcohol when imbibed is quickly absorbed into the circulatory system. About one-fifth of the quantity taken passes into the blood from the stomach, and one-tenth from the uppermost section of the small

[1] "Alcohol: its Action on the Human Organism." H.M. Stationery Office, 1918." (Quoted by permission of the Controller.)

intestine; but the main absorption, equal to about one-half of the whole dose, occurs in the middle portion of the small intestine. The remaining one-fifth is absorbed from the third and last section. By the time the alimentary contents reach the large intestine, all the alcohol has been taken up from them into the blood. The rate of absorption appears to vary with the conditions, such as the degree of dilution of the alcohol, the form in which the latter is taken, and the time in relation to meals; but the evidence respecting these factors is not clear enough to warrant a definite statement as to their precise effects.

Excretion.—A small proportion of the imbibed alcohol is excreted unchanged, mainly through the lungs and in the urine. The actual quantity thus lost is variable. Any influence which hastens absorption into the blood, or stimulates the production of urine, or augments the vigour of respiration, will tend to increase the quantity of alcohol eliminated in an unchanged form. The loss, however, never exceeds 10 per cent. of the quantity of alcohol swallowed, and is usually much less—about 2 per cent. on an average. As little as 1 per cent. of a moderate dose may escape where habitual drinkers are concerned.

There is no evidence that alcohol is ever eliminated to any appreciable extent in the perspiration. It has been detected in the milk of women addicted to alcohol, but probably it does not occur in the milk except when large doses are taken, and even then the amount excreted is too small to affect the health of the infant.

In this connection, it may be noted that the available evidence does not support the popular belief that alcoholic beverages promote the secretion of milk, and are therefore beneficial to nursing mothers. Whether in the form of spirits or beer, alcohol does not seem to have any effect whatever on either the quantity or the quality of the milk secreted.[1]

Oxidation.—Except for the small proportion excreted unchanged, alcohol taken into the body is oxidised therein as completely as the carbohydrates are. Definite proof of this has been obtained by analysing the air inspired and that expired by subjects treated with experimental doses of alcohol, and thus determining the effect of the treatment upon the value of the "respiratory quotient." This quotient is the ratio:—

$$\frac{\text{volume of carbon dioxide produced}}{\text{volume of oxygen used up}};$$

and for the oxidation of carbohydrates its value is unity.

[1] Rosemann, *Pflüger's Archiv*, 1889, **78**.

This will be seen from the following equation, denoting the oxidation of a sugar :—

$C_6H_{12}O_6$	+	$6O_2$	=	$6CO_2$	+	$6H_2O$.
Dextrose		Oxygen, 6 vols.		Carbon dioxide, 6 vols.		Water

The volume of the carbon dioxide produced is equal to that of the external oxygen supplied and used up in the oxidation, so that, for carbohydrates, the above ratio = 1.

With alcohol, however, a larger proportion of oxygen is required :—

C_2H_6O	+	$3O_2$	=	$2CO_2$	+	$3H_2O$.
Alcohol		Oxygen, 3 vols.		Carbon dioxide, 2 vols.		Water

Hence the respiratory quotient for alcohol is only 2/3. Its value is in fact lower, not only than that for carbohydrates, but for fats and other ordinary foodstuffs.

Thus if alcohol is oxidised in the body, the addition of alcohol to the diet should be followed by a fall in the value of the respiratory quotient. This, in fact, is found to occur (Atwater and Benedict).[1] It has been shown further that the energy liberated by this oxidation of alcohol is not lost as mere superfluous heat. Up to the extent of one-fifth of its total needs, the body can utilise energy derived from the metabolism of alcohol.

Energy so utilised will conserve that supplied by carbohydrates and fats in the diet. Of this there is experimental proof. Thus a man was kept on a standard measured diet, rich in carbohydrates, and his respiratory quotient was determined. A ration of alcohol was then added to the diet. The respiratory quotient fell promptly, and to such an extent as to show that, while the alcohol was being oxidised, carbohydrate was being economised and added to the food reserve of the man's body.

Similarly as regards fats ; if a fixed diet sufficient for maintenance is given, an addition of alcohol protects some fat from oxidation, and allows more fat to be added to the body's reserve supply.

Thus alcohol can to some extent replace foodstuffs such as sugars, starches, and fats in the nutrition of the body. Moreover, unlike starch and fat, it requires no preliminary digestion, but passes unchanged to the tissues which utilise it. Since, however, it contains no proteids, alcohol is not a food in the sense of being a flesh-forming material. Nevertheless, it can apparently serve in

[1] "Physiological Aspects of the Liquor Problem," New York, 1903.

some degree to economise protein, by reducing to a minimum the amount which the body requires.

Excess of protein in the diet, over the amount necessary to repair tissue-waste, is oxidised to furnish energy, and alcohol can supply the place of this excess, so that a smaller ration of protein suffices. Whilst the experiments made to determine this point are not all in agreement as to the results, the general conclusion is that stated above.

The method of experiment is to put the subject on a mixed ration, containing known amounts of protein, carbohydrate, and fat. The nitrogen excreted in the urine is determined; this indicates the amount of protein that is being oxidised and used up merely as a source of energy. The diet is so adjusted that a reduction of carbohydrates or fat will lead to increased oxidation of protein, which will be shown by a larger amount of nitrogen excreted. If now, instead of simply reducing the carbohydrate, a chemically equivalent amount of alcohol is substituted for it, and if it is found that there is no increase in the quantity of excreted nitrogen, the result is evidence that the alcohol has taken the place of the carbohydrate as an economiser of protein. Most of the experimenters are agreed that this is, in fact, the effect produced, though there are some exceptions, believed to be due to the fact that the subjects of the experiments in these cases were not accustomed to taking alcohol.

The conclusion is that alcohol has a certain food-value in a limited sense, namely, as a fuel or supplier of energy. This, however, is not the whole story. Its theoretical value as a food is in practice limited and counterbalanced by its other properties; and in any case it has, from the point of view of its food-value alone, no advantages over a foodstuff like sugar.

Concentration in the blood.—During the first few hours after it is imbibed, alcohol passes into the blood more rapidly than it is oxidised. The concentration therefore rises, reaches a maximum value, and usually remains at about that level for some time. The interval before the maximum is reached varies with the amount of the dose and other conditions. During the phase of unaltered concentration the oxidation and the absorption practically balance each other. Then the oxidation begins to preponderate, the concentration decreases, and after about twenty-four hours no more alcohol is detectible in the body.

The degree of maximum concentration attained is important. It bears a regular relation to the dose given. With an animal receiving alcohol equivalent to 1 cubic centimetre per kilogram of body-weight, the maximum subsequently found in the blood was about 0·1 per cent.; with 2 cubic centimetres, the maximum was about 0·2 per cent., and so on.[1] This maximum concentration does not, of course, represent the whole of the alcohol; it is the balance of absorption over destruction. Some of the alcohol has already been destroyed, whilst some is still unabsorbed. The correspondence between the one, or two, parts per thousand of alcohol administered and alcohol found in the body is an accidental coincidence.

Thus it is possible, from the percentage found in the blood, to calculate approximately the minimum quantity of alcohol taken. Suppose, for example, that the blood of a man weighing 10 stone is found to contain 0·5 per cent. of alcohol. This, from what precedes, represents at least 5 c.c. per kilogram of body-weight, and as 10 stone = 63·6 kilos., the minimum quantity of alcohol drunk = 5 × 63·6 c.c. = 318 c.c., or 11·2 fluid ounces.

Chabanier and Loring,[2] using the Nicloux method of analysis, have determined the concentration of ethyl alcohol (and also of methyl alcohol) in the blood and in the urine of subjects who had ingested these alcohols. They found that the concentration was practically the same in the urine as in the blood. They conclude, therefore, that there is no accumulation of alcohol by the kidneys, since it is eliminated at substantially the same degree of dilution as is found in the blood.

Lethal dose.—According to Dr. A. W. Blyth,[3] quantities of one or two ounces of absolute alcohol given in the form of brandy, gin, etc., would be a highly dangerous and probably fatal dose for a child below ten or twelve years of age; while the toxic dose for adults is somewhere between 2½ and 5 ounces.

This, however, appears to be a very low estimate. The Central Control Board Committee, already mentioned, give it as being "generally accepted" that with a content of alcohol in the blood exceeding 0·6 per cent. there is a considerable likelihood of death.[4] If this is taken as being approximately the alcoholic concentration in dangerous poisoning, it follows from Gréhant's results noted above that the dose taken would be about 6 c.c. per kilo. of body-weight. This, for a man of 10 stone weight, works out to about 13½ fluid oz. of absolute alcohol. The fatal dose is put, in fact, at "about 14 oz. of absolute alcohol, or nearly a pint and a half of

[1] Gréhant; *Compt. rend. Soc. Biol.*, 1881, 1886, 1889.
[2] *Ibid.*, 1916, **79**, 8.
[3] "Poisons," p. 144, 1906 edition.
[4] "Alcohol, its Action on the Human Organism," pp. 87, 88.

proof spirit," on the assumption mentioned. But it is to be remembered that some persons are much more susceptible than the average person to the action of alcohol.

It has been suggested that the amount of the lethal dose in cases of direct alcoholic poisoning may depend upon the degree of dilution of the spirit, as strong alcohol will act almost corrosively on the mucous membrane of the stomach, and so aid the more remote effects. But even when alcohol kills (by acute poisoning), it kills through its action on the brain and the rest of the nervous system, and not by directly injuring any other bodily organ. Thus, for instance, to depress the action of the heart to an appreciable degree alcohol must be present in the blood to the extent of about 0·5 per cent., which would imply an original dose of more than 11 oz. of absolute alcohol for a man of 10 stone weight. With such a dose, in an ordinary individual, the direct effect on other organs would be negligible in presence of the symptoms of profound and dangerous poisoning of the central nervous system.[1]

Quantity producing intoxication.—Alcohol gets to the central nervous system by passing from the blood into the cerebro-spinal fluid, and the amount which enters this fluid is strictly proportional to the amount in the blood. From experiments on animals and from observations on man, it has been found that the onset and intensity of the symptoms of intoxication are roughly dependent on the quantity of alcohol present in the circulation. Dogs and horses began to be slightly affected when the proportion reached 0·12 per cent.; with higher proportions, the symptoms became more marked, and profound stupor, frequently ending in death, ensued when the alcohol content of the blood rose to 0·72 per cent.[2] Similarly with man, in one case of drunkenness the blood was found to contain 0·153 per cent. of alcohol; and in another instance, where the intoxication was more pronounced, 0·227 per cent. was found.[3] These quantities are roughly equivalent, respectively, to total doses of 3½ oz. and 5 oz. for a man of 10 stone weight.

"From the evidence at present available, it may be said that any form of alcoholic liquor, weak or strong, can cause drunkenness if such a quantity of it is taken, either at once or within a short period, as will lead to the presence of alcohol in the blood to an extent greater than a certain proportion, which in the case of the

[1] *Loc. cit.*, p. 86.

[2] *Loc. cit.*, p. 87; quoted in Kobert, "Lehrbuch der Intoxikationen," Vol. 2, p. 986. Stuttgart, 1906.

[3] Schweisheimer, *Deutsch. Archiv f. Klin. Med.*, 1913, **109**, 271.

average healthy adult may be put provisionally at from 0·15 to 0·2 per cent."[1] The weaker the alcoholic beverage taken, the greater must be the quantity drunk before this proportion is reached; so that the use of the more dilute beverages instead of the stronger is an important safeguard against intoxication.

It will be noted that all these calculations of the total dose from the alcoholic concentration found in the blood depend upon the accuracy of Gréhant's experimental results mentioned above.

Chronic alcoholism.—There is an important distinction between the effects of a single excessive dose of alcohol, and those produced by immoderate quantities frequently repeated, even though these quantities may be, and usually are, smaller than the single dose which gives rise to intoxication. From the single excessive dose proceed intoxication-effects which, as will be shown later on, are mainly apparent in disturbance of the functions of the brain; but when the alcohol is eliminated from the system these symptoms disappear, and the subject soon returns to his normal state. It is quite otherwise with chronic alcoholism. In this there are changes of the drinker's tissues which persist long after all the alcohol has been eliminated, and which may be, and often are, permanent in character. Moreover, these changes are not limited to the nervous centres, but in one way or another may affect most of the organs of the body. They are complex changes, only partially the *direct* effect of alcohol. Largely they are brought about through its detrimental action on the lining membrane of the stomach and bowel, causing chronic catarrh and failure in the action of the digestive secretions, and so promoting the absorption from the alimentary canal of digestive and microbial toxins, which in healthy conditions of the mucous membrane would be formed in lesser amount, or not at all, and in any case would not pass so freely into the system.

It is, indeed, a question whether many of the morbid changes which occur in other organs in the course of chronic alcoholism may not really be secondary to these local disorders in the gastro-intestinal tract. In some recent experimental inquiries it has been found that when alcohol was administered to guinea-pigs by *inhalation*, instead of by the mouth, no visible alterations were produced in the animal's tissues, even when the intoxication was kept up for periods as long as three years.[2]

There are two essential factors in the causation of chronic

[1] *Loc. cit.*, p. 90.

[2] Stockard, *Amer. Naturalist*, 1913, **47**; *Proc. Soc. Exp. Biol. Med.*, 1914, **11**.

alcoholism. First, the drug must be taken in sufficient quantity to exercise an injurious action on the tissues; and secondly, that action must be more or less continuous. Excess of dose alone, without continuity of action, does not give rise to persistent tissue changes: an isolated bout of intoxication does not leave lasting after-effects. On the other hand, chronic poisoning is not induced by even the regular use of alcoholic beverages so long as only moderate quantities are taken. As to *how much* alcohol there must be in the blood, and *how long* its action must be kept up, in order to exercise a detrimental effect on the vitality of the tissues, nothing very definite can be said. The available data are insufficient, or are not exact enough, to justify more than the foregoing general statement.

Different individuals show wide variations of susceptibility to the injurious effects of alcohol in chronic alcoholism. Moreover, they differ also very widely as regards the tissues or organs most prone to suffer. In one subject the liver may be specially attacked, in another the nervous system, and so on.

Mental disorders.—Some affection of mind is usually present in chronic alcoholism. Commonly it is moderate in degree, and may be shown only in weakened will-power and failure of memory. In *delirium tremens,* more intense, but transitory, disorders occur; and in relatively rare instances alcoholism seems to be responsible for a chronic insanity with persistent delusions, usually of persecution and jealousy. "In general, however, the part which alcoholic excess plays in the causation of the ordinary forms of mental disease is of secondary importance: it has been shown that when the two things are associated, intemperance is more usually a symptom of insanity than its cause."[1]

Morbid changes in nervous system.—These are very variable in character and degree. Most commonly there is some thickening of the membranes, with wasting of the nervous tissues, notably in those parts of the brain which are supposed to be specially related to the higher mental activities. These appearances, however, are not distinctive of alcoholism. Further, the diseased conditions seen in the brain of patients dead of *delirium tremens* are quite similar to those found in cases of alcoholism where there is no *delirium tremens,* and they are neither constant nor very definite. Hence it appears that in chronic intoxication the nervous tissues may be damaged in ways which, while pro-

[1] Mott, *Arch. of Neurol.,* 1907, **3**, 424, quoted in "Alcohol, its Action on the Human Organism," p. 98.

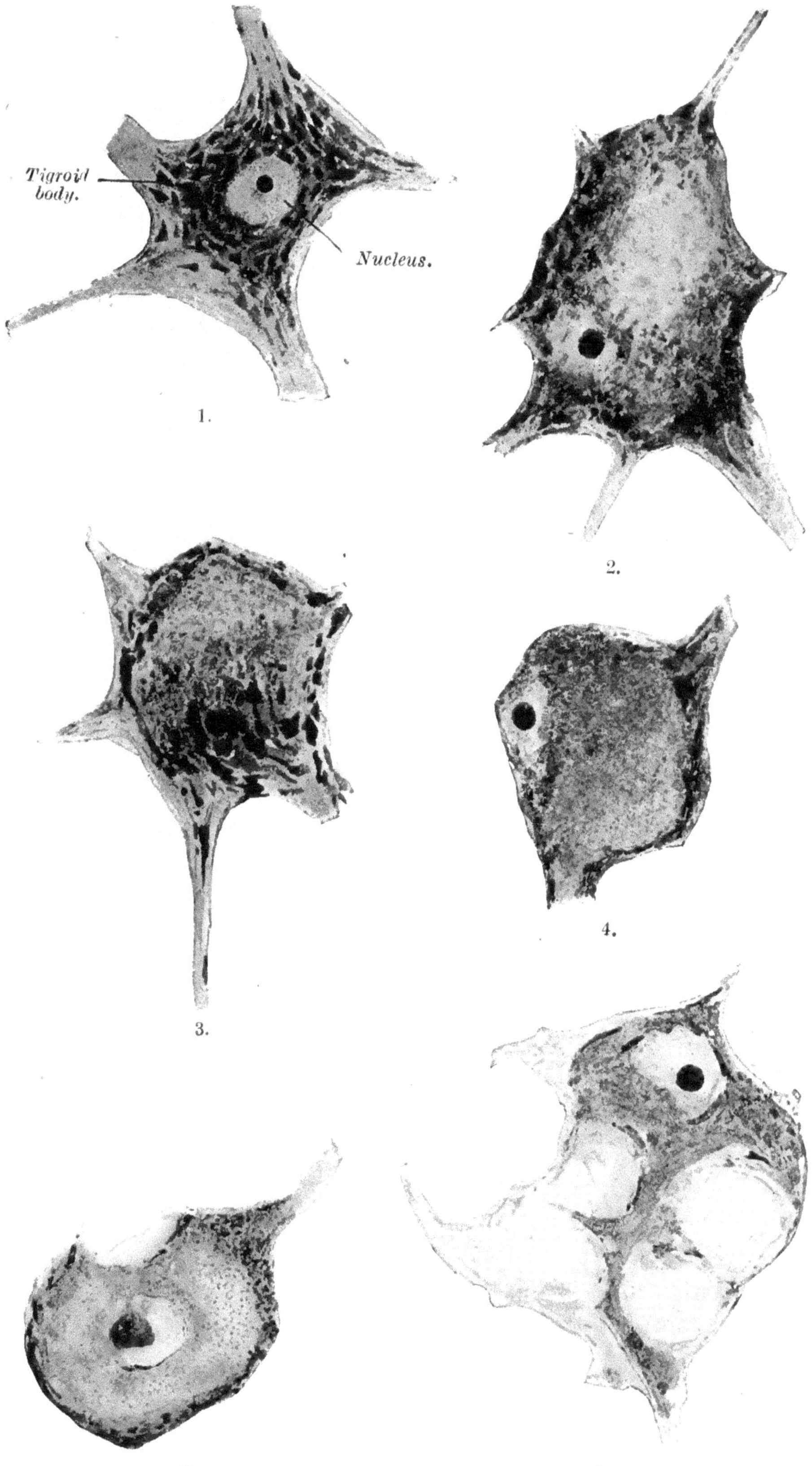

Tigroid body.

Nucleus.

1.

2.

3.

4.

5.

6.

FIG. 47.—DRAWINGS OF NERVE-CELLS

(Stained with methylene-blue), showing degenerative changes. No. 1, a normal cell. No. 2 shows disappearance of colouring matter and displacement of nucleus. Nos. 3, 4, 5, and 6 show varying degrees of degradation of the cells. (Horsley and Sturge.)

foundly affecting their healthy functioning, are not revealed in any visible structural change.

In alcoholic peripheral neuritis, degenerative changes are found in the nerve-fibres, and also not infrequently in the related cells of the spinal cord. Such alterations of the nerve-cells and -fibres are demonstrable through the microscope, and even in some degree to the naked eye. The diseased cell becomes swollen, its nucleus is displaced towards the margin, its extensions shrivel and vanish, empty spaces occur in the protoplasm, and finally the cell disappears.

"The explanation of these changes seems to be that alcohol is a powerful protoplasmic poison, having a selective affinity for the delicate cells of the nervous system, with whose functions and capacity it interferes at a very early stage, finally causing gross alterations in the tissue."[1]

Disorders of the digestive system.—Chronic gastritis is met with in heavy drinkers, especially those who take large quantities of spirits. It precedes, and is in great measure responsible for, the disease of the liver known as "cirrhosis." The inflammation of the mucous lining of the stomach sets up degenerative changes in the cells which secrete the gastric juice, and as a result the hydrochloric acid of the latter, essential for digestion and for the prevention of bacterial fermentation, may be completely absent. Toxins elaborated by microbial action are absorbed from the alimentary canal into the blood and pass with the latter through the portal vein, so that the liver contains these poisons in a special degree. They bring about prolonged irritation and inflammation of the connective-tissue supporting the portal vein and its ramifications in the liver, inducing a swelling of the hepatic cells and leading to an enlargement of the whole liver. Subsequently, the process of fatty degeneration may set in, the protoplasm of the cells being transformed into globules of fat. This enlargement in many cases persists until dropsy supervenes; or there may be a more complete conversion of the chronic inflammatory tissue into fibrous-tissue cells, leading to the formation of what is known as "scar tissue." This permanently replaces some of the active hepatic cells, and results eventually in cirrhosis, involving shrinkage of the liver and formation of the knobby projections or nodules which characterise the "hob-nailed" liver of drunkards. Such an interference with the normal activities of this important organ naturally gives rise to many ill effects, among which may be anæmia, indigestion, and jaundice.

[1] Horsley and Sturge, "Alcohol and the Human Body," p. 133.

Effects on the kidney and heart.—Changes of a similar type may be brought about in the kidney by the action of imbibed alcohol in immoderate and continued quantities. There is a similar sequence of cellular changes—cloudy swelling and fatty degeneration of the tubule-cells, increase of fibrous tissue, and eventual shrinkage, with formation of what is termed "granular"

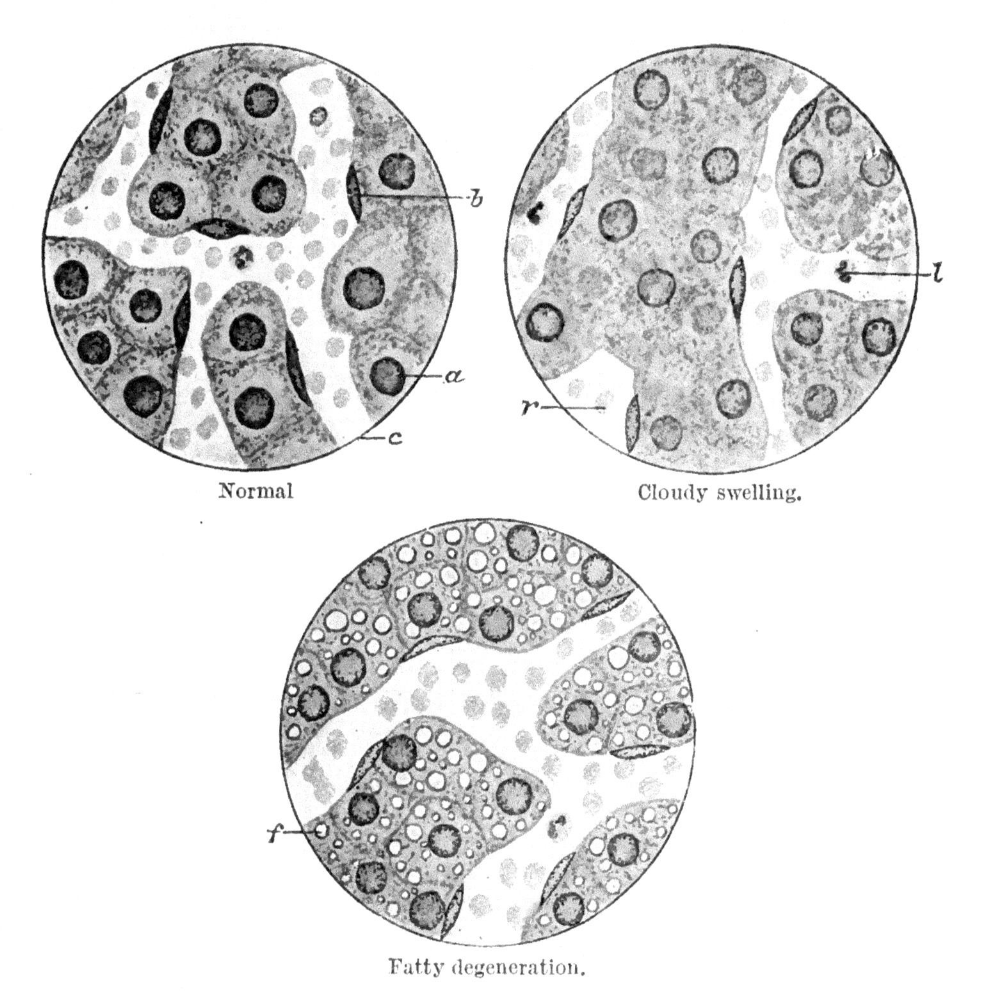

FIG. 48.—MICROSCOPICAL SECTIONS OF HUMAN LIVER.

Showing changes which occur in the course of fatty degeneration. (Horsley and Sturge.)

a, Nucleus of liver cell; *b*, nucleus of cell forming wall of *c*; *c*, a capillary blood-vessel; *l*, leucocyte or white blood corpuscle; *r*, red blood corpuscle; *f* fat droplet.

kidney of the "coarse red mottled" variety. Among other disorders, the degeneration of the blood-vessels which leads to apoplexy; and albuminuria, giving rise later to diminished excretion of urine as the kidney shrinks, and eventually to Bright's disease, have been recognised as frequent concomitants of alcoholic excess. On the muscle fibres of the heart the effect is to promote protoplasmic change which leads to deposition of fat and eventually to dilatation of the heart, with a consequent weakening of its propulsive power. It is to be noted, however, that all these diseased conditions are found, and very often found, in persons who never take alcohol; they may be brought about by many deleterious agencies, operating singly or in combination. Alcoholism is merely one of these agencies.

Lessened resistance to infection.—Chronic alcohol poisoning, by devitalising the tissues, weakens the power of the body to ward off microbial attacks. Alcohol affects the structure of the red corpuscles of the blood, and diminishes their power of resistance towards hæmolytic agents (Laitinen). It exerts a paralysing effect upon the leucocytes, and thus interferes with their functions as destroyers of infective micro-organisms that may have gained access to the blood. On the blood-plasma, also, alcohol, has an injurious action, bringing about a decrease in its bactericidal power. The obvious conclusion from these observations is that alcohol lessens the ability of the blood to combat disease. Indeed, as regards its effects upon the leucocytes, Horsley and Sturge remark that "the seriousness of this adverse influence . . . cannot be over-estimated. Herein lies the explanation of many infections, many prolonged illnesses, much chronic ill-health, and many premature deaths."[1] A slight general depressing influence such as a chill or a local injury may be most dangerous to a chronic alcoholic; whereas upon a healthy individual there might be no harmful effect even if micro-organisms were present, because the vital reaction of the normal healthy tissues would prevent a general infection.

Action on the reproductive cells.—Berthelot and Weichselbaum have shown independently that in the majority of male alcoholic patients dying in the prime of life there is atrophy of the testicles and absence or scanty production of spermatozoa. In the female subject alterations of a similar character may be discovered in the ovaries. Morbid changes of the same type can be produced in the genital glands of experimental animals (rabbits, dogs, guinea-pigs) by continued administration of alcohol; and further, there is direct experimental evidence that parental alcoholism may react injuriously upon the vitality and normal development of the offspring. Alcohol was administered to guinea-pigs by inhalation; and the progeny of the alcoholised animals, in comparison with the young of "control" animals of the same stock, were found to be conspicuously inferior in strength and vitality, and in many instances presented gross abnormalities of

[1] "Alcohol and the Human Body," p. 206.

organisation. These ill-effects were transmitted through several generations, and were, indeed, more pronounced in the later generations than in the immediate offspring of the alcoholised subjects. Even when there are no structural changes visible in the germ-cells, the injurious influence of the intoxication may be manifested in the progeny.[1] In view of the great importance of these results, indicating as they do a possibility of the deterioration of the race through parental alcoholism, it is considered well to suspend judgment on these experiments until the conclusions have been verified by further investigation.[2]

Effects of single doses.—Such, then, are the main physiological effects of alcohol taken in sufficient quantity and with sufficient frequency to cause chronic alcoholism. Let us turn now to the effects produced when these conditions are not fulfilled—by far the more usual case. What are the results when the quantity imbibed, whether large or small, is essentially an isolated quantity, not repeated at such short intervals, or over so long a period, as to cause an act to merge into a more or less continuous habit?

The answer to this question involves consideration of the mental effects, the influence on muscular work, and the results produced by alcohol on the digestive, respiratory, and circulatory systems. These will now be reviewed in the order given.

Mental effects.—On the brain and nervous system alcohol acts as a narcotic. If a dose is taken sufficiently large to produce intoxication, then, although the successive phases of inebriation cannot be sharply distinguished and each case has its own peculiarities, yet, broadly, three main stages can be made out.

In the first stage, there is a weakening of self-control, and a blunting of the power of self-criticism. In the second, the nervous functions controlling skilled movements and sense-perceptions are involved; there is a certain clumsiness of behaviour, an impairment of vision, hearing, etc., and also emotional instability; while as the narcosis proceeds, dulness and heaviness, dreamy somnolence, or actual sleep may supervene. In the third stage, "the intellectual processes of judgment and self-criticism and control are virtually suspended; the functions of sense-perception and skilled movement are grossly impaired; and the emotional tendencies themselves are invaded and weakened, so that only strong appeals to them suffice to evoke any response, and, in their absence, the drinker sinks inert and nerveless into a heavy sleep, which lasts until the

[1] Stockard; *American Naturalist*, 1913, **47**; 1916, **50**; *Proc. Soc. Exp. Biol. Med.*, 1912, **9**; 1914, **11**.

[2] "Alcohol, its Action on the Human Organism," p. 104.

alcohol absorbed by the nervous system has been oxidised or carried away in the blood and consumed by other tissues."[1]

These three main stages correspond with the invasion by the narcotic of the three principal levels of cerebral function, namely (1), the higher intellectual faculties, the latest acquired in the development both of the individual and of the race; (2), the sensory and skilled motor functions and their nerve-centres; and (3), the emotional capacities, a very ancient endowment, situated in the basal ganglia—the part which is alone represented in the brains of the lower vertebrates. Alcohol successively weakens and suspends these functions in the order given, from above downwards. The higher intellectual faculties are the first to suffer; then follows the narcotising of the sensory and skilled motor centres, and finally even the emotional faculties are weakened.

There appears to be no certain evidence that alcohol acts as a stimulant on the nervous system. The passing phase of initial exhilaration or excitement often observed in the early stages of intoxication may, not improbably, be attributed to the influence of festive environment acting upon the emotions, the control of which by the intellect and by the will has been diminished through the action of the alcohol taken. Apart from a possible exception as regards a small or moderate dose of alcohol acting on the respiratory nerve-centres, the conclusion arrived at from a study of the experiments recorded is that the direct effect of alcohol upon the nervous system is, in all stages and in all parts of the system, to depress or suspend its functions. In short, alcohol acts as a narcotic drug from first to last.

To explain the successive stages of the action of alcohol on the brain, as above described, the following hypothesis has been put forward. Alcohol acts primarily and most powerfully, not upon the nerve-cells themselves, or on the nerve-fibres, but upon the junctions (*synapses*) between nerve-cells. The nervous system may be regarded as made up of a large number of cells, each consisting of a central body and one or more fibres, and each cell having no anatomical continuity with others, but only a functional one. The points of contact of the cells are the weak points of the nervous pathways. They are the points which give way most readily under strain or shock and under the influence of fatigue, and of various paralysing drugs. Further, there is good reason to believe that in the lower levels of the brain the points of junction are relatively firm and open to the passage of the nervous current, whereas those of the higher and later-developed levels are less solidly organised,

[1] "Alcohol, its Action on the Human Organism," pp. 35, 36.

and therefore offer more resistance to the current. (Merely as an illustrative analogy, we may picture an electric current passing through a copper rod divided into a large number of segments; if at one end of the rod the segments are pressed firmly together the current passes easily; if, at the other, the segments barely touch one another the current passes the junctions only with difficulty.) If it is assumed that alcohol acts equally on all the synapses (nerve-cell junctions), equally increasing their resistances, it will first raise the resistance to the point of non-conductivity at those junctions where the normal resistance is already greatest—that is, in the later-developed levels, where the mental functions are highest; and it will progressively effect a similar paralysis of the other nerve-paths. Thus the higher intellectual centres would be the first paralysed, then the sensory and skilled motor centres, and finally the emotional centres; which is the order actually observed to occur.[1]

Experimental investigations.—A short outline may here be given of some of the researches undertaken during recent years on the mental effects of alcohol, taken for the most part in small or moderate doses. It will serve to exemplify the methods adopted and to indicate the general results obtained.

Kraepelin of Munich has carried out a long series of careful investigations respecting the influence of alcohol, taken in moderate or small doses, upon the mental functions. The amount of the dose varied, but as a rule was about an ounce, diluted with water. Sometimes one-half, or one-quarter, of this quantity was used. In fact, the amounts were often far below those frequently taken at meals by ordinary individuals. Such mental processes as reading aloud, adding columns of figures, calculating arithmetically, memorising words or numbers, and associating ideas with words, were employed in the tests. In certain of the experiments the rate of mental action was measured by means of time-recording apparatus designed to indicate accurately the reaction-period—*i.e.*, the time occupied in making a response to a given signal. In other experiments, the ability to add figures correctly was tested upon subjects sometimes taking alcohol, sometimes refraining from it. The outlines of one such experiment may be given as a simple example:—

First six days, no alcohol taken. Practice in adding figures for half an hour daily. The ability to add increased every day.

Next twelve days, alcohol taken. In spite of the influence of the previous days' practice, the capability of adding did not increase. On the contrary, it began to decrease very rapidly.

[1] "Alcohol, its Action on the Human Organism," p. 37.

Nineteenth day, alcohol stopped. Immediate improvement shown.

Twenty-sixth day, alcohol resumed. A decided decrease in the power of adding figures was again shown.

The general results arrived at from all the experiments were that in the simpler, more or less automatic work, mental activity was slightly quickened at the outset under the influence of alcohol, but in most cases began to slow down after a few minutes, the diminution becoming more and more marked, and enduring as long as the alcohol was in active operation in the body, namely, four to five hours. When, on the other hand, the higher powers of the mind, *e.g.*, those involving association of ideas and the formation of judgments, were called into play, there was no real quickening of the brain activity under alcohol. The slowing effect began from the first, and continued throughout. Moreover, not only does alcohol, according to this observer, delay the rapidity of cerebral association. It alters the quality also, favouring the inferior kinds of mental association and weakening the higher associations. In other words, even small doses of alcohol influence adversely, from the very first, the finer work of the brain-cells.

Aschaffenburg made a careful series of observations upon the work of compositors, done when alcohol was taken in " dietetic " quantity, and also without alcohol. He found that there was a distinct impairment of mental activity, amounting to about 9 per cent. as measured by the output of work, when alcohol was taken. The impairment was absent in one case only out of eight.

Other investigators have studied the duration of the effect produced by alcohol. Fürer used amounts such as are contained in two litres of strong beer or half a litre of wine. The effects were found to last all the following day, causing a dulling of mental labour, although the subject was under the impression that his work was just as good as usual. Kürz, taking 80 grams of alcohol in water on twelve successive evenings, found that there was a decided diminution in the day's work (calculating and studying) as compared with that done on alcohol-free days, and that this effect persisted until the fifth day after ceasing to take alcohol. A single large dose acts for twenty-four or even forty-eight hours.

W. McDougall, describing a " method for the study of concurrent mental operations and mental fatigue,"[1] investigated the effect of dietetic quantities of alcohol upon subjects performing a certain task—namely, accurately marking dots driven past an opening at a known rate. In one series of experiments he found that the

[1] *British Journal of Psychology*, 1.

errors under the influence of alcohol compared with the normal errors were as 583 to 379. In another (shorter) series they were as 351 to 298. Three ounces of whisky caused 53 per cent. more errors than when the brain was under normal conditions. On the other hand, the errors when tea was taken were less than the normal.

The general results of these and other experiments go to show that, as regards the effects of small or moderate doses of alcohol upon the nervous and neuro-muscular system :—

(1).—Alcohol lengthens the time taken to perform complex mental processes, although the person experimented upon imagines that his psychical activities are rendered more rapid.

(2).—There is an initial stage of temporary stimulation or exhilaration, chiefly due to a slight numbing of the higher nerve-centres ; but this is followed by a prolonged depressant after-stage.

Action on the neuro-muscular system.—Experiments have been made in order to test the action of alcohol on the muscles themselves, separated from the nervous system.[1] With doses ranging up to the equivalent of about 70 c.c. for man, administered through the blood, no obvious effect was produced upon the contractile power or other functional properties of muscle. It is therefore inferred that any influence which alcohol in ordinary quantities exerts upon the performance of muscular acts must be referred to its effects upon the nerve-centres concerned with activating the muscle.

Alcohol depresses simple reflex reactions of the nervous system. A dose of 30 c.c., taken one to one and a half hours before the test was applied, was found to lessen the speed and amplitude of the reflex knee-jerk. As an average obtained from observations on six men, this dose of alcohol reduced the speed of commencement of the responsive movement by 9·6 per cent., and diminished the extent of the movement by 48·9 per cent. A larger dose, 45 c.c., impaired the reaction-speed and amplitude still more.[2] Somewhat similar results, though of smaller percentage magnitude, were obtained with the reflex speed and amplitude of the eyelid movement when an involuntary blink was evoked by a sudden loud sound.

A slight quickening of the pulse rate commonly follows upon the taking of a moderate dose of alcohol. This acceleration appears to be due to a depression in degree of the reflex cardio-inhibitory

[1] Furth and Schwarz, *Pflüger's Archiv*, 1909, **129**, 525.

[2] Dodge and Benedict, "Psychological Effects of Alcohol." Washington, 1915.

tone which, normally, acts in restraint of the heart-beat.[1] It does not, apparently, occur in all cases.

The depression caused by alcohol in all the foregoing instances indicates a specific lowering of the powers of the lower nervous centres, similar to that produced by drugs like chloroform, though of much less intensity.

Voluntary movements, as distinct from reflex actions, are much more complex matters for investigation. Experiments have, however, been made which, without attempting to analyse the willed act, and accepting the movement made as index of that act's success, indicate how its efficiency changes with varying conditions. For example, the ergograph can be used to examine the power of a muscular act and its ability to withstand fatigue. In one form of this instrument the middle finger is commonly used to raise a weight by means of a string and pulley. The finger is fitted into a ring of leather, to which the string is attached; the weight is one of about 9 lb. The forearm and hand being at rest, this one finger is bent at intervals of from one to two seconds, the weight being lifted as high as possible. The movements are registered, and are kept up until exhaustion occurs.

Special caution, however, has been found necessary in interpreting the results obtained with the ergograph. The subject's mental conditions are liable to affect the records to a marked degree. Fleeting states of his mind, such as varying concentration of attention, and greater or lesser interest in the repetition of the movement at one time than at another, may distinctly influence the performance. The mere knowledge that he has or has not received a dose of alcohol may affect the subject's action, and thus obscure any effects produced by the alcohol itself.

Rivers,[2] amongst others, has carried out investigations in which precautions have been taken definitely to guard against such sources of error. Experimenting upon two persons, he found that single doses of 5, 10, or 20 c.c. of alcohol left no indubitable traces upon muscular action, as recorded by the ergograph. With the dose increased to 40 c.c., a small increase in the number of contractions performed was shown by one of the subjects, who, previously, had been an abstainer from alcohol. The increase appeared about one and a half hours after administration of the dose. On the other hand, the second subject showed a slight decrease of work; but the investigator was not satisfied that this was a clearly-established effect due to the alcohol.

[1] Dodge and Benedict, "Psychological Effects of Alcohol." Washington, 1915.

[2] "Influence of Alcohol and other Drugs on Fatigue." London, 1907.

It was noted, however, that the 40 c.c. dose of alcohol did in one of the two subjects impair the execution of some skilled movements (adjusting the apparatus, etc.) incidental to the experiments, though not recorded on the ergograph. Also, within half an hour of taking the dose, "there came on a subjective feeling of lassitude and disinclination for activity, either of body or mind. It was doubtful how far the state of lassitude was preceded by one of exhilaration, but, if the latter occurred, it was certainly of very brief duration."

Oseretzkowsky and Kraepelin,[1] giving a single dose of 50 c.c., likewise found no obvious effect of alcohol upon the ergographic record. Hellsten,[2] using a form of ergograph in which the movement registered is executed with the two arms, and employing as the subject of the experiment an athlete of 90 kilos. weight, found similarly that single doses of 25 c.c. and of 50 c.c. of alcohol produced no clear and unequivocal effect on the record. The alcohol was given in appropriate dilution with water five to ten minutes before the test began. With a dose of 80 c.c., there was a slight and short increase in the recorded muscular work, followed by a marked decrease. When this dose was taken half an hour before the test began, the decrease observed amounted to 20 per cent. of the normal performance done without alcohol. When the alcohol was taken one hour previously, the decrease was 17 per cent., and when taken two hours before the test, 11 per cent.

The effect of alcohol on the muscular effort involved in walking uphill has been investigated by Dürig.[3] The conditions of the ascent—route, time of day, etc.—were kept as far as practicable the same for a number of successive tests, but on some days alcohol was added to the food ration, and on others it was omitted. The dose was 30 c.c. of alcohol in 150 of water, given at breakfast just before starting. It was found that although the walker, who was accustomed to moderate use of alcohol, felt in himself no difference between his condition on the alcohol days and on the non-alcohol days, the ascent per minute was on the alcohol days less by 12 to 14 per cent. than that on the non-alcohol days. This was so, although more energy was expended by his body on the former than on the latter days. The investigator was inclined to attribute this deterioration to impairment of the skill with which movements are directed: the effect of the alcohol tended to undo the results of previous training.

On a different scale, and of a different character, are the muscular

[1] "Psycholog. Arbeiten," 1901, **3**, [iv], 587
[2] *Skand. Arch. Physiol.*, 1904, **16**, 160.
[3] *Pflüger's Archiv*, 1906, **113**, 314.

movements involved in adjusting the eyballs to the focussing of the sight on an object brought closer and closer to the observer. The effects of alcohol on such movements have been studied by Guillery.[1] He found that a dose of 20 c.c. did not affect the facility of adjustment, but one of 40 c.c. very distinctly weakened and slowed the movement. The impairment was first detectible about twenty minutes after taking the dose. Normal speed and power were regained about forty minutes later. A greater impairment was shown with 60 c.c. of alcohol; it came on sooner (in ten to fifteen minutes), and lasted longer (one and a half hours).

Similarly, Dodge and Benedict found that a dose of 45 c.c. of alcohol measurably influenced the speed of starting the movement required in directing the gaze to a fresh object. Such a movement involves not only the motor centres directing the muscular action, but also the sensory nerve centres, information from which (as to the posture of the eyeballs and the direction in which they have to be turned) is a factor in the guidance and alertness of the motor centres themselves. The dose of 45 c.c. was found, an hour and a half after imbibition, to increase the normal delay in starting the movement by 15 per cent., taking the average for the six subjects tested. The same observers found also that a dose of 45 c.c. of alcohol reduced the rapidity of a simple to and fro finger movement by 8·8 per cent., taking the average for the same six persons as before. This test was likewise made one and a half hours after the alcohol was drunk.

Whilst, therefore, deductions must be cautious on account of the relatively small number of suitable experiments, the available evidence indicates that a single dose of less than 40 c.c. of alcohol has but little, if any, effect upon the performance of simple, "unskilled" muscular acts by an adult accustomed to moderate use of alcohol. On the other hand, the performance of acts requiring skill tends to be temporarily impaired by a dose of even 30 c.c., the effect being shown especially in a diminution of the speed and nicety of the performance. There seems to be no trustworthy evidence showing that, in normal circumstances, alcohol improves the efficiency of any muscular performance, skilled or unskilled.

Effects on the digestion.—Respecting the effect of alcohol on the process of digestion a good deal has been written, both as to the favourable and the detrimental results produced; but the consensus of modern opinion seems to be distinctly against the view that for the ordinary healthy individual there is, on the whole, any particular benefit to be obtained by the use of alcohol

[1] *Pflüger's Archiv*, 1899, **79**, 597.

as a dietetic beverage. Some beneficial action there may be, but it is liable to be set off by undesirable consequences in other parts of the system. It is only in certain acute diseases that any desirable effects produced by alcohol on the stomach are worth obtaining.

Certainly the common notion that alcohol in moderate quantity is a useful aid to gastric digestion does not receive very much support from digestion-experiments made *in vitro*. Some of the earlier of such experiments, carried out by Sir W. Roberts[1] more than a quarter of a century ago, may usefully be quoted. The digestion-mixture studied was composed of 2 grams of beef-fibre, 1 c.c. of glycerine extract of pepsin, hydrochloric acid sufficient to give 0·15 per cent. of HCl, and varying proportions of alcoholic liquors, the whole being made up with water to a volume of 100 c.c. The time in which the digestion of the beef was completed was compared with the time (one hundred minutes) required without alcohol. The results may be summarised as follows :—

ROBERTS'S EXPERIMENTS ON PEPTIC DIGESTION.

Proportion of alcoholic liquor. Per cent.	Time required (normal, one hundred minutes).					
	Spirits. Minutes.	Sherry. Minutes.	Port. Minutes.	Burton ale. Minutes.	Table beer. Minutes.	Lager beer. Minutes.
5	100	115	100	—	—	—
10	115	150	115	115	100	100
15	—	200	150	—	—	—
20	135	300	180	140	115	115
30	180	—	200	—	—	—
40	300	—	—	200	140	140
60	—	—	—	—	180	180

The "spirits" used comprised proof spirit (plain), brandy, whisky, and gin.

Roberts considered that the wines and malt liquors contained some retarding agent besides alcohol, as the effect produced on the digestion was out of proportion to the amount of alcohol present.

If the total gastric charge of food is taken as 2 lb., 20 per cent. of this would be about 6½ oz., so that according to these results less than a glass of beer exercises a perceptible, though not a considerable, effect upon peptic digestion.

Coming to more recent work, Chittenden's experiments may be quoted. This observer found that when the percentage of alcohol in the digestive mixture used was as low as 1 or 2 per cent. there was sometimes a slight acceleration of the rate of digestion. When, however, the proportion of alcohol was raised, retardation or inhibition of digestive action occurred, though this was ordinarily not

[1] "Collected Contributions on Digestion and Diet," 1891.

very pronounced until the digestive mixture contained 5 to 10 per cent. of alcohol, or more. Further, with a weak gastric juice, where the amount of ferment present is small and the digestive action consequently slow, or where the proteid material is difficult of digestion, the retarding effect of a given percentage of alcohol is far greater than where the digestive fluid is more active. It may be noted, in passing, that a concentration of 10 per cent. of alcohol can rarely, if ever, be present in the stomach of a living man for more than a few seconds.

The foregoing experiments do not, of course, take into account all the factors concerned in actual digestion *in corpore*. In addition to the effects of alcohol upon the action of the enzymes as just described, its influence upon the secretion of the digestive juices, and upon the churning movements of the stomach which normally aid digestion, have also to be considered.

There is no doubt that alcohol placed in the mouth does, like other sapid fluids, increase the flow of saliva, but this action is of no very great importance. There is also no doubt that on reaching the stomach alcohol evokes a considerable secretion of a kind of gastric juice. This juice, however, differs from the normal gastric juice, inasmuch as it is deficient in pepsin, though it contains the normal amount of hydrochloric acid. In fact, whatever pepsin this juice contains is what has been washed out of the cells ; alcohol apparently causes no fresh secretion of pepsin. Hence the increased supply of juice is of no particular value in improving the digestion, although, on the other hand, there is no evidence that it has any detrimental effect. The flow of the other digestive juices—the pancreatic juice and the bile—is also stated to be increased by alcohol, and this may be in part due to some action on the stomach, since it is known that an increase of gastric secretion often leads to augmented activity of the pancreas. As tested by experiments on dogs, the amount of increased gastric secretion is greatest when relatively small doses are given, such as produce in the stomach a concentration not greater than 10 per cent. Larger proportions lead to the formation of much mucus, with less total juice.

As Roberts's experiments and those of Chittenden show, the peptonising power of the gastric juice is not much affected by small doses of (plain) alcohol, but is distinctly retarded by large doses. Some authorities have considered that the effects on pancreatic digestion are more favourable, and even that alcohol accelerates the digestion of fats ; but there is evidence to show that as tested *in vitro* the enzymes of the pancreas are yet more susceptible to the action of alcohol than are those of the stomach. In concentrations as low as 2 to 3 per cent. alcohol may retard the digestion of albuminous substances. But be that as it may, the probability is that, in the organism, alcohol reaches the intestine in such relatively small proportions and in such a low degree of concentration, and moreover is so rapidly absorbed there, that its action on pancreatic digestion is of comparatively small importance.

As regards the churning motion, it is often stated that alcohol "promotes greater activity in the muscular layers of the stomach,"[1] and thus tends to accelerate digestion. It does not appear, however, that this increased activity can be accepted as satisfactorily demonstrated, and some observers have failed to obtain any confirmation of the statement. Carlson,[2] for instance, saw no increase of churning movement when diluted alcohol, brandy, and wines were introduced into a man's stomach through a fistula; but on the contrary, the rhythmical movements and the bracing of the muscular coats, which are associated with hunger, were arrested. Doses of 50–100 c.c. of 10 per cent. alcohol sufficed to stay the hunger-contractions for two hours, and 200 c.c. of beer had the same effect for half an hour to an hour. Chittenden,[3] in experiments on dogs, did not find that the presence of alcohol materially lessened the time during which food remained in the stomach. There appears, indeed, to be at present no good evidence that gastric movement is increased by alcohol, whilst some forms of stomach-contraction are even arrested by it. Horsley and Sturge consider that lessened vigour of the muscular movements of the stomach is a consequence of alcohol depressing the nervous system, since the nerves which control the muscles are enfeebled.[4]

Similarly, there seems at present to be no trustworthy evidence that moderate doses of alcohol have any important effect, one way or the other, upon the process of absorption of the digested food-stuffs into the blood. In general, it may be said that apart from its taste and its tendency to increase gastric secretion and mucus, alcohol itself, in moderate doses, has not been proved to affect the digestive organs to any appreciable degree. On the other hand, there is a consensus of opinion that some of the alcoholic beverages may be more deleterious than others. Some wines, for instance, do not "agree" with certain people, though other persons can take them without digestive ill-effects. The extractive matters—tannins, acids, sugars, and other solids—as also the volatile secondary

[1] *Encycl. Brit.*, article "Alcohol."
[2] *Amer. J. Physiol.*, 1913, **32**, 252.
[3] "Physiological Aspects of Liquor Problem," **1**, 294. Boston, 1903.
[4] "Alcohol and the Human Body," p. 164.

constituents, namely, esters, higher alcohols, aldehydes, and acids, have been suggested as the possible causes of disturbed digestion in these cases ; but at present there is nothing actually and definitely known about the effects produced by these substances.

Action on the respiration.—Alcohol has long been held in repute as a respiratory stimulant. Many observers have noted a small increase in the activity of the lungs following upon the administration of a moderate dose of alcohol, even when care has been taken to keep the subject in repose after the dose. Not all the experimenters, however, agree in this conclusion. Thus Loewy[1] gave, separately, doses of 35 c.c. and 60 c.c. of alcohol to each of two subjects, one habituated to alcohol, the other not ; but only in the case of the latter subject, taking the larger dose, was any increased respiratory activity detected.

More modern researches point in the same direction. They indicate that in normal conditions there is probably no stimulant effect of any practical importance produced on the respiration by a moderate quantity of alcohol.

An outline of a recent research carried out by Higgins[2] may be given. The nervous centre governing the respiration acts normally in response to the stimulating action of the carbon dioxide in the blood, increasing or decreasing the respiratory activity in such manner as to keep the proportion of carbon dioxide practically constant. If alcohol affects the respiratory nervous centre, increasing its excitability to the normal proportion of carbon dioxide and therefore augmenting the respiration, the proportion of this gas in the blood will fall. But the gases of the blood are in equilibrium with those of the alveolar air of the lungs, and this air can be analysed. If the analysis shows that the proportion of carbon dioxide diminishes after alcohol has been taken, the inference (leaving other factors out of account for the present purpose) is that the alcohol has stimulated the nervous centre and increased the respiratory activity.

Higgins experimented on seven subjects, including both abstainers from and regular users of alcohol. Doses of 30 c.c. and of 45 c.c. were given, suitably diluted with a flavouring mixture, and each experiment was controlled by another in which the subject took the same flavouring mixture without the alcohol. The patients were kept carefully at rest, to guard against production of carbon dioxide through muscular activity. It was found that in some of the experiments there was, in fact, a small reduction of carbon

[1] *Pflüger's Archiv*, 1890, **47**, 601.
[2] *J. Pharm. Expt. Ther.*, 1917, **9**, 441.

dioxide in the alveolar air after the alcohol had been taken, indicating a slight increase in the excitability of the respiratory centre. This effect, however, was counterbalanced by a diminished production of carbon dioxide by the body, so that the net result on the breathing was almost *nil*. The volume of air breathed per minute was either unchanged or slightly diminished.

Practically, therefore, the effect of a moderate dose of alcohol on the respiration would appear to be trivial. "The only important effect of alcohol on respiration is the paralysis of the respiratory centre by large doses, which is the cause of death in (alcoholic) poisoning."[1]

Effect on the circulation.—It has been very generally supposed that alcohol acts as a stimulant upon the heart, increasing the frequency and power of its beat. The matter has been much debated, and many experiments have been made with a view to ascertain what the effect of alcohol on the heart-beat really is. In a recent survey of the whole question the conclusion arrived at is that "it has yet to be proved that the heart-muscle can be stimulated by alcohol."[2]

Most of the observers, however, agree that an increase in the pulse-rate, lasting about half an hour, follows the taking of a moderate dose of alcohol, and there seems to be no doubt that this does commonly occur, although not always. In Higgins's investigation on the respiratory activity, quoted above, a slight quickening of the heart-beat was recorded in about one-half of the experiments; no change was detected in the other cases. Apparently different persons react differently to alcohol, in this respect as in others. Probably also the quantity taken and the degree of dilution have some influence on the result.

There is reason to believe, however, that this quickening of the pulse, where it occurs, is not in the main due to a *direct* action of alcohol on the heart, since most of the observations made on the isolated heart, free from nervous control but still beating, have shown no quickening or strengthening of the beat under the influence of alcohol. It has been suggested that the accelerating effect noted above is probably an indirect result of alcohol acting on the nervous inhibitory centre which restrains the heart-beat, and weakening that restraint. The quickening effect has been observed when fairly strong alcohol (50 per cent.) has been simply placed in the mouth and rejected, without being swallowed.

A single dose of fairly strong alcohol, such as brandy, may

[1] *Loc. cit.*, p. 70.

[2] "Alcohol and the Cardio-Vascular System," by Drs. Munro and Findlay, of Glasgow Royal Infirmary.

produce useful reflex effects in cases of fainting or syncope, causing the heart to beat more rapidly. But as regards this it has been urged that the mere act of swallowing, even if the liquid is only water, produces a similar reflex action. Alcohol perhaps acts simply by virtue of its irritant action on the mucous membrane of the mouth and throat, much in the same way as the fumes of ammonia, or of ether, or of burnt feathers, will act as an irritant or stimulant when inhaled. That the effect is a local and indirect one is evidenced by the fact that it appears almost at once, before there has been time for any significant quantity of alcohol to be absorbed and carried to the heart. In other cases, where there is more protracted weakness of the heart, a beneficial effect of alcohol is attributable to its narcotic and sedative action on the nervous centres which affect the action of the heart.

Alcohol when swallowed produces a general relaxation of the small arteries which carry blood to the skin. It thus causes a slight general flushing of the body surface. It appears, however, to have only a small and not very definite effect upon the arterial blood-pressure. A small rise of pressure has been detected by some observers after intravenous injection of alcohol ; others have noted either a slight fall, or no definite effect.

Effect on the body temperature.—It has just been noted that alcohol produces a relaxation or dilatation of the blood-vessels which ramify through the skin. The dilatation is due to the alcohol causing a slight paralysis of the nerves which control the size of the blood-vessels, thus allowing them to distend a little. A consequence of this is that the general body temperature is lowered. More blood reaches the surface of the body, and more heat is radiated or conducted away. Any feeling of warmth experienced after drinking alcohol is explained by the fact that this flow of blood to the surface warms the skin and the ends of the sensory nerves in the skin, and these convey to the brain a sensation of warmth. But the sensation is illusory ; the body as a whole has not really been made warmer.

The fact that alcohol actually lowers the temperature of the body was first announced by Sir B. Ward Richardson in 1866 to the British Association. His observations showed a fall of temperature ranging from three-quarters of a degree (F.) to 3 degrees, the depression persisting not merely for minutes or hours, but even for days. Various observers have since found that ordinary quantities of alcohol taken as a beverage depress the temperature of the body, usually by less than half a degree in healthy men ; but large doses may cause a fall of five or six degrees.

The increased loss of heat at the periphery of the body is therefore not compensated by any increased production of heat internally. There is, in fact, no evidence to show that alcohol has any special effect in directly increasing the rate of heat-production in the body, though indirectly it may do this to a small extent—namely, in so far as it favours muscular restlessness by weakening the control exercised by the brain.

The popular belief in alcohol as being a good thing to take in order to "keep out the cold" does not, therefore, appear to have much justification. No doubt to a normal healthy person, well clad, and exposed to a moderate degree of cold for only a short period, the discomfort of chilliness may be alleviated by a small quantity of alcohol without risk of incurring a dangerous fall of internal temperature. But to take alcohol in quantity when the exposure is likely to be prolonged or the cold considerable may be decidedly dangerous, and all the more so because any sensation of warmth which may be produced masks the perception of the real effect, which is a general cooling of the body.

On the other hand, alcohol may be of distinct value after the body has been chilled by exposure to cold such as an immersion in cold water. When the patient has been wrapped in hot blankets, the administration of alcohol is useful, since the liquid, by promoting the return of blood to the surface, can now assist in the absorption of external heat and thus help to restore the general body temperature.

Use of alcohol in treatment of fevers.—Alcohol has long been regarded as a valuable remedy in typhoid and other fevers, partly by reason of its cooling effect, but perhaps still more because it is capable of serving in some degree as a foodstuff, replacing starches and sugars. In fever the higher temperature of the body has been considered to favour the oxidation of the alcohol, so that a larger quantity can be utilised than could be used up in normal circumstances. During its administration, however, the effects must be carefully watched to guard against injurious action on the nervous system, which may occur with certain classes of patient.

In modern medical practice alcohol is used much more sparingly than formerly, even in the treatment of fevers. Evidence of this is found in the decreasing amount of money spent on alcoholic stimulants by certain hospitals during recent years. Thus in seven of the large London hospitals the aggregate expenditure on alcoholic liquids was £3,740 during the year 1892; but in 1912, with more patients under treatment, it had decreased to £1,238, or less than one-third of the former amount.

Use as antiseptic.—Alcohol at a strength of about 10 per cent. and upwards acts as a preservative of many organic substances, and is often added to medicinal preparations, extracts, wines, etc., to prevent putrefactive deterioration. In the absence of better antiseptic remedies it may serve as a useful application to wounds if used somewhat freely and of not too low a strength—say 50 to 80 per cent. In many spirituous liniments the alcohol, apart from any purpose which it may serve as solvent or antiseptic, has a mild effect as a counter-irritant, since when well rubbed into the skin it dilates the blood-vessels. When, on the other hand, it is used as a lotion merely to bathe the surface of the skin, and allowed to evaporate, it produces a cooling effect and diminishes the amount of sweat excreted. Hence its use, in the form of Eau de Cologne, Florida water, lavender water, and so on, to soothe certain forms of headache.

Strong alcohol absorbs water from animal and vegetable tissues, thereby hardening them ; it is therefore employed for dehydrating histological specimens preparatory to cutting sections therefrom for microscopical examination.

According to Russell and Buddin,[1] neither methyl alcohol nor ethyl alcohol is nearly so effective in sterilising soil as might be supposed, the minimum effective doses being, respectively, 3·2 and 4·6 per cent. of the weight of the soil.

A. Beyer[2] has found that alcohol of 70 per cent. strength by weight (76·9 by volume) is more effective as a bactericide than alcohol of any other strength. At above 80 per cent. (by weight) it is almost useless as a disinfectant, since strong alcohol preserves bacteria by drying them. Even absolute alcohol does not kill dry bacteria. The addition of chloroform, ether, benzene, acetone, glycerine, carbon disulphide, or petroleum ether, does not increase the bactericidal power of alcohol ; but Eau de Cologne—a spirituous solution of perfume oils—has a more powerful disinfectant action than plain alcohol. Comstock, however, has investigated the germicidal action of alcohol on the organisms *Bacillus subtilis*, *B. anthracis*, *B. coli communis*, and *Streptococcus pyogenes aureus*, and concludes that it has but little value as an antiseptic against these micro-organisms, whether the strength is 95 per cent. or 70 per cent.[3]

[1] *J. Soc. Chem. Ind.*, 1913, **32**, 1138.
[2] *Apoth. Zeit.*, 1912, **27**, 28
[3] *Chem. Abst.*, 1915, **9**, 2661.

BIBLIOGRAPHY

ENZYMES AND FERMENTATION.

Baylis, W. M., "The Nature of Enzyme Action." London (Longmans), 1908.

Beatty, J., "The Method of Enzyme Action." London (Churchill), 1917.

Boulard, H., "Études et recherches sur les levures." Paris (Vigot), 1915.

Delbrück and Schrohe, "Hefe, Gärung, und Fäulnis." Berlin (Parey), 1904.

Effront, J., "Les Enzymes et leurs Applications." Paris, 1899.

—— "Les Catalyseurs Biochimiques." Paris, 1914.

Effront and Prescott, "Biochemical Catalysts in Life and Industry." New York (Wiley), 1917.

Fowler, G. J., "Bacteriological and Enzyme Chemistry." London (Arnold), 1911.

Green, J. R., "The Soluble Ferments and Fermentation." Cambridge, 1899.

Hansen, E. C., "Practical Studies in Fermentation." London (Spon), 1896.

Harden, A., "Alcoholic Fermentation." London (Longmans), 1911.

Jörgensen, A., "Micro-organisms and Fermentation." 4th ed. London (Griffin), 1911.

Klöcker, A., "Fermentation Organisms." London (Longmans), 1903.

Oppenheimer and Mitchell, "Ferments and their Action." London (Griffin), 1901.

Slator, A., "Studies in Fermentation." *Trans. Chem. Soc.*, London, 1906, 1908, 1910.

BREWING AND MALTING.

Bailey, R. D., "The Brewer's Analyst." London, 1907.

Brown, A. J., "Laboratory Studies for Brewing Students." London (Longmans), 1904.

Delbrück, M., "Brauerei Lexikon." Berlin, 1910.

Faulkner, F., "Modern Brewing." London, 1888.

Hooper, E. G., "Manual of Brewing." London (Shepherd), 1891.

Mann and Harlan, "The Morphology of the Barley Grain," *U.S. Dept. Agric. Bulletin No.* 183, 1915.

Michel, C., "Lehrbuch der Bierbrauerei." Augsburg, 1900.

Moreau and Lévy, "Fabrication des Bières." Paris, 1905.

Moritz and Morris, "Text-Book of the Science of Brewing." London (Spon), 1891.

Southby, E. R., "Practical Brewing." London (Brewing Trade Review), 1889.

Stopes, H., "Malt and Malting." London (*Brewer's Journal*), 1885.

Sykes and Ling. "Principles and Practice of Brewing." London (Griffin), 1907.

Thatcher, F., "Practical Brewing and Malting." London, 1905.

ALCOHOL PRODUCTION: DISTILLATION.

Barbet, E., "La Rectification et les Colonnes Rectificatrices en Distillerie." Paris, 1895.

Brannt, W. T., "Distillation and Rectification of Alcohol." Philadelphia, 1904.

Bucheler et Légier, "Traité de la Fabrication de l'Alcool." 2 Vols. Paris (Fritsch), 1899.

Dejonghe, G., "Traité complet de la Fabrication de l'Alcool et des Levures." 3 Vols. Lille, 1899.

Lévy, L., "Les Moûts et les Vins en Distillerie." Paris, 1903.

Maercker-Delbrück, "Handbuch der Spiritusfabrikation," 9th Aufl. Berlin (Parey), 1908.

Moewes, "Destillierkunst," 9th Aufl. Berlin (Parey), 1892.

Nettleton, J. A., "Manufacture of Whisky and Plain Spirit." Aberdeen (Cornwall and Sons), 1913.

Sorel, E., "La Distillation." Paris (Gauthier Villars), 1895.

—— "La Rectification de l'Alcool." Paris, 1894.

ALCOHOL: INDUSTRIAL USES, ETC.

Brachvogel, J. K., "Industrial Alcohol." London (Crosby Lockwood and Son), 1907.

Calvet, M. L., "Alcools." Paris (Béranger), 1911.

Duchemin, R., "La Dénaturation de l'Alcool, etc." Paris, 1907.

Herrick, R. F., "Denatured or Industrial Alcohol." New York (Wiley), 1907.

McIntosh, J. G., "Industrial Alcohol." London (Scott, Greenwood and Son), 1907.

Report of *Departmental Committee on Industrial Alcohol.* London, 1905.

Siderski, D., "Les usages industriels de l'Alcool." Paris (Baillière), 1903.

WINE: SPIRITS: ANALYSIS.

Babo and Mach, "Handbuch des Weinbaues." 4th Aufl. Berlin (Parey), 1910.

Coste-Floret, P., "Vinification." 3 Vols. Paris, 1903.

Duplais and McKennie, "Manufacture and Distillation of Alcoholic Liquors." Philadelphia (Baird), 1871.

Gayon and Laborde, "Vins." Paris (Béranger), 1912.

Girard and Cuniasse, "Manuel Pratique de l'Analyse des Alcools." Paris (Masson), 1899.

Portes et Ruyssen, "Traité de la Vigne." Paris, 1889.

Post and Neumann, "Traité Complet d'Analyse Chimique." French Edition by MM. Chenu and Pellet. Paris (Hermann), 1910.

Report of *Royal Commission on Whisky*, etc. London, 1909.

Report on (i) *Analysis of Potable Spirits*, and (ii) *Standards for Whisky*: Commonwealth Papers. Perth, Western Australia, 1915.

Scarisbrick, J., "Spirit Assaying." Wolverhampton (Whitehead), 1898.

Thudichum and Dupré, "Origin, Nature, and Varieties of Wine." London (Macmillan), 1872.

Vasey, S. A., "Analysis of Potable Spirits." London (Baillière), 1904.

Walker, E., "Manual for the Essence Industry." New York (Wiley), 1916.

PHYSIOLOGICAL EFFECTS.

Central Control Board Committee (Liquor Traffic), " Alcohol : its Action on the Human Organism." London (H.M. Stationery Office), 1918.

Dodge and Benedict, " Psychological Effects of Alcohol." Washington, 1915.

Horsley and Sturge, " Alcohol and the Human Body." London (Macmillan), 1915.

Kraepelin, E. " Über die Beeinflussung einfacher psychischer Vorgänge durch einige Arzneimittel." Jena, 1893.

—— Psychologische Arbeiten, 1901.

Kobert, " Lehrbuch der Intoxikationen." Stuttgart, 1906.

" Physiological Aspects of the Liquor Problem " (various contributors). Boston, 1903.

Rivers, " Influence of Alcohol and other Drugs on Fatigue." London, 1907.

Roberts, Sir W., " Collected Contributions on Digestion and Diet." London, 1891.

GENERAL WORKS OF REFERENCE AND PERIODICALS.

Allen's " Commercial Organic Analysis." Vol. I. London (Churchill), 1909.

Dammer, O., " Chemische Technologie der Neuzeit." Stuttgart, 1910.

Journal of the Society of Chemical Industry.

Journal of the Chemical Society.

Journal of the Institute of Brewing.

Journal of the American Chemical Society.

Journal of Industrial and Engineering Chemistry.

Journal of Pharmacology and Experimental Therapeutics.

Journal of Physiology.

Ost, H., " Lehrbuch der Chemisches Technologie." 8th Aufl. Leipzig, 1914.

Pflüger's Archiv fur die gesammelte Physiologie.

The Analyst.

The Biochemical Journal.

Thorpe, T. E., " Dictionary of Applied Chemistry." London (Longmans), 1912.

Ullmann, F., " Enzyklopädie der technischen Chemie." Berlin, 1914.

Wagner and Gautier, " Traité de Chimie Industrielle." Paris (Masson), 1903.

Zeitschrift für Spiritusindustrie.

ALCOHOLOMETRY: SPECIAL MEMOIRS.

Blagden and Gilpin, " Report on the best method of proportioning the Excise on spirituous liquors, and tables in connection therewith." *Philosophical Transactions,* 1790, **80**, 321; 1792, **82**, 425; 1794, **84**, 275.

Tralles, " Untersuchungen über die spezifischen Gewichte der Mischungen von Alkohol und Wasser." *Gilbert's Annalen der Physik,* 1811, **38**, 349.

Gay Lussac, " Instruction pour l'usage de l'alcoomètre centésimal." Paris, 1824.

Fownes, " On the value in absolute alcohol of spirits of different specific gravities." *Philosophical Transactions,* 1847, **137**, 249.

Drinkwater, " The preparation of absolute alcohol and the composition of proof spirit." *Memoirs of the Chemical Society,* 1848, p. 447.

McCulloh, " Hydrometers," Report on, to U.S. Government, 1848.

Baumhauer, " Mémoire sur la densité, la dilatation, etc., de la vapeur de l'alcool." Amsterdam, 1860.

Mendeléef, " Über die Verbindungen des Alkohols mit Wasser." A German summary by Richter of Mendeléef's research. *Poggendorff's Annalen,* 1869, **138**, 103, 230.

Squibb, " Absolute Alcohol." *Ephemeris of Materia Medica,* 1884, p. 541.

Homann and Loewenherz, " Das Gewichtsalkoholometer und seine Anwendung." Berlin, 1889.

Kaiserliche Normal Eichungs Kommission. Data obtained by this Commsision appear in Homann and Loewenherz's work just mentioned, and in the " Physikalisch-Chemische Tabellen " of Landolt-Börnstein.

ADDENDUM

Alcohol as Motor Fuel.—An inter-departmental Committee was appointed in October, 1918, to consider questions relating to the supply of alcohol, its manufacture, cost, method of denaturing, and suitability for use in internal-combustion engines.[1] The report of this Committee appeared whilst the present volume was in the final stages of printing. Some of the chief conclusions are indicated hereunder.

The Committee consider that action should be taken to ensure close investigation of the questions of production and utilisation, in all their branches, of alcohol for power and traction purposes.

A large-scale practical trial, extending over a period of about 26 weeks, of alcohol–benzol and alcohol–benzol–petrol mixtures in a complete fleet of London motor-omnibuses, running under daily service conditions, was arranged for by the Committee. An experimental research for the purpose of obtaining accurate data as to the combustion of various mixtures was also instituted. Neither of these investigations, however, had been completed when the report was published.

As regards supply, there are within the British Empire vast existing and prospective sources of alcohol from vegetable products. For example, evidence was received concerning production, costs, and yield of "power alcohol" from the flowers of the Mahua tree (*Bassia latifolia*), which flourishes in the Deccan and the Central Provinces of India. The sun-dried flowers of this tree contain 60 per cent. of fermentable sugars, and yield, per ton, about 90 gallons of 95 per cent. alcohol. They can be pressed, packed, exported, and stored for long periods without deterioration.

The prospective production of alcohol from maize and other cereals in the overseas Dominions and other parts of the Empire is considered to be "encouraging, both as regards quantities and cost."

[1] Report Cmd. 218; 1919.

No satisfactory method for utilising peat as an economic source of " power alcohol " was brought to the notice of the Committee, but the potential value of peat as a raw material for the purpose should not be overlooked.

In the United Kingdom the production of power alcohol on a commercial basis from such articles as potatoes, artichokes, sugar beet, and mangolds does not appear practicable except under some system of State subvention. So far as vegetable sources of raw material are concerned, the conclusion is that we must rely mainly or entirely on increased production in tropical and sub-tropical countries.

Synthetic production in considerable quantities, however, especially from coal and coke-oven gases, is regarded as promising. The evidence as to the synthetic conversion of ethylene into alcohol indicates that this gas is a large potential source of power alcohol in Great Britain; but further investigations are necessary before definite figures as to quantities and price can be given.

The Committee suggest that the cost of denaturing power alcohol might be diminished by lowering the proportion of wood-naphtha at present employed, the difference being made up, wholly or partially, by petrol, benzol, or other nauseous substance. Improved facilities for importation and distribution of power alcohol are also recommended.

INDEX

INDEX OF NAMES

INDEX OF SUBJECTS

F

G

H

N

O

P

Lightning Source UK Ltd.
Milton Keynes UK
UKHW050802240720
367047UK00013B/426